- Images assoc. w/ the
acc O.
Why are they?

JON BALSERAK

(0131) 556 5751

07867 538 758

07888 736 644

The
Unaccommodated
Calvin

OXFORD STUDIES IN HISTORICAL THEOLOGY

PRIMITIVISM, RADICALISM, AND THE LAMB'S WAR
The Baptist-Quaker Conflict in Seventeenth-Century England

T. L. Underwood

THE GOSPEL OF JOHN IN THE SIXTEENTH CENTURY
The Johannine Exegesis of Wolfgang Musculus

Craig S. Farmer

CASSIAN THE MONK

Columba Stewart

HUMAN FREEDOM, CHRISTIAN RIGHTEOUSNESS
Philip Melanchthon's Exegetical Dispute with Erasmus of Rotterdam

Timothy J. Wengert

IMAGES AND RELICS
Theological Perceptions and Visual Images
in Sixteenth-Century Europe

John Dillenberger

THE BODY BROKEN
The Calvinist Doctrine of the Eucharist and the Symbolization
of Power in Sixteenth-Century France

Christopher Elwood

THE UNACCOMMODATED CALVIN
Studies in the Foundation of a Theological Tradition

Richard A. Muller

The
Unaccommodated
Calvin

■ ■ ■

Studies in the Foundation of a
Theological Tradition

RICHARD A. MULLER

New York   Oxford

OXFORD UNIVERSITY PRESS

2000

Oxford University Press

Oxford   New York

Athens   Auckland   Bangkok   Bogotá   Buenos Aires   Calcutta
Cape Town   Chennai   Dar es Salaam   Delhi   Florence   Hong Kong   Istanbul
Karachi   Kuala Lumpur   Madrid   Melbourne   Mexico City   Mumbai
Nairobi   Paris   São Paulo   Singapore   Taipei   Tokyo   Toronto   Warsaw

and associated companies in
Berlin   Ibadan

Published by Oxford University Press, Inc.
198 Madison Avenue, New York, New York 10016

Oxford is a registered trademark of Oxford University Press

Library of Congress Cataloging-in-Publication Data
Muller, Richard A. (Richard Alfred), 1948–
The unaccommodated Calvin : studies in the foundation of a
theological tradition / Richard A. Muller.
p.   cm.—(Oxford studies in historical theology)
Includes bibliographical references and index.
ISBN 0-19-511681-X
1. Calvin, Jean, 1509–1564.   I. Title.   II. Series.
BX9418.M79   1999
230'.42'092—dc21   98-18788

1 3 5 7 9 8 6 4 2

Printed in the United States of America
on acid-free paper

For Gloria

_____

wife, companion, and friend

PREFACE

There is truth in the saying that history is rewritten by each generation. Of course, few historians would claim to have entirely rewritten history—and those who have made the claim have usually been less than successful in convincing others of the validity of their conclusions. The task of rewriting or, more precisely, of reinterpreting history typically assumes the advances of the past, attempts to build on them, and, either through an increased precision or through the attainment of a different vantage point, moves on not to a new history but to a new perspective on a history already fairly well known. Recognition that the writing of history always involves a process of reinterpretation builds humility among historians. The young recruits of today are the old war horses of tomorrow. The latest reappraisal soon becomes grist for the mill of reevaluation. Once the historiographical task has been relativized and deprived of its finality, it nonetheless remains the case that the reexamination of sources with a view to greater precision in detail and with an altered sense of the legitimate context of investigation brings a certain kind of forward movement in study: if we never attain to finality, we at least can state with relative certainty that faulty or partial older perspectives have been set aside.

In the last decade, we have clearly come to such a shift—or to a series of shifts—in the interpretation of Calvin and Calvinism. Without making any claim to finality, we can review the history of recent scholarship and note that an older model, typical of the heyday of Barthian studies of Calvin, has become outmoded, albeit not entirely set aside. Movement away from the Barthian or neo-orthodox approach has taken at least two directions, the one quite promising, the other (to borrow a phrase from Calvin and his contemporaries) pressing deeper into a labyrinth of twentieth-century theologizing.

The positive, promising shift in Calvin historiography is a movement, evidenced among historians of ideas as well as among social and political historians, away from the dogmatically motivated study of Calvin's theology and from the related assumption that the primary purpose of an exposition of Calvin's doctrine is to provide a significant point of departure for contemporary theologizing. The other direction, into the labyrinth, moves away from the Barthian approach only to offer alternative modernisms as grids through which to read Calvin's work: thus, it is variously argued that Calvin should be read through a Schleiermacherian, or a "sapiential," or an existential and psychologizing glass; or perhaps his foundation in Renaissance rhetoric should be used to draw him into dialogue with twentieth-century theologies in which rhetorical webs of language have replaced objective theological substance.

It is my hope in the present volume to underline the importance of an examination of Calvin's ideas in their sixteenth-century context and, as part of a movement away from various dogmatic readings of Calvin, to emphasize the importance of understanding Calvin's methods and procedures as a point of departure for understanding his thought. Over against such contemporary oxymorons as "postmodern" and "deconstructionist historiography"—and equally against the systematic theologians who, long before "postmodern" and "deconstructionist" became terms in our vocabulary, practiced their trade of deconstructing texts in the name of their own theological program—the plea for an "unaccommodated Calvin" embraces the intransigence and irreducibility of the historical text. The past is not, of course, totally recoverable. In our search for the historical Calvin, we are burdened by numerous layers of interpretive accretion (not the least of which is the apparatus of modern critical editions and the translations based on them) and by irrecoverable gaps in our documentation—but Calvin's text itself and the express statements that Calvin made about the nature, content, method, and arrangement of his work are still available for us to examine. And where there is text, there is hope.

In the context of this last sentiment, some comment must be made concerning the texts consulted. I have tried, as far as possible, to cite the text of Calvin's *Institutes* from the sixteenth-century editions. Throughout the volume, all subsequent short references to the sixteenth-century editions offer both a short title form and the date of the edition cited. Thus, the Latin text of the *Institutes* is cited, example, as *Institutio* (1539) or *Institutio* (1550); the French text as *Institution* (1541) or *Institution* (1560). Whereas the notes consistently provide the Latin or French titles of Calvin's works, I have consistently used English titles in the main text of the essay. I have also, for the convenience of those who do not have access to the sixteenth-century editions, made regular reference to the *Calvini Opera* (identified as *CO*) in the *Corpus Reformatorum*, and I have offered collateral citation of the 1559 edition of the *Institutes* where no modern edition of the text is available. I have also used the *Corpus Reformatorum* (identified as *CR*) for the citation of Melanchthon's writings. For reasons that will be apparent from the argument of the following work, particularly as found in chapters 4, 6, and 8, much of my analysis of Calvin's methods and thought patterns rests on sixteenth-century editions of his writings: this is particularly true in the case of the *Institutes*. For the same reasons, I have not relied on the Barth/Niesel *Opera selecta* unless it offers a text not easily accessible elsewhere. As my apparatus indicates, a considerable number of editions of the

Institutes, both in Latin and in French, from 1536 to 1590, have been examined in preference to modern critical editions.

I have also availed myself of the standard translations—the often cited McNeill-Battles translation of Calvin's *Institutes* and the multivolume translation of the commentaries, tracts, treatises, and letters, undertaken in the nineteenth century by the Calvin Translation Society. I find the more recent translation of Calvin's commentaries on the New Testament less than satisfactory, and I have not used it in the present volume. I have also consulted the older translations of the *Institutes*, namely those of Norton, Allen, and Beveridge, in view of both the accuracy of those translations and the relationship in which they stand to the older or "precritical" text tradition of Calvin's original. Both in its apparatus and in its editorial approach to the text, the McNeill-Battles translation suffers from the mentality of the text-critic who hides the original ambience of the text even as he attempts to reveal all of its secrets to the modern reader.

Profound thanks go to David C. Steinmetz, of Duke University, and to Susan E. Schreiner, of the University of Chicago. Both read the manuscript with considerable discernment at various stages of its progress, and both listened with care and careful critique to many of the musings that were eventually incorporated in the book. John L. Thompson, of Fuller Theological Seminary, has placed me deeply in his debt with his discerning reading of the book and his insightful suggestions in matters of form and content. There are times when John has the ability to frame my thoughts far more adroitly than I can. To my friend and colleague Timothy J. Wengert, I offer profound thanks for our fruitful dialogue about another far more significant conversation—the theological conversation that went on between John Calvin and Philip Melanchthon—and for the impact of our dialogue on this book. Indeed, I have drawn from him my use of the term "conversation" as a way of describing theological and exegetical interchange. To Raymond A. Blacketer, my graduate assistant, I also owe a deep note of appreciation for an ongoing, discerning dialogue on many of the ideas and issues reflected in the following pages. Colleagues at the University of Utrecht and at the Free University of Amsterdam receive my thanks for their most helpful reflections on chapters 3 and 6.

I also must offer my thanks to Paul Fields and Karin Maag, respectively the curator and director of the H. Henry Meeter Center for Calvin Studies at Calvin College and Seminary in Grand Rapids, for their help in obtaining and using materials related to the study of Calvin and Calvinism. The many rare editions of the *Institutes* and of other works of Calvin examined in the following chapters were made available to me at the Meeter Center, as were virtually all of the older monographs and essays needed for my work. I also offer thanks to the editors at Oxford, particularly to my virtuoso copyeditor Jeri Famighetti—her work has clarified the line of argument in many places and has removed a host of minor problems. Finally to my wife, Gloria, go the profoundest thanks of all, for supporting and sustaining me during so many times and in so many places. Without her, there would be no book at all.

Grand Rapids, Michigan   R. A. M.
December 1998

CONTENTS

Part II

Text, Context, and Conversation: The *Institutes* in Calvin's
Theological Program, 99

The
Unaccommodated
Calvin

An Approach to Calvin

On Overcoming Modern Accommodations

Theological Approaches to Calvin: The Problem

The life and thought of John Calvin (1509–1564), the great Reformer of Geneva and one of the principal founders of the Reformed tradition, have been presented on so many pages in such a wide variety of books that, at first glance, one might well wonder whether anything new can be said. Reams of pages have been written on Calvin's *Institutes* alone. Nonetheless, even cursory examination of works written in the second half of the twentieth century reveals less than a consensus. One can read, for instance, that Calvin's *Institutes* is not a theological system but a theology of piety or a theology of rhetoric or a rhetoric of piety or a pastoral theology—or that it is indeed a theological system. Or that Calvin was a humanist rhetor who opposed scholastic theology in all its forms—or that Calvin stands in continuity with several of the scholastic theological currents of the later Middle Ages. Or that Calvin was a rigid logician; on the contrary, Calvin was a theologian or, better, not a theologian, but a rhetor of piety. Calvin's theology rested on the divine decrees as a central principle; Calvin's theology rested on the principle of the sovereignty of God; Calvin's theology centered on the doctrine of the Trinity; Calvin's thought was christocentric. Calvin's thought was a gathering and juxtaposition of opposites or perspectives, having no central principle. So, too, we can read that Calvin was not a "covenant theologian" and that he taught only a unilateral concept of covenant in contrast to Bullinger's bilateral concept—or that Calvin held the doctrine of covenant in high esteem and did teach a bilateral view of covenant.

The list of contemporary interpretive antitheses could be continued indefinitely. There is no use in reciting further examples—and there is even less in attempting to explain such antitheses in terms of tensions, bifurcations, or contradictions inherent in Calvin's own thought or personality. Most, if not all, of these antitheses, at least in one of their members, are the result of the particular set of theological spectacles through which Calvin has been viewed by writers of rather varied interests and intentions, and most of them fail to recognize the extent to which the antithesis itself is resident in modern scholarship—not in the thought of the sixteenth century. Calvin's thought has, in short, been avidly deconstructed by nineteenth- and twentieth-century writers in search of a theological or religious ally or, occasionally, in search of a historical source for the theological trials of the present.

The solution to such problems resides in the documents. The historical Calvin ought not and, ultimately, cannot be accommodated to modern theological programs without considerable distortion of his intention and meaning. Of course, the proponents of the various accommodations of Calvin's thought have also read the documents—and this fact points to the underlying burden of the present essay. Approaching Calvin in his proper historical context is not simply a matter of reading the text of Calvin as found in modern critical editions: rather, it is a matter of establishing the specific sixteenth-century context within which various sixteenth-century documents ought to be read. And it is often also a matter of overcoming perspectives impressed on the documents either by entrenched patterns of scholarly and theological analysis or by the modern apparatus in its function as an interpretive grid superimposed on the text. In the case of many contemporary analyses of Calvin's theology—typically based on the *Institutes* with little more than collateral or confirmatory reference to his commentaries, sermons, and treatises—both of these problems obtain. Moreover, this problem of modern interpretive grids can be just as apparent in a nominally biographical essay as in theological investigations.[1]

Dogmatic Accommodations of Calvin: A Critique

Although several of his essays on Calvin's theology indicate a kinship with the Barthian reading of the Reformer,[2] T. H. L. Parker has more consistently pointed his readers toward the text of Calvin and has labored to illuminate the patterns of Calvin's work, particularly in the areas of exegesis and preaching.[3] In a penetrating essay written some five decades ago, Parker pointedly critiqued the nineteenth-century tendency to analyze Calvin's thought in terms of specific dogmatic centers or as a strictly logical working out of a series of fundamental concepts. This was, certainly, the theological method of the nineteenth-century commentators on Calvin's work, many of whom pressed their own understanding of theology onto the work of their sixteenth-century subject. "Such a method," Parker observed, "was abhorrent to [Calvin's] mind."[4] Calvin did intend to give "a comprehensive summary and orderly arrangement of all the branches of religion" based entirely on the interpretation of Scripture, but this, comments Parker, "is a very different matter from building a system of theology starting from one foundation."[5]

Not only have many writers failed to heed Parker's warning and have continued to search for central motifs around which Calvin's thought crystallized,[6] but also much of the writing on Calvin's thought continues to be exclusively doctrinal, with the result that a collection of such works could be arranged on a shelf so as to constitute a fairly extensive system of theology—including topics not otherwise easily located in Calvin's writings! So, too, the studies that examine a particular doctrine or complex of doctrines as Calvin's central motif are invariably organized and argued in ways that do not reflect either the patterns of organization found in Calvin's own text or statements that Calvin himself makes concerning the argumentation of his work. Here, in particular, doctrinal statements made in the *Institutes* tend to be harmonized with statements made in the commentaries, sermons, and treatises, with the explicit intention of uncovering theological structures not revealed by Calvin to his readers. This is not to argue that one ought not to study Calvin's doctrine. The point is, simply, that there are both useful and fundamentally misleading ways in which to examine Calvin's doctrine—and that, unfortunately, all too many studies of Calvin's doctrine have opted for patterns of analysis that are misleading, insofar as they are also dogmatically motivated.

Although much of the emphasis of the present volume is therefore on Calvin's *Institutes*, the burden of our examination of the *Institutes* is to understand it in the context of the early sixteenth-century Protestant analysis and reconstruction of what might be called the "body of Christian teaching." Such an examination, moreover, while maintaining the *Institutes'* identity as a sixteenth-century form of theological system, must point away from modern dogmatics and toward Calvin's exegetical task as the proper context for understanding the document. Calvin, after all, did not think of himself as a dogmatician in the modern sense of the term: rather, like most of the other theologians of his time, he understood himself as a preacher and exegete, and he understood the primary work of his life as the exposition of Scripture. The *Institutes* is equaled in size by Calvin's sermons on Job and dwarfed by the sermons on Deuteronomy, as well as by the individual commentaries on Psalms, Isaiah, Jeremiah, and the Pentateuch.

One might fairly argue that Calvin never set out to produce a theological system in the modern sense of the term. At the same time, it must be emphasized (against several modern accommodations of his work) that he certainly did intend to produce a theological system or body of doctrine in and for his own time. Specifically, he determined in his *Institutes* to develop a fairly cohesive set of theological topics and disputations that would guide theological students in their approach to Scripture—and he expanded the text in the light of insights gained in his work of preaching and exegesis and in the course of his polemical defense of the Reformation.[7] Again, we find a significant parallel with the work of his contemporaries: theological system in the sixteenth century most frequently took the form of a gathering of theological topics drawn out of the work of exegesis and disputation, a set of *loci communes*, or "commonplaces"—an approach found in the work of Melanchthon, Musculus, and Hyperius and superimposed on Vermigli's theology by his editor, Massonius.[8]

Dogmatically motivated studies of Calvin's thought, like the old systematic method for the study of the history of Christian doctrine, as practiced by Neander, Hagenbach, and Shedd,[9] have typically been conceived according to a topical, dogmatic method that locates the meaning or significance of the historical issue being examined in the doctrinal consciousness of the historian's or dogmatician's present rather than in the intellectual, exegetical, polemical, or political context of the historical issue itself. Such studies tend to follow the approach to dogmatic topics current in the historian's present, rather than the series of topics recognized in the era under examination. Thus, dogmatic studies of Calvin's theology have often cited his commentaries but have seldom inquired into the impact of Calvin's exegetical efforts on his formulation of theological topics. Indeed, the dogmatic study of Calvin has virtually never examined the formation of theological topics or *loci* in the sixteenth century. Such studies have succeeded in telling their readers much about what a specific thinker said on particular doctrinal topics, albeit with little or no insight into the relationship of their subject either to the thought of his contemporaries or to the teachings of the broader Christian tradition.[10]

The exposition of Calvin's thought is certainly one object of all of these works. But the majority of these studies also present Calvin's thought in a twentieth-century Barthian, rather than in a sixteenth-century Reformation, context and thereby submerged much of the meaning of Calvin's theology under their own contemporary agendas.[11] Characteristic of such works were an absence of specific attention to Calvin's medieval roots and to the thought of Calvin's contemporaries and the assumption that a generalized picture of the Middle Ages, Renaissance, or Reformation was sufficient backdrop for the presentation of Calvin's thought. In addition, these works embody a somewhat problematic method: the exposition of the theology of Calvin by means of a harmonistic reading of texts from his biblical commentaries, treatises, sermons, and *Institutes* into a predetermined dogmatic *locus*. The largely unintended result of such argumentation is a series of doctrinal portraits of Calvin that present his thought not only garbed in rather neo-orthodox clothes but also, even when the sixteenth-century meaning of Calvin's arguments is reasonably well conveyed, as a dogmatic monolith, with no attention to its relative originality or, indeed, to its frequent lack of originality.

More specifically, when Calvin's interpretation of a particular biblical passage or of a particular point of doctrine is not set against the background of specific patristic and medieval antecedents and of specific contemporary parallels, the ideas and interpretations that are uniquely Calvin's cannot be identified nor, indeed, can the continuities between Calvin's thought and the catholic tradition. Similarly, when the texts of Calvin's commentaries, treatises, sermons, and *Institutes* are harmonized for dogmatic purposes, the actual intention underlying Calvin's arguments can be obscured, the context of a remark can be lost, and the meaning and significance of a point mistaken.[12] A superb example of the problem is the fairly large number of essays devoted to the theological question of whether Calvin held to a doctrine of "limited atonement." The worst of these studies utterly ignore the fact that the term "limited atonement" is not accurately descriptive of the themes of sixteenth- or even seventeenth-century theology. Others, of a slightly more historical cast, recognize this first problem but then attempt either to wedge Calvin into the thought-world of the Synod of Dort or to extract him from it without fully acknowledging that the problem of the limited application of Christ's all-sufficient satisfaction to the elect alone was not a problem debated by Calvin. Virtually all of these studies exist primarily for the sake of enlisting Calvin's support in the establishment or justification of a contemporary theological program—and their method consists in the gathering of comments from various of Calvin's works for the sake of reframing them into a full-scale doctrine either of limited, or universal, or, indeed, hypothetically universal atonement.[13]

It is also the case that discussions of "Calvin's doctrine of man," "Calvin's doctrine of predestination," or "Calvin's doctrine of word and sacrament" have the somewhat ironic effect of reifying or giving present solidity to something that was not precisely obvious in the sixteenth century. On the one hand, Calvin himself might well object to the notion of "Calvin's doctrine" of anything, inasmuch as the doctrines that Calvin held and taught were, in large part, not his own! When his contemporaries, particularly when those who (like Bullinger) stood within the same confessional trajectory, criticized Calvin's doctrine, they were, typically, pointing toward disagreements concerning the discrete elements of Calvin's thought or concerning the precise identification of what they viewed as the normative teaching of Scripture, all within a spectrum of fairly traditional definition. On the other hand, one may well speak of "Servetus's doctrine of the Trinity," for that was a rather unique teaching easily identifiable as Servetus's own. And Servetus was burned for it.

What Calvin intended to teach was the church's doctrine, not his own doctrine. To the extent that he was successful, his originality must be sought more in his manner of presenting Christian doctrine, in the way he received, incorporated, or modified forms and arguments of patristic and medieval theology, in his particular fusion of older theological substance either with his own exegetical results or with Renaissance rhetorical forms, and in the nuances that he gave to the elements of extant tradition. Thus, when Calvin and one of the other founders of the Reformed tradition, like Bullinger, differed on a doctrinal nuance—as is evident in their views on predestination and the Lord's Supper—both had clear patristic and medieval antecedents and, particularly in the case of their disagreement on predestination, neither offered a radically new perspective.[14] On the other hand, even in those cases in which Calvin produced a doctrinal tractate on a particular subject—predestination, the Lord's Supper—the treatise is so lodged in a specific sixteenth-century context and, therefore, so defined by polemical debate and exegetical practice that a modern synthesizing or dogmatic approach will either distort or lose much of its meaning and implication.

The decline of neo-orthodoxy as a major force in Protestant theology in the twentieth century has led to a corresponding decline in interest in the neo-orthodox reading of Calvin's theology.[15] The failure of this particular approach to Calvin's thought, unfortunately, has led not to the rejection of theological grids but to the replacement of the Barthian or Brunnerian grid with other dogmatic constructs, such as a tension between "sapiential" and "evangelical" approaches in theology[16] or a Schleiermacherian patterning of the theological themes of grace, Word, Christ, and revelation.[17] The former approach assumes that these terms, only one of which (namely, evangelical) stands in any significant relationship to Calvin's own usage, can be useful constructs for comparing and contrasting issues or identifying "tensions" in Calvin's thought. Tensions arise, not because Calvin's own arguments actually conflict with one another but because a theme reinterpreted under the rubric of "sapiential" does not quite merge with another theme now read out under the rubric "evangelical." The resulting theorizations are particularly removed from Calvin's intellectual realm when "sapiential" is used to correspond roughly to a Thomistic view and "evangelical" to a Reformation perspective: only generalizations survive, for both the genuine later medieval background and the legitimate sixteenth-century context are lost.

The latter approach similarly permits its practitioners to avoid the issue of Calvin's antecedents, whether in the Middle Ages or in the Reformation itself, and to avoid consideration of Calvin's sixteenth-century context. Failure to identify context is particularly apparent in the claim that Calvin's polemics reveal little about the central concerns of his theology[18] and in the global generalizations used to identify similarities between Calvin and Schleiermacher, as if they were merely a pair of christocentric preachers of the Word. Thus, it is argued that both center their theological "systems" on "the Word made flesh" and on the doctrines of the Person and work of Christ; both have a "sacramental" understanding of the Word and, therefore, of the activity of preaching as a re-presenting of Christ to the congregation; both also manifest little interest "in historical grounding of biblical texts."[19] Yet, beneath these exceedingly broad and undifferentiated categories of comparison, there are vast differences between the two thinkers, many of which can be properly understood only in and through examination of the historical context. Although this global dogmatic approach offers a counterbalance to Bouwsma's claim that Calvin was not a systematic theologian,[20] its systematic interest is clearly a twentieth- and not a sixteenth-century interest. Indeed, it is of little use to claim that Calvin was (or, alternatively, was not) a "systematic theologian" when no attention is given to the systematizing or codifying task as understood by the theologians of the sixteenth century.

It may also be worth mentioning what is certainly the most flagrant attempt in recent years to press Calvin into the service of a modern theological agenda—Reist's *Reading of Calvin's Institutes.*[21] The title and the preface of the book identify it as an introduction to theology by way of a survey of Calvin's classic work, and yet Calvin has been obliterated: we meet here instead the child of Derrida, an essay for which "there is no text" even when text is cited and in which the only context of interpretation is the contemporary theological scene. One example will suffice: Reist cites the passage, "Hence, it was necessary for the Son of God to become for us 'Immanuel, that is, God with us' and in such a way that his divinity and our humanity might by mutual connection grow together."[22] The phrase "by mutual connection grow together" (*mutua coniunctione . . . inter se coalescerent*), Reist comments, is of particular significance:

> Dare we say that for Calvin it was becoming clear that as God grows, so do we? If so, dare we say that in the light of Calvin's insights we may now risk the view that our own growth is the result of, even a clue to, God's growth? We may, but only with tools now available to us. Here we encounter the *processive* character of Calvin's Christology.[23]

The sixteenth-century framework of meaning disappears, along with Calvin and his text. The Latin, which is cited by Reist, might just as easily be rendered "by being brought into mutual connection unite": *coalesco* can be rendered "grow together" in the sense of "unite"—but not in the sense of personal growth or personal change in union, such as Reist indicates. I am not quite sure what a "processive Christology" is— but I am quite certain that Calvin did not have one, nor did it ever cross his mind to claim that God could "grow." Other examples of textual abuse are to be found throughout Reist's essay.

Accommodation to Partial or Overly Generalized
Historical Contexts

The attempt to overcome the problems of the dogmatic approach by presenting Calvin's thought against a generalized background of the later Middle Ages, Renaissance, and Reformation often serves only to exacerbate the problem, inasmuch as the background is often too generalized to enlighten any particular aspect of Calvin's thought and insofar as presentation of the background all too often becomes the excuse for reverting to a harmonistic doctrinal discussion of Calvin's thought. Broad, generalized notions of "scholasticism" and "humanism," posed against the specificity of Calvin's thought or, indeed, against the thought of his successors, often fail to consider major streams of scholarly reappraisal, such as the work of scholars like Oberman and Courtenay on the theology of the later Middle Ages or the work of historians like Kristeller, Trinkaus, and Margolin on the Renaissance.[24] The result is that many studies of Calvin have tended to set a humanistic and reformatory Calvin in contrast with a dark, obscurantistic, superstitious, and scholastic Middle Ages[25]—or, alternatively, they indicate two "conflicting" sides of Calvin[26] or argue theological "tensions" between different aspects of Calvin's thought.[27] Such essays typically fail to set Calvin into any specific currents of French humanism, or later scholastic thought, or the ongoing exegetical tradition—each of which had profound impact on Calvin and in each of which he participated.[28]

Characteristic also of such works has been their distaste for Calvin's medieval scholastic antecedents and Protestant scholastic successors, whose purported rigid dogmatism and "Aristotelianism" they were wont to contrast with Calvin's warm piety and humanism, as if Calvin could not be dogmatic or display profound influences of Aristotelianism even in the context of his piety—or as if his successors had no warm piety and were uninfluenced by humanism—or, again, as if Calvin never criticized humanists with a vehemence comparable to that of his attacks on scholastics.[29] For all his humanist training, Calvin refused the gambit of a Valla in giving rhetoric the ultimate place, just as he refused the Erasmian model that, in Chomarat's words, "always placed piety above dogmas."[30] Along similar lines, many historical presentations of the history of biblical interpretation have contrasted the exegetical approach of the Reformers with the systematizing approach of their successors—as if the Reformers did not think in dogmatic categories and their successors either did not do or radically deemphasized exegesis.[31]

Just as recent scholarship has indicated many theological continuities as well as discontinuities between the later Middle Ages and the Reformation and has shown that the radical dichotomy between medieval scholastic thought and Renaissance humanism cannot be supported, so, also, has the much of the recent work on Calvin's thought been able to overcome a strict separation between Calvin's theological teachings and late medieval theology without losing sight of or in any way diminishing his reliance on the linguistic and rhetorical emphases of the Renaissance. Similarly, the assumption of a disjunction between Calvin and his successors has been undercut by recent scholarly investigations of doctrinal, exegetical, methodological, and philosophical continuities between the Reformation and the post-Reformation eras.

Often, in relation to the exposition of Calvin's humanistic training, a radical contrast was created between the supposed central dogma predestinarianism of the Protestant scholastics with the Christocentrism of Calvin—as if predestinarianism were the natural result of "scholastic" tendencies and warm christocentric piety the natural analogue of "humanism." Here, too, a dogmatic and specifically neo-orthodox reading of Calvin's thought has tended to abstract him from his times and, in so doing, make his theology appear less like the temporally proximate work of his late sixteenth- and seventeenth-century successors than like the temporally and culturally remote work of the twentieth-century neo-orthodox theologians. And once he had been abstracted from the detail of his historical context, the incredible unlikelihood of a greater similarity between Calvin's thought and the post-Kantian, post-Kierkegaardian theological forms of neo-orthodoxy could be (and, in the case of the works noted earlier, often was) ignored.

Failure to establish the proper context for examination of Calvin's text is not an exclusive property of historical and systematic theologians. The recent biographical study of Calvin by Bouwsma, for example, despite its rather existential and psychologizing tone, proceeds on the assumption that Calvin's words, set against a generalized background of the Renaissance, are context enough for a discussion of Calvin's life and thought. Indeed, Bouwsma often appears so concerned to portray Calvin against a nontheological humanistic background that Calvin's theology and his relation to the theological tradition disappear from Bouwsma's roster of significant issues in Calvin's life. Although ostensibly "biographical," the book virtually ignores issues of the chronology and the immediate historical context of Calvin's works. In contrast, moreover, to the method and approach of researchers in the history of exegesis, Bouwsma makes no comparisons of Calvin's thought with the earlier exegetical tradition—and thereby places himself on very unsure ground when he moves from the more seemingly existential comments that Calvin makes on various texts in Scripture to the conclusion that Calvin had thereby bared his soul to the public. Such a conclusion cannot be reached legitimately without examination of other exegetes' readings of the same text—or, indeed, without consideration of the text itself. Bouwsma's method leaves us with the distinct possibility that some of the more "existential" statements found in Calvin's commentaries and sermons may in fact lay bare the soul of Nicholas of Lyra or some other medieval exegete, rather than the soul of John Calvin! In addition, Bouwsma's reading of Calvin's text and his identification of fundamental motifs in Calvin's thought tends to proceed from broad concepts generated by Bouwsma against the generalized "anxiety" of the age, rather than from the texts as set into their actual literary and historical context—with the result that the generalizations do not often conform to Calvin's actual usage.

It might be objected that this critique of the methods and assumptions of much earlier scholarship and the strictly historical and contextual approach advocated here make impossible any significant understanding of Calvin's impact or potential impact on the theology of the twentieth century. Response to such an objection may take two directions. First, it is arguable that a failure to approach Calvin's thought from the perspective of its historical context converts any attempt to assess its impact on the present into an essay in deconstruction. The historical task necessarily precedes the systematic and, moreover, retains its integrity through an independence from the systematic task.[32] Second, contemporary theologians who desire historical and textual accuracy in their representations of Christian doctrine need to be prepared to acknowledge that, on any given point, Calvin may have no direct influence and, indeed, no clear relevance to contemporary discussion. In any case, the genuine usefulness of Calvin's thought to the present can be assessed only when his thought is rightly understood.

Locating the Historical Calvin: A Glance at Some Alternatives

A series of works published since the late 1980s by rather diverse authors and from fairly diverse perspectives have all, in one way or another, attempted to reach into the sixteenth-century context of Calvin's thought for clues to its direction and intention. The contrast between these studies and those works in which the dogmatic models prevail is significant. By way of example, studies of Calvin by Steinmetz, Schreiner, Thompson, Lane, and Millet, albeit quite different in their choice of specific subjects, are united in offering a detailed contextual approach to their subject, intended specifically to understand Calvin in and through the intellectual currents of the sixteenth century, rather than to impose twentieth-century theological concerns on the past. Even when these studies examine particular doctrines, they cannot be classed as primarily dogmatic analyses.

Thus, Steinmetz, Schreiner, and Thompson have raised the issue of Calvin's exegetical context and have indicated more thoroughly and fully than was done before the medieval as well as the patristic roots of Calvin's biblical interpretations.[33] In these studies, the originality of Calvin's exegesis is not merely asserted globally but demonstrated with precision, through the examination of Calvin's predecessors, while at the same time claims for the breadth and scope of his originality have been reduced through the recognition that, more often than not, Calvin worked with and reflected the exegetical tradition of the church. Lane has closely examined texts used by Calvin in order to evaluate Calvin's much-vaunted interest in and use of Bernard of Clairvaux, and he has also studied the way in which the Reformers complied and used handbooks or anthologies of patristic citations in their work.[34] And Millet's vast and erudite study of Calvin's rhetoric documents at a level previously unattempted the close relationship between Calvin's theology of the Word and his humanist understanding of the dynamics of language—in the context of a detailed discussion of the rhetorical tradition and the contemporary rhetorical training on which Calvin drew.[35]

Whereas exegetical, theological, and rhetorical or methodological studies of Calvin against his medieval and humanistic background serve to locate him in historical context, studies of the various forms of his thought, notably the commentaries and the sermons, serve to locate him in the immediate context of his own theological project—as either dogmatic analyses of the *Institutes* or harmonistic studies of the theology of the *Institutes*, commentaries, and treatises cannot. Here we note not only the exegetical analyses mentioned in the preceding paragraphs but also work on Calvin's sermons as a distinct source of his thought. The sermons become a focus of interest, particularly in cases where they reveal interests or present issues not as easily identified or developed from his other works.[36] The publication of previously unpublished sermons and the location of several volumes of the "lost" sermons of Calvin has also stimulated interest in the homiletical aspects of his theology,[37] often accompanied by a sense of the way in which Calvin's approach to the biblical text in his sermons can illuminate his expository and exegetical work—particularly by way of contrast with his commentary or lecture on the same text.[38] Armstrong has made the important point that Calvin's sermons were so central to his life-work that their style and content must also be examined as central to our understanding of his theology.[39]

Of course, these approaches to Calvin are not without antecedent: nearly all of these writers have profited from the superb presentation of Calvin's thought by Wendel,[40] which offers a richly historical and contextual approach to Calvin's thought and, therefore, a significant alternative to dogmatic essays like Niesel's *Theology of Calvin*. So, too, does the contextual approach draw on the very careful text-studies of Calvin done earlier in this century by Lefranc, Pannier, and Benoit.[41] There have been studies of Calvin's use of patristic and medieval sources,[42] and there have been earlier studies of Calvin's style and rhetoric, albeit none so rich in its sense of context as Millet.[43] In addition, as Oberman has recently pointed out, there are also clear antecedents for the interest in the history of exegesis evidenced in several of the works just noted.[44] The point of this initial exercise in defining the task is, thus, not to claim an utterly new direction for Calvin studies but to acknowledge and then to follow useful precedents— while at the same time to identify and then avoid the cul de sac of various unfruitful accommodations of Calvin's thought to contemporary interests.

Among these approaches—the textual, rhetorical, and exegetical—it is perhaps the exegetical approach that most easily exemplifies the shift in perspective that overcomes the accommodation of Calvin's thought to twentieth-century interests and concerns. As Steinmetz has pointed out, the primary significance of a carefully contextualized examination of issues in the history of "precritical" biblical exegesis may well be, quite simply, the recognition that precritical exegesis is fundamentally different in its method and assumptions from modern, "critical," or "historical-critical" exegesis.[45] Before the close examination of Calvin's actual exegetical practice in the context of the exegetical efforts of his contemporaries and in the context, also, of the medieval background to Calvin's conclusions about particular texts, it was all too easy to draw a generalized picture of Calvin's understanding of the Bible that enlisted him as an antagonist of all things medieval and as a clear predecessor of the historical-critical method. This problematic reading of his work is evident in many of the older essays on Calvin's exegesis and in a few more recent works as well. So, too, unless Calvin's actual patterns of approach to biblical texts are placed in their sixteenth-century exegetical and dogmatic context, it becomes all to easy to accommodate his view of Scripture to a neo-orthodox or Barthian notion of the Bible as a "witness" to the Word.[46]

The alteration of perspective evident in the textual and rhetorical study of Calvin has a less direct but no less significant impact on the study of Calvin's theology. Lane not only offers us a clearer understanding of Calvin's use of the writings of Bernard of Clairvaux but also provides us with a perspective on the way in which Calvin actually approached and learned from medieval and patristic authors. Not only does Lane identify with some certainty precisely which florilegia and editions of Bernard's work Calvin examined; he also demonstrates that Calvin came to the substantive use of Bernard fairly late in his development and that, far from being a general admirer of Bernard's theology, Calvin remained quite selective in his appropriation of ideas and materials. Lane's findings confirm Ganoczy's arguments concerning the relatively late development of Calvin's knowledge of medieval theology.[47] The overly optimistic assumption, characteristic of the work of Reuter and of Torrance, that, from the beginning of his career, Calvin had a profound and detailed acquaintance with the medieval tradition[48] is, therefore, to be set aside—and a picture emerges of a Calvin who learned his theology in the act of writing it over the course of decades. This conclusion, in turn, militates against the harmonistic reading of Calvin's theology found in the doctrinal or dogmatic studies noted earlier and demands an alternative approach. Calvin's theology must be read in its development in dialogue with the past and with his contemporaries.

Millet also provides Calvin studies with a series of insights and details that demand an altered paradigm for the examination of Calvin's thought. Whereas earlier works by Breen, Willis, and Bouwsma tend to present Calvin against a generalized background of humanistic rhetoric and to use the humanistic connection as a facile argument for severing Calvin's relationship to scholastic or, in Bouwsma's case, systematic theology,[49] Millet provides a highly specified context of early sixteenth-century rhetoric against which to examine Calvin's thought and, very precisely, indicates how the tools of rhetoric were placed at the service of theology in Calvin's writings, particularly in the *Institutes*. Like Lane, Millet presses on us the importance of Calvin's actual sources and antecedents and, in addition, confirms the need to examine Calvin's use of the technical language of rhetoric in order to establish clearly the form taken by Calvin's work.

At issue here is also the relationship between what might restrictively be called "Calvin studies" and the broader realm of specialized works dealing with such issues as the continuity between the Middle Ages, Renaissance, and Reformation. The study of Calvin, in other words, must take into consideration developments in the analysis of scholasticism and humanism, in the study of the progress of rhetoric in the sixteenth century, and in the broader field of the history of biblical interpretation. This consideration, as implied earlier, must examine not only influence but also context and what has been called the theological or exegetical "conversation" in which Calvin was engaged—understanding "context" as a broader issue than "influence" and "conversation" as, if not a narrower, certainly a more specified one.[50]

The "context" of Calvin's thought includes the works and ideas of individuals whose works Calvin most probably did not read, but whose thought, by way of its impact on the culture, on theology, philosophy or rhetoric, exegesis, method, and so forth, not only stands in the background of Calvin's thought but also frames it significantly. By way of example, medieval scholasticism (although the identity and nature of Calvin's actual sources still elude us) must be considered as part of the context within which Calvin's thought evolved. The late medieval debate over the relationship of Scripture and tradition, whether or not Calvin ever read the works of Wessel Gansfort or John Pupper of Goch, frames Calvin's understanding of the issue. So, too, the medieval, Renaissance, and early Reformation exegetical tradition—the writers to whom Calvin so often refers obliquely as "some" (*quidam*), in agreement and disagreement—is part of Calvin's context, as is the late medieval and Renaissance revision of rhetoric and logic. Works like Denis the Carthusian's *Enarrationes* on the Pentateuch, which Calvin never cites but may have read as a source of medieval exegetical and theological opinion, and Rudolph Agricola's *De inventione*, which he probably did know, are examples of "set pieces" that define the context.[51]

The theological and exegetical "conversation" in which Calvin was involved is far more specified than the issue of "context." It is at times exceedingly clear from Calvin's prefaces and from references in the text of his letters as well as his printed works that his theology was constructed in dialogue with certain thinkers and certain books. Calvin sought advice and counsel from Farel, Viret, and Bucer. He engaged in extended discussions with Bullinger and Melanchthon. He framed his exegetical method with specific reference to the alternative approaches of Bucer, Melanchthon, Bullinger, and others. As I hope to show, there is also a mass of evidence that Calvin engaged in an ongoing methodological dialogue with Melanchthon's theology, quite distinct from their major disagreement on the issue of human free choice and election. This conversation included, moreover, not only living authors: Calvin's exegetical and rhetorical work engaged the medieval tradition and classical rhetorical texts like Cicero and Quintilian, whose writings he had ready to hand.[52] The point of identifying this relationship to other authors as a "conversation" is to emphasize that Calvin did not merely cite, use, and agree or disagree with these thinkers but rather developed his thought in an ongoing exercise of learning from and, in some cases, with them.

The Unaccommodated Calvin: A Prospectus

The essays in this volume are all concerned with understanding Calvin in his sixteenth-century context, with attention to the continuities and discontinuities between his thought and that of predecesors, contemporaries, and successors. In several of the essays, the exegetical context of Calvin's thought is examined and, in virtually all of the essays, some attempt is made to analyze the interplay between theological and philosophical themes common to Calvin and the medieval doctors and developments in rhetoric and argument associated with humanism. All of the chapters are interwoven. In addition to the themes that distinguish the chapters, there are also more or less unifying themes that recur throughout the book and that could, perhaps, have been brought together into relatively independent essays—such as the relationship between Calvin and Melanchthon. Nonetheless, each chapter is intended to offer an argument that can stand on its own and that can be accessed independent of the other chapters. Hence, there is necessarily a greater degree of repetition of certain themes than some might desire.

I have endeavored throughout to examine Calvin's text in its sixteenth-century context. The title of the resulting book, suggested to me by colleagues, points toward my own encounter with a Calvin who does not fit neatly into the dogmatic, existential, or psychological paradigms of much twentieth-century scholarship. Nor does this Calvin fit into the all-too-neat approach of those scholars who juxtapose categories like "scholastic theologian" and "humanist rhetor" and then demand that Calvin be wedged into one or the other. The sixteenth-century Calvin, the Calvin who was born Catholic, whose theology was learned primarily in and through his work as a commentator and Reformer, whose work evidences the impact of humanist philology and rhetoric, of patristic study, but also, both positively and negatively, of the categories of medieval scholastic thought, and whose conclusions, together with those of a group of contemporary Reformed and Lutheran thinkers, became a basis for much of later Protestant theology—this Calvin cannot easily be accommodated to the needs and desires of modern Barthians or Schleiermacherians. Nor does this Calvin admit of intellectual or psychological bifurcation along the lines of twentieth-century prejudice. A reading of

Calvin's thought in its sixteenth-century context, in other words, yields the picture of a theology at once intriguing and intractible to twentieth-century concerns. This intractible and unaccommodated Calvin is important to our historical understanding in direct proportion to the level of distortion found in several generations of modern dogmatic analysis of his thought.

Part I, "Perspectives on Calvin's Text" (chapters 2–5), moves beyond the critical burden of this introductory chapter to a discussion of Calvin's own view of his theological task as presented in the prefaces and "arguments" to a series of his works. The section then moves on to analyses of three issues that confront the modern reader of Calvin's *Institutes*: first, the scholastic past of sixteenth-century theology with specific reference to the difficulty of defining Calvin's relationship to an older theology, in which he was not schooled, for which he expressed a pointed distaste, and to which he was nonetheless often indebted. Then, we examine the understanding of Calvin's *Institutes* in the sixteenth century, as evidenced in the efforts of his colleagues, contemporaries, and successors to provide a suitable apparatus for the understanding and use of Calvin's text. Here we see also the confluence of humanism and scholasticism in sixteenth-century theology. It is one of the premises of this study that, if it is possible to claim for a humanist scholar like Erasmus a relative isolation from as well as antipathy to scholastic theology,[53] the problem of the relationship and tension between humanist and scholastic method becomes increasingly complex as we move out of the world of the philologist into the province of the theologian-exegete. Finally, this section glances at the literary, humanistic setting of the *Institutes* by way of a critique of Bouwsma's biography of Calvin.

Accordingly, chapter 2 frames and defines the task of the volume as a whole by examining a series of major prefaces written by Calvin throughout his career. Particular attention is given to the content and thrust of the early prefaces inasmuch as they offer precise indications of the project that Calvin, early on in his life, designed for himself and then, with astonishing stamina and intensity, maintained for the remainder of his life. The prefaces point, certainly, toward the humanist aspects of Calvin's work—whether the closely defined method of the commentaries, the philological and rhetorical learning presumed by his varied tasks, the critical advocacy of the *locus* method, or the careful attention to questions of literary genre in the identification of the various forms of his work.

Among the accommodations of Calvin's thought to twentieth-century perspectives we must rank the tendency to identify Calvin as a humanist rhetor in isolation from scholastic, dogmatic, and what can only be called "systematic" concerns—as if Calvin can be saved from the scholastic past and detached from the increasingly scholastic future of Reformed theology in the sixteenth century.[54] We point, therefore, (in chapter 3) toward the scholastic background of Calvin's thought—without, however, setting aside the profound impact of humanist logic and rhetoric on his teaching. Specific attention is given to the way in which the scholastic and the Aristotelian elements in Calvin's theology are frequently mediated to him in his examination of the exegetical tradition. Calvin's explicit distaste for "scholastic" theology and for Aristotle is thereby balanced against his use and appropriation, often without comment, of materials that are both scholastic and Aristotelian. Here, too, the blending of humanistic methods in rhetoric and philology with nominally scholastic materials is evident.

The fourth chapter deals with a very specific point of continuity between Calvin's thought and the thought of his immediate successors: their understanding of the *Institutes* as framed by its elaborate sixteenth-century apparatus. One of the themes that links this essay to all of the following chapters is the understanding of the *Institutes*, present in this older apparatus, as a set of theological *loci* and *disputationes*. Here the methods of humanist logic and rhetoric, in a line of fairly continuous development from the methods of scholasticism, are transmitted to Calvin's successors. The underlying methodological point of the essay concerns the character of continuities that link the medieval, Reformation, and post-Reformation eras: continuity is not to be measured by precise reproduction, discontinuity by change; rather, both continuity and discontinuity need to be assessed in terms of the development of traditions in method and in teaching and in terms of the awareness and use of various streams of thought in one's predecessors by later generations. In this particular case, the apparatus of the *Institutes* points toward a keen awareness of the method, structure, and implication of Calvin's thought on the part of his succesors. Once again, we address one of the modern accommodations of Calvin—this time with regard to the reception of the *Institutes* itself, which has been determined, in the "critical" editions, by the mentality of modern text editors and, in the translations, by the neo-orthodox theological assumptions of the authors of modern subheadings and discursive footnotes.[55] The sixteenth-century apparatus offers a dramatically different perspective on Calvin's thought.

Chapter 5 looks in detail into the language of the "abyss" and the "labyrinth" found in Calvin's writings, in order to test the claims of Bouwsma's biography of Calvin but also for the sake of pointing toward other, potentially more significant, language used by Calvin in the exposition of his theology. Here, again, we raise the issue of the humanist context of Calvin's work, now with specific reference to a pair of literary *topoi* common in the usage of Calvin's time (viz., the "abyss" and the "labyrinth"). Both metaphors illustrate the literary side of the humanistic *ad fontes* and, in particular, point toward a primary stylistic characteristic of Calvin's Latin *Institutes* to which we will return in the eighth chapter: Calvin's assumption that his learned audience will recognize, without any explanatory citation, a host of references from classical and biblical literature—whether the biblical chaos imagery of the *abyssus* or *tehom* and the classical mythic imagery of the labyrinth of Knossos, of Theseus and the Minotaur, or, more generally, the vast number of biblical allusions not identified by Calvin (albeit noted, for the sake of our biblically illiterate age, by several generations of accommodating modern editors).

The four chapters of part II (chapters 4–9) are united by the theme of the place and significance of the *Institutes* in Calvin's theological program. Indeed, although examination of the *Institutes* is a focus of all four chapters, the thrust of their argument is to place the *Institutes* alongside the commentaries and sermons and to argue both its dependence and its intrinsic relationship to the central task that Calvin had appointed for himself, that of biblical commentator. If the *Institutes* is a theological system, it is not a theological system that was ever intended to have a function independent of the work of exegesis. Nor was it ever intended to take the place of the commentaries as a synopsis of all theological points made by Calvin in the course of his exegesis.

Accordingly, the sixth essay takes us to the question of Calvin's method. Although quite sympathetic to the thought that Calvin was indeed a systematic theologian, the essay offers no solace to the dogmatic student of the *Institutes* and resists the accommodation of sixteenth-century theological form and method to modern understandings of theological system, particularly as they have been brought to bear on the question of whether Calvin was a "systematic theologian." The essay places Calvin's *Institutes* into the context of the methods of the sixteenth century, namely the gathering of *loci communes* and *disputationes*, and makes a case, based both on Calvin's preface to the 1539 *Institutes* and on textual evidence within the *Institutes*, not only that this sixteenth-century method was used by Calvin in the composition of his theological system but also that Calvin selected this method in the light of his life-work as commentator on the text of Scripture.

Chapter 7 continues the theme of the method and arrangement of the *Institutes* with specific reference to the crucial expansions of the text that took place between 1539 and 1559. Central to the argument of the chapter is the place of Melanchthon in the sixteenth-century context of Calvin's theological formulation. Here, too, the importance of the 1539 *Institutes* to the understanding of Calvin's impact on his contemporaries is outlined, as is the character and carefully conceived "Pauline" ordering principle added to the structure of the 1539 edition.

The eighth essay, "*Fontes argumentorum* and *capita doctrinae*" (Sources of argument and heads of doctrine), provides further discussion of Calvin's method, now in its application to specific texts and to the theological result of exegesis in *loci* and *disputationes*. This essay also raises the issue of the editorial techniques and the apparatus developed by modern editors and translators of the *Institutes* that have often obscured the actual nature of Calvin's work and created barriers to a full understanding of the interrelationship between the *Institutes* and Calvin's other work, notably his work as an exegete.

Chapter 9 reviews a single issue in Calvin's theology in the hope of applying some of the fruits of research in previous chapters to a theological or doctrinal analysis of Calvin's teaching on faith. The problem of dogmatic accommodations of Calvin's theology remains in focus, particularly in the critique of Kendall's discussion of Calvin on faith and assurance: Kendall's intention, laden with theological agenda, was to pose the "intellectualist" Calvin against his "voluntarist" successors, without ever asking what precisely "intellectualism" and "voluntarism" could indicate in and for the background and context of Calvin's thought. In addition, the essay attempts to put into practice an analysis of Calvin's thought in the light of the interrelation of commentaries, sermons, and the *Institutes*—in other words, to illustrate one of the underlying theses of the book.

The epilogue returns to theme of the proper way of approach to Calvin's thought in an effort to gather together the methodological issues raised in the preceding chapters. More explicitly here than in the preceding chapters, we take up the issue of debate between the older scholarship, with its strong theological tendency, and the newer scholarship and its varied trajectories of reappraisal. At the heart of the chapter is a series of premises or proposals intended to define and to further the task of examining Calvin's thought in its proper context.[56]

■ P A R T   I ■

PERSPECTIVES ON CALVIN'S TEXT

Of Prefaces, "Arguments," and Letters to the Reader

Calvin's Testimonies to His Intention and Method

In Search of Calvin's Intention and Method

Although the broad contours and even the day-to-day activities of Calvin's life are well documented, and although we know a great deal, from his vast correspondence, about the issues and individuals, the debates and personal trials that concerned Calvin throughout his life, even to the extent of identifying personal likes and dislikes, tribulations of career, and digestive problems, we know little from his writings of the inward or "existential" life of the Reformer. Calvin was not a man to tell much about himself. The autobiographical comments that we have from him are few and sometimes difficult to interpret.[1] References to contemporary events found in his sermons are rare, and, when they can be identified, they tend to be oblique.[2] Even Calvin's letters to close friends tend to discuss matters of significance concerning the reform, Geneva, theological disputes, and so forth, and only seldom do they meditate on purely personal matters. The crises of calling and worries about direction of which Calvin writes to his closest colleagues—notably Farel and Viret—are hardly testimonies to Calvin's ongoing psychological state.[3] Nor do we have from the pens of his friends and companions any documentation even slightly reminiscent of Luther's Table-talk.[4] Those, therefore, who attempt to reconstruct the trials and tribulations or to identify inward bifurcations of Calvin's psyche from the similies and metaphors chosen by Calvin to illustrate his arguments or from the seemingly "existential" comments that appear here and there throughout Calvin's writings run the risk that, as was said of Adolph Harnack, they will peer down the well of history and see their own faces reflected back at them. The problem becomes particularly intense when the modern mind seeks out "motifs" in the writings of Calvin or a Melanchthon—such as references to abysses and labyrinths—and then anachronistically assumes that mention of such things carries with it a psychological freight in the sixteenth century that parallels twentieth-century usage.[5]

This problem of sources and materials ought not, however, to surprise us greatly. It is Luther who is the great exception to the rule of sixteenth-century documentation. Unlike their nineteenth- and twentieth-century descendants, the people of the sixteenth century did not understand the individual ego or psyche as the primary locus of meaning in their world.[6] Their writings tell us a great deal about what and how they thought concerning significant issues in their world—but the twistings and turnings of personal biography or of inward personal struggle were seldom understood as so significant. And, given that most of Calvin's productive life was spent in the creation of a framework for the reform of the church, whether intellectual, social, or political, we ought not to be surprised that his writings address these and not personal matters. In this he is little different from Bullinger, Musculus, Melanchthon, Vermigli, or other of his contemporaries involved in work similar to his own.

Calvin, however, did leave a series of precise and careful descriptions of his life-work and his chosen methods. His early *Letter to All Those Who Love Jesus Christ* (1535) offers a perspective on the history of redemption that identifies central issues in Calvin's theology that would not only remain significant to Calvin in later years but that would be definitive of his view of the theological task.[7] Similarly, Calvin's prefatory letter to the reader, affixed to the Latin versions of the *Institutes* from 1539 on and the "argument" prefaced to the French *Institutes* (1541–57),[8] together with the preface to his Romans commentary of 1540 offer insight into the exegetical and theological agenda that Calvin undertook at quite an early age and prosecuted with remarkable consistency until his death in 1564. So, too, from the perspective of the apologetic task itself as distinct from method, does his 1536 letter to Francis I identify directions and purposes in his work.[9] There are occasional remarks concerning method in the prefatory materials to various of Calvin's theological treatises, and the prefaces to the *Harmony of the Evangelists*, Psalms, Isaiah, Genesis, Daniel, and the *Harmony of the Four Last Books of Moses* are notable for the insight they offer into the methods and directions taken by Calvin's later writings. The preface to Calvin's *Commentary upon the Book of Psalms* is of particular importance because it so intimately combines a few biographical details with a survey of Calvin's work.[10]

From Basel to Geneva: Letters and Prefaces of 1532–1536

Calvin's earliest published writing and, therefore, his earliest published prefatory exercise is the commentary on Seneca's *De clementia* (1532).[11] Although scholars still debate its relationship to his "conversion," the commentary on *De clementia* and its preface not only mark Calvin's debut as a writer, but also offer evidence of a series of themes that belong to Calvin's entire life-work, whether or not he was converted to the reform of the church in 1532. Should it be the case, as many have argued, that the conversion occurred after the writing of the commentary, then the work bears witness to the elements of humanistic method that carried over into Calvin's later career and that remained at the foundations of his method, despite his theological critique of other elements of the humanist program. First, Calvin praises the "unlabored" style of Seneca's prose but criticizes his subject's "luxurious verbosity." In addition, Calvin notes a lack of "orderly arrangement" or proper *dispositio* in the work, a characteristic of great importance to him in his own literary efforts.[12] Proper *dispositio* and right *ordo* or *via* would remain Calvin's recommendation for a suitable *methodus* through the abysses, labyrinths, and "thorny places" encountered by scholars, theologians, and laity alike.

In a letter most probably written in 1534 from the home of his friend Du Tillet in Angoulême, Calvin identifies his health and relative repose as an "inducement" to keep him "continually mindful to cultivate those common pursuits of study for the sake of which so great a value is put upon me."[13] Yet another letter from 1534 or early 1535, written after Calvin's arrival in Basel, documents his two earliest writings and offers some insight into his sense of theological method: Calvin responds to the criticisms of Christopher Fabri concerning a draft of his *Psychopannychia*, noting that additions have been made and, more important, that the whole treatise has been recast in "an altogether different form and method." In the same letter, Calvin speaks of "an essay . . . given to Olivetan to read" that contained "first thoughts . . . thrown together in the shape of memoranda" but not fully "digested after any definite and certain method."[14] Calvin's language here is important: his initial exercise in the draft essay sent to Olivetan followed the humanistic pedagogy of gathering topics in a book of memoranda or *loci communes*,[15] prior to the task of finding a proper *methodus* or "way through" the materials.[16] The "essay" sent to Olivetan could be a draft of the *Institutes*, but, in view of Calvin's involvement in the production of Olivetan's French translation of the Bible, also noted in the letter to Fabri, the more likely candidate is his *Épitre à tous amateurs de Jésus-Christ*. Interest in a proper *methodus* appears, significantly, in Calvin's comment on both documents.

Calvin's often-neglected *Épitre a tous amateurs de Jésus-Christ*, "Letter to All Those Who Love Jesus Christ," rightly stands at the head of any gathering of the theologically and methodologically significant prefaces penned by the Reformer. The letter was written as a preface to the New Testament of Olivetan's French Bible, published in Neufchâtel in 1535, and stands as the earliest printed work by Calvin in French and his earliest published theological treatise.[17] The text of the letter presents a survey of salvation-history from the creation of human beings according to the image of God to the coming of Christ in the New Testament, in which Calvin's theology parallels Bullinger's earlier treatise on the covenant.[18] Calvin continues by indicating the application of the promises to believers:

> All these things are announced, manifested, written, and sealed in this [New] Testament: through Jesus Christ we are made heirs of kingdom of God his Father, and [through Jesus Christ] he declares his will, as a testator to his heirs, that it might be executed. For we are all called to this inheritance without respect of persons, male or female, small or great, servant or lord, master or disciple, clergy or laity, Jew or Greek, French or Latin, no one shall be rejected who, by a sure pledge, receives what has been sent to him and embraces what had been given to him, in short, who acknowledges Jesus Christ as the one who has been given by the Father.[19]

There is little directly revealed here of Calvin personally other than the vibrancy of his biblical piety,[20] but much can be elicited concerning the focus of his understanding of

Scripture on the historical plan of salvation as witnessed in the unity of the two testaments. Nor is it without significance that the sole explicit biblical reference in the letter is to Paul's Epistle to the Romans. Romans provides ground for the assumption that God has never left his fallen world "without testimony"—not even among "those on whom he has bestowed no knowledge of his word"—inasmuch as he has "engraved" on the very substance of the universe "the splendor of his power, goodness, wisdom, and eternity."[21] The earth resounds, Calvin continues, with testimonies of the greatness of God—nor was God "content" with this general revelation: "in order more fully to reveal his infinite goodness and mercy . . . he especially caused a particular people to hear his voice . . . and by his good will and free grace elected and selected [esleu and choisy] them from among all the nations of the earth."[22]

We have, thus, from Calvin's earliest major preface, a glimpse of significant directions that his thought would take and, probably, a pointer toward his first choice of a biblical book for major expository consideration: Calvin's emphasis on the fullness of salvation-history adumbrates his lifelong task as an expositor of nearly the whole of Scripture. In a highly stylized sense, Calvin's *Épitre* as a whole could be argued to follow out the order of topics in Romans from general revelation and the problem of sin to the historic promise of redemption and the salvation of the elect. This focus on the Epistle to the Romans points directly toward the beginning of his exegetical task and obliquely toward topics in the later editions of the *Institutes*. So, too, we encounter the soteriological theme of grace and election, so central to his thought, and the theme of salvation-history that he would express in the language of the unity and distinction of the testaments, in his hermeneutical approach to such issues as Christology and the kingdom of God in his exegesis, and in the covenantal interest evidenced primarily in his commentaries and sermons. Nor, we add, was the significance of Calvin's presentation of salvation-history lost on his successors: the *Épitre à aux tous amateurs de Jesus-Christ* appears in Genevan Bibles of the seventeenth century as "Preface monstrant comment Christ est la fin de la loi: par Maistre Iean Calvin."[23]

The context and purpose of the first edition of the *Institutes* received Calvin's specific attention in two documents separated by the space of some twenty years—the prefatory letter to Francis I written for the first edition of the *Institutes* and the preface to the *Commentary upon the Psalms*. Dedication of a Protestant theological essay to the king of France had the precedent of Guillaume Farel's *Sommaire et briefve déclaration d'aucuns lieux fort nécessaire à ung chascun chrestien pour mettre sa confinace en Dieu et ayder son prochaine* (Basel, 1525) and Huldrych Zwingli's *De vera et falsa religione commentarius* (1525).[24] The letter to Francis I was also viewed by Calvin as a document significant enough in its own right to merit separate publication: he accordingly translated it into French and published it as his *Epistre au treschrestien roy de France, Francoys premier de ce nom: en laquelle sont demonstreés les causes dont procedent les troubles qui sont auiourd'huy en l'Eglise*, at approximately the same time that he issued the first French edition of the *Institutes*.[25] The letter was also included by Calvin in all succeeding editions of the *Institutes*, both Latin and French.

Nor should it be at all surprising that the letter to Francis I remained an integral part of the *Institutes*, despite the somewhat different historical and theological context of the later editions: a large portion of the text of the 1536 *Institutes* remained in the later editions, and virtually the entire text of 1539 is preserved, with only minor editorial adjustment, in the 1559 edition. Calvin edited and, indeed, developed his thought primarily by augmentation. Of course, it is simply not correct that Calvin did not edit the text of the letter as he edited the text of the *Institutes*.[26] If Calvin did not alter the text of the letter to the extent that he altered and augmented the *Institutes* as a whole, he certainly did make changes, some to the length of a paragraph, others consisting merely in the addition of a word or two of clarification. The most substantive changes date from the 1539 edition of the *Institutes*, although some significant editing also occurred in 1543. Calvin, however, left the early date (1535/36) at the conclusion of the address, offering no indication at this point that there had been changes in the later editions.[27] One suspects that the relative stability of the text of the letter derives more from its genre than from its content: introductory *argumenta* and letters to readers in general are as readily alterable as text, whereas a letter addressed to an individual, whether sent by post or placed at the beginning of a book, would presumably not be as subject to broad changes and restructurings, particularly after the death of the addressee in 1547.

In the preface to his *Commentary upon the Psalms*, the only major personal statement from the Reformer's pen,[28] Calvin notes the autobiographical context in which the first edition of the *Institutes* arose: he had fled both notoriety and persecution, had left his homeland and had found himself an "obscure corner" in Basel in which to pursue his scholarly work. In the background to this flight was not only the rising threat of persecution but also Calvin's own beginnings as a teacher following his "unexpected conversion" to the Protestant cause: as it became known that the young Calvin was increasingly adept at the explanation of Christian doctrine, many of those "who had any desire after purer doctrine were continually coming to [him] to learn." In his shyness, Calvin had initially fled this acclaim as well. News from France of persecution and of the burning of Protestants reached Basel, where, Calvin continues, profound "indignation was kindled against the authors of such tyranny."[29] In response, the French persecutors and their allies circulated pamphlets identifying the objects of the persecution as "Anabaptists and seditious persons, who, by their perverse ravings and false opinions, were overthrowing not only religion but also all civil order." The intention of the pamphlets, quite clear to Calvin but hidden from the sight of the citizens of Basel and of Germany, was to mask "the disgrace of shedding so much innocent blood" and to make it possible for further persecution of "the poor saints" to occur "without exciting compassion towards them in the breasts of any."[30]

At this juncture, Calvin recognized that further silence on his part would indicate both "cowardice and treachery." "This," he continues, "was the consideration which induced me to publish my Institute of the Christian Religion."[31] Calvin follows these comments with the most concise and probably the clearest statement that we have anywhere in his writings concerning the purpose of the 1536 *Institutes*:

My objects were, first, to prove that these reports were false and calumnious, and thus to vindicate my brethren, whose death was precious in the sight of the Lord; and next, that as the same cruelties might very soon after be exercised against many unhappy individuals, foreign nations might be touched with at least some compassion towards them and solicitude about them. When it was published, it was not that copious and labored work which it now is, but only a small treatise containing a summary of the principal truths of the Christian religion; and it was published with no other design than that men might know what was the faith held by those whom I saw basely and wickedly defamed. . . . That my object was not to acquire fame, appeared from this, that immediately after I left Basle, and particularly from the fact that nobody there knew that I was the author.[32]

These remarks are confirmed from the time of the first edition of the *Institutes* by Calvin's own dedicatory letter to Francis I of France—although it is clear that Calvin had the fundamental instructional or catechetical task of the first edition of the *Institutes* more clearly before him at the time that he first set pen to paper than he did later on, in retrospect. He notes that his initial intention had not been to present the result of his labors to the king: "my purpose was solely to transmit certain rudiments by which those who are touched with any zeal for religion might be shaped to true godliness . . . especially . . . our French countrymen, very many of whom I saw to be hungering and thirsting for Christ."[33] The comment comports well with his later acknowledgement that fame was never his object: a catechetical manual outlining the faith, first published anonymously, served Calvin's purpose better than a life of public instruction: "the book itself witnesses," he continues, "that this was my intention, adapted as it is to a simple and, you may say, elementary form of teaching."[34] In addition, the initial comment indicates that Calvin had begun to compose the *Institutes* as a catechetical manual some time before his decision to address the volume to Francis I and that the apologetic thrust of the address was in fact secondary to the original intention of the document.[35]

Calvin thus seems already to have begun his project when he became aware of "the fury of certain wicked persons" in France directed against his reformatory countrymen. This fury, he continues, had "prevailed so far" that there seemed to be "no place for sound doctrine" in all of France.

> Consequently, it seemed to me that I sould be doing something worthwhile if I both gave instruction to them and made confession before you with the same work. From this you may learn the nature of the doctrine against which those madmen burn who today disturb your realm with fire and sword. And indeed I shall not fear to confess that here is contained almost the sum of that very doctrine which they shout must be punished by prison, and fire, and be exterminated on land and sea. . . . But with what right has it been condemned? Now the very stronghold of [our] defense was not to disavow this very doctrine but to uphold it as true.[36]

Calvin's letter to Francis I reflects this fundamentally apologetic intention but also makes clear the basic, positive instructional purpose of the *Institutes*, a purpose that would increasingly dominate Calvin's approach to and recasting of the work.[37] By contrast, Calvin's preface to the Psalms commentary recognizes, if tangentially, what the *Institutes* had become—no longer a "small treatise" offering a "summary of the principle truths of the Christian religion" but a work that, to use a favored humanist term, was now a "copious" treatise expressing the larger, richer frame of Christian teaching.

It is entirely possible, therefore, that Calvin altered his design at a very early stage in the writing of the *Institutes*: what may have begun as a purely instructional exercise became an apologetic treatise.[38] Some justification of this perspective may be drawn from Calvin's catechetical *Instruction et confession de foy* of 1537, translated into Latin in 1538 as *Catechismus, sive christianae religionis institutio,* a work that not only reflects the 1536 *Institutes* in its title but also draws on it for its content.[39] In any case, Calvin's instructional or "catechetical" intention yielded not a typical catechism in the 1536 *Institutes* but a somewhat more elaborate expository form of instruction, lacking the question-and-answer form of shorter catechisms and considerably longer than Luther's *Large Catechism.* At the same time, Calvin's catechetical impulse did produce an alternative to the larger form of the *Institutes* in the two catechisms of 1537–38—albeit still not the brief question-and-answer form of catechisms for the young.[40]

Prefaces and *Argumenta,* 1538–41: Strasbourg and the Inception of a Program

Calvin's ejection from Geneva and his subsequent stay in Strasbourg provided him with a brief respite from the intense ecclesial and political struggles of Geneva and, in that respite, a time for thought and literary composition that would not only give clearer direction to his career as as Reformer but also ensure his place among the major formulators of Protestant theology. This is not to say that Calvin's stay in Strasbourg was without deep concerns, even tribulations, but, as his letters from those years reveal, his perturbation, particularly concerning his calling, took place in a context in which his ministry was well received, his pen productive, and his engagement with other Reformers, whether in Strasbourg itself or at the Diet of Worms in 1540, fruitful.[41] Much of the concern over calling, moreover, came toward the end of his stay in Strasbourg as the Genevan church implored him to return.[42]

A revealing comment is found in a letter of 1540 from Calvin to Farel: Calvin comments on the renewed call from Geneva and wonders to "what avail will be the exertions of a single individual, hampered by so many . . . hindrances on every side?" He then contrasts this memory of his Genevan experience with his work in Strasbourg: "here . . . I have only to take the oversight of a few, and the greater number hear me, not so much as a pastor, as with the attention and reverence due to an instructor."[43] It does not take a great stretch of the imagination to relate this esteem for the work of an instructor in the faith in the French congregation at Strasbourg to Calvin's work as a commentator and to his recasting of the *Institutes.*

From this time at Strasbourg we have Calvin's preface to a projected edition of the sermons of John Chrysostom.[44] Here Calvin writes of the importance of making Scripture available to all people and, after having stressed the primary role of the Holy Spirit in the understanding and interpretation of Scripture, notes the usefulness of various interpretive "instruments" (*instrumenta*) or "supports" (*adminicula*). Calvin's own purpose in making available the sermons of Chrysostom is "to pave a path (*viam sternere*) to the reading of sacred Scripture for the unskilled and uneducated."[45] The advantage of Chrysostom's sermons is not only their "straightforward," nonallegorical approach to the "genuine, simple sense" of the text but also their method—which is a "continuous exposition" that explains each verse. The sole major problem posed by Chrysostom for Christians is his "excessive" interest in human free choice, a tendency that Calvin explains on the basis of the problematic philosophies of Chrysostom's day.[46] Of interest here is Calvin's sense of the need for a "path" or "way,"[47] a theme that would be echoed in the 1539 *Institutes*, and his preference for a commentary that not only looked to the "genuine" and "simple" sense of the text but also offered a "continuous exposition," themes that Calvin would take up in his own work, as emphasized in his 1540 preface to the Romans commentary.

Calvin's prefaces to the 1539 *Institutes* and the 1540 *Commentaries on the Epistle to the Romans* not only were written in close temporal proximity to each other but also reflect similar concerns. Indeed, Calvin's prefaces to the two major editions of the *Institutes* (Latin, 1539; French, 1541) and to the commentary on Romans (1540) should be regarded as an interrelated set of statements concerning not only the method he chose to follow in his work but also the program of writing that he began with the 1539 *Institutes* and the Romans commentary—the program that he followed, with little alteration, for the remainder of his life. The relationship between Calvin's letter to the reader from the 1539 *Institutes* and the preface to his 1540 Romans commentary is particularly significant: in the latter Calvin argued forcefully the rectitude of his adoption of the form of a running commentary on the text of the Bible without recourse to the logical and methodological device of identifying the *loci* or *topoi* addressed by the biblical authors in the course of their argument, while in the former, he noted that his *Institutes*, as recast in 1539, was to be constructed in such a way as to relieve him of the necessity of developing either *loci communes* or *disputationes* as part of his approach to the text in his commentaries.[48] Given, moreover, his critique of Bucer and Bullinger for placing *loci* into their commentaries after they had provided a running exegesis of the text and his critique of Melanchthon for offering only the *loci* and not the running commentary, the thrust of the two prefaces is not to disparage the work of gathering *loci* as part of the process of biblical interpretation but rather promote the establishment of a proper division of labor.[49]

Once the division of labor and Calvin's positive assessment of the *locus* method is rightly understood, then the full significance of his differences with Bucer and Melanchthon becomes clear as well. On the one hand, Calvin countered Bucer's rather burdensome style with his emphasis on *brevitas* and *facilitas*. Calvin's method would hold to the text but would do so expeditiously.[50] Yet, like Bucer and like Bullinger as well, Calvin would comment on the whole text, for, in reserving his *loci* for the *Institutes*, Calvin also assumed, against Melanchthon, that the commentator had more to do than analyze the text rhetorically and elicit the topics. Indeed, the chief task of the commentator was to examine the entire text of Scripture, not omitting a single verse.[51] This approach to the text was to be characteristic not only of Calvin's early commentaries but of his entire exegetical and homiletical output. In addition, as Wengert points out, the divergent Melanchthonian and Calvinian approaches to the task of commentator have significant hermeneutical and theological implications and result in major differences in theological result between the two thinkers.[52]

Not to be ignored, once the significance of the methodological language of Calvin's opening letters has been registered, is the *argumentum* placed by Calvin at the beginning of his exposition of the Epistle to the Romans. We see here another dimension of Calvin's approach both to the text of Scripture and to theological formulation. His humanistic training pressed him to understand that the preliminary identification of the *argumentum, dispositio, scopus*, or *methodus* of a text was integral to the work of interpretation. In the case of the *argumentum* of the Epistle to the Romans, Calvin offers his readers the initial insight, which he held in profound agreement with Melanchthon, that "the entire Epistle is so methodically arranged" that it is a model of the art of rhetoric and dialectic.[53] The understanding of this Epistle, given its excellence in substance and arrangement, provides the proper "entrance . . . to all the most hidden treasures of Scripture."[54]

We have here, in a nutshell, Calvin's theological method: the running exposition of the biblical text in commentary and sermon, coupled with the elicitation of theological *loci* from the text and the gathering of those *loci* together with the important dogmatic *disputationes* of Calvin's time into the form of a basic instruction or *institutio* in theology. In practice, Calvin's pattern of homiletical exposition would differ from the method followed in the commentaries: whereas the commentaries held to the model of *brevitas* and *facilitas*, the sermons tended toward a more amplificatory model of oratory, often reaching three or four times the length of the comment on the same text and drawing on more collateral texts for the sake of broader hortatory, topical, and polemical development.[55] All that needs to be added is the theme of establishing the right order of expression or teaching, the *ordo recte dicendi* and the *methodus* or *via*,[56] according to which the *loci* would be organized—and that emphasis also appears in the 1539 *Institutes*, as does Calvin's development of a Pauline ordering of topics in conjunction with the original catechetical order.[57] So, too, in 1539, could Calvin state that "the arrangement of divine wisdom" was so "ordered and disposed" that it evidenced a most "beautiful agreement among all its parts."[58] The identification and exposition of that order and disposition can be identified as the "systematic" aspect of Calvin's method in the *Institutes*,[59] but it is clearly an aspect of his larger method, in which the topical and organizational drive cannot be separated from the exegetical effort.

Calvin's training in humanist rhetoric and dialectic exerts a pervasive influence over the form and methodological direction of these prefaces. This influence is clear in Calvin's concern for proper method, in his rhetorical focus on *persuasio* rather than *demonstratio*, in his quite specific interest in the presentation of *loci communes*, and in his very strict observance of the boundaries of literary genre—characteristics of hs work to which we will return frequently in the following chapters. It can even be argued that much of Calvin's dispute with Melanchthon's method arose out of the issue of literary genre: to Calvin's mind, a *commentarius*, strictly defined, was a running analysis of an entire text consisting in brief annotations and explanations, unencumbered by digressions or expansions. From this perspective, Melanchthon's "commentaries," given their refusal to comment on the entire text and their emphasis on the identification of *loci*, were in bad form.[60] Nevertheless, it is certainly both an unwise and a partial explanation of Calvin's thought to imply, as several recent essays have done, that Calvin's authorial identity is somehow entirely exhausted by descriptions of him as a Christian humanist rhetor, or that his theology is virtually entirely an exercise in rhetorical piety.[61] This confuses the vehicle with its cargo and, moreover, offers an incomplete picture of the vehicle.

Parker comments that these developments of 1539–40 belong to Calvin's lifelong search "for the form that would best express his theology."[62] In 1539, Parker continues, Calvin "abandoned" the catechetical form of the first edition of his *Institutes* for the form that he would use for two decades: "in spite of its freshness and brilliance, in spite

of the clarity and certainty of its French translation, this edition only narrowly escaped
being a set of unrelated *loci communes*."[63] Calvin certainly did not intend to "escape"
from writing a set of *loci communes*—this appears to have been his precise intention,
perhaps under the inspiration of the greatly developed 1536 edition of Melanchthon's
Loci communes theologici, a work not available for his examination during the preparation
of the first edition of the *Institutes*.

What Calvin did escape, as Parker well recognizes, was the creation of an "unrelated"
set of *loci*—but neither the original contents of the *Institutes* nor the probable Melanchthonian model for the 1539 revision would have guided Calvin away from the use
of broad themes to bind his essay together on a larger scale.[64] Indeed, Melanchthon
had indicated in his analysis of the rhetorical flow of Romans that, "since the best mode
of interpretation is to reveal the disposition of the speech, we have discussed the order
of all the topics, propositions, and arguments. . . ."[65] Melanchthon also had made an
explicit connection in his 1532 Romans commentary between his discussion of topics
in the commentary and his development of the doctrinal topics in the *Loci communes
theologici*.[66] The point, in fact, adumbrates Calvin's comment in the 1539 *Institutes* to
the effect that one ought not to look in his commentaries for *loci communes*—albeit,
in critique of Melanchthon, Calvin drew the line of distinction between *commentarius*
and *loci communes* far more sharply.

The methodology and program of Calvin's work is made still clearer by the alterations he made in his Latin letter to the reader in his process of transforming it into a
formal "argument" for the French translation of 1541. Any reader of the 1541 *Argument*
will note close parallels in structure and phraseology to the "letter to the reader" from
the 1539 Latin *Institutio*. The subject matter of the Latin letter and that of the latter
half of the French "argument" are virtually identical. Thus, in the letter Calvin speaks
of the contents of the *Institutes* and then notes that "if, after this road . . . has been
paved . . . I shall publish any detailed expositions of Scripture, I shall always condense
them, because I shall have no need to undertake long dogmatic disputations, or to
wander about in the basic topics." In the "argument" from 1541, he writes "if our
Lord gives me the means and opportunity to write commentaries, I will use the greatest
brevity of which I am capable: for it will not be necessary to make long digressions,
inasmuch as I have here treated at length almost all of the articles that belong to
Christianity." In the letter he indicates that the *Institutes* should help to "prepare and
instruct candidates in sacred theology for the reading of the divine Word" inasmuch as
it has "embraced the sum of religion in all its parts," and in the "argument" he states
that his work is, first, "a summary of Christian doctrine" and, second "a profitable
point of entry into the reading of both the Old and New Testaments."[67]

Whereas the thrust of the French "argument" parallels closely that of the Latin
"letter," particularly when one looks to the initial form of the letter in the 1539 *Institutio*, the literary genre of the "argument" is somewhat different from that of the
"letter"—just as the "argument" reflects Calvin's rhetorical sensitivity to the difference
between the French and the Latin *Institutes*. Both essays serve as prefatory statements
to prospective readers intended to display in brief the purpose and content of the book,
but the "argument" stands as a somewhat more formal introduction. Rather than trace
the movement of the work from its early, shorter form, to the expanded form of 1539,
Calvin presents the work as an established text that has proved its value in one venue,

now offered to a new audience. He acknowledges the perfection of teaching in Scripture but notes the need for instruction, particularly for novices. His purpose, he continues, was to present "the doctrine of salvation" first in Latin for the learned people of all nations and now to offer the same teaching in such a way as to "bear fruit in our French nation."[68] The 1541 "argument," stands, in short, as an alternative to and also a replacement of the "letter" and bears the same relationship to the 1541 and the subsequent French editions that the "letter" bears to the 1539 and subsequent Latin editions.

The "argument," moreover, also signals the relative independence of the developing French text from the Latin: although the 1541 translation generally follows the Latin text of 1539, there are occasional differences in arrangement of text and slight alterations of content. There are also points at which the 1541 French reflects not the emended Latin text of 1539 but the original Latin of 1536, indicating that Calvin may have begun the translation of the *Institutes* before he completed the 1539 Latin text—a thesis probably confirmed by a letter to François Daniel dating from 1536.[69] In addition, in many places where Calvin is clearly working from the 1539 Latin, the 1541 French text offers considerable augmentation and explanation, often intended to accommodate the text to an audience both more pious and less erudite than his Latin readers.[70] One cannot simply follow the text and the paragraphing of the 1539 text and expect to find an identical flow of material in the French. And, whereas the "argument" is reproduced verbatim in the subsequent French editions of 1545, 1554, and 1557, there was no attempt made to transfer it to the Latin editions of 1543, 1550ff., and 1559. The reason that the "argument" never appeared in a Latin version of the *Institutes* is clear: it was written specifically for the French versions and intended to replace and parallel the "letter to the reader" of 1539. Just as all of the Latin texts from 1539 on offer first the letter, then the address to Francis I, and then the text of the *Institutes*, so do all the French editions from 1541 to 1557 offer first the "argument," then the address to Francis I, followed by the text of the *Institutes*.[71]

In Geneva, 1541–1559: The Implementation of Calvin's Design

The prefaces and *argumenta* written after 1541 offer a series of brief, sometimes oblique, but nonetheless significant comments on Calvin's sense of direction. A letter to Viret from 1542 counsels that all "unreasonable" teaching be set aside and that one ought not "to complicate by ambiguous and obscure language what requires the utmost lucidity and perspicuity."[72] The dedicatory epistle of his commentary on Titus (1549), addressed to Farel and Viret, formally acknowledges Calvin's indebtedness to them and his sense of a profound bond among them arising from their common task. He also compares them to Paul, himself to Titus: as Titus finished the work begun by Paul in Crete, it has been his task to to take up and complete in Geneva the work begun by his dear colleagues.[73] So also does Calvin dedicate his commentary on I Thessalonians (1550) to Mathurin Cordier, from whom he learned the "true method of teaching" that prepared him for his later work.[74]

At the very beginning of the *argumentum* to his commentary on I Corinthians (1546), Calvin comments that "the advantages of this epistle are various and manifold, for it contains many significant topics (*insignos loci*), the handling of which successively in their order will show how necessary they are to be known."[75] We have here, surely, a reflection of the 1539–41 prefaces and their critical interest in Melanchthon's method. At the end of the *argumentum*, Calvin reiterates his point: the epistle is most "profitable" for Christians inasmuch as it presents "disputations on so many important topics" (*multis praeclaris locis disputationes*).[76] The topics and their order: Calvin's common ground with Melanchthon again is clear—although, as he declared in the prefaces of 1539 and 1540, he will isolate and develop no theological topics in the commentary itself: his interest in the commentary is in the exposition of the *loci* understood as *fontes*—sources or grounds of argument—not in the amplification of the *loci* into full *loci communes*.[77]

More explicit is Calvin's preface to the treatise on free choice against Pighius: the work as a whole is dedicated to Melanchthon. On the one hand the preface signals the beginning of Calvin's personal debate with Melanchthon over the latter's synergistic leanings: Calvin here praised Melanchthon for his defense of the truth, only to receive a firmly worded notice of their differences in a reply from Melanchthon.[78] On the other hand, and at much greater length, Calvin grounds the dedication in their common intention to defend the truth in a "clear and open manner" free from "pretense and sophistry" and extraneous embellishment. This, Calvin, comments, has always been the central characteristic of Melanchthon's work.[79]

This indication of a common interest is also surely reflected in Calvin's prefatory recommendation of the French translation of Melanchthon's *Loci communes theologici* into French.[80] Calvin there praises Melanchthon as a scholar and as a Christian, indicating that, had the volume been printed in Latin, any introductory letter would have been superfluous, indeed, presumptuous. Part of Calvin's rationale for providing the prefatory latter refects the logic of his own *Argument du livre* in the 1541 French *Institution*: the author, Calvin comments, is renowned among "les gens de lettres" but remains unknown "among those of our nation who have never received instruction in the schools." It therefore "seemed expedient," Calvin continues, to apprise potential readers of "the fruit that they might gather from the present volume" in order to encourage them to study it carefully. Perhaps most striking, particularly given Calvin's feelings on the matter and the intensity of his epistolary critique of Melanchthon, is the restraint with which he notes his differences with Melanchthon over predestination.[81]

The years immediately preceding the 1550 *Institutes* were marked by a significant shift in Calvin's homiletical endeavor: his preaching was regularized, and, in 1549, Denis Raguenier began the work of transcribing the sermons. This transition from unrecorded to recorded preaching may have led Calvin to meditate on his style of exposition: in a letter of 1549, he criticized Farel for having an "involved" and "tedious" style and also noted, perhaps to soften the criticism, that he was quite dissatisfied with Augustine's style as well, given its prolixity. Calvin then comments, "perhaps my style, in the meantine, is overconcise."[82] The comment ought not to be taken as a proposal of prolixity as an antidote to the treasured *perspicua brevitas* of the early commentaries. Yet it is the case that the sermons transcribed by Raguenier and his successors evidence a rhetorical copiousness quite distinct from the style of the commentaries—and the later commentaries themselves did become increasingly elaborate.

Several of the prefatory essays from this time are of importance to an understanding of developments in Calvin's theology and method. The commentary on Isaiah bears two dedicatory letters (the first, from 1551, addressed to Edward VI of England, the second, from the second edition of 1559, to Elizabeth I) and a preface on the nature and character of Isaiah's prophecy. As Calvin indicated in his preface to Queen Elizabeth, he had taken "so much care and industry" in his revisions that the second edition "ought justly to be reckoned a new work."[83] Apart from his revision and augmentation of the Romans commentary, this was the only time that Calvin saw fit to pause in his progress through the text to make substantial revision—in this case because he had initially only superintended the editing of Des Gallars's transcription of his lectures. Indeed, Calvin had indicated to Dryander that the "composition" was actually the work of Des Gallars, who "jots down to my dictation and arranges his materials afterwards at home."[84]

Calvin not only offers here a clear testimony to his sense of the direct address of Old Testament prophecy to the church, he also indicates his understanding of the prophets as expositors of the Law as "a perpetual rule for the church . . . to be observed in every succeding age." Understood in the larger sense, as transcending the chronological bounds of the Old Testament Israel, the Law is to be understood as "the doctrine of life," the "threatenings and promises," and "the covenant of grace."[85] The point reflects conclusions that Calvin had already drawn in his 1539 discussion of the Old and New Testaments and in various additions made at that time to his presentation of the Law; the same point is also reflected in the augmentations Calvin made to these sections of the *Institutes* in 1559.[86]

The prefaces or *argumenta* to the commentaries on John (1553) and on the Gospel harmony (1555) also provide significant insight into Calvin's approach to scripture and theology. For, although Calvin recognized that the Johannine account could not be easily conflated with that of the three other Gospels, he believed that God had "dictated to the four Evangelists what they should write, in such a manner that, while each had his own part assigned to him, the whole might be collected into one body." Given this divinely established relationship between the four accounts, Calvin continued, "it is now our duty to blend the Four by a mutual relation, so that we may permit ourselves to be taught by all of them, as by one mouth."[87] Right order of exposition, here as in the *Institutes* and confessional declarations,[88] provides clarity and better inculcates the message of the Gospels. What is more, the order in which Calvin did his exegesis and produced the two commentaries paralleled his understanding of their theological relationship:

> As to John being placed the fourth in order, it was done on account of the time when he wrote; but in reading them, a different order would be more advantageous, which is, that when we wish to read in Matthew and the others, that Christ was given to us by the Father, we should first learn from John the purpose for which he was manifested.[89]

Calvin's perspective is precisely the reverse of Bucer's, in that the Strasbourg Reformer understood his commentary on John as supplementary to the more exhaustive treatment of theological questions raised in his harmony of the Synoptic Gospels.[90]

The issue of order and the clarity it offers appears from another perspective in Calvin's prefatory remarks to the treatise against Westphal, published in 1556: here Calvin laments not only the inability of the Reformed and Lutherans to come to any agreement but also the lack of clarity brought on by ill-organized polemic. In this very treatise, Calvin indicates, it had been his desire "to pursue the point directly, and to treat it with a minimum of digression," but his opponent's haphazard method prevents the more lucid approach of a regular "order." Calvin resigns himself to a rebuttal of Westphal following the outlines of the latter's treatise—but, by way of preface, he first offers an orderly synopsis of the problem at issue.[91] The point is interesting not only in view of Calvin's stress on an *ordo recte docendi* but also in view of his exchange with Beza in 1552 over the method followed in Calvin's second response to Pighius: Beza had criticized Calvin for following Pighius' text rather than the logic of his own argument.[92] Here, Calvin attempted to rectify the problem.

The sermons on Psalm 119, preached in 1553 and published in French in 1554,[93] offer important documentation of Calvin's understanding of the central purpose of biblical exposition—what he called in his commentary on 2 Timothy "instruction in the shaping of life," energized by "exhortations and reproofs."[94] The prefatory letter to "faithful readers," perhaps not by Calvin himself, indicates the transition from pulpit and transcript to printed form: "by way of a full recommendation, as much of the author as of the book, I hope for nothing less than the same fruitful result among those who will read [these sermons] in the future than has already been gathered by those who have already seen them." The book has been produced because "there are some people who prefer to have such books as can be easily carried about in the hand," and this particular book had the virtue of providing a "lively meditation . . . on the holy law and good will of God" without "vain repetitions."[95] The text of the sermons reinforces the theme by emphasizing the pedagogical nature of the Psalm, constucted as it was, in an acrostic on the Hebrew alphabet, an "ABC" of God's law to be used for edification in the "school of God."[96]

Calvin's preface to his Psalms commentary of 1557 not only presents the crucial biographical materials already noted but also contains several significant notices of its author's method. He writes, in the first place, for the "edification of the church," by which he means "all the people of God," and not merely those versed in theology. To this end, Calvin proposes to examine the ways in which the Psalms can instruct Christians in prayer, right worship, and Christian life.[97] Inasmuch as Calvin assumed, consistently, the direct address of the text to the people of God, the pattern of his exposition often reflects a movement from exposition of the text to the particular lesson inculcated by the text for Christian belief or practice,[98] albeit never in the form of digression from the flow of the text for the sake of developing a topic or *locus*.

In commenting at some length on the Psalms as offering models for prayer, Calvin indicates that teachings on "the true method of praying will be found scattered throughout the whole" of his commentary and that he will pause only briefly in his preface to indicate the various points of discussion: he will not, in other words, gather together any *loci* either in the preface or in the commentary itself.[99] The dual task of running exposition of text in the commentary over against exposition of *loci* in the *Institutes* remains in the forefront of his method. So, too, at the very end of his preface, Calvin notes that he has "observed . . . a simple style of teaching" and has "generally abstained from refuting the opinions of others" in the course of his exposition: the *facilitas* advocated at the beginning of his career remains a prominent value, and the *disputationes*, like the *loci*, will be placed elsewhere.[100] Calvin did not, however, take the occasion of these methodological comments to echo his 1540 preface to the Romans commentary and offer a less than favorable critique of the work of other exegetes—in fact, Calvin offers warm praise of Bucer's work on the Psalter and indicates his respect for Musculus' commentary, despite the predilection of both these exegetes for the presentation of theological *loci* in the text of the commentary.[101]

Prefaces, Letters, and *Argumenta*, 1559–1564: Refinements and Modifications

In the modified form of his letter to the reader, edited in 1559 for the final edition of the *Institutes*, Calvin noted that, after the second edition of 1539, he had "enriched" the text with "additions" in each new printing. He then commented that he did not "regret the labor spent" on these augmentations of the text but that nonetheless he "was never satisifed until the work had been arranged in the order now set forth."[102] Just as the 1539 edition of the *Institutes* had marked a major alteration and solidification of direction, so did the 1559 edition indicate for Calvin a point of fruition: the organization of the text now finally fulfilled the more dogmatic intention of the 1539 shift from catechetical manual to a set of theological *loci* presented in close relation to Calvin's exegetical project. His somewhat self-deprecating comments about the augmentations of 1543 and 1550 indicate that Calvin had been sensitive to the loss of form occasioned by the addition of topical sections generated by his work as an exegete and polemicist from the time of his fundamental recasting of the *Institutes* in 1539 to the final revisions of 1559. The text of 1539 marked a clear departure from the style and shape of a catechetical manual, but neither in 1543 nor in 1550 had Calvin worried greatly about the overall shape of the book—he had simply augmented the text as necessitated by his other concerns. In 1559, however, he considered the whole, specifically, the whole in view of what it had become by way of massive augmentation, and, for the first time since 1539, attended to the question of the outline or *ordo* of the work.

The French translation of 1560, now fairly universally recognized to be Calvin's own work,[103] represents Calvin's first (and, of course, final) attempt to bring the texts of his Latin and French *Institutes* into full harmony with each other. The French text now follows the organization of the Latin, while the Latin text, for the first time, incorporates several of the substantial additions made independently to the French. Perhaps the clearest sign of Calvin's coordination of the two texts is his treatment of the prefatory material in the French: the 1541 *Argument* is missing from the French text of 1560, and we are presented, for the first time, with a translation of the emended "letter to the reader." Calvin offers no explanation for this change—and one would not expect him to. But the rationale for the change is probably quite clear. The 1541, 1545, 1554, and 1557 French editions had a relative independence from the Latin text—with 1545, 1554, and 1557 building on the French of 1541 by making additions in parallel, but also in addition, to those made in the Latin augmentation of 1550.[104] The 1560 French translation, however, conformed the French text almost exactly to the text, the marginalia, and the index of the 1559 Latin.[105] And Calvin had edited and augmented his letter to the reader considerably for the 1559 Latin edition. Thus, by translating the augmented "letter to the reader" and by supplying at the end of the French text of 1560 a French version of the Colladon index to the 1559 Latin,[106] Calvin saw to the establishment of the French version of his great work in precisely that form and "order" with which his "letter to the reader," as of 1559, had expressed such full satisfaction. Unfortunately, the 1541 "argument" stood in relation to a form that had now been superseded, and it passed out of use even in subsequent sixteenth-century editions of the French text.

In the year following the appearance of his final French *Institutes*, Calvin published his lectures on Daniel—accompanied by one of his more extended dedicatory epistles. We find here a backward glance at the homeland he had left some twenty-six years before, a clear conviction of the divine purpose behind his departure, and a profound hermeneutical meditation relating the prophesies of Daniel to the faith and life of his beloved countrymen. His absence from France, Calvin declares, has enabled him to pursue a life of study, and that has been an advantage to the faith of his countrymen. "The contemplation of this advantage," he continues, "has not only deprived my banishment of its sting, but has rendered it even pleasant and joyful."[107] Calvin, now nearing the end of his career, has been confirmed in his work, and he has clarified his initial intention and method. Specifically, in the case of these lectures, Calvin recounts what can only be called a personal, even existential, confirmation of his approach to the text of Scripture. He identifies a distinct parallel between the situation of God's people related in the book of Daniel and the situation of God's people in France: the French kingdom is, according to Calvin, "a region from which the truth of God, pure religion, and the doctrine of eternal salvation are banished, and the very kingdom of Christ laid prostrate," while the book of Daniel offers a "mirror" reflecting to the French the way in which "God proves the faith of his people . . . by various trials, and how with wonderful wisdom he has taken care to strengthen their minds by ancient examples."[108] Both in France and in the history of Daniel, God has given over "the choicest flower of his elect . . . to extreme calamity"—so that, as "the goodness of God shines forth at the close of this tragedy," it also can "arm us with invincible confidence."[109] After a lengthy, nearly apocalyptic declamation against ungodly rulers and the evils of the papacy, Calvin declares, "the similarity of the times adapts [Daniel's] predictions to ourselves, and fits them for our own use."[110] Therefore, Calvin concludes, "remember that your course has been defined by a heavenly Master of the contest, whose laws you must obey the more cheerfully, since he will supply you with strength unto the end."[111]

We have here a classic statement of one of Calvin's underlying interpretive principles—the direct speech of Scripture to the living church. Calvin makes the point explicit: "the prophet, then, not only animates us to hope and patience, but adds an exhortation dictated by the Spirit, which extends to the whole reign of Christ, and is applicable to us."[112] This conviction of the direct address of the text to the church relates immediately to Calvin's entire task: it animates his preaching, it fuels his exegesis, and it is the engine that generates theological *loci* in his exegetical encounter with the text.[113]

Calvin began work on his massive *Harmony of the Four Last Books of Moses* in 1559, at about the same time that he was preparing the final edition of the *Institutes* and his

Commentary on the Minor Prophets for the press. Whereas the *Commentary on the Minor Prophets* does not contain a methodologically significant preface, the *Harmony* most certainly does—and if the juxtaposition of the preface to the *Harmony* with the preface to the 1559 *Institutes* is not nearly as striking in result as the juxtaposition of Calvin's prefaces to Romans and to the 1539 *Institutes*, there are still some important lessons to be learned concerning Calvin's theological trajectory by an examination of the preface to the *Harmony* as it fits into the theological context defined (at least in part) by the most mature version of the *Institutes*.[114]

Calvin begins his preface to the *Harmony* with a sentiment much like the one expressed in his earlier *Harmony of the Evangelists*: he worries that some of his readers might object to the harmonizing approach.[115] Here, however, in the exposition of the Pentateuch, the problem was somewhat more intense: most exegetes recognized that the need for comparative examination of the evangelists, and Bucer in particular, had offered Calvin a significant precedent, but, in the case of the Pentateuch, there was little precedent and not nearly as much parallel or duplication of material. In addition, whereas a harmony of the Evangelists could easily echo the basic order of the narrative of Matthew, Mark, and Luke, a harmony of the last four books of Moses would need to depart fairly radically from the order and arrangement of the Pentateuch. Calvin notes that he has not "inconsiderately . . . altered the order which the Holy Spirit himself has prescribed" but has only offered an aid to the "unpracticed reader" to facilitate the understanding of the object and plan of Moses' work. The biblical books ought still to be studied separately, as written.[116]

The pattern or *methodus* of Moses' teaching was, Calvin indicates, to offer both a "historical narrative" and a doctrinal instruction, the latter intended to inculcate "true piety, comprising faith and prayer," as well as "the fear and worship of God." This distinction between narrative and doctrine, although obvious in the content of the books, had not been observed by Moses, who neither presented the "history in a continuous form" nor offered the doctrine in a continuous discourse but "unconnectedly, as opportunity occurred."[117] If Calvin's description of Moses' doctrinal plan echoed Calvin's own project in the *Institutes*,[118] his approach to the problems of Moses' arrangement of materials echoed the old critique of Melanchthon's and Bucer's methods. Here was a series of biblical books presented as largely the work of a single author in which narrative and doctrinal topics were intermingled and in which the doctrinal topics were arranged not in a logical order for teaching but rather "as opportunity occurred" in the course of the narration. Calvin's own method virtually demanded that he offer a running commentary on the narrative and a separate commentary on the Mosaic doctrinal *loci*, presented, as nearly as possible, in an order suitable for teaching.

Two points, then, can be made by way of conclusion concerning Calvin's methodological development on the basis of Calvin's preface to his *Harmony on the Last Four Books of Moses*. First, Calvin's methodological premise of 1539–40 remains in force: he resists to the end any mingling of tasks. The running commentary on the *historia* or narrative sense of the text must not be mingled with the construction of theological *loci*, and neither task must give way to the other. Second, the presence of doctrinal topics in the Mosaic text itself leads Calvin to a variation on his own method: inasmuch as the *loci* are not Calvin's gatherings of texts or disputed issues in Calvin's own time, they can and must be dealt with as *loci* in the commentary. The exposition of materials prefatory to the law in Exodus and Deuteronomy, of the law itself, and of the promises and threats attached as sanctions to the law stands both parallel to and independent of the *Institutes*—indeed, it dwarfs the exposition of the law found in the *Institutes*.[119]

This presence of large-scale theological statement in the commentary may be regarded as the extension of a tendency already present in the commentaries on Psalms and Isaiah, in which the *facilitas* of Calvin's early method remains, but the *brevitas* is partially set aside. Yet, in one of the final dedicatory letters of Calvin's life, a letter of 1563 addressed to Henri Duc de Vendôme and placed at the head of the full edition of the commentary on the Pentateuch,[120] Calvin offers a somewhat existentially phrased description of his method that manifests consistency to the very end: given his failing health, he "preferred giving a succinct exposition to leaving a mutilated one behind," but he nonetheless took care not to "pass over" any difficult passages. Those who delight in "verbosity" should "seek some other master" than Calvin! There is what amounts to a last reference to the balance of his own method between different genres: "I do not see why one should complain of brevity, unless he wishes to derive his knowledge exclusively from commentaries."[121]

Perhaps the most striking conclusion imbedded in the comments on the intention and method of his theology in Calvin's prefaces and *argumenta* concerns the single-mindedness with which Calvin approached his task. Once he had been positioned, so to speak, in his theological and ministerial career, he set for himself a pattern of working that would guide him for the remainder of his life. This positioning, which can be identified at least in part with his decision to set aside plans for a life as a humanist studying, teaching, and editing classical texts, can surely be located during his exile in Strasbourg, in the contact with Bucer and Capito, and in the renewal of reformist energy associated with his *Letter to Sadoleto* and the decision to return to Geneva, and it can surely be confirmed in the profound and interrelated declarations of intention that appear in his prefaces of 1539 and 1540—his *Letter to the Reader* in the 1539 *Institutes* and his *Letter to Grynaeus* in the Romans commentary. The final documentation of this singleminded approach to the theological task and of the rigor with which Calvin carried it out can, of course, arise only out of an analysis of his actual practice throughout his career,[122] but the prefaces and *argumenta* offer a guide to the method itself and, as a group, testify to his fundamental intention.

Scholasticism in Calvin

A Question of Relation and Disjunction

The Problem of Calvin's Relationship to Scholasticism

Patterns in Scholarship

The name of John Calvin and the term "scholasticism" have seldom been stated positively in the same breath. The reasons for assuming a profoundly negative relationship between Calvin and the scholastic doctors of the Middle Ages literally abound on the pages of Calvin's *Institutes*, in the form of his running diatribe against the "schoolmen." Nonetheless, Calvin's theology—whether from the perspective of its methods or from the perspective of its contents—did not arise in a sixteenth-century vacuum. Not only did Calvin formulate his theology in distinct opposition to elements of late medieval and early sixteenth-century Roman Catholicism; he also quite subtly felt the influence of the medieval as well as the patristic past. It is worth recognizing from the outset that the Reformation altered comparatively few of the major *loci* of theology: the doctrines of justification, the sacraments, and the church received the greatest emphasis, while the doctrines of God, the trinity, creation, providence, predestination, and the last things were taken over by the magisterial Reformation virtually without alteration. In addition, many of the differences between the theological methods of the Reformation and those of the Middle Ages can be attributed to the development of logic and rhetoric and to their impact on the relatively stable *disputatio*, rather than to a vast rebellion in academic approach.[1]

As much recent scholarship has shown, moreover, the relationship of the Reformation to the eras immediately preceding and immediately following it cannot be reduced to a simple contrast between scholasticism and reform or scholasticism and humanism. The Reformation should not be reductionistically described as a humanistic phenomenon. Scholasticism or, more precisely, aspects of scholastic thought should not be viewed as incapable of rapprochement with aspects of humanist methods or, indeed, as contributing to the theological and methodological assumptions of an individual trained in the humanistic philology and dialectical method.[2] And, of course, these rapprochements and interrelationships occurred in the thought of the same "humanist" writers who took up their polemical cudgels against the "scholastics."[3] Nor can we discount the profound impact of the humanist method on the trajectory of scholasticism through the sixteenth century, particularly in terms of its gravitation toward the *locus* method. In Calvin's case, there is no absolute contradiction between his use of humanistic methods and his appropriation of elements of scholastic theology, nor are his attacks on the scholastics to be taken as creating a clear dichotomy between "humanism" and "scholasticism."

Thus, the frequently cited study by LaVallee comes to the still useful conclusion that Calvin perhaps "did not think of the Scholastics in terms of schools of thought" and that the generalized "scholastic theologian" of Calvin's critique is more likely than not a variety of late medieval nominalist such as Calvin might well have encountered around the edges of his education in Paris.[4] In addition, LaVallee concluded that the scholastic theologian of Calvin's critique is very much "the reversed image" of Calvin, very much a rhetorical foil for Calvin's positive exposition of the teachings of the Reformation—and he also offered a critique of the editorial practice of citing various scholastics in the apparatus of the *Institutes* without any clear indication that Calvin had read their works.[5] The more subtle question of continuities between Calvin's thought and medieval scholastic theology—particularly in those places where Calvin *does not* offer negative comments about the older theology but simply formulates a doctrinal point—was addressed in a massively erudite manner by Reuter, who points quite convincingly to elements of late medieval Scotistic and Augustinian thought, specifically in the works of John Major and Gregory of Rimini, that are parallel to Calvin's teaching.[6] Reuter's detailed study of the medieval background of Calvin's thought has, however, been criticized for its assumption that Calvin studied theology in Paris under John Major and had direct and positive access to late medieval scholastic theology from the beginning of his intellectual career. There was also a notable lack of medieval "Augustinian" material in the library of the Academy: one volume only of Gregory of Rimini (the commentary on *Sententiae* I and II), and nothing by either Giles of Rome or Thomas Bradwardine. So, too, of Scotus, only the commentary on the *Sentences* was held by the Academy, and there was nothing of Bonaventure.[7]

As LaVallee argued and as Ganoczy has clearly demonstrated, not only is it impossible to determine that Calvin studied with Major (indeed, the evidence points in the opposite direction); it is also not at all clear that Calvin's earliest theology evidences direct influence scholastic thought and method.[8] Reuter's response to Ganoczy has been subjected to almost microscopic scrutiny by Lane—with the result that the views of LaVallee and Ganoczy have been confirmed.[9] Thus, despite its insight into the positive relationship between Calvin's teaching and that of the medieval doctors, Reuter's work may not be able to identify either the definitive source of Calvin's inherent scholasticisms or their precise trajectory in and through Calvin's thought. Similarly, T. F. Torrance's occasionally insightful essay on Calvin's "hermeneutics" assumes as a basic premise of its argument the early positive connection with scholasticism by way of Major, with the result that the modified scholastic background and framework that it constructs for Calvin's theory of knowledge and interpretation lacks clear and demonstrable contact with Calvin's own work.[10] The scholastic influences remain, but their source or sources are obscure: whereas it is quite instructive to identify scholastic distinctions in Calvin's thought and then inquire into their medieval background, it is not useful—indeed, as Torrance's work demonstrates, it is quite perilous—to assume a particular late-medieval scholastic background and to understand Calvin's thought through its detailed and often technical language.

Recent essays by Steinmetz, Schreiner, Thompson, Oberman, and Faber have looked in detail at aspects of the scholastic background and at Calvin's dialogue with it.[11] On the one hand, all of these scholars have taken up the question of Calvin's encounter with several themes from Scotist and nominalist theology—notably the distinction between *potentia absoluta* (absolute power) and *potentia ordinata* (ordained power)— against a background of recent reappraisal of Scotism and nominalism, in which a theme of divine transcendence has been emphasized at the same time that the claim (found in older scholarship) that the language of *potentia absoluta* indicated an utterly arbitrary God.[12] On the other hand, all five have indicated that, despite the significant impact of Scotism on Calvin, the Reformer also distanced himself at crucial points from the older theology and rejected not only interpretations or abuses of scholastic distinctions but the some of the distinctions themselves.[13] Schreiner and Steinmetz have also indicated similarities and differences between Calvin's interpretation of select passages in Scripture and the Thomistic literal trajectory in medieval exegesis.[14] Actual sources have remained obscure, while, at the same time, a predominantly "Scotist-nominalist" background to Calvin's assumptions concerning divine transcendence and hiddenness has been identified alongside what can be called the "Thomistic" trajectory of literal exegesis. (We remember, of course, that the Franciscan Nicholas of Lyra also stands in this trajectory.[15]) In addition, more subtle relationships than scholarship has previously recognized have been outlined between Calvin's use, acceptance, or rejection of the terms and concepts from earlier theological tradition and their use by medieval theologians and exegetes.[16] An essay by Paul Helm, written from a theological and philosophical rather than from an exegetical perspective, draws on some of the conclusions of these exegetical studies and points toward continuities in the use of theological distinctions and definitions between the later Middle Ages, the Reformation, and the post-Reformation eras.[17]

Crucial in these last noted studies has been the increasing recognition on the part scholars of the Reformation that the theological polemics of the sixteenth and seventeenth centuries served to obscure the positive relationships that obtained between the thought of the Reformers and their genuine "forerunners" in the Middle Ages[18]—and, moreover, that these positive relationships are recoverable only when study is carried out in exegetical detail and, indeed, when the exegesis done by the Reformers is examined with a view to its antecedents. Thus, the positive relationships, as well as specific antagonisms, between the thought of the Reformers and their medieval predecessors appear quite clearly in examination of particular passages, such as Genesis 18:13; 25:29; Romans 9:19; and Isaiah 23:9 (with reference to the divine *potentia absoluta* and *potentia ordinata*);[19] Job 2:4; 23:1–7; 34:12 passim, with reference both to absolute power and *duplex iustitia*;[20] Exodus 3:14, with its traditionally "essentialist" reading of the divine "I am Who I am"; or Isaiah 28:21, on the basis of which medieval theologians made a distinction between the "proper" and the "alien" work of God. Still, the historiographical problem remains: given the varieties of late medieval theology and exegesis, the vagaries of polemical argument, and the absence of citation, precise sources and antecedents of the Reformers' thought—Calvin's in particular—frequently cannot be determined.

The Identification of "Scholasticism"

The problem of the relationship of scholasticism to Calvin (and to later Calvinism as well) is complicated, moreover, by the tendency of much twentieth-century Protestant theology and historiography to view scholasticism as a highly speculative and rationalistic system of thought bound to Aristotelianism and to certain specific theological and philosophical conclusions characteristic of the thirteenth, fourteenth, and fifteenth centuries, the primary goal of which was to produce a synthesis of Christian theology and Greek philosophy.[21] When, however, scholasticism is rightly defined as a dialectical method of the schools, historically rooted in the late patristic period, particularly in the thought of Augustine, and developed throughout the Middle Ages in the light of classical logic and rhetoric, constructed with a view to the authority of text and tradition, and devoted primarily to the exposition of Scripture and the theological topics that derive from it using the best available tools of exegesis, logic, and philosophy,[22] a rather different picture emerges. In other words, if we oblige the understanding (characteristic of generations of scholarly study of medieval thought) of "scholasticism" as a method that, in itself, did not necessarily prejudice theological conclusions, we are pressed to offer a series of qualifications. Some distinction becomes necessary between the relationship of the substance Calvin's thought to aspects of older theology (method notwithstanding) and the relationship of Calvin's expository methods to the methods used by the older theology.

So, too, the relationship between ideas and method must not be overlooked: recourse to the ideas of a particular thinker or thinkers may result, if only minimally, in some acceptance of the method through which the ideas were conveyed—or vice versa. One of the points of overlap between these issues of method and content is, of course, the use of distinctions: the scholastic method resolved problems and seeming contradictions by generating distinctions—and the use of these distinctions, in turn, affected the content of theology. Nonetheless, the caveat remains in force here as well: the acceptance of distinctions (like those between absolute and ordained power, proper and alien work, the decree and its execution, the sufficiency and efficiency of Christ's death) does influence content, primarily in terms of patterns of exposition and the identification of various subissues as identified by the distinction, but it *does not* determine the final result of an argument. All of the distinctions just noted fit as easily into Semi-Pelagian as into strict Augustinian argumentation or, in the era of the late Reformation, into Arminian as well as Reformed theology.[23]

An added incentive to join the discussion of Calvin and "scholasticism" comes to us from several generally neglected sources related to Calvin's own life and work. The first of these is the preface by Jean Budé to Calvin's lectures on the Minor Prophets, dated February 14, 1557. Budé writes,

> [Calvin] preferred to advance the edification and benefit of his hearers by eliciting the true sense and making it plain, rather than by vain pomp of words to delight the ears, or to regard ostentation and his own glory. I would not, at the same time, deny, but that these lectures were delivered more in the scholastic than in the oratorical style. If, however, this simple, though not rude, mode of speaking should offend any one, let him have recourse to the works of others, or of this author himself, especially those in which, being freed from the laws of the school, he appears no less the orator than the illustrious theologian.[24]

We see a similar usage in the *Statutes of the Genevan Academy*, written probably by Calvin, for its official establishment in 1559: the young *éscholiers* or *scholastici* are enjoined to study and then write out, every month, "positions that are neither curious nor sophistic, nor contain false doctrine."[25] Students in the Academy would study, in addition to their theological subjects, logic or dialectics, defined in the *Statutes* as "the classification of propositions," the identification of "figures" or rhetorical forms of "argument," and, more generally, as "the science of predications, categories, topics (or *loci*), and disputes (*elenchus*)." On the first Friday of each month, these budding Genevan *scholastici* would engage in formal theological disputation.[26] Beza's rectoral address, delivered at the formal inauguration of his tenure and of the newly constituted academy, also identifies the students as *scholastici* and defines the Academy as a place of "scholastic" learning, indeed, a *respublica scholastica*, or academic commonwealth.[27] Protestant writers of the Reformation era could use the term "scholastic" with favor—or at least not pejoratively—simply indicating their own academic exercise.

The reason for this usage is not that Beza and others were subtly reintroducing medieval scholasticism under the noses of their antischolastic colleagues—or that the usually antischolastic and humanistic Calvin gave in to dark scholastic urges as he devised the course of study for the Genevan Academy. Rather, Beza's—and Calvin's—positive references to "scholastics" are indications of one of the fundamental efforts of Renaissance humanism. What is at issue here is that the Latin noun for "school," *schola*, had not changed—nor had the Latin adjective applied to the things, attitudes, and persons associated with the school, *scholastica*. The Latin adjective *scholasticus* translates, quite simply, not as "scholastic" in any highly technical or restrictive sense, but as "academic"—with all of the positive and negative connotations that we today find in the word. Thus, *scholasticus* used to refer to "academic standards" or "academic method" has a positive sense, whereas the same term used to refer, for example, to "the merely academic theology that has no reference to faith and life" has a negative implication.

The sixteenth-century materials themselves point toward a dual use of the term "scholastic." On the one hand, it could refer to "school-theology" in the worst sense, a theology invested in academic quibbles, divorced from the needs of the Christian community, arcane and, as the humanistic mind of the Renaissance would add, barbaric in its use of language. On the other hand, however, the term could be (and was) used in a neutral sense, referring to the life of the academy, its classroom work, and its honored methods in discourse and argument.[28] Thus, there was certainly a sense, current in Calvin's own time and evidenced in Calvin's own writings, in which the term "scholastic" could be applied positively to the work of humanistically trained Reformers. Thus, finding a positive relationship between Calvin and things "scholastic" does not at all entail an unwillingness to take his polemic seriously—instead, it entails a willingness to examine both his negative and his positive uses of the term and, in addition, to examine Calvin's relationship to the scholasticism of the past and of his own present, particularly in those places where he uses its forms without mentioning it by name.

One aspect of the Renaissance humanist program, not without late medieval parallels, was the reform of the school and of student life, including a reform of the study of logic and disputation along classical lines.[29] So, too, the student dialogue or *colloquium scholasticum*, which had been a standard teaching form in the classical age and which had not entirely disappeared in the Middle Ages, experienced a major revival at the hands of Renaissance educators, notably in the *Colloquies* of Erasmus and Vives. Mathurin Cordier, Calvin's teacher in Latin at the Collège de la Marche and later one of the professors at the Academy in Geneva, published his own set of *Colloquia scholastica* in 1564.[30] So, too, does one find among the various academic orations of Melanchthon an *oration* in praise of the "scholastic life."[31] Humanism was not posed against all things scholastic. It was posed against scholastic problems, notably the absence of a refined use of classical languages and rhetoric that was rooted in the absence of sound philological training and against excessively speculative theological argument.[32]

This, too, is why the term "scholastic" gradually crept back into the prefaces and even the titles of Protestant theologies: it was the term universally recognized as denoting, in quite a neutral sense, the academic enterprise, not only of the Middle Ages but of the Renaissance and Reformation as well.[33] We ought, in fact, to reconsider our typical translation of the term *theologia scholastica* as it appears in the titles of sixteenth- and seventeenth-century Protestant works and render it not "scholastic theology" but "academic theology." By the end of the sixteenth century, the irony of the language had pressed various Protestant writers carefully to distinguish between a right-minded and rightly constructed Protestant "school theology" and a problematic, which is to say medieval, or Roman Catholic one—recognizing, at the same time, that not all and perhaps not even most of what the medieval scholastics had said was problematic.[34]

Scholasticism in Calvin: Relation and Disjunction

According to Ganoczy's measured conclusions, "the first edition of the *Institutes* reveals only a very limited and superficial knowledge of scholastic theologians," as indicated by Calvin's very unsystematic and polemical use of Lombard and Gratian. At an early stage in his development, Calvin evidences no knowledge of major scholastic theologians like Aquinas, Scotus, Occam, Gregory of Rimini, or Pierre d'Ailly and, indeed, no knowledge of the thought of John Major.[35] Ganoczy also argues that, both in style and in content, Calvin's references to Lombard and Gratian can be traced to his study of Luther, particularly of the German Reformer's *Babylonian Captivity of the Church*, rather than to a detailed study of the medieval writers. At an early stage in his thought, Calvin probably "assimilated—without knowing it—diverse elements of the scholastic system" through his reading of Luther. In addition, the scholastic philosophy, to which Calvin was most surely introduced in the basic course of study at the Collège de Montaigue, "contributed to the dialectical structure of Calvin's thought and indirectly to the elaboration of his theological doctrine." At the same time, however, "his conscious position was characterized from the start by an indignant refusal to accept this 'theology of the sophists.'"[36]

To this we may add that the study of philosophical matters by the identification of topic or *locus*, prevalent after the fifteenth-century work of Rudolf Agricola, together with the determination of conclusions through the process of academic disputation, also surely had its impact on Calvin. LaVallee quite convincingly hypothesized that Calvin studied scholastic theology privately after his conversion and that much of what Calvin knew came from contemporary Roman Catholic commentaries on the *Sentences* (in which, presumably, the opinions of major teachers of previous centuries were summarized).[37]

In addition, Calvin most certainly read medieval theology after 1536, and, we may hypothesize, he read more fully in the work of biblical commentators like Nicholas of Lyra and Denis the Carthusian than he did in the dogmatic writings of the period. This last hypothesis arises both from the character of Calvin's own work as primarily exegetical and from the indication of a greater interest in scholastic distinctions in relation to particular texts of Scripture (as evidenced by Calvin's commentaries) than in relation to the writing of theological *loci* and *disputationes* (as found in the *Institutes*).[38]

Calvin and Scholastic Method

If scholasticism is narrowly (and, I would argue, correctly) defined as a method, it remains the case that the medieval scholastics were able, by means of the method, to draw elements of biblical teaching, patristic theology, and classical philosophy together into a relatively coherent theological whole—and that, therefore, later theologians who had recourse to the method or to aspects of it (such as the use of *loci* and *disputationes* as forms of presentation and argument) also frequently absorbed elements of the older theology and philosophy along with its method. We must, therefore, be very careful in what we identify as scholastic: Calvin's positive use of the Aristotelian fourfold causality does not necessarily indicate that Calvin was scholastic or drew on aspects of scholasticism—though it does indicate a positive reflection in Calvin's theology of the thought-world of many of the medieval scholastics and a significant degree of continuity between the thought-world of the sixteenth-century Reformers and that of the medieval scholastics. In addition, it reveals a basis in Calvin's thought on which successors like Beza might develop a more overtly scholastic form of "Calvinism." At the methodological level, we point to Calvin's presentation in the *Institutes* of his *loci communes* and *disputationes dogmaticae* in which an *ordo recte docendi* was established[39]: here the parallel between the purpose of Calvin's *Institutes* and that of Lombard's *Sententiae in IV libris* is noteworthy.[40]

The pattern of argument in many of the chapters of the *Institutes*, moreover, reflects a fairly strict observation of the form of scholastic disputation, moving from the initial statement of a point to various objections and replies to objections. It is worth noting that this structure has often been obscured by the apparatus or lack of apparatus in modern editions of the *Institutes*, beginning with the *Corpus Reformatorum* and continuing in the *Opera Selecta*, along with the Weber and the McNeill-Battles translations—

whereas it was clearly noted in many places in the vast alphabetical collation of theological *loci* by Nicholas Colladon that appeared as an index to the 1559 *Institutes* and in the marginal subheads of the late sixteenth- and seventeenth-century editions of the *Institutes*.[41] Thus, *Institutes* II.xii divides into two groups of arguments—sections 1 through 3 offer reasons why the mediator was necessarily both divine and human; sections 4 through 7 offer a series of twelve objections and answers, culminating in a brief summation of the orthodox doctrine. Similarly, *Institutes* II.xiii can be understood as a statement of the doctrine of Christ's true humanity (section 1), followed by series of objections and refutations (sections 2–4). The pattern of statement, objections, and answers is also evident in *Institutes* II.xiv, where Servetus is the principal contemporary objector to the doctrine of the two natures, and in *Institutes* III.xi, where sections 1 through 4 define justification, sections 5 through 21 offer a series of objections and answers, and sections 22 and 23 resolve and confirm the doctrinal result of the disputation. Examples can easily be multiplied.

It is also clear from Calvin's usage that technical *distinctiones* occupied virtually the same place in his theological method as they did in the development of Lombard's *Sententiae*: the *distinctio* offered a means of dealing with difficulties and even potential contradictions in the text of Scripture or between a biblical statement and a truth known from some other perspective. When, for example, Calvin addresses the knotty problem of the providential ordination of all things and the apparent existence of chance and contingency in our world, he notes, "since our minds rest far beneath the height of divine providence, we must have recourse to a *distinctio* which may assist them in rising."[42] Similarly, when addressing the question of Christ's merit, Calvin argues that Christ's saving work cannot be paralleled with our good works: the priority of "the free favor of God" or "ordination of God" as the cause of Christ's merit and its efficacy for us places Christ's work entirely in the order of grace. "It is a well-known rule," Calvin writes, "that subordinate things are not incompatible [with first principles or first causes]."[43] He goes on to state that "this *distinctio* is found in numerous places in Scripture."[44] So, too, the problem of bearing one's cross is resolved through a distinction "between philosophical and Christian patience."[45] In both of these places, moreover, Calvin follows the standard pattern of achieving resolution in a disputation through the use of a distinction—a point noted full well by Colladon and his associates in the creation of the sixteenth-century apparatus to the *Institutes*.

Calvin's Polemics against Scholasticism: Indications of Relationship, Positive and Negative

Calvin's polemical references to the scholastics or, as he also identifies them, the sophists are nearly all general attacks that, except for the occasional reference to Lombard, seldom identify the scholastic theologians to whose teaching Calvin objects. In some cases, Calvin appears to attack as "scholastic" views not held by the major medieval doctors—and, after his attack, to adopt positions that actually reflect teachings of the medieval scholastics. Bierma, for example, notes that Calvin's early attack on the scholastic distinction between the moral and the ceremonial dimensions of Sabbath observance miss the point of the distinction: Albert the Great and Aquinas could distinguish between the moral obligation to set aside time for worship and the ceremonial designation of a particular day of the week as the Sabbath. Calvin's polemic views the distinction as a useless identification of the moral obligation to set aside one day and the ceremonial duty to worship on the seventh day. Then, as Bierma indicates, Calvin goes on to make his own distinction between "the truth of the precept" and "the ceremonies" or "outward rite," a distinction quite parallel to that made by Albert and Aquinas.[46] This particular remark offers little positive indication of the nature and direction of Calvin's polemic against scholasticism, but it does raise, from an early point in Calvin's career (1536), questions concerning the extent of Calvin's knowledge of the scholastic past and the precise object of his polemic.

Quite notable among Calvin's mature attacks on scholasticism is his sharp declamation against the distinction between *potentia absoluta* and *potentia ordinata*, and his related attack on the use of this and similar distinctions to define the divine transcendence as *ex lex* or beyond the law.[47] In the sermons on Job (the original of which exists in French only), Calvin speaks of the teaching of "the doctors of the Sorbonne" as "a devilish blasphemy forged in Hell"[48] because it identifies the "absolute" power of God as "lawless"—indeed, because it violates the fundamental assumption of the inseparability of the divine attributes: God is not a tyrant whose power can run contrary to his righteousness.[49] There is, surely, a divine "righteousness more perfect than that of the Law"—but there is no divine power beyond or outside of the divine righteousness.[50] By way of contrast, "we must say that God as an infinite or endless power which, notwithstanding, is the rule of all righteousness . . . for it would be to rend God in pieces to make him almighty without being all-righteous."[51] In these arguments, Calvin is clearly attacking not scholasticism in general but a specific excess of late medieval nominalist speculation concerning the limits of divine transcendence and the *potentia absoluta*. What is notable here is not only the specification of "Sorbonistes," and the association of their theology with a notion of God as *ex lex* (not characteristic of the theology of the great scholastics of earlier times), but also the fact that Calvin opposes this particular "scholastic" or Sorbonnistic teaching with equally "scholastic" assumptions concerning the divine simplicity and the essential identity of the divine attributes. It is also the case that Calvin can argue that God sometimes overrules secondary causes and the order of nature, a point resembling one of the implications of the *potentia absoluta/ordinata* distinction,[52] again indicating a considerable degree of specification in what, superficially, might appear to be a general denunciation of scholastic theology.

Similarly, Calvin had little sympathy with traditional distinctions between God's positive will and God's permissive willing, although his critique of such distinctions not only placed him clearly in the tradition of medieval Augustinianism but also drew positively on other scholastic distinctions, such as those concerned with the hidden and manifest will or wills of God (*voluntas Dei beneplaciti/signi*). Thus, Calvin can insist that "though to our apprehension the will of God is manifold, yet he does not in himself will opposites, but, according to his manifold wisdom, transcends our senses, until such time as it shall be given us to know how he mysteriously wills what now seems adverse to his will."[53] (We note here an underlying acceptance of the concept of divine simplicity—a concept available from the fathers but enunciated with clarity only by the scholastics.) Some distinction must be made between the "secret counsel" of God that ultimately governs and guides the world order and the precepts of the revealed law: in the *Institutes*, Calvin notes how Scripture in general and the book of Job in particular keep us "humble" by noting the theme of the hidden will of God.[54] Nonetheless, the standard distinction between positive and permissive willing falls short inasmuch as nothing can happen "without the will of God," although Calvin can, if pressed, accept the Augustinian qualification that the permission of God must be understood as a "willing" rather than an "unwilling" permission.[55] In a sense, therefore, Calvin's assault on the distinction occurs within the bounds of rather traditional constructions—constructions that he shared with many medieval theologians.

His discussion of the object of faith, perhaps more than any other part of the *Institutes*, evidences either an unwillingness to deal with the details of scholastic theology or a certain degree of ignorance of its content—or, as will be elaborated, a rather specific protest, masked by vague language, against a particular form of scholastic teaching. In other words, his lack of formal theological training may be most evident here. Calvin writes,

> when faith is discussed in the schools, they identify God as the object of faith *simpliciter*, and by a fleeting speculation . . . lead miserable souls astray rather than direct them to a definite goal. For, since "God dwells in inaccessible light" Christ must become our intermediary. . . . This evil, then, like innumerable others, must be attributed to the Schoolmen, who have, as it were, drawn a veil over Christ to hide him. Unless we look straight toward him, we shall wander through endless labyrinths.[56]

On the one hand, Calvin's point that medieval theology—probably, late medieval theology—tended toward speculative formulations of the doctrine of God and drew attention away from Christ is a truism of the Reformation that underlined its own sense of direct access to God in Christ through faith against speculations about the absolute power of a transcendent deity hidden behind his ordained and revealed will and underlined also the Reformers' replacement of the intricacies of the sacramental system with a more immediate sense of Christ's presence to faith in justification.[57] On the other hand, it falls considerably short of being a description of scholastic theology either in general or in particular. Few medieval scholastics claimed, without qualification, that God is the object of faith.

For instance, Scotus's identification of God *qua Deus* (God considered as God) as the "object of theology" was intended to contrast with his identification of God *qua Ens* (God considered as Being) as the object of metaphysics—and, therefore, to indicate a distinction between theological enquiry and philosophical speculation.[58] Quite arguably, moreover, Scotist and nominalist use of the distinction between *potentia absoluta* and *potentia ordinata* could create a barrier to speculation about God and pressed theologian and believer alike to consider means.[59] In addition, Calvin's very polemic here partakes of a scholastic distinction concerning the nature of theology, namely whether theology is a speculative discipline, the teachings of which are to be known as a goal in themselves, or a practical discipline, the teaching of which are to be known insofar as they conduce to a particular goal.[60]

Similarly, Hugh of St. Victor had declared that the proper subject of theology was the work of redemption—and the theological tradition of the Augustinian order, as presented in the work of Giles of Rome and Gregory of Rimini, came very close to Calvin's perspective when it identified the subject or object of theology as God, the creator and redeemer or God, creator, redeemer, and glorifier.[61] Not only do these latter definitions have a clear affinity with Calvin's insistence that faith looks to God in Christ; they also surely point directly toward Calvin's theme of the twofold knowledge of God, the so-called *duplex cognitio Dei*, according to which God is known primarily as Creator and Redeemer. Calvin might even have seen the point made in summary form in Altenstaig's much used *Vocabularius theologiae*.[62] On this issue, then, we may fairly ask whether Calvin knew of the variety of scholastic formulation—or whether he ignored it for the sake of polemic. If the *duplex cognitio Dei* offers any indication of an answer, we may hypothesize here that Calvin knew and, very quietly, without citation, drew on scholastic views of the object of theology and then turned about to polemicize broadly about what he knew to be either a caricature or, at best, a minority opinion. Perhaps, too, the polemic was more pointed and specific than Calvin's Latin "scholastici" indicates: the 1560 French text offers "théologiens Sorboniques."

Later in the same passage, Calvin accuses the scholastics of "wearing down all the force of faith and almost annihilating it by their obscure definition."[63] Here, too, the point is generalized and overstated for the sake of polemical rhetoric—at the same time that Calvin's own definition of faith carries with it clear reflections of traditional, scholastic definition. Thus, following the traditional Aristotelian distinction of "mind" into faculties of intellect and will,[64] Calvin insists that faith addresses the whole person in both faculties: "the heart," he writes, must be "strengthened and supported" even as the intellect is illuminated, given that "faith is much higher," and, we add, broader, "than human understanding (*intelligentia*)."[65] Once he has offered this perspective on the relationship of faith to the faculties of soul, Calvin adds the following polemical remark:

> The Scholastics go completely astray, who in considering faith identify it with a bare and simple assent (*assensum*) arising out of knowledge (*notitia*), and leave out confidence and assurance of heart (*cordis fiducia et securitate*). . . . How very dull men are to perceive the mysteries of God; partly because they do not have regard to that firm and steadfast constancy of heart which is the chief part of faith.[66]

As an aspect of Calvin's attack, first on the Roman Catholic doctrine of implicit faith and, by extension, on an excessive identification of "faith" with *fides quae creditur* (faith, understood as the normative teaching of the church), the polemic functions well—but as an evaluation of scholastic theology, it falls rather short of the mark.

Indeed, Calvin's inclusion of *fiducia* in his definition (particularly given his identification of "heart" as the will) places him in direct accord with most scholastic definitions, where faith is typically distinguished into a twofold act of intellect (knowledge of a truth and the judgment that it is indeed true) and an act of the will (assent to or apprehension of the truth for one's self). Thus, Aquinas distinguishes "between faith and all other intellectual operations" on the ground that, whereas the intellect "first conceives a simple meaning" and then, in "an act of judgment," recognizes the meaning to be either true or false, faith consists in this but also in something more, namely an assent of the will to the truth. Aquinas writes:

> "The author of faith," is he who produces the believer's assent to the truth declared. Mere hearing is not a sufficient cause. The assent is caused by the will, not by any

necessity of reason. And therefore a preacher or herald cannot produce faith. God is the cause of faith, for he alone can alter our wills.[67]

As Augustine, Lombard, and Aquinas and virtually all other scholastics comment, it is one thing to "believe concerning God (*credere Deo* or *de Deo*)," another to "believe God (*credere Deum*)," and yet another to "believe in God (*credere in Deum*)"—which is to say, to believe that what is said about God is true, to believe that God exists (both of which levels of belief are found in good and evil people alike), and to believe in or cling to God in love, which last is the character of the faith the justifies.[68] Faith is the virtue or power by which one believes what cannot be seen: as such, it is both intellectual and volitional, and it is the ground or "foundation . . . through which Christ dwells in the heart."[69] Scotus, too, insisted that faith consists not merely in knowledge but in knowledge and assent—and he insisted that the volitional aspect of assent rested on the grace of God.[70] Calvin's generalized polemic against scholasticism and the "scholastics," therefore, frequently points in two directions—toward a strong distaste for specific scholastic formulae and also toward an appropriation of other elements of medieval scholastic theology, often as the means by which elements of scholastic thought viewed by Calvin as problematic might be refuted.

These (and other) significant discrepancies between Calvin's claims in his critiques of *scholastici* and the actual teachings of the "scholastics" raise the historical and analytical question of how literally we ought to understand Calvin's terms. On the one hand, some license must be granted to his polemic. On the other hand, some insight may be again provided by Calvin's French usage: in the 1560 French *Institutes* and in Calvin's French sermons, the target of his critique is often identified, not as the "scholastici," but, with considerably greater specificity, as the "théologiens Sorboniques."[71] There are several possible explanations here: Calvin may, at times, have been ignorant of the breadth of scholastic definition and opinion—or he may have been attacking, as LaVallee hypothesized, a particular form of late medieval theology under a generalized rubric. Alternatively, he may have simply borrowed a particular language of antischolastic polemic: the focus of attack in a work like Erasmus's *Ratio seu mathodus compendio perveniendi ad veram theologiam* (1519) is clearly Paris and the Sorbonne.[72] Given Calvin's own early experience of the fate of reform in Paris, this language was also surely reflective of his sentiments, if not of a profound knowledge of medieval documents. His antagonism to the Sorbonne, moreover, was something more worthy of expression to a French audience than to a broader European Latin readership.

Indeed, when one examines the texts of the 1559 and 1560 *Institutes*, a surprising difference of usage appears. Calvin refers to the "scholastici" twenty-six times in the edition of 1559; all of the instances of the word in the 1539 edition passed over into 1559 and have their parallels in the French of 1560.[73] Of the twenty-six (or, if we include the "quae in scholis" = "Sorbonistes" of III.ii.8, twenty-seven) references to "scholastici" found in the Latin text of the 1559 *Institutes*, fifteen are rendered precisely as "scolastiques" in the 1560 *Institutes*, while twelve are altered in their passage into the French of 1560. Of these twelve Latin references to "scholastici," one is rendered "théologiens romanistes," two are translated as "Sophistes," and the remaining nine appear as "théologiens Sorboniques" or "Sorbonistes." There are also four references to the Sorbonne and its teachers found in the 1539 *Institutes*: all carry over verbatim into the French in 1541 and are retained in 1559 and 1560. One other reference appears in the 1543 Latin text, is translated verbatim in the 1545 French version, and is retained in the final editions (1559 and 1560).[74]

The polemic against the Sorbonne, therefore, although resident in Calvin's Latin text from 1539 on, intensifies in the French of 1541 and retains that intensity in the subsequent French editions through 1560. It is also principally a polemic directed toward the French audience: the rendering of "scholastici" as "théologiens Sorboniques" represents a reading characteristic of Calvin's movement from Latin to French, as seen from the texts of the 1539 and 1559 *Institutes* and is largely focused on materials found in Book III of the *Institutes*. Calvin also never moves from the Latin "sorbonistae" to a French "scolastiques" or some other equivalent. Thus, the word "scholastici" does not appear at all in *Institutes*, Book I (despite the several attacks on medieval theology and philosophy), and the references to "scholastici" in Book II are all rendered "scolastiques." It is in Book III, however, that the term "théologiens Sorboniques" appears, with the result that of the fifteen Latin references to "scholastici," eight are rendered "théologiens Sorboniques," one (III.iv.26) alters syntax and renders "universi scholastici" as "toutes leurs écoles," and two are rendered "Sophistes"—leaving only three references to "scolastiques" in the French. In the Latin of Book IV, there are five references to "scholastici"; two appear in French as "scolastiques," one as the synonymous construction "docteurs de l'école," one as "théologiens romanistes," and one as "théologiens Sorboniques."

Beyond these variations, two other stylistic features characteristic of the translation process should be noted. First, in all cases where Calvin's Latin reference is to Peter Lombard and other (unidentified) scholastics—II.ii.4; II.ii.16; II.xvii.6; III.iv.26—the French translation gives "scolastiques." The single exception to this generalization appears to be *Institutes*, III.iii.43, where Lombard's teaching is mentioned but then contrasted with the greater abuses of the later schools: here, "in scholis" is rendered "ez escolles des Sophistes, c'est à dire Sorboniques." And, second, in the few cases in which Calvin's reference to "scholastici" is not entirely negative—his reference to scholastic use of Augustinian definition (II.ii.4), the two references to "saniores scholastici" (II.ii.6 and III.xiv.11) and one to a more "modest" formulation of the scholastics (IV.xvii.13)—he translates "scholastici" as "scolastiques," never as "Sorbonistes." When Lombard's formulations are cited and, therefore, when the older scholasticism is identified in debate, Calvin typically uses "scholastici" or "scolastiques." In cases where Lombard is not mentioned, and potentially where a more recent scholastic abuse is indicated, Calvin's French quite frequently specifies the theology of the Sorbonne. Thus, while "scholastici" can occasionally function as a neutral term, "théologiens Sorboniques" is invariably a term of reproach.

We have already noted the concentration of the French usage "théologiens Sorboniques" in book III of the *Institutes*. It is also the case that the usage is largely confined to the discussions of faith (III.ii), repentance, confession, and penance (III.iv), righteousness and justification (III.xi.15; xiv.11–12; xvii.15), and one reference in the discussion of the relationship between predestination and sin (III.xxiii.6). Even so, three out of the four references to the Sorbonne that carry over from 1539 into the later editions (i.e., III.xv.7; III.xviii.8; III.xviii.9) indicate a similar pattern of reference. If we add to this list the numerous references in the sermons on Job—where the issue is the problem of divine transcendence and the ramifications of speculation on the *potentia absoluta* for the discussion of divine and human righteousness—it becomes possible to identify, in the midst of Calvin's seemingly unspecified attacks on "scholastici" and, in particular, in several places where the general language and argument of the Latin *Institutes* could be faulted for imprecision, a rather pointed and precise attack *not* on the older scholastic tradition but on a strain of contemporary scholastic theology viewed by Calvin as especially problematic in view of its extreme nominalism.

What is significant here is that a large number of the references to "Sorbonistes" in Book III of the *Institutes* are not the result of Calvin's heated dispute with the Paris doctors over the articles drawn up by the Sorbonne at the behest of Francis I (to whom Calvin had dedicated the first edition of his *Institutes*). The articles appeared in 1543, and Calvin responded with his *Articuli a facultate sacrae theologiae Parisiensi determinati super materiis fidei nostrae hodie controversis: Cum antidoto* in 1544.[75] Most of the polemic against the Sorbonne in *Institutes*, Book III, originated in the 1539 Latin and was intensified in the 1541 French translation. (The added polemics of the 1543–59 Latin and 1545–60 French text, largely belonging to *Institutes*, Book IV, with their references to "les Sorbonistes," can surely be traced to the debate over these condemnatory articles.)

Calvin's distaste for the Sorbonne was evident, therefore, before his major conflict with the Paris doctors: it may be related to his earlier conflict with the sometime Reformer and apostate Pierre Caroli, beginning in 1536: Caroli had a doctorate from the Sorbonne.[76] Or, as already noted, it is possible that Calvin's anti-Sorbonnist language reflects the rhetoric of Erasmus's *Ratio seu methodus* of 1519, in which there is a tendency to aim antischolastic polemic at Paris and the Sorbonne as exemplifying the worst "scholastic" abuses of the day. There was, certainly, an intensification of Calvin's problems with the Sorbonne after 1543—and his French usage then certainly takes on the accents of what Oberman has identified as the "refugee" mentality and the theology of an "underground" church,[77] for it was on the ground of the royally sanctioned Sorbonne articles that many of Calvin's French associates and students were executed for heresy. What we cannot conclude, however, is that his distaste for the Sorbonne, any more than Calvin's status as a refugee, was a later phenomenon caused by the articles of 1543. Beginning in 1521, with its condemnatory *Determinatio* on Luther, the faculty of the Sorbonne had engaged in a series of censures and condemnations of reformatory or "evangelical" authors and writings.[78] From the very beginnings of his association with the Reform, around 1532, Calvin would have known the Sorbonne as an obstacle. For his French audience, therefore, Calvin portrayed the Sorbonne as the extreme and abusively scholastic adversary from the outset in 1539, and he specifically linked his polemic to certain doctrinal issues.

Calvin's Positive Appropriation of Scholastic Distinctions

Of course, once the "scholastic" opponents are specified in this manner, Calvin's theology appears less overtly antagonistic to medieval scholasticism in general. Indeed, by way of contrast with the preceding examples, we can look to elements of Calvin's Christology as indicators of the positive side of his relationship to scholastic theology. Although Calvin's identification of Christ as Mediator according to both natures appears quite contrary to traditional Catholic doctrine, it finds echoes in the medieval discussion of the problem of mediation, particularly among the Franciscan doctors: Bonaventure could, for example, declare "truly he could not be Mediator, unless he were in between (*medius*)" and that Christ was *medius*, or in between, by reason of the union of the two natures.[79] Scotus offers much the same argument.[80] Of course, neither Bonaventure nor Scotus departs from the argument that Christ is Mediator according to his human nature—nevertheless, the *medius* concept precedes and governs the *mediator* concept. Bonaventure's perspective, moreover, is not only normative for Scotus but stated as definitive for the nominalist theologians by Biel. The *medium*, argues Biel, has something in common with two extremes: to this concept the term *mediator* adds the idea of a work of reconciliation. Christ is thus *medium* between extremes "by the participation of both natures, divine and human" but "He is however Mediator: according to the human nature only."[81] Calvin's Christology, arguably, reflects the medieval discussion by pressing the question of Christ's median status to the point that he could conclude that Christ must be understood as mediator according to both natures.[82] Similarly, Calvin's way of arguing the sufficiency of Christ's merit on the ground of the divine decree may be an extension of the Scotist critique of Anselm's satisfaction theory: whereas Scotus had argued that Christ's merit could not be infinite because it rested on the obedience of the human nature and that God merely accepted it as payment, Calvin appears to argue that the payment was infinite because God decreed that it would be so.[83]

There are also numerous instances in which Calvin either appropriates a scholastic distinction without comment and incorporates it into his own theology or, to his credit, identifies the distinction as belonging to the older theology and its method and acknowledges its correctness and its usefulness to his own thought. Thus, the distinction between the eternal decree and its execution in time occupies a fairly prominent place in Calvin's discussions of the relationship between God and world and is used both in the commentaries and in the *Institutes* as a way of focusing attention on God's revelation rather than on God in himself. We read in the *Institutes* "that God is the disposer and ruler of all things,—that from the remotest eternity, according to his own wisdom, he decreed what he was to do, and now by his power executes what he has decreed."[84]

So, too, in his discussions of providence and of the divine-human person of the Mediator, Calvin reflects on scholastic distinctions between levels of necessity.[85] In the former instance, he notes the difference between "necessity *secundum quid*" and "absolute necessity," or between "consequent necessity" and a "necessity of the consequence." Calvin notes, "that which God has determined, though it must come to pass, is not, however, precisely, or in its own nature, necessary." In other words, whereas there must be a "secret impulse" or "secret agency of the hand of God" underlying all contingent events, an event understood "in its own nature" or as part of the world of temporal causality remains in some sense contingent. By way of example, Calvin argues that John 19:33 and 36 should be understood to mean that God made Christ's bones breakable, like all human bones, but "in reference to the necessity of his counsel," God "exempted them from actual fracture." It was neither an absolute necessity nor a necessity of the consequence that Christ's bones were not broken, but a necessity *secundum quid*, a consequent necessity resting on a specific divine willing and not on the nature of the bones themselves. There is, Calvin concludes, "good ground for the distinction which the Schoolmen made" between different kinds of necessity.[86] Not only the distinction but certainly also the question of the sort of necessity belonging to the "infrangibility" of Christ's bones are points that arise out of a theological consderation of the divine intention underlying the fulfillment of prophecy and are almost certainly reflections of medieval scholastic analysis of such biblical texts.[87] What is more, the presence of these comments in such detail in the *Institutes* rather than in the commentary expresses Calvin's method: the *locus* or *disputatio* appears in the *Institutes* and in fact reflects the development of Calvin's polemics.[88]

In the latter instance, Calvin notes that there was no "simple or absolute" necessity that the Mediator be both divine and human but that the constitution of the Mediator "flowed from the divine decree on which the salvation of man depended"—in other words, a necessity of the consequence.[89] Here, Calvin certainly echoes the Scotist critique of Anselm's *Cur Deus homo*—specifically, to the point that God must not be understood as subject to necessity. Although Calvin argues the suitability of the divine-human Mediator to the work of redemption, he does not agree that the nature of the problem of human sin can dictate the nature of the Mediator: rather, it is the divine will that the Mediator be the God-man that provides the necessity of the incarnation.[90]

Given the formal and methodological importance of the exegesis of Scripture both to the genesis of medieval scholastic theological system and to the creation of Calvin's *Institutes*, we turn to several examples of the biblical or exegetical foundations of theological *loci* treated by Calvin and by the medieval scholastic doctors.[91] First, Calvin's reading of Exodus 3:14, both in the *Institutes* and in his commentary on the text, falls precisely into the traditional, "essentialist" reading of the text and indicates Calvin's continuity with both the patristic and the medieval past: God's "eternity and self-existence are announced by that wonderful name," declares Calvin in the *Institutes*.[92] He elaborates at considerable length on this issue in his commentary, noting the future tense of the divine declaration "I will be what I will be" but arguing that its meaning differs little from the usual translation into the present, except insofar as the future tense even more forcibly "designates the perpetual duration" of God. Calvin also assumes that God here "attributes to himself alone divine glory, because he is self-existent and therefore eternal." Further, Calvin concludes that God "gives existence and subsistence to every creature" while at the same time retaining his own distinct predicates or attributes: "eternity is proper to God alone." Thus, "all things in heaven and earth derive at his will their essence or subsistence from the One who truly is."[93]

Again, for comparison's sake, we look first to Aquinas. First, in response to the objections offered against the existence of God, Aquinas responds, "On the contrary, It is said in the person of God, *I am who I am*."[94] Or, in close parallel to Calvin's statement that the essence or subsistence of things rests on the One Who Is, Aquinas writes, "the existence of created things does not spring from their inner essential principles, and consequently no created form or nature is its existence. God's proper name, however, is *I am*, and that denotes his very form."[95] Similarly, Bonaventure speaks of two "modes" of contemplating God—one looking to the "essential attributes" and resting on the Old Testament revelation, the other looking to the Trinity and resting principally on the New Testament. The first mode "looks primarily and essentially to God's being, and says that God's foremost name is 'He Who Is'; or again, "the first approach looks more to the Old Testament, which stresses the unity of the divine essence, for it was said to Moses: 'I Am Who Am.' " As "the most absolute being," God is "the very first and the last . . . the origin and final end of all things."[96] So, too, Duns Scotus:

> O Lord our God, true teacher that you are, when Moses your servant asked you for your name that he might proclaim it to the children of Israel, you, knowing what the mind of mortals could grasp of you, replied, "I am who am," thus disclosing your blessed name. You are truly what it means to be, you are the whole of what it means to exist.[97]

A further example: Calvin did know and accept, with limitation, the medieval distinction between the "sufficiency" of Christ's satisfaction for all sin and its "efficiency" for the "elect" or "believers" alone. (We do not raise, at this point, the perennial question of whether or not Calvin held a doctrine of "limited atonement"—we only illustrate one of the difficulties involved in coming to grips with Calvin's use of scholastic distinctions.) In commenting on the text of I John 2:1–2, Calvin recognized that verse 2, "and not for ours only, but also for the sins of the whole world," raised the question of the universality of Christ's satisfaction. These phrases, he indicates, expand upon the first verse "in order that the faithful might be assured that the expiation made by Christ, extends to all who by faith embrace the gospel."[98] The expiation, he explains, extends only to the faithful, not merely to the faithful known to those addressed by the Apostle but to all who "by faith who embrace the gospel," wherever and whenever that may be. Once this limitation is expressed, then the question again arises concerning the universalizing language of the text: what is the meaning of the word "*all* or whole," or, as Calvin comments, "how have the sins of the whole world been expiated"? Calvin now turns to the "monstrous" error—so monstrous, indeed, that he states, rhetorically, that it "deserves no refutation"—of various "fanatics" who use the text as a "pretense" to "extend salvation to all the reprobate, and therefore to Satan himself."[99] The text does not indicate universal salvation resting on the infinite value of the sacrifice: even so, in order to "avoid this absurdity," the exegetical tradition had often resolved the problem of this and similar texts with the time-honored distinction that "Christ suffered sufficiently for the whole world, but efficiently only for the elect." "This solution," Calvin adds, "has commonly prevailed in the schools."[100]

Having stated the distinction—presumably because he recognized it to be the standard solution to the problem of the text and therefore assumed that he ought to mention it at this point—Calvin proceeds to indicate that the proffered solution does not apply to this particular text, while at the same time indicating the theological correctness of the distinction: "Though then I allow that what has been said is true, yet I deny that it is suitable to this passage, for the design of John was no other than to make this benefit common to the whole church."[101] Calvin thus accepts the standard scholastic distinction but appears to indicate that the text itself did not intend to speak either in general theological terms of the sufficiency of Christ's sacrifice for all sin or of the restriction of that sufficient payment by efficient application to the elect only; rather, the text intended to speak directly to the question of the application of Christ's propitiatory work to the church in general. Just as Calvin's reading of the text does not fully resolve the question of his relationship to the later Reformed doctrine of "limited atonement," so, also, does it not fully resolve the question of his relationship to scholastic theology and its distinctions. He surely noted the distinction at this point because he encountered the distinction in the exegetical tradition.[102]

Calvin's comments on Isaiah 28:22 offer a similar reference to a scholastic distinction. Calvin here remarks that "some" of the interpreters explain the "strangeness" of God's destructive work as a contrast between the divine anger that makes God seem "to act against his will" or nature—given the revelation of God's "proper" nature and work as the merciful pardoning of sins.[103] Others, Calvin comments, explain the passage as distinguishing between the former defense and protection of his people that has here been succeeded by a "strange" or "alien" work of God, as if his people were now his enemies. For himself, Calvin identifies the strangeness as the "uncommon," "wondrous," or "rare" character of the work of God described in the text.[104] In his unidentified citations of previous commentators and in his own remarks, Calvin has simply reflected, without editorial comment or polemic, the medieval tradition of understanding a necessary distinction here between the divine *opus proprium* (proper work) and *opus alienum* (alien work). The scholastic or medieval exegetical tradition and its understanding of problems and seeming contradictions as distinctions has in fact set the agenda for Calvin's comments on the text.[105]

Calvin's later exegetical work, some of which had an impact on the 1559 *Institutes* (and some of which was done so late in his career that it did not) was largely devoted to the exposition of the Old Testament—Genesis, the Harmony of the Pentateuch, Psalms, the Prophets. Here, Calvin experienced, as he surely did not experience in his interpretation of the New Testament, great theological problems involving the status of the literal meaning of the text anad its relation to the doctrines of God, creation, and providence. As Schreiner has shown, this problem is evident in the sermons on Job,[106] and we have seen it also from the vantage point of the commentaries on Exodus 3:14 and Isaiah 28:22. Had Calvin examined the commentaries of Nicholas of Lyra or Denis the Carthusian, he could have drawn on a digest of scholastic exegetical opinion extending back to Thomas Aquinas.[107] And it was perhaps here, apart from the polemical context of debate, that Calvin encountered both many of the traditional scholastic distinctions and the rationale, in the biblical text, for their enunciation by the medieval doctors.

Some Conclusions

It often appears from the *Institutes*, commentaries, treatises, and sermons that Calvin held a fundamentally negative view of scholastic theology, at times to the point of caricature, at the same time that his theology contained a measure of positive allusion to and indirect reliance on scholastic formulations. In several of the cases noted, the appearance of caricature may be related to the disparity between Calvin's Latin and French usage: many of the places in which Calvin's critique of scholastics seems exaggerated or misapplied give a rather different impression when the target of the critique is understood as the theologians of the Sorbonne identified by Calvin's French text. The hypothesis that "scholastici" and "théologiens Sorboniques" are not simple equivalents and that the latter is more precise and specific than the former is confirmed to a certain extent by Calvin's consistent rendering of phrases like "Peter Lombard and the scholastics," "the Master of the *sentences* and the scholastics," and "the more sound scholastics" with precise verbal equivalents. Lombard and the "more sound" scholastic thinkers were not the object of Calvin's most heated attacks. Indeed, if the language of the French text is accepted as Calvin's meaning, the critiques are often quite specific and, indeed, quite contemporary—and no longer directed against such luminaries of the scholastic past as Bonaventure, Aquinas, or Duns Scotus. In addition, Calvin clearly tended to reserve his most angry and specified polemic for his French audience, for the sake of reminding them (if reminder was needed!) that the faculty of the Sorbonne was the chief theological barrier to the reform of Christianity in France.

Calvin's knowledge of scholastic theology certainly also increased as he prepared his lectures on Scripture, his commentaries, and the successive editions of the *Institutes*. It may well be the case that his more positive use of scholastic distinctions arose by way of his encounter with them as explanations of difficulties and seeming contradictions in the biblical text, an encounter largely related to his reading of major medieval commentators in preparation for his writing of lectures and commentaries on Scripture. This hypothesis is supported by the findings of Steinmetz, Schreiner, and Thompson and accounts for his continuing negative assessment of the scholastic theological system, his fairly consistent but also rather vague reflection of the scholastic tradition in many of his central arguments (such as his discussion of the merit of Christ and his great theme of the twofold knowledge of God), his occasional misunderstanding or intentional distortion of the import of a scholastic argument, and his increasing nonpolemical notice of scholastic distinctions in his writings.

In addition, with a view toward scholarly writing on the subject, the way of framing the problem permits Reuter's correlation of Calvin's views with those of the medieval scholastics to be held in tension with the problem of Calvin's access to their thought: the relation and disjunction between Calvin's theology and medieval scholasticism reflects the variegated process by which Calvin assimilated their ideas—polemically through explicit negative reference in the writings of predecessors like Luther and Bucer who were learned in the older theology, positively but vaguely and without reference to specific scholastic thinkers (or even to scholasticism as such) through the reading of these same works, and more dialogically (with clearer reference to the sources of the concepts) through the reading of medieval commentators. We are also able to accept and refine many of LaVallee's arguments, particularly his conclusions concerning the identity of the "scholastici" as "théologiens Sorboniques"—but now in only certain of Calvin's most concentrated polemical arguments. This understanding leads, in turn, to the possibility of finding a place in Calvin's developing thought for the positive impact of earlier strains of medieval thought and even for Calvin's participation in the long-term development of a doctrinal theme, as in the Christological examples we have noted.

In short, Calvin's overtly negative reaction to the "scholastici" conveys only a small part of his relationship to medieval scholastic theology, its method, themes, and distinctions. Alongside the rejection, there is also appropriation, sometimes explicit, but often unacknowledged. There are also parallels in method and intention, notably between Calvin's approach to system and commentary and the approach of Peter Lombard—moreover, there is the exegetical tradition to which Calvin became increasingly attentive and through which he received the insights both of the patristic and of the medieval periods. Finally, there is also the issue of Calvin's and his contemporaries' positive understanding of their own "scholastic" enterprise, an academic effort framed by the late medieval and Renaissance recasting of logic and rhetoric, that would permanently alter the course and shape of "scholasticism" in the sixteenth century. It is to this latter investigation, the detailed relationship between Calvin's exegesis and the western exegetical tradition, that study will need to turn in order to clarify fully the relation and disjunction between Calvin's theology and the thought of the medieval doctors.

Appendix

A. *References to scholasticus* and its French equivalents in Calvin's *Institutes*, 1539–60.

II.ii.4—(1539/59): "Itaque Petrus Lombardus et Scholastici Augustini definitionem magis amplexi sunt . . ."; (1541/60): "Pourtant le Maistre des Sentences & les docteurs scolastiques ont plustost receu celle de S. Augustin . . . Thomas d'Aquin pense que ceste définition seroit bonne. . . ."[108]

II.ii.6—(1539/59): "iam, lector, quantum a sanioribus Scholasticis disentiam. Longior enim intervallo a recentioribus Sophistis differo" (1541/60): "en quoy je discorde d'avec les docteurs scolastiques qui ont tenu une doctrine plus entiere que n'ont faict les Sophistes qui ont venuz apres. . . ."

II.ii.16—(1539): "coactus est magister Sententiarum . . ."; (1559): "coacti sunt Magister sententiarum et scholastici ut gratiuta homini dona post lapsum"; (1541): "laquelle le Maistre des Sentences a esté contrainct d'approuver"; (1560): "Car ceste sentence que nous avons alleguée de S. Augustin est tresvraye, laquelle le maistre des Sentences & les Scolastiques ont esté contreints d'approuver."[109]

II.ii.26—(1539/59): "Nam et scholastici fatentur nullam esse liberi arbitrii"; (1541/60): "Car les theologiens Scolasticques mesmes confessent qu'il n'y a nulle action du franc Arbitre."[110]

I.ii.27—(1539/59): "ab Origene, et veterum quibusdam sumptam, Scholastici communiter amplexi sint"; (1541/60): "Il n'y a point de doubte que les scolastiques n'ayent communement receu ceste opinion, comme elle leur estoit baillée de Origene."[111]

II.viii.56—(1539/59): "Vel ignorantiae, vel malitiae fuit, quod Scholastici ex praeceptis de non appetenda vindicta"; (1541/60): "Parquoy ce a esté une ignorance, ou malice pernitieuse, que les docteurs scolastiques, des commandements que nostre Seigneur a baillez. . . ."[112]

II.xvii.6—(1559): "sibi ipse meruerit (quod faciunt Lombardus et scholastici) non minus stulta est . . ."; (1560): "si Iesus Christ a rien merité pour soy, comme font le Maître des sentences et les scolastiques. . . ."[113]

III.ii.1—(1559): "imo quum in scholis de fide disputant, Deum eius obiectum simpliciter vocando"; (1560): "mesmes quand on dispute de la foy aux escoles de Theologie, en disant cruement que dieu en est l'obiet. . . ."[114]

III.ii.2—(1539): "Quod malum, ut alia innumera, scholasticis sophistis acceptum referri par est: qui praeterquam quod calignosa sua definitione totam vim eius deterunt";

(1559): "Ergo hoc malum; ut alia innumera, scholasticis acceptum referri par est. . . ."; (1541): "Lequel mal, comme autres innumerables, se doibt imputer aux Sophistes et Sorbonistes: lezquelz, oultre ce qu'liz amoyndrissent la vertu d'icelle par leur obscure et tenebreuse diffinition"; (1560): "Ce mal donc, comme d'autres infinis, doit estre imputé aux theologiens Sorboniques, lesquels ont couvert tant qu'ils ont peu Iesus Christ comme d'un voile."[115]

III.ii.8—(1559): "Ac primo refutanda est, quae in scholis volitat nugatoria fidei formatae et informis distinctio"; (1560): "En premier nous avons à refuter la distinction qui a eu tousjours en vogue entre les Sorbonistes, touchant la foy qu'ils appellent Formée et Informée."[116]

III.ii.33—(1539/59): "In quo, tota terra, scholastici aberrant: qui in fidei consideratione nudum ac simplicem e notitia assensum arripiunt . . ."; (1541/60): "En laquelle chose les Theologiens Sorboniques faillent trop lourdement: qui pensent que la Foy soit un simple consentement à la parolle de Dieu. . . ."

III.ii.38—(1539/59): "Hinc iudicare licet quam perniciosum sit scholasticum illud dogma"; (1541/60): "De là peut-on iuger, combien la doctrine des theologiens Sophistes et pernicieuse: c'est que nous ne pouvons rien arrester en nous de la grace de Dieu. . . ."[117]

III.ii.41—(1539/59): "Quod enim tradunt Scholastici, charitatem fide ac spe priorem esse"; (1541/60): "Or ce que les sorboniques enseignent, que la charité précède la foi et l'esperance, n'est que pure rêverie."[118]

III.ii.43—(1539/59): "O magistrum talibus dignum discipulis quales in insanibus rabularum scholis nactus est!"; (1541/60): "Mais un tel maistre est digne des disciples qu'il ha eu ez escolles des Sophistes, c'est à dire Sorboniques."

III.iv.1—(1539/59): "Nunc venio ad excutienda ea quae de poenitentia scholastici sophistae tradiderunt"; (1541/60): "Je viens maintenant à discuter ce ques les Sophistes ont enseigné de la Pénitance."[119]

III.iv.4—(1539/59): "ingens fuit pugna inter Canonistas et Theologos scholasticos"; (1541/60): "Touchant la Confession: il y a tousjours eu grande controversie entre les Canonistes et les Theologiens scolastiques."[120]

III.iv.26—(1539/59): "nec unus aut alter, sed universi scholastici. Nam ipsorum magister, postquam Christum . . ."; (1541/60): "non seulement un ou deux d'entre eux; mais toutes leurs Escoles? Car leur maistre après avoir confessé . . ."[121]

III.iv.38—(1539/59): "cum dogmaticus tamen scholasticis conciliari nunquam poterunt"; (1541/60): "jamais ne se pourront accorder avec la doctrine des Scolastiques."

III.xi.15—(1539): "His pravis dogmatibus orbem imbuerunt scholastici. Sed illi dupliciter falluntur. . . . Scholae in in deterius semper aberrarunt"; (1559): "*Crassius paulo scholastici, qui praeparationes suas miscent . . .* Quod ad vulgares Papistas et Theologos scholasticos, dupliciter hoc falluntur. . . . Scholae in in deterius semper aberrarunt"; (1541): "Ce ont esté les Theologiens Sorboniques qui ont abreuvé le monde de ceste faulse opinion . . . mais ilz s'abusent doublement. . . . Les escholes Sorboniques sont tousjours allées de mal en pis"; (1560): "*Les theologiens Sorboniques sont un peu plus lourds en meslant leurs preparations . . .* Quant est des Sorboniques, ils s'abusent doublement. . . . Les escoles Sorboniques sont toujours allées de mal en pis. . . ."[122]

III.xiv.11—(1543–59): "iustificationis nihil inter nos et saniores scholasticos pugnae est"; (1545–60): "il n'y a nul débat entre nous et les docteurs scolastiques qui ont quelque sens et raison."[123]

III.xiv.12—(1539/59): "Quae ad evadendum, subterfugia quaerunt hic scholastici, eos non expediunt"; (1541/60): "Les subterfuges que cherchent icy les Sorbonistes pour evader, ne les despechent point."[124]

III.xiv.15—(1539/59): "non quid in scholis et angulis fabulari possumus"; (1541/60): "ou mentir, en quelque anglet d'une Sorbonne."

III.xvii.15—(1539/59): "Quo non tantum intelligimus quod tradunt scholastici: a gratia acceptante . . ."; (1541/60): "Par lesquelles parolles, nous n'entendons pas seulement ce qu'enseignent les Scolastiques."[125]

III.xxiii.6—(1539/59): "Scholastici vero in ea quiescunt . . ."; (1541/60): "Les Sorboniques s'y arrestent entierement. . . ."[126]

IV.xiv.14—(1539/59): "Magno enim consensu sophisticae scholae tradiderunt, Sacramenta novae legis . . ."; (1541/60): "Car les escholes des Sophistes d'un commun consentement ont determiné, que les Sacremens de la nouvelle Loy. . . ."[127]

IV.xiv.23—(1539/59): "Scholasticum autem illud dogma . . . quo tamen longum discrimen inter veteris ac novae legis sacramenta notatur . . ."; (1541/60): "Au surplus ce que les Docteurs de l'eschole mettent une grande difference entre les Sacremens de la vielle et nouvelle Loy. . . ."[128]

IV.xvii.13—(1543–59): "Verecundius Scholastici, quos tam barbarae impietatis horror . . ."; (1545–60): "Les theologiens scolastiques ayant horreur d'une impiété si barbare parlent un peu plus sobrement. . . ."[129]

IV.xvii.30—(1559): "Tritia est in scholis distinctio, quam me refere non pudet. . . . Atque utinam Scholastici ipsi vim huius sententiae probe expedissent . . ."; (1560): "Il y a une distinction vulgaire entre les theologiens Sorboniques, laquelle ie n'auray pas honte de reciter . . . que ces poures gens poisassent bien que vaut ceste sentence"[130]

IV.xviii.1—(1539/59): "Quomodo initio dogma istud acceperint saniores Scholastici, nihil moror"; (1560): "comment elle a été traitée des docteurs scolastiques, qui ont parlé un peu plus passablement. . . ."[131]

IV.xix.15—(1543–59): "Romanenses autem at Scholastici (quibus solenne est omnia perperam . . .)"; (1545–60): "Or les theologiens romanistes, qui ont cette bonne coutume de corrompre et de dépraver tout par leurs belles gloses. . . ."[132]

B. References to the Sorbonne and Sorbonnists in Latin and French

II.iii.13—(1539/59): "ne aetatis nostrae Pelagiani, hoc est sorbonici sophistae totam vetustatem nobis adversam"; (1541/60): "à fin que les Pelagiens de nostre temps, c'est à dire les Sophistes de Sorbonne . . . que tous les docteurs anciens nous sont contraires."

III.xv.7:—(1539/59): "Ita Sorbonicae scholae, errorum omnium matres" (1541/60): "Voila comment les Sophistes des escoles Sorboniques meres de tous erreurs."

III.xviii.8—(1539/59): "Hic unus syllogismus amplo documentus est: scholas omnes Sorbonicas ne summis quidem labris"; (1541/60): "Ce seul argument est suffisant pour nous donner à coignostre, que toutes les escholes Sorboniques n'ont jamais gousté. . . ."

III.xviii.9—(1539/59): "Nolo singula persequi, quae hodie stulti Sorbonistae arrepta ex Scripturis temere"; (1541/60): "Je ne veulx point poursuyvre tous les tesmoignages que les accariastres Sorboniques prenne inconsiderement cà et là de l'Escriture. . . ."

IV.xix.24—(1543/59): "ineptos istos rabulas, Sorbonistas et Canonistas"; (1545–60): "ces badeaux de theologiens Sorboniques & Canonistes."

In the Light of Orthodoxy

The "Method and Disposition" of Calvin's
Institutio *from the Perspective of Calvin's*
Late-Sixteenth-Century Editors

Explaining the *Institutes*: A Sixteenth-Century Apparatus and Its
Displacement

A small, largely neglected, but far from negligible aspect of the relationship between
the Reformed theology of the mid-sixteenth century and the Reformed orthodoxy of
the seventeenth century is the understanding of Calvin's thought as it was received by
later Reformed theologians. The numerous editions, translations, and synopses of the
Institutes printed during the late sixteenth and the seventeenth centuries testify to its
continuing use and importance to later Reformed theology.[1] Moreover, as Brian Armstrong has shown, Calvin's teaching was subject to several possible interpretations during
the era of orthodoxy and, indeed, capable of being cited with significant effect by Moyse
Amyraut against his Reformed opponents.[2] One index to the understanding of Calvin's
thought in the sixteenth and seventeenth centuries and, indeed, a significant index to
the commonalities and differences between Reformation- or post-Reformation-era and
twentieth-century understandings of Calvin,[3] is the apparatus added to the *Institutes* by
editors in the late sixteenth century—notably, the detailed description of the "method
and disposition" of the "argument" of the *Institutes* and the system of marginal subheads
found in many of the older editions and translations but omitted from all of the more
recent editions and translations—as if it had never existed—presumably on grounds of
authorship.[4]

The 1590 edition of the *Institutes*, as will become apparent shortly, must be regarded
as the culmination of the sixteenth-century process of creating an apparatus. It placed
eleven items between the title page and the first line of the text of Book I: (1) Calvin's

letter to the reader, (2) an alphabetical list of "principal topics" keyed to the books and chapters of the *Institutes* and related to the main topics elaborated at length in the index of theological *loci* appended to the text, (3) Calvin's preface to Francis I of France, (4) an "admonition to the reader" detailing the major sources of the apparatus constructed by the 1590 editors, (5) a "method and disposition, or argument" of the entire *Institutes*, (6) a set of "one hundred aphorisms briefly embracing the summary and order of the four books of the *Institutes*," (7) a detailed index of theological *loci* by Nicholas Colladon, in which each of the topics of the *Institutes* is summarized with reference to the relevant chapters and subsections, (8) a letter to the reader from Augustinus Marloratus explaining his work of biblical and topical indexing, (9) Marlorat's detailed index to Old and New Testament texts (including the text of each verse cited in canonical order), (10) Marlorat's index of "subjects and names" as augmented by the 1590 editors, and (11) an "argument" or analytical summary of book I. Analytical summaries or *argumenta* are also prefaced to books II, III, and IV, and the entire text is supplied with analytical synopses of the chapters and with marginalia identifying the topics and structure of Calvin's numbered subsections and the sources cited in the text. Following the text, the reader finds a table of contents of the books and chapters in numerical order.[5]

Comparison of this structural aspect of the older editions and translations with those produced after 1860 reveals that the various tables, indices, and "argumenta" of the sixteenth-century edition, which were of course not provided by Calvin himself, have either not been replaced or have been replaced by new annotations and chapter headings. These new annotations and headings are also, of course, not provided by Calvin himself.[6] The historical dividing line, both for editions of the Latin text and for translations, is the publication of the *Calvini Opera* in the *Corpus Reformatorum* with barely a hint of the older apparatus.[7] Thus, Müller's 1909 translation offers only the titles of the books and chapters—the numbered subsections are given, as in the *Corpus Reformatorum*, without headings.[8] The editing of the *Corpus Reformatorum* had a similar effect on the Dutch translations of Wijenberg and Sizoo and on the French version of Benoit.[9] Other translations, notably the German of Weber and the French of Cadier and Marcel, do not look back behind the *Corpus Reformatorum*, but supply an entirely new set of sub-heads as an aid to the reader.[10] To be sure, all the more recent editions and translations supply indices of biblical texts and of subjects and names, and they retain Calvin's own prefatory materials. But they have excised and discarded the initial alphabetical list of chapters, the letter of the 1590 editors, the "method and disposition," the "hundred aphorisms," the four *argumenta* and the analytical synopses of chapters, the index of theological *loci*, and Marlorat's letter on the composition of indices—plus, of course, the extensive topical and structural marginalia. Not counting the marginalia, this amounts to a deletion, without replacement by comparable materials, of more than ninety double-column pages of closely set folio Latin text.

Such editorial modification, not of the text but of what might be called the frame into which the text is placed, is arguably of considerable methodological and theological significance: as a wise painter and teacher once noted to me, the frame is nearly as important as the picture—mediocre art beautifully framed often appears admirable to the passing observer, while superb art badly framed may be passed by as uninteresting. Alternatively, almost any painting can be accommodated to Baroque surroundings by being placed in a wide, ornately carved frame or to the modern context by being set in a narrow, plain frame. Without altering by one iota the words of Calvin's teaching, the sense of the whole and the relationship of its parts can be altered greatly by the provision of a new interpretive framework. And just as the interpretive framework offered by modern annotations and chapter headings can serve to distance Calvin's thought both from his own mid-sixteenth-century context and from the teachings of the era of Protestant orthodoxy, so, too, might the older *argumenta* offer a framework that serves to place the *Institutes* more clearly into the atmosphere of sixteenth- and seventeenth-century Reformed thought. And, indeed, whatever one's ultimate judgment on the quality of the sixteenth-century interpretive apparatus, it is undeniable that the work of the sixteenth-century editors did serve to frame the understanding and interpretation of Calvin during the era of Reformed orthodoxy—and is therefore of considerable significance to the historical discussion of the development of Reformed theology in the sixteenth and seventeenth centuries.

In other words, the question of continuity and discontinuity between Calvin and the so-called "Calvinism" of his successors is only partially answered when modern interpretations of the structure, argument, and implication of Calvin's *Institutes* are juxtaposed with modern interpretations of later Reformed theology: it may very well be the case that late-sixteenth-and seventeenth-century Reformed theologians understood their own efforts as standing in clear continuity with the work of Calvin (and his contemporaries) on the ground of a late-sixteenth-century framework for understanding Calvin's thought and method. The importance of this point not only to grasping the relationship between Calvin's thought and later Reformed theology but also to understanding Calvin's thought in its own sixteenth-century context becomes clear when we recognize that at least two elements of the late-sixteenth-century apparatus of the *Institutes* (the much of the marginalia and the initial statement of argument) derived from the work of Nicholas Colladon and Caspar Olevianus, both of whom were acquainted with Calvin himself. The late-sixteenth-century apparatus, thus, evidences not only a historical but also a personal proximity to Calvin and his work.

The Development of an Apparatus for the *Institutes*, 1559–1667

The modern reader who has not examined sixteenth-and seventeenth-century editions and epitomes of Calvin's *Institutes* can have little sense either of the considerable attention paid to apparatus in these older editions or of the rather different approach to apparatus characteristic of sixteenth- and seventeenth-century editors of Calvin. These early editions are, in the first place, indexed in great detail and typically offer careful collations of chapter titles in their prefatory or concluding material. There were, of course, indices to the *Institutes* prior to 1559: the 1550 and 1553 editions boast exhaustive indices of biblical texts, disputed points, patristic references, and topics—as well as marginal citations of Scripture and the fathers.[11] These earlier apparatus were, however, rendered useless by Calvin's large-scale revision of 1559. In their place, the reader finds at the end of the 1559 and 1561 editions a synopsis of the four books listing the individual chapter titles and a lengthy alphabetical list of *loci communes*—it is, in effect, an elaborate topical index, prepared by Nicholas Colladon.[12] This index of *loci* also appears in the French translation of 1560.[13] The Colladon index marks a significant new departure, inasmuch as it contains an alphabetical listing of *loci communes* and, under each topical heading, a synopsis of the relevant chapters with references to the numbered subsections. In the 1562 and subsequent French editions, as well as in the next Latin edition (1568/69),[14] the reader finds an exhaustive index of biblical passages, compiled and carefully checked by Augustine Marlorat against the text of Scripture and a substantial *index rerum* or index of briefly identified topics, issues, and some names (not to be confused with the Colladon index of *loci*). In all of these editions, the scripture references together with some references to the fathers are virtually the only marginalia. The editions of 1568 and 1569 follow the same basic pattern in their apparatus.[15]

That these indices and brief marginalia were ultimately unsatisfying and that additional explanatory and interpretive devices were viewed as necessary is suggested by the major development of analyses, analytical abridgements, and apparatus that occurred at the same time as the publication of the London and Lausanne editions of 1576.[16] These efforts were virtually necessitated by Calvin's own expansion of the *Institutes* from the original form of the editions of 1536 and 1539–50—which remained, even at its greatest expansion, a rather manageable form of instruction instruction in twenty-one chapters—to the large-scale four-book, eighty-chapter structure of 1559. Bunnie confessed that he found the final edition of *Institutes* daunting in its density.[17] For, although Calvin's 1539 preface to the reader clearly indicated the direction of this development (the addition of *loci communes* and *disputationes* written in the course of exegesis and debate), the expansion of the *Institutes* from 1543 onward was not paralleled by any effort on Calvin's part to offer a synopsis: he provided no summaries, analyses, or headings for the numbered subsections of his burgeoning chapters.[18]

The first major movement in this direction occurred in 1576 in the London and Lausanne editions of the *Institutes*. Summaries or "arguments" of the four books of the *Institutes* and the comments on the structure of the chapters written by Edmund Bunnie were appended to the Vautrollier edition of 1576.[19] These materials were also published in the same year in a much augmented form as an abridgement or *Compendium* of Calvin's work.[20] Vautrollier's *Institutes* offered a significant advance toward a major apparatus: in addition to appending Bunnie's *argumenta*, it reproduced the Colladon and Marlorat indices to the Geneva editions and added, albeit somewhat inconsistently, marginal subheadings and an elaborate system of cross-references at various points in the text. Bunnie's *Compendium*, moreover, offered a full-scale independent analytical apparatus for Calvin's text that could be placed next to the text of the *Institutes* as a guide. Bunnie summarized each of the numbered subsections of the *Institutes*, often retaining Calvin's precise system of numbers while at the same time reducing the argument typically to single-sentence synopses. He also offered, perhaps for the first time, summaries of the "argument" of each book of the *Institutes*, prefaced to the text of each book, and charts of an Agricolan or Ramist character designed to manifest the structure of the *Institutes*.[21] In addition, Bunnie frequently prefaced his compend of individual chapters of the *Institutes* with introductory analyses of the argument of the chapter, noting, for example, that a particular chapter had "three principal parts" and then noting both the content of each part and the sections of the chapter belonging to each.[22] The Latin version of Bunnie's "arguments" and initial analyses of the chapters were highly influential: these devices were edited, augmented, and incorporated into the Geneva editions published by Le Preux beginning in 1590,[23] retained in the Geneva *Opera Omnia* of 1617,[24] and incorporated into the famous Schipper edition of the *Opera* in 1667,[25] whence they were carried over into Tholuck's nineteenth-century editions and into the Allen and Beveridge translations.[26]

The Lausanne edition published by Franciscus Le Preux in 1576 also offers, for the first time among the continental editions, a significant analytical apparatus. The Lausanne edition indicates on its title page the nature of the added materials.[27] In the Lausanne edition, moreover, a new prefatory letter by Nicholas Colladon (addressed to Blasius Marcuardus, professor of Scripture in Lausanne) offers a lengthy description of the various elements of the marginalia, and Colladon identifies himself as the author or at least chief editor—with Calvin's blessing—of the apparatus.[28] These new marginalia describe in brief the topics found in the various numbered subsections of the *Institutes* and include marginal characterizations of Calvin's argument in such phrases as "obiectio contra nostrorum doctrina" and "obiectio & eius solutio." Unlike the Vautrollerius edition, the Lausanne Le Preux edition inaugurates a standardized pattern of marginal subheadings for every section each chapter. This identification of the structure of Calvin's *loci communes* and *disputationes* is characteristic of the various Le Preux editions and is a significant indication of the way in which Calvin's gathered or codified polemic was understood in the sixteenth century as part of a process of formal scholastic disputation. Among these marginalia, the Lausanne edition also provides cross-references to Calvin's other works.[29]

Of significance nearly equal to the addition of the *argumenta* by Bunnie was the introduction of one hundred numbered "aphorisms," descriptive of the contents of Calvin's work and arranged in the order of the outline of the *Institutes*, placed as an introductory synopsis together with the other prefatory materials in several of the Latin and French editions from the era of orthodoxy.[30] These aphorisms are based on the work of Gulielmus Launeus (William Delaune) in his "epitome" of the *Institutes*. Launeus not only summarized the *Institutes*, for the most part using Calvin's own language, offering a view of the contents of all four books in a single volume; he also formally identified Calvin's pattern of polemical argumentation to meet the requirements of late-sixteenth-century polemic: each disputative chapter of the *Institutes* appears as a series of objections and replies.[31] Launeus also attempted to explicate the logic of Calvin's order and argument in the *Institutes* in detailed charts of an Agricolan or Ramist character. The charts are both organizational, showing the structure of the four books and the relationship of the chapters to each other, and interpretive, offering an indication of the way in which the *Institutes* was perceived and understood in the era of the greatest systematizing efforts of the late Reformation. The aphorisms are based on the headings in the charts, augmented slightly as demanded by syntax.[32] Thus, Launeus's chart contains the following divisions:

> Vera sapientia sita est in cognitione Dei. 1. creatoris, (1) naturaliter insita, (2) aliusdem comparata nempe (a) totius mundi fabrica . . . , (b) scripturis . . . ; 2. redemptoris ad cuius cognitionem nota, (1)lapsum hominis . . . (2) causam materialem redemptionis nempe Christum, ubi considerato, (a) Quomodo exibetur hominibus. (b) quomodo recipitur ab hominibus (c) quomodo Deus in societate Christi nos retinet. . . . [33]

The relevant aphorisms from the 1590 Geneva edition are:

1. Vera hominis sapientia sita est in cognitione Dei Creatoris & Redemptoris.
2. Haec cognitio est nobis naturaliter insita. . . .
4. Aliunde etiam est comparata: nempe totius mundi fabrica & sacris scripturis.
14. Cognitio Dei redemptoris colligitur ex lapsu hominis, & ex materiali redemptionis causa.
21. Materialis causa redemptionis est Christus, inquo consideranda tria: 1. Quomodo exhibeatur hominibus. 2. Quomodo recipiatur. 3. Quomodo in eius societate homines retineantur.[34]

The first three aphorisms cited here belong, of course, to the first book of the *Institutes* and represent, respectively, the underlying structural theme of the *Institutes*,[35] the theme of chapter three, and the themes of chapters five and six; the fourteenth aphorism is the first aphorism pertaining to the second book, and the twenty-first brings the argument to Book II, chapter six, "The Redemption of Lost Human Beings Is to Be Sought in Christ."

The 1590 Geneva *Institutes* notes clearly the sources of the various elements of its apparatus in its prefatory "admonition to the reader": the hundred aphorisms are drawn out of the chart or *tabula* of Gulielmus Launeus; the annotations that appear throughout the text of the *Institutes* are drawn "in part from the labors of Nicholas Colladon and Edmund Bunnie" and "in part from our own observations" of "the order and connection of arguments" and the author's "responses to objections from adversaries":[36] Colladon's exhaustive index of *loci communes* was based on summary statements of doctrinal subtopics with reference to sections of the *Institutes*, Bunnie's (and Launeus's) compendia provided material for marginal heads, and Bunnie's text provided summaries of sections. The 1590 Geneva edition, therefore, marks a considerable development past the use of Bunnie's *argumenta* in the Vautrollerius edition of 1576: there Bunnie's synopses had appeared as a appendix; here they are set into the text of the *Institutes* as apparatus prior to each book and chapter. In fact, the editors of the 1590 edition not only edited Bunnie's initial summaries of argument but provided similarly structured summaries for those longer chapters that Bunnie had not anaylzed, thereby offering a consistent model of analytical introduction for all of the chapters.[37] Even so, many of the marginalia draw on Launeus's marginal summaries of sections, some draw on the Colladon index's summaries of the *loci*, while other marginalia continue to reflect the patterns of citation, cross-reference, and comment found in earlier editions of the *Institutes*, and still others appear to have been added in 1590. At all levels, moreover, the index of loci, the various compendia, and the marginalia reflect the words of Calvin's 1559 text and evidence a variety of textual interrelationships: thus, for example, Bunnie's compendium frequently uses or adapts phrases from the Colladon index. In addition, among these added marginalia are characterizations of subsections, sometimes echoing the Lausanne edition of 1576, that identify places where Calvin encounters the "objection" of an adversary and offers his response.[38] Indeed, the 1590 Johannes le Preux edition (published in Geneva) consciously takes up the task of developing an apparatus at the point reached by the 1576 and 1577 Franciscus Le Preux editions (published in Lausanne), incorporating materials from the epitomies that had been written after the 1576 and 1577 editions had gone to press. (2From the perspective of the printers, these developments may simply represent the transfer of the task of providing a definitive edition of the *Institutes* from the press of the older brother in Lausanne to the burgeoning business of the younger brother in Geneva.[39])

The prefatory "admonition" of the 1590 edition also attributes the remaining element of the apparatus—namely the initial analysis of the "method and disposition, or argument of the entire work"—to Caspar Olevian, whose own epitome of the *Institutes* appeared in 1586.[40] In the order of their appearance, the prefatory materials of the *Institutes* now included Calvin's original prefatory letter to Francis I, his letter to the reader, Olevian's *Methodus et dispositio*, the hundred aphorisms drawn from Launeus, and the *argumentum* for Book I taken from Bunnie, followed by the text edited 1559 of the *Institutes* with the Colladon-Launeus organizational marginalia and the Bunnie *argumenta* for Books II–IV. Also present are the Colladon index of *loci*, the Marlorat index of biblical texts, and a version of the Marlorat *index rerum*, now augmented with references to all of the citations from the fathers, referencing first the patristic author, then the title of the work cited. As of the 1590 edition, then, we have complete the apparatus characteristic of nearly all subsequent editions prior to the *Opera Calvini* in the *Corpus Reformatorum*.[41]

Thus, the 1590 edition of the *Institutes*, followed in virtually all of the seventeenth-century editions with only minor revisions, including the *Opera* of 1617 and the Schipper edition of 1667, is certainly the preeminent edition of Calvin's work in and for the era of Reformed orthodoxy—and, arguably, the most fully and clearly interpreted edition in the entire history of the *Institutes* from the sixteenth century to the present. The well-known nineteenth-century Tholuck edition offers the *argumenta* and many of the initial structural analyses of chapters but omits the marginalia and the hundred aphorisms. The Allen translation provides only the basic *argumenta*, while Beveridge alone gives his readers a version of the entire late-sixteenth-century apparatus, with the marginal subheads gathered together at the beginning of each chapter immediately following a translation of the logical analysis—although Beveridge deviates from the older model in his relegation of the "hundred aphorisms" to the end of his second volume and removes the biblical and historical references from the subheads to bracketed references in the text.

Methodus et Dispositio: The Understanding of the *Institutes* in the Early Orthodox Era

Whereas it is certainly useful to identify the Protestant theology of the last three or four decades of the sixteenth century (ca. 1565–1600) as belonging to the "early orthodox" era, we dare not forget that periodizations are historical constructs or generalizations, the chronological boundaries of which are difficult if not impossible to document precisely. Even so, the transition from the theology of Calvin and contemporaries like Melanchthon, Bullinger, Musculus, Vermigli, and Hyperius to the thought of the next Reformed generation—Beza, Ursinus, Olevianus, Zanchi, Danaeus—was quite gradual. The fairly intense attention paid by the later sixteenth-century theologians to the method and the topics of theological system, although characteristic of the development of a scholastic Protestant theology, is rooted not simply in a reappropriation of late medieval patterns of argument by later generations of Protestants but also in the inter-related development of scholastic method, humanistic rhetoric and logic, and Renaissance Aristotelianism during the sixteenth century itself. Thus, the attention to *methodus* characteristic of the later theology stands in continuity with the descriptions of theological *methodus* in the writings of Melanchthon and Hyperius. So, too, the interest of the early orthodox theologians in the *loci communes* or universal topics of theology, elicited from Scripture by exegesis, and in the development of those topics through a process of academic and polemical disputation looks back to the efforts of Melanchthon, Musculus, and, indeed, Calvin.

From 1539 on, Calvin had, after all, described his patterns of doctrinal formulations in the *Institutes* as "dogmatic disputations" (*disputationes dogmaticae*) and "standard topics" or "commonplaces" (*loci communes*).[42] What Colladon provided in his index was, in effect, the summary of Calvin's theological *loci* and their subtopics, arranged in alphabetical order. The Colladon index is not only an exhaustive list of topics; it is also an alphabetical compendium of the theology of the *Institutes*, based on Calvin's own assumption that the *Institutes* was a systematically ordered series of *loci* and *disputationes*. From the perspective of later editors, the use of phrases from the Colladon index as part of a marginal apparatus summarizing and highlighting the topics and subtopics of the *Institutes* was surely a most natural step toward the creation of an apparatus, given both Calvin's identification of the *Institutes* as a series of *loci* and his at least tacit approval of Colladon's work as it appeared in the several editions of the *Institutes* overseen by him and issued between 1559 and his death in 1564.

By way of example, Colladon's brief locus "Of the Merit of Christ" follows closely the argument and the language of *Institutes* II.xvii:

> It is truly and properly said that Christ merited for us the grace of God and salvation: where it is shown that Christ is not merely the instrument or minister of salvation, but its author and principal agent: nor in speaking this way is the grace of God obscured, since the merit of Christ is not opposed to the mercy of God, but indeed depends on it. For whatever is subordinated does not conflict, Book 2, cap. 17, sect. 1.
>
> This distinction between the merit of Christ and the grace of God is proven from many places in Scripture, sect. 2.
>
> Many testimonies of Scripture are presented, from which it is surely and solidly concluded that Christ, by his obedience, has truly acquired and merited for us the Father's grace, sect. 3.4.5.
>
> It is foolish curiosity to inquire whether Christ merited anything for himself, and truly rash to assert this, sect. 6.[43]

Not only does the Colladon summary reflect Calvin's argument closely; it also reflects (as indicated in the note) the language of Calvin's chapter.

Similarly, both in his 1539 preface to the reader and in many of his commentaries, Calvin evidenced a concern, typical of both late scholastic and Renaissance humanist method,[44] for the "order" or "method," "scope," and "argument" of texts and topics under examination. Thus, the title of the 1559 *Institutes* indicates that the treatise is "now for the first time arranged into four books, and divided into definite chapters, according to a most suitable *methodus*," while its preface speaks of an *ordo* into which the material has been "digested" and of the focus or *scopus* in or through which the teaching of Scripture ought to be understood.[45] Calvin also quite frequently presented his readers with a synopsis or *argumentum* as a prolegomenon to his commentary. The point of these prefatory discussions was to summarize analytically the central issue of the book: thus, in the commentary on Romans, Calvin indicates that "the subject" of chapters 1–5 is "that man's only righteousness is through the mercy of God in Christ, which being offered by the Gospel is apprehended by faith" and then summarizes the remaining chapters as developments of this theme, which, among other things, record and answer objections to the Apostle's basic argument.[47] What the editors of later editions of the *Institutes* provided by including Olevianus's *Methodus et dispositio seu totius operis argumentum* was this basic analytical summary of contents—an introductory exercise not provided for the *Institutes* by Calvin himself but clearly related in its approach to Calvin's own methods. Writes Olevianus:

> The central intention (*scopus*) of this Christian Institution, is twofold: first, that knowledge of God which leads to blessed immortality: and second, in connection with this, [the knowledge of] ourselves. In order that we might understand this *scopus*, he simply sets before us the arrangement (*methodus*) of the Apostle's Creed as something most familiar to all Christians.[47]

Olevianus's view of the credal order of the 1559 *Institutes* can hardly be called arbitrary—indeed, it rests directly on a perception of the way in which Calvin reorganized his materials for what would be the final edition of his treatise—at least in part by separating and repositioning the three credal chapters of 1543 as organizational anchors for the four books of the final edition.[48]

As already noted, Calvin himself had identified the contents of the *Institutes* as *disputationes*; furthermore, Colladon's overview of the *loci* frequently identified responses and counterarguments, and, in 1576, the Lausanne edition had identified the internal structure of Calvin's disputations as consisting in the statement of a position followed by objections, and replies. Similarly, Launeus' *Compendium* (1583) had attempted to identify the disputative portions of the *Institutes* by summarizing "objections" and "replies" in a dialogical form. Probably with these precedents in view, the editors of the 1590 *Institutes* provided a more detailed marginal apparatus to illustrate the pattern of Calvin's numbered chapter sections as reflective of the style of the disputation or dogmatic *locus*. Various elements of the new apparatus—the aphorisms based on Launeus, the structural analyses drawn from Bunnie, and the other marginalia taken from Colladon's index of *loci*—indicate the resources used by the editors: they had before them previous editions, with their indices and marginal references; Bunnie's *Epitome* with its charts, its analyses, and its propositional summaries of Calvin's subsections; a version of what would become Olevianus's *Epitome;* and Launeus's *Epitome*, with its exhaustive structural charts and its disputative patterning, usually in Calvin's own words. And, of course, the editors had Calvin's final title and his preface to his readers with their language of method, order, disputation, and *loci communes.*

In the following analysis of portions of several chapters (II.xv.6; III.xxiii.1–6), a superscripted "1559" indicates marginalia from the first stratum of marginal apparatus to the 1559 text, the Genevan and Strasbourg editions, 1559–69; "Coll," reflections of the Colladon index of *loci;* "LePr," language taken over from the Lausanne Le Preux editions; "Bunn," elements taken from Bunnie's *Compendium;* "Laun," apparatus from Launeus's *Epitome;* unmarked words are assumed to be material added by the editors of the 1590 edition, whether from other, as yet unidentified sources or of their own composition. Parallel marginalia, indicating, for example, the reliance of the 1590 J. le Preux edition on the 1576/77 F. Le Preux text are be indicated in footnotes. Calvin's subsection numbers appear with a section sign (§) preceding the number; further subdivisions of subsections characteristic of the 1590 edition are given in parentheses—for example, (1). In addition, since marginalia found in an earlier edition are typically taken over into the later editions, no indication is given of repetitions: thus, the biblical and patristic texts referenced in "1559" are also noted in the margins of "LePr," and so forth. Of course, only an analysis of the complete marginalia could indicate the relative importance of the various sources to the final composition.

Analysis of the 1590 Edition of the *Institutes*

II.xv.

§6. *Quod ad sacerdotium Christi,[ut ad nos perveniat eius efficacia & utilitas].*[Coll/49]
[Psal. 110.4.][1559]

[*A morte Christi incipiendum est.*][Coll] *unde sequitur (1) eiusdem in tercessio pro nobis. (2)*
  [*precandi fiducia.*][Coll] *(3)* [*conscientiarum tranquillitas.*][Coll/50]

(4) *Christiani per Christum fiunt sacredotes, seipsos & sua omnia Deo accepta offerentes.*
[Apoc.1.6.][1559]
[Iohan.17.19.][1559]
[Dan.9.14.][1559]
[*Hinc sequitur Papistas graviter peccare qui Christum se immolare iactitant.*][Bunn/51]

III.xxiii.

Constat caput quatuor partibus, quae praecipuas obiectiones variasque adversariorum instantias & exceptiones ab his obiectionibus pendentes, refellunt. His praemittitur 1 sect. refutatio eorum qui electionem fatentur, reprobationem negant.

1. Primae obiectionis adv. doctrinam de electione & reprobatione consideratio, sect. 2.3.4. & 5.
2. Ad secundam obiectionem responsio, sect. 6.7.8. & 9.
3. Obiectionem tertiam, eiusdemque confirmationem diluit sect. 10. & 11.
4. Quarta refellitur sect.12. & 13. addita sect. 14. utili & necessaria cautione.[52]

§1. *Falluntur qui reprobationem negant.*[53] [vid. Bernard. in die ascens. Serm.2.][LePr]
(1) [*Electio enim nisi reprobtionis opposita non stat.*][Laun]
(2) *Proteruè agunt cum Deo, cuius consilia angelis ipsi adorant.* [Rom.9.20.][1559]
(3) *Expressis Scriptura testimonia refelluntur.* [Mat.15.13.][1559]
(4) *Deo obstrepunt, per Apostolorum consilia sua aperienti.* [Rom.9.22.][1559]
[*Exceptio. 1*][LePr/54]
Responsio.
[Li.5. Contra Iul. cap.5.][1559]
[*Exceptio.*][LePr/55]
Responsio.

Augustinus voce confirmata. [Lib.1.de praedest. Sanct. c.2.][1559]

§2. [*Obiectio.*][LePr] *Deum immeritò iraces in quos exitio, citra proprium metirum, devovet.*[56]
Responsio 1 à consideratione divinae voluntatis.
[Hoc ex August. sumptum lib.1.de Gen. contra Manic. c.3.][1559]
Qua sit illa voluntatis, & quomodo consideranda.[57]
[Psal.51.6.][1559]

§3. [*Resp.*][LePr] *2. eàque trimembris.*[58]
Deus nihil homini debet.
[*Aequissima iustitiae ratione*][Bunn/59] *peccato corruptos odio prosequitur.*
Suae ipsorum conscientia sensus & iudicio reprobi omnes morti destinari iusto Dei iudicio
  agnoscunt.

§4. [*Exceptio.*][LePr] *Ad peccatum reprobos praeordinatos videri.*[60]
Responsio.
Eiusd. expositio.
[Rom.9.20.][1559]
Instantia.
Solutio, textum Apostolicà calumnis praeclarè vendicans.
[Prov.26.10.][1559]
[I.Tim.5.21.][1559]

§5. *Eadem solutio,* [*Augustini authoritate confirmatu*].[Bunn]
[Epist.106.][LePr]
[*Prosopopeis*][Bunn] *item egregia illustratatur.*
[Psal.36.7.][1559]
Et praeclaro [*August. dicto, de verbis Apost. Serm.20*].[1559]

§6. [*Obiectio*].[LePr/61] [*Deus imputare non debet hominibus peccata quorum necessitatem suae*
  praedestinatione imposuit].[Coll/62]
Prima [*responsio*],[Coll/63] *veterum, quae infirma censentur.*[64]
Ratio.
[Prov. 16.4.][1559]
Secunda responsio, etiam diluta.
Tertia responsio quam Valla proposuit, probata.[65]

The Theological and Methodological Significance of the Older Apparatus: A Comparison of Scholarship Old and New

Given the detail and the intensely structural and analytical character of the older apparatus, it should be clear that its loss has affected our understanding of Calvin—and it is hardly surprising that the rediscovery of its insights has been both intermittent and gradual. Perhaps the most striking illustration of this problem is the understanding of Calvin's distinction of the knowledge of God into a knowledge of God the Creator and a knowledge of God the Redeemer. This theme of the *duplex cognitio dei* or "twofold knowledge of God," highlighted in the twentieth century by Dowey's now classic study, was hardly an idea unique to Calvin.[66] Not only was it used by contemporaries of Calvin (such as Viret) and later Reformed theologians (including Polanus and Du Moulin); it probably also reflects the medieval Augustinian identification of the *obiectum theologiae* as God the Creator and Redeemer (Giles of Rome) or God the Creator, Redeemer, and Glorifier (Gregory of Rimini).[67]

In any case, given its rather wide circulation, it is not surprising that the concept and its organizing function were clearly noted in the late-sixteenth-century apparatus of the *Institutes*. The first aphorism abstracted from Launeus reads, "True human wisdom consists in the knowledge of God the Creator and Redeemer." The subject of Book I is clarified in the second, third, and fourth aphorisms: "(2) This knowledge is naturally implanted in us . . . (3) But this seed is corrupted . . . (4) It is also provided from another source: from the fabric of the entire world, and [by] the Holy Scriptures."[68] Nor is the organizational character of the distinction lost: the fourteenth aphorism, marking the beginning of Book II, reads, "The knowledge of God the Redeemer is gathered from the fall of man, and from the material cause of redemption."[69] Of even more significance for the early orthodox understanding of the structure and logic of the *Institutes* is Launeus's chart, in which the initial distinction between the knowledge of God the Creator and the knowledge of God the Redeemer provides the basic structural division of the *Institutes*, with the subjects of Books III and IV being subsumed under the theme of redemptive knowledge initiated in Book II. Launeus's view of the organization of the *Institutes* is virtually identical to Dowey's thesis—although it stands definitively in the way of Dowey's assumption that Reformed orthodoxy lost sight of Calvin's conception of the orgainzation of theology.[70]

Dowey's work was almost immediately rebutted by Parker, who argued for a credal order in the *Institutes*—and, some time later, ably defended by Dowey.[71] It is, of course, impossible to discover how the sixteenth-century editors of the *Institutes* would have responded to this debate. What we can say, however, is that the sixteenth-century editors knew and in some measure accepted *both* views of the organization of the *Institutes*, given the fact that Olevianus's *Methodus et dispositio* and Bunnie's *argumenta* for the individual books, also ensconced in the text, offered the credal explanation of the plan of the four books of the *Institutes*. We may infer at least that they did not view the two explanations as mutually exclusive or as contradictory. On the one hand, Launeus did not understand the architectonic use of the *duplex cognitio Dei* as creating an imbalance: his Ramistic or Agricolan divisions of the topic assume the relative brevity of the discussion of the knowledge of God as Creator in comparison to the three-book discussion of the knowledge of God as Redeemer, wherein the "restoration" of humanity in Christ must be provided (Book II), received (Book III), and maintained (Book IV).[72] This, moreover, is precisely the view of Köstlin, Wendel, and Dowey: given the logical and theological grounding of the arguments of Books III and IV in the objective work of redemption in Book II, the *Institutes* divides, in effect, into two parts—the knowledge of God the Creator and the Knowledge of God the Redeemer. Köstlin describes the twofold knowledge of God, as Creator and as Redeemer, as the *Gesammtanordnung* of the *Institutes* into two "objective, theological moments over against the anthropological" and, presumably, subjective aspects of theology.[73]

This understanding is not absent from Olevianus's credally patterned *Methodus et dispositio*. He notes that the first article of the creed deals with "God the Father" and that, therefore, "the first book is concerned with the knowledge of God, inasmuch as he is the Creator, Conserver, and Governor of each and every thing. It teaches both what the true knowledge of the Creator is and the goal toward which it leads."[74] This knowledge of God the Creator is, however, vitiated by sin—which also made necessary the redemption of humanity through Christ. Therefore, the next article of the Creed and "the second book of the *Institutes* deal with the knowledge of God as the Redeemer in Christ"—in short, it "shows the fall of humanity and leads human beings to Christ the Mediator."[75] Just as Launeus held that the connection between Book II and Book III was the reception or application of the revelation of Christ as Redeemer, so too does Olevianus argue:

> As long as Christ is separated from us, there is no benefit to us. We must be engrafted into him, as branches into the vine. Thus, after the doctrine of Christ, *I believe in the Holy Spirit* follows as the third part of the Creed: inasmuch as the Spirit is the bond of union between us and Christ.[76]

Nor is it enough to speak generally of this engrafting, since, Launeus reminds us, we need to understand how we are "held in relationship to Christ"—as Olevianus notes, "the Holy Spirit does not engraft all people into Christ, or give faith to all; and to those to whom he does give it, he does not ordinarily give it without means, to which end he uses the preaching of the Gospel and the celebration of the Sacraments, with the full admininstration of [ecclesial] discipline."[77] Therefore, both the creed and the *Institutes* conclude with a discussion of the church. In Olevianus's credal model, as in Launeus's discussion of the *duplex cognitio Dei*, the implication or logic of the revelation of God as Redeemer leads to the personal receiving of salvation and the corporate administration of means: Books III and IV are not independent articles but the logical outcome of the subject of Book II. In both forms of the argument, moreover, we witness not an imbalance or lack of symmetry in the *Institutes* but only the expected increase of detail as the argument moves from creation and sin to soteriological topics, redemption and the means of redemption. The symmetry revealed, moreover, in Launeus's chart is a symmetry generated not by relative size of books and chapters but by the flow of argument (and the horizontal flow of the chart) from the knowledge of God, to the subdivision of the knowledge of God into knowledge of the Creator and knowledge of the Redeemer in Books I and II, and then, given the completion of the argument concerning God the Creator, to the further subdivision of the knowledge of God the Redeemer into the two resultant categories of the application of Redemption (Book III) and the continuance or maintenance of Redemption through the established means (Book IV).

Yet another highly significant feature of the apparatus, already noted in the discussion of its development, is the structural and analytical analysis of each chapter deriving from Bunnie's work and from the efforts of the 1590 editors. Here, unlike the reflection of the structural insights of Dowey and Parker in the work of the early editors, we find a considerable difference in approach and result. Indeed, whereas it has been the effect of the work of Otto Weber, John T. McNeill, and Ford Lewis Battles to emphasize the discursive character of the *Institutes* by inserting topical headings, often with little concern for the rhetorical mode of the text—that is, whether it is a positive exposition, a polemical statement of opposing opinion, or the rebuttal of an opponent—it was characteristic of the sixteenth-century editors to note these rhetorical issues and, frequently, to indicate the organization of a chapter in terms of positive statement, objections and replies. Moreover, this movement from statement, to objections, and then to replies indicates, if not a fundamentally scholastic pattern in the discursive flow of the *Institutes*, at least the clear possibility of understanding the flow of Calvin's argument in terms of scholastic as well as humanistic models.[78] Indeed, inasmuch as Calvin's rhetoric can be understood as fundamentally syllogistic—consisting in statement, adversative modifier, and conclusion—the assumption of a conflict between humanistic rhetoric and scholastic disputation may not apply at all to Calvin's work.[79] This is particularly the case inasmuch as Calvin's understanding of the *disputatio*, like his use of rhetoric and logic and his variant of the *locus* method, partook of the shifting forms of discourse characteristic of their passage through the sixteenth century: thus, Calvin's highly discursive *disputationes* reflect the altered classroom practice of beginning not with a *quaestio* but with a thetical statement of the issue to be debated.[80]

By way of example, the apparatus for *Institutes*, II.xiv, Calvin's chapter on "How the Two Natures Constitute the Person of the Mediator," presents, first, the analytical argument adapted from Bunnie, followed by a series of marginal heads, some of which follow Bunnie's *Compendium*, some of which draw on the Colladon index of *loci*, and others that probably originated with the editors of the 1590 Le Preux edition: "This chapter contains two principal parts: I. The doctrine of Christ's two natures in one person is briefly expounded, sec. 1–4. II. The heresies of Servetus, which destroy the distinction of natures in Christ, and the eternity of the divine nature of the Son are refuted."[81] The marginalia for this chapter are as follows (numbers correspond to subsections; biblical references are omitted):

§1. The first part, demonstrating that there are two natures in Christ, the human and the divine. / Confirmation, by analogy drawn from the union of body and soul. / Application of the analogy.[82]

§2. Second confirmation, drawn from testimonies of Scripture which declare a distinction between the two natures. / Testimonies concerning the communication of properties.[83]

§3. Third confirmation, from testimonies that show the conjunction of both natures. A rule worth being observed in this disputation.[84]

§4. Utility and use of the above doctrine concerning the conjunction and distinction of two natures in Christ. / Against the double Christ imagined by the Nestorians. Also against the confusion or destruction of the natures by the Eutychians. / Both justly condemned by the church.[85]

§5. The second part of the chapter, in which Servetus' heresies negating the eternal deity and two natures of Christ are refuted. / General response or sum of the orthodox doctrine of Christ. / What is meant by the hypostatic union. / First objection of Servetus to the eternal deity of Christ. / Response. / Second objection. Response.[86]

§6. Third objection. / Response. / Christ the true, natural, and only Son: on which ground he is distinguished from [God's] adopted sons, which is to say, from all of those elected by God in Christ. / The twofold filiation of Christ: namely, of God and of man.[87]

§7. Fourth objection. / Response. / Confirmation from the testimonies of the fathers.[88]

§8. Conclusion to the preceding objections, leading to the terrible consequence, as if Christ had a human nature drawn out of God himself. / Why the other pestilential heresies of Servetus are not refuted here. / The impure intentions of this heretic.[89]

Two differences between this analysis of the chapter and the analysis offered by McNeill are immediately apparent: the sixteenth-century apparatus divided the chapter differently, and it noted the technical shape of a *disputatio*, moving from positive statement or proof based on definition, analogy, and biblical argument to a statement of the usefulness of the doctrine against two ancient heresies to a series of contemporary objections and replies, in this case all in debate with Servetus. McNeill argues two subdivisions but identifies them as sections 1–3 and sections 4–8, respectively and his subheads offer little indication of a formal structure of disputation.

An examination of Calvin's text supports the sixteenth-century editors' division: the chapter begins with Calvin's classic statement of the meaning of the incarnation: "He who was the Son of God became the Son of man, not by confusion of substance, but by unity of person," which Calvin then proceeds to elaborate in terms of the analogy of the union of soul and body and in consistent reflection on the Chalcedonian formula and the doctrine of the communication of proper qualities. The Chalcedonian definition is then argued biblically first (section 2) from passages that refer either to the divinity or to the humanity of Christ and thereby distinguish the natures and then (section 3) from passages "which comprehend both natures at once." At this point—the end of section 3—Calvin has justified the traditional dogma through examination of Scripture. If we follow McNeill, the positive section of the chapter has been concluded, and five sections in "condemnation of the errors of Nestorius, Eutyches, and Servetus" follow, finishing out the chapter. But Calvin begins section 4 with the words, "This observation, if the readers apply it properly, will be of no small use in solving a vast number of difficulties."[90] He is clearly drawing out conclusions from the preceding argument. This linkage with the preceding is clear from his brief condemnations of Nestorius and Eutyches, both of which conclude with references to the biblical arguments of sections 2 and 3, in which Calvin had justified the Chalcedonian definition in terms that undercut both the Nestorian and the Eutychian heresies. In a sense, the basic argument of the chapter has come full circle—Calvin began with the Chalcedonian definition and concludes his formulation with specific reference to the usefulness of his formulation in defeating the two archetypal christological heresies. The old marginalia, here looking back to the Colladon index, refer to the usefulness of the definitions in combatting the ancient heresies.[91] The remainder of the chapter deals with the contemporary problem of Servetus—sections 5 through 8 stand as a relatively coherent unit. In other words, in this particular case, the older apparatus more clearly identified the shape of the chapter.

What is more, the modern subheads often serve to obscure rather than indicate the disputative character of the chapter. Section 5 thus begins, "But in our age, also, has arisen a not less fatal monster, Michael Servetus, who for the Son of God has substituted a figment," offering an introductory statement of Servetus's heresy and then returning to the orthodox position by way of refutation—"Meanwhile, however, the definition of the church stands unmoved. . . ."[92] Whereas the sixteenth-century apparatus describes this argument with the phrases "The heresies of Servetus refuted" and "General answer or sum of the orthodox doctrine," McNeill, following Weber, offers only, "Christ is the Son of God from everlasting." Similarly, section 6 introduces Christ's eternal filiation, notes that "Servetus, and others similarly frenzied, hold . . . ," and continues, "Let them now answer me." The old apparatus reads, "Another objection and answer . . . the twofold filiation of Christ"—while the Weber-McNeill apparatus states, "Christ as Son of God and Son of man."[93] When this contrast of old and new apparatus is multiplied by many chapters throughout the *Institutes*,[94] the cumulative effect is virtually the creation of two different documents—one of which explicitly outlines the pattern of the scholarly disputation as practiced throughout the high Middle Ages, the Reformation,[95] and the era of orthodoxy, the other often passing over the textual evidence of disputation; the one indicating a relative continuity of formal exposition and refutation from the Middle Ages through the Reformation and orthodoxy, the other obscuring that continuity; the one showing an element of scholastic structure in the humanistic rhetoric of Calvin, the other often concealing the scholastic model while emphasizing the discursive aspect of Calvin's style.

Conclusions

Examination of the late-sixteenth-century apparatus of Calvin's *Institutes* reveals a rather sophisticated insight into the structure and argument of Calvin's theology, some aspects of which have found echoes in modern scholarship, notably the work of Dowey and Parker, and other aspects of which have been overlooked—particularly when they relate to the continuities between Calvin's work and that of the early Reformed orthodox. The architectonic structure of the *Institutes* and the internal patterns of disputation— statement of doctrine, objections, and reply—can, in fact, appear as bridges to the structures and patterns of early orthodox theology: Wendel has commented that the *Institutes* was immensely successful during Calvin's lifetime, was "never discredited" afterwards, and "was indubitably one of the causes of the very rapid rise of a Calvinist orthodoxy" because of the stability and clarity of its doctrinal formulas.[96] Similarly, the clarity of its disputative style was surely also one of the roots of Reformed orthodoxy and, inasmuch as it carried the scholastic model forward into the realm of humanist rhetoric, also one of the sources of the renewed and modified scholastic forms that emerged in the era of early orthodoxy.

The accuracy and the detail of the older apparatus indicate that the theologians of the late sixteenth and seventeenth centuries had available to them a finely designed framework for the interpretation of Calvin, much of which came from the hand of Nicholas Colladon, the close friend and biographer of Calvin—one of the few, in Walker's words, who "enjoyed [Calvin's] full confidence."[97] Colladon's work on the apparatus between 1559 and 1576 binds its phrases and outlines to Calvin, indeed, often to the phrases of the *Institutes*. Other materials incorporated from Olevian, Bunnie, and Launeus also reflect a theological context not far from that of Calvin. Our own brief analysis has indicated several points at which the older apparatus parallels the best recent scholarship on the structure and implication of the *Institutes* or at which it is

markedly superior to the interpretive apparatus of several modern editions and translations.

The larger issue here, beyond the question of the apparatus (and, therefore, an issue
only partially resolved by the present investigation) concerns the proper context and
framework for understanding Calvin's thought and work. Much of the scholarship in
this century has tended to view Calvin's theology as (miraculously!) providing its own
context, and either a rather generalized view of the thought and culture of the sixteenth
century or the dogmatic assumptions of a particular twentieth-century school of thought
(like neo-orthodoxy) as providing a suitable backdrop or foil for the interpretation of
Calvin. And, although this scholarship has produced many notable works and has, in
many ways, advanced our understanding of Calvin's thought, it has also frequently
obscured the detail, direction, and immediate context of Calvin's work for the sake of
offering a normative dogmatic portrait of the Reformer. Thus, for example, examinations of Calvin's teaching on human nature, Christology, church, and sacraments have
often neglected questions concerning the sixteenth-century understanding of particular
texts of Scripture, the precise relationship between Calvin's exegetical and theological
views and either the exegetical tradition or Calvin's own contemporaries, and (as illustrated by the present essay) the understanding of Calvin's thought and method lodged
in the materials of the sixteenth century, offered by and available to Calvin's contemporaries and immediate successors.[98] The problem inherent in such works—even when
they achieve a genuine understanding of Calvin's thought, as is the case with Dowey's
and Parker's studies of Calvin's doctrine of the knowledge of God—is the absence or
loss of sixteenth-century context, as illustrated by Launeus's reading of the *duplex cognitio Dei* and Olevian's perspective on the credal organization of the *Institutes*.

One may, of course, debate whether the late-sixteenth-century apparatus, with its
disputative and even scholastic overtones, moves Calvin's thought ever so slightly into
the early orthodox frame of the next generation of Reformed thought, rather than
merely giving the next generation a thoroughly valid sense of continuity between its
own theological enterprise and Calvin's patterns of thought and argument. But, of
course, any alternative apparatus, such as the Weber-McNeill system of subheads and
chapter divisions, will also have its theological *tendenz*. In the case of the Weber-McNeill
apparatus, the reader most surely will see Calvin through the eyes of the neo-orthodox
theology and historiography of the mid-twentieth century. When, however, we view
the *Institutes* through the eyes of Colladon and Olevianus, whatever the variance between their theological understanding and the document itself, we view it through eyes
that looked into the eyes of Calvin.

Beyond the Abyss and the Labyrinth

An Ordo recte docendi

The Perturbed Calvin: A Problematic Portrait

Since its appearance in 1988, William Bousma's *Portrait of Calvin* has received much positive attention, and quite a few reviewers and commentators have indicated that it has marked out a new direction in Calvin studies.[1] There have, of course, been a few doubts raised by reviewers and commentators about the method and the conclusions of the book, but, for the most part, its picture of a deeply troubled Calvin, suspended in an "age of anxiety" between the abyss and the labyrinth, has gone unquestioned.[2] This way of portraying Calvin offers, in fact, an extended case study for Bouwsma's earlier characterization of the Renaissance as an age of anxiety, a characterization that has broad ramifications for Calvin's theology.[3] In place of the orderly, disciplined, and highly systematized Calvin of so much past scholarship, Bouwsma presents a terrified Calvin, profoundly at odds with himself and incapable of producing anything like a system of theology.

Bouwsma's Calvin was beset by anxieties in "a world out of joint"—he "was a singularly anxious man, and, as a reformer, fearful and troubled." This anxiety was so profound that, Bouwsma alleges, "there were . . . psychologically and culturally not one but (at least) two Calvins."[4] This anxiety, this "distrust of the world" ran so deep that Calvin, "so committed to *sola scriptura*," still "tended to employ, in his treatment of sin, a vocabulary not only of good and evil but also of order and disorder, concepts alien to biblical discourse."[5] So, too, Calvin had a profoundly fearful and constant association of water with a threat to his existence: because of his acceptance of "traditional physics," which regarded water as lighter than earth, Calvin believed that "only

79

the power of God . . . restrains water from submerging the whole earth."[6] Echoing these fears and terrors, Calvin's theology was a mass of unresolved tensions.

Bouwsma cites, at considerable length, statements from Calvin's sermons, commentaries, treatises, and *Institutes* that manifest the world as a place of anxiety and confusion and then focuses on two of Calvin's "favorite images" for describing situations of extreme spiritual discomfort"—the abyss and the labyrinth. These images of anxiety are significant because "they help to identify tensions and contradictions in [Calvin's] thought." The abyss, Bouwsma contends, was "a symbol for Calvin's horror of the unlimited," while the " 'labyrinth' suggested the anxiety implicit in the powerlessness of human beings to extricate themselves from a self-centered alienation from God."[7] Perhaps by way of extension, Calvin also "associated the labyrinth primarily with the papal church he sought to leave behind, its theology, and the cultural assumptions of his past"—the "abyss," however, "conjured up a more personal terror."[8]

In a transition that is itself obscure from these two metaphors to the somewhat more concrete assumption of scholastic and humanistic influences on Calvin's thought, Bouwsma concludes that there are in fact "two Calvins" in tension and, indeed, at war within the person of the Genevan Reformer. On the one side, characterized by fear of the abyss, "Calvin was a philosopher, a rationalist and a schoolman in the high Scholastic tradition represented by Thomas Aquinas, a man of fixed principles, and a conservative."[9] The "other Calvin," the Calvin dominated by a dread of the labyrinth, "was a rhetorician and a humanist, a skeptical fideist in the manner of followers of William of Ockham, flexible to the point of opportunism, and a revolutionary in spite of himself."[10] Why he links Calvin to Aquinas rather than (as most scholars have done) to Gregory of Rimini or Duns Scotus, why "rhetorician" and "humanist" are categories juxtaposed with "philosopher" and "rationalist" and having "fixed principles," Bouwsma does not indicate. Nor does he show why abysses should be the terror of scholastics and labyrinths the bane of humanists. Underlying these obvious problems with Bouwsma's paradigm, however, is the more fundamental question of whether, using the language of abyss and labyrinth, he is actually able to document tensions in Calvin's psyche—and whether, therefore, the proposal of "two Calvins," humanist and scholastic, rationalist and fideist, conservative and revolutionary, philosopher and rhetorician, or any other set of neat bifurcations, offers a suitable picture of the life and work of the reformer.[11]

A salutary note of caution in the face of Bouwsma's arguments was offered by Francis Higman, who noted one location in the *Institutes* where the word "labyrinth" appears but once, while "light" appears twice, "road" and "path" some seven times. To drive the point home that "the image of the Way is omnipresent in Calvin" and that the way or road "is linear," Higman indicates that "labyrinth" occurs four times in the 1539 *Institutes*, twelve times in 1559; "abyss" twelve times in 1539 and twenty-six in 1559, whereas *via*, the "road" or "way," occurs some one hundred and twenty-nine times in 1539 and one hundred and seventy-six times in 1559.[12] The statistics themselves ought to give us pause. From a different perspective, one that takes up Bouwsma's gambit in order to move discussion beyond the place where Bouwsma left it, Oberman has elaborated on Calvin's use of the terms "abyss" and "labyrinth," with particular emphasis on the biblical and exegetical basis of many of Calvin's references to the "abyss"—a point entirely missed by Bouwsma despite his consistent recourse to Calvin's sermons and commentaries.[13] It is also worth noting that at least one earlier scholar had observed the often sharp juxtapositions of ideas in Calvin's thought that Bouwsma sees as unresolved tensions arising from anxiety but explained them as an association or connection of opposites (*complexio oppositorum*), juxtaposed within a rationally presented structure, in order to illustrate the nature of theology itself as permitting no single organizing principle.[14]

Beyond these points of criticism, Bouwsma's own discussion of the two words raises warning flags. There are not only citations in which Calvin speaks of the frightful abysses of idolatry, wickedness, and death, but also citations referring to the "abyss of God's goodness" and the abyss of God's will and universal governance: in the latter two cases, "abyss" certainly indicates something unlimited, but the connotation is hardly one of "horror" and "anxiety."[15] Similarly, Calvin indicates that those who are alienated from God "must necessarily be blind and wander in a labyrinth." Wherever such men turn, "a labyrinth of evils surrounds them."[16] Surely the term, in these two usages, indicates something like what Bouwsma calls "the anxiety implicit in the powerlessness of human beings to extricate themselves from a self-centered alienation from God"—but Calvin also speaks quite frequently of the grace of God that extricates human beings from their plight. It is, in fact, one of the basic themes of Calvin's theology that, in the midst of their own sinful inability, human beings are reconciled to God by grace alone. This particular use of "labyrinth," then, points not to a problem for believers but to the anxiety of the lost. Against the anxieties of the lost, Calvin can discourse on the certitude of faith and the certainty of salvation in Christ.[17] Calvin's usage, therefore, does not quite provide the images of anxiety and horror that Bouwsma presents—not even in the citations given by Bouwsma. But do a few objections to Bouwsma's extended list of citations indicate a flaw in his argument? Or can the terms *abyssus* and *labyrinthus* be used as indicators of a generalized and pervasive anxiety in Calvin's thought?

Calvin's Use of "Abyss" and "Labyrinth" in the *Institutes*

Although the survey of Calvin's thought that it provides cannot be viewed as absolutely definitive, the *Institutes* surely provides a fairly representative sampling of Calvin's thinking, covering as it does most of the topics in his theology and offering glimpses of his piety, his exegesis, his polemic, and his rhetorical style, particularly of the various literary *topoi*.[18] The words *abyssus*[19] and *labyrinthus*[20] do appear, albeit comparatively infrequently, in the *Institutes*: no one who has read carefully through Calvin's doctrine of predestination can fail, for example, to be impressed by his warning against speculation into the relation of one's one salvation to the depth of the dreaded decree. Anyone who engages in such speculation, Calvin asserts, will be lost in a labyrinth.[21] But Bouwsma's contention that these terms offer deep insight into a broad and abiding anxiety in Calvin's thought is offset by the fact that other terms, descriptive of Calvin's theological enterprise and of his faith, such as "order," "path" or "way," "truth," and "clarity," far outnumber statements concerning the abyss and the labyrinth. These latter terms appear to be far more pervasive indicators of Calvin's approach to Christian life and thought. Thus, *ordo* appears 180 times in the 1559 *Institutes* and *via* 176; *veritas* occurs 258 times, *claritas* 22, and *clarus* 138.

More important, examination of the contexts in which Calvin's use of the terms "labyrinth" and "abyss" is found does not confirm Bouwsma's claims but instead reveals to the reader a complex relationship between Calvin's literary style and rhetoric and his theological method.[22] As Calvin himself indicated in the *Argument du livre* prefaced to the 1541 French *Institutes*, he had intended the Latin text for "men of learning, to whatever nation they belonged."[23] Calvin's Latin text was, on this account, rather different from his French version: as Marmelstein documented at some length, the 1541 French text frequently augments and explains classical references, as if Calvin recognized a need to accommodate his style to a less learned audience.[24] Conversely, the Latin text of the *Institutes* assumes a high level of erudition—Calvin's humanistically trained readers will (or should) be aware of the implications of a host of classical and patristic allusions and ought to experience the full impact of those allusions when they belong to set literary *topoi* and contribute to the high rhetoric of Calvin's argument. This richness of allusion and consistent recourse to established *topoi* not only points toward the relationship between Calvin's method and the humanist rhetoric of his day but also points away from Bouwsma's understanding of a particular set of literary *topoi* as indications of personal anxiety.

Thus, in the first of his references to the labyrinth in the *Institutes*, Calvin speaks of the prevalence of idolatry and of the variety of false views of God among the nations of the earth. The reason for this plethora of falsehoods is the labyrinthine nature of the human mind: we have here an image of confusion among the corrupt and false religions of the world, not of anxiety on Calvin's part. Nor does the text offer any reference either "primarily" or secondarily either to "the papal church" or to "cultural assumptions of [Calvin's] past": rather, the references are to the "nations," "the rude and untutored crowd," "the Stoics," and "the Egyptians."[25] By way of contrast, Calvin's next reference is to the "splendor of the divine countenance" that is "for us like an inexplicable labyrinth unless we are conducted into it by the thread of the Word." The context here is Calvin's exhortation to find "true knowledge of God" in Scripture— the assistance of the Word overcomes the forgetfulness and fallenness of the human mind.[26] The third and last reference in the *Institutes*, Book I, echoes the second: Calvin cautions that people who "indulge their curiosity" concerning distinctions in the divine essence "enter a labyrinth." He advises his readers to "use great caution" in such matters and not to allow either thoughts or speech to "go beyond the limits to which the Word of God itself extends."[27] If we may hazard a guess about the logic behind these second and third appearances of the term, it most probably arises not so much out of Calvin's need to reiterate a major "labyrinth" motif in his theology as out of the classicist dimensions of humanist rhetoric: the text is ornamented with a literary reference to the legend of Theseus. The motif, which is indeed present and which is illuminated by the metaphor of the labyrinth, is the contrast between the inherent difficulties confronting human investigation into things divine and the need for Holy Scripture as a guide, a rule, or a light to the mind.[28]

Virtually the same theme is found in Calvin's dictum that "we must learn humbly to seek, otherwise than by our own understanding, the true way of knowledge," inasmuch as "without the word nothing is left for men but darkness."[29] Nor does Calvin's usage indicate fear or apprehension on his part: well guided by "the thread of the

Word," he fears no labyrinth of the untutored human mind—and he warns his readers to take up the Word rather than run afoul of the Minotaur. The operative issue, for Calvin, is not a personal fear of confusion but the establishment for his readers of the right foundation and right order of teaching so that they do not lose themselves on the twisted byways of the human imagination. Precisely this point is made in Calvin's comment that "a man's life cannot be ordered aright unless it is framed according to the law of God . . . without this [law] he can only wander in crooked bypaths."[30]

One's sense of the importance of Calvin's use of "labyrinth" as a metaphor for prevalent anxiety is considerably diminished by the thought that the reader of the *Institutes* must move through the remaining five chapters of Book I and the entirety of Book II before encountering another reference to the term. In *Institutes*, Book III, Calvin finds an occasion to introduce the term that parallels, to a certain extent, the use in Book I: whereas there the labyrinthine confusion of the mind was identified as a problem arising from the use of the fallen mind unaided by revelation, in the beginning of Book III, the labyrinth is characteristic of the error of Roman Catholic theology, which has "constructed" an unbiblical "labyrinth" with its doctrine of implicit faith: such doctrine draws "a veil over Christ to hide him" that "ruinously" deludes "simple folk." Those who follow this doctrine rather than the Christ revealed in Scripture "shall wander through endless labyrinths."[31]

Here we find an element of sound observation in Bouwsma's reading: the labyrinth refers to the problems of "papal" or Roman Catholic theology. What is absent from Calvin's sentiments, however, is the deep fear hypothesized by Bouwsma. The metaphor of the labyrinth belongs to an argument in which Calvin indicates a way of moving past delusion toward clarity: "thus they fancy that in error they possess truth; in darkness, light; in ignorance, right knowledge."[32] Calvin is quite certain that truth, light, and right knowledge, and not the toils of the labyrinth, belong to his teaching. It can also be fairly easily documented that Calvin's use of "labyrinth" as an image for error and his proposal, in effect, of a spiritual parting of the ways—the choice of path, one toward an inextricable maze of error and the other out of the maze and into the light of the Gospel—is not his own but a classical and, indeed, patristic metaphor, used by such writers as Hippolytus of Rome, Prudentius, Jerome, and Augustine to characterize the errors of paganism and heresy.[33] Ambrose wrote of God's commandments as providing a paved road past the winding paths of error and warned of the danger of falling off the way into a labyrinth,[34] and Augustine specifically opposes the mazes and circuitous tracks of error to the true way of Christ and the straight path of Christian doctrine.[35] So, also, do Augustine, Jerome, and Boethius write of labyrinthine disputations or arguments.[36] Arguably, Calvin's purpose here was not to indicate anxiety at all but rather, in the course of a polemical disputation, to apply a well-known patristic *topos* describing heresy to the teaching of his Roman adversaries.

The next two references to the labyrinth may be taken together. Here Calvin addresses not so much the inward snares of the fallen intellect or the difficulties faced by the mind in an unaided and unbiblical penetration into the divine mysteries as the tribulations of the world. "Though we had been dispersed like lost sheep through the labyrinth of the world," Calvin writes, [God] has gathered us together again to join us with himself."[37] Even so, Calvin can also state that "in harsh and difficult conditions, regarded as adverse and evil, a great comfort comes to us: we share in Christ's sufferings in order that as he has passed from a labyrinth of all evils into heavenly glory, we may in like manner be led through various tribulations to the same glory."[38]

In both cases, the world is certainly understood as a terrifying place, full of snares and troubles for those outside of Christ. But the burden of the passages is not the terror but rather deliverance from it. If in these places " 'labyrinth' suggested the anxiety implicit in the powerlessness of human beings to extricate themselves from a self-centered alienation from God,"[39] then Calvin's text clearly points its readers beyond their human inability toward the power of divine grace. These are not words of anxiety and fear in "a world out of joint" but words of comfort and assurance in divine promises that do not depend on the world. Nor does this usage indicate a newly developed language on Calvin's part: as in the previously noted use of "labyrinth," we encounter here as well an established literary or rhetorical *topos*. The description of world and life as a maze might easily have been learned by Calvin from his early philosophical interest, Seneca;[40] and the specific understanding of the world as a labyrinth of evils from which Christ alone can extricate us Calvin could have found in the writings of Gregory of Nyssa.[41] (This particular usage of labyrinth was made famous in Protestant literature of the seventeenth century by Johannes Comenius.[42])

Institutes, III. xix.7, returns us to the toils awaiting the human mind and heart apart from a right knowledge of God. Here the problem, once again, is Roman Catholic theology, specifically the burdens placed on the conscience by the loss of Christian liberty in the face of superstitious adherence to such *adiaphora* or "indifferent things" as feasts and fasts, holy days and vestments. Knowledge of Christian liberty, writes Calvin,

> is also very necessary for us; for without it we shall have no tranquillity of conscience, nor will there be any end of superstitions. . . . For once the conscience has fallen into the snare, it enters a long and inextricable labyrinth, from which afterward it is difficult to escape. . . . The necessary consequence [of such dispute over adiaphora] is, that some are hurried by despair into a vortex of confusion, from which they see no escape; and some, despising God, and casting off all fear of him, make a way of ruin for themselves.[43]

Once again, Calvin certainly sees deep anxiety as the necessary result of Roman Catholic piety—but the anxiety is clearly not Calvin's, and the contrast is not between an abyss on the one side and a labyrinth on the other but between a labyrinth wrought for the conscience by faulty theology and piety and a way toward liberty and assurance. And here, moreover, in Calvin's emphasis on a way—a *via* or an *ordo*—grounded in right knowledge of God and obedience to God's law, we have returned to one of the fundamental themes of the *Institutes*, the interrelationship of the right knowledge of God with the right knowledge of self.[44] Oberman quite rightly notes that "the 'labyrinth' marks the point of departure, namely the perplexities of the confessional, too heteronomous to assuage and redirect the conscience"[45]—but it is a departure that Calvin has already accomplished for himself and that he now recommends to others.

The most famous use of "labyrinth" in Calvin's writings, the warning against invading the labyrinth of the divine decree found in his doctrine of predestination,[46] has only a tangential relationship to the problem of "the powerlessness of human beings to extricate themselves from a self-centered alienation from God" and no clear relation to Bouwsma's "primary" association of the term, "papal church." Rather, this particular usage ought to be read in the context of similar recourse to the problem of a labyrinthine speculation—a speculation resting on false premises—identified both in Ochino's *Labyrinthus*, written as a protest against Calvin's doctrine, and in Beza's *Tabula praedestinationis*, written in defense of Calvin's teaching. In both of these documents, the term appears not as a sign of personal psychological distress but as a term indicating a problem arising from *someone else's* mistaken understanding of or approach to an issue.[47] So, too, Calvin's other reference to the "labyrinth" in the context of his doctrine of predestination urges attention to the Word of God. We ought, writes Calvin, to be satisfied with the 'mirror' and its 'dimness' until we see [God] face to face" rather than be drawn by speculative "allurements . . . more and more deeply into the labyrinth."[48] This passage and the others dealing with the involuted mazes of misguided minds finds significant parallel in Augustine, whose early *Contra Academicos* warned students to shun the all too attractive "labyrinths" of "contentious" and "obscure" philosophical prose.[49]

The two final references to "labyrinth" in the *Institutes* belong to Calvin's ecclesiology and are of a somewhat different order. In the former, Calvin notes a spiritual difficulty encountered by Gregory the Great in his life as a bishop: Gregory found that his public role as bishop drew him more consistently toward worldly things than had his earlier existence as a layman: "because he cannot simply devote his whole self to the office of bishop, he seems to himself to be in a labyrinth."[50] Calvin sees a parallel between Gregory's complaint and the troubles of the sixteenth-century church: "Judge, then, what he would have said, if he had fallen upon these times."[51] Similarly, in the latter reference, Calvin notes the complaints of Gregory the Great and of Bernard of Clairvaux against the evils of their times, indicates the greater evils present in the church in his own day, and laments "yet this labyrinth is praised as if nothing better ordered and disposed could be found."[52] In the first case, the term points to a personal spiritual difficulty, in the latter, somewhat mockingly, to a corporate one. The labyrinth, the maze of problems, belongs to the troubled life of the church, particularly to the church of Rome—and the term appears in Calvin's diatribe in the second section of his discussion of "the power of the church," just prior to his discussion of the limitation of churchly power by the Word of God.[53] We have seen the underlying point before: the Word of God is the only sure guide out of the labyrinth of human confusion.

When we turn to Calvin's use of "abyss," we encounter a similar result—the deep anxiety detected in the term by Bouwsma is seldom, if ever, Calvin's present personal anxiety. But here, our understanding of Calvin's usage must also be weighed against the biblical rootage of the term and its usage as a literary *topos* in Augustine's works. Thus, all of the three appearances of "abyss" in *Institutes*, Book I, are governed by particular biblical texts. The first of these references appears in a citation of Psalm 106: 26 conflated with the central point of Deuteronomy 30:12–14: "Say not in your heart, who will ascend into heaven, or who will descend into the abyss: behold the word is in your mouth."[54] The third and final appearance of "abyss" in *Institutes*, Book I, rests on a biblical reference and its application, indeed, the same text in Deuteronomy: "Moses proclaims that the will of God is to be sought not far off in the clouds or in abysses, because it has been set forth familiarly in the law." This point leads Calvin to a collateral citation of Romans 11:33–4 and a contrast between the "abyss" of God's hidden will and the revealed law.⁵⁵ Calvin's remarks here parallel his use of "labyrinth" with regard to the unfathomability of the divine decree (also grounded on Romans 11:33–34): we must not inquire into what God has not revealed but rather look to his revelation.

Calvin's second use of "abyss" in *Institutes*, Book I, is again governed by a biblical text: "the testimony of Moses in the history of the Creation is very clear, that 'the Spirit of God was extended over the abyss,' or formless matter."⁵⁶ The context of this reference is Calvin's discussion of the divinity of the Holy Spirit—and so the point of Calvin's argument here is quite different from the point being made with the other two citations. Here Calvin identifies the power of the Spirit in creation; there he urged attention to the revealed Word over against attempts to penetrate the inaccessible depth of the divine mystery. Since there are two different points of reference and two different meanings presented here, it becomes impossible to argue a common existential or psychological motive behind the citation of texts that share a particular word. None of these references to the "abyss," moreover, has anything to do with fear or anxiety. They are not used as symbols to conjure up for the reader "Calvin's horror of the unlimited."

Of the three appearances of the word "abyss" in *Institutes*, Book II, one falls into the rather neutral category of biblical citation: "Zechariah . . . compares the Babylonian disaster, into which the people had been cast, to a deep, dry pit or abyss, and at the same time teaches that the salvation of the whole church is a release from the nether depths."⁵⁷ The context of the reference is Calvin's discussion of Christ's descent into hades and what he feels to be the erroneous interpretation of biblical references to Sheol as the *limbus patrum*. A related reference to "abyss" takes its departure from the biblical notion of Sheol and belongs to Calvin's interpretation of Christ's descent as the profound spiritual suffering of Christ on the cross: "he does not pray to be spared death, but he prays not to be swallowed up by it . . . and surely no more terrible abyss can be conceived than to feel yourself forsaken and estranged from God; and when you call upon him, not to be heard."⁵⁸ Here, surely, we have finally found a reference to the "abyss" that is connected with anxiety and, indeed, that is stated somewhat existentially—but its immediate context is not Calvin's own fear or even the fear of a hypothetical believer but rather Calvin's reading of Christ's anguished cry "My God, my God, why hast thou forsaken me" as Christ's own spiritual descent into the torments of hades.

There is one other appearance of the word "abyss" in *Institutes*, Book II. Here, for the first time, we have an instance of Calvin selecting the word as an indication of the depths of the human predicament: "The natural man refuses to be led to recognize the diseases of his lusts. The light of nature is extinguished before he even enters upon this abyss."⁵⁹ What is significant to our investigation in this reference is that "abyss" does not indicate a problem or fear distinct from the "labyrinth" but is in fact used virtually as a synonym. Like the understanding of "labyrinth" typical of Book I of the *Institutes*, this reference to "abyss" in the preredemptive context of the second chapter of Book II directs our attention to the spiritual failure of the unregenerate human being. And the point of Calvin's argument is not that human beings are necessarily destined to be swallowed up in an abyss of their own making but that, like David, they must pray to God for understanding in order that God will "restore that which he had given at the beginning, but which had been taken away from us for a time."⁶⁰

By far the greatest number of appearances of the word "abyss" is in Book III of the *Institutes*, but even here we do not have a great concentration of uses and certainly not a uniform implication of the word. In several places the word does indicate anxiety caused by the failure of faith, but the direction and counsel of Calvin's text indicates assurance rather than profound fear or worry. Thus he writes, "Nor if we are troubled on all sides by the agitation of unbelief, are we for that reason immersed in its abyss . . . the end of the conflict is always this: that faith ultimately triumphs over those difficulties which besiege and seem to imperil it."[61] A sense of "personal terror" does indeed accompany Calvin's similar statement that "God's saintly servants give proof of huge torments . . . when they speak of uttering their plaintive cry to the Lord from the deep abyss, and from the very jaws of death." Even so, Calvin indicates, "great anxiety should kindle in us the desire to pray."[62] Similarly, Calvin can hold that it would be preferable to be plunged into "abysses and chasms" than to "stand for a moment before" the final wrath of God against the wicked.[63]

There are, of course, nuances of meaning here: the ultimate abyss of unbelief troubles believers "on all sides," yet they are never fully "immersed" in it—on the one hand, there is an "abyss" of doubt and torment from which the saints daily cry out to God, while, on the other, there are the abysses and chasms, the dark hiding places, into which the wicked would rather be placed rather than face the judgment—a thought that finds reflection in the final scene of Marlowe's *Dr. Faustus:* "mountains and hills, come, come and fall on me / And hide me from the heavy wrath of God, / No, no—/ Then I will run headlong into the earth: /Earth, gape! O no, it will not harbor me."[64] In neither case does Calvin's usage evidence Bouwsma's sense of "a symbol for . . . horror of the unlimited." Rather, the word indicates a place of torment, doubt, anxiety, and, specifically, a place in which God appears to be absent—the biblical language of Sheol. In addition, these several uses offer rather distinct referents: an ultimate terror of doubts that believers never need face, the ongoing doubts and struggles of believers, and a pit in which the wicked might hide. In only one of these instances, the second, does "abyss" refer to an anxiety that affects Calvin.

Here, in what is usually referred to as the "problem of assurance," one does find a series of tensions in Calvin's thought and even what some writers have identified as contradictions. Calvin argues that faith is "firm conviction" and a "sure and certain knowledge" and yet warns that "unbelief is, in all men, always mixed with faith." This unbelief "is so deeply rooted in our hearts" that only "hard struggle" can lead us to confess "that God is faithful." Thus, while "every man's wavering uncovers hidden weaknesses," there is nonetheless a "full assurance" that belongs to faith.[65] Despite the length of Calvin's discussion—*Institutes*, III.ii runs to forty-three subsections, one of Calvin's longer chapters—the word abyss appears only twice.[66] What is more, despite Calvin's emphasis throughout the chapter on the problem of assurance and the trials of faith, only one of these references comes close to Bouwsma's thesis.[67] "Abyss" is clearly not the primary term or symbol for Calvin for indicating these problems.

Nor are the other uses of "abyss" in Book III uniform. In one place, it refers to David's recognition of the depth of "the abyss of our sins": here Calvin argues against the Roman Catholic doctrine of confession, that it is impossible to "catalogue" all of our sins. Rather, we should emulate the example of David, admit that we are overwhelmed by our sin, and pray to be drawn out of the pit.[68] So, also, Calvin notes that, if salvation were to depend on the absolution of a priest, there is an "abyss": "for where confession is not complete, the hope of pardon is also impaired."[69] In both instances, the "abyss" indicates the hopelessness of unremitted sin, specifically the hopelessness engendered by confessional and penitential practice. Here it is not the "labyrinth" that is associated with the abuses of late medieval Catholicism but the "abyss"—once again, "abyss" is not an opposite problem to "labyrinth" but a nearly identical one. And it is hardly an indication of "tensions and contradictions" in Calvin's thought, but instead an indication of a tension and contradiction in which Calvin's readers are liable to be immersed if they do not follow his direction. If, moreover, we look for precedent, we need look no farther than Augustine, who referred to the "abyss" of "worldly life" with its "depth of sin" from which we are extricated by the grace of Christ.[70]

Related to these uses is Calvin's paraphrase of Luke 18:13, "Lord be merciful to me a sinner," as "May the abyss of thy mercy swallow up this abyss of sin."[71] Or, again, "The Lord [has] rescued man from the abyss of his perdition."[72] Sin is an abyss, but an abyss from which there is divine deliverance. What is more, if we ask the question of usage, the abyss of sin may well be overwhelming and terrible, but the abyss of God's mercy is a great comfort: the word "abyss" does not of itself represent terror or anxiety to Calvin. And here, too, the understanding of human sinfulness as an abyss is a typically Augustinian usage.[73]

In another passage, the usage comes from Augustine, not Calvin, and it refers to "some depth or other of God's judgments" according to which God either initiates faith in a person or does not initiate it. Faith, declares Calvin, is a gift—"To sum up: Christ, when he illumines us into faith by the power of his Spirit, at the same time engrafts us into his body that we become partakers of every good" by means of the "abyss of the cross."[74] Here, "abyss" refers not to anxiety or to chaos and disorder but simply to the mystery of God's working. A similar reference appears in Calvin's citation of Psalm 36:6 as an indication that "the judgments of God are beyond measure" and are called by the Psalmist a "profound abyss." "What good will it do you," Calvin continues, "in your mad search to plunge into [this] abyss, which your own reason tells you will be your destruction?"[75] A virtually identical usage appears in Calvin's statement that "if we try to penetrate to God's eternal ordination, that deep abyss will swallow us up,"[76] and in his warning that anyone who "attempts to break into the inner recesses of divine wisdom . . . buries himself in an abyss of sightless darkness."[77] In each of these three instances, the abyss of the divine will is something not to be penetrated by human curiosity—and here, too, we find clear parallel in Augustine and in the later Augustinian tradition.[78]

Calvin's usage here certainly indicates a sense of dread or awe before the unlimited majesty and mystery of God, but once again we find a parallel rather than a contrast to Calvin's use of "labyrinth." In fact, we are barely a chapter distant from Calvin's famous warning to avoid speculation into the labyrinth of the decree.[79] The issue is not anxiety or terror per se but the limitation of human capability and the need to adhere strictly to what has been revealed by God—inasmuch as undue speculation will lead not to consolation but to anxiety. Such speculation, Calvin comments, is a "wicked desire to inquire outside of the way"—*extra viam*.[80] Analogous to these references is the final reference to "abyss" in the *Institutes*. Calvin here warns against misreading of the words of institution of the Lord's Supper: "when foul absurdities come forth from this fiction, because they have already with headlong hast ensnared themselves, they plunge into the abyss of God's omnipotence to extinguish by this means the light of truth."[81] Again, the usage is parallel to the use of "labyrinth." Arguably, it is Calvin's entire purpose in these warnings concerning the labyrinth or the abyss of the divine decree to emphasize not the dread and anxiety brought about by taking the wrong path but to point past problematic quests for assurance to to the right way, to the right order of teaching.

Chaos, Anxiety, and the Exegetical Basis of Calvin's Theology

Beyond the problem of Bouwsma's exaggeration of the importance accorded by Calvin to the terms "abyss" and "labyrinth" and to the anxieties and problems indicated by them, there is also a problem underlying Bouwsma's readings of Calvin's exegesis—a problem placed in clear focus by Bouwsma's amazement that Calvin, who was "committed to *sola scriptura*," nonetheless "tended to employ, in his treatment of sin, a vocabulary not only of good and evil but also of order and disorder, concepts alien to biblical discourse."[82] Whereas Bouwsma's portrait of Calvin, like his many earlier writings, evidences a vast knowledge of the culture of the Renaissance, it also manifests a profound ignorance of Scripture and of the Christian exegetical tradition. Far from being "alien to biblical discourse," the concepts of order and disorder—of a godly, providential order set against the impending threat of chaos, the *tehom* of the creation narrative—are intrinsic to the theology of biblical text and, indeed, are linked with the problem of human righteousness and human sin in such passages as the stories of creation and of the flood.[83] Nor was this near-truism of modern biblical theology lost on the older exegetical tradition: the Latin exegetical tradition tended to render the "deep," in Hebrew, *tehom*, as *abyssus* and to recognize its threatening character.[84] Indeed, the various understandings of the biblical usage "abyss" that are found in Calvin's exegetical efforts mirror the tradition: the abyss of chaos and disorder, the abyss of the human heart in its sinful predicament, the abyss of the divine justice and mercy, the abyss of death and hell.[85]

For example, Calvin dwells on the text of Psalm 42:7, "One abyss cries out to another abyss at the noise of thy waterspouts: all the waves and floods have passed over me."[86] The Psalmist's words express the "grievousness" of his sufferings, writes Calvin—the "temptations by which he was assailed" are compared to the depths of the sea. So, too, the floods passing over David in the second part of the verse refer to the overwhelming weight of affliction: the Psalmist was, "as it were, swallowed up." Sinful people are so "insensible" of their predicament, Calvin concludes, that they fail to "stand in awe of the threatenings of God" and fail to see that, "once his anger is kindled against us, there will not only be one depth to swallow us up, but depth will call unto depth."[87] This interpretation of the text might pass for an indication of considerable anxiety on Calvin's part were it not for the reflection on the divine mercies that follows immediately in the discussion of verse 8—and, more important still, were it not for the exegetical tradition behind Calvin that found similar meanings in the same text. Thus, Augustine notes that "abyss" indicates "a depth that cannot be reached or comprehended"; in this case, the abyss is the human heart and its inward thoughts. When the abyss calls to the abyss, moreover, Augustine writes, it is the abyss of the human heart trembling out of fear of divine judgment: " 'Abyss calls to abyss with the voice of thy waterspouts,' in that Thou threatenest; Thou sayest that there is another condemnation in store even after those sufferings."[88] When Calvin's reading so mirrors that of Augustine, one may fairly ask precisely whose anxiety is mirrored in Calvin's comment on the text—Calvin's, Augustine's, some fifteen centuries of churchly anxieties, or (if we are dealing here with a reasonable exegesis of a biblical text) perhaps the anxieties of the Psalmist himself?

Similarly, in his meditations on the creation narrative of Genesis 1, Calvin understands the "darkness on the face of the abyss" as an indication of "confused emptiness . . . in opposition to all those created objects which pertain to the form . . . and perfection of the world."[89] He also describes the sin of Adam as a "defection . . . whereby the order of creation was subverted" and insists that the "chaos" of the first verses of Genesis could be given order and sustained in that order only by the Spirit of God, so that the removal of the Spirit results in dissolution and the return of disorder.[90] Augustine, too, understands the darkness and the deep—the abyss—as a chaos and disorder that not only stand against the divine creative activity in the beginning but that also stand, in view of sin, against the redemptive work of God. The "formless" and "darksome deep" of the beginning are an image of the "spiritual deformity" later manifest in the "children of Adam" who "hide themselves from [God's] face, and become a darksome deep."[91]

There is, similarly, a traditional association of the impending chaos of unrestrained seas with the problem of human sinfulness in Calvin's reading of the story of the flood.[92] In this place, and in other passages that indicate either the threat of chaos or the restraining of the waters, Calvin does—as Bouwsma indicates—reflect on the fact, inexplicable by the science and philosophy of his day, that water does not cover the earth. This confinement of the sea, says Calvin, is nothing less than a revelation of the sovereign power of God. Human experience of floods teaches, in a small way, what water can do unless it is restrained.[93] Yet in none of these passages does Calvin speak of terror: rather, his explicit point concerns the power of God that makes human habitation possible in a miracle beyond the grasp of philosophy. Indeed, in one of the texts that Bouwsma singles out to indicate Calvin's terror that "the survival of the human race from moment to moment . . . depends on God's keeping the seas under an *unnatural* control,"[94] Calvin comments, "in this we certainly perceive that God, who is ever attentive to the welfare of the human race, has inclosed the waters within certain invisible barriers, and keeps them shut to this day."[95]

As Bouwsma notes, Calvin often referred to death and hell as the abyss, reflecting patristic usage.[96] Of course, it is worth noting that both Calvin and the fathers here reflect biblical usage and that Calvin's references to death and hell as the abyss are, more often than not, generated by the text itself, rather than by personal anxieties. So, too, the association of sin with disorder is hardly a product of the overanxious psyche of John Calvin: it is an association imbedded in Scripture and tradition to which Calvin, together with numerous other theologians throughout history, was attracted—just as he was profoundly attracted to the equally biblical association of the creative and re-creative or redemptive power of God with order. Surely this is the sentiment reflected in Calvin's comments on the divine restraint of the seas.

What is more, Calvin does not dwell excessively on the danger of death and hell: in the passages cited by Bouwsma, he consistently juxtaposes the punishment of sin with the gift of God's mercy. Thus, in the sermons on Deuteronomy, where he prays that he and his hearers will be "delivered from the abyss of death," he has stated immediately beforehand,

> When [God] sees our feebleness, he reaches out to us his hand and calls us to him, and comforts us, inasmuch as he in his mercy does not charge any of our sins against us. Therefore you may see how the faithful do not cease to be of good cheer, even though in themselves, they are condemned.[97]

Indeed, in this passage, cited by Bouwsma as an example of anxiety, the larger part of Calvin's sermon has to do with the comfort offered by God's gratuitous justification of sinners. The single reference to the "abyss of death" points not to our anxiety in the face of death but our deliverance from it.

Far from emphasizing anxiety, many of the places in which Calvin refers to the "abyss" are passages filled with comfort. Not only from a theological perspective, according to which the grace and promise of God overcome the fear of death and hell, but also from a linguistic and rhetorical perspective, the passages cited in part by Bouwsma, when seen in their entirety, tend to disprove his argument. So, also, Calvin's recourse to images of disorder in his discussions of sin, far from being generated by a troubled psyche all too ready to abandon its biblicism in the face of the terrors of daily life, was the result of the biblical text itself as understood in and through an age-old Christian tradition of interpretation. What Bouwsma is unable to tell us, in other words, is whether Calvin's expressions of anxiety (or any other intense feelings in relation to the biblical text) image forth Calvin's own anxieties or simply manifest the anxieties of the author of the text—or, indeed, whether they are the textually generated expressions of anxiety of centuries of Christian exegetes in whose works Calvin had immersed himself.

The *Ordo recte docendi*: A *Via* Through the *Tentationes* and the *Topica*

Calvin certainly did experience the problem of the labyrinth, whether in the context of the spiritual or of the intellectual difficulties encountered by the academically trained and ecclesially committed Christian reformer of the early sixteenth century. It is perhaps worth noting that the phrase "age of anxiety" can be applied to nearly any era in human history[98] and that the typical response to various forms of confusion and disorder—a response characteristic, moreover, of both the "scholastic" and the "humanist" educational cultures—is to establish a method that brings order out of chaos. And it may also be worth noting that Christian theology and spirituality, whether scholastic or humanist, have traditionally found a significant paradigm for overcoming their own varied encounters with disorder and its religious analogue, sin, in the biblical revelation of the God whose first act is to bring cosmic order out of pre-cosmic chaos and whose ultimate act is to bring soteriological order out of hamartiological chaos.

Our examination of Calvin's references, not to global and undifferentiated terrors but to the various and distinct abysses, thorny places, and labyrinths that confront both Christians and Christian theologians, has consistently found these several spiritual and intellectual problems juxtaposed with solutions. In addition, more often than not, Calvin's solutions reside in his identification of a right order, method, or path, an *ordo*, *methodus*, or *via*, through which both clarity (*claritas*) and truth (*veritas*) are attained. Early on in his career, Calvin had indicated that his initial step in writing was to compile "memoranda" or *loci communes* and then to set them in a proper order.[99] This emphasis on the correct method or way through problems and materials can be seen not only in the frequent references to "order," "method," or "path" found in his *Institutes*, but also in the twin poles of his methodological proposal of 1539/40—to present his exposition of the text of Scripture with *clarity* and *brevity* and, by direct implication, to gather his *loci communes* and *disputationes* together into one place, namely the *Institutes*.

Thus, Calvin regards highly the God-given gift of understanding as evidenced in "the invention and methodical teaching of [the] arts."[100] The phrase itself, moreover, looks directly to the tradition of rhetoric and dialectic in its division of the task into *inventio* and *methodus*, the former term indicating the technique of discovering arguments or the materials of argument within the *topoi* or *loci*, the latter pointing toward the proper, expeditious, or compendious path or way through the arguments and the various *loci*.[101] Melanchthon specifically defined *methodus* as "the right way or order for investigation and explication, whether of simple questions or of subjects for discourse" and, more fully, as "the disposition, which is to say, the knowledge or technique, of making a path by means of sound reasons, that is, [the disposition] which discovers and identifies a path through impassible topics overgrown, as it were, with briars, and which brings to light especially the material related to the theme of the discourse or discloses its order."[102] Calvin echoes Melanchthon's definition of method when he declares that the church needs to return to the ancient custom of proper catechesis, namely the memorization of a "formulary . . . containing . . . all the articles of our religion, in which the universal church of believers ought to agree" on the ground that this "discipline" would promote "harmony of faith" and prevent "ignorance and want of information" inasmuch as, then, "all would have some methodical instruction in Christian doctrine."[103] And he echoes Melanchthon's metaphor in his commentary on Psalm 19, where he warns against "wandering in crooked bypaths."[104]

One of Calvin's uses of *via* is particularly instructive: in concluding his discussion of the believer's eternal hope and immediately before turning to the fate of the reprobate before God's wrath, Calvin writes "let this be an advantageous path (*viae compendium*) for us: to be content with the mirror and the mystery until we are able to see face to face."[105] This directive follows immediately upon Calvin's warning against being "drawn more and more deeply into the *labyrinthus*." Doubly significant, moreover, is that this juxtaposition of *labyrinthus* and *via* at the conclusion of the paragraph parallels the statement at its beginning: "As all the pious will receive this with one consent, because it is sufficiently attested in the Word of God, so also will they bid farewell to those thorny questions (*spinosus quaestionibus*) which they recognize as obstacles, and will not transgress the prescribed bounds" of discourse or investigation. The Word of God sets bounds on investigation and sets aside the "distressing" or "thorny questions" (*spinosae quaestiones*), just as it provides a way around the labyrinth. We also find an echo here of Melanchthon's comment that method moves one through briar-ridden topics.[106]

Parallel in rhetorical shape to this argument is the flow of discourse in *Institutes*, IV.viii.13, where Calvin declares that the church ought not attempt to be wise "through its own . . . divisings" (*non ex se cogitet . . . rationis suae inventis*) but should be "taught by the Holy Spirit through God's Word": the church should "never doubt that the Holy Spirit is . . . its best guide in the right path" (*optimum rectae viae ducem*). The rhetorical flourish that juxtaposes "abyss," "labyrinth," or "thorns" with the right path is absent, but the meaning is the same. Or, again, in another place, "consider how unsafe it is . . . to leave the pure Word of God for the reveries of our brains" specifically, "if it be the design of the sacrament to assist the mind of man, which is otherwise weak, that it may be able to rise to discover the sublimity of spiritual mysteries,—those who confine themselves to the external sign, wander from the right way of seeking Christ (*recta Christi via*)."[107]

The imagery and usage in all of these places reflects not so much personal anxieties as the identifiable sources and antecedents of Calvin's method: the theological tradition, including the methodological struggles of the later Middle Ages, and the rhetorical tradition, particularly as recovered and appraised by Renaissance humanists. After citing Erasmus's comment to Budé "Your aim is to conquer; mine to inform or to persuade," André Hugo remarks:

> If one glances at any of [Calvin's] *Tractatus Minores*, or at the *Institutes*, and remarks there the beautiful Ciceronian periods set off by terse little Senecan sentences, and the wealth of patristic and scholastic Christian terminology varied with picturesque, often playful, idioms and metaphors and proverbs taken from classical mythology and history, then one hardly need ask in what school he had learnt this amazing art. It was the school of Erasmus.[108]

As Millet points out, one of Calvin's favorite rhetorical techniques was the posing of a "dilemma" by means of "oxymorons and relations of words, points, [and] distinctions . . . which, in a binary parallelism opposed terms one against another, two against two, three against three" in a single argument or phrase.[109] Radical antitheses between good and evil, positive and negative, were used by Calvin as a simple rhetorical device to encourage the faithful to accept his teaching and to reject that of his opponents—as Higman notes, this basic binary pattern is Calvin's typical way of making analogies and forcing conclusions.[110] A classic case of this antithetical pattern of argument, stated for the reader in the form of a dilemma, is Calvin's repeated statement that if the right *via* is not chosen, the reader will be irretrievably lost in a labyrinth or, indeed, an abyss of error.[111] Indeed, what better way to press on a reader the necessity of choosing between two *viae*, the one disastrous, the other salvific, than to draw on the image of a labyrinth or maze, which traditionally takes the form of a *bivium* or division of the ways, one leading to entrapment, the other to the light?

It is a hallmark, moreover, of Calvin's style to press his point through the use of adversatives, like the standard rhetorical form of the *correctio* (identified by such phrases as "*I do not mean* [merely] false and perverse opinion, *but* vast and horrifying blasphemies") or the simple intensifier "not only . . . but also," often used as vehicles for hyperbolic denunciation of false teaching—none of which, as Higman points out, can be taken as definitive indicators of a "personal element" or of "feeling and emotion," inasmuch as the entire syntactical structure has been carefully constructed for the purpose of persuasion.[112] Of less rhetorical value but expressive of the same argumentative impulse is the constant juxtaposition of "true" with "false" in several of Viret's works.[113] In the light, also, of Calvin's declared apologetic purpose in the *Institutes*—to inform and persuade Francis I of the rectitude of the reform—the biblical and patristic usage of "abyss," the classical mythological references to a "labyrinth," the somewhat more mundane but nonetheless picturesque references to "thorny places," the scholastic theological issues for which such terms provide an argumentative setting, and Calvin's own insistence on the correct order or path for comprehension all fall into place as characteristic forms not of disturbed psyche but of the pedagogical intentions of a humanistic rhetor.

Calvin drew these references and metaphors out of the rich literary resources of his classical, patristic, and medieval heriitage. Nor, as Hugo and Millet remind us, was the use of such rhetorical devices in the sixteenth century unique to Calvin. Just as the image of briars and thorny places appears in Melanchthon's definition of *methodus*, so, too, do images of dark caves and labyrinths frequently appear in discussions by other sixteenth-century writers of the human mind, the difficulties of life in the world, free choice, and predestination, and so forth. As Erasmus indicated in his *Adagia*, "labyrinth" was among the standard literary *topoi* to be used in the rhetorical amplification of argument. "A labyrinth," Erasmus writes, "was a name in old days for any speech or course of action which was excessively complicated or hard to unravel, as for instance if one were to call the study of philosophy 'a labyrinth' because those who have once entered can never find the way out."[114]

Even so, Luther commented to Spalatin that he had, in raising questions about indulgences, entered a "dangerous labyrinth of disputation" only to be beset by "six hundred Minotaurs."[115] In his *Diatribe or Discourse concerning Free Choice*, Erasmus argued:

> There are some secret places in the Holy Scriptures into which God has not wished us to penetrate more deeply and, if we try to do so, then the deeper we go, the darker and darker it becomes, by which means we are led to acknowledge the unsearchable majesty of the divine wisdom, and the weakness of the human mind. It is like that cavern near Corycos of which Pomponius Mela tells, which begins by attracting and drawing the visitor to itself by its pleasing aspect, and then as one goes deeper, a certain horror and majesty of the divine presence that inhabits the place makes one draw back. So when we come to such a place, my view is that the wiser and more reverent course is to cry with St. Paul: 'O the depth . . . !' "[116]

Still more like Calvin's metaphor is Melanchthon's comment in his discussion of the many impediments to free choice: first among these impediments are the "great many things [that] happen to a man caught in the hopeless mazes (*inextricabilia*) of human intentions." In a parallel phrase, Melanchthon speaks of a third impediment as "the confusion of this life, a great mountain of difficulties and dangers, in which, daily, are presented to us many unforeseen [difficulties] and insurmountable mazes (*inextricabilia*) which exceed all human conjecture.[117] So, too, does Melanchthon state that excessive curiosity and love of argument will lead to "infinite labyrinths of disputation."[118] Not only do these usages provide parallels with Calvin's description of the human mind as a "labyrinth"; they also point toward the long-established use of such phrases as "a quandary impossible to unravel" (*inextricabilis negotium*) as synonyms for labyrinth, particularly when the labyrinth is understood not as a physical maze but as the bewildering intricacy of human error.[119]

On the subject of free choice and predestination, we also have Ochino's treatise *On the Labyrinth*, pointing both in its title and in its consistent metaphor to the inextricable maze of these problems.[120] And, in addition, there is the declaration, paralleling and probably borrowing from Calvin, found in Beza's *Tabula praedestinationis* that those who "imagine either a bare and indifferent [divine] permission or a twofold counsel of God" will

> from these errors . . . necessarily fall into an infinite number of other utterly absurd mistakes, partly to deny the relationship of these intimately connected issues, partly to contrive many futile and obscure distinctions [of their own] which they advance at great length and in which they inextricably entangle themselves—with the result that they shall never emerge from the labyrinth.[121]

In each of these cases, not only does the metaphor used by other authors parallel Calvin's precisely; it also stands juxtaposed with the assumption that the labyrinth or, in Erasmus's case, the cave may be avoided if the reader follows the advice of the author.

At several key points in the *Institutes*, moreover, Calvin specifically refers to an "order" of teaching as his basic concern: after offering his criticism of the "ecclesiastical constitutions" of the Papacy, he comments, "I shall now endeavor to collect a summary of the whole, in the best order I can."[122] More important, at the very beginning of the *Institutes*, in his statement of method to the reader, Calvin comments that he has presented "a comprehensive summary and orderly arrangement of all the branches of religion" such that any reader will be able to identify "the principal objects" and the proper "scope" or "goal" of biblical study.[123] So, also, at the outset of his discussion of the knowledge of God and self, he states, "the proper order of instruction (*ordo recte docendi*) requires us first to treat of the former, and then proceed to the discussion of the latter."[124] Similarly, a few chapters later, Calvin comments on "the most proper way" and "most suitable order" for seeking God in theology.[125] Or, again, Calvin indicates that the discussion of faith must be related to the issues of repentance and forgiveness of sin; he comments, further, that faith is the source of both repentance and forgiveness and that, "as a consequence, reason and the order of teaching (*ratio et docendi series*) require me, under this topic (*hoc loco*), to begin to discuss both" issues in sequence.[126] In the preface to his commentary on the Psalms, Calvin similarly recommends the clear or simple "method of teaching" (*docendi ratio*).[127]

Some Conclusions

Examination of Calvin's usage does not point us toward a deep and consistent worry about an "abyss" or a "labyrinth." In the first place, Calvin uses these terms comparatively infrequently. When juxtaposed with his insistence on discerning a right "way," his declarations concerning the "clarity" and the "truth" of God's Word and his interest in establishing a "right order of teaching," the "abyss" and the "labyrinth," even if they were used consistently and in tandem, do not appear to indicate a major motif in Calvin's thought. When, moreover, the number of uses of "abyss" that are governed by the presence of the word in a biblical text—particularly given that the citations of such texts or the comments on them frequently focus on other issues rather than singling out the terrors of the abyss as an issue—the possibility of understanding the "abyss" as a major motif in Calvin's thought is still further decreased. In addition, the high rhetoric contrasting "abyss" and "labyrinth" with "method," "order," "reason," and "path" hardly dwells on the terms "abyss" and "labyrinth." Indeed, like Melanchthon and others trained in the humanist rhetoric of the day, Calvin also liked imagery of briars and thorns potentially blocking the way through the *loci*. The sixteenth-century rhetorical context of Calvin's language as distinct from the imposed Bouwsmian existential and psychological context is thus illuminated by a series of other usages parallel to both "abyss" and "labyrinth."

In the second place, when Calvin does use the words "abyss" and "labyrinth" as indicators of problems, they are more likely to indicate dangers and problems that his theology and piety prevent or avoid than anxieties with which he was beset—certainly not anxieties with which he was beset after his conversion to the evangelical faith and cause. In fact, once one excludes the biblical verses in which "abyss" occurs only tangentially to Calvin's motive for citing the text, nearly all of the occurrences of these terms in the *Institutes* belong to discussions in which Calvin attempts to point out a clear or illuminated way or to establish a right order of teaching that will enable others to see and avoid the abysses and the labyrinths into which sinful and deluded people may fall. The abyss and the labyrinth are encountered by those who ignore the truth of God's Word and, especially, those who ignore the *via* or the *ordo recte docendi* provided for them by Calvin in the *Institutes*.

Third, when we move beyond the *Institutes* to the sermons and commentaries, use of the term "abyss" in particular does not seem to have consistent reference to anxiety, whether Calvin's or anyone else's. In most instances, Calvin's usage simply refers either to the text of Scripture or to the exegetical tradition. Unlike Bouwsma, Calvin and the earlier exegetical tradition recognized that sin and disorder were related in the text of Scripture itself and that chaos or the abyss awaits those who transgress God's order. Nowhere, in the instances examined, does either word refer to "tensions and contradictions" in Calvin's own theology—and if there are such tensions and contradictions (none of which have been delineated by Bouwsma, who studiously avoids examining theological topics), they do not appear to be identified by Calvin's references to the abyss or the labyrinth.

Finally, it must be noted of these several references to abyss and labyrinth in the *Institutes* that the terms never appear in pairs. Nor have I often found them paired in other places—either in the sermons or the commentaries.[128] Whether or not they refer to human inabilities, confusions, or difficulties, the abyss and the labyrinth do not appear, as Bouwsma's thesis appears to demand, as juxtaposed hazards, one to the right, the other to the left, like a theological Scylla and Charybdis between which the anxious Calvin must pass. Indeed, sometimes "abyss" and "labyrinth" mean virtually the same thing. Nor does either term appear to have a single worrisome implication related to a particular problem, either in Calvin's own psyche or in the Christian psyche generally.

Calvin warns against various dangers and misapprehensions, sometimes using the terms "abyss" and "labyrinth," frequently using other words—and he typically offers his warnings in the context of abundant solace. He can also use the word "abyss" to indicate a great depth without negative connotation—as in his references to the abyss of God's mercy. The interpretive problem here is akin to the "root fallacy" that possessed the mind of at least a g.   .ation of biblical theologians in the middle of the present century: theologically laden words in the Old and New Testaments were understood in terms of their etymology rather than in terms of the context of their usage. Meaning is thereby imported, often incorrectly, from a theoretical level of investigation to a particular context.

Thus, in the case of Bouwsma's reading of the terms "labyrinth" and "abyss," broad categories of existential or psychological distress become the presumed frame reference for interpreting specific passages in Calvin's writing—whereas, as we have seen, the specific passages, taken in their own context, do not invariably or even frequently point back toward such global fears. Moreover, we have no evidence that Calvin used these particular literary *topoi* in a way that was very different from the use of these and similar metaphors by his predecessors and contemporaries. Not only, therefore, do these two terms fail to offer a means of identifying a troubled Calvin in an age of anxiety; they also fail to offer indications of two poles or two aspects of a bifurcated personality. We have no evidence, in Calvin's use of these terms, of "two Calvins"; no evidence of an anxiety-induced departure from *sola Scriptura*. Calvin's references to the "abyss" moreover, inasmuch as they often reflect both the biblical text itself and, frequently, a traditionary reading of the text, consistently point us away from Bouwsma's psychologized or existentialized interpretation. Or ought we to say that Bouwsma's psychologized and existentialized interpretation consistently points his readers away from Calvin?

Without diminishing the impact of Calvin's personal anxieties and tensions on his work, whether related to assurance in faith or the difficult task of maintaining his vision of the Reformation in Geneva, and while giving full recognition to his concern for the trials and tribulations of his readers, the language of terrors, of abyss, of labyrinth, of chasm, and so forth, found throughout the *Institutes* and Calvin's other writings, must be placed fully into the context of Calvin's rhetoric and logic and into the context of Calvin's dialectical and apologetic intentions. Calvin's rhetorical penchant for argument by sharp juxtaposition of the labyrinths and abysses caused by his opponents' error stands in close stylistic relation to his theological penchant for drawing opposites together in theological formulations. That this imagery is, moreover, a rhetorical device and not an indication of deep psychological worry is confirmed by its absence from the one place where Calvin does reveal profound personal turmoil—his letters from Strasbourg to Farel and other friends in which he worries at length over the call to Geneva and over his personal calling in the light of his earlier troubled experience in that city. Here we have a Calvin torn between two alternatives, puzzling over his life and its direction, but no reference to an *abyssus* or a *labyrinthus*![129]

What is perhaps most surprising in Bouwsma's account of the humanistic Calvin is that this aspect of Calvin's high rhetoric has been taken out of the context of rhetoric and placed into the context of existential trauma. Inasmuch as the underlying purpose of the rhetorical forms used by Calvin, the basic thrust of the topical logic, was persuasion, how better might Calvin present the case for his order of materials, his way through the problems, his theological and religious path, than to depict the alternatives as thorny places, chasms, impassible abysses, and impenetrable labyrinths, or, to borrow Melanchthon's somewhat less terrifying image, roads overgrown with briars? Beyond the abyss, through the labyrinth, and past the briars and the thorny places, there was, truly and clearly, an *ordo recte docendi*.

TEXT, CONTEXT, AND CONVERSATION

The *Institutes* in
Calvin's Theological Program

To Elaborate on the Topics

The Context and Method
of Calvin's Institutes

Calvin's *Institutes* as a Theological System: The Present Question

Calvin's *Institutes* is a theological system—to the extent the term can be applied to the forms used to frame and present Christian doctrine between the twelfth and the seventeenth centuries.[1] The *Institutes* is certainly an example of the sixteenth-century antecedent of what came to be called a "system of theology" in the seventeenth century. This point must be made, given the apparent vogue of statements to the effect that Calvin was not a "professional theologian" and wrote no "formal theology,"[2] or that he was "a biblical theologian" who "despised what passed for systematic theology in his own time" and who was interested primarily in "the right order of teaching,"[3] that he was "not a systematic thinker" and "did not even aspire to the construction of a system."[4] Calvin's *Institutes* is said to lack a "unified theological methodology" and to function as an "ad hoc collection of many methods and systems."[5] It is a "pastoral" rather than a dogmatic theology.[6] Bouwsma comments that "a systematic Calvin would be an anachronism; there were no 'systematic' thinkers of any significance in the sixteenth century,"[7] and he points his readers toward the earlier comments of Dillenberger that Calvin was "the least systematic of systematic theologians," but rather a "biblical theologian" whose "*Institutes* are like a wheel without a rim, a hub full of spokes" with "some spokes longer than others," certainly "no system in the sense in which we use it."[8]

These statements are, of course, quite contrary to the view of earlier scholarship: Wendel, for example, refered to the *Institutes* as a "manual of dogmatics . . . complementary to [Calvin's] courses in exegesis . . . in which he . . . developed his dogmatic convictions." Nor did Wendel view this purpose of the later editions of the *Institutes* as in any way contradictory to Calvin's earlier intention to provide the faithful with a basic statement of doctrine and a foundational apologetic.[9] Doumergue identified the second edition of the *Institutes* as the "manual of theology" in which Calvin began to develop the "theological system" already adumbrated in the first edition of 1536. For Doumergue, moreover, the *Institutes*, as a manual or system, stood head and shoulders over works like Zwingli's *Commentarius de vera et falsa religione* or Melanchthon's *Loci communes*.[10] Loofs spoke of the opening chapters of the 1539 *Institutes* as "the first Protestant prolegomena to dogmatics."[11] Seeberg discusses Calvin as a "dogmatician" as well as an exegete and characterizes his theological efforts as "a remarkable work [of] organizing dogmatic materials."[12] Others identify Calvin as a systematic thinker who so subjected himself to the exegetical task that he refused to impose his own logic on the teachings of Scripture and therefore retained the ambiguity or, indeed, the mystery of the biblical message.[13] There is, in other words, no shortage of older, indeed, eminent older works that place the *Institutes* into the genre of systematic or dogmatic theology and that do so without indicating any apology for or qualification of these terms. Of course, "systematic" and "dogmatic theology" were not terms available in Calvin's time—as they were not available in the era of Lombard's *Sentences* or Aquinas's *Summa theologiae*. This historical problem of the term, however, ought not to stand in the way of an examination of the substance of the issue—the place of Calvin's *Institutes* within the sixteenth-century forms of the historical discipline that has come to be known as "systematic theology."

Loci communes and *disputationes:* The Method and Intention of Calvin's *Institutes*

The 1539 edition of Calvin's *Institutes* marks a crucial solidification of purpose and yet a significant alteration of direction.[14] It was at this point that the *Institutes* ceased to be a brief, catechetical work and took on a new appearance—arguably the appearance of what one might call a sixteenth-century "system" of theology. The first sign of this development is the fairly radical alteration of the title. In 1536, the title had read, "Of the Christian Religion, an Institution [or Instruction], embracing nearly an entire summary of piety and what is necessary to know of the doctrine of salvation: a work most worthy to be read by all those zealous for piety."[15] The verb "embracing" (*complectens*) refers both to the "summary of piety" and to the "necessary . . . doctrine": the initial proposal of the *Institutes* was not simply to offer a summary or a system of piety but to inculcate both piety and doctrine and to do so in the form of a catechetically organized compendium.[16] Much of the original title, and, to that extent, of the original intention also, carried over in the first French edition (1541), the title of which deleted only the final clause of the 1536 version, namely "a work most worthy to be read by all those zealous for piety."

Calvin pointedly indicated his change of direction in the title of the 1539 Latin *Institutes*: he removed the entirety of the early subtitle—both its reference to piety and its reference to necessary doctrine, altered the word order of the main title from "Of the Christian Religion, an Institution" to "An Institution of the Christian Religion," and then added the significant new statement "now at last truly corresponding to its title."[17] Alteration of title also occurs in the French in the transition from the 1541 to the 1545 edition, at which point the reference to a "summary of piety" also drops out, yielding "Institution of the Christian Religion . . . in which a summary of all Christianity is contained." This remained the form of the French title until 1560, when all trace of the early subtitle was removed.[18]

There are several levels at which the editorial alteration must be considered. At the first and perhaps the most superficial level, the alteration probably stems from Calvin's assertion of his own personality over that of his editors: as Doumergue hypothesized, the newly established Basel publisher Platter and Lasius decided to enhance the significance of this new volume by a virtually unknown author by aumenting its simple title, *Christianae religionis institutio*, with a flowery and laudatory description of its contents.[19] The 1539 title, *Institution of the Christian Religion, now for the first time truly corresponding to its title*, represents a critique of the 1536 title, which Calvin himself felt did not properly represent his intentions or, as Doumergue argues, did not reflect his own natural reserve and modesty.[20] Parker, by way of contrast, is surely incorrect in his assessment of the clarifying second clause of the 1539 title as indicating that "not the whole of the Christian religion had been treated in 1536," for the 1536 title did not claim to offer a presentation of "the whole of the Christian religion."[21] The common element in the 1536 and 1539 titles, moreover, is not any claim to completeness but rather the claim to offer an *institutio* or fundamental instruction—and, in 1539, no longer an instruction in piety.

At the next level, some attention must be paid to the relationship between the excised phrases and the purpose of the *Institutes* as indicated in the dedication and the letter to the reader: the 1539 excisions removed references to the *Institutes* as a "sum of piety" and a gathering of all the teachings "necessary to know for salvation," but the preface now identified the work as embracing "the sum of religion in all its parts" primarily for the purpose of instructing "candidates in sacred theology in the reading of the divine Word."[22] The catechetical model, in other words, was deemphasized, and the identification of the *Institutes* as part of a large-scale theological "instruction" became central.[23] (Parker overstates the point somewhat, arguing that the alternation represented a complete shift from a catechetical arrangement to a "systematic arrangement of the main doctrines of Holy Scripture."[24]) In 1539, Calvin turned to full instruction by way of the standard form of *loci communes*, but he did not set aside the catechetical arrangement. The "sum of religion" offered in 1539 adds a series of Pauline topics by interspersing new chapters between the chapters of the orignal catechetical model—significantly, without altering the order of the original chapters.[25]

At a third and even more profound level, the continuity between the 1536 and the 1539 titles is found principally in the identification of the work as an *institutio* and the claim of 1539 that now, presumably, the work for the first time has become an *institutio*—a profound issue for Calvin, given his attention to precise literary genre. Not only was Calvin dissatisfied with the initial title of the work as augmented by the printers; he was also somewhat dissatisfied with the contents and direction of his own work. The 1536 edition was conceived in some relationship to the early catechism, written shortly afterward for use in Geneva, also called an "institution" or "instruction": the first edition of the *Institutes* followed the order of Luther's *Small Catechism*, and

Calvin's *Catechismus, sive christianae religionis institutio* of 1538 paralleled the 1536 *Institutes*, albeit with significant addition of topics, adumbrating the new materials of the 1539 *Institutes*.[26] So, too, Calvin's catechism written for the French congregation in Strasbourg, ca. 1538–41, was entitled *L'Institution puérile de la doctrine chrestienne*. The new catechism of 1541 and its Latin translation of 1545, however, omit the term *institution* or *institutio*.[27] Thus, as of 1539/41, Calvin ceased to identify catechetical works by the term *institutio* and reserved it for his ever-expanding theological "summa." In addition, in his "Letter to the Reader" of 1539, Calvin described the earlier edition as having dealt "lightly" with the subject of Christianity. Presumably, the purpose, noted in the 1539 preface, of instructing not catechumens but theological students (that is, candidates for ministry) has taken the place of the initial catechetical purpose—and the term *institutio* has become associated with that task.[28]

The import of the phrase "now for the first time truly corresponding to its title" can therefore be inferred both from the meaning of *institutio*—"institution" or, as it is typically rendered, *institutes*—and from the reflections added to the 1539 version of Calvin's preface. The term *institutio* was well known to Calvin from the titles of Quintillian's *Institutio oratoria* (ca. A.D. 90), Lactantius's *De divinis institutionibus* (ca. 310), an Erasmus's *Institutio principis christiani* (1516), and perhaps from the introduction to Luther's *Larger Catechism* (1529).[29] In each of these cases, *institutio* indicates a fundamental instruction. In the first two, it does so with the added connotations from classical usage of a proper disposition or arrangement and a statement of principles or methods. The term itself, therefore, can point either to a basic instruction or to a work of greater depth and development. Calvin's initial choice of the term in 1536 could certainly have echoed Luther, whereas his retention of the term while at the same time setting aside the early "Lutheran" catechetical model may point to the classical and the patristic sources—Quintillian and Lactantius—and to a more fully developed "instruction."[30] There is also the tantalizing possibility that Calvin knew of Melanchthon's early *Theologica institutio in Epistolam Pauli ad Romanos* (1519), even as he associated his 1539 revision of the *Institutes* with topics drawn from the exegesis of Romans.[31]

In his 1539 preface to his readers—corresponding to the change in title—Calvin offered a modified description of his work and an indication of the pattern of theological work that would occupy him for the remainder of his life. The crucial passage reads:

> It has been my purpose in this labor to prepare and instruct candidates in sacred theology for the reading of the divine Word, in order that they may be able both to have easy access to it and to advance in it without stumbling. For I believe I have so embraced the sum of religion in all its parts (*religionis summam omnibus partibus*), and have arranged it in such an order, that if anyone rightly grasps it, it will not be difficult for him to determine what he ought especially to seek in Scripture, and to what end (*scopum*) he ought to relate its contents. If, after this road has, as it were, been paved, I shall publish any detailed expositions (*enarrationes*) of Scripture, I shall always condense them, because I shall have no need to undertake long doctrinal disputations (*dogmatibus longas disputationes instituere*), or to wander about in the basic topics (*in locos communes evagari*).[32]

Although Calvin does not directly state in this passage that his *Institutes* is a set of *loci communes* and "dogmatic disputations," he points his readers toward this conclusion, particularly when these introductory remarks are placed into the context of various methodological statements in the *Institutes* and into the context of Calvin's ongoing exegetical project.[33] It is significant here that when Calvin speaks of *undertaking* or introducing "long dogmatic disputations," he uses the verb "to instruct" (*instituere*): the result of such an undertaking would, as the verb implies, be an "instruction" (*institutio*). Also interesting is his use of the verb *evagari*, translated as "digress" (Battles), "dilate" (1539/Beveridge), or "enlarge" (1559/Beveridge): the basic meaning of "wander" or "manoeuvre" not only refers, negatively, to what Calvin sought to avoid in his commentaries—a wandering through topics that could be viewed as digressive from the basic purpose of the commentary—it also reflects, in its more positive indication of the purpose of the *Institutes*, Calvin's (and Melanchthon's) consistent metaphor for rightly ordered *loci communes*, the identification of a *via* through difficult topics.

That Calvin, from 1539 on, did understand his *Institutes* as a gathering of *loci communes* and *disputationes* appears also from the even more explicit statements presented in his introductory "Argument" to the French translation of 1541. Calvin paraphrases the 1539 Latin preface, repeating the comment "if our Lord gives me the means and opportunity to write a few (*quelques*) commentaries, I will use the greatest brevity of which I am capable" and continues, now explicitly identifying the contents of the *Institutes*, "for it will not be necessary to make long digressions, inasmuch as I have recited here at length (*j'ay icy desduict, au long*) almost all of the articles that belong to Christianity."[34] The words "*desduict, au long, quasi tous les articles*" correspond with the words of the Latin "I shall have no need to undertake long dogmatic disputations" and state expressly what the Latin implies: the lengthy discourses omitted from the commentaries are collected "here," in the *Institutes*. In this "argument," Calvin once again indicates the purpose of the *Institutes* and, this time, omits all reference to piety, identifying his purpose, first, as providing a "sum of Christian doctrine" and, second, as offering a point of entry into the study of the Old and New Testaments.[35] Some contemporary attestation to this understanding is also found in Colladon's index to the 1559 and 1560 *Institutes*, where the explanatory heading identifies the major theological topics of Calvin's work as *loci*.

These introductory comments, moreover, must be read in the light of Calvin's insistence in several places in the *Institutes* on the establishment of "a proper order of expression" or "right order of teaching," with the primary reference coming from the 1539 text.[36] The construction of doctrinal *loci* as a product of the work of exegesis and the composition of doctrinal disputations in the course of polemic yields the contents of a theology, but not its order and arrangement. Thus, the compiler of a set of *loci communes* needs also to attend to the ordering of the topics, as Philip Melanchthon, Heinrich Bullinger, and Andreas Hyperius had all pointed out in their essays on the study and method of theology.[37] The result of these two concerns—the identification of the basic topics for discourse and the identification of a right order or *methodus* through which the relationships between the *loci* and the broader organizational patterns of the discipline might be elucidated—can be seen in the transition from the simple catechetical forms of early-sixteenth-century Protestant theology to the more elaborate forms of *Loci communes theologici*, *Methodus theologiae*, and *Institutio christianae religionis* that belong to the work of the mid-sixteenth-century codifiers of Reformation theology.

This characterization of Calvin's *Institutes* has become both a point of departure and a stumbling block to many of those who have attempted to survey and explain his theology. When, for example, these comments are placed together with Calvin's statement that he "was never satisfied until the work had been arranged in the order now [1559] set forth," the conclusion has been drawn that Calvin understood the final form of the *Institutes* to be the primary source for any understanding of his theology.[38] Imbart de la Tour described the commentaries and treatises as "forward buttresses intended to defend the central position" of Calvin's theology, namely the *Institutes.* Calvin, he wrote, is "entirely comprehended" (*est tout entire*) in the *Institutes.*[39] Parker argues that, although the commentaries and treatises sometimes offer fuller expression, "there is nothing in the commentaries that does not also come in the *Institutes.*"[40] Fuhrmann, by way of contrast, remarks that Calvin never emphasized the *Institutes* "at the expense of other expositions."[41] Yet none of these writers identified the *Institutes* as but one part of a larger project or argued an integral relationship between the development of the *Institutes* and the writing of the commentaries.[42]

A significant exception to these generalizations was Stauffer's insistence on the importance of the sermons to Calvin's life work. The *Institutes,* Stauffer commented, neither exhausted Calvin's genius nor, more important, stood as a sufficient explanation of his importance to the sixteenth-century audience. Stauffer pointed toward the nearly eight hundred of Calvin's sermons published during his lifetime and the fifteen hundred more preserved in manuscript form after his death in Geneva.[43] The *Institutes* stands, surely, in the midst of Calvin's work, but its place and purpose was hardly separable from the other efforts in which he engaged—most notably, his exposition of Scripture, whether in sermon or commentary.

A somewhat different perspective on Calvin's own characterization of his *Institutes* arises when it is recognized that the instructional purpose of the work was first set originally in the form cited earlier in the 1539 edition of the *Institutes,* as Calvin prepared his first commentary (on Romans) for publication. In a recent essay, McKee has taken careful note of the probable identification of the *Institutes* as a set of *loci* and has made the point that Calvin's statement concerning its purpose indicates not a priority but a complementarity of position and a "symbiotic relationship" between the *Institutes* and the commentaries.[44] Calvin's statement of purpose, moreover, fits extraordinarily well with the highly topical arrangement of the work in 1539—and, like the omission of the 1536 phrase *summa pietatis* from the title, it marks the transition of the *Institutes* from its early form as a theologically or dogmatically expanded catechetical exercise to its later form as a series of *loci communes* and *disputationes.*[45] It also looks forward to Calvin's exegetical method, soon to be made evident in the commentary on Romans. There, Calvin avoided the expansive approach of Bucer, Bullinger, and others, where theological *loci* and *disputationes* were placed into the text, much like *scholia* in the medieval commentaries.[46] Indeed, Calvin's commentary on Romans offers a rather sparse examination of the text when compared with other commentators of the age, while the *Institutes* often contains the broader frame of biblical and traditionary reference found in the commentaries of Calvin's predecessors and contemporaries without, however, exegetical detail.[47] Calvin did not, moreover, change the wording of this description of his project in subsequent editions of the *Institutes.*

Examination of the various terms used by Calvin in the *Institutes* to describe his task itself bears out this understanding of his introductory statements. Simpson's essay on piety in the *Institutes* notes the many instances of the term *pietas* but fails to recognize that, unlike the deleted title, virtually none of these usages gives an indication of the task or genre of Calvin's work.[48] Calvin continually exhorts his readers to piety and consistently criticizes authorities and teachings that stand in the way of piety or of the teaching of piety (*doctrina, exercitia,* or *studium pietatis*),[49] but he never describes what he is doing as a form of piety. Piety was to be conjoined with "teaching" or "doctrine" (*doctrina*): Calvin did not understand it as an exercise separable from his teaching, preaching, and debating. By way of contrast, he often refers to the genre of his work, indeed, to the form of specific chapters and subsections, as a *disputatio* or a *locus*.[50] for example, he begins his discussion of false sacraments by stating that "the disputation on the sacraments immediately preceding ought to have been enough to persuade teachable and sober folk. . . ."[51] So, too, in his analysis of the problem of merit, Calvin refers to his earlier "disputation on free choice."[52] Or, again, in opening his discussions of repentance and the forgiveness of sins, Calvin comments that "any disputation concerning faith" would be useless if "these two heads" (repentance and forgiveness) were omitted.[53] The phrases "this disputation" and "in this disputation" occur throughout the *Institutes*.[54] So, also, when Calvin published his discussion of human knowledge from the 1550 *Institutes* as a separate treatise, he identified it as a disputation.[55]

A similar result appears when Calvin's use of the term *locus* is examined. Quite frequently, Calvin refers to the biblical text he is about to examine as a *locus*.[56] He also, albeit less frequently, identifies his own discussions of particular issues as *loci*: thus, in broaching the subject of the division of the Decalogue into two tables, Calvin comments that "it is necessary for us to deal with this *locus* in order that our readers might not . . . wonder at the division."[57] Or, again, when raising the issue of the Mediator in his discussion of the Trinity, Calvin notes that he will discuss the point more fully in its proper *locus*.[58] So, too, in discussing the power of the church, Calvin comments that "now follows the third *locus, de ecclesiae potestate*" and then that the "*locus* concerning [this] doctrine has two parts."[59] It is worth noting that the phrases *locus de ecclesiae potestate* and *locus de doctrina* have a far more technical implication than is conveyed by their translation as "the section" or "division" on "the power of the church" and "the doctrinal side":[60] in both cases, Calvin specifically refers to sections of his own work as formal presentations of set topics in debate—and does so by using the traditional, technical language of dialectic.

The *Institutes* thus contains the *loci* or topics and the *disputationes* that, had Calvin followed the style of Bullinger or Bucer, would have appeared in commentaries. The successive editions of the *Institutes* must be regarded as expansions and augmentations of the 1539 *loci* and *disputationes* in the light of issues that arose in the process of Calvin's great exegetical work of commenting on nearly the entire Bible. As McKee has argued, the biblical citations in the *Institutes* ought frequently to be understood as "cross-references" to the commentaries.[61] Indeed, when the biblical citations in the *Institutes* are not cross-references to Calvin's own commentaries, they probably should be viewed as references to the exegetical tradition and not as "proof-texts" in the sense of texts wrested out of their context in violation of the principles of biblical interpretation.[62] The term "summary" or "comperd of religion" *summa religionis*, moreover, points not toward a final, exhaustive summation but toward a summary—indeed, toward a body, gathering, or collation of *loci communes* or *disputationes dogmaticae*.[63] The *Institutes* must not be read instead of the commentaries, but with them: the commentaries and the *Institutes* together provide, in what Calvin thought to be a better arrangement of materials, what one would find in the commentaries of other writers. Indeed, if one wishes to ascertain the biblical basis of Calvin's topical discussions and disputations, one *must* read the commentaries. And, arguably, this is precisely what Calvin meant by his introductory characterization of the *Institutes*.

It is also the case that Calvin's disputative comments on Scripture and doctrine, as offered in the *Institutes*, frequently fail to indicate the entirety of his teaching—and, as any study of the historical development of the *Institutes* in the light of the ongoing work of Calvin as commentator and preacher will show, the *Institutes* typically manifests a dependence on the thought of the commentaries, rather than vice versa.[64] At the same time, the exegetico-theological conclusions embodied in the commentaries frequently lack either systematic elaboration or illustration on the basis of other biblical texts, historical example, or dispute with variant theological views—all of which occur at the relevant point in the *Institutes*.

As T. H. L. Parker and others have observed, the methodological comments offered by Calvin at the beginning of the *Institutes* offer an insight into Calvin's exegetical method in its distinction from the methods of his contemporaries.[65] But the point must also be made that these comments offer an insight into Calvin's theological method in the *Institutes* in its relation to the *loci communes* and "systems of theology" of Calvin's contemporaries and successors[66]—and, indeed, a explanation of why the *Institutes* sometimes argues a point not commonly found in later theological systems and why it often fails to discuss issues present both in the scholastic theological systems of the Middle Ages and in the theological systems of the Reformed theologians of the late sixteenth and seventeenth centuries. The commentaries frequently shed light on the meaning of a passage in the *Institutes*, sometimes offer indications of why topics are augmented in certain ways in the *Institutes*; sometimes, when topics has been expanded in the *Institutes* prior to the examination of a related text, the commentaries explicitly refer the readers to extended discussions in the *Institutes*.[67] Contemporary or occasional issues, particularly those generated by polemic, transfer from the work of the exegete to the pages of the *Institutes*—and the commentaries often provide positive theological argumentation, typical of earlier and later theological systems, that Calvin chose not to duplicate in the *Institutes*.

The *Locus* and the Methods of Theology in the Sixteenth Century

The prominence of the *locus* or *topos* in the logic and dialectic of the later Middle Ages, the Renaissance, and the Reformation rested in no small degree on the perception that the elicitation of topics or *loci* from the subject under examination provided the optimal point of departure for the examination of the subject.[68] Melanchthon commented that Cicero's *Topics* described "the method of locating arguments" and of "amplifying or explaining discourse."[69] He owed his point to the efforts of Rudolf Agricola (1443–

85), whose *De inventione dialectica libri III* (1480/1515) had been championed by Erasmus and echoed in Erasmus's popular treatise on argument and the gathering of materials for argumentation, *De copia* (1512).[70] Agricola was not, by intention, a creative thinker: his hope was rather to renew interest in the classical disciplines. But his emphasis on grounding logic in rhetoric and on deriving the rules of logic from the examination of the works of great classical orators led to the view of logic as an art of probabilities rather than a science of necessities—"dialectics," he wrote, "is the art of speaking in a probable way"—based on the examination of fundamental topics or *loci*. The basic work of this rhetorical logic, "invention," was defined by Agricola as the location of proof or grounds of argument in and through the identification of the *loci*, which is to say the "places" or *topoi* in which they might be found.[71]

As Stump has argued, the movement of later medieval logic prior to Agricola had tended away from a logic of probabilities toward a logic of necessary conclusions. With reference to Aristotle's and Cicero's *Topics*, a "concentration on the nature of the rules for consequences"[72] tended to subsume the logic of the *Topics* under the stricter models of the *Analytics*. (Of course, Aristotle himself did not make a strict division between logic and rhetoric: in the rhetorical forms of the *Topics*, logic is applied to persuasion, with the result that its structures are not quite as strict but still belong to the realm of logic.) Agricola, by emphasizing the logic of Aristotle's and Cicero's *Topics*, pressed in the opposite direction: in Agricola's model, dialectic focused on the *Topics* and, therefore, on probability and the persuasive use of probable propositions. Agricola thus echoed a Ciceronian use of logic in persuasion and identified the "sources" or "seats" of argument (*fontes* or *sedes argumentorum*) as the knowledge found in basic *loci* or *topoi* and defined the dialectical study of the *loci* as "the art of establishing the probability or credibility of whatever had been proposed."[73]

From the perspective of the Northern Renaissance, the Agricolan method freed rhetoric from the procrustean bed of logical forms and Aristotelian categories and allowed logic to follow out, in high discursive style, the patterns and implications inherent in the materials of debate. Nonetheless, Agricola also held to the Augustinian assumption that the primary function of the rhetor was to teach and that the rhetorical skill of moving and pleasing the mind was secondary—and therefore he refused to subordinate logic fully to rhetoric, as Valla did.[74] The scholastic sense of an intimate relationship between categories of predicates and the work of argumentation was replaced by a more strict separation of logic and the philosophy of properties and relations (i.e., physics and metaphysics)—with the similar result that the methods of interpretation could assume rhetorical and philological forms distinct from the stricter logic of demonstration. In early-sixteenth-century debate over curricula, the change was viewed as vast: from a humanist perspective, the stylistic "barbarism" of medieval dialectic, as represented by the famous manual by Peter of Spain, could be juxtaposed with the "more elegant" flow of Agricolan argumentation—whereas from the more traditional and nominally scholastic perspective, clarity of line had given way to stylistic subtlety.[75]

Nonetheless, a strong element of continuity must also be noted in this development of dialectic: the basic connection between *loci* or *topica* and the academic exercise of *disputationes* remained unchanged during this development of place logic. In Stump's words, "the scholastic tradition of dialectic has its roots in Aristotle's *Topics*," the large part of which "is devoted to a method for finding arguments useful in dialectical dis-

putations."[76] Whether understood as providing the grounds for arguing logical consequences or as understood in the more rhetorical (i.e., the Agricolan) sense of establishing
probabilities for the purpose of persuasion, the examination of *loci* or *topica* was foundational to argument and, therefore, to the construction of *disputationes*. Moreover,
from a methodological perspective, the virtual identity of the "maxims" of dialectic,
the *sententiae* or "maxims" of theology, and the *loci communes* of rhetoric was noted
specifically by Alain of Lille at the end of the twelfth century—just as the application
of the *locus* method to theology was noted by both Erasmus and Melanchthon in the
early sixteenth century.[77] This connection between the several exercises and methods,
altered little by the Renaissance restructuring of the relationship between logic and
rhetoric, remains in force in the theological *loci communes* and *disputationes* of the
sixteenth-century Reformers and of their seventeenth-century successors, as well.

If Agricola, as recommended by Erasmus, was the mediator and interpreter of the
dialectical *locus* or *topos* to the Renaissance and Reformation, Melanchthon was the
mediator and interpreter of the *locus* or *topos* for the Protestant theological tradition.
Agricola had noted the applicability of his dialectic to theology and had also noted that
his concentration on probable argumentation was "most aptly" referred to faith, but
he had not elaborated any application of the *locus* method to theology.[78] In his biblical
commentaries and in his theological system, the *Loci communes rerum theologicarum seu
hypotyposes theologicae* (1521), Melanchthon bridged the gap between the scholastic
method of deriving doctrinal topics or *scholia* from the work of exegesis and the dialectical examination of topics or *loci* as "seats" or "sources of argument." For Melanchthon, crucial biblical texts are (or provide) *loci* in the sense of "seats" or "grounds
of arguments" (*sedes argumentorum*), while the elicited topics, organized by recourse to
a proper method into a coherent sequence, are *loci* in the sense of theological topics.[79]
Melanchthon can also insist that theology, unlike philosophy, rests not on demonstra-
tions but on "the clear and certain testimonies" of God: the right method of theology,
therefore, will be the ordered exposition of *loci* and not philosophical demonstration.[80]

It is surely this Melanchthonian approach to the *loci*—both as biblical seats or sources
of argument and as theological topics—that carried over into the *Institutes* in Calvin's
gathering of *loci communes* and *disputationes*, although Calvin may well have first encountered Agricolan logic in Claude Chansonette's *Topica juris civilis*.[81] What is more,
the internal style of Calvin's *loci* and *disputationes* also follows in the tradition of the
medieval and Renaissance *topics*. In the first place, inasmuch as he was engaged in
persuasion rather than simple demonstration, Calvin understood the basic logical form
of the *locus* as the enthymeme (a partially stated rhetorical form of syllogism), rather
than the full syllogism, a clear point of continuity with the Aristotelian past, whether
with the original patterns of Aristotle's *Topica*, with the medieval elaboration of the
Topica for purposes of disputation, or with Agricola's dialectic.[82] In the second place,
as Battles has shown, Calvin's pattern of argument in disputation evidences a certain
tendency to bifurcation, a point that Battles associated with the somewhat later development of Ramism[83] but that ought, more rightly, to be associated with basic patterns
in the dialectics of Rudolf Agricola and of Erasmus.[84] Here, too, we see a close relationship between Calvin's logic and the place-logic of the later Middle Ages and the
early Renaissance. The specific pattern of argument that Battles documents—an initial
bifurcation between untrue or defective teaching and true teaching, followed by a sec-

ondary bifurcation between an extreme or excess of statement and the true teaching rightly stated[85]—also obliges standard patterns of argument in the older dialectic, both scholastic and humanistic, and particularly the Agricolan approach to *topoi*.[86]

Whereas Breen was certainly correct, therefore, in associating Calvin's rhetoric with Ciceronian forms, he certainly overstated his case by making a strict contrast between the dialectic and the syllogistic forms of the scholastics on the one hand, and the rhetoric of the humanists, characterized by a use of the enthymeme, on the other.[87] Admittedly, Calvin's Ciceronian tastes pressed him toward an understanding of the *locus* or *topos* as an investigation of the "seats" or "sources of argument." Nonetheless, in view of the dominance of Agricolan dialectic, his attention to the logic of the topic constituted not so much a choice of rhetoric over dialectic as the choice of a rhetorical dialectic. Even so, the use of the enthymeme was characteristic of the Aristotelian (and Ciceronian) topical logic of the high scholastic era:[88] Calvin's use of the enthymeme as opposed to the syllogism points not away from dialectic or, indeed, away from scholasticism but rather toward the logic of the *Topica*, whether of the scholastic era or of the Renaissance. Indeed, the choice of one form over the other might well relate to the genre of the document: in his Pauline commentaries, Calvin, like Melanchthon, often noted syllogisms or other specific figures of speech in tightly stated summaries of the argument, whereas, in sermons on the same text, Calvin's arguments tend to be far more discursive and not at all intent on filling out the form of the syllogism or stating the figure.[89]

Nor ought the Renaissance emphasis on topical or place-logic in the context of persuasive discourse be understood as a fundamental rejection or exclusion of the more strictly syllogistic forms of argument: this was not the case with Agricola, nor was it the case with members of the faculty of the University of Paris in Calvin's time,[90] nor was it the case with Melanchthon's formal rhetoric. Indeed, Melanchthon discussed the use of the enthymeme as the conclusion to his chapter on the forms of syllogism.[91] Even so, the distance between the syllogism and the enthymeme—like that between many scholastics and many humanists—is not vast: the enthymeme, as defined by various medieval and Renaissance logicians is a syllogistic form that implies rather than states its middle term. According to these logicians and dialecticians, the purpose of the *topos*, with its investigation of the sources of argument, was to supply the materials of the missing proposition of the enthymeme. As Agricola comments, *loci communes* are "nothing other than the major propositions for argumentation."[92] They are, in Melanchthon's words, "the principal topical divisions, which comprise [both] the sources and the fruition of the art [of argumentation]" and which therefore provide the major premises of syllogisms or enthemymes.[93]

Brevitas and *facilitas* versus *dogmatibus longas disputationes.*
The Impact of Calvin's Exegetical Method on the
Contents of the *Institutes*

If Calvin's statement of intention in the preface to the 1539 *Institutes* pointed toward the correlation of his doctrinal task with his future exegetical work, specifically toward the commentary on Romans in which he was then engaged, his methodological statement in the commentary (1540) surely points back to his work on the text of the

Institutes. Calvin there proposed an approach not only to the text of Scripture but also to the genre of commentary, characterized by such terms as "perspicuous brevity" (*perspicua brevitas*) and "ease" or "smoothness of exposition" (*facilitas*).[94] These terms resonate strongly with the methodological context of Calvin's work. On the one hand, they reflect the values of classical rhetoric and of humanist expository models, notably those of Lefèvre and his circle.[95] On the other hand, the demand for concision and ease or simplicity was not at odds with the medieval scholastic technique of glossing the text—and it was specifically identified by Calvin's contemporary, Hyperius, as a characteristic of the "scholastic" method of biblical exposition.[96] So also did Jean de Budé characterize the plain and simple style of Calvin's commentary on the Minor Prophets as "scholastic" and suited to the life of the school, rather than "oratorical" in style.[97] This usage, offers, therefore, further evidence of the confluence of humanist and scholastic methods in the work of Reformers like Calvin (and Hyperius).

Calvin's application of the principles of *perspicua brevitas* and *facilitas* was quite specific: he had objected strenuously, on aesthetic and methodological grounds, to the elaborate, diffuse, and highly dogmatic style of Martin Bucer, which was followed in large part, albeit without quite as much verbiage, by contemporary exegetes like Bullinger, Musculus, and Pellican. The Bucerian model had presented lengthy dogmatic excurses or *loci communes* whenever the text indicated a major doctrinal issue. Indeed, certain segments or pericopes were understood as the basis for dogmatic treatises: as Bullinger's practice indicates, the title of the treatise could even be inserted into the text of the commentary to indicate the transition from exegesis proper to the dogmatic formulation of a *locus*—just as, in an alternative pattern of organization sometimes used by Calvin, an introductory analysis of the argument or scope of an epistle could be set prior to the initial citation of verses to be examined.[98]

The *Loci communes theologici* (1560) of Calvin's contemporary, Wolfgang Musculus were a gathering of precisely these kind of postexegetical doctrinal discussions out of a lifetime of exegetical labor into a single theological summation.[99] Calvin's call for *brevitas* and *facilitas* stood quite specifically against this practice—not, of course, against the elaboration of the *loci* but only against their insertion into the commentary. The contrast between Calvin's procedure and that of Musculus is striking, as much in its dogmatic result as in the form of the commentary: Musculus consistently included topical *observationes* in his commentaries but never attempted a full, independent set of theological *loci* until the end of his career.[100] The result is a work in which some topics are developed in vast detail and others are given only brief treatment. Calvin, by way of contrast, began with the entire project in mind, including an initial outline for his *loci*.[101] The result was a lifetime of exegetical labor coordinated not only with the writing of the individual *loci* but also with years of effort towards the establishment of the most suitable order of teaching.

In view of Calvin's methodological statements and the nature of *loci communes* as theological topics related to particular texts, not only must the *Institutes* be understood as a gathering of *loci*, but the contents of these *loci* must also be regarded as primarily exegetical *both* in origin *and* in their continuing frame of reference.[102] Even those chapters understood as *disputationes* rest on fundamental exegetical considerations, albeit in the immediate context of Calvin's polemic. This exegetical understanding coincides, of course, with the basic intention of the *Institutes* as an instruction in religion introductory to the study of Scripture. But it also means that the *Institutes* as a whole and the contents of its individual *loci* must be understood not only in the history of theological system but also in the history of exegesis. The individual chapters and sections of the *Institutes*, understood as *loci communes*, must therefore be read in the context of their exegetical point of origin—which is to say, in the context of the commentary and of the specific biblical *loci classici* or *sedes doctrinae* that generated them in the first place.[103] As indicated earlier, this assumption can be gathered not only from Calvin's preface but also from the consistent internal identification both of major texts under examination and of their positive doctrinal elaborations as *loci*. When, moreover, the nature of the *Institutes* as a set of *loci communes* is taken seriously and the various *loci* are examined in the context both of Calvin's own commentaries and of the exegetical tradition, only then does it become clear precisely why certain issues are addressed, why particular collateral texts are employed as fundamental to explanation, and even (on occasion) why the specific section of the *Institutes* under examination takes on one particular argumentative cast rather than another.[104]

The terms *brevitas* and *facilitas* thus function as a parallel to the phrase "long dogmatic disputationes" (*dogmatibus longas disputationes*) that described both method and the genre of the *Institutes*. From a purely linguistic perspective, it is the case not only that *brevitas* of exposition in the commentary contrasts with "length" (*longitudo*) of discourse in the *Institutes* but also that the term *facilitas*, with its broad implication of ease, directness, and absence of contest, contrasts with the style of the *disputatio* that is also characteristic of the *Institutes*. The one major qualification that must be placed on this model arises from the changing style of Calvin's commentaries. Calvin's identification, in 1540, of *brevitas* and *facilitas* as primary stylistic characteristics of his commentaries, although paralleled by his declaration of a "simple method of teaching" in the 1557 Psalms commentary,[105] was an initial stylistic proposal not always followed by Calvin in his later writings. In the preface to Psalms, he elaborates on the phrase "simple manner of teaching" with the comment that he has "for the most part, abstained from refutations" and has avoided mention of "contrary opinions" unless necessary to the clarity of his exposition.[106] *Facilitas* remains unaltered. But the Psalms, like Calvin's other commentaries on the Old Testament, evidence a tendency toward the fuller elaboration of theological concepts, so that *brevitas* is perhaps less in evidence. The later commentaries—most notably the *Harmony on the Last Four Books of Moses*—tend to bear an increasing portion of Calvin's positive theological formulations, with the result that the identification of Calvin's later doctrinal positions often rests as much on the commentaries as on the *Institutes*, or more.[107]

The understanding of Calvin's *Institutes* as a set of *loci communes* that stands in profound relation to the history of exegesis must also be balanced with the issues raised by Calvin's references to *disputationes* and to the "right order of teaching." In its beginnings, the *Institutes* was formally rooted in the catechetical tradition, and Calvin's subsequent efforts to establish the right order for his teaching must be understood in part as a maintenance of the basic catechetical topics as doctrinal *loci* and in part as an attempt to move beyond the restrictions and the less-than-systematic ordering of the catechism.[108] The content of the *Institutes* was thus determined by the Creed, the Decalogue, and the Lord's Prayer, with the various expansions reflecting both exegetical development (*loci communes*) and theological debate (*disputationes dogmaticae*). Doctrinal debate and polemic, largely absent from the commentaries, pervade the *Institutes*. And whereas the catechetical foundation assured inclusion in the *Institutes* of the basic theological topics, its disputative purpose, like the process of gathering exegetical *loci*, gave it an unmistakably occasional character. The *Institutes* does not provide an exhaustive set of positive *loci*: its development and expansion reflects the history of Calvin's debates and of his exegetical work as much as it does a desire for systematic exposition. And its limitation points back to the initial topical limitation of a catechetical exercise. When Calvin's topics extend beyond those dictated by the original catechetical model, they typically derive either from the commentaries as dogmatic *loci* (as is clear in the case of providence and predestination in 1539)[109] or from the debates or disputations in which Calvin and his contemporaries were—often unwillingly—embroiled (as illustrated by Calvin's intense polemic against Andreas Osiander in the *Institutes*).[110]

Given this continuing interrelationship and interplay between the *Institutes* and the commentaries (and to a certain extent the semons), Calvin's comments on any given topic tend to vary, in form and in place, among exegetical reflection, topical expansion, and (in the case of the sermons) discursive amplification.[111] This distinction, in turn, gave rise in the course of Calvin's theological work to several different patterns of address to any given theological issue. On the one hand, it should not be surprising that certain of the theological issues raised and even developed in some exegetical depth by Calvin in his commentaries are not brought over into the *Institutes* as *loci communes*. Apparently, the issue was not present in current debate or was not one that fell easily into either the catechetical topics of the 1536 or the added Pauline topics of the 1539 *Institutes*. A case can be made, along these lines, for the absence of discussion of the divine essence and attributes or of the doctrine of covenant from the *Intitutes*. On the other hand, readers of the *Institutes* in 1539 ought to have taken Calvin's introductory remarks on *loci communes* and dogmatic disputations as an invitation from the author to seek out the exegetical basis for the new chapter on providence and predestination in his Romans commentary of 1540. What is more, those who attempt to elicit Calvin's views on predestination from the commentary alone will be somewhat disappointed by the calculated *brevitas* of the exposition, which follows strictly the line of the text rather than attempting to explicate the doctrinal topic in full.[112]

Similarly, the rather harsh impression given by Calvin's commentary on Romans 13:1–7 arises, at least in part, from his close attention to the issue addressed by the text—obedience to the civil authorities—and his unwillingness either to expand his comment to include other issues traditionally raised in the *scholion* or *locus* developed from this text or to raise qualifications arising from the theological interrelationship of a particular pericope to other pericopes, even those in the same book of Scripture. Thus, the qualifications on obedience found in the more elaborate commentaries of Calvin's contemporaries, such as the traditional citation of Acts 5:29, "We ought to obey God rather than men," are absent from Calvin's commentary. They appear, however, in the *locus* on civil government found in the *Institutes*.[113]

By the same token, the chapters against Servetus and Osiander appear in the *Institutes* as evidence of Calvin's careful division of labor: the chapter against Servetus stands as a disputative *locus* that Calvin did not offer in his commentaries, not even in the commentary on John, despite the pressing need there to identify Servetus's interpretation as erroneous.[114] The initial chapter of Calvin's Christology is also largely polemical.[115] Here Calvin devotes four out of seven sections to an attack on Andreas Osiander's doctrine of the necessity of incarnation apart from sin. The tone and, indeed, the theological emphasis of the chapter are not at all representative of the christological discussions in the commentaries, where the positive soteriological purpose of incarnation is clearly the dominant theme, and the polemic against Osiander passes unnoticed.[116] This pattern is, of course, precisely what Calvin forecast in his preface to the *Institutes*: the dogmatic disputations do not generally find a place in the commentaries.

These considerations, in turn, point toward the fundamentally problematic character of theological arguments that assume, first, that Calvin's *Institutes* can be evaluated as a full system of theology in the modern sense and, second, that Calvin's omission or inclusion of a given topic offers a perspective on what Calvin viewed as theologically legitimate.[117] Thus, the absence of any extended treatment of such topics as natural theology or the divine essence and attributes from the *Institutes*, together with Calvin's frequent attacks on excessive speculation, ought not to be interpreted as implicit denials on Calvin's part of the legitimacy of those topics. In certain cases, this kind of interpretation of the *Institutes* has been thrust back upon the commentaries, to the loss of the larger content of Calvin's thought. An example of this problem is Parker's denial of any natural theology in Calvin's comment on Psalm 104—largely on the basis of Calvin's negative comments on the noetic effects of sin in the *Institutes*.[118]

It can similarly—and erroneously—be argued that Calvin did not hold to a traditional, albeit not particularly speculative, view of the divine essence and attributes, when, in point of fact, the commentaries contain many indications that Calvin held thoroughly traditional views on the subject of divine essence and attributes, even though he did not (presumably because of the absence of controversy on these issues) move from his commentaries to the creation of extensive *loci* or *disputationes* in the *Institutes*.[119] Calvin's sense of the *loci* properly belonging to the *ordo recte docendi* probably also accounts for the presence of the chapters on the relationship of Old and New Testament and for the reservation of other aspects of the discussion of biblical covenant language to commentaries and sermons.[120]

These considerations do, of course, point toward a rather complex way of approaching Calvin's thought—not so much via the *Institutes* or via the *Institutes* and the commentaries taken as a whole and compared topically as via a historical and developmentally conditioned reading of the successive editions of the *Institutes* and of the changes made in them in the light of the commentaries and controversies that had intervened between the editions or that were in progress at the time that Calvin was also looking toward a new edition of the *Institutes*. The picture is made somewhat more complicated when we recognize that, in many cases, Calvin first preached through a book or lectured on it and then developed his commentary—so that the appearance of a commentary often indicated a long period of study through a book of the Bible.[121] (The point can also be made, in reverse, concerning Calvin's late sermons on the New Testament.) So, also, did significant editing sometimes occur in strata of the *Institutes* that follow a series of sermons: this is certainly true in the case of Calvin's sermons on Job.[122] And it remains the case that these additions to the *Institutes* serve only to point the reader back to the exposition of Scripture—and to the rather extensive exposition of various theological topics like the "twofold righteousness" (*duplex iustitia*) in Calvin's Job sermons.[123]

This rather complicated picture of the development of Calvin's thought and, equally important, of the exegetical, polemical, and doctrinal context of the various strata of the *Institutes* comports also with the identity of Calvin as an interpreter of Scripture—the identity that is most clearly indicated by his career and work. Calvin was not, after all, a teacher of systematic or dogmatic theology: his system of *loci communes* and *disputationes* stands alongside, and is, in a sense, preparatory to his readers' encounter with, the text. As Steinmetz notes, Calvin did not offer lectures on doctrine in the academy; his *Institutes*, quite unlike the commentaries, did not arise directly out of his work in the classroom. Instead, the exegetical work was primary, while the *Institutes* arose out of the further discussion of exegetical results and, in some sense, "remained subordinate" to the work of biblical interpretation.[124]

Once it is recognized that the *Institutes* must be read in a developmental relationship with Calvin's exegetical and interpretive work, the issue of Calvin's relationship to the history of exegesis rises in importance as a key to the understanding of his theology. As scholars like Steinmetz, Schreiner, and Thompson have shown, Calvin's exegetical theology frequently reflects the older tradition: Calvin not only studied the exegetical works of contemporaries like Bucer, Bullinger, and Oecolampadius; he also read carefully in the commentaries of fathers like Ambrose, Augustine, and Chrysostom and quite possibly of medieval exegetes like Nicolas of Lyra and Denis the Carthusian. Calvin's exegetical conclusions are not universally or even usually original—they rise out of a venerable catholic tradition and, in their typically nonpolemical mood, seldom indicate indebtedness directly or explicitly.[125] (The citation of sources, whether negatively or as authorities, belonged far more to the work of compiling *loci* and *disputationes*.) In any case, no claim about Calvin's originality can be sustained without comparative exegesis.

These considerations do not, of course, stand in the way of doctrinal studies of Calvin. They point, however, to a necessary refinement in the task of compiling doctrinal studies, along lines similar to those indicated by McKee and Armstrong. The *Institutes* must be read in the light of the commentaries and on the assumption that Calvin's basic, positive theological formulations are at least as likely to appear in the commentaries as in the *Institutes*. Conversely, passages in the *Institutes* ought not to be abstracted either from the ongoing polemic in which Calvin was involved or from the sermons, lectures, and commentaries that led to them—given that the express intention of the *Institutes* was to state only one part of Calvin's doctrine. What must be ruled out is any attempt either to abstract dogmatic definitions from the commentaries as if Calvin's comments were not strictly limited by the text under examination or to cite the *Institutes* without recognition either of its polemical dimensions or of the background of its formulations in Calvin's exegetical and polemical works. This type of exposition of Calvin's thought—once quite prevalent—ignores the very nature of the *Institutes* and disregards Calvin's division of labor.[126]

In this context, the significance of Armstrong's cautions concerning a "systematic" approach to or reading of the *Institutes* is most evident. What is more, our identification of the *Institutes* as a set of *loci communes* and *disputationes* takes a middle ground between the most strident of the objections to its systematic character noted at the outset and the most extreme of the older dogmatic understandings of Calvin's text. We rule out as untenable both the denial that the *Institutes* is a theological system and the modern dogmatic or systematic reading of the text of the *Institutes* without reference to the highly contextual character of its contents and the ongoing dialogue—recorded only in part in its pages!—between Calvin's ample exegetical and dogmatic labors.

Establishing the *Ordo docendi*

The Organization of Calvin's
Institutes, *1536–1559*

Examining the *Institutes*: The Importance of 1539

The text-history and theological development of Calvin's *Institutes* has been the subject of considerable scholarly discussion—from the foundational essays prepared by the nineteenth-century editors of the *Opera Calvini* and the refined theological and textual analyses of Köstlin, Autin, and Marmlestein to the now-classic essay of Warfield and the highly focused studies of Pannier and Benoit.[1] Most of the detailed efforts to understand Calvin's thought processes and intentions, however, have been focused on either the origins of his work in the 1536 *Institutes* or the final form of his work in the 1559 Latin and 1560 French *Institutes*.[2] There have been but few examinations of the intervening editions from 1539 to 1557,[3] and there have been virtually no concentrated analyses of the form and content of the great transition from the first edition of 1536 to the edition of 1539 and those that immediately followed it.[4] Attention has, perhaps, been diverted from these editions of the *Institutes* because of the virtual fixation of historical theologians on Calvin's comment, in his 1559 letter to the reader, "though I do not regret the labor previously expended, I never felt satisfied until the work was arranged in the order in which it now appears."[5] These comments have been used to taking the 1559 *Institutes* as the primary gauge to Calvin's thought, sometimes even to the exclusion of the commentaries and theological treatises.[6]

This approach to the document is unfortunate, inasmuch as Calvin's editorial work of 1539 gave the *Institutes* a form with which he remained basically satisfied for some twenty years, during what was surely the most theologically productive and, perhaps, theologically formative period of his life.[7] (By way of contrast, the catechetical model of 1536 satisifed Calvin for less than four years, and the great revision of 1559 served him for only the five years between its printing and his death.) Indeed, once we take seriously Calvin's indication, given in his 1539 letter to the reader, that the *Institutes* was restructured and augmented in order that it might serve as the repository of the *loci communes* and *disputationes* that might otherwise have appeared in the commentaries, it is precisely the several Latin and French editions of the *Institutes* published between 1539 and 1557 that best illustrate Calvin's theological method. And it is in the topical expansion of the relatively stable form selected in 1539 that we can most clearly see the relationship between various branches of Calvin's theological effort—the sermons, commentaries, treatises, and the *Institutes*.

Accordingly, when the question of the "*initia Calvini*" or of Calvin's final theological result is posed, the 1536 and 1559 editions of the *Institutes* loom large. But when the question concerns the method and development of Calvin's theology, the intervening editions provide by far the clearer index. In the encounter with these intervening editions of the *Institutes*, moreover, there are two main directions for inquiry: first, the examination of Calvin's ordering or reordering of the topics and, second, the examination of the nature and character of various particular additions to the text. The present chapter examines the structure of the successive editions of the *Institutes*, with emphasis on the first of these two directions, in order to understand Calvin's quest for the *ordo recte docendi* in the successive editions of the *Institutes*, 1536–1559. In the chapter 8, "*Fontes argumentorum* and *capita doctrinae*," we take up the latter direction of inquiry.

From Catechesis to *Loci communes*: The *Institutes*, 1536–1539

The organizational development of Calvin's theology in his early years in Geneva can be traced through three documents: the famous *Christianae religionis institutio* (1536) and the lesser-known *Instruction & confession de Foy dont on use en l'Eglise de Genève* (1537) along with its sister document, the *Catechismus, sive christianae religionis institutio* (1538). These works, in turn, point toward the *Institutio christianae religionis* of 1539, edited during Calvin's brief exile in Strasbourg. The first three works are catechetical in their format: the latter marks a transition in Calvin's work to another theological form. We have already seen how this alteration of literary genre is reflected in the movement of Calvin's titles and, beginning in the work of 1539–41, in the reservation of the term *institutio* or instructions for the larger instructional form. With reference to the *Institutes* itself, this alteration was both substantive and organizational.

In 1536, Calvin's *Institutes* was constructed as a basic catechetical manual, in six chapters:

1. De Lege, quod Decalogi explicationem continet
2. De Fide, ubi et Symbolum (quod Apostolicum vocant) explicatur
3. De Oratione, ubi and oratio dominica enarratur
4. De Sacramentis
5. Sacramenta non esse quinque reliqua quem pro sacramentis hactenus vulgo habita sunt, declaratur: tum qualia sint, ostenditur
6. De libertate christiana, potestate ecclesiastica, & politica administratione.[8]

As has often been observed, Calvin's form is very close to the form of Luther's *Small and Large Catechism*,[9] although, even from a purely formal perspective, the catechetical model was readily available to Calvin from other sources, and he chose it, arguably, because it was a standard and not a revolutionary form—contrary to Barth's characterization of the work as "a dark and threatening forest" and an "emergency structure."[10] Even the final chapter of the 1536 *Institutes*, which moves beyond the usual catechetical topics to discuss Christian freedom, church powers, and political administration, has its analogue in the "table of household duties" (*tabula oeconomica*) appended by Luther to the *Small Catechism*.[11] This initial catechetical or confessional purpose was seconded by a closely related apologetic motive, indicated in Calvin's prefatory letter to King Francis I of France.[12]

The 1539 *Institutes* departs from the catechetical model adopted by Calvin in his earlier compendia of Christian teaching.[13] This change of genre is marked by Calvin's comment to Farel that in Strasbourg he was viewed "not so much as a pastor" as an "instructor."[14] Nonetheless, the new *Institutes* took much of its substance not only from the first edition but also from the intervening catechetical exercises.[15] Particularly significant are the eight topics that appear in the catechisms of 1537–38 that were not found as distinct topics in the 1536 *Institutes*: the universal fact of religion, the distinction between true and false religion, free choice, election and predestination, church offices, human traditions, excommunication, and the civil magistracy. The chapters on free choice, election and predestination, church offices, human traditions, excommunication, and the civil magistracy are, of course, mirrored directly in the 1539 *Institutes*. The discussion of religion found in the catechism, which marks a point of departure somewhat different from the knowledge of God/knowledge of man (*cognitio Dei/cognitio hominibus*) distinction of 1536, carries over into the 1539 *Institutes* as a new subtopic belonging to the elaborated chapter on the knowledge of God.

Arguably, Calvin's choice to pursue his instructional task not on the intermediate level of the "larger catechism" but on both the more simple and the more complex levels—the catechetical instruction of children and the *institutio* now understood as an instruction of candidates for the ministry—is reflected not only in his decision to recast the *Institutes* but also in his decision to recast the subsequent catechisms. In the work of 1537–39, this decision is reflected in the movement of the added eight catechetical topics out of the expanded catechetical form and into the *Institutes*.[16] These topics become an integral part of the new shape of the *Institutes* and, at the same time, as of 1541, they disappear from Calvin's catechetical instruction.[17] When Calvin expanded the *Institutes* in 1539, he expanded the substance of both the fourth chapter and the sixth chapter into two series of three chapters each (10–12 and 14–16), and added eight entirely new chapters, bringing the total number of chapters to seventeen. What is also significant, but not often noted, is that Calvin retained the order of the original topics, leaving at the core of the vastly expanded 1539 *Institutes* a basic catechetical structure, interspersed with new chapters, some of which were based directly on themes in the original six chapters. Thus:

1. De cognitione Dei
2. De cognitione hominis and libero arbitrio
3. De lege; Explicatio Decalogi (i)

4. De fide; Expositio symboli Apostolici (ii)
5. De poenitentia
6. De iustificatione fidei, and meritis operum
7. De similitudine ac differentia veteris ac novi testamenti
8. De praedestinatione and providentia Dei
9. De oratione (iii)
10. De sacramentis (iv.a)
11. De baptismo (iv.b)
12. De coena Domini (iv.c)
13. De libertate Christiana (vi.a)
14. De potestate Ecclesiastica (vi.b)
15. De politica administratione (vi.c)
16. De quinque falso nominatis sacramentis (v)
17. De vita hominis Christiani.[18]

In addition, apart from the rearrangement of the order of discussion of the false sacraments, there was no rearrangement of the original chapters. We must therefore take minor exception to Parker's claim that Calvin here moved definitively from a catechetical to a systematic order: the catechetical order remained in 1539 and itself accounts for some of the arrangement and development of the work.[19]

Yet Parker is certainly correct to the extent that the shape of the 1539 *Institutes* represents so important an alteration of genre and purpose that the direction of the new edition can in no way be inferred from the original work of 1536 or even completely deduced from the expanded catechetical forms of 1537–38. It is certainly fruitless to ground the entire structural development of the *Institutes* in a single complex of meanings found in Calvin's early experience and presented in almost cryptic summary form in the 1536 text. No more than the argument of Calvin's *Letter to All Those Who Love Jesus Christ* can the opening declaration of 1536 be read as a "restatement" of Calvin's conversion experience—nor can this declaration that sacred doctrine largely consists in "knowledge of God and knowledge of ourselves" be pressed into service to explain either role of the "twofold knowledge of God" (*duplex cognitio Dei*) or of the credal model in ordering the final edition of the *Institutes*.[20]

Rather, one must ask why Calvin chose to elaborate some topics and not others, why there are also chapters, such as those on predestinaton and the two testaments, that have no significant topical precedent in the 1536 text, and whence Calvin derived the distinctively different model for the identification and arrangement of the chapters that were conflated with the original catechetical model in Calvin's theological essays of 1537–1539. There are at least four identifiable grounds for the development of new chapters and topics and for the recasting of the work in a new genre. First, as Parker well notes, Calvin built on themes resident in the 1536 edition that had, even there, pressed his argument beyond a simple exposition of the catechetical topics.[21] Thus, the first sentence of the 1536 edition, in which "sacred doctrine" was identified as consisting in "two parts, the knowledge of God and the knowledge of ourselves,"[22] has become the substance of two introductory chapters, "On the Knowledge of God" and "On the Knowledge of Man."[23] So, too, has the discussion of repentance found in the 1536 edition become in 1539 a separate chapter.[24] The single chapter on Christian freedom and ecclesiastical and civil powers has become three separate chapters, and the implication of these issues for Christian life, resident in the original discussion, has developed into a new final chapter.[25]

A sense of the embryonic presence in 1536 of issues developed in subsequent editions does not, however, account for all of the additions made in 1539 or in the further recasting of the document in 1543 and 1550. Although the new chapter on justification by faith could be viewed as a necessary elaboration of the earlier discussion of faith, this relationship does not fully explain the logic of creating a separate chapter, and it does not at all account for the new chapters *De similitudine ac differentia veteris ac novi testamenti* and *De praedestinatione and providentia Dei*.[26] Nor does it account easily for all of the shorter additions to the text that are characteristic of the second, third, and fourth major redactions of the *Institutes*. Nor, indeed, does the internal logic of the 1536 text account for its being recast in a different literary genre in 1539. Other grounds or bases for elaboration and development now come into play: thus, in the second place, Calvin's own theological development as chronicled in his sermons, commentaries, catechisms, and treatises; third, alterations and developments in Calvin's reformatory work that contributed to an altered sense of his task, as documented in part by his efforts to organize the worship and instruction in the church both in Geneva and Strasbourg; and, fourth, Calvin's evolving appreciation and appropriation of theological models from predecessors and contemporaries.

Calvin's own theological development, particularly as it took place in his work preaching, lecturing, and commenting on Scripture, is the one basis for the development and expansion of the *Institutes* that was mentioned explicitly by Calvin. It was in the *Institutes*, as he declared in his preface to the 1539 edition, that he would place the theological *loci* that arose out of the work of exegesis.[27] This exegetical trajectory certainly accounts for the inclusion of a *locus* on predestination in the 1539 edition, a *locus* most surely written in conjunction with Calvin's production of the commentary on Romans (1540). The task of commenting on Romans may also explain, at least in part, Calvin's interest in developing an entire *locus* on justification by faith: like the *locus* on predestination, this was a significant topic broached by the Epistle to the Romans and thus something that Calvin, in contrast to contemporary commentators like Bucer, Bullinger, and Melanchthon, would have felt obliged to place in his *Institutes*, rather than in his commentary. Perhaps, too, the work on Romans, with its strong contrast of law and gospel, also raised the question of the relationship between the Old and New Testaments.

Nonetheless, neither the internal logic of the 1536 edition nor the exegesis of Romans explains Calvin's juxtaposition of providence with predestination in one chapter, and the exegesis of Romans does not offer an utterly compelling reason for the inclusion of the chapter on the Old and the New Testaments. Nor do these two grounds for development explain the order and arangement of the newly added topics—and it is unlikely that Calvin's major recasting of the *Institutes* in 1539 was not the result of careful consideration of the purpose and, especially, of the literary and theological genre of the document. We can conclude from Calvin's carefully phrased letter to the reader of 1539, from the related "argument" prefaced to the 1541 French translation of the *Institutes*, and from the rather pointed editing of the title of the work that Calvin understood the transition from 1536 to 1539 as a major shift in the genre of the document. As argued in chapter 6, Calvin understood his 1539 *Institutes* as an expandable set of *loci communes* and *disputationes*. Nowhere, however, does Calvin state the logic of his arrangement of the chapters. He could assume the intelligibility of the catechetical series (which remained unchanged)—but he offered no explicit *argumentum* or *methodus* to explain either the new shape of the whole work or the presence of the new chapters at beginning, middle, and end, which, by their mere presence, now redefined the nature of the work as no longer simply catechetical.

Third among the grounds for Calvin's alteration and development of his text, therefore, is the negative aspect of Calvin's 1539 editorial decision. In the midst of his work of writing the Romans commentary and editing the *Institutes*, Calvin was also involved in the composition and reworking of a series of catechisms for Geneva and Strasbourg: in part the recasting of the *Institutes* involved a decision concerning what it was not to be—namely, a catechetical instruction.[28] As already noted, the French and Latin catechisms of 1537 and 1538 can account for several of the alterations of content in the 1539 *Institutes*.[29] What is more, the titles of these works indicate, albeit obliquely, a minor quandary concerning literary genre: we have the extended catechetical essay of 1536, the *Christianae religionis institutio*; the French catechism of 1537, *Instruction et confession de foy*; the Latin version of 1538, *Catechismus, sive christianae religionis institutio*; the 1539 revision of the 1536 essay, *Institutio christianse religionis nunc vero demum suo titulo respondens*; and the catechism *L'Institution puérile de la doctrine chrestienne*, written in Strasbourg between 1538 and 1541. At the very least, the titles generated a confusion: the Latin catechism of 1538 was not the *Institutes* of 1536—although that might certainly be inferred from its title! Beginning in 1541, Calvin altered the titles of his catechisms: the French title now identifies the work as a "formulaire d'instruire les enfants," and the Latin of 1545 echoes the point in its phrase "formula erudiendi pueros."

In 1536, Calvin published a document that offered a basic instruction but that functioned neither at the foundational level of a catechetical *institutio* nor at the level of an academic *institutio*. In his literary projects of 1537–41, Calvin abandoned this middle ground in favor of the foundational and the academic levels. He also appears to have determined in his own mind the proper literary genre of an *institutio*, just as, at the same juncture, in critical dialogue with Bucer, Melanchthon, and Bullinger, he had satisfied himself concerning the proper literary genre of the *commentarius*.[30] After his extensive catechetical efforts, resulting in five different editions—three French (1537, 1538/41, and 1541) and two Latin (1538, 1541)—the term *institutio* disappears definitively from the titles of the catechisms—this, at the time that the new edition of the *Institutes* adds the pointed phrase "now for the first time truly corresponding to its title."[31] So, too, is the catechetical order of the original *Institutes* augmented and developed for the sake of approaching the more comprehensive order of an academic theological exercise.

The fourth ground for Calvin's alteration of the shape and content of the *Institutes* was certainly his awareness and assessment of several significant models for the theological task that he found among his predecessors and contemporaries: he tells us as much in the prefatory letters to the 1539 *Institutes* and the 1540 Romans commentary. Thus, the key to understanding the new organization of Calvin's *Institutes* in 1539 lies in Calvin's own prefatory remarks, where he indicates that the projected life-work of commenting on Scripture will not offer *loci communes* or *disputationes* embedded in commentaries: these topical discussion will henceforth be found in his *Institutes*. In this establishment of the *Institutes* as a series of theological *loci* or *topoi*, Calvin probably looked for precedent in the works of significant predecessors and contemporaries—just as he had done in the selection of a catechetical model for the first edition of the *Institutes*.

Hovering somewhere in the background of Calvin's desire, in 1539, to establish an *ordo recte docendi* or "correct order of teaching" according to which the various *loci* of theology might be presented was Erasmus's *Ratio seu methodus compendio perveniendi ad veram theologiam*.[32] As already noted, Calvin's polemic against scholasticism has Erasmian echoes, as does his interest in the elicitation of theological *loci* or *topoi* from Scripture. Yet is it clear from any comparative examination of the structure and order of Erasmus's *Ratio* and Calvin's *Institutes* that the two documents present widely different conceptions both of the order and arrangement of the topics and of the specific topics to be identified: Erasmus enumerates faith, fasting, patience consolation of the sick, respect of authority even when those who exercise it are evil, avoidance of offense or scandal, biblical study, parental devotion, charity—a list that overlaps Calvin's in part but that reflects neither the catechetical interest of the 1536 nor the more doctrinal interest of the 1539 *Institutes*.[33] More important, Calvin's sense of the specific source both of the *loci* and of their *methodus* or *ordo* is different from that of Erasmus—as we will see, Calvin's source is not the New Testament in general, as is the case for Erasmus, but the Epistle to the Romans. The influence of Erasmus is present, but it is indirect.[34]

Following Blanke and Ganoczy in their rebuttals of the old claims of Seeberg and Lang that Calvin did not find any great inspiration in Zwingli's thought, Büsser has argued, on grounds of theological content and of humanistic inclinations, that one of Calvin's models was Zwingli's *De vera et falsa religione commentarius*.[35] Both works, of course, are dedicated to Francis I of France. The clearest theological resemblance, certainly, is at the very beginning of the *Institutes* where Calvin juxtaposes the knowledge of God with the knowledge of man and discusses the meaning of "religion" at some length.[36] Calvin indicated, in the additions made to the 1539 *Institutes*, that the knowledge of God and the knowledge of man or self are so interrelated that "it is not easy to discern" which form of knowledge "precedes and brings forth the other."[37] After discussing the problem at some length, Calvin concludes that "however the knowledge of God and of ourselves may be mutually connected: the right order of expression requires that we discuss the former first, then proceed afterward to treat the latter."[38] Zwingli not only discusses God and man in the context of the problem of religion and religious knowledge; he also understands the correct order as placing the discussion of God prior to the discussion of humanity.[39] Given, moreover, the relationship between these topics and the topics added to Calvin's catechisms of 1537–38, the case for a Zwinglian impact on the first two chapters of the revised *Institutes* is quite strong.

It is also certainly the case that there is a continuity of theological argument on the definition of covenant and on the problem of the relationship of the testaments between the Zürich theology of Zwingli and Bullinger and the theology of Calvin. Zwingli argued the substantial identity of the salvific testament or covenant of God in the Old and New Testaments. In a striking argument against the Anabaptists, Zwingli pointed to the differences between the testaments as founded not in the promise itself but in the historical character of our "human infirmity"—in the Old Testament, Christ is promised; in the New, Christ is given. This fundamental difference points toward distinctions between types or figures and the thing signified by them, between shadows and the full light of revelation, between the limited offer of the promise to Israel and the universal offer of salvation to all nations.[40] The doctrinal continuity between Zwingli's teaching and Calvin's statements of more than a decade later is undeniable.[41]

Nonetheless, the structure and content of Zwingli's *Commentarius* can at best provide only a partial model for the 1539 *Institutes*, and the treatise against the Anabaptists offered no model for the order and arrangement of theological topics. Moreover, the movement of topics from God to human nature is so common in theology that Calvin did not need to examine Zwingli to derive this particular element of his *ordo recte docendi*. If Zwingli provided a model for the initial opening sentence of 1536 and for the two new opening chapters of 1539, the "cognitio Dei ac nostri," Zwingli did not juxtapose chapters on the Old and the New Testaments and predestination or on the sacraments and Christian freedom, as Calvin most certainly does. Of course, these features could have arisen simply out of Calvin's own sense of the order and organization of the *loci* or *topoi* of theology—but such a conclusion ought not to be posed before the obvious alternative, a reliance on the order of Melanchthon's *Loci communes theologici* of 1535, has been examined.

The result of Calvin's early reading of Melanchthon's work was an initial meeting followed by a lifelong dialogue, only part of which can be reconstructed from their letters. Nor ought it to assumed, in a facile manner, that this was an amiable camaraderie based on engagement in a common task. On the one hand, there was a profound and positive methodological relationship between the two thinkers, while, on the other hand, there was an equally profound disagreement over free choice and predestination accompanied by a tense interchange over the doctrine of the Lord's Supper and the problem of "things indifferent," or *adiaphora*.[42] Melanchthon is said to have referred to Calvin as "the theologian,"[43] and Calvin wrote a largely laudatory preface to the French translation of Melanchthon's *Loci communes* despite the presence in that very edition of the doctrinal points on which the two most strongly disagreed. (Indeed, given that Melanchthon's synergism was not all that different from Bolsec's, the context of debate could sometimes be as important as the doctrinal point at issue: Calvin's public debate with Melanchthon, unlike the row with Bolsec, remained oblique.) Between Calvin and Melanchthon there was, on the one side, an intellectual bond grounded in the methodological dialogue in which the two engaged, during the decades in which both men, trained in humanist rhetoric and philology, learned theology on the fly, as each engaged in the work of the commentator and the compiler of theological *loci*. The other side of the relationship, however, as revealed in their letters and in the occasionally grudging remarks in their published writings, was an angry debate over a series of theological points, exacerbated by citation of Melanchthon in the writings of Calvin's adversaries.[44]

What is most curious is that scholars have often deemphasized the influence, whether positive or negative, of Melanchthon's *Loci communes* on Calvin.[45] Pannier places Melanchthon's *Loci communes* of 1521 among the influences on Calvin's intellectual formation, but without further elaboration.[46] Lang, Doumergue, and Wendel, of course, note theological continuities, but none indicates any Melanchthonian influence on the organization of the *Institutes*—nor do Lang and Doumergue raise the issue of influence after the 1536 *Institutes*.[47] A partial explanation for this omission, from the perspective of the history of scholarship, can be found in the Köstlin's unappreciative dismissal of Melanchthon's *Loci communes* as poorly organized and of far less theological interest than Calvin's *Institutes*. Köstlin's essay, moreover, referred to the final editions of the *Loci communes* and the *Institutes* as end-points of editing processes, without manifesting any interest in comparing the earlier editions.[48] It is also the case that, of the additions to the 1539 *Institutes*, the *loci* on justification and predestination had more affinity with Bucer for its positive doctrinal content than with Melanchthon (or with Zwingli).[49]

There is also Calvin's negative reference to Melanchthon's methods in the 1540 Romans preface, which could be interpreted broadly as a dismissal of Melanchthon's method, rather than as a specific rejection of its application to commentaries as distinct from sets of *loci communes* and *disputationes*. Calvin did, however, express admiration for Melanchthon's work, perhaps most notably in his preface to the 1546 French translation of Melanchthon's *Loci*, and he also understood his new approach to the *Institutes* in 1539 as the construction of *loci communes* and *disputationes*.[50] And, although various scholars have taught us that Calvin eventually overcame an initial reluctance to view Zwingli as a great reformer, it remains clear that Calvin never chose to praise Zwingli's theology as he had praised Melanchthon's. Nor is it the case that the humanistic aspects of Zwingli's work outshone the humanistic elements of Melanchthon's.

Büsser argues that "at least" an "indirect influence" of Zwingli underlies Calvin's addition of a chapter on the distinction between Old and New Testaments in 1539: the sources of this Zwinglian influence are probably, according to Büsser, Bullinger's *De testamento seu foedere Dei unico and aeterno* (1534) and his *De scripturae sanctae authoritate* (1538).[51] Yet, there are several significant reasons that we ought to look elsewhere for Calvin's model for this discussion. On the one hand, little can be gleaned concerning the problem of the testaments from the chapters on Gospel and Law found in Zwingli's *Commentarius*—not only does Zwingli, unlike Calvin, move from Gospel to Law, but he also separates these chapters with a chapter on repentance. Zwingli's theological interest, moreover, is not in the problem of the similarity and distinction of the Testaments. Nor should it be forgotten that Bullinger's emphasis is on the unity of the one covenant, not on the relationship and the distinction between the testaments. Not that there is a vast difference between Bullinger's conception of covenant and Calvin's: indeed, it is incorrect to claim a dipleuric concept of covenant for Bullinger and a monopleuric concept for Calvin,[52] and it would also be incorrect to deny the strong influence of Bullinger's *De testamento* on Calvin's general view of covenant.[53] Nonetheless, Bullinger's influence was largely doctrinal rather than formal, and Bullinger's treatises cannot account well either for the architectonics of the 1539 *Institutes* or for the way in which this particular new chapter relates to those around it.

On the other hand, a nearly parallel chapter can be found in Melanchthon's *Loci* from 1521 on: "De discrimine Veteris ac Novi Testamenti."[54] Melanchthon (followed in 1539 by Calvin) begins his discussion with the unity of Scripture in both testaments and moves on to the examination of the distinction between Old and the New Testament as contrasted with and measured by the distinction between Law and Gospel. It is easily arguable that Calvin's famous definition, added to the *Institutes* in 1539—"The covenant made with all the patriarchs in no way differs from ours in substance and reality, so that it is actually one and the same. The administration, however differs"[55]—reflects Melanchthon's opening remark in his later versions of the *locus* that "there is one continuing church of God . . . from the creation . . . to the present day; but the promulgation of its teaching has differed under different forms of governance."[56] Despite the significant differences between Melanchthon's distinction between Law and Gospel and Calvin's own, Melanchthon's insistence that both Law and the "promise of grace" or the Gospel belong to the substance of the entire Bible clearly parallels Calvin's understanding of the unity of the two testaments.[57]

So, too, if one asks the question of the method and disposition (*modus et dispositio*) of theological topics, without discounting Büsser's suggestion of a Zwinglian influence on Calvin, Melanchthon's various prefaces to the *Loci communes theologici* and several exegetical approaches to Romans offer a series of clues to Calvin's arrangement of topics in the *Institutes*. All of Melanchthon's prefaces address the issues of the identification of *loci* and the establishment of a right *methodus* or *ordo*, quite in contrast to the prefatory remarks to Zwingli's *De vera et falsa religione*.[58] Melanchthon could insist, on the one hand, that the optimal order for the topics of theology was the credal order, but he could also indicate, on the other, that such topics as sin, the promises of God, law and gospel (topics that do not appear explicitly in the credal order) ought to be elucidated in their historical order, as revealed by the Prophets and Apostles.[59] Unlike Zwingli, Melanchthon could not conceive of placing Gospel prior to Law, either on theological or on historical grounds; nor, indeed, as all editions of the *Institutes* testify, from first to last, could Calvin.[60] In addition, Melanchthon (and, subsequently, Luther as well) had argued the centrality of Romans to the understanding of the biblical message and, therefore, the priority of the Epistle to the Romans in any attempt to identify the basis of Christian theology.[61]

The positive relationship between Melanchthon's and Calvin's understandings of Gospel, Law, and other *loci* arising out of exegetical consideration of the Epistle to the Romans points toward the probable influence of Melanchthon's rhetorical analysis of the epistle on Calvin's exegesis: whereas Calvin rather pointedly repudiated the method of Melanchthon's commentary, examination of Calvin's *Argumentum* to his commentary and of aspects of his exegesis indicates a positive use of Melanchthon's *Dispositio orationis in Epist. Pauli ad Romanos* (1529/30).[62] Of course, it needs also to be noted that the wellspring of Melanchthon's several early theological essays was his exegesis of Romans: the early *Theologica institutio in Epistolam Pauli ad Romanos* (1519)[63] led both to a series of commentaries and analyses of the epistle and to Melanchthon's *Loci communes theologici* of 1521.[64] So, too, was the exegesis of Romans at both the inception and the heart of Calvin's establishment of his theological program—just as Calvin's encounter with the weighty content and the organization of Romans was arguably the occasion for his bifurcation of the theological task into a series of commentaries lacking theological *loci* and the developing *Institutes*, designed to contain the theological *loci*.

Melanchthon understood the initial "narration" (*narratio*) (1:18–3:31) of Romans as an argument leading to the establishment of the fundamental proposition that "we are justified by faith." To this end, according to Melanchthon, the argument of epistle begins (1:18) with the statement of a negative or counter proposition, namely that "all people are under sin (*sub peccato*)."[65] The first section of Romans, in Melanchthon's view, concludes with a confirmation of the argument on faith and justification (chapter

4) and an epilogue (5:1–11).[66] Melanchthon argues that the second section of the epistle has an entirely different form: rhetoric now passes over into dialectic for the formal disputation of the topics presented in the inintial argument: thus, the topic of sin (*peccatum*) follows in Romans 5:11–19, law (*lex*) in 5:20–7:25, and grace (*gratia*) in 8:1–8. Within the discussion of *lex*, Melanchthon also locates an excursus on the need to do good works (6:1–7:6). Melanchthon identifies a third section of the epistle (chapters 9–11), as concerned with the "people of God," specifically with the relationship of Israel and the Jewish people to "the calling of the Gentiles," and as centered on the *locus of predestination*. The fourth section of the epistle (chapters 12–15) deals with a series of ethical and moral issues: good works (12), the civil authorities (13), Christian liberty and offense (14).

The soteriological argument of the Epistle to the Romans presents justification by faith as the center and results in a series of theological *loci* in the following order: sin, law, grace, the people of God and the call of the Gentiles, predestination, good works, civil authority, Christian liberty, and the problem of offense or "scandal."[67] When these topics are expanded ever so slightly to include both issues directly implied by the Pauline *loci* and related topics demanded for the full churchly discussion of the Pauline topics, the structure of Melanchthon's 1521 *Loci communes* and, with slight variation, of Melanchthon's 1535/6 *Loci communes*, emerges: free choice and sin; various kinds of laws (divine and human) juxtaposed with the gospel; grace, justification, and faith; the fruits of salvation in faith, love, and hope; the people of God, now understood in terms of the problem of the Old and the New Testaments; Christian life and good works under the rubrics of the "old man and the new," "mortal and daily sin," the sacraments, and Christian love; the magistrate; and scandal or offense.[68] One wonders whether those who have found Melanchthon's order and topics less than satisfactory would say the same of his Pauline source.[69]

Be that as it may, we have found in the fundamentally Pauline order of Melanchthon's *Loci communes* a probable answer both to several questions concerning the chapters added by Calvin to the 1539 *Institutes* and to the crucial question of the ordering of Calvin's new chapters as they fell into place in between the original catechetical *loci*. In the first place, Calvin shared with Melanchthon an overriding sense of the importance of Romans as a didactic center and therefore as a point of departure for exegesis and theology.[70] Thus, the chapter on the "similarity and distinction of the Old and New Testaments" appears as a topic added in the light of the exegesis of Romans, but only as elicited first by Melanchthon from the argument of Romans 9–11 concerning the people of God throughout history. We may surmise here that Calvin read not only the 1521 but also the 1536 *Loci communes*: for, in 1536, Melanchthon here specifically derives the topic of the two testaments from the theme of the people of God.[71] It was also in his 1536 *Loci communes* that Melanchthon first identified predestination as a separate *locus* and placed it, in Pauline fashion, in immediate relation to the *locus* concerning the relationship of the Old to the New Testament.[72]

We have already seen hints of Calvin's sense of the centrality of Paul's Epistle to the Romans in his *Letter to All Those Who Love Jesus Christ* of 1535.[73] But it was the Pauline pattern of argument, as identified in Melanchthon's *Dispositio orationis* and *Loci communes* of 1521 and 1536, that accounts for the addition of these two crucial chapters to Calvin's 1539 *Institutes* and that accounts, moreover, for the seemingly odd placement of predestination following the discussion of the Old and the New Testaments. As Beza would later comment in the explanation to his famous *Tabula praedestinationis,* "unless there is some significant reason to do otherwise," a teacher ought to follow "Paul in the Epistle to the Romans," inasmuch as "this is the proper path (*methodus*) through all of theology: he proceeds from the Law to the remission of sins and then, gradually, to the highest degree."[74]

Also characteristic of Melanchthon's 1535/6 *Loci communes* is the development of three, as opposed to merely two, uses of the law. The clear distinction between the pedagogical function and the normative function of the law was not evident in 1521 but arose out of Melanchthon's debates in the early 1530s. It is therefore of some significance that Calvin's discussion of the law and its uses in the 1536 and the 1539 *Institutes* also reflects the Melanchthonian model.[75] In 1536, Calvin followed a pattern much like that of Melanchthon's 1535/6 *Loci communes,* placing the uses of the law after the exposition of the Decalogue, as the point of transition to the doctrine of justification. In 1539, while adopting the broader outlines of the Pauline-Melanchthonian *loci,* Calvin retained the concept of the three uses of the law as the conclusion to his discussion of the Decalogue, although, given the other changes that took place in 1539, the third use of the law no longer led to the discussion of justification.[76] Also in 1539, justification no longer immediately follows law but is separated by the chapters on faith and creed and on justification.[77] Calvin has echoed Melanchthon's Pauline order of law, gospel, grace (justification and faith), and the distinction of the Old and the New Testaments by moving from law to faith and creed, repentance, justification, and the distinction of Old and the New Testaments, but he has also managed to retain, as a broader and fuller discussion of the gospel, an expanded version of his chapter on faith and creed. The catechetical model is retained but bracketed and explained by the Pauline *loci.*

The order of *loci* identified by Melanchthon in Paul's Epistle to the Romans thus established a standard for the organization of Protestant theology.[78] It was, of course, but one *methodus* among others but, unlike the catechetical method, it did have the advantage of offering a suitable systematic placement for such topics as sin and grace, the gospel, Old and New Testament, and predestination. In addition, the early chapters of Romans, in which Paul introduces the problem of the universal knowledge of the law in the context of a sinful human race left without excuse in its idolatry, also provide the basis for Calvin's expansion of the themes of knowledge of God and knowledge of man into two larger chapters preparatory to the *loci* on sin and the law. The shift of topic from knowledge to sin, moroever, marks the shift in Pauline argument from the introductory sections of the epistle to the more formal development of theological *loci*—a shift that would become still more pronounced in the 1559 *Institutes.*

Once this Pauline "method" is seen as providing the *ordo recte docendi* already sought by Calvin in 1539, we are in a position to dispel one of the modern dogmatic myths concerning the order of Calvin's *Institutes.* Calvin did not, as has often been stated, remove the doctrine of predestination from the doctrine of God and place it in an a posteriori position in order to avoid the theological problems of the "*Deus nudus absconditus,*" speculative determinism, and central dogmas.[79] Calvin had never wrestled with these nineteenth- and twentieth-century problems—and, indeed, he had never placed the doctrine of predestination anywhere until he located it in the Pauline series of topics added to his 1539 *Institutes*. (And, as will be indicated in detail later, that placement is also where he left the doctrine in his final reorganization of the *Institutes*.) His motive in adopting this order was hardly the motive assigned by the modern dogmatic theorists—rather, it was the desire to transform the *Institutes* from primarily a catechetical exercise into a series of *loci communes* based on the Melanchthonian understanding of the Pauline model. We are thus also in a position now to object strenuously both to McGrath's unsubstantiated assertion that the 1539 edition was "poorly organized" and to Bouwsma's comment that Calvin's "*Institutes* is not logically ordered."[80] The organization is finely tooled and, indeed, has a clear and commanding logic: to perceive the organization, however, one does need to look to its sixteenth-century context.

The topics added to the 1539 *Institutes* are, for the most part, the very topics or *loci* generated by the exegesis of Romans, particularly in view of the Melanchthonian understanding of the structure of the epistle. But Calvin chose, in agreement with Melanchthon's sense of *ordo* and *methodus* and at the same time in disagreement with Melanchthon's approach to the commentary, to write a running commentary on the text and to place all of the theological *loci* in the *Institutes*. The augmentation of the *Institutes* in 1539, from a structural perspective, ought to be described not as a movement from catechism to system but as an integration of the catechetical topics and order with the topics and order of Pauline soteriology. This development was, moreover, already a step beyond the Melanchthonian model for *loci communes*, even as it was a step beyond the original catechetical order of the *Institutes*: by retaining the catechesis at the heart of his *loci*, Calvin created a series of theological topics at once more neatly organized and more comprehensive than Melanchthon's *Loci communes theologici*, not to mention Zwingli's *Commentarius*. The work is certainly not "poorly ordered," and it is also clearly "logically ordered" if one accepts the soteriological logic of the Apostle Paul.

Expansion of the *Institutes* 1543–1550/57

Calvin's augmentation of the *Institutes* in 1539 created a model in which the traditional catechetical *ordo* and the still older Pauline *ordo* tended to create not only a juxtaposition but also an occasional problematic separation of topics. The latter problem was precisely what he had sought to avoid by presenting his exegesis in one place and his theological *loci* in another. We may hypothesize that these new problems of order and arrangement—together, of course, with the continuing process of eliciting *loci* or the materials for *loci* from his ongoing series of commentaries—was the source of the internal but nonetheless significant shuffling and rearrangement of materials that belonged to Calvin's editorial process between the Latin text of 1543 and the French text of 1557.

The problems of order caused by the expansion of a catechetical exposition of theology, particularly by the presence of themes taken up in the credal discussion in added soteriological *loci*, was not, moreover, a problem unique to Calvin's work. Although we do not find it in Melanchthon, who never did reflect catechetical models in his *Loci communes theologici*, we certainly see it in the outline of Bullinger's *Compendium christianae religionis* of 1556 and, to a lesser extent, in Bullinger's *Decades* as well. The ten books of Bullinger's *Compendium* follow a series of doctrinal topics from Scripture (I), to God and his works (II), sin and its punishment (III), the law (IV), grace and justification through Christ (V), faith and the Gospel (VI), prayer (VII), the sacraments (VIII), good works (IX), and death and the last things (X).[81] Whereas Book IV plus Books VI through VIII point toward the order of the catechism, Books III through VI and IX surely reflect the Pauline order from Romans. Since the subject of Book VI (faith) presents both the concept of faith and the doctrines of the creed, doublets are created by the initial discussion of God and Trinity in Book I, the discussion of faith in relation to grace and justification in Book V, and the discussion of Christ and his work, also in Book V.

Whereas Bullinger was content to leave the *Compendium* as an augmented catechetical model, Calvin remained unsatisfied and, already in 1543, began to adjust the materials of his *Institutes* by ordering of chapters as follows:

1. De cognitione Dei;
2. De cognitione hominis;
3. De lege (i);
4. De votis;
5. De fide;
6. Explicatio primae partis symboli (ii.a);
7. Explication secundae partis symboli; tertia pars (ii.b);
8. Quartae partis symboli expositio (vi.b; ii.c);
9. De poenitentia;
10. De iustificatione fidei et meritis operum;
11. De similitudine et differentia V. et N.T;
12. De libertate christiana (vi.a);
13. De traditionibus humanis;
14. De praedestinatione et providentia Dei;
15. De oratione (iii);
16. De sacramentis (iv.a);
17. De baptismo (iv.b);
18. De coena Domini (iv.c);
19. De quinque falso nominatis sacramentis (v);
20. De politica administratione (vi.c);
21. De vita hominis christiani.

Here, some of the original catechetical ordering has begun to give way: most notably, the discussion of Christian freedom, originally part of the sixth chapter of the *Institutes* and retained in relation to the other two parts of chapter 6 in the expansion of 1539, has now been moved to a place immediately following the chapter comparing the Old and the New Testaments. The chapter on false sacraments has, however, been returned to its original juxtaposition with the true sacraments and is, as before, followed by civil government.

In the movement from the seventeen chapters of 1539 to the twenty-one of 1543, only one entirely new *locus* has appeared: the chapter *De votis*, on vows. The position of the chapter, moreover, is significant: vows are discussed not in the context of the other ecclesiological topics toward the conclusion of the *Institutes* but following the law and prior to the discussion of faith. This model stands in direct contrast to the positioning of the discussion in Zwingli's *Commentarius*, which offers Calvin a rather remote model at best.[82] Once again, we are presented with a far closer model in Melanchthon's 1535/6 *Loci communes*, where the discussion "concerning monastic vows" appears as a subtopic of the *locus* on the law, following a section on counsels and connected with the discussion of judicial and ceremonial laws, and prior to the *loci* on the Gospel and faith.[83]

Crucial, also, is the division of the chapter on the creed into three major chapters reflective of the traditional four-part gathering of credal articles. As Parker has noted, Calvin explicitly taught a fourfold division of the *Apostles' Creed* in the Geneva Catechism of 1545.[84] This division of the credal articles was already reflected in the 1543 edition of the *Institutes*, where Calvin divided his chapter on the creed into three, not four, segments, yielding a chapter (6) on faith, God, and creation; another (7) on Christ and the Spirit; and a final credal chapter (8) on the church, forgiveness of sins, and the resurrection. The title of chapter 7 indicated that its subject was the second and third parts of the creed, namely the articles concerning the Son and the Spirit.

Certainly, the order and content of Melanchthon's 1535 *Loci communes theologici* does not fully explain either the order and content of the 1539 *Institutes* or the nature of the methodological movement from the 1536 to the 1539 *Institutes*. But Melanchthon's work certainly provides part of the answer. This is particularly the case given the nature of Calvin's methodological remarks in his prefaces of 1539, 1540, and 1541. For, there, Calvin both criticizes the method used by Melanchthon in his commentaries and adopts as his own the approach used by Melanchthon in his *Loci communes*.

From 1550/57 to 1559: Achieving the Final Arrangement

Although Calvin's letter to the reader does not appear to have undergone any revision either in the editions of 1543 and 1545 or in the edition of 1550, the 1550 edition was a signifcantly altered work. Calvin had retained his 1539 title, *Institutio christianae religionis nunc vere demum suo titulo respondens*, in the editions of 1543 and 1545. In 1550, however, the title was altered to read *Institutio totius christianae religionis*—surely indicating the massive augmentation of the text. In addition, Calvin saw to the revision and expansion of the indexing apparatus: the index to biblical and patristic texts was expanded, a major topical index added, and, equally important, the increasingly lengthy chapters were now, for the first time, divided into into numbered paragraphs.[85] This system of paragraphing carried over into the French revision of 1551.[86]

The title of Calvin's final edition of the *Institutes* reads: *Institution of the Christian religion, newly presented in four books: and divided into chapters according to a most suitable [order and] method: also augmented by such additions that it ought properly to be regarded as a new book.*[87] Calvin clearly viewed the reorganization of the work in 1559 as the most significant revision and augmentation that he had undertaken. The *Institutes* was now virtually a new work. Calvin also went out of his way to emphasize in his title that the chapters were now arranged according to a suitable *methodus* or, in the French version, a suitable *ordre et méthode*. Nonetheless, far too much has been made of Calvin's prefatory comments concerning his satisfaction with the final order and arrangement of the topics in his *Institutes*,[88] though he surely found the four-book arrangement of 1559 to be a significant advance over previous editions. We have absolutely no indication that he foresaw any further structural shifts in the work. His comments indicate that, on the large scale, he viewed the massive rearrangement of materials in the 1559 edition as finally establishing the *ordo recte docendi* that had been his quest since his initial identification of the *Institutes* as a set of *loci communes* and *disputationes* in 1539. Yet even these comments offer no reason to assume that the revised *Institutes* has now become the centerpiece of Calvin's theological enterprise, rather than, as he continued to describe it, the set of *loci communes* and *disputationes* that stood in a complementary relationship with his central effort of commenting on the text of Scripture.

What has changed, and changed considerably in the movement from the last major Latin rescension of 1550 and the French version of 1557, is the relationship between Calvin's credal exposition and his overarching *ordo docendi*. As has often been noted, the key to this four-book model was Calvin's dispersion of the four credal topics, elicited from the three credal chapters of 1543–57, to strategic places in the document as structural markers. The four credal topics of Father, Son, Spirit, and church, formerly gathered in one place, are now dispersed, as foci of the four books, among the remaining topics of the catechetical model (law, the Lord's Prayer, and the sacraments) and the topics of the Pauline order (sin, law, grace, the people of God in the Old and the New Testaments, predestination, good works, civil authority, Christian liberty, and offenses). Indeed, all the elements of the catechetical and the Pauline model are now logically related to (albeit not lost within) the four article credal structure. Yet, the "knowledge of God and ourselves" and the "twofold knowledge of God" remain as elements in the ordering of the material[89]—and, as discerned by Packer, the Pauline order of 1539 continues to remain significant to the organization of the *Institutes* as well.[90]

As Benoit observed, "the parallelism between the plan of the Creed and that of that last *Institutio* edition is only relative": the resurrection is treated at the end of Book III before Calvin arrives at his ecclesiology in Book IV.[91] But this "relative" parallel to the Creed, rather than pointing away from the credal model, only serves to show that Calvin approached the problem of the credal model through the precedent of earlier theologies and through the glass of his earlier assumptions concerning the ordering of the *Institutes*. At first glance, one might conclude that the new *locus* on the final resurrection was added in 1559 because of the new prominence given to the expanded discussion of credal articles. The creed itself, in fact, causes a problem for credally ordered theological systems, since it introduces eschatological issues at the end of the second article, when Christ is confessed as coming "to judge the quick and the dead," and then returns to eschatology at the close of the third article with the phrase "the resurrection of the dead and the life of the world to come." Calvin, however, chose neither of these specifically credal options but placed his thoughts on the final resurrection after his doctrine of predestination. Once again, clear precedent, based on a concern for the Pauline *ordo docendi*, is offered by Melanchthon's eventual placement of the doctrines of Christ's reign and the final resurrection precisely at this point in his 1543 *Loci*.[92] Nor does a credal model explain the new placement of Calvin's discussion of faith close to the beginning of Book III. Even so, the fourth book of the *Institutes* can be only partially explained by the credal pattern, which indicates a discussion of ecclesiology and eschatology but does not indicate any discussion of civil government, scandal, or, needless to say, vows.

In addition to the creed, it therefore remains important to emphasize the various structures from the 1536 and 1539 *Institutes* that contribute to the order of the 1559 text. Indeed, twentieth-century debate over the primary ordering principle of the *Institutes* has obscured the internal patterning of the *Institutes*, particularly when it has occurred at a more detailed level than the large-scale credal patterning or the *duplex cognitio Dei*. Just as the movement from the 1536 *Institutes* to the editions of 1539 ff. was not a simple setting aside of a catechetical for a systematic ordering, so was the movement from the augmented 1550 text to the greatly revised structure not a simple setting aside of an interim systematic ordering *either* for a purely credal model *or* for a model based on the theme of the twofold knowledge of God as creator and redeemer. Note, too, that a practice of retaining elements of earlier patterns and of modification or development mostly by augmentation was also Calvin's approach to the words of the text. Calvin did not work by excision and replacement: virtually the entirety of the 1536 *Institutes* remains in the 1559 edition.[93]

Parker is certainly correct in arguing against Dowey that the initial and most basic twofold knowledge in the *Institutes* is not the "twofold knowledge of God" but the "knowledge of God and ourselves"[94] the knowledge of God and self that was identified as basic to Calvin's thought in the first sentence of the 1536 text and that became the two foundational introductory chapters in 1539: this introductory structure remains in 1559. In addition, a rigid understanding of the *duplex cognitio Dei* as the primary ordering principle of the *Institutes* leads Dowey to the rather curious conclusion that Calvin sometimes misunderstood the implications of his own model.[95]

Contrary to Dowey's view that *Institutes*, Book II, properly begins with the fourth chapter, with the first three chapters (the discussion of sin) serving as a "last look to the *cognitio Dei creatoris*" of Book I (thus in some distinction from Parker's insistence on the utter priority of a credal order),[96] the beginning of Book II with the problem of sin surely represents Calvin's continued use, together with the more clearly identified credal patterning of 1559, of the Pauline *ordo* of 1539. As Melanchthon had indicated in his *Dispositio*, the Pauline series of *loci* following the initial argument or *narratio* of Romans is a redemptive *ordo*, beginning with sin and moving toward the other topics concerned with redemption. Parker, therefore, is substantially correct in his sense of the intimate theological relationship between the topics of sin and redemption at the beginning of *Institutes*, Book II.[97] What he misses, however, is the Pauline and Melanchthonian rationale for the relationship and the fundamental continuity in organizational principle between the 1539 and the 1559 editions of the *Institutes*.

Indeed, inasmuch as the soteriological discussion of *Institutes*, Book II, continues to follow the Pauline *ordo* added by Calvin to the 1539 edition, it becomes clear that neither Dowey's stress on the *duplex cognitio Dei* nor Parker's emphasis on the credal model fully accounts for the order and arrangment of the 1559 edition, because the one point that the *duplex cognitio Dei* model and the credal model have utterly in common is that both begin their second division with the Person of the redeemer, having moved from creation to redemption without any clear indication of the precise location of the problem of sin. The same must be said for the identification and placement of other topics in the 1559 *Institutes,* specifically those not handled by the creed. Neither the credal order nor the *duplex cognitio* accounts either for the presence or for the location of such topics as free choice, the relationship and distinction of the two testaments, predestination, Christian freedom, the magistrate, or the subsections on offense or scandal—all of which were generated in 1539 by consideration of the Pauline *ordo* and all of which remain in 1559 in basically the same relation to one another as they held in 1539, albeit now interspersed with the expanded and repositioned credal sections. Similarly, contrary to Battles' claim that in 1559 the discussions of the law and of the Old and the New Testaments were "relocated" to a place "within the christological sequence," recognition of the Pauline *ordo* not only reveals the continued placement of law in basic relation to the 1539 sequence but also underlines the impropriety of identifying this placement as "christological": the placement of the law was and remains subsequent to sin and prior to faith.[98]

The discussion of the Old and New Testaments has been placed in relation to the law, now prior to faith, repentance, and justification. The movement of chapters is noteworthy: a first step toward juxtaposition of the chapters on law with those on the Old and the New Testaments was achieved merely by the removal and dispersion of the four chapters on faith and creed. Calvin also removed the remainder of the intervening chapters—repentance and justification—placing them together with faith at the beginning of Book III. From the Melanchthonian perspective, faith, repentance, and justification belonged to Paul's initial *narratio,* not to the series of *loci* that followed: in 1559, Calvin moved to integrate these topics with the other Pauline *loci.* Although no explicit rationale for the arrangement is anywhere stated, the final model moves quite easily, in a historical pattern, from the discussion of the Old and the New Testaments to the christological chapters taken from the credal exposition—and then, at the beginning of Book III, from an allusion to the third article (the Spirit) to a soteriological series of faith, repentance, Christian life, justification, Christian freedom, prayer, and predestination. Although the movement from Book II to Book III certainly reflects the movement from the second to the third article of the creed, the creed cannot explain the location of changes made in individual chapters.[99] The Pauline order remains determinative: the original order of sin, law, grace, Old and New Testaments, predestination has been interspersed with other topics but not altered. What is more, the original complex of soteriological chapters of the 1537/8 catechisms (predestination, faith, justification, sanctification, repentance/regeneration, and righteousness) has been restored, albeit in a different order, probably reflecting 1539: the movement from repentance to justification, characteristic of 1539ff. has been retained, as has the posterior placement of predestination.[100]

With specific regard to the placement of the doctrine of predestination in the 1559 edition, we can now safely conclude not only that it remains determined by the Pauline *ordo* of the 1539 *Institutes* but also that the twentieth-century discussion of Calvin's definitive movement of the doctrine "out of the doctrine of God" in order to argue one doctrinal implication rather than another is an utterly anachronistic argument that remains ignorant of the underlying motives for the arrangement of the *Institutes.*[101] Indeed, as the *Synopsis Editionum Institutionis Calvinianae* offered by the editors of the *Calvini Opera* indicates so graphically, it is the chapters on faith and creed, the similarity and difference of the Old and the New Testaments, human traditions, providence, and prayer that were moved, while at the same time the location of predestination remained stable.[102] What Calvin did with his discussion of predestination and providence was, in fact, to move the section on providence into his discussion of God, conflating the relevant sections of the 1550 chapter on predestination and providence with the comments on providence already in place in his 1550 chapter on the "first part of the creed," thereby excising a duplication of materials.[103]

The one significant structural movement of the *locus* on predestination that occurred in the text-history of Calvin's instructional efforts occurred in the transposition of the doctrine from the catechetical model of 1537/8 into the *Institutes* of 1539. In the 1537/8 catechetical form, the discussion of election and predestination was not bound to a discussion of providence—in addition, it was lodged within the discussion of faith, prior to the topics of justification, sanctification, repentance, and righteousness that preceded the credal section of the catechism.[104] In the 1539 *Institutes*, Calvin shifted the credal discussion forward and placed a revised order of repentance, justification, the testaments, and predestination (now juxtaposed with providence) after his exposition of the creed—and the best explanation for this arrangement remains his accommodation to the Pauline *ordo* modeled on Melanchthon. In 1559, Calvin moved his doctrine of providence, leaving predestination still within the Pauline *ordo*, now only slightly posterior to its 1539 placement and still in relation to the topics of faith, justification, sanctification, repentance, and righteousness that had framed its original placement in the 1537 catechism.

Finally, some comment must be made concerning the actual topics found in the 1559 *Institutes*. As already indicated, Calvin's chapter on the final resurrection was new to the 1559 edition. New as a separate chapter—but the topic had already appeared, albeit briefly, in chapter 2 of the 1536 edition at the conclusion of the credal exposition, tripling in length in 1539, and developing into five numbered sections in the 1550 edition.[105] For those who would argue a rigid credal model in 1559, there is an irony in the fact that Calvin observed the credal placement of the resurrection in all editions up to 1559 and then, in 1559, when the discussion of the resurrection became a separate *locus*, opted to place it according to the 1539 Pauline *ordo*, rather than in a credal location. If, moreover, one asks which chapters are utterly new in 1559, the answer is that very few represent new topics: in all of Book I, all but two chapters—*Institutes*, I.ii and xviii, "What it is to know God" and "God so uses the Works of the Ungodly . . . that He remains Pure"—are previously extant subsections now separated out as chapters with their own headings.[106] Similarly, the only utterly new chapter topic in *Institutes*, Book II, is chapter 9, "Christ . . . was known . . . under the Law [but] clearly revealed only in the Gospel." There are no new chapter topics in Book III and IV but—again— only chapters based on previously extant subsections or series of subsections. The sense of radical newness rests largely on the fact that the numbered subsections of 1550 were untitled, so the titles (as distinct from the content) of the chapters constructed out of the 1550 subsections are new. The text of these chapters, albeit often greatly expanded, does not indicate the addition of new topics in 1559. Thus, for all the reorganization that took place, the topics themselves reflect, by way of the expansions of 1543 and 1550, the fundamental expansion of the *Institutes* that took place in 1539, when Calvin added the Pauline *loci*. In other words, Calvin's views on the actual topics or *loci* to be developed in theology altered little after 1539.[107]

Conclusions: The *Ordo recte docendi* in the Final Edition of the *Institutes*

What, then, did Calvin probably mean when he wrote of the 1559 *Institutes* that he "was never satisfied until the work had been arranged in the *ordo* now set forth"?[108] It should be fairly clear by now that he did not mean that all previous arrangements and relationships had been discarded or that he had successfully established either the four principal credal topics or the "twofold knowledge of God" as the sole overarching organizational structure. What he probably meant was that, in 1559, the credal model already resident within the *Institutes* had, for the first time, been successfully integrated with the remaining elements of the catechetical model and, above all, with the basic outline of the Pauline *loci* drawn from Melanchthon's *Dispositio* and *Loci communes*. In 1539, Calvin added the Melanchthonian-Pauline *ordo*, probably under the impact of studying Melanchthon's work, specifically the *Dispositio*, as he prepared both the Romans commentary and the *Institutes*, dividing carefully the task that Melanchthon had never divided—namely the preparation of a commentary and the gathering of the *loci* identified in the commentary. Calvin also surely looked at Melanchthon's 1536 *Loci communes*, accepting its understanding of the problem of Old and New Testament in relation to the Pauline *loci*. He did not, however, add all of the topics from Melanchthon's *Loci communes* but emphasized the loci based directly on the analysis of Romans. In 1559, when Calvin separated out and fully developed his *locus* on the final resurrection, he seems, once again, to have looked to Melanchthon as his model. Indeed, as we have seen from the comparison of new chapter headings added in 1559, Calvin actually added very little in the way of new topics. His sense of the significant *loci* in theology remained determined, even in 1559, by the topics of the catechetical and Pauline models as identified originally in 1536 and 1539.

Thus, the reordering of the *Insitutes* in 1559, although in part determined by the division and rearrangement of the credal chapters, was not merely a credal reorganization. The four-book structure only imprecisely follows the articles of the creed, inasmuch as the transition from Book I to Book II no more precisely obliges the movement from the first to the second article of the creed than it obliges the *duplex cognitio Dei*: Book II still reflects the Pauline *ordo* in its initial reflections on sin. The shifting of the credal chapters was as much a removal of doublets, like the duplicated discussion of providence, as it was the imposition of a new ordering principle. Even in 1559, the dominant ordering principle is the Pauline order as inaugurated in 1539—as is seen by an assessment of the relative balance of the various patterns of organization present in the *Institutes*. The initial division of subject into the knowledge of God and knowledge of self, certainly accounts for the initial chapters of Book I, but, if the Pauline *ordo* is also seen as present, this initial division accounts for the entirety of Book I of the *Institutes*, understood as the basic argument of Romans: the relationship of God to humanity, the character of the human predicament, and the fact that humanity is left "without excuse" in the presence of the revelation of God in nature.

The *duplex cognitio* accounts for the movement from Book I to Book II of the *Institutes*, particularly when Dowey's understanding of the term is set aside in favor of a view that recognizes the beginning of the knowledge of God the redeemer in the right understanding of sin[109]—and, moreover, subsumes the *duplex cognitio* under the Pauline *ordo*. The *duplex cognitio*, in other words, makes sense as a way of describing the move-ment from Paul's initial description of humanity in the presence of the Creator and nature but bereft of the saving revelation of God's grace in Christ to the series of *loci* concerned with the work of salvation. What is more, once the *duplex cognitio* is under-stood as a reflection on the Pauline *ordo*, then it also points toward not only Book II, but also toward Books III and IV of the *Institutes*, as DeLaune and, eventually, Dowey argued.[110] Nonetheless, the *duplex cognitio* itself does not account for the identity and the order of the topics—that function belongs to the Pauline *ordo*.

As for the credal model—it has long been recognized that the final order of the *Institutes*, despite the significance of the dispersion of the credal chapters to that order, does not at all reflect the actual shape of the Apostle's Creed. The Creed alone cannot account for the chapters on the Decalogue, the sacraments, and Prayer: the credal sections, like these other catechetical topics, were remnants of the original catechetical model that Calvin merged with and subsumed under the Pauline *ordo* of 1539. Calvin's rearrangement of topics in 1559 did not structure Book I around the theme of "God the Father Almighty, maker of heaven and earth," any more that it constructed Book II as a meditation on the christological section of the creed. Book III does begin with the Holy Spirit—but it also contains the catechetical (not credal) topic of prayer, and it concludes with the final resurrection, which no longer belongs to the credal exposition. Book IV does present the doctrine of the church, but it also offers the catechetical topics of the sacraments. All of these noncredal characteristics of the four-book model of 1559 appear to be results of the integration of the catechetical with the Pauline *ordo* in 1539. Certainly, the placement of the final resurrection in 1559 disobliges the creed entirely in favor of the Pauline model—and the continuing relationship of sin to law, followed by the problem of the two testaments and the work of redemption; placement of pre-destination prior to the last things, the church, and the civil magistrate all stands as reflections of the Pauline *ordo*.

Why should this be our conclusion? Because, quite simply, it does justice to the text of Calvin's *Institutes* in its mid-sixteenth-century context. As we have seen in our dis-cussion of the successive editions of the *Institutes*, it is not the case that one arrangement superseded or replaced another: elements of the 1536 order remain in all editions of the *Institutes*, including the 1559 edition. More important, the Pauline patterning of *loci* that Calvin incorporated in 1539 served both to preserve crucial elements of the catechetical order and to supply a significant *methodus* or "way through" the four-book structure of the final edition. We are left with the impression, moreover, that the unaltered language of *loci communes* and *disputationes* found in the 1559 version of the letter to the reader continues to be the primary characterization of the *Institutes*. After all, the work ceased to be a catechetical exercise in 1539, and the revisions of 1559, for all their use of the organizational patterns drawn from the Apostles' Creed, did not turn Calvin's theology into a commentary on the Creed: the *Institutes* remains a gathering of topics, determined largely by the work of exegesis and the controversies of the day, and the organizational question remains a matter of identifying a suitable *ordo docendi*.

This understanding of the order and arrangement of the *Institutes* also relates to what Benoit, Parker, and others have long understood as Calvin's manner of elaborating his arguments: Calvin never retracted any of his original positions, and he virtually never set aside any materials. Nearly the entire text of the 1536 *Institutes* remains within the

1559 edition—indeed, as does the larger portion of the 1539, 1543, and 1550 texts.[111] Calvin worked, in short, by the elaboration and augmentation of his arguments. He modified primarily by addition and rearrangement and did so in a way that lost virtually none of his initial insights. This manner of working extends also to the organization of the *Institutes* and to Calvin's quest for the *ordo recte docendi*.

Fontes argumentorum and *capita doctrinae*

Method and Argument in Calvin's Construction of loci *and* disputationes

The Commentaries, the Sermons, and the *Institutes*: Distinction of Genre and Division of Labor

The reader of any modern edition of Calvin's *Institutes* could easily infer, from the most cursory glance at the text, that Calvin envisaged a profound relationship between the study of his *Institutes* and the understanding of Scripture, for citations of Scripture abound on every page.[1] By pursuing the investigation a bit farther, the reader might fasten on Calvin's introductory letter, in which the purpose of the *Institutes* is set forth, and find significant confirmation of his observations: Calvin's purpose was to train theological students in the substance of the biblical message. The *Institutes*, Calvin comments, was designed to "pave" or "make smooth" the "way" for a reading of Scripture and, more specifically, for a reading of his own expositions of Scripture.[2] Furthermore, Calvin quite clearly indicates that he does not intend to duplicate efforts: the *Institutes* stands in the place of the dogmatic disputations and the "commonplaces" or *loci communes* often found in the biblical commentaries of the time. Readers will not find dogmatic elaborations in his commentaries: they ought to look for these in the *Institutes*.[3] These comments did not, of course, free Calvin's readers from the task of examining his commentaries: they only point toward the very different purposes of the commentaries and the *Institutes*.

All of these points are stated quite clearly, and the text of the *Institutes* offers so many biblical references that the modern reader might proceed no further in attempting to decipher the meaning of Calvin's statements of purpose, or what one might call the "mentality" behind the biblicism of the *Institutes*. In other words, the reader might never be forced to ask the question of precisely how Calvin understood the text of Scripture and its relation to theological statement or the equally significant question of precisely how Calvin understood the relationship between the text of his *Institutes* and the text of his many commentaries and sermons on Scripture.[4] One rather striking clue in the search for answers to these kinds of questions about the theological mentality of Calvin, the exegete and theologian, lies in the fact that more than half of the citations of biblical texts found in modern texts of the *Institutes* (e.g., the Barth/Niesel edition in the *Opera selecta* or the McNeill/Battles translation),[5] simply do not appear either in the original editions of the *Institutes* (1536–59) or in the major editions offered during the late sixteenth and seventeenth centuries—this, despite the concerted attempt on the part of Calvin's immediate associates and editors to provide the rather naked text of the 1559 *Institutes* with an extensive apparatus suitable to the task of a detailed understanding of Calvin's work. By way of example, the McNeill/Battles edition offers references to seven biblical texts in *Institutes*, III.xx.1, whereas the original text of the 1559 *Institutes* cites only one, and subsequent editions, beginning with the 1560 French and the 1561 Latin editions, cite only two. The NcNeill/Battles version of *Institutes*, III.xx.2, offers one citation, the sixteenth-century editions offer none. Or, to sample citations of a particular biblical book, NcNeill/Battles note some sixty-seven references to Job—but Calvin actually cited the text of Job only twenty times by chapter and verse plus five broad references to issues raised by the book.[6] And these are not isolated examples—they are, in fact, typical.

Let us make the point again, bluntly, so as not to lose its force: *the majority of the biblical citations found by the modern reader in twentieth-century editions of Calvin's "guidebook" to the Bible are not found in the original edition or in any of the sixteenth- and seventeenth-century editions.* To press the point a bit harder, none of the quotation marks placed around biblical citations in order to mark them off clearly from Calvin's text are found in the sixteenth- or seventeenth-century editions—such marks are a more recent invention. And, what is more, none of Calvin's actual biblical citations are noted in the text of the early editions of the *Institutes*: they all appear in the margins, juxtaposed with blocks of text. The sixteenth- or seventeenth-century reader of the *Institutes* thus approached a book that was, visually, quite different from any of the modern printings. Where the modern reader sees biblical texts, neatly blocked off from Calvin's own words by quotation marks and bracketed citations of biblical texts between the closing quotation mark and the final punctuation, the sixteenth- or seventeenth-century reader saw only the text of the *Institutes*, in which no visual differentiation had been made between Calvin's text and the biblical text, juxtaposed with a free-standing marginal citation of a biblical passage. The biblical references are, therefore, posed marginally against whole sentences and paragraphs in which some biblical phrase or allusion appears that Calvin (or his editorial assistants) wished to highlight—and in which other biblical phrases and allusions may appear that Calvin did not see fit to highlight. This obvious visual difference, moreover, points toward a profound difference in understandings of the relationship between theology and Scripture, between the exegete and the text of Scripture, and between the exegete turned dogmatician and his task of formulation, a difference that has arisen between the end of the seventeenth century and our own times.

Before we enter into a more detailed examination of Calvin's text, some preliminary observations are in order. First, Calvin's readers had a more profound knowledge of the text of Scripture than does the contemporary audience: the absence of quotation marks around biblical verses and phrases and the absence of a system of referencess attempting to identify all biblical allusions would not have deterred Calvin's sixteenth- and seventeenth-century readers from identifying his biblical references and allusions. They knew the Bible well enough to recognize its language when they saw it. And Calvin's most educated readers similarly could identify his classical allusions without recourse to a system of explicit references. Second, only the editions of the *Institutes* published after 1555 could have made use of the Stephanus versification—and at the time of the 1559 edition, Stephanus's versification had not yet become the standard pattern.[7] Thus, Calvin's identification of particular verses did not provide a form of reference to all of the Bibles and commentaries of the day—and, indeed, some of the citations offered in the modern critical editions offer a level of specification foreign to the original text of the *Institutes*.[8] Third, given both his readers' extensive, albeit perhaps theologically naive, acquaintance with the biblical text and Calvin's own failure to identify most of the allusions and brief citations found by modern editors, it should be quite clear that the citations offered by Calvin as precise identifiers of certain biblical texts used or referenced in the *Institutes* were not simply and certainly not primarily for the sake of identifying such texts for his readers![9] Fourth, Calvin's very selective procedure of identifying certain texts and not others can, arguably, be attributed to his intention to alert readers not merely to particular texts, and not only to the texts that were particularly germane to his argument, but also to texts on which he and his contemporaries had commented on fairly extensively as the grounds or "seats" of theological argumentation. In other words, Calvin sought not so much to identify all possible references and allusions as to point his readers from a particular place or topic (i.e., a *locus*) in the *Institutes* to a particularly significant biblical text (also a *locus*) where the reader would gain further insight, especially if the reader looked in the right commentaries. To borrow a modern term that Calvin would not have used, the issue was not so much citation as intertextuality.

The correspondence between the text of Scripture, understood as a offering topical *loci*,[10] "sources of argument" (*fontes argumentorum*), or "heads of doctrine" (*capita doctrinae*) and the text of the *Institutes*,[11] understood as a gathering of biblical *loci* based on consideration of various biblical texts, can be seen from Calvin's patterns of biblical citation. Whereas many of the chapter and verse references to biblical texts found in the *Institutes* are simply identifications of particular texts cited in full or in part, other chapter (and/or chapter and verse) references in the *Institutes* point the reader not to a single numbered verse but to larger units of text,[12] while still other references lead the reader to extended discussions of particular verses in the commentaries.[13] For Calvin, as for Melanchthon, the humanistic movement *ad fontes* is, therefore, not merely a generalized movement toward the biblical and classical sources in their original languages but a rather specified movement toward the sources of argument—*ad fontes argumentorum*—for the sake of the elaboration of theological topics.[14]

With these considerations in mind, the reader of Calvin's commentaries, sermons, and *Institutes* ought not only to recognize a division of labor and a rather precise distinction of genre among these three forms of theological exposition but also to note significant consequences for the understanding of Calvin's work. As strongly implied in his prefaces to the Romans commentary and the 1539 *Institutes*, Calvin felt constrained by the genre of the commentary to place theological topics in his *Institutes*. Concomitantly, he also assumed that the genre of the sermon permitted him more freedom for theological exposition than was suitable to the commentary, but in a more popular and accessible style than was requisite in the formal *loci communes* and *disputationes* that made up his *Institutes*. It hardly needs to be observed, moreover, that the issue of literary genre was, for Calvin, not merely a formal issue: the genre of a work—commentary, sermon, *institutio*, catechesis, tract—related specifically to an identifiable context in which particular instructional or polemical issues were faced or in which a particular exegetical or theological "conversation" was taking place.[15]

Differences in content, therefore, could rest as much on the distinction of genres as on either the occasion of the work or the stage of development of Calvin's thought.[16] Movement from a sermon or commentary to the *Institutes*, from a sermon to a commentary on the same text, or from a commentary to a sermon may well offer insight into the development of Calvin's thought—but, equally, such seeming "movement" may only reveal different aspects of his approach to any given subject. Whereas, for example, *brevitas* was a stylistic virtue emphasized by Calvin in his early commentaries,[17] a virtue corresponding to the more "scholastic" approach of the commentary or academic lecture, *brevitas* was not a stated characteristic of the *Institutes*—and less so of the sermons. The *facilitas* of the commentaries, to the extent that it indicated an unencumbered or nonpolemical flow of argument, was also less evident in the sermons, where polemic against "popery" and extended hortatory discourse is frequently found, as well as in the highly polemical or disputative sections of the *Institutes*.

In these latter genres, the strict commitment to *brevitas* was offset by an interest in the rhetorical technique of amplification (*amplificatio*) or abundance (*copia*), understood as an elaboration of the theme drawing on historical, poetic, philosophical or, indeed, biblical references, images, or allusions, less for the sake of rhetorical ornamentation than for the sake of topical development.[18] Indeed, as distinct from the commentaries, Calvin's sermons are often devoted to the exposition of the doctrines of Scripture, often to the point of pressing beyond a specific text and a series of collateral references to a doctrinal issue and its hortatory application.[19] Calvin explicitly indicates that "rhetoric and exquisite verbiage" used in order to bring praise to the speaker ought to be "banished" from the church—because the divine intention embedded in the Word is that the people be "edified."[20] Calvin's opposition to frivolous rhetoric was so intense that it led to his several attacks on the more profane forms of humanism.[21] And as for secular rhetoric, Calvin was convinced that the words of Scripture were "immeasurably superior" to greatest classical oratory,[22] inasmuch as they evidence no "affected language" or "extravagant speculations" and partake of no "frivolous rhetoric" but speak to us in "pure simplicity."[23]

Indeed, it was a reflection of the Agricolan and Melanchthonian model to identify the "copious" and "varied" treatment of *loci* as the central task of Christian teaching and to associate *amplificatio* or *copia* less with ornamentation than with edification.[24] Such stylistic difference appears particularly in a comparison of the commentaries with the sermons, insofar as, in the latter, the "oratorical" style has fully replaced the "scholastic," and the task of edification in the "school of God" has led to considerable theological, polemical, and pastoral amplification.[25] Yet the sermons and the commentaries follow similar patterns of argument, often moving from the presentation of a unit of text, translated into French for the sermons and into Latin for the commentary, to an exposition of the text in which philological or syntactical issues could be raised, to a more theological elaboration in which the doctrinal or moral meaning of the text could be addressed.[26]

Thus, for example, Calvin's sermons on Galatians were delivered in Geneva as Calvin's Sunday sermon series between November 14, 1557, and May 15, 1558—a full decade after he had published his commentary on the epistle to the Galatians (1548) and immediately before he began his series on Ephesians.[27] As is typically the case with Calvin's sermons, the homiletical treatment of the text of Galatians is far more expansive than the exegetical treatment: the sermons are nearly five times the length of the commentary—reflecting the contrast, made by Jean Budé in his preface to Calvin's commentary on the Minor Prophets, between the tightly argued and unadorned "scholastic" style of the Calvin the comentator and the highly developed "oratorical" style cultivated by Calvin in other works. Thus, in a commentary, Calvin could state an enthymematic Pauline argument in neat syllogistic form and then, in a sermon on the same text, offer a broad expansion of the theme or argument without the neat, syllogistic exposition.[28]

Not only was Calvin more expansive verbally in his sermons; he also allowed himself in his sermons more freedom to range throughout the whole of Scripture in search of examples and theological explanations than he did in his commentaries. In his comments on Galatians 1:3–5, he offers only four collateral references, one from Romans, two from the Gospel of John, and one other from I John. In the sermon on the same text, however, he offers some eighteen collateral references, including four from the Psalter. The comment and the sermon have in common their explanatory citations of I John 5:19 and John 3:16 as Calvin explains the meaning of the word "world" and the saving will of God in Christ. The sermon, moreover, in contrast to the commentary, offers a highly developed discussion of the meaning of the phrase "gave himself for our sins" (verse 4) in which Calvin indicates that Christ's "sacrifice," understood as the "obedience" of Christ's "death and passion," was a "full satisfaction" according to which "God receives us as his own children." In the detail of the homiletical exposition, Calvin juxtaposes the "person of Jesus Christ" in his mediatorial office with "the person of Adam"—a theme not registered in the commentary.[29] Thus, just as the sermons follow more an "oratorical" than a "scholastic" style, so also do they move toward a copious, amplificatory model of exposition rather than follow the commentary model of *brevitas* and *facilitas*.

The implication of this greater theological development in the sermons is certainly that Calvin engaged in intense preparation for his preaching, a point that correlates precisely with his extemporaneous style of delivery. As Stauffer has argued, Calvin's insistence to the Lord Protector Somerset that "preaching ought not to be lifeless but lively, to teach, to exhort, to reprove" and his related objection to the English style of reading sermons "from a written discourse"[30] must be understood in the light of his comment "if I should step into the pulpit, without vouchsafing to look at any book, and fondly imagine [that] . . . God will give me enough whereof to speak, at the same time that I scorn to read or to study beforehand what I shall say, and come hither without minding how to apply the holy Scripture to the edification of the people, . . . I should play the presumptuous fool, and God also would put me to shame for my overboldness."[31] Calvin stressed the liveliness and, indeed, the persuasive character of his oratory, assuming that his extemporaneous delivery was buttressed both by a mastery of the tools of rhetoric, particularly by techniques of topical amplification, and by an immersion in the text of the sermon as well as in the text of Scripture as a whole, the grounds or *fontes* of his amplificatory practice.

Perhaps no better illustration of the difference between Calvin's homiletical style and the style of his commentaries can be found than a comparison of his readings of Galatians 3:3ff. and 4:21ff. Calvin's commentary on Galatians 3:3–5 takes up only a few paragraphs, whereas the same text serves as the basis for an entire sermon. What is more, the commentary dwells on the problem of the Galatians' distortion of Paul's preaching and reserves discussion of faith until the flow of Paul's argument focuses on that issue in the next unit of text (verses 6–9), whereas the sermon expands the reference to faith in verse 5 into an elaborate discourse that anticipates the remainder of the chapter. Thus, in the sermon, verse 5 becomes the basis for a broader definition of faith posed polemically against the doctrine of the "papists" and explained in terms of the similarity and difference of the testaments and the unity of God's covenant and promise. The commentary opens none of these doors and, as one would expect from Calvin's definition of the genre, follows the text in a manner both *brevis* and *facile*, without polemic.[32] If the *brevitas* of the commentary genre stood in the way of the development of *loci communes* and the *facilitas* of the genre barred the way to polemical dispute, the absence of these norms from the sermon could lead Calvin both to the development there of themes similar to those of the theological *topoi* and to the inclusion of far more polemic than permitted in the commentary.[33] Nonetheless, neither the commentary nor the more elaborate sermon approaches either the fullness of definition or the detailed level of polemic found in the *Institutes*.[34]

Calvin the commentator recognizes Galatians 4:21ff. as the *locus classicus* for the justification of allegorical exegesis and declaims at length against the way in which Origen and many who followed him had taken the Pauline identification of Sarah and Hagar as an allegory of the two covenants, law and gospel. The sermon on Galatians 4:21–25 does not mention Origen by name and only briefly indicates that this text ought not to be used "to abolish the natural sense of holy Scripture."[35] On the other hand, the sermon elaborates at far greater length, and with far more allusion to other texts in Scripture, on the way in which the law brings bondage and the gospel brings freedom in salvation. The sermon also includes a barrage against the Papacy. The distinction of genres is clear: in the commentary Calvin speaks crisply and technically to a learned audience, whereas in the sermon he speaks with a less technical but far more expansive oratory, employing a wider variety of images, to all types and classes of believers for the sake of their spiritual edification.[36]

Biblical *fontes* and Dogmatic *loci*: The Sequence of Exposition and the Strata of the *Institutes*

The relationship between the *Commentaries on Romans* (1540) and the *Institutes* of 1539 has already been noted. In the years before these works appeared, Calvin had preached and lectured in Geneva, probably on Romans and perhaps other Pauline epistles (1536–38), and in Strasbourg, on the Gospel of John and I Corinthians (after 1538). Parker argues that much of the decade following 1540 was occupied with lectures on the New Testament.[37] By the time that Calvin had completed the third major revision of the *Institutes* (1543), in which he added four new chapters (on vows, faith, Christian freedom, and human traditions) and divided the credal exposition into three separate chapters, his work as an interpreter of Scripture had not moved forward greatly in terms of printed result: an exposition of Jude appeared in 1542, but other lectures and expositions, probably on the Gospel of John and I Corinthians, were not yet published.[38]

The expansion of the *Institutes* in 1543, largely through added citations, in the form of either simple quotations or glossed texts, was, however, considerable. Comparison of the 1539 with the 1543 texts indicates, moreover, that Calvin's profound association with Paul's Epistle to the Romans had nearly as much effect on the 1543 edition as on that of 1539. In the case of the 1539 additions, it is certainly reasonable to trace the major interest in predestination to work on the commentary, as is also the case with sizable additions to the discussion of the law.[39] But Calvin was at work on the commentary both during and just after the completion of the 1539 *Institutes*. The additions of 1543 evidence the further impact of Romans, now in the form of a large number of brief augmentations of argument.[40] Also to be factored in at this and at the next stage of development of the *Institutes* is Calvin's treatise on free choice against Pighius, published in 1543.[41]

An exposition of I–II Peter followed in 1545,[42] and the commentary on I and II Corinthians in 1546–47.[43] Commentaries on Galatians, Ephesians, Philippians, and Colossians (1548) and Hebrews (1549) followed. In 1550, Calvin published his commentaries on I–II Timothy, Titus, and James, while the commentary on I–II Thessalonians and Philemon, although probably complete in 1550, waited until the following year for its publication.[44] We know little about Calvin's preaching during this time: the printed expositions of Jude and I–II Peter are quite distinct from the commentary of 1551 and may be the result of preaching or lecturing.[45] There are also two collections of early sermons published in 1546 and 1552, respectively.[46]

The situation changed radically in 1549, when a new schedule for preaching called for a sermon on every weekday and two on Sunday and a determined program of transcription was begun under order of the deacons by Dennis Raguenier: Calvin completed a series on Hebrews and preached through Acts (1549–52) on Sunday mornings and on the Psalms in the afternoon; on weekdays he continued to preach through Jeremiah. The beginning of the series on Jeremiah, preached before the advent of Raguenier, was only partially transcribed.[47] The picture of a Calvin commenting on and preaching through nearly the entire text of Scripture in a highly disciplined manner is only beginning to emerge—but the presence of the stenographer has probably served, in Calvin's mind, to integrate the work of preaching into his larger theological project.

Between the fourth (1550) and the fifth (1559) editions of his Latin *Institutes*, Calvin continued his work as a commentator with considerable energy, producing commentaries on Isaiah (1551/59), the Canonical Epistles (1551), Acts (1552–54), John (1553), Genesis (1554), the Harmony of the Evangelists (1555), Psalms (1557), Hosea (1557), and the Minor Prophets (1559). Merely the list of commentaries indicates a vast exegetical effort at this stage of Calvin's work. When juxtaposed with the trajectory of Calvin's weekday sermon series, moreover, the impression of an enormous effort and of a corresponding increase in grasp of the text of Scripture is only enhanced: Calvin completed a series of sermons on Jeremiah and passed on to Lamentations in September 1550; he then surveyed the Minor Prophets (Micah, Zephaniah, Hosea, Joel, Amos, Obadiah, and Jonah) in an effort that took him into the summer of 1552. Ezekiel followed from the summer of 1552 to February 1554, followed by Job (until March 1555). The sermons on Deuteronomy occupied the remainder of 1555 and half of 1556, succeeded by Isaiah (until September 1559).[48] Virtually all of these sets of sermons, moreover, can be juxtaposed with commentaries: those on the Minor Prophets, Jeremiah, Lamentations, Ezekiel, and Deuteronomy point toward Calvin's exegetical publications from 1559 to the time of his death, while the series on Isaiah, occupying as it does much of the time between the two editions, points toward Calvin's renewed effort to understand the text and to move toward revision.[49] And, if the recitation of Calvin's commentaries and sermons implies a fury of activity, his own comments to Farel concerning publication dates and writing projects—engaged, postponed, and delayed—give the impression of a Calvin awash in his work.[50]

In 1559, at the time of the final edition of the *Institutes*, he had completed his exegetical work on the New Testament: the Catholic Epistles—I and II Peter, James, I John, and Jude (1551), Acts (1552–54), John (1553), and the *Harmony of the Evangelists* (1555). Calvin had, by this time, defended his doctrine of predestination against Bolsec,[51] Pighius,[52] and Castellio[53] and had contributed to and signed the *Consensus Tigurinus*. Calvin had also begun his series of lectures and commentaries on the Old Testament, with the first edition of the *Commentary on Isaiah* appearing in 1551 and the Genesis commentary in 1554; although the commentary on the Psalms would wait until 1557 before it appeared in print, Calvin had preached on various Psalms beginning in 1549 and had lectured through the Psalter in 1552. Calvin also preached on the minor prophets from November of 1550 to November of 1552, on Ezekiel in 1553, and on Job in 1554 and early 1555. From March of 1555 until June 1556, he preached on Deuteronomy. This preaching saw its eventual fruit in the commentaries on Hosea (1557) and on all the Minor Prophets (1559). We also know that Calvin lectured on Daniel and began to compile his *Harmony of the Books of Moses* in 1559.

Several patterns of interrelationship between the *Institutes* and the commentaries and sermons can be identified. In the first place, there is a host of issues that Calvin did not address in the *Institutes*, some of which are often found in fully developed systems of theology. In many cases, these issues are addressed in the commentaries and sermons but never became either the subject of a controversy and therefore of a disputation or the subject of an extended theological locus. In the second place, there are doctrinal topics and issues that appear both in the *Institutes* and in the commentaries, treatises, or sermons and that receive different emphases, depending on their location, literary genre, and the context (whether exegetical or polemical) of Calvin's writing. Just as Calvin's biblical citations in the *Institutes* often point the reader to his commentaries, so are there explicit places in the commentaries where Calvin directs his readers to the development of a topic in the *Institutes*.[54] Once again, the reader must look to each of the sources rather than to one of them—and certainly not to the *Institutes* alone if the breadth of Calvin's thought is to be grasped. In the third place, there are also patterns of interrelationship between the *Institutes* and the commentaries or sermons, so an issue not found in one stratum of the *Institutes* will appear as a fully developed new topic or as an augmentation of an extant topic after having been examined exegetically in sermons or in a commentary completed between the successive editions of the *Institutes.*

Of course, there are also significant developments that occur as Calvin moves from the exegetical effort entailed for a sermon to the exegesis required in a lecture and a commentary (or, in some cases, a movement from commentary to sermon)—a development that can be documented from Calvin's work on Deuteronomy and Genesis.[55] As Nicole and Rapin have demonstrated in the case of Calvin's work on Isaiah, theological insights gained from a homiletical exercise that intervenes between two editions of a commentary can alter the argument of the second edition.[56] In these last instances, the relationship between Calvin's exegesis and his doctrinal formulation is most evident. Of interest here, also, is Calvin's emphasis on the New Testament as a basis for his Sunday sermons—given that it led to a return to the text of the New Testament in homiletical form after Calvin had written and published commentaries on the same texts. Perhaps the most notable cases in which sermons have survived are the sermons on the Pastoral Epistles (1555), I Corinthians (1555–57), Galatians (1557–58), Ephesians (1558–59), and Genesis (1559–61)—of which only those on Galatians and Ephesians and on the Pastoral Epistles were published complete during Calvin's lifetime. Also to be considered are those instances in which Calvin did not comment on a book but did produce a series of sermons—notably Job (1554), Deuteronomy (1555–56), I Samuel (1561–52) and II Samuel (1562–53): of these series of sermons, those on Job and Deuteronomy were early enough to have an impact on the final edition of the *Institutes.*[57]

From the Biblical *fontes* to *loci* in the *Institutes*: Patterns of Relationship

That the sequence of Calvin's expository efforts did in fact have a significant impact on the development and expansion of the *Insitutes* can easily be documented from an examination of his editorial work on the text of the *Institutes.* This is not, of course, a claim that every one of Calvin's commentaries or each of his series of sermons had a major impact on the recasting of chapters and subsections in the *Institutes.* One could easily produce a negative list—passages in sermons or commentaries that raised no new doctrinal nuances for inclusion in the *Institutes* or issues raised in raised in sermons and commentaries that Calvin did not see fit to incorporate into the *Institutes* either as new *loci* or as new elements of extant *loci.*[58] Nonetheless, there is undeniable evidence of movement from biblical exposition to the construction and augmentation of doctrinal topics in the *Institutes* along the lines indicated by Calvin in his prefaces of 1539 and 1540.

A nearly perfect example of the interrelationship between Calvin's commentaries and the text of the *Institutes* is found in the chapter on prayer (*Institutes*, III.xx), in which various changes found in editions of the *Institutes* from 1543, 1550, and 1559 rest on Calvin's preaching, lecturing, and commenting on the Psalms (1549–57). In addition, major augmentations of the section on the Lord's Prayer occur in the 1559 *Institutes* close on the completion of Calvin's commentary on the *Harmony of the Evangelists*

(1555). Thus, the first section of Calvin's chapter on prayer contains a single major addition, which belongs to the 1543 expansion of the text:

> Hence the Apostle, to show that a faith unaccompanied with prayer to God cannot be genuine, states this to be the order: As faith springs from the Gospel, so by faith our hearts are framed to call upon the name of God [Rom. 10:14]. And this is the very thing which he had expressed some time before—viz. that the *Spirit of adoption*, which seals the testimony of the Gospel on our hearts, gives us courage to make our requests known unto God, calls forth groanings which cannot be uttered, and enables us to cry, Abba, Father [Rom. 8:26].[59]

Not only are the thoughts expressed here explicitly Pauline; they are also, as Calvin's citations indicate, drawn from meditation on Romans—namely from a commentary that appeared in 1540, between the original writing of the passage and the augmentation of 1543.

The passages from Romans cited in this passage also illustrate the way in which Calvin understood the construction of his *locus* on faith and prayer: he draws together insights from two places in the epistle and uses them to amplify his extant discussion. Calvin has, in fact, illustrated the point made in his 1539 letter to the reader of the *Institutes*: the *Institutes* "paves the way" for the reader of the commentaries and enables Calvin, as writer, to avoid inserting "long dogmatic disputations" and *loci communes* in the commentaries. Nonetheless, as examination of the commentary makes clear, the exegetical elaboration in the commentary of the individual verses cited in the *Institutes* is no duplication. Given Calvin's strict distinction of genres, the content and thrust of the commentary differs from and supplements that of the *Institutes*.

These particular citations also point toward a logic of reference that is evident in several places in the *Institutes*. Given that the reference to Romans 10:14 in *Institutes* II.xx.1 is a reference to the first verse of a pericope (Rom. 10:14–17) identified by Calvin in his commentary, the reference in the *Institutes* probably directs the reader not to a particular verse but, instead, to the beginning of the pericope and, thereby, to Calvin's exegetical essay on the relationship of faith to the calling of the Word. The point is confirmed to a certain extent by Calvin's second citation, Rom. 8:26. Whereas McNeill/Battles here adds references to Rom. 8:15 and 16 because Calvin's use of the phrases "Spirit of adoption" and "Abba, Father" recalls those verses, Calvin cites only Rom. 8:26. Examination of the texts themselves and of Calvin's commentary supplies the probable reason for Calvin's (as distinct from McNeill/Battles's) pattern of citation: although he reminds his readers of the Apostle's words at Rom. 8:15–16, these verses do not refer to the work of the Spirit in relation to prayer, whereas Rom. 8:26 does precisely that, and, what is more, Calvin's comment on the pericope, identified as Rom. 8:26–27, offers an extended expository discussion of that subject. In other words, Calvin's citation of texts in the *Institutes* is quite frequently a reference not to isolated verses but instead to the initial verse of an identifiable pericope on which Calvin has commented at length. (This is not, of course, the invariable intention of Calvin's citations—some are simply identifications of texts quoted in the *Institutes*—but it is one pattern of citation that appears when a particular stratum of the *Institutes* follows and then points back toward Calvin's production of commentaries on a book or books of Scripture.)

In the same chapter of the *Institutes* (III.xx), there is also an extensive addition to Calvin's discussion of various kinds of prayer (vows, supplications, petitions, and thanksgivings) that belongs largely to the editorial effort leading toward the final edition of the *Institutes*.[60] Here, in the editorial work concluded in 1559, Calvin cites a battery of biblical passages, notably in one of the added portions of the text, a concentration of verses from the Psalter coupled with citation of Isaiah, Jonah, Hosea, and Philippians. Only the citation of Phil. 4:6 represents a text commented on by Calvin before the appearance of an earlier edition of the *Institutes*, namely the 1550 edition: all of the citations from the Psalter and the prophets point toward the work done by Calvin as commentator between 1550 and 1559 and thus represent an addition to the *Institutes* relating directly to Calvin's efforts in exegesis. Of these citations, moreover, the citations of Ps. 18:1, 106:47, 116:1, and 116:12 may also be citations of comments on pericopes rather than simply individual texts. This is certainly the case with the citation of Ps. 106:47, inasmuch as Calvin's commentary identifies verses 47–48 as a unit dealing with the historical situation of a dispersed and afflicted Israel (verse 47), followed by the general application or "regulation" of corporate prayer (verse 48) as a way of drawing near to God both publicly and privately in times of adversity. This appears also to be true of Calvin's citation of Ps. 116:12–13: Calvin's commentary on Ps. 116:12–14 is a fairly unified discussion of solemn thanksgivings and vows.

So, also, the block addition on sincere confession of guilt and plea for pardon, added to same chapter in the 1559 edition,[61] identifies four texts: Ps. 25:7, 25:18, 51:5, and 1 John 1:9, all of which are drawn from commentaries written in the years intervening between the 1550 and the 1559 editions of the *Institutes*. None of these citations points toward the beginning of a pericope isolated by Calvin, but they certainly represent a gathering of topically related texts, in other words, the basis for a *locus* such as Calvin chose not to offer in his commentaries but indicated that he would place in the *Institutes*—and the commentary on 1 John 1:9 is a fairly extended exposition that supplements rather than duplicates the exposition in *Institutes* III.xx.9.[62] A discussion of the relation of prayer to faith, based on references to the Epistle of James (1:5 and 5:15), also appears in this chapter of the 1559 edition—once again from a commentary that appeared between the 1550 and the 1559 editions. As is typical, the *Institutes* does not duplicate the commentary. In the *Institutes*, Cavin uses the text only to indicate that "prayer of faith" is a term for genuine prayer and that nothing is gained apart from faith—whereas in the commentary he looks to the preceding verse (5:14), where James refers to anointing with oil. Calvin concludes that the "special gift" of anointing and the promise connected with it are of no avail if not accompanied by faith: the anointing practiced by the "papists," he concludes, is therefore "spurious." Calvin also rests his argument on the view that healings belonged to the era of the New Testament and that anointing did not pass over into the era of the church as a sacrament.[63] Still, the pattern we have been describing is not invariable: the 1559 additions also include new citations from Romans.[64]

Similar conclusions about the relationship of the *Institutes* and the commentaries can be drawn from changes made to the chapters on providence and predestination in the 1559 *Institutes*. These changes bear examination both in the light of Calvin's controversies and in the light of significant exegetical or homiletical efforts following 1550, notably in commentaries on the Canonical Epistles, Acts, Ephesians and the Gospel of

John and in sermons on Ezekiel, Job, the minor Prophets, and Deuteronomy. First, there does not appear to be any evidence that the polemical encounters with Bolsec, Pighius, or Castellio—unlike those with Servetus and Osiander—had a substantive impact on the text of the *Institutes*.[65] In each of these debates, Calvin had tended to defend what he had already formulated in 1539 rather than to break new doctrinal ground, and his defense was largely accomplished in point-for-point polemical reductions of his opponent's arguments. The defensive additions to the *Institutes* generated by these debates are brief. Thus, certainly in response to issues raised in the Bolsec controversy and in the subsequent debate with Bern, Calvin added a comment on the importance of preaching predestination: the damage done to "weak souls" by preaching the doctrine is nothing compared to the problem of hiding the doctrine and subjecting God's plan to reproach.[66] Calvin appears to have found his discussions of providence and predestination to have stood the test of time.

In these chapters, however, he did add substantive text references from (or to!) his exegetical labors.[67] By way of example, one of the few major changes in the doctrine of predestination after its insertion into the *Institutes* in 1539 is a lengthy addition that stands as *Institutes*, III.xxii.6, ad fin. and xxii.7, in which Christ is identified as the "author of election." Calvin's own citations of text in the new material for *Institutio* (1559), III.xxii.6, comprise single citations from Romans, Acts, and II Timothy and two citations from I Peter: three of the citations, therefore, derive from books on which Calvin had commented after 1550—and, in fact, the basic argument of the passage rests on these texts.[68] The entire exegetical basis for III.xxii.7 (which appeared as a block of new material in 1559) derives from the Gospel of John (1553) and represents a collation of thoughts on the relationship between Christ and election generated by a series of passages throughout the Gospel but not immediately available in the exposition of the passages in their immediate textual locations.[69] Indeed, *Institutes*, III.xxii.7, should probably be understood as a theological *locus* developed in the process of Calvin's exegetical examination of the Fourth Gospel and abstracted from the commentary on the ground enunciated in Calvin's preface to the 1539 *Institutes*.

Even so, much of the initial argumentation on the topic of the universal call of the gospel and the special calling of the elect (*Institutes*, III.xxii.10, added in 1559) derives from Amos and Isaiah.[70] Similarly, on the subject of God's foreknowledge and the election of Israel, several paragraphs appear in the 1559 edition that rest entirely on Old Testament texts, most notably on Deuteronomy and the Psalter—both of which represent exegetical efforts undertaken by Calvin after his editorial work on the *Institutes* in 1550, the former in a series of sermons from 1555, the latter in a major commentary from 1557.[71] This pattern continues in the next section of Calvin's argument, another block of new material, in which the citations are from the Psalter and from Malachi.[72] What is more, the citations from Deuteronomy in *Institutes*, III.xxi.5 and those from the Psalter in *Institutes*, III.xxi.5 and 6, occur in blocks of material that could easily be understood as topical collations on themes identified by Calvin in his work as expositor of text but not placed in a commentary or developed in quite the same way in his sermons. None of these collations are technical exegetical comments or lengthy expository arguments—that was the work of the commentaries and sermons: rather, they are elaborations of a point already found in the *Institutes* by way of substantive addition to or modification of text on the basis of insights drawn from the exposition of a series of topically related passages. The absence of utterly new *loci* (as distinct from subtopics of extant *loci*) points to the conclusion, noted in the preceding chapter, that Calvin viewed the basic *loci* of his theology as derived from the catechetical and the Pauline models and tended not to add new topics that rested on other materials.

When one examines Calvin's citations of the book of Job, a similar process of exposition and topical development appears—movement from Calvin's extensive preaching through the book of Job (1554) to the 1559 *Institutes*. These sermons, perhaps more than any other series that Calvin preached, plumb new theological depths and, in addition, offer evidence of Calvin's concern for correct teaching on the major doctrinal issues of providence and the decrees.[73] The Job sermons may in fact contain Calvin's final word on the issues raised in the Bolsec controversy—for it is here that Calvin takes up the problem of God as tyrant and the problem of a hidden divine justice distinct form the revealed justice of God.[74]

It is here that Calvin pointedly identifies these problems, which Bolsec had claimed belonged to Calvin's own theology, as the views of the "Sorbonne theologians." Indeed, whereas the citations from Job belonging to the 1539 and 1543 strata of the *Institutes* are often perfunctory and seldom of high significance to the argument,[75] the citations from Job found in the 1559 *Institutes* are virtually all substantive. Several references were added to the chapter on providence to indicate that the "lofty theme" of the "secret providence of God" was central to the book of Job.[76] The extension of divine providence even to ills brought about by Satan is also referred in 1559 to the text of Job, and the problem of "contrary wills" in God is resolved in the same manner.[77] There is even one instance of a text from Job, cited virtually without comment in 1539, to which a significant explanatory comment was added in 1559: "he refers," Calvin now writes with reference to Job 10:15, "to that spotless righteousness of God, before which even angels are not clean . . . when brought before the bar of God, all that mortals can do is to stand dumb."[78]

So, too, the extensive christological work done for the 1559 edition reflects both exegetical and polemical efforts undertaken by Calvin after the editorial work done on the preceding edition (1550) of the *Institutes*. Reflected here is Calvin's reaction to Osiander's christology and to the trinitarian and christological heresies of Servetus and Gentile.[79] Beyond these polemical issues, the development of the concept of a threefold office of Christ by the rearrangement and augmentation of the discussion of the offices clearly reflects the enormous emphasis on Old Testament exegesis in the decade following 1550—a point largely overlooked by Jansen, who seeks in vain in the exegesis of the New Testament for confirmation of Calvin's doctrine and understands the prophetic office as a purely dogmatic construct.[80]

Beyond the *Institutes*: Expository Issues and Themes Not Presented as *Loci*

Of course, it may not always be possible to draw out relationships between the *Institutes* and Calvin's work on sermons, lectures, and commentaries—if only because many of the theological arguments that developed in the exegetical context were left there and never reflected in the *loci* or *disputationes* found in the successive editions of the *Institutes*.

In addition, the ability to document Calvin's pattern of working ceases, in a sense, in 1559: in the absence of subsequent editions of the *Institutes*, we can no longer move from the commentaries and the sermons to the text of the *Institutes* in search of topical additions. Nonetheless, substantive theological issues are raised by Calvin, sometimes for the first time, in his later commentaries and sermons. Thus, in the *Institutes*, Calvin provides no extended examination of the divine attributes and offers only an occasional reference to the divine essence and self-existence, such as the brief comment that God's "eternity and self-existence are announced by that wonderful name" Jehovah or the statement that Scripture uses the word "God" in such a way as "to denote the unity of the divine essence."[81] Readers of the *Institutes* might easily gain the impression that Calvin had little interest in discussion of the divine essence and attributes. Quite to the contrary, Calvin elaborates at considerable length on these issues in his commentaries—most notably in the *Harmony of the Last Four Books of Moses*, which was begun in 1559 and therefore is not reflected in editorial strata of the *Institutes*. Calvin's comment on Exodus 3:14 observes the traditional interest in the divine essence:

> The verb in Hebrew is in the future tense, "I will be what I will be"; but it is of the same force as the present, except that it designates the perpetual duration of time. This is very plain, that God attributes to himself alone divine glory, because he is self-existent and therefore eternal; and thus gives being and essence to every creature. Nor does he predicate of himself anything common, or shared by others; but he claims for himself eternity as peculiar to God alone, in order that he may be honored according to his dignity. Therefore, immediately afterwards, contrary to grammatical usage, he used the same verb in the first person as a substantive, annexing it to a verb in the third person; that our minds may be filled with admiration as often as his incomprehensible essence is mentioned. But although philosophers discourse in grand terms of this eternity, and Plato constantly affirms that God is peculiarly τὸ ὄν; yet they do not wisely and properly apply this title, viz., that this one and only Being of God absorbs all imaginable essences; and that, thence, at the same time, the chief power and government of all things belong to him. . . . Wherefore, rightly to apprehend the one God, we must first know, that all things in heaven and earth derive at his will their essence or subsistence from the One who truly is. From this being all power is derived; because, if God sustains all things by his excellency, he governs them also at his will.[82]

These comments are significant to the discussion of continuity and discontinuity between Calvin and later Reformed theology (as well as between Calvin and the medieval tradition), inasmuch as Calvin here demonstrates that he shared traditional assumptions concerning the divine being and essence with medieval scholastic tradition. In other words, this is not a biblicistic Calvin who avoids the traditional essentialist reading of Exodus 3:14, but a biblicistic Calvin in the process of making the transition to systematic or dogmatic theology by way of *loci communes*—and his successors deviate barely a hair's breadth from his thought when they look to this text as the basis for the more metaphysical considerations belonging to the *locus de Deo*.

To be sure, Calvin does evidence caution about metaphysical speculation concerning the tetragrammaton that was not always present, in either the earlier or the later exegetical tradition, in his comment on the name of God in Psalm 8:1—where many commentators had offered extensive analysis of the relationship of "Jehovah" to the verb "to be":

> I do not approve of the subtle speculations of those who think the name of God means nothing else but God himself. It ought rather to be referred to the works and properties by which he is known than to his essence. David, therefore, says that the earth is full of the wonderful glory of God[83]

But, even here, Calvin's emphasis on the relationship between God and his people that is indicated by the holy name stands in continuity with the English and Dutch Reformed—that is, with the Puritan and *Nadere Reformatie*—emphasis on the practical or homiletical application of exegesis and of doctrine. Nor does Calvin intend by these comments to rule out an essentialist understanding of the divine name when that understanding is developed exegetically, without philosophical speculation: of the phrase "thy name Jehovah" in Psalm 83:19, Calvin writes, "this implies that *being*, or *really to be*, is in the strict sense applicable to God alone."[84]

Beyond this particular example, Calvin's commentaries on the Psalms and the prophets contain a vast array of discussions of the divine attributes, none of which were transferred to the *Institutes*. Thus, for example, the eternity and immutability of God are contrasted with the temporality and mutability of creatures in the exegesis of Psalm 90:2 and 102:24–25: the "everlastingness" of God, Calvin comments "is to be referred not only to the essence of God, but also to his providence . . . although he subjects the world to many alterations, he remains unmoved."[85] In meditating on the Psalmist's complaint "Hath God forgotten to be merciful?" Calvin buttresses his sense of the abiding truth of God's mercy with a comment that could have been drawn from a scholastic commentary on the *Sentences*: "the goodness of God is so inseparably connected with his essence as to render it impossible for him not to be merciful."[86]

Similarly, a reader of the *Institutes* could easily assume that Calvin wished to expand on the relationship of God as Creator to the created order without presenting anything like the traditional doctrine of creation. In the *Institutes*, Calvin's brief comment on the six days of creation serves only to underline the power, love, and goodness of the Creator and to stress the "obedience of faith" necessary to the contemplation of the created order as a revelation of God.[87] Nonetheless, the first two chapters of the Genesis commentary develop at length a theological approach to creation ex nihilo, the six days, the *imago Dei*, the creation of Adam, the institution of marriage, and the establishment of order as evidenced both in the creation itself and in the gift of law to Adam.[88] Since the commentary was written after the 1550 edition but before the 1559 edition of the *Institutes*, we may at least infer that Calvin did not view the doctrine presented in the commentary as in need of further elaboration in a positive *locus* or in need of defense against error in a disputation, and that—again, as indicated in the 1539 preface to the *Institutes*—that both the commentary and the *Institutes* must be read in order for Calvin's teaching on creation to be understood.

So, too, must Calvin's doctrine of covenant be recovered largely from sermons, commentaries, and his preface to Olivetan's French New Testament.[89] Although Calvin had completed his Genesis commentary and his sermons on Deuteronomy, in which much of his most concentrated discussion of the covenant appears, well before the appearance of the final edition of the *Institutes*, he did not alter the sections on the similarities and diffferences between the Old and the New Testaments appreciably, and he did not add any other covenantal passages to the *Institutes*.[90] By far the larger portion of these chapters (*Institutes*, II.x–xi) came forward unaltered from the 1539 edition, with the two sections (II.xi.13–14) on divine justice and freedom dating from 1543. There is some material in the discussion of the faith of Abraham (II.x.11) that was added in 1559, probably indicating the impact of the commentary on Genesis. Here, again, the exposition in the commentary is far larger and cannot be regarded as duplication—and, whereas the commentary consistently follows the flow of the text the *locus* in the *Institutes* represents a gathering of texts, specifically related to the faith of Abraham from the entire series of chapters on Abraham.[91]

The *Institutes* does not, in other words, reflect either the extended discussion of the covenant with Abraham in the commentary on Genesis 17, the highly significant bilateral covenant language of the Deuteronomy sermons, or the careful definition of the Psalms commentary in which Calvin notes how from one perspective the covenant is unconditional and from another, conditional.[92] Inasmuch as the chapters on the two testaments in the *Institutes* deal very little with the theme of covenant—except to offer Calvin's classic definition of the covenant as one in substance but twofold in administration—the commentary and the sermons stand as the primary source of his teaching. The focus of the chapters of the *Institutes* from which Calvin's "covenant" doctrine is frequently drawn was initially (and remained) the unity and distinction of the testaments. Neither the covenant of grace nor the nature of human responsibilities in covenant was Calvin's subject here.[93] Indeed, even the definition finds more extended explanation in the commentary.[94] So, too, Calvin offered a fairly brief discussion of the third use of the law in the *Institutes*, with little application of the concept to the law itself, its promises, and its sanctions and therefore again left to the commentaries and sermons his larger but somewhat less topically ordered presentation of the law as the standard and norm for human responsibilities in covenant.[95] (Baker's analysis of Calvin's covenant theology takes none of these issues into consideration. Following the pattern of Trinterud's thesis concerning the origins of covenant theology, Baker poses Calvin's purportedly rigid adherence to a unilateral concept of covenant against Bullinger's so-called bilateral or two-sided concept, without examining either the numerous bilateral covenantal arguments that appear in Calvin's sermons and commentaries or the fully monergistic intention of Bullinger's teaching.[96])

If pressed to explain this seeming gap in the *Institutes*, we may can note that, on the one hand, Calvin—considering the dates of the sermons, lectures, and commentaries that deal at length with the subject, either shortly before or after the publication of the 1559 *Institutes*—came late to his understanding of the importance of the concept of covenant, just as he came late to study the Pentateuch in depth—and, on the other, that covenant did not take on for the Calvin the dimensions of a *locus* or *disputatio*. The large-scale development of covenant theology, after all, came later, and the older theological systems—*Sentence* commentaries and *Summae*—with which Calvin was acquainted did not single out covenant as a separate topic.

In the same way, the lectures on Jeremiah (1563), commentary on Joshua (1564), the *Harmony of the Last Four Books of Moses* (1564), and the *Lectures on Ezekiel* (1565) all appeared after the final edition of the *Institutes* and thus promise to add dimensions to our understanding of the theology of Calvin that is not available to the reader of the

Institutes. By way of example, the lectures on Ezekiel contain cosmological meditations, specifically discussions of the cosmic spheres, that are more detailed than any parallel discussions in Calvin's earlier works. But it is equally clear that Calvin's ongoing meditations on various theological problems can move the reader from an argument in the *Institutes* to its fruition in a later commentary. Such is the case with Calvin's elaborate discussion of the doctrinal form of the law codes in the Pentateuch—where a preliminary step is taken in the *Sermons on Deuteronomy* (1555), a fuller definition established in the 1559 *Institutes*, and a large-scale discussion and implementation of the definition executed in the *Harmony of the Books of Moses.*

A significant point of contact between Calvin's teaching and both medieval cosmology and the medieval exegetical tradition occurs in his lectures on Ezekiel 1:4–24 and 10:8–16. Not only did Calvin respect the Aristotelian language of causality; he also could argue the mediated character of the divine impetus behind the events of the world. The point is important, if only as an indication that it is not as simple as some writers imagine to contrast the Aristotelianism of Calvin with that of Beza: in this particular case, Beza's discussion of the celestial spheres in terms of a metaphor of a clock and its wheels must be recognized as a point of continuity rather than of discontinuity with Calvin's thought.[97] So, also, Partee's study of *Calvin and Classical Philosophy* restates the traditional view that, although Calvin knew Aristotle "rather well," his citations of Aristotle "are more literary than substantial." Aristotle's influence on Calvin, Partee concludes, "is slight."[98] Partee never asks the question of latent Aristotelianism in Calvin's thought, particularly in places where Calvin does not cite Aristotle. Similarly, Dowey's now-classic study of Calvin's views of our knowledge of God indicates that a complete analysis of Calvin's doctrine of predestination would require examination of "Calvin's use of the Aristotelian terminology of essential and accidental relationships and of primary and secondary causation" and then immediately proceeds to dismiss these Aristotelianisms as "lame theodicy-like formulations" and "questionably used . . . terms" less than central to Calvin's thought.[99]

If it is difficult to justify such statements on the basis of a careful reading of the *Institutes*, it is surely impossible to make them once the commentaries are brought into consideration, especially his last works, notably the commentary on Ezekiel. There Calvin argues the transmission of motion from God as first mover to the angelic movers of the spheres and thence to the nexus of temporal causes and effects. The words of the prophet "And when the living creatures proceeded, the wheels went beside them . . ." indicated to Calvin that "all the changes in the world depend on celestial motion" and that "the living creatures represent to us angels whom God inspires with a secret capacity (*virtus*), so that he works by means of their hands." It is thus by the "motion and inspiration" of the angelic movers that "things in themselves motionless are borne along."[100] Calvin's fairly frequent use of terms for the "celestial machinery" (*orbis machina* and *caelestis machina*) ought probably, therefore, to be understood as references to this transmission of motion from God as First Mover through the spheres to the order of nature.[101]

Quite significantly, in these last lectures, Calvin has more positive recourse to the concepts of a divine agency in the order of the cosmos and of the mediation of divine willing through the agency of secondary causes than he had evidenced in his earlier works.[102] Calvin writes:

Whenever the confusion of our affairs urges us to despair, let us try to remember this sentiment, that the spirit of the living creatures is *in the wheels.* And truly, when we tremble in doubtful circumstances, what can we do but acquiesce in this doctrine— namely, that the end of everything will be as God decrees, because nothing is carried on apart from his will, and that there is no motion, no agitation under the heavens, unless he has inspired it by his angels. . . . On the whole, the Prophet here says that angels so move all things that are done under heaven, that no proper motion ought to be ascribed to them. And why? because God presides over them and govern their actions.[103]

The point is not incompatible with Calvin's more typical language of presumably un- mediated sovereign divine causality, but it offers a nuance not offered in the *Institutes* or the polemical treatises. The difference, presumably, is generated by the cosmological and exegetical as distinct from the specifically soteriological and highly charged polem- ical context for his remarks. Nor ought it to be assumed that this positive appropriation of Aristotle either is restricted to the lectures on Ezekiel or is a feature of Calvin's later meditations only: a careful, positive use of Aristotelian causality is characteristic of Calvin's 1551 reading of Ephesians, chapter one, it is quite pervasive in his early (1543) treatise against Pighius on the problem of free choice, and, as Backus has shown, it is present also in the *Institutes* in Calvin's trinitarian terminology.[104] Rather, therefore, than view the Aristotelianism of the *Institutes* as incidental or "lame," we ought to recognize it, like the many other scholastic echoes, as integral to Calvin's thought. What should have been evident from a variety of statements made in commentaries and polemical treatises is presented in detail as a normative view of the cosmos in Calvin's last lectures—and, in any case, the fullness of Calvin's thought on the subject of sec- ondary causality cannot be inferred from the *Institutes* alone.

Some Conclusions

Calvin's identification of the contents of his *Institutes* as *loci communes* and *disputationes* placed him in continuity with theological developments in his time and at the center of a significant confluence of nominally humanistic and nominally scholastic patterns of discourse. The *locus* method and the organization of *loci communes* into theological systems so characteristic of the Reformation and of Protestant scholasticism were, after all, the result of modifications introduced into logic by the humanist Rudolf Agricola in the fifteenth century. The *disputatio*, by way of contrast, was typical of the older scholastic educational model and, in its movement from statement of premise to ob- jections and replies, was taken over with perhaps less formal change in Calvin's *Institutes.*

This identification of the contents of the *Institutes* also pointed Calvin's readers to- ward the proper context within which the *Institutes* needed to be read and understood. From one perspective, this context was the task of training ministerial candidates in the teachings of Scripture and in basic forms for the presentation of those teachings, namely positively stated topics and polemically argued disputations. From another perspective, this context was Calvin's larger work of the exposition of Scripture within which the *Institutes* had a specific role. As Calvin had argued, his readers ought to use the *Institutes* as a background to the study of Scripture *and* to the study of the commentaries. Still, the commentaries themselves and the sermons must be read in order to gain a full understanding of Calvin's thought, specifically with relation to the biblical *fontes* of his topical argumentation.[105] The topic that arises from the expository work in a commentary can point the reader to the *topos* or *locus* in the *Institutes*. Equally so, the texts cited in the *locus* in the *Institutes* point the reader to the exposition offered in the commentary. In many cases, the same relationship obtains between Calvin's sermons and the *Institutes*. So, too, must the sermons be examined for indication of Calvin's pastoral and theological amplification in the context of the congregation. Not only, therefore, does the text of the *Institutes*, taken by itself, offer a partial view of Calvin's thought; it offers only a partial picture of Calvin's theological project. In order for any given point in Calvin's theology to be understood in its proper context, one must examine all of Calvin's chosen forms of expression. And, more than that, each form must be allowed to speak out of its own context, whether defined by its genre, its immediate historical environment, or by the interpretive conversation in which Calvin was taking part as he produced his text.

Fides and *Cognitio* in Relation to the Problem of Intellect and Will in the Theology of John Calvin

The Problem of "Intellectualism" in the Study of Calvin's Definitions of Faith

Virtually all of the studies of Calvin's concept of faith have declared, and rightly so, that Calvin could not conceive of faith apart from knowledge.[1] In his continuous polemic against the scholastic doctrine of *fides implicita*, Calvin had defined faith as "a certain and from knowledge"[2] or, in the more familiar form given in the *Institutes* from 1539 on, "a firm and certain knowledge of divine benevolence toward us."[3] Nonetheless, from the very beginning of his theological career, Calvin had indicated another dimension of faith, trust or "fiducia."[4] Calvin insisted that faith not only was a matter of "believing God" but consisted also in "believing in God": to have faith was "not only to count as true all that has been written and said about God and Christ, but to place all hope and trust in God and Christ."[5] Indeed, he could define faith as a "firm and solid confidence of heart" as distinct from a mere knowledge lodged in the "brain."[6]

Recent scholarship has emphasized Calvin's association of faith (*fides*) with knowledge (*cognitio*), but has neglected the implications of his reference, from nearly the beginning of his theological work, to the fiducial aspect of faith. Among the more recent monographs, that of Schützeichel denominates knowledge as essentially a synonym for faith in Calvin's thought and argues that the concept of "certainty" is the center of Calvin's teaching.[7] Shepherd's study calls knowledge "essential" to faith in Calvin's theology.[8] We note also Krusche's thesis that the underlying thrust of all of Calvin's teaching is "cognitive."[9] One study in particular, R. T. Kendall's *Calvin and English Calvinism to 1649*, draws on this "cognitive" aspect of Calvin's theology in order to argue for a fundamental difference between Calvin's thought and that of later Calvinism:

where Calvin was intellectualist in his doctrine of faith, his successors were voluntarist and experiential.[10]

In Kendall's analysis of Calvin, intellectualism is taken to mean not only a priority of intellect but an emphasis on intellect to the virtual exclusion of the will in matters of faith. Kendall points to Calvin's use of terms like "science," "recognition," "illumination," and "knowledge" (*scientia, agnitio, illuminatio*, and *cognitio*) in passages that discuss faith and attempts to argue that, since Calvin never identifies faith as "man's act," he must also exclude all "voluntarism."[11] Later Calvinists, Kendall argues, turned the equation completely about and defined faith in terms of will rather than intellect and, by implication, viewed the inception of faith as a human act.[12] In other words, the identification of faith with the intellective function relates, in Kendall's view, to monergism; identification of faith with the voluntary function, to a form of synergism. But this is hardly a necessary relationship—note, for example, the radically monergistic soteriology of Augustine, who nonetheless assumed the priority of the will.

Compounded with this fundamental misunderstanding of the implications of "intellectualism" and "voluntarism" is Kendall's flawed analysis of Calvin's vocabulary. Of the terms cited, only *cognitio* occupies a central place in Calvin's definition. The other terms do not function as "synonyms" for faith in any real sense. Calvin does say that "faith" is "frequently called" *agnitio* ("recognition") in Scripture and is called *scientia* ("knowledge") by John—but in the same passage,[13] he cites Eph. 3:18–19, drawing the conclusion that faith is "far beyond understanding" (*esse omni intelligentia longe sublimius*) and that "the knowledge of faith (*fidei notitiam*) consists of assurance (*certitudine*) rather than apprehension (*apprehensione*)." The thrust of these statements is not to construct a definition of faith around the terms *agnitio* and *scientia*, nor does Calvin's language offer an exclusively intellectualistic perspective: the "knowledge" that belongs to faith (*fidei notitia*) takes the form of certitude or assurance—and faith extends beyond mere understanding (*intelligentia*). Of these terms, only *intelligentia* is strictly a matter of intellect, and Calvin here speaks of it as transcended by faith.

In the passage where Kendall sees faith designated *illuminatio*,[14] "illumination" is in fact identified as a Spirit-given "keenness of insight," parallelled by Calvin with *lux*, "light . . . given [to] the sightless." The text indicates that the Spirit leads believers "by faith into the light of the gospel": again, faith is neither precisely identified with nor exhausted by illumination. Calvin's pattern of definition precludes the identification of faith with "keenness of mind." Nor is there any reason to conclude from this text that faith is solely a matter of intellect. We are left with *cognitio* as the basic term of definition, and we are left with the question of the relationship between intellect and will in Calvin's understanding of faith.

Beyond these basic caveats, the questionable character of Kendall's thesis points to the need for a more detailed inquiry into the relation of intellect and will in to Calvin's concepts of *fides* and *cognitio*. Several of the older discussions of Calvin's theology do, in fact, point toward dimensions of *fides* and *cognitio* not noted by Kendall. Blondiaux indicated the importance of "moral confidence" while rightly identifying the volitional element in Calvin's doctrine.[15] Doumergue, for one, cautioned against the assumption that Calvin's thought was "intellectualistic": since, for Calvin, "theology ought to be comprehensible to all" and is, therefore, in a certain sense "anti-intellectualistic" and essentially "practical," then (according to Calvin) "faith itself will be, for the strongest of reasons, both practical and anti-intellectualist."[16] Lobstein similarly pointed out that *cognitio* itself has an "experimental and practical character" in Calvin's usage, and that Calvin's definitions all indicated, more than mere intellectual adherence, "an act of trust, a submission of the will to the holy and merciful God."[17] Dee noted that Calvin sometimes referred faith to mind (*mens*) but with equal frequency to heart (*cor*), and he stressed the volitional or affective side of Calvin's teaching over the "intellectualism" of late medieval Catholic doctrine.[18] Dee also pointed, with some reservation, toward parallels between Calvin's doctrine and affective elements in the teaching of Alexander of Hales and Bonaventure.[19] Leith notes that "the knowledge of God," according to Calvin, is not "abstract knowledge" or sense knowledge but a knowledge that "consists more in certainty than in comprehension."[20]

Several recent essays, moreover, follow lines of argument similar to those of Blondiaux, Lobstein, Dee, Doumergue, and Leith: Vos, for example, in his comparison of Calvin with Aquinas, has noted that Calvin viewed faith as neither "merely" nor "primarily" intellectual and that Calvin, like Aquinas, hardly ignored "the role of the will" in faith.[21] More recently, along lines similar to Doumergue's concern for the practical emphasis in Calvin's theology and to Leith's emphasis on Calvin's address to the whole person, Armstrong has noted that a "spiritual purpose" undergirded Calvin's theology and, specifically, that faith ought to be understood as providing "a new dimension by which the believer is able to penetrate to a deeper, spiritual level."[22] Schreiner indicates that Calvin refers the certainty of faith to the work of the Spirit in "both mind and heart."[23]

If these considerations did not provide ground for reappraisal, it can also be noted that Kendall's essay, for all its chronological arrangement of thinkers, is hardly historical: Kendall makes no attempt to place Calvin's thought in its historical context or to examine its possible development. Indeed, among the previous essays on the subject, only Dee's and Schreiner's examine Calvin's context and give some notice to the development of Calvin's thought. Lobstein, Stuermann, Schützeichel, and Shepherd fail to consider either context or development: instead, they move freely between the final edition of the *Institutes* and the commentaries and treatises to create a harmonistic, dogmatic account of Calvin's thought.

A Context for Interpretation: Calvin's Vocabulary in Relation to the Intellectualist and Voluntarist Traditions

Although Calvin addressed both faith and the spiritual faculties of human beings as significant issues or topics for theological discussion and himself raised the issue of the relationship of intellect and will to faith and knowledge by the manner in which he defined faith, he certainly never singled out the problem of intellect and will as a distinct *topos*. Among other things, this means that the relationship between intellect and will in Calvin's theology appears at the edges of discussion, as an adjunctive consideration, rather than in statements offered for the precise definition of a specific issue. Given, moreover, the medieval background of the language of faith, Calvin not only was drawn to the problem of intellect and will at the edges of his definitions of faith; he also came to the issue with a certain polemical predisposition. In addition, Calvin's discussion of faith, knowledge, intellect, and will clearly reflects a development from the brief comments in the 1536 *Institutes*, through the increasingly extensive analysis of aspects of these topics in his early New Testament commentaries and the 1539 *Institutes* to the detailed examination and rather precise definition in the exegetical works following 1550 and in the final edition of the *Institutes*.[24]

Before we proceed any further, we must pay some attention to the range of meaning of "intellectualism" and "voluntarism." From the very first, colloquial meanings are ruled out: intellectualism and voluntarism do not refer to an excess of ratiocination in theology, on the one hand, and to an emphasis on freedom of choice, on the other: this point was recognized by Dee,[25] but neglected in most of the more recent studies, disastrously in Kendall's work. The terms refer to the two faculties of soul, intellect and will, and to the question of which has priority over the other: intellectualism indicates a priority of the intellect; voluntarism, a priority of the will. In a technical theological and philosophical sense, however, intellectualism indicates a view of soul that denominates intellect the nobler of the two faculties because it is the intellect that apprehends the final vision of God as being and truth, whereas voluntarism denominates the will as the nobler faculty and assumes that its ultimate cleaving to God as the highest good (*summum bonum*) addresses the highest object of human love. (The intellectualist position would respond that such union with God is possible only when the intellective vision of the divine essence has been attained and the connection between the divine esence and all "particular goods" is perceived.[26]) Neither view leads naturally to the assumption of a human act prior to the work of grace. Intellectualism, so defined, tends to view theology as primarily contemplative or speculative; voluntarism tends to view theology as primarily practical. It is this more technical sense of the terms in their relation to faith that provides us with the focus of our inquiry.

Equally important and illuminating—particularly in view of these alternative approaches to Calvin's concept of faith—is the probable background of Calvin's thought on these issues. In addition to the broad Augustinian basis for Calvin's theology, quite a few scholars have argued a Scotist tendency in the thought of the Reformer.[27] Both the Augustinian and the Scotist psychologies are voluntaristic, not intellectualistic, inasmuch as both place will prior to intellect in the inward human causality.[28] Nor can Calvin's frequent pairing of *fides* with *cognitio* definitively distinguish him from the voluntarist tradition, for *cognitio*, without any modifier, does not necessarily refer exclusively to the intellect, even in the usage of an intellectualist thinker like Thomas Aquinas. Gilson comments of Aquinas's teaching that "the understanding and the will reciprocally include and move each other."[29] It is also the case that Aquinas's intellectualism in no way prevented him from defining faith as a matter of will as well as of intellect.[30] The will is not unknowing—and even in the voluntaristic psychology of Scotus, the will has "a natural tendency" to assent to the known good, even though the intellect is not "the efficient cause of volition."[31] The near equation of *fides* and *cognitio* in Calvin's thought, far from solving the problem of the relationship of intellect and will, actually raises it in a rather pressing manner: for, if *cognitio* can relate to will and to the affections of the will as well as to intellect, then *fides* can also have a voluntaristic as well as an intellectualistic side.

Returning to Calvin's text, we can detect hints of his later definition of faith in the 1536 *Institutes*. Here Calvin writes of true faith as "not only" a belief "that God and

Christ are" but also a belief "in God and Christ, truly acknowledging Him as our God and Christ as our Saviour."[32] Here, too, he defines faith as a "firm persuasion of the rational soul" (*firma animi persuasio*).[33] Taken in isolation from Calvin's later statements, the definition lacks the clearly stated balance of mind and heart, of intellective and affective faculties, that is characteristic of Calvin's subsequent definition—although even here, the language of "truly acknowledging" God and Christ, followed by the characterization of faith in terms of hope (*spes*) and trust (*fiducia*), probably implies the relation of faith to both faculties. So, too, does Calvin's early definition lack the emphasis on *fiducia*, trust or faithfulness, that permeates his later discussion. Absence of language of the heart (*cor*) and trust (*fiducia*) from the 1536 *Institutes* also creates a contrast with at least two of Calvin's potential early Reformation models, Melanchthon's *Loci communes theologici* and Zwingli's *De vera et falsa religione commentarius*, both of which tend to define faith as belonging to heart as well as mind and consisting in trust as well as certainty.[34]

The alteration of definition came almost immediately: we find it in the *Catechismus, sive christianae religionis institutio* of 1537/8:

> Faith, in the Christian sense, is to be conceived neither as a bare knowledge of God nor an understanding of Scripture that flits around in the brain with minimal impact on the heart: such may be the common opinion of this issue confirmed to us by rational argument. Rather [faith] is a firm and solid confidence of heart, through which we rest securely in the mercy of God as promised to us in the Gospel.[35]

In 1539, Calvin augmented the discussion of faith still more substantially, drawing both on his 1536 *Institutes* and the 1537/8 catechism. The need for a broader definition certainly reflects the shift in genre of the document itself: the 1536 *Institutes* offered a definition that was suitable to the needs of a catechetical document in which "faith" provides a prologue to the substance of the *Credo*. The 1539 *Institutes*, by way of contrast, sought to provide a definition and discussion of faith representing the *locus* or *topos* elicited both from a reconsideration of the needs of Christian instruction and from Calvin's exegetical efforts, notably the commentary on Romans in which he was concurrently engaged. And, if we are correct that Calvin saw Melanchthon's *Loci communes*, and, in particular, its Pauline *ordo*, as a model for the gathering and organization of biblical *loci*, he would have had not only the fiducial emphasis of the 1521 *Loci communes* at his disposal, but also the finely tooled intellective-volitional balance of the the 1535/6 *Loci communes* to credit for the development that took place between 1537 and 1539.[36] We may even hypothesize that Calvin read Melanchthon's 1535/6 *Loci communes* between his work on the 1536 *Institutes* and his composition of the 1537/8 catechism.

Significantly, the emphasis on *cor* and *fiducia*, so central to Melanchthon's argument, is not as prominent Zwingli's *Commentarius*. Melanchthon's *locus* was grounded specifically on the text and structure of Romans, whereas Zwingli's was not. Nor is Bullinger a likely source of inspiration: his *Decades* do contain a strong fiducial emphasis in their exposition, albeit not as much in their initial definition of faith as in its elaboration—but the *Decades* (1549–51) could not have influenced the 1539 *Institutes*.[37] Bullinger's 1533 Romans commentary,[38] however, is another matter. When Bullinger arrives at the key text of Romans 5:2, "we have access by faith into this grace," he insists, against the attempt of "papal religion" to obscure the meaning of faith, that faith (*fides*) here indicates trust (*fiducia*).[39] So, also, at Romans 10:10 ("for with the heart [a person] believes unto righteousness") Bullinger speaks of faith as "constancy and certitude" and then indicates that the reference to "heart" indicates that faith requires and "intergity and sincerity in the seat of the feelings," that also excludes all hypocrisy.[40] The language of *cor* and *fiducia* is present and based firmly on the Pauline text, but not nearly with the emphasis found in Melanchthon. Nor does Bullinger draw these terms into a theological *locus* in the commentary. Calvin's approach appears more Melanchthonian than Bullingerian, although Bullinger's exegesis surely supported the line of argument found in Melanchthon's work.

In accordance with the alteration of genre, the 1539 stratum of the *Institutes* drew more fully on the New Testament in order to support the flow of Calvin's argument with numerous biblical phrases. The added references, moreover, reflect Calvin's pre-occupation with the Pauline epistles and the Gospel of John between 1536 and 1539. Specifically, the new definition of faith retains the sense of "firm conviction" found already in 1536 in the phrase "firm and certain knowledge" but adds both in the preceding sentence and in the definition itself a reference to the "heart" that balances the original emphasis on "mind": the "mind of man" is blinded and the "heart" wavers—"therefore our mind must be otherwise illumined and our heart strengthened." Faith is "a firm and certain knowledge (*cognitionem*) . . . both revealed to our minds (*mentibus nostris*) and sealed upon our hearts (*cordibus obsignatur*)."[41] This added emphasis is reflected in and, perhaps, directly caused by Calvin's encounter with Romans. There we read that "faith is not a changeable persuasion . . . but . . . it sinks deep into the heart" and that "the seat of faith is not in the brain, but in the heart."[42] Calvin also indicates that his point is concerned with not so much a "part of the body" as the biblical association of "heart" with "serious and sincere feeling," leading to the conclusion that faith is fundamentally *fiducia*, "a firm and effectual confidence."[43]

The language of these definitions itself points toward a particular relationship intellect and will in traditional Christian faculty psychology. The soul is understood to be *rational* in both of its faculties. This "sealing" of faith on the heart ought not therefore to be interpreted as experiential to the exclusion of cognition. Calvin does not oblige any neat "head/heart," intellective/affective, rational/experiential dichotomy: what is "sealed upon our hearts" is the "firm and certain understanding" or "cognition." Nor can there be genuine "persuasion," "sincere feeling," or "effectual confidence" unless heart as well as mind is involved in the cognitive act. We are here directed toward the assumption of the traditional faculty psychology that the will is itself rational—and to the question of Calvin's views on the relationship of intellectual and voluntary elements in cognition itself.

The Problem of Intellect and Will in Calvin's Theology

As is the case with most of the issues debated in detail by the medieval scholastics, the problem of intellect and will receives little explicit attention in Calvin's theology but, instead, hovers in the background of Calvin's thought as a necessary presupposition of major doctrinal formulations. Calvin, typically, refuses to engage in "scholastic" speculations, but his doctrinal stance is always formulated in the context of an extant approach to theological and philosophical issues and with particular reference to the aspects or elements of that approach that prove troublesome to him in his own less speculative meditations on the problem.

Calvin clearly held to the traditional Aristotelian "faculty psychology," according to which the soul (*anima*) could be distinguished into the faculties or parts (*partes*) of intellect (*intellectus*) and will (*voluntas*) and could be viewed as the seat of the affections of the will.[44] In addition, Calvin held that the "whole person" (*totus homo*) was fallen and that sin had affected both parts of the soul, both intellect and will.[45] This perception of the fallenness of the soul in both its faculties provides a convenient point of entry into Calvin's view of the relation of intellect and will.

In his initial statement of the problem in 1539, Calvin presents the intellectualist position both as ideally correct and as typical of the Greek philosophers:

> The human soul consists of two faculties. . . . Intellect and will. Let the office, moreover, of the intellect be to distinguish between objects, as each seems worthy of approval or disapproval: while that of the will, to choose and follow what the intellect pronounces good: but to reject and flee what it disapproves. . . . Let it be enough for us, that the intellect is as it were the leader and governor of the soul. The will depends on its command (*nutum*) and in its own desires awaits its [i.e., the intellect's] judgment.[46]

What is significant here, more than the definition itself, is its placement following the discussion of original sin in the order of Calvin's theology, coupled with Calvin's rather sardonic comment "we shall presently see just how well the intellect governs the direction of the will."[47] In the original form of the discussion (1539), Calvin's treatment of the prelapsarian condition of intellect and will followed his analysis of original sin and was immediately juxtaposed with his presentation of the distortion of the faculties by sin.[48] The problem of the traditional faculty psychology is that its entirely correct definition of the relationship of intellect and will applies only to the prelapsarian condition of humanity. The philosophers did not understand grasp the problem of sin and therefore did not perceive the degree to which sin subverts the right ordering of the faculties. Calvin's arrangement of materials in 1539 makes his arguement all the more trenchant.

Calvin continues his discussion by noting that, according to Aristotle, "the mind has no motion in itself (*nullam esse menti per se motionem*), but is moved by choice."[51] This choice Aristotle called the *intellectus appetitivus*, the appetitive intellect. Calvin refuses to enter into Aristotelian minutiae and comments only that there is no "power of soul" (*animam potentiam*) beyond intellect and will, that the inclination toward concupiscence comes from sense and the inclination toward good from the intellect, and that—when the will follows the intellect—will may be regarded as the "affection of the intellect" (*affectio intellectus*).[50] Calvin then states that choice belongs to the will, including the choice to follow or to disregard the intellect: surely his point is that this inherent capability of the will makes possible the vast upheaval of the faculties that occurs in the fall.[51]

What Calvin does not say in this basic statement of the problem is that his own construction, despite his customary unwillingness to follow Aristotle into labyrinthine speculations, partakes substantively of the medieval scholastic debate over the meaning of Aristotle's rather vague reference to an *intellectus appetitivus*. Aquinas had specifically identified Aristotle's "appetitive intellect" as the will, and as subordinate in function to the intellect.[52] Scotus, on the other hand, had offered alternative terms that avoided the intellectualistic implications of *intellectus appetitivus*, such as "rational power" (*potentia rationalis*) or "rational appetite" (*appetitus rationalis*), and had indicated that the will is rational in and of itself and not merely as a spiritual function subordinate to the intellect.[53] Scotus's definition, moreover, was specifically designed to protect the freedom of the will against the intellect: intellect naturally exerts influence on the will, but the will as *appetitus rationalis* is not bound, as Bonansea comments, to "follow the dictate of the intellect."[54] For Scotus, then, the will is not merely an intellective appetite that receives directions from the intellect but a formally distinct and coordinate faculty of soul that, by its freedom of choice, determines even the extent of our knowledge of any given object.[55] Scotus's view may be seen to follow Augustine more closely than did Aquinas on this point.[56]

When placed into the context of this debate, Calvin appears to echo the voluntarist tradition insofar as he places choice in the will and does not make the intellect either efficiently or finally the cause of the will's choice, despite the intellect's role as "governor."[57] Rather, under ideal conditions, the free choice (*liberum arbitrium*) of the will becomes the basis for a decision in favor of the good known to reason rather than of the evil inclination of sense.[58] The will "stands in between reason and sense" (*inter rationem et sensum medium locant*) with the capacity to turn toward either.[59]

Calvin is not, however, interested in elaborating an analysis of the freedom of the will or of its relative primacy over the intellect: instead, he inquires into the problem of human inability to will the good, the problem of the restriction of free choice. Human beings are "not deprived of will" (*non voluntate privatus*) but they are deprived of soundness of will (*voluntatis sanitate*).[60] Like Augustine and Luther, Calvin does not deny the basic freedom of will: the faculty is free from external compulsion, although it operates under certain necessities belonging to its nature, whether under God or under sin. He therefore argues the restriction of choice to sinful choice.[61] We find here, in other words, not a philosophical but a soteriological voluntarism that not only recognizes the necessity of grace to all good acts of the will but also recognizes that, in the soul's present sinful condition, the will most certainly stands prior to the intellect.[62]

The voluntaristic perspective appears fully when Calvin addresses the issue of the relation of the fallen will to rational knowledge of the good. Under the terms of Calvin's ideal or philosophical definition,[63] reason ought to announce the good and the will ought to follow the dictates of reason, albeit freely and of its own choice. The will occupies a place between the intellect and the senses and is capable of following either. In fallen humanity, however, the will freely follows the senses into lust—indeed, "the natural man refuses to be led to recognize the diseases of his lusts."[64] Reason itself, after the fall, only vaguely and indistinctly perceives the truth of God—like a distant lightning flash in the darkness, comments Calvin—and it never, of its own, either "approaches" or "strives toward" God.[65] Reason has become a weak guide, and the will, in any case, is no longer inclined to follow reason.

Calvin thus moves toward a soteriological rather than a purely metaphysical or philosophical voluntarism: the problem of salvation centers on the freedom of the will in its sinning and the inability of the freely sinful will to choose the good.[66] We cannot will the good, nor can we will to have faith. Both result only from the gracious activity of the Spirit that changes the will from evil to good.[67] In Calvin's Augustinian model, *voluntas* (understood not as an activity but as the fundamental faculty that wills) is defined as incapable of being coerced while nonetheless bound by its own sinful nature and, therefore, free in its inability to choose the good.[68] Since will therefore is free even from the coercion of the intellect, the beginning of the redeemed life and of faith must be such that the will—"insofar as it is will" (*quatenus est voluntas*)—retains its primal integrity and its essential freedom. The evil will is abolished by grace in such a way that, without suffering even a momentary abridgement of its uncoerced willing, it may now will the good.[69]

Faith in Relation to the Faculties of the Soul

As in his discussion of intellect and will, Calvin indicates also in his discussion of faith that sin provides a barrier to the free choice of truth. Here again, we see the balancing of mind and heart (probably resulting from the exegesis of Romans) that is so characteristic of the 1539 stratum of the *Institutes*. The Word ought to be "amply sufficient to engender faith," but the mind in its perversity "is always blind to the light of God's truth."[71] The Word has no effect "apart from the illumination of the Holy Spirit"— nor can this illumination be restricted to the mind: "the heart" must "also be strengthened and supported," inasmuch as "faith is much higher than human understanding (*intelligentia*)."[71] Calvin continues:

> In this matter, the Scholastics go completely astray, who in considering faith identify it with a bare and simple assent (*assensum*) arising out of knowledge (*notitia*), and leave out confidence and assurance of heart (*cordis fiducia et securitate*). . . . how very dull men are to perceive the mysteries of God; partly because they do not have regard to that firm and steadfast constancy of heart which is the chief part of faith.[73]

Calvin's polemic here and in parallel passages in the Romans commentary closely reflects that of Melanchthon's early *Loci*—indeed, the parallel is so close that one is tempted to see this as a borrowed point, rather than a reference to a broad field of scholastic arguments with which Calvin was directly acquainted.[73] On the other hand, this is also a place where Calvin's French versions of the *Institutes* point angrily at "les theologiens Sorboniques"—a specificity of attack that argues for Calvin's knowledge of one type of scholastic formulation, while at the same time allowing for his relative ignorance of the details of the medieval tradition. The virtual duplication of the polemic in Calvin's 1558 sermons on Galatians, now with his adversaries identified as "papists," serves to confirm the contemporary rather than the historical object of Calvin's attack.[74])

Against these scholastics, Calvin insists that only when the Spirit illuminates "the mind and the seat of feeling (*mentem et animo*)" are we "drawn beyond our understanding" to the truth of God in Christ.[75] Similar language appears in the commentary on Ephesians (1548), where Calvin speaks of a "twofold effect of the Spirit on faith" that is directly related to the "two principal parts of faith," inasmuch as the Spirit both "illuminates the mind" (*mentes illuminat*) and "confirms the seat of our feelings" (*an-*

imos confirmat).[76] In both of these definitions, the terms are *mens* and *animus*—and the pairing appears to indicate not so much "mind" and "soul" as the two faculties of soul (*anima*), the intellect or mind and the will, or, as the masculine, *animus*, often indicates, the seat of the feelings and affections.[77]

The whole human being receives the benefit of this illumination—for faith must be lodged both higher and deeper than understanding: "the Word of God is not received by faith if it flits about in the top of the brain, but when it takes root in the depth of the heart."[78] In 1559 Calvin would explicitly reference this distinction between the empty speculation of the "brain" (*cerebrum*) and the true "knowledge of God" rooted in the heart (*cor*) in what had then become a fairly disparate passage.[79] Although neither of these passages cites Romans directly, the passage from 1539 probably reflects the new emphases that we have associated both with Melanchthon's influence and with Calvin's exegesis of Paul's epistle.[80] In any case, Calvin does not intend to argue a purely cerebral meaning of faith when he identifies faith as *cognitio* (knowledge). Even so, Calvin speaks of a "sense of the divine" engraved not on the mind or brain but upon the heart. As Stuermann suggested, "heart" is frequently used by Calvin as a synonym for "soul" (i.e., *animus*), but particularly when juxtaposed with "mind" (*mens*), the term also refers to "the seat of the emotions" or "the whole range of human affections," or, indeed, the faculty that reaches out toward known objects, which is to say, the will.[81]

Calvin added considerable subtlety and clarification to his understanding of the biblical language of mind and heart and the faculty psychology as he moved forward with his exegetical project after 1539 and increasingly encountered the Hebrew text of the Old Testament and began to juxtapose his knowledge of Greek with Hebrew terminology. Calvin was aware of the breadth of meaning accorded by Scripture to the term "heart": in the Old Testament, he comments, "heart" often "includes mind," particularly when used in connection with "soul" (*anima*). This sensitivity to the difficulties of translation blurs the neat lines of the faculty psychology (and rightly so) in commentaries on the Old Testament, although his interest in the whole person remains quite clear, and the commentaries typically attempt to bridge the linguistic gap by drawing on the language of faculty psychology that was surely a commonplace to Calvin's audience.[82] The sermon on Deuteronomy 6:4–9 (dated July 20, 1555) illustrates how Calvin went about this task. There, Moses commands, "Tu aimeras le Seigneur ton Dieu de tout ton coeur, de tout ton ame, et de toute ta force." Calvin immediately interprets the text as indicating by "heart" (*coeur*), "soul" (*ame*), and "strength" (*force*) what would be called in his own time "soul" (*ame*), "spirit" (*esprit*), and "strength" (*force*). In other words, he expands the intellective function of "heart" by offering "soul" as its French equivalent and relegates the remaining spiritual functions to what the text calls "soul"—explaining this latter term as "spirit."[83] Christ, he continues, adds a single word to the series, not to alter the meaning but to explain more clearly what Moses intended by the words "soul" (*ame*) and "spirit" (*esprit*). Christ offers "soul" (*ame*), "heart" (*coeur*), and "mind" (*pensee*):

> We recognize from this that our souls possess primarily the power (*vertu*) of thinking, when we grasp objects for the sake of judgment or discernment: this is the primary faculty of the soul. That is, after having seen objects, we enter into deliberation and judgment, and we conclude either this or that. . . . And thus, the soul is not under-

stood only as life, but is an intermediary between our thoughts and our heart. For the heart indicates affections, desires, volitions: there is a difference between thinking of a thing and striving for it. . . .[84]

When, therefore, the Great Commandment enjoins us to love God with all our heart and soul, it intends that we understand the love of God to entail a devotion to God with all of our powers. The form of the Great Commandment given in Matthew, which adds to heart and soul the devotion of mind, points toward "the higher seat of reason from which all purposes and thoughts proceed."[85] In the Greek of the New Testament, therefore, heart and mind are frequently contrasted as representing different faculties of the soul. Indeed, Calvin assumes that the language of the New Testament corresponds with the terms given him by classical and scholastic faculty psychology and that the Old Testament, despite the differences between its language and that of the New Testament, offers much the same perspective:

> Scripture is accustomed to divide the soul of man, as to its faculties, into two parts, the mind and the heart (*mentem et cor*). The mind means the intelligence (*intelligentiam*), while the heart denotes all the affections or wills (*omnes affectus: aut voluntates*). These two terms, therefore, include the entire soul (*totam animam*).[86]

Significantly, the *Harmony of the Evangelists* dates from the same year as the *Sermons on Deuteronomy*, with chronological precedence probably belonging to the *Harmony*: that the one text reflects the other is not surprising. In 1559, Calvin drew on these exegetical conclusions of 1555 when he added a line of definition to the *Institutes* indicating that the faculties are located in the "mind and heart."[87] Strictly speaking, then, *mens* (or *cerebrum*) and *cor* indicate not only the faculties but also their place or seat in the human being, whereas intellect (*intellectus*) will (*voluntas*), and the affections (*affectiones*), indicate the faculties themselves in a more abstract sense—a feature of the usage that, in addition to the biblical source of the mind/heart (*mens/cor*) distinction, explains Calvin's tendency to use "mind" and "heart" as his primary terms of reference.

In the light of this explanation of biblical language, Calvin's linkage of mind and heart in faith appears to be a statement concerning the necessity of involving the whole person, or, more precisely, the entire spiritual side of the person, the soul in both its faculties, intellect and will, in faith. Were this not so, Calvin would not be able, under the terms of faculty psychology, to explain the positive impact of faith on the affections of the will, which is to say, upon love and hate, mercy and cruelty: without faithfulness to God, he writes, the heart "fluctuates amidst its own affections."[88] Even so, Calvin states that the gospel "is not indeed a doctrine of the tongue, but of life; nor is it, like other disciplines, apprehended by the memory and understanding alone, but it is received only when it is possessed by the *entire soul* and finds a seat and a refuge in the most profound affection of the heart."[89]

Indeed, Calvin's 1539 polemic against those "scholastics" who identify faith "with bare and simple assent arising out of knowledge" can only be interpreted as a polemic against an excessively intellectualistic view of faith, specifically against the reduction of faith to an assent to church doctrine: the "chief part of faith" (*praecipuam fidei partem*) is the "firm and steadfast constancy of heart" (*firmam illam stabilemque cordis constantiam*).[90] Far from departing from all scholastic definitions of faith, Calvin actually succeeds in reflecting the older tradition, while at the same time polemicizing against what he views as an abuse or distortion of doctrine. Many scholastics had, in fact, distinguished faith into knowledge (*notitia*), assent (*assensus*), and trust (*fiducia*). Calvin equally clearly follows the division of those aspects of faith into functions of intellect (*notitia* and *assensus*) and, given his frequent identification of the heart as the will, into a function of the will (*fiducia*). It is the intellect that knows and recognizes its knowledge to be true and assents to that truth; only when the heart—that is, the will and its affections—grasps that truth in trust can the truth be appropriated savingly by the individual.[91] Here, again, Calvin's polemic not only appears to be secondary or derivative; it also bears a distinct resemblance to Melanchthon's emphases on the heart and on *fiducia* in polemic against the scholastics.[92]

Calvin therefore balances the functions of intellect and will in his conception of faith, rather than argue either a purely intellectualist or a purely voluntarist definition: in other words, if faith is knowledge (*cognitio*), then this *cognitio* is not to be restrictively understood as a function of intellect. Faith is not "a naked or frigid apprehension of Christ, but a lively and effective sense of his power" that persuades the heart and is sealed on the heart.[93] Calvin has in fact borrowed the larger range of significance of the term *cognitio* that we have already noted in the medieval background.

When this pattern of definition is set into its soteriological context, a solution to the issue of priority of intellect or of will begins to emerge. In the order of temporal priority, the intellect must come first, insofar as the will must have a ready object for its act of trust. Nonetheless, temporal priority is not causal priority: the will is free to accept or to reject the knowledge presented by the intellect—not to the extent that will can eradicate the contents of intellect but rather to the extent that will need not appropriate in a personal and fiducial way the object of knowing. On the level of causal priority, Calvin clearly recognizes that knowledge and intellectual assent, apart from a "firm and steadfast constancy of heart"—indeed, apart from the will's fiducial apprehension of the truth presented by the intellect—do not constitute faith.[94] Since, moreover, *cognitio* indicates the spiritual apprehension of an object, there can be no severance of the will's apprehension of truth from the cognitive act: as already noted, the will is not unknowing. Calvin's conception of faith as *cognitio*, then, draws together intellect and will or, in the language of the scholastics, combines intellective knowledge (*cognitio intellectiva*) with affective knowledge (*cognitio affectiva*).

Intellectualism, Voluntarism, and Calvin's View of Faith

At this point, we have arrived at a view of faith surprisingly like that of the great medieval doctors, virtually none of whom actually fall under Calvin's critique of a purely intellectualistic definition of faith. For Aquinas, "faith is lodged in the intellect," but in such a way "as to receive its specification and motivation from the will."[95] Thus, not even for the philosophical intellectualist is faith purely a matter of assent to knowledge: faith is primarily and properly grounded in the intellect, but it remains also a voluntary act of love and trust in God; "to believe is an act of the intellect moved to yield its assent by the will."[96] According to Thomas, two spiritual dispositions conjoin in belief—faith, the habit of the intellect, and *caritas* or love, the habit of the will. The latter *habitus* is necessary to press the intellect, in and by the love of God, beyond mere assent or "unformed faith" to a faith informed by love.[97]

In the medieval tradition, given this effective conjunction of intellect and will in the act of faith, the question of the priority of one faculty over the other has to be determined not so much by the question of efficient as by the question of final causality. Thus, in the intellectualist perspective of Thomas, although intellect and will conjoin in faith, it is ultimately the intellect, made perfect in love, that rests upon God in the *visio Dei*.[98] In the voluntarist perspective of Scotus, however, even though the intellect remains the subject of faith, the choice of the will is nobler—inasmuch as final blessedness is attained not in intellectual vision but in an act of will that identifies the highest good (*summum bonum*) as the proper and ultimate object of will (*summum volendum*).[99] On this point, as in his discussion of the temporal problem of salvation, Calvin appears to lean toward the voluntarist model: for Calvin, it is the heart, not the mind, that is "the chief part of faith" and that is ultimately "established" in the "truth of God."[100] Calvin's eschatology is so pastoral and nonspeculative that it is impossible to determine whether this establishment of the heart (which is to say, the will) in God carries over as the primary characteristic of eternal blessedness. On the one hand, Calvin's discussion of the passage from faith to sight may indicate a rather intellectualistic approach to the vision of God.[101] On the other hand, however, Calvin calls God "the source of all good" and appears to identify God as the *summum bonum*, or at least union with God as our highest good, and to view love, the highest of the affections of the will, as "the principal part of true godliness," since it is the source of the highest and best worship of God.[102]

Calvin's antispeculative approach and his disdain for scholasticism, not to mention his lack of training in the intricacies of medieval thought,[103] held him back from discussing such issues as the intellectualist and voluntarist views of final blessedness. We cannot, therefore, make an absolute determination concerning the relationship of Calvin's views on intellect and will to the philosophical and speculative forms of intellectualism and voluntarism found in medieval thought—nor can we argue that this ultimate and rather speculative distinction would have been of any great concern to Calvin. Nonetheless, we can conclude that Calvin's theology falls, in its basic attitude toward the problems of human knowing and willing in their relation to the temporal working out of salvation, into a voluntarist rather than an intellectualist pattern. This conclusion is, moreover, supported by the practical, antispeculative character of Calvin's theology as a whole. The will, not the intellect, stands at the center of the soteriological problem: the sinner knows the good but does not will it. Even so, intellectual knowledge is not ultimately constitutive of the *cognitio* that is faith. For this "knowledge" to occur, the heart must apprehend what the intellect knows. Unlike Aquinas, Calvin does not lodge faith in the intellect and place only the capability of choice in the will. Faith, for Calvin, is a matter of intellect and will in conjunction—with the highest part, not merely the instrumental part, of faith belonging to the will.

It can also be noted that both Calvin's expansion of the definition of faith to include "heart" as well as "mind" and Calvin's polemic against various "scholastic" aberrations date from the 1539 stratum of the *Institutes* and from his meditation through Romans—with the result that the revised definition was integral to his theology from fairly early on and that, in addition, the basic polemic arose at a stage in his development at when

Calvin probably had little detailed knowledge of the scholastic tradition. If, however, our conjectures concerning the specificity of Calvin's most bitter antischolastic polemic are correct,[104] the identification of the object of this particular polemic as the faculty of the Sorbonne indicates that Calvin would probably not have muted the attack at a later stage of his development even if he had gained a broader knowledge of medieval teaching concerning faith.[105] In addition, we find that we are able to trace an increasing solidification of the relationship of Calvin's doctrine of faith to a biblically interpreted faculty psychology, rooted in his ongoing work of exegesis and reflected in additions to the doctrine made at various points in the editing process of the *Institutes*. On the specific point, moreover, of the right correlation of the biblical language of mind and heart with the language of the faculty psychology, the commentaries and sermons offer the clearer and fuller account of Calvin's thought—surely because this is a linguistic and exegetical point and not one of the *loci* that Calvin chose to abstract for specific discussion in the *Institutes*.

Against the tendency of some recent scholarship—particularly against the view advanced by Kendall—to identify Calvin's definition of faith as *cognitio* with a purely "intellectualist" position, we must view Calvin as holding to a nonspeculative, soteriological voluntarism that carries over into the language of faith. Nor is this simply a single point made by Calvin: it is the result of a meditation on the problem of the biblical language of mind and heart that took place across several decades. Calvin, it is true, does use terms like *cognitio* and occasionally *scientia* for faith, and he does call faith an *illuminatio*, but—in accord with the approach to Calvin evident in the work of Leith, Vos, and Armstrong—we find that these are balanced by an equally strong insistence on the assurance (*securitas*) that belongs to faith as faith addresses the human heart and passes beyond mere intellectual comprehension to grasp the whole person.[106] This voluntarism has certain affinities with a Scotist perspective but ought probably to be traced to Calvin's generally Augustinian view of the problem of sin and salvation, rather than to any intentional appropriation of Scotist theology. Kendall was correct in his argument that Calvin excluded any view of faith as a human act, insofar as Calvin refuses steadfastly to charaterize faith as a merit and consistently identifies it as a gift of God.[107] Nonetheless, Kendall either ignored or misunderstood the basic issue between intellectualism and voluntarism in the Western tradition, particularly as it treated the question of the relation of understanding and will to faith and salvation. As a consequence, Kendall also misses the central thrust of Calvin's argument by hypothesizing an almost exclusively intellectualist understanding of faith in Calvin's theology: faith is a gift that awakens all the powers of the soul, intellect and will, so that both are enlightened and moved, each in its own way, to grasp the gift of God in Christ.

These conclusions confirm the basic insights of Dee, Doumergue, and Lobstein concerning the "experimental and practical character" of Calvin's thought and indicate the need to modify somewhat the frequent claim that Calvin equates faith with knowledge and adopts an essentially cognitive approach to doctrine: Calvin's language of faith as *cognitio* tends to balance intellect and will, rather than to emphasize intellect alone, while Calvin's soteriological interest creates in the doctrine of faith itself an emphasis on the primacy of the will in the cognitive act. It is also clearly the case that, with Calvin, "voluntarism" in no way implies human autonomy, self-initiated preparation for grace, or synergism—nor, when the traditional problem of intellectualism and vol-untarism is rightly understood, ought one to expect any such implication. Finally, if this perspective on Calvin's concept of faith is accepted, then the attempt to create a contrast between Calvin's thought and the voluntaristic leanings of later Reformed theology must also be reassessed and, probably, set aside.[108]

The Study of Calvin

Contexts and Directions

Calvin's Theology in Its "Humanistic" and "Scholastic" Context

The burden of the preceding chapters has been the elucidation of the context of Calvin's theology for the sake of providing a basis for further discussion of his teaching. The effort has taken both negative and positive directions. Stated negatively, the burden of the work has been to set aside several of the dogmatic (or antidogmatic) grids that have been placed over Calvin's text as well as over his thought. Stated positively, it has been to set the elements of Calvin's theology into the context of the intellectual dialogues and debates within which he worked as correlated with a fairly close textual study of his thought.

Central both to the understanding of Calvin's intellectual context and to the argument of the book is the relationship of humanism and scholasticism in Calvin's world of thought. If the humanist and the scholastic elements in Calvin's theological method were to be weighed, the one against the other, the resulting formula would certainly lodge Calvin in a context that was primarily humanistic—at least insofar as its fundamental methodological concerns were drawn from humanistic training in logic and rhetoric. From a purely methodological perspective, the elements of scholastic disputation that flowed over into Calvin's writings had been filtered through the late medieval and Renaissance revision of the disciplines of logic and rhetoric and of their relation one to another. But even this conclusion concerning the historical process by which materials and methods were transmitted to exegetes and theologians in the sixteenth century indicates a high degree of continuity between scholastic and humanistic concerns.

Beyond this broad conclusion, the specific character of Calvin's own method, exegesis, and theology offers an instance in which usual generalizations concerning "scholasticism" and "humanism" are confounded by the particular. If we allow that humanism ought to be understood, as Kristeller indicated, primarily as a philological and linguistic method, an approach to the sources and the methods of argument, the term itself is inadequate to the task of explaining Calvin's work. Calvin provides, instead, a theological and exegetical example of the confluence of intellectual cultures that Schmitt outlined so convincingly with reference to Renaissance Aristotelianism: if it is possible to argue in the abstract for distinct humanistic and scholastic cultures, the concrete realm of individual human existence blurs the edges of these generalizations.[1] Calvin, like Melanchthon, stood within the humanistic culture but drew so heavily on the exegetical and theological tradition that scholastic patterns of thought and exposition inevitably were reflected in and modified by the humanistic models of philology and rhetoric that he emulated. And, just as Calvin rejected the excesses of medieval scholastic theology, so did he reject the teachings of humanists that went beyond philological method to the praise of ancient pagan virtues.[2]

A series of more specific reflections are therefore in order: first, it was characteristic of the Reformers to admire the older tradition, from Augustine to the close of the twelfth century. For instance, both Luther and Calvin spoke highly of the theology and piety of Bernard of Clairvaux. Early on, Luther could distinguish between the order, arrangement, and implication of Lombard's *Sentences* and the problematic speculation that had appeared in the tradition of commentary on Lombard.[3] Calvin's contemporary Andreas Hyperius of Marburg wrote positively of the early scholastics, up to and including Peter Lombard, as providing models for theological formulation—at the very same time that he recommended a humanist approach to the classical languages and a humanist understanding of the relationship of rhetoric and logic.[4] Another contemporary, Wolfgang Musculus, regularly cited Lombard's definitions, noted points made by Scotus and Occam, and used various distinctions, such as that between the *voluntas beneplaciti* and the *voluntas signi Dei*, the *opus alienum* and the *opus proprium Dei*,[5] and did so as an integral part of a theology based on exegesis of the biblical *fontes* in the original languages and on the extraction of *loci* from the sources. Students of the sixteenth-century materials must also recognize that Protestant attacks on "scholastics" may refer to perceived abuses in the theology of their Roman Catholic contemporaries more than to earlier forms of scholastic theology.

Calvin's own polemic against scholasticism reflected a moderate level of disagreement when the older scholasticism of Lombard was in view but a far more bitter antagonism when the contemporary scholasticism of the Sorbonne was under consideration—the latter representing to Calvin not only a problematic theology but also an entrenched opposition to reform. It is necessary, therefore, to add to the contemporary discussion of Calvin and scholasticism the Reformers' own distinction between the older forms of medieval scholasticism, the forms that developed in the thirteenth century, and the still later aspects of the scholastic heritage that remained current in the theological world of the sixteenth century.[6] So, too, did Calvin employ distinctions inherited from scholasticism, albeit without offering positive reference to individual works, such as found in Musculus's *Loci communes*. And Calvin, like many humanistically trained authors, referred to the academic style and context, without pejorative implication, as "scholastic."

Second, given that the scholastic tradition both in general and in the persons of its major teachers—Alexander of Hales, Bonaventure, Aquinas, Duns Scotus—assumed that the primary and basic task of the theologian was the exposition of the *sacra pagina* and of the theological topics elicited from it, the discussion of Calvin and scholasticism must look to the medieval exegetical tradition as well, to the *Glossa ordinaria,* and to the work of eminent individual exegetes still read in the sixteenth century, including Thomas Aquinas, Hugh of St. Cher, Nicholas of Lyra, and Denis the Carthusian.[7] This examination of the work of medieval exegetes reveals quite clearly that the textual, literal, and grammatical emphasis of the Reformers, together with specific exegetical results of that emphasis, stood in clear continuity with the literal trajectory of medieval scholastic exegesis. Indeed, as Mülhaupt and Parker have noted, Calvin's approach to sermons and lectures—the verse-by-verse or pericope-by-pericope exposition of the text—has roots not so much in medieval preaching as in the medieval scholastic practice of biblical exposition.[8] Calvin and his contemporaries evidence continuity of interpretation not only in style but also in specific interpretive result and even in their identification of pericopes—and indeed, Calvin was wont to call the task of expository preaching in the congregation "the school of God," where Christians could learn the A, B, Cs of faith and practice.[9]

Third, there remains in the theology of the Reformers, despite their antagonism to the development of a more speculative theological system based on the *loci* extracted from Scripture and the use of philosophical argumentation, a reliance on the thought forms and the technical distinctions found in this later scholastic theology and, indeed, in its use of philosophy. In the case of Calvin's theology, there are, as many scholars now recognize (and however their origin is explained), numerous positive reflections of the theological and epistemological concerns of late medieval Scotism and Augustinianism. Calvin also evidences certain major gaps in his knowledge of scholasticism, as indicated by the occasional misplaced criticism—thereby demonstrating, however inadvertently, that in his appropriation, critique, and adaptation of scholastic ideas he was not always the most careful or the most learned student of the older theology. A similar point must be made concerning Calvin's approach to Aristotelian patterns of thought: whereas the larger portion of his references to Aristotle, particularly in the *Institutes,* is highly negative in implication, his actual use of Aristotelian categories offers a very different picture. Whether one examines Calvin's use of fourfold causality or his conception of angelic movers, the positive impact of medieval Aristotelianism is undeniable.

Fourth, some contrast must be made between the historical understanding of "scholasticism" as the method of theology used during the high Middle Ages and the late sixteenth and seventeenth centuries (an understanding of the term present in the historical sources themselves, including those of the Protestant orthodox era) and the polemical use of the terms "scholastic" and "scholasticism" by the Reformers and, indeed, by Protestant scholastic theologians of the seventeenth century. The polemical usage denounces not the *method* but, instead, the theological and philosophical *content* of the writings of the scholastic era. In other words, Calvin seldom, if ever, inveighs against the use of distinctions in theological argumentation. He does, in fact, use quite a few traditional scholastic distinctions, either without comment or with explicit agreement. And, not infrequently, he begins a discussion or section of a discussion in the

Institutes with explicit reference to a "distinction" necessary for the proper understanding of a subject. The polemic is nearly invariably directed against the use of particular distinctions and their implication in theology. Similarly, Calvin does not object to the centerpiece of scholastic education, the *disputatio*. Indeed, he describes the centerpiece of his own theological project, the *Institutes*, as a series of theological *loci* and *disputationes dogmaticae*.[10]

Yet, it is here that Calvin's humanism also presents itself not as a counter to his scholasticism but rather as its interpreter and mediator: his *loci* and *disputationes* have been adjusted to and modified by the humanist development of rhetoric. Indeed, his entire approach to the *loci* evidences not only the impact of Agricolan logic but, more concrete and more significant, the impact of a continuing dialogue with Melanchthon. It is very important to the understanding of Calvin's work to recognize these sources: Calvin is not simply following ancient rhetorical norms like Cicero and Quintillian; he is involved in adaptations and interpretations of classical rhetoric characteristic of the Northern Renaissance.[11] Specifically, Calvin's Agricolan and Melanchthonian understanding of rhetorical categories like *amplificatio* or *copia* more as supports for the elaboration of theological *loci* than as forms for the ornamentation of a discourse points him away from the Erasmian "*theologia rhetorica*" and toward the development of a didactic theology suited to the Protestant schools.

The *Institutes* and Calvin's "Systematic" Task

Examination of Calvin's own statements concerning the task undertaken in the *Institutes* leads ineluctably to the conclusion that the older scholarship was largely correct in its identification of the work as a theological system. But the examination also presses us to qualify the point: the *Institutes* is a sixteenth-century form of theological system that presents *loci communes* or "commonplaces" and *disputationes* in a coherent order. This description of the *Institutes* as a set of commonplaces and disputations follows both from Calvin's statements in his preface and from numerous statements in the text of the *Institutes* itself in which Calvin continues to identify his own work as disputation and discussion of *loci*. It is also crucial to the right understanding of Calvin's larger theological task to see the relationship between the changes he made to the preface of the *Institutes* in 1539 and the comments that he made concerning his exegetical style in the preface to his Romans commentary: in the preface Calvin refers to his work as a commentator and states that he will not place either *loci* or lengthy *disputationes* in the commentaries but will gather them into the *Institutes*, thereby freeing his style in the commentaries to be brief and direct. And, at the same time that he presented this coordinated description of his exegetical and dogmatic output, he also edited the title of the *Institutes*, noting its passage from its early catechetical form, a *summa pietatis*, to its later more systematic form, in effect, a *loci communes*. Unfortunately, the three modern English translations—Allen, Beveridge, and Battles—obscure Calvin's use of these technical terms and thereby obscure also the character of his theology and the nature of his theological task.

Dillenberger was, of course, quite correct in arguing that the *Institutes* was not a system in the modern sense of the term—although his simile of the hub with spokes and no rim falls considerably short of the mark.[12] Bauke's phrase "combination of opposites" (*complexio oppositorum*) is perhaps less literary, but it is surely more accurate.[13] Dillenberger's simile certainly ought not to be understood as an argument for a dogmatic center in Calvin's theology—for the *Institutes* is clearly not a theological system comparable to Schleiermacher's *The Christian Faith* or Tillich's *Systematic Theology*, inasmuch as it does not move deductively from premises to their logical conclusions or inductively from evidences to general principles and does not have a "central dogma." Calvin followed either a catechetical pattern (1536) or a fourfold credal pattern (1559),[14] in the latter case respecting as well Melanchthon's *series . . . dogmatum ab ipso ordine historiae* from creation to the judgment and in both cases following *linear* patterns of argument.[15] Certainly, the *Institutes* is not a theological system in the modern sense— and it would be quite anachronistic to make such a claim. Once this is recognized, however, it becomes important to acknowledge precisely what kind of theological system the *Institutes* is—and particularly important to avoid the confusion that can result from the simple claim that it is not a theological system at all.

The term "theological system" or "system of theology" was not, of course, available to Calvin or to any of his contemporaries. One of the earliest instances of the term, perhaps its first use, is Bartholomaus Keckermann's *Systema sacrosanctae theologiae*, published in 1602 and reissued on several occasions in the early seventeenth century.[16] Inasmuch as Keckermann followed an inductive or analytical order in his theology, there can be no implication in his use of the term *systema* of a deductive or synthetic model. The term, arguably, correlates with other usages of the seventeenth century— notably body (*corpus*), marrow (*medulla*), and, in some cases, marrow of the marrow (*medulla medullae*)[17]—that connote larger or smaller gatherings of material characterized by a broad thematic, indeed, "organic" completeness. *Corpus* and *systema* were used synonymously with the implication of a full "gathering" or *collegium* of topics.[18] (The term *corpus* or "body" had, of course, a long history of use with this connotation.[19]) Both terms point specifically to the complete or relatively complete presentation of materials and therefore have a connotation similar to that of the alternative usages, *Loci communes* and *Collegium* or *Sylloge disputationibus*.[20] *Medulla* ("marrow") indicates a central core, potentially topically complete but pared down to the essence of the materials—similar to the time-honored term *Compendium*, often indicating a still smaller and more essential gathering of arguments.[21] In these contexts, the term *loci* referred specifically to the theological "topics" usually drawn from the text of Scripture in the process of exegesis, whereas the term *disputatio* typically indicated a context of classroom discussion and debate.[22]

It can, moreover, be easily shown that none of the theological systems written between 1150 and 1700—whether entitled *Systema, Loci communes, Summa, Corpus, Medulla*, or *Compendium*—fall into a category of system patterned like Schleiermacher's or Tillich's systems.[23] The order of topics in these older theological "systems" follows a credal or catechetical model or proceeds in a more or less historical, soteriological, and biblical series from God and creation to the church and the last things—approaches similar to those adopted by the Reformers. Theological topics result not from a process of logical argument but from a fairly traditional extraction of theological *loci* from Scripture. The topics and their arrangement, after all, had changed but little for centuries: there remains in all of these works evidence not only of a basic credal pattern but also of some of the more elaborate developments of that pattern found in such later patristic doctrinal works as Augustine's *Enchiridion* and, especially, John of Damascus's *De fide orthodoxa*—or, in the Middle Ages, Lombard's *Sententiarum libri quatuor.*[24]

In all of these logical and theological developments there are, certainly, discontinuities as well as continuities. Calvin and his contemporaries rejected many definitions and distinctions from medieval theology even as they appropriated and adapted numerous others. Their use of the *locus* or *topos* had medieval roots, but it also reflected the Renaissance modification of dialectic and rhetoric. By the same token, the Renaissance and Reformation use of topical logic and the Reformers' adaptation of the model to theological argumentation forever changed the shape of theology; but it did so subtly, with the result that the techniques of the Renaissance commonplace method—further developed, refined, and adapted by later generations of Protestant theologians—became one of the staples of post-Reformation scholasticism and thus another example of the continuities and discontinuities to be examined in the development of Protestant thought.[25] Characterizations of Calvin's theology as purely "humanistic" and therefore as in fairly radical contrast with both the theology of the later Middle Ages and the theology of Protestant orthodoxy fail to do justice not only to the diverse sources— patristic, medieval, renaissance—of Calvin's thought; they also fail to do justice to the nature of the humanistic influences themselves.[26]

When we come, therefore, to Bouwsma's remarks that Calvin "despised what passed for systematic theology in his own time" and that "there were no 'systematic' thinkers of any significance in the sixteenth century," we encounter a major historical and theological gaffe: certainly there was a discipline that not only "passed for" systematic theology in the sixteenth century but that also was, quite clearly, the sixteenth-century version of what began to be called a "system" of doctrine or theology in the seventeenth century. It was the discipline that gathered together theological topics or *loci* that arose in the process of one's exegetical, dogmatic, and polemical labors either into a set of "universal topics" (*loci communes*) or into a series of academic exercises or or debates (*disputationes*). Representatives of this discipline in the sixteenth century—as testified by the titles of their more systematic theological works—included Philip Melanchthon, Wolfgang Musculus, Andreas Hyperius, Martin Chemnitz, and (through the efforts of Robert Masson) Peter Martyr Vermigli,[27] none of whom ought to be written off as insignificant. Nor did Calvin disdain their work. Indeed, he penned a laudatory preface, including a few mild theological disclaimers, to the 1546 French translation of Melanchthon's *Loci*.[28]

What is more, the question of "the right order of teaching" was one that Calvin shared with other gatherers of *loci communes*. Melanchthon's prefaces raise this question and answer it with the suggestion of a historical series of doctrines,[29] while Hyperius's *Methodus theologiae* (1568) devoted considerable space to the issue of order and arrangement in dogmatic theology. As we have seen, Calvin probably conceived his *Institutes* as a series of *loci communes* and *disputationes*: he also insisted on seeking out the "*ordo recte docendi*" for their arrangement.[30] In this, Calvin was at one with his contemporaries both in their view of what constituted dogmatic or systematic theology and in their sense of its relation to the work of exegesis.

If Calvin was not trained as a theologian, he certainly became one in the eyes of his contemporaries—and, given the parallel between the systematic or dogmatic task envisioned by his contemporaries and Calvin's work of preaching, lecturing, refining commentaries, and extracting or abstracting theological *loci* and *disputationes* for inclusion in the *Institutes*, he certainly functioned as a theologian—in precisely the sense that Melanchthon, Bullinger, Musculus, and Vermigli did. Given that the *Institutes* was crafted intentionally as a set of theological *loci* and *disputationes*, Calvin surely did write a "formal theology." Far from despising "what passed for systematic theology in his own time," he both aspired to and succeeded in "the construction of a system." Even so, it is less than useful to argue that Calvin's *Institutes* was not intended "to meet the demands of a rationally acceptable and defensible system but to assist the faithful in understanding God's revelation."[31] After all, the *disputationes* included in the *Institutes* imply the defensible character of Calvin's theology and the concerted use of rhetoric and logic in its defense. *Loci communes* and *disputationes* do assist the faithful—and there is a profound strain of piety in the *Institutes*, often precisely in the context of disputation.

There is, on this count, a significant parallel to be noted between the rise of Protestant dogmatics in the sixteenth century and the rise of a more systematized approach to theology in the twelfth century: there is a significant parallel, in other words, between Calvin's *Institutes* and Lombard's *Sententiae*.[32] The development of books of "sentences" by Peter Lombard and his contemporaries was grounded in part on the problem of teaching theology in the basic course on Scripture. At many points in the course of study, as evidenced by the lengthier *scholia* in the *Glossa ordinaria*, doctrinal themes arose out of exegesis, but, given the association of numerous texts with particular doctrines, each major doctrinal topic would need to be discussed many times during the survey of Scripture. Lombard and his contemporaries were pressed to distinguish between the exegetical study of the *sacra pagina* and the examination of the topics of *sacra doctrina* and to draw together the contents of related *scholia* into doctrinal *loci*.[33] In other words, the rise of systematic theology in the Middle Ages, as evidenced preeminently in Lombard's *Sententia*, was the result of the extraction of doctrinal *loci* from the commentary and of the organization of these *loci* into a coherent sequence. On the one hand, the *Gloss* and the basic course on Scripture would not be burdened with massive doctrinal *loci* and *disputationes*, while, on the other, the many topics developed out of exegesis, its interaction with the tradition, and the resulting queries (e.g., seeming contradictions between authorities, the meaning of equivocally used terms) were coordinated into a coherently ordered body of doctrine. The motivation for the medieval theological system was, accordingly, almost identical to Calvin's stated motive in constructing the *Institutes* and to the similar motives behind the *Loci communes* of Melanchthon, Musculus, Hyperius, and Vermigli.

In sum: the *Institutes* was not a theological system in the sense of Schleiermacher's *The Christian Faith* or Tillich's *Systematic Theology*, but it was surely a theological system in the sense not only of the many *loci communes theologici* of the sixteenth century but also in the sense, nearly the precise sense, of Peter Lombard's *Sententiae in IV libris*. Given, moreover, Calvin's use of the well-defined forms of the *locus* and *disputatio* and his emphasis on an internal logic or method employing the enthymene and the scholastic technique of finding the truth between excess and defect, his was truly a "formal theology" for the sixteenth century.

This conclusion in no way diminishes the humanistic training and emphases present in Calvin's work—but it does undercut any reading of Calvin's humanistic training as productive of an antisystematic or antidogmatic attitude on his part, just as it undercuts rigid separation of "scholastic" and "humanist" forms of thought. Ineed, it was Calvin's humanist training in rhetoric that he brought to bear on the nominally scholastic task of constructing disputations. Moreover, taken together with the understanding of most of the systematic theology of the sixteenth and seventeenth centuries as in large part *loci communes* related to the work of exegesis, this conclusion undercuts the claim that Calvin was a "biblical" and not a "systematic" theologian. The complexity of the problem is illustrated also by the continuance of the nominally "humanistic" place-logic of Agricola as the standard form of Protestant "scholastic" theological argument, the *Loci communes*. The real anachronism here is to misunderstand the character of "systematic theology" in the sixteenth century, to create an exaggerated distinction between the methods of humanism and those of the earlier theological tradition,[34] and to ignore the eighteenth-century origins of "biblical theology" as a discipline distinct from systematic theology.[35]

Calvin against the "Accommodators": Some Theological Implications

Each of the chapters in this volume has pointed, in one way or another, toward the historical context of Calvin's theology as the foundation for any definitive analysis of that theology itself. One might assume that such a premise is self-evident. Yet the premise has been ignored by numerous essays on Calvin's thought, many of them quite recent. At the most general level of response to such misidentifications of context, there is simply the complexity and specificity of Calvin's own theological program—which stands in the way of the various accommodations of Calvin's work to modern theological agendas. This general statement of principle can be elaborated under several specific points.

First, it is simply not helpful to declare that Calvin's *Institutes* is not a theological system, that it is a "pastoral" rather than a "dogmatic theology," that it is a "theology of piety" or a "theology of rhetoric." Calvin's theology was certainly pastoral, even in many places in the *Institutes;* it certainly contains elements of piety throughout; and it virtually nowhere loses sight of the rules of classical rhetoric—but it also has profound dogmatic concerns throughout, even as it has elements of rather pointed polemic that do not easily speak to us with pious voice. To call Calvin a "theologian of piety" or a "theologian of rhetoric" is as vacuous as to call him a "theologian of polemic." The modern notion of "genitive theologies"—theologies of this, theologies of that—is a twentieth-century imposition on the sixteenth-century mind, as is the radical dichotomization of pastoral or biblical and dogmatic or polemical forms of theology. For Calvin, certainly, there was a clear distinction of literary genre among *institutio, commentarius, praelectio, tractatus,* and *sermo*—distinctions that often account for both stylistic and substantive differences among his works. His *Institutio* was surely intended as a formal instruction in Christian religion, containing *loci communes* and *disputationes,* arranged in a suitable order of teaching—with the result that it was dogmatic, polemical, and pastoral as required by each issue addressed.

Second, investigation of the interrelationship of the various literary forms used by Calvin in the accomplishment of his larger theological task offers no clear sense of the priority of one form over another. In other words, the theological arguments found in the *Institutes* ought no more to be viewed as the primary index to Calvin's thought than the arguments found in his commentaries, sermons, or treatises. Specifically, when there are differences in content between a sermon or commentary and a portion of the *Institutes*, the reader ought not to conclude that one content is more representative of Calvin's thought than another. At times, the differences may indicate a development in Calvin's thought—but the possibility of development must be carefully assessed in the light of differences in genre between the documents. It is clear that Calvin moves in one direction in the *Institutes*, in another in a commentary, and in still another in a sermon, primarily because particular forms of discourse offer places to locate particular kinds of subject matter or particular forms of argument. One cannot, in other words, reject or disparage the significance of a position taken in a commentary or sermon (such as Calvin's exegetical and homiletical interest in the conditional aspects of divine covenants) simply because that view is not treated in the *Institutes*. To know the whole Calvin one must read the whole Calvin, and then some!

Some details of the relationship among the sermons, commentaries, and the *Institutes* can also be specified. Although there is a relationship between sermons and commentaries and there are clear instances in which a point that Calvin raised in one of these forms carried over into the other, it is also the case that development is seldom easily identified. The form of the sermon led Calvin to be more expansive than he felt was suitable to the commentary. Sermons seek more widely and more copiously after collateral texts for illustration of argument, and sermons also present theological arguments more broadly, with greater interest in the major themes of Christian doctrine. Calvin's Old Testament sermons often belie the christological restraint of the Old Testament commentaries—and they abundantly refute the Lutheran accusation that Calvin was an exegetical "Judaizer." This broader use of texts and theological themes and this less-restrained christological reading of the Old Testament appears in sermons delivered both before and after Calvin's commentary on the same text.

As for the relationship between the expository works and the *Institutes*, it appears that Calvin consistently held the *Insitutes* in mind just as much as he did his exegesis. On the one hand, the later commentaries often refer the reader to a point already made in the *Institutes*, while, on the other, the *Institutes* was fairly consistently expanded in the light of Calvin's exegetical and expository work. These expansions, moreover, fall into two basic categories: first, there is evidence in the text of the *Institutes* that Calvin collated texts thematically from throughout a biblical book as he wrote his commentaries and then, at the point of editing the text of the *Institutes*, added blocks of text, in effect *loci* or parts of *loci*, based on these collations. His method, after all, discouraged him from obtruding these *loci* upon his commentaries. Next, Calvin also added or substantively augmented comments in the *Institutes* on individual texts of the Bible—often after having commented on or preached through a book of the Bible. In this latter category of addition, the more expansive theological treatment often appears in the running commentary on the passage, rather than in the *Institutes*. It is also worth reminding ourselves that Calvin's commitment to *brevitas* lessened somewhat in the later commentaries, where the comment on units of text can become very elaborate indeed, as illustrated by his exposition of the law in his *Harmony on the Last Four Books of Moses*.

Third, the problem of the relationship between Calvin and "covenant theology" can now be seen to be (as several scholars have already indicated on other grounds) a problem of twentieth-century approaches to theology, rather than a problem of theological definition lodged in Calvin's text. It is, to say the least, quite curious that McNeill went so far as to identify *Institutes* II.x as the place where Calvin "unfolds the doctrine of the covenant" and that Baker concludes, from his reading of this discussion of "covenant," that "Calvin's covenant theology . . . was really a theology of testament" lacking Bullinger's clarity of distinction between the terms "covenant" and "testament."[36] Calvin, after all, identified the chapter as a discussion not of covenant but of the "similarity between the Old and New Testaments," only one aspect of which is the continuity of the covenant of grace or adoption. Calvin did not include a covenant *locus* in the *Institutes*—and, as we have already noted, the larger portion of his views on covenant, *pace* McNeill and Baker, must be sought elsewhere. When the commentaries and sermons are examined, textual ground for the neat twentieth-century bifurcation between unilateral and bilateral covenant theories governed by different views of predestination simply disappears.

Fourth, the problem of the placement of Calvin's doctrine of predestination in the *Institutes*, noted frequently in twentieth-century discussions of "Calvin and Calvinism," now appears in an entirely different light. It is simply not the case, as is often claimed, that in 1559 Calvin definitively "moved" the discussion of predestination "out of the doctrine of God" and into a soteriological location in order to make a particular theological point concerning the meaning of the doctrine. Calvin did not move the doctrine of predestination at all in 1559: he left it in approximately the same place that he had located it in 1539. What is more, the 1539 location probably represented Calvin's identification of Melanchthon's reading of Romans as the basis for a suitable order of teaching in his reorganized *Institutes*. Calvin's placement of the doctrine of predestination, both in 1539 and in 1559, had little or nothing to do with a redefinition of the doctrine and a great deal to do with the establishment of a proper order of teaching. Moreover, as we have noted, Beza actually echoed Calvin when he explained the difference between his diagram of the order of causes of election and reprobation and the proper method of teaching the doctrine: Beza was quite ready, in his *Tabula praedestinationis*, to offer a diagram of the decree and its execution, beginning with the first cause and extending through all intermediate causality to the final cause of election and reprobation—but he was equally ready, in his discussion of the very same *Tabula*, to advise that the doctrine be taught following the Pauline order, beginning with sin and ascending toward the decree by means of the revealed causes of salvation. In neither case does the sixteenth-century discussion of the placement of the doctrine in the order of teaching imply a redefinition of the doctrine.

Calvin and the "Problem" of Protestant Scholasticism

These last considerations bring us to yet another aspect of the problem of Calvin's theological context, namely the increasingly regular recourse to the theological and philosophical usages of the medieval and Renaissance scholastic tradition associated with the rise of scholastic method and the increasingly institutionalized (indeed, "catholic") forms in the thought and work of Reformation and post-Reformation Protestantism.[37] Particularly given the development of the sixteenth-century apparatus of Calvin's *Institutes*, we not only must come to respect the generation following Calvin for its sophisticated reading of the *Institutes* and of Calvin's exegetical corpus; we may also understand the "scholasticism" of this early orthodox era as an extended context for the interpretation of the conflict and confluence of scholastic and humanisic themes in Calvin's own work. Calvin's work provides us with an avenue of apporach to the later materials, a way of identifying both continuity and change, just as the later materials offer a view of one setting—clearly different from the modern setting—in which Calvin's thought has been interpretively reflected.

As in the discussion of the medieval scholastic background, some distinction must be made here as well between scholastic method and the theology that it served: traditional theological issues could be and were dealt with by the Protestant scholastics in works, notably their commentaries, that did not employ a scholastic method. And their use of the method itself, as evidenced in their recourse to disputation and careful distinctions, did not determine either how the distinctions were used or a particular theological outcome of the disputation. The question of Protestant scholasticism (which is, of course, a vast question in its own right[38]) contributes to an understanding of the relationship between Calvin and scholasticism in several ways. In the first place, Calvin's own theology, including its scholastic elements, belongs to an era of transition between the more fluid theological and exegetical forms of the early Reformation and the more systematized and established patterns of the later sixteenth century. As Wendel remarked, Calvin's clarity of definition "was indubitably one of the causes of the very rapid rise of a Calvinist orthodoxy, strictly adherent to the formulas of the *Institutes*, which even the later controversies have only with difficulty managed to modify."[39]

In the second place, Calvin (as a result) was not only one of the significant mediators of the theology of the Reformation to later Protestantism; he was also one of the significant mediators of aspects of later scholasticism, together with a frequent and stringent critique of its teachings.[40] In assessing the transition between the time of Calvin and his contemporaries and the era of Protestant orthodoxy, the ways in which Calvin's thought (and the thought of his contemporaries) was mediated must be examined—particularly when the *Institutes* is seen to be only one of the several forms through which Calvin's theology became known. Of paramount importance to our understanding of the developing Reformed tradition, therefore, is the ongoing exegetical and homiletical task. There are profound continuities in the Protestant expository and interpretive tradition. Thus, the ways in which Calvin dealt with elements of later medieval thought and method and, in general, received and modified the earlier theological tradition (particularly when this aspect of his work is understood in the context of the similar efforts of contemporaries like Musculus, Vermigli, Bullinger, and Hyperius) can and must be measured at least to some degree against later Protestant usage. There is, in other words, a transmission of both scholastic and humanistic methods from the later medieval period, through the Reformers, to their successors.[41]

Finally, as indicated in the apparatus that they supplied for the *Institutes*, Calvin's orthodox or scholastic successors not only paid considerable attention to his work but also explicated it with considerable insight and finesse. On the one hand, the apparatus offers a refined understanding of the patterns of argument found in the various *loci* and *disputationes* that Calvin placed in the *Institutes*. And, on the other hand, the apparatus clearly anticipated the modern analyses of the structure and organization of the *Institutes* by Parker and Dowey—to the point that Dowey's claim that later Reformed theologians failed to see the *duplex cognitio* and the cognitive ordering of topics must be laid at the feet of the editors of the *Corpus Reformatorum*, rather than at the door of the Reformed orthodox.

Conclusion: Premises for the Examination of Calvin's Theology

We conclude with some words of admonition—premises, one might say, for the examination of Calvin's theology:

1. Although "scholasticism" and "humanism" can and ought to be defined as distinct methods that have bearing on our understanding of the debates within and the development of Protestant thought in the sixteenth century, these terms ought not to be used as hermetically sealed containers into which historians may place sixteenth-century people. Inasmuch as most of the Reformers were both recipients of the patristic and medieval theological tradition and exponents of the philological method associated with humanism, crucial elements of both approaches will be found in their work. It is also the case that classical logical and rhetorical patterns were shared by the scholastic and humanistic methods and that the humanistic return to classical sources in the sixteenth century brought about alterations in the scholastic method itself. Such humanistic recasting of scholastic forms is intrinsic to Calvin's theological method, as it is to the work of his successors.

2. Even so, the specifics of Calvin's thought ought to be read not against a generalized background of the "Reformation" and "Renaissance movements" or of the "Middle Ages" but rather against a background of specific ideas, documents, and individuals that impinged on or influenced Calvin's thought. On the one hand, generalized conceptions of the Middle Ages, Renaissance, and Reformation fail to do justice to the complexity of history—and, on the other hand, they fail to illuminate the very specific trajectories of thought that bear directly on the specifics of Calvin's own work.

3. Calvin's humanistic foundations and method must be examined with specific reference to the humanism of his teachers and partners in theological conversation. For example, it is of little use to compare Calvin's rhetoric to Cicero's without also examining in some detail the ways in which classical rhetorical forms were understood in Calvin's own time and the context in or through which he appropriated those forms. Calvin's appropriation of humanist method, like his appropriation of scholastic categories, was not uncritical. Thus, Calvin was adamantly opposed to the reverence for ancient paganism that he observed in a Guillaume Budé or a Johannes Sturm, more amenable to what has been called the "biblical humanism" of the mature Erasmus, and still more attached to the precise use of the *locus*, of *amplificatio* for the purpose of edification, and of the Pauline center of biblical interpretation characteristic of the method of Melanchthonian humanism. Simply to identify Calvin as a humanist rhetor is to obfuscate his relationship to the philological methods of humanism and to the humanist evaluation of ancient sources.

4. Calvin's theology cannot simply be read out of the *Institutes*. Nor, indeed, can it be read out of a harmonization of texts found in Calvin's *Institutes*, commentaries, treatises, and sermons. Calvin himself indicated that his thought was rooted in two parallel exercises—in the ongoing work of preaching, lecturing, and commenting through the text of Scripture and in the related work of developing disputations and *loci* based on exegetical insight and presented to particular contexts of positive thought and debate. The *Institutes* cannot be rightly understood apart from Calvin's exegetical and expository efforts, nor can his exegetical and expository efforts be divorced from his work of compiling the *Institutes*.

5. By extension, the *Institutes* is an incomplete source for the analysis of any particular doctrine taught by Calvin—even those doctrines that Calvin considered as specific *topoi* or *loci* in theology. His strict distinction of literary genre presses his readers to recognize that certain aspects of a given doctrinal issue are treated in one place, while other aspects of the issue are treated elsewhere. Broad, topical exposition that collates texts from throughout Scripture and deals with points of dispute occurs in the *Institutes*; careful textual study that avoids disputation and broad topical development in order to follow the line and logic of a text occurs in the commentaries and lectures; and more fully developed oratory that expands a particular text topically in the interest both of edification and of piety occurs in the sermons. When, moreover, a given doctrinal issue was not understood by Calvin as a specific *locus* in theology—for example, such issues as the positive extent of natural theology in a Christian context or the covenant of grace—the *Institutes* provide either an untrustworthy measure or no measure at all of Calvin's thought on that issue.

6. With specific reference to the *Institutes*, this understanding of Calvin's pattern of working points toward the central importance of the 1539 edition and the order of argument established therein. Calvin departed from the 1536 framework in barely three years—at which point he indicated in his revised title that the 1539 work was, finally, a genuine *institutio*. The 1539 order, in its two major expansions of 1543 and 1550, was the order of the *Institutes* that served him for twenty years, during his most productive period. It was also the primary form by which his theology was known and assessed by his contemporaries, and it was the place where Calvin most clearly and precisely identified the theological *loci* that he believed ought to be elicited from Scripture and gathered together into a "right order of teaching." If the order changed somewhat in 1559, the actual identification of topics or *loci* altered but little, and, in fact, much of the 1539 Pauline *ordo* remained in the 1559 edition. The 1539 *Institutes*, therefore, must become a focus for the investigation of Calvin's thought.

7. Related to this recognition of the 1539 *Institutes* as the principal text of that work to be examined for a sense of Calvin's impact on his own time is the necessity to recognize the years 1537 through 1541 as the crucial moment of development in Calvin's theological career. The 1536 *Institutes* was a considerable accomplishment for the young Calvin, particularly considering the elementary state of his theological learning at the time of its composition. But the crucial development, leading to the crystallization of his sense of the theological task as evidenced in the methodological balance achieved between the *Institutes* and the commentaries, began in his quest for a more

comprehensive and cohesive order of topics in the 1537/8 catechism and reached fruition in the larger exegetical and instructional model described in the prefaces of 1539 and 1540. One of the keys to this development is surely his reading of Melanchthon's 1535/6 *Loci communes* at the point of preparing the catechisms of 1537/8 and his subsequent clarification of the task of *institutio* as consisting in the orderly presentation of *loci* and *disputationes* rather than as basic catechetical instruction. Calvin's clarification of his theological task between 1537 and 1541 led, in summary, to the recasting of the *Institutes*, the publication of the Romans commentary, and, indeed, to his attendance at the Frankfurt colloquy of 1539 with the express intention of meeting Melanchthon, with whom he had corresponded for approximately a year.

8. So, too, must the complex of Calvin's theological program—the *Institutes*, commentaries, sermons, lectures, and treatises—be set into the context of the exegetical and theological tradition on which he consistently drew and the contemporary intellectual movement of which he was a part. Calvin's originality (or lack of originality) can be discerned only through examination of the work of his predecessors and contemporaries, not only those whose works he cites but particularly those whose works he probably examined and did not cite but with whom he surely engaged in a fairly consistent and continuous dialogue. Nicholas of Lyra and Philip Melanchthon are but two of the most significant examples.

9. Calvin's theology must be understood not as a finished product but as a theology in development—specifically, a theology that was learned in the course of a life of exegetical, homiletical, and ecclesial labor in close dialogue, positive and negative, with a definable group of partners in conversation. There must, in other words, be a comparative element in any discussion of Calvin's thought, but it must not be a broad and generalized comparison—much less an eclectic one!—set by the agenda of the modern author. Projects that compare Calvin and Barth or of Calvin and Schleiermacher will not enlighten us particularly about Calvin—nor probably about Barth or Schleiermacher, for that matter. Neither will a broad comparison of Calvin and Luther or of Calvin and Bullinger be particularly helpful to our understanding. The comparison must examine actual partners in the ongoing sixteenth-century theological conversation and be sensitive to the fact that ideas held in common may not be evidence of direct conversation but may instead indicate a shared acceptance of the tradition or, indeed, of the common use of an esteemed older source.

10. As a corollary to our recognition of Calvin's place in a sixteenth-century theological conversation, we must refrain from a tendency to absolutize the documents unless they explicitly require us to do so: specifically, Calvin's own explicit identification of sources or of polemical opponents provides only a partial access to his theological conversation. Even when his doctrinal statements appear at their most objective and apodictic they remain rooted in his time, determined by the materials he read, the individuals with whom he conversed and debated, and the broader work in which he was engaged.

11. We can not have reliably clear or direct access to Calvin's thought either through the standard modern translations or through the modern critical editions on which they are based. The approach of the "critical edition" often fails to present Calvin's thought as he intended to present it: when the critical edition does offer *what* Calvin said, it almost invariably fails to indicate *how* he intended to say it or, indeed, how he intended

his words to be read. Therefore, scholars and theologians of the next century must have recourse to the original editions, either in the research facilities that preserve the sixteenth-century printings or in the form of photographic reproductions. A new translation, embodying a suitable approach to the text and a credible apparatus, is also to be desired.

12. Many, if not all, of the attempts to discover or identify "tensions" in Calvin's thought have arisen out of anachronistic claims of inconsistencies or problems—claims grounded in modern dogmatic concerns, such as what the center of Calvin's theology should have been;[42] which elements of Calvin's teaching can be easily harmonized with a given modern context (and which cannot); or what views expressed by Calvin do not fit a particular grid imposed on his thought.[43]

13. Even so, we cannot develop a suitable understanding of the "systematic" character of Calvin's thought without close attention to his method—with its concern for the elicitation of doctrinal *loci* from Scripture, including its assumption that the *ordo* itself ought to be biblical or, at least, biblically grounded. Only when Calvin is recognized as a sixteenth-century formulator of an orderly series of theological *loci* and *disputationes* does the true character of his *Institutes* emerge. His quest for a "right order of teaching" was inseparably related to an exegetical task—a task in which establishment of the *scopus* and *dispositio* of a biblical book is as integral to the effort as the exposition of text and as a result of which the *scopus* and *dispositio* of the Epistle to the Romans could become determinative of Calvin's "systematic" order.

14. These strictures do not stand in the way of theological studies of Calvin's work—but they do stand in opposition to the use of contemporary theological grids—whether Barthian, Schleiermacherian, or "rhetorical"—as indices or heuristic guides to Calvin's world of thought. The strictures point, instead, to the necessary of discerning the textual and contextual framework in and through which Calvin's work can be rightly understood. A clever theologian can accommodate Calvin to nearly any agenda; a faithful theologian—and a good historian—will seek to listen to Calvin, not to use him.

NOTES

CHAPTER ONE

1. Thus, William J. Bouwsma, *John Calvin: A Sixteenth-Century Portrait* (New York: Oxford University Press, 1988) as an example of an interpretive grid laid over the matarials. Also note Suzanne Selinger, *Calvin Against Himself: An Inquiry in Intellectual History* (Hamden, Conn.: Archon, 1984), and J. Wayne Baker, *Heinrich Bullinger and the Covenant: The Other Reformed Tradition* (Athens, Ohio: Ohio University Press, 1980). Baker, "Heinrich Bullinger, the Covenant, and the Reformed Tradition in Retrospect," in *Calvin Studies VIII: The Westminster Confession in Current Thought*, papers presented at the Colloquium on Calvin Studies (Davidson College, January 26–27, 1996), pp. 58–75, exemplifies the failure to examine any of Calvin's writings beyond the *Institutes*. I deal with both of these issues: Baker's thesis appears in review in chapter 8, "*Fontes argumentorum . . . ,*" and the underlying problematic of Bouwsma's study is the subject of chapter 5, "Beyond the Abyss and the Labyrinth."

2. Thus, T. H. L. Parker, *The Doctrine of the Knowledge of God: A Study in the Theology of John Calvin* (1952; rev. ed., Grand Rapids, Mich.: Eerdmans, 1959) and Parker, *The Oracles of God: An Introduction to the Preaching of John Calvin* (London: Lutterworth, 1962).

3. T. H. L. Parker, *Calvin's New Testament Commentaries* (London: SCM/Grand Rapids: Eerdmans, 1971); Parker, *Calvin's Old Testament Commentaries* (Edinburgh: T. & T. Clark, 1986); Parker, "Calvin the Exegete: Change and Development," in *Calvinus Ecclesiae Doctor*, ed. W. H. Neuser (Kampen: J. H. Kok, 1980), pp. 33–46; Parker, "The Sources of the Text of Calvin's New Testament," in *Zeitschrift für Kirchengeschichte* 73 (1962), pp. 272–298; and Parker, *The Preaching of John Calvin* (Louisville: Westminster/John Knox Press, 1992).

4. T. H. L. Parker, "The Approach to Calvin," *Evangelical Quarterly* 16 (1944), p. 169.

5. Ibid., p. 171, citing Calvin's "Letter to the Reader" from the 1559 *Institutes;* cf. the similar conclusions of John H. Leith, "Calvin's Theological Method and Ambiguity in His Theology,"

Reformation Studies: Essays in Honor of R. H. Bainton, ed. F. Littell (Richmond: John Knox, 1962), pp. 106–14.

6. For example. Alain-Georges Martin, "La Place de la trinité dans l'institution chrétienne de Calvin," in *Revue Reformée* 30 (September 1979), pp. 131–49; Charles Partee, "Calvin's Central Dogma Again," *Sixteenth-Century Journal* 18 (1987), pp. 191–199; Philip W. Butin, *Revelation, Redemption, and Response: Calvin's Trinitarian Understanding of the Divine-Human Relationship* (New York: Oxford University Press, 1995); Brian A. Gerrish, *Grace and Gratitude: The Eucharistic Theology of John Calvin* (Minneapolis: Fortress Press, 1993); and Guenther H. Haas, *The Concept of Equity in Calvin's Ethics* (Waterloo, Ontario: Wilfrid Laurier University Press, 1997).

7. See further, chapters 6 and 8.

8. Thus, Philip Melanchthon, *Loci communes theologici* (Wittenberg, 1521, 1536, 1543); Wolfgang Musculus, *Loci communes* (Basel: Iohannes Hervagius, 1560, 1561, 1573); Andreas Hyperius, *De theologo, seu de ratione studii theologici, libri IIII* (Basel, 1556, 1559); and Peter Martyr Vermigli, *P. M. Vermilii loci communes* (London, 1576; 2nd ed., 1583).

9. Johann August Wilhelm Neander, *Lectures on the History of Christian Dogmas*, trans. J. Ryland, 2 vols. (London: Bohn, 1858); Karl R. Hagenbach, *A History of Christian Doctrines*, trans. E. H. Plumptre, 3 vols. (Edinburgh: T. & T. Clark, 1880–81); W. G. T. Shedd, *A History of Christian Doctrine*, 2 vols. (New York: Scribner, 1889; repr. Minneapolis: Klock & Klock, 1978).

10. Notable examples of this method include Wilhelm Niesel, *The Theology of Calvin*, trans. Harold Knight (London: Methuen, 1956); Heinrich Quistorp, *Calvin's Doctrine of the Last Things*, trans. Harold Knight (Richmond: John Knox Press, 1955); and Thomas F. Torrance, *Calvin's Doctrine of Man* (Grand Rapids, Mich.: Eerdmans, 1957). See also, Torrance, "Calvin's Doctrine of the Trinity," *Calvin Theological Journal* 25/2 (November 1990), pp. 165–93; Edward A. Dowey, *The Knowledge of God in Calvin's Theology* (New York: Columbia University Press, 1952; 3rd ed. Grand Rapids, Mich., Eerdmans, 1994); Paul Van Buren, *Christ in Our Place: The Substitutionary Character of Calvin's Doctrine of Reconciliation* (Edinburgh: T. & T. Clark, 1957); Ronald S. Wallace, *Calvin's Doctrine of the Word and Sacrament* (Grand Rapids, Mich.,: Eerdmans, 1957); Wallace, *Calvin's Doctrine of the Christian Life* (Edinburgh: Oliver and Boyd, 1959); and Wallace, *Calvin, Geneva and the Reformation: A Study of Calvin as Social Reformer, Churchman, Pastor and Theologian* (Grand Rapids, Mich.,: Baker Book House, 1988).

11. Note the protest of Basil Hall in "Calvin Against the Calvinists," in *John Calvin*, ed. Gervase E. Duffield (Grand Rapids, Mich.: Serdmans, 1966), pp. 22–23.

12. Cf. the comments of Harro Höpfl, *The Christian Polity of John Calvin* (Cambridge: Cambridge University Press, 1982), p. 4.

13. For example: M. Charles Bell, "Was Calvin a Calvinist?" *Scottish Journal of Theology* 36/4 (1983), pp. 535–40; Bell, "Calvin and the Extent of Atonement," *Evangelical Quarterly* 55 (April 1983), pp. 115–23; James B. Torrance, "The Incarnation and 'Limited Atonement,'" *Scottish Bulletin of Evangelical Theology* 2 (1984), pp. 32–40; Robert A. Peterson, *Calvin's Doctrine of the Atonement* (Phillipsburg, N.J.: Presbyterian and Reformed Publishing Co., 1983); Jonathan H. Rainbow, *The Will of God and the Cross: An Historical and Theological Study of John Calvin's Doctrine of Limited Redemption* (Allison Park, Pa.: Pickwick Publications, 1990).

14. On these debates, see the essays by Paul Rorem, "Calvin and Bullinger on the Lord's Supper: Part I. The Impasse," *Lutheran Quarterly* NS 2 (1988), pp. 155–84, and "Calvin and Bullinger on the Lord's Supper: Part II. The Agreement," *Lutheran Quarterly* NS 2 (1988), pp. 357–89; and Cornelis P. Venema, "Heinrich Bullinger's Correspondence on Calvin's Doctrine of Predestination, 1551–1553," *Sixteenth Century Journal* 17/4 (1986), pp. 435–50. Note the telling comparison between Calvin's views on predestination and those of Augustine and Aquinas in J. B. Mozley, *A Treatise on the Augustinian Doctrine of Predestination*, 2nd ed. (New

York: E. P. Dutton, 1878); see the parallels between Calvin's thought and late medieval theology in Karl Reuter, *Das Grundverständnis der Theologie Calvins* (Neukirchen: Neukirchner Verlag, 1963); and see David C. Steinmetz, *Calvin in Context* (New York: Oxford University Press, 1995), for an extensive description of Calvin's relationships to the earlier exegetical tradition.

15. Cf. the critique of Barthian readings in Haas, *The Concept of Equity in Calvin's Ethics*, pp. 3, 128.

16. Thus, Peter Wyatt, *Jesus Christ and Creation in the Theology of John Calvin* (Allison Park, Pa.: Pickwick Publications, 1996); see my review in *Calvin Theological Journal* 31/2 (November 1996), pp. 618–20.

17. Cf. Brian A. Gerrish, *Grace and Gratitude: The Eucharistic Theology of John Calvin* (Minneapolis: Fortress Press, 1993); Dawn DeVries, *Jesus Christ in the Preaching of Calvin and Schleiermacher* (Louisville: Westminster John Knox Press, 1996); see the more detailed critique in my reviews of Gerrish in *Journal of Religion* 75/1 (1995), pp. 119–21, and of DeVries in *Calvin Theological Journal* 31/2 (November 1996), pp. 603–07.

18. Gerrish, *Grace and Gratitude*, pp. 126, 144.

19. DeVries, *Jesus Christ in the Preaching of Calvin and Schleiermacher*, p. 41; cf. p. 89.

20. See Bouwsma, *John Calvin*, pp. 5, 238, note 24, citing Calvin, *Institutes*, I.i.3; cf. Bouwsma, "The Spirituality of John Calvin," in *Christian Spirituality: High Middle Ages and Reformation*, ed. Jill Raitt (New York: Crossroad, 1987), pp. 318–19.

21. Benjamin A. Reist, *A Reading of Calvin's Institutes* (Louisville: Westminster/John Knox Press, 1991).

22. Calvin, *Institutes*, II.xii.1.

23. Reist, *Reading*, p. 43.

24. Paul Oskar Kristeller, *Renaissance Thought: The Classic, Scholastic, and Humanist Strains* (New York: Harper & Row, 1961); Jean-Claude Margolin, *Humanism in Europe at the Time of the Renaissance*, trans. John L. Farthing (Durham, N.C.: Labyrinth Press, 1989); Charles Trinkaus, *In Our Image and Likeness: Humanity and Divinity in Italian Humanist Thought*, 2 vols. (Chicago: University of Chicago Press, 1970). Also note the discussion of contemporary perspectives on the Renaissance and Kristeller's role in their formation in Charles G. Nauert Jr., *Humanism and the Culture of the Renaissance* (Cambridge: Cambridge University Press, 1995), pp. 8–17, 218.

25. Thus, Quirinius Breen, *John Calvin: A Study in French Humanism* (Grand Rapids, Mich.: Eerdmans, 1931), Breen, "John Calvin and the Rhetorical Tradition," in Breen *Christianity and Humanism: Studies in the History of Ideas* (Grand Rapids, Mich.: Eerdmans, 1968), pp. 107–29; Hall, "Calvin Against the Calvinists," pp. 19–37; Hall, "Calvin and Biblical Humanism," in *Huguenot Society Proceedings* 20 (1959–64), pp. 195–209; E. David Willis, "Rhetoric and Responsbility in Calvin's Theology," in *The Context of Contemporary Theology: Essays in Honor of Paul Lehmann*, ed. Alexander McKelway and E. David Willis (Atlanta: John Knox Press, 1974), pp. 43–63, and Willis, "Persuasion in Calvin's Theology," in *Calvin and Christian Ethics*," papers and responses presented at the Fifth Colloquium on Calvin and Calvin Studies, sponsored by the Calvin Studies Society, May 8–9, 1985, ed. Peter De Klerk (Grand Rapids, Mich.: Calvin Studies Society, 1987), pp. 83–94.

26. Thus, Bouwsma, *Calvin*, pp. 32–34, 45–8, 230–31; Brian G. Armstrong, "*Duplex cognitio Dei*, Or? The Problem and Relation of Structure, Form, and Purpose in Calvin's Theology," in *Probing the Reformed Tradition: Historical Essays in Honor of Edward A. Dowey, Jr.*, ed. Elsie Anne McKee and Brian G. Armstrong (Louisville: Westminster/John Knox, 1989), pp. 135–53, and Armstrong, "The Nature and Structure of Calvin's Theology: Another Look," in *John Calvin's Institutes: His Opus Magnum*, ed. B. van der Walt (Potchefstrom: Institute for Reformational Studies, 1986), pp. 55–81.

27. See, for example, John H. Leith, "Calvin's Theological Method and Ambiguity in his

Theology," in *Reformation Studies: Essays in Honor of R. H. Bainton*, ed. F. Littell (Richmond: John Knox, 1962), pp. 106–14; H. Jack Forstman, *Word and Spirit: Calvin's Doctrine of Biblical Authority* (Stanford: Stanford University Press, 1962); Brian G. Armstrong, "*Duplex cognitio Dei*, pp. 135–53; Armstrong, "The Nature and Structure of Calvin's Theology: Another Look," pp. 55–81; Peter Wyatt, *Jesus Christ and Creation in the Theology of John Calvin*, pp. xix–xxiii, et passim. Cf. the discussion of this line of argument and the attempt to move beyond it in Mary Potter Engel, *John Calvin's Perspectival Anthropology* (Atlanta: Scholars Press, 1988), pp. x–xii.

28. See, at greater length, Richard A. Muller, "Calvin and the Calvinists: Assessing Continuities and Discontinuities Between the Reformation and Orthodoxy, Part I," in *Calvin Theological Journal* 30/2 (November 1995), pp. 345–75; "Part II," in *Calvin Theological Journal* 31/1 (April 1996), pp. 125–60.

29. Calvin's antagonism to certain forms of humanism was well documented in the older scholarship by Pierre Imbart de la Tour, *Les Origines de la réforme*, 4 vols. (Paris: Hachette/Firmin-Didot, 1905–35), IV, pp. 322, 366, 606–7; Henri Hauser, *Études sur la Réforme française* (Paris: Alphonse Picard et Fils, 1909), pp. 52–64; Josef Bohatec, *Calvin et humanisme* (Paris: Revue Historique, 1939); Bohatec, *Budé und Calvin: Studien zur Gedankenwelt des französischen Frühumanismus* (Graz: Herman Böhlaus, 1950); François Wendel, *Calvin et l'humanisme* (Paris: Presses Universitaires de France, 1976); also note the discussion in Mary Potter Engel, *John Calvin's Perspectival Anthropology* pp. 199–205.

30. On Valla, see Jerrold E. Siegel, *Rhetoric and Philosophy in Renaissance Humanism* (Princeton: Princeton University Press, 1968), p. 168; and see J. Chomarat, *Grammaire et rhétorique chez Erasmus* (Paris, 1981), p. 1162.

31. See Muller, "Calvin and the Calvinists," Part I, pp. 364–75; Part II, pp. 126–29, 140–47.

32. See the further discussion of this point in James E. Bradley and Richard A. Muller, *Church History: An Introduction to Research, Reference Works, and Methods* (Grand Rapids, Mich.: Eerdmans, 1995), pp. 48–62.

33. David C. Steinmetz, *Calvin in Context*, pp. 95–109, 122–56. Steinmetz, "Calvin as an Interpreter of Genesis," in *Calvinus Sincerioris Religionis Vindex*, ed. Wilhelm Neuser and Brian G. Armstrong (Kirksville, Mo.: Sixteenth-Century Journal Publishers, 1997), pp. 53–66; Susan E. Schreiner, "Through a Mirror Dimly: Calvin's Sermons on Job," *Calvin Theological Journal* 21 (1986), pp. 175–193; Schreiner, "Exegesis and Double Justice in Calvin's Sermons on Job," *Church History* 58 (1989), pp. 322–38; Schreiner, *Where Shall Wisdom Be Found? Calvin's Exegesis of Job from Medieval and Modern Perspectives* (Chicago: University of Chicago Press, 1994); John Lee Thompson, *John Calvin and the Daughters of Sarah: Women in Regular and Exceptional Roles in the Exegesis of Calvin, His Predecessors and His Contemporaries* (Geneva: Droz, 1992); Thompson, "The Immoralities of the Patriarchs in the History of Exegesis: A Reappraisal of Calvin's Position," *Calvin Theological Journal* 26 (1991), pp. 9–46; and Thompson, "Patriarchs, Polygamy and Private Resistance: John Calvin and Others on Breaking God's Rules," in *Sixteenth-Century Journal*, 25/1 (1994), pp. 3–28.

34. Anthony N. S. Lane, "Calvin's Sources of St. Bernard," *Archiv für Reformationsgeschichte* 67 (1982), pp. 258–78; Lane, "Bernard of Clairvaux: A Forerunner of Calvin?" in *Bernardus Magister*, ed. John R. Sommerfeldt (Kalamazoo, Mich.: Cistercian Publications, 1993), pp. 533–45; Lane, "Calvin's Use of Bernard of Clairvaux," in *Bernhard von Clairvaux: Rezeption und Wirkung im Mittelalter und in der Neuzeit*, ed. Kaspar Elm (Wiesbaden: Harrassowitz, 1994), pp. 303–332; Lane, "Justification in Sixteenth-Century Patristic Anthologies," in *Auctoritas Patrum: Contributions on the Reception of the Church Fathers in the 15th and 16th Century*, ed. Leif Grane, Alfred Schindler, and Markus Wriedt (Mainz: Verlag Philipp von Zabern, 1994), pp. 69–95; and Lane, "Calvin's Use of the Fathers and the Medievals," *Calvin Theological Journal* 16 (1981), pp. 159–65.

35. Olivier Millet, *Calvin et la dynamique de la parole: Etude de rhétorique réformée* (Paris: Libraire Honoré Champion, 1992).

36. See, e.g., Susan E. Schreiner, "Through a Mirror Dimly: Calvin's Sermons on Job," pp. 175–93; Schreiner, "Exegesis and Double Justice in Calvin's Sermons on Job," pp. 322–38; D. Fischer, "L'Élément historique dans la prédication de Calvin: Un aspect original de l'homilétique du Réformateur," in *Revue d'Historie et de Philosopie Religieuses* 64 (1984), pp. 365–86.

37. See Richard Stauffer, "Les Sermons inédits de Calvin sur le livre de la Genèse," *Revue de Théologie et de Philosophie*, 3 ser., 15 (1965), pp. 26–36; Stauffer, "Un Calvin méconnu: Le Prédicateur de Genève," *Bulletin de la Societé d'Histoire du Protestantisme Français* 123 (1977), pp. 184–203; and Stauffer, *Dieu, la Création et la Providence dans le prédication de Calvin* (Bern and Frankfurt: Peter Lang, 1978); Max Engammare, "Calvin Incognito in London: The Rediscovery in London of Sermons on Isaiah," *Proceedings of the Huguenot Society* 26/4 (1996); pp. 453–62; and Engammare, "Le Paradis à Genève. Comment Calvin prèchait-il la chute aux Genevois?" *Études Théologiques et Religieuses* 69 (1994), pp. 329–47.

38. P.-D. Nicole and C. Rapin, "De l'exégèse à l'homilétique, evolution entre le Commentaire de 1551, les sermons de 1558 et le commentaire de 1559 sur le prophète Esaïe," in *Calvinus Ecclesiae Genevensis Custos*, Wilhelm Neuser ed. (Frankfurt am Main: Peter Lang, 1984), pp. 159–62; note also Max Engammare, "Calvin connaissait-it la Bible? Les citations de l'Écriture dans les sermons sur la Genèse," *Bulletin de la Societé d'Histoire du Protestantisme Français* 141 (1995), pp. 163–84.

39. Brian G. Armstrong, "Exegetical and Theological Principles in Calvin's Preaching, with Special Attention to His Sermons on the Psalms," in *Ordentlich und Fruchtbar: Festschrift für Willem van't Spijker*, ed. Wilhelm Neuser and Herman Selderhuis (Leiden: J. J. Groen en Zoon, 1997), pp. 191–203.

40. François Wendel, *Calvin: The Origins and Development of His Religious Thought*, trans. Philip Mairet (New York: Harper & Row, 1963).

41. Abel Lefranc, *Grands écrivains français de la Renaissance* (Paris: Librairie Honoré Champion, 1914); Lefranc, "Introduction," in *Institution de la religion chrestienne de Calvin*: Texte original de 1541 réimprimé sous la direction de Abel Lefranc par Henri Chatelain et Jacques Pannier (Paris: Librairie Honoré Champion, 1911), pp. 1*-57*; Jacques Pannier, *Calvin écrivain. Sa place et son rôle dans l'histoire de la langue et de la littérature française*, 2nd ed. (Paris: Fischbacher, 1930); Pannier, *Recherches sur la formation intellectuelle de Calvin* (Paris: Alcan, 1931); Pannier, "Notes historiques et critiques sur un chapitre de l'*Institution* écrit Strasbourg (1539)," *Revve d'Histoire et de Philosophie Religieuses* (1934), pp. 206–229; Pannier, "Introduction," in John Calvin, *Institution de la religion chrestienne* (1541), I, pp. vii–xxxi; Jean-Daniel Benoit, "The History and Development of the *Institutio*: How Calvin Worked," in *John Calvin: A Collection of Distinguished Essays*, ed. Gervase E. Duffield (Grand Rapids, Mich.: Eerdmans 1966), pp. 102–17.

42. Luchesius Smits, *Saint-Augustin dans l'oeuvre de Jean Calvin*, 2 vols. (Assen: Van Gorcum, 1956–58); and R. J. Mooi, *Het Kerk- en Dogmahistorisch Element in de Werken van Johannes Calvijn* (Wageningen: H. Veenman & Zonen, 1965), dealing with Gregory the Great, Gratian, Lombard, and Bernard (pp. 297–338); Johannes van Oort, "John Calvin and the Church Fathers," in *The Reception of the Church Fathers in the West: From the Carolingians to the Maurists*, 2 vols., ed. Irena Backus (Leiden: E. J. Brill, 1997), pp. 661–700.

43. See, for example, Jean Plattard, *La Renaissance de lettres en France de Louis XII à Henri IV* (Paris: Librairie Armand Collin, 1925), pp. 70–78; Plattard, " 'L'Institution chrestienne' de Calvin, premier monument de l'éloquence française," *Revue des Cours et Conférences* 37 (1935/6), pp. 495–501; Plattard, "Le beau 'style' de Calvin," *Bulletin de l'Association Guillaume Budé* 62 (January 1939), pp. 22–29; Abel Lefranc, *Calvin et l'éloquence française* (Paris: Fischbacher,

1934); Quirinus Breen, *John Calvin: A Study in French Humanism*; Breen "John Calvin and the Rhetorical Tradition," pp. 107–29; Ford Lewis Battles, "The Sources of Calvin's Seneca Commentary," in *John Calvin: A Collection of Distinguished Essays*, ed. G. E. Duffield (Grand Rapids, Mich.: Eerdmans 1966), pp. 38–66; the introductory essays in *Calvin's Commentary on Seneca's De Clementia* with intro., trans., and notes by Ford Lewis Battles and André Malan Hugo (Leiden: E. J. Brill, 1969); Francis Higman, *The Style of John Calvin in His French Polemical Treatises* (London: Oxford University Press, 1967); Rodolphe Peter, "Rhétorique et prédication selon Calvin," *Revue d'Histoire et de Philosophie Religieuses* 2 (1975), pp. 249–72; E. David Willis, "Rhetoric and Responsibility in Calvin's Theology," pp. 43–63; Claude-Marie Halbritter Baldwin, "Calvin s'attaque à la persécution: Une étude comparative de son style français," Ph.D. dissertation: Michigan State University, 1984; and William J. Bouwsma, "Calvinism as *Theologia Rhetorica*," in *Calvinism as Theologia Rhetorica*, ed. Wilhelm Wuellner (Berkeley: Center for Hermeneutical Studies, 1986), pp. 1–21.

44. See his remarks in *Biblical Interpretation in the Era of the Reformation: Essays Presented to David Steinmetz in Honor of His Sixtieth Birthday*, ed. Richard A. Muller and John L. Thompson (Grand Rapids, Mich.: Eerdmans, 1996), pp. xi–xii, with reference to the series *Beiträge zur Geschichte der biblischen Exegese* (Tübingen: Mohr-Siebeck, 1959ff.); and note my survey of the bibliography in this field of Reformation research in *Biblical Interpretation in the Era of the Reformation*, pp. 3–6.

45. See David C. Steinmetz, "The Superiority of Pre-Critical Exegesis," in *Theology Today* 37 (1980–81), pp. 27–38; and Steinmetz, "John Calvin on Isaiah 6: A Problem in the History of Exegesis," *Interpretation* 36 (1982), pp. 156–70.

46. An accommodation performed with reckless abandon in J. K. S. Reid, *The Authority of Scripture: A Study of Reformation and Post-Reformation Understanding of the Bible* (London: Methuen, 1962); cf. the critique in Richard A. Muller, *Post-Reformation Reformed Dogmatics*, 2 vols. (Grand Rapids Mich.,: Baker Book House, 1987–93), pp. 90–94.

47. See Alexandre Ganoczy, *The Young Calvin*, trans. David Foxgrover and Wade Provo (Philadelphia: Westminster, 1987), pp. 173–78.

48. Karl Reuter, *Das Grundverständnis der Theologie Calvins*, Reuter, *Vom Scholaren bis zum jungen Reformator* (Neukirchen: Neukirchner Verlag, 1981); Thomas F. Torrance, *The Hermeneutics of John Calvin* (Edinburgh: Scottish Academic Press, 1988).

49. Thus, Quirinius Breen, *John Calvin: A Study in French Humanism*; Breen, "John Calvin and the Rhetorical Tradition," pp. 107–29; E. David Willis, "Rhetoric and Responsibility in Calvin's Theology," pp. 43–63; Willis, "Persuasion in Calvin's Theology," pp. 83–94; and William J. Bouwsma, "Calvinism as *Theologia Rhetorica*," pp. 1–21.

50. The problem of a generalized understanding of humanistic rhetoric also persists in Serene Jones, *Calvin and the Rhetoric of Piety* (Louisville: Westminster/John Knox, 1995). See my review of Jones in *Calvin Theological Journal* 31/2 (November, 1996), pp. 582–83.

51. Cf. Steinmetz, *Calvin in Context*, pp. vii–viii; see Alexandre Ganoczy, *La bibliothéque de l'Académie de Calvin* (Geneva: Droz, 1969), pp. 104 (the extensive holdings of Denis' works) and 187 noting only a *De formando studio Rodolphi Agricolae, Erasmi Roterodami et Philippi Melanchthonis rationes* (Cologne: J. Ossenburg, 1555).

52. Note the work of Pieter A. Verhoef, "Luther's and Calvin's Exegetical Library," *Calvin Theological Journal* 3 (1968), pp. 5–20, Richard C. Gamble, "Sources of Calvin's Genesis Commentary: A Preliminary Report," in *Archiv für Reformationsgeschichte* 84 (1993), pp. 206–21, and A. N. S. Lane, "Did Calvin use Lippoman's *Catena in Genesim?*" *Calvin Theological Journal* 31/2 (1996), pp. 404–19.

53. But note John B. Payne, *Erasmus: His Theology of the Sacraments* (Richmond Va.: John Knox Press, 1970), pp. 12–14, 19–23, 238–39; E.-W. Kohls, *Die Theologie des Erasmus*, 2 vols.

(Basel, 1966), I, pp. 193–96, 223; and Christian Dolfen, *Die Stellung des Erasmus von Rotterdam zur scholastischen Methode* (Osnabrück: Meinders & Elstermann, 1936), pp. 64–82.

54. So Willis, "Persuasion in Calvin's Theology," p. 83; cf. Bouwsma, *John Calvin*, pp. 2–5, 113–27.

55. See, for example Johannes Calvin, *Unterricht in der christlichen Religion: Institutio christianae religionis*, übersetzt und bearbeitet von Otto Weber (Neukirchen: Moers, 1936); John Calvin, *Institutes of the Christian Religion*, ed. John T. McNeill, trans. Ford Lewis Battles, 2 vols. (Philadelphia: Westminster, 1960).

56. These premises stand in conscious reflection of the argument of my essay on "Calvin and the Calvinists: Assessing Continuities and Discontinuities Between Reformation and Orthodoxy, Part I," pp. 345–75; "Part II," pp. 125–60. There the ten premises point from Calvin and his context toward the thought of the next several generations; here the premises point toward Calvin and his historical context with a view to medieval and Renaissance antecedents.

CHAPTER TWO

Several paragraphs of this essay have been adapted from Richard A. Muller, "Calvin's *Argument du livre* (1541), An Erratum to the McNeill/Battles *Institutes*," *Sixteenth Century Journal* 29/1 (1998), pp. 35–38.

1. Cf. the comments of François Wendel, *Calvin: The Origins and Development of his Religious Thought*, trans. Philip Mairet (New York: Harper & Row, 1963), p. 15. The sole significant exception here is the preface to Calvin's commentary on the psalter, written in 1557: see Calvin, *Commentary on the Psalms*, preface, in *CO*, col. (*CTS Psalms* I, p. xxxv–xlix). Also see the discussions of the autobiographical value and potential use of the preface in T. H. L. Parker, *John Calvin: A Biography* (Philadelphia: Westminster, 1975), pp. 162–65 and, especially, Alexandre Ganoczy, *The Young Calvin*, trans. David Foxgrover and Wade Provo (Philadelphia: Westminster, 1987), pp. 49–106, 241–66.

2. See Francis M. Higman, "Introduction," in Jean Calvin, *Sermons sur le Livre d'EsaïeChapitres 30–41* (Neukirchen-Vluyn: Nerkirchner Verlag, 1995), pp. x–xiii; cf. Max Engammare, "Calvin incognito in London: The Rediscovery in London of Sermons on Isaiah," *Proceedings of the Huguenot Society* 26/4 (1996), pp. 457–59.

3. Note the cautionary comments of Heiko A. Oberman, "The Conversion of John Calvin," in *Reformiertes Erbe, Festschrift für Gottfried W. Locher zu seinem 80. Geburtstag*, ed. H. A. Oberman, E. Saxer, A. Schindler, and H. Stucki, *Zwingliana* 19/2 (1992), p. 279.

4. Cf. Theodore Beza, *L'Histoire de la vie et mort de [M. Iean Calvin]*, in *Commentaires de M. Iean Calvin, sur le livre de Iosué* (Geneva: François Perrin, 1564), also in *CO* 21, col. 1–50; Beza, *Ioannis Calvini Vita* (Geneva: Petrum Santan dreanum, 1575), also in *CO* 21, col. 119–172; Nicholas Colladon, *Vie de Jean Calvin* (Geneva, 1564), also in *CO* 21, col. 51–118.

5. This is the fundamental flaw in William J. Bouwsma, *John Calvin: A Sixteenth Century Portrait* (New York: Oxford University Press, 1988), a problem that will be taken up at some length in chapter 5.

6. Cf. the discussion of the self and self-understanding in the Renaissance in Debora K. Shuger, *Sacred Rhetoric: The Christian Grand Style in the English Renaissance* (Princeton N.J.: Princeton University Press, 1988), pp. 232–35.

7. Jean Calvin, *A tous amateurs de Iésus Christ, et de son S. Evangile, salut* in *CO* 9, cols. 791–822; and note the discussion in Wulfert De Greef, *The Writings of John Calvin: An Introductory Guide*, trans. Lyle D. Bierma (Grand Rapids, Mich.: Baker Book House, 1993), pp. 90–93.

8. See Jean Calvin, *Institution de la religion chrestienne* (Geneva: Michel du Bois, 1541), fol. A1v–A2v, entitled *Argument du livre;* also (Geneva: Jean Girard, 1545), fol. A2r–v, here and

henceforth entitled *Argument du present livre;* (Geneva: Jean Girard, 1551), a2r; (Geneva: Jean Girard, 1553), fol. *2r–v; (Geneva: Philibert Hamelin, 1554), fol. A2 r–v; (Geneva: François Iaquy, Antoine Davodeau, & Iaques Bourgeois, 1557), fol. *1r-v. I have also consulted Jean Calvin, *Institution de la religion chrestienne de Calvin:* Texte original de 1541 réimprimé sous la direction de Abel Lefranc par Henri Chatelain et Jacques Pannier (Paris: Librairie Honoré Champion, 1911) and, for the 1560 text, Jean Calvin, *Institution de la religion chrestienne,* edition critique avec introduction, notes et variants publiée par Jean-Daniel Benoit, 5 vols. (Paris: J. Vrin, 1957–63), which also includes an edited text of the *Argument.* Contrary to the attribution of J. T. McNeill, the document does not appear in the 1560 French text: see Calvin, *Institutes* (1559/Battles), I, pp. 6–8.

9. On Calvin's letter to Francis I, see J. W. Marmelstein, *Étude comparative des testes latin et français de l'Institution* (Groningen: J. B. Wolters, 1923), pp. 25–30; Jean Calvin, *Épitre au roi François Ier: Préface de la première édition française de l'Institution de la religion chrétienne, 1541.* Texte publié, pour la première fois, d'après l'exemplaire dela Bibliothèque Nationale, avec Introduction et Notes par Jacques Pannier (Paris: Fischbacher, 1927); Ford Lewis Battles, "Introduction," in *Institutes* (1536), pp. xxxviii–xl; François Wendel, *Calvin: The Origins and Development of His Religious Thought,* trans. Philip Mairet (New York: Harper & Row, 1963), pp. 144–46; and I. John Hesselink, "The Development and Purpose of Calvin's Institutes," *Reformed Theological Review* 24 (1965), pp. 65–72.

10. I have not attempted to outline all of Calvin's prefaces, nor have I discussed here the specifically doctrinal or theological content of the biblical prefaces, which is considerable.

11. I follow here *Calvin's Commentary on Seneca's De Clementia,* with intro., trans., and notes by Ford Lewis Battles and André Malan Hugo (Leiden: E. J. Brill, 1969).

12. Calvin, *De clementia,* pp. 10–11; cf. the comment in Jacques Pannier, *Calvin écrivain. Sa place et son rôle dans l'histoire de la langue et de la littérature française,* 2nd ed. (Paris: Fischbacher, 1930), p. 10.

13. Calvin to François Daniel, 1534?, in *CO* 10, col. 36 (*Selected Works Letters* I, p. 41). Note the discussion in A. Lefranc, *Grands écrivains française, de la Renarssance* (Paris: Liberarie Honré Champion, 1914), pp. 354–57, of the emphasis on order and method evidenced in Calvin's literary style.

14. Calvin to Christopher Fabri (Libertet), 11 September [1534/35?], in *CO* 10, col. 52 (*Letters* I, p. 43).

15. Cf the recommendation in Erasmus, *Ratio seu methodus compendio perveniendi ad veram theologiam,* in *Ausgewählte Werke,* pp. 291–93. Also see the classic studies of Calvin's relationship to humanism, Josef Bohatec, *Calvin et humanisme* (Paris: Revue Historique, 1939), and Bohatec *Budé und Calvin: Studien zur Gedankenwelt des französischen Frühumanismus* (Graz: Herman Böhlaus, 1950); and François Wendel, *Calvin et l'humanisme* (Paris: Presses Universitaires de France, 1976).

16. Cf. Melanchthon, *Elementa rhetorices,* in *CR* 13, col. 573, and Melanchthon, *Loci theologici* (1543), in *CR* 21, col. 886.

17. In the following discussion I have used Jean Calvin, *Épitre a tous amateurs de Jésus-Christ: Préface à la traduction française du Nouveau Testament par Robert Olivetan (1535) . . . avec Introduction sur une édition française de l'Institution dès 1537?* ed. Jacques Pannier (Paris: Fischbacher, 1929); the text, with a significant introduction, is also found in Irena Backus and Claire Chimelli, *Le Vraie Piété: Divers traités de Jean Calvin et confession de foi de Guillaume Farel* (Geneva: Droz, 1986). Calvin also wrote the less theological Latin preface to the whole Olivetan Bible.

18. Cf. Heinrich Bullinger, *De testamento seu foedere Dei unico et aeterna . . . brevis expositio* (Zürich: Froschauer, 1534), with the comments in Backus and Chimelli, *La Vraie piété,* pp. 17–23.

19. Calvin, *Épitre a tous amateurs,* p. 48.

20. Contra Ford Lewis Battles, "Calculus Fidei," in *Interpreting John Calvin*, ed. Robert Benedetto (Grand Rapids, Mich.: Baker Book House, 1996), pp. 147–49, where the *Épistre* is presented as a commentary on Calvin's conversion experience!

21. Calvin, *Épitre a tous amateurs*, pp. 38–39.

22. Calvin, *Épitre a tous amateurs*, pp. 39–40.

23. See *La Bible, qui est toute la Saincte Escriture du Vieil et du Nouveau Testament: autrement l'anciene & la Nouvelle Alliance. Le tout reveu & conferé sur les textes Hebrieux et Grecs par les Pasteurs & Professerus de l'Eglise de Geneve* (Geneva: Pierre et Iaques Chouët, 1638), fol. *6v–*8r: the text is unaltered until the second column of fol. *8r, where, at line 12, a different conclusion is inserted in order to allow the letter to serve as a preface to the whole bible.

24. Cf. De Greef, *Writings of John Calvin*, p. 196.

25. See Pannier, ed., *Épitre au roi François Ier*, pp. xxx–xxxii; also see the analysis of the French style of the letter in Claude-Marie Halbritter Baldwin, "Calvin s'attaque à la persécution: Une étude comparative de son style français," Ph.D. dissertation, Michigan State University, 1984, pp. 39–80.

26. Contra the comments in Serene Jones, *Calvin and the Rhetoric of Piety* (Louisville: Westminster/John Knox, 1995), pp. 50–51. Jones holds that Calvin used the "original, unaltered form" of this letter "to introduce each successive edition of the *Institutes*" and that the "shifts in context" from one edition to another "prompt us to ask why Calvin used an outdated preface to introduce a new, updated edition of the *Institutes*." Since Calvin did in fact edit the prefatory letter, Jones's subsequent speculation is rendered purposeless.

27. Yet even in the matter of precise date there are changes: the original date given in 1536 was "10 Kalendas Septembras" or August 23, without indication of the year. The French editions of 1541 and 1545 respect the March 1536 publication date of the volume and state "the twenty-third of August, one thousand, five hundred and thirty-five," as the date of the letter to Francis. With the 1539 Latin edition, the date shifts to August 1, and the year is altered, perhaps inadvertently, to 1536.

28. From 1557, but discussed here in order to preserve the chronology of Calvin's life—methodological elements of this preface are discussed later, with other materials from the time of its production. On this document and the problem of Calvin's "conversion," see Wendel, *Calvin*, pp. 21, 37–39; Ganoczy, *Young Calvin*, pp. 260–66; and Wilhelm H. Neuser, "Calvin's Conversion to Teachableness," in *Calvin on Christian Ethics: Papers and Responses Presented at the Fifth Colloquium on Calvin and Calvin Studies*, ed. Peter De Klerk (Grand Rapids, Mich.: Calvin Studies Society, 1987), pp. 57–77.

29. Calvin, *In Lib. Psalmorum Comm., Calvinus lectoribus*, in *CO* 31, col. 21, 23 (*CTS Psalms* I, pp. xl–xli).

30. Ibid., in *CO* 31, col. 23 (*CTS Psalms* I, pp. xli–xlii).

31. Ibid.

32. Ibid., *CO* 31, col. 23 (*CTS Psalms* I, p. xlii).

33. Calvin, *Christianae Religionis Institutio* (Basel: Thomas Platter & Balthasar Lasius, 1536), *Epistola nuncupatoria*, p. 3 (*CO* 1, col. 9); also *Institutes* (1536/Battles), p. 1.

34. Ibid.

35. Cf. Parker, *John Calvin: A Biography*, p. 33.

36. Calvin, *Institutio* (1536), *Epistola nuncupatoria*, pp. 4, 6 (*CO* 1, col. 9, 11); also *Institutes* (1536/Battles), pp. 1–2.

37. Cf. Hesselink, "Development of Calvin's *Institutes*," pp. 68–69.

38. Cf. Ford Lewis Battles, "Introduction," in *Institutes: 1536 Edition*, p. xxxvi–xxxviii, xlv.

39. *Le Catéchisme français de Calvin, publiée en 1537, reimprimé pour la première fois*, avec deux notices par Albert Rilliet & Théophile Dufour (Geneva: H. Georg, 1878), also in *CO* 22, cols. 33–96; Johannes Calvinus, *Catechismus, sive christianae religionis institutio* (Basel: n.p.,

1538), also in *CO* 5, cols. 317–62; note the text and translation offered in *Catechism or Institution of the Christian Religion*, trans., and intro. by Ford Lewis Battles (Pittsburgh: Pittsburgh Theological Seminary, 1972; rev. ed., 1976). On these works, see De Greef, *Writings of John Calvin*, p. 124–5. The texts of the two editions of the *Institutes* and the texts of the two catechisms are interrelated and there remains some debate over the relationship of the French to the Latin Catechism. Herminjard (*Correspondence*, IV, pp. 185–86) and E. Doumergue, *Jean Calvin, les hommes et les choses de son temps* (Lausanne: G. Bridel, 1899–1927), II, p. 229, n. 4, Marc Boegner, *Les Catéchismes de Calvin: Étude d'histoire et Catéchétique* (Pamiers: L. Labrunie, 1905), pp. 25–26, and Battles, "Preface," p. vi, argue the priority of the Latin, while others, acknowledging the latinate nature of the French prose and its probable source in a Latin original (viz., the 1536 *Institutes*), accept the declaration of the preface to the Latin catechism, that it was a translation from the vernacular: thus, the editors of the document in their "Notice préliminaire," *CO* 22, cols. 7–18; and Louis Gonin, *Les Catéchismes de Calvin et d'Ostervald: Étude historique et comparative* (Montauban: J. Granié, 1893), pp. 20–21.

40. Cf. Lefranc, *Grands écrivains français*, pp. 323–24; and note the considerable variety of catechetical forms in Ferdinand Cohrs, *Die Evangelischen Katechismusversuche vor Luthers Enchiridion*, 5 vols. (Berlin: A. Hofmann, 1900–1907; repr., 2 vols., Hildesheim and New York: George Olms, 1978).

41. In addition to the chapters in the biographies by Doumergue, Walker, and Parker, see Jacques Pannier, *Calvin à Strasbourg* (Strasbourg: Imprimerie Alsacienne, 1925).

42. Cf. Calvin to Farel, 21 [27] October 1540, with Calvin to the Seigneury of Geneva, 12 November 1540, and Calvin to Bernard, 1 March 1541, in *CO* 11, col. 90–93, 104–06, 165–66 (*Selected works . . . Letters*, I, pp. 210–17, 234–37).

43. Calvin to Farel, 27 October 1540, in *CO* 11, col. 91–92 (*Selected works . . . Letters*, I, pp. 212).

44. John Calvin, *Praefatio in editionem Homiliarum Chrysostomi*, in *CO* 9, cols. 831–38; translated in W. Ian P. Hazlett, "Calvin's Latin Preface to His Proposed French Edition of Chrysostom's Homilies: Translation and Commentary," in *Humanism and Reform: The Church in Europe, England, and Scotland, 1400–1643. Essays in Honour of James K. Cameron*, ed. James Kirk (Oxford: Basil Blackwell, 1991), pp. 129–50. Note also "John Calvin, Preface to the Homilies of Chrysostom," trans. John I. McIndoe, *Hartford Quarterly* (Winter 1965), pp. 19–26. The date of the document is uncertain: many writers have dated it early, ca. 1535 or 1540 (cf. De Greef, *Writings of John Calvin*, p. 90), whereas Walchenbach argued for 1559: see John R. Walchenbach, "John Calvin as Biblical Commentator: An Investigation into Calvin's Use of John Chrysostom as an Exegetical Tutor," Ph.D. dissertation, University of Pittsburgh, 1974, pp. 201–06. As Hazlett points out, Walchenbach's argument is based entirely on the similarity of themes enunciated in the *Praefatio Chrysostomi* and in Calvin's prefatory letter to his Isaiah commentary (1559). Hazlett's case for 1538–40 rests firmly Calvin's own manuscript, taking into consideration idiosyncrasies of Calvin's early hand and the watermark of the paper. See the discussion in Johannes van Oort, "John Calvin and the Church Fathers," in *The Reception of the Church Fathers in the West: From the Carolingians to the Maurists*, 2 vols., ed. Irena Backus (Leiden: E. J. Brill, 1997), pp. 691–93.

45. Calvin, *Praefatio Chrysostomi*, in *CO* 9, col. 832–33.

46. Ibid., *CO* 9, col. 835. On the significance of Chrysostom to Calvin as an exegetical and hermeneutical model, see John R. Walchenbach, "John Calvin as Biblical Commentator," and Alexandre Ganoczy and Klaus Müller, *Calvins Handschriftlighe Annotationen zu Chrysostomus: Ein Beitrag zur Hermeneutik Calvins* (Wiesbaden: F. Steiner, 1981).

47. The phrase "ad scripturae sacrae lectionem . . . *viam sternere*" from the preface to Chrysostom (*CO* 9, col. 833) is echoed in the 1539 preface to the *Institutes*, fol. *1v: "Itaque hac veluti *strata via*, si quas posthac scripturae enarrationes edidero."

48. Calvin, *Institutio* (1539), "Epistola ad Lectorem," fol. *1v (*CO* 2, col. 3–4); Calvin, *Commentarii ad Romanos* (1540), "Calvinus . . . Grynaeo," fol. A4r–v, A5v: in *CO* 10, col. 403–05 (*CTS Romans*, p. xxv–xxvi); cf. Hesselink, "Development and Purpose of Calvin's Institutes," pp. 69–70.

49. On the humanistic stress on the identification and ordering of *topoi* or *loci communes*, see Manfred Hoffmann, *Rhetoric and Theology: The Hermeneutic of Erasmus* (Torono: University of Toronto Press, 1994), pp. 6, 8, 25, 37–38, 145–48. Also note Jerry H. Bentley, *Humanists and Holy Writ: New Testament Scholarship in the Renaissance* (Princeton, N.J.: Princeton University Press, 1983).

50. See Richard Gamble, "*Brevitas et facilitas*: Toward Understanding of Calvin's Hermeneutic," *Westminster Theological Journal* 47 (1985), pp. 1–17. It is worth noting that the comparison between Bucer's wordiness and Calvin's *brevitas* can be readily made in the context of Calvin's 1540 Romans commentary compared to Bucer's vast *Metaphrases et enarrationes perpetuae Epistolarum D. Pauli Apostoli . . . Tomus primus . . . in Epistolam ad Romanos* (Strasbourg: Wendelin Rihel, 1536)—whereas Calvin's later commentary on the Gospel of John is comparable in size to Bucer's, Bucer was here less and Calvin, more expansive.

51. Calvin, *Commentarii ad Romanos* (1540), "Calvinus . . . Grynaeo," fol. A5v: in *CO* 10, col. 404–05 (*CTS Romans*, p. xxvi).

52. Timothy J. Wengert, " 'We Will Feast Together in Heaven Forever: The Epistolary Friendship of John Calvin and Philip Melanchthon," in *Melanchthon in Europe: His Work and Influence Beyond Wittenberg*, ed. Karin Maag (Grand Rapids, Mich.: Baker Book House, 1999), pp. 19–44. Calvin, it should be noted, frequently observed in polemic that his opponents had not paid attention to "the whole of Scripture": cf. Calvin, *Response à certaines calomnies et blasphemes*, in *CO* 58, col. 202, where Calvin is also dismissive of an appeal to Melanchthon by Castellio.

53. Calvin, *Commentarii ad Romanos* in *CO* 49, col. 1 (*CTS Romans*, p. xxix); cf. Melanchthon, *Elementa rhetorices*, in *CR* 13, col. 431–32.

54. Calvin, *Commentarii ad Romanos* in *CO* 49, col. 1 (*CTS Romans*, p. xxix).

55. See chapter 8, *Fontes argumentorum*. . . .

56. Calvin, *Institutio* (1539), fol. 2: note that Calvin's phrase in 1539 is *ordo recte dicendi*, "right order of expression or speech." This form is retained in the 1543 edition but altered to *ordo recte docendi*, "right order of teaching," in Calvin, *Institutio* (1550), I.3, ad fin. The change ocurred earlier in the French: Calvin, *Institution* (1541), fol. 3, reads simply "ce que l'ordre requiert," but the very next edition, Calvin, *Institutio* (1545), fol. 3, offers "ce que l'ordre d'enseigner requiert."

57. Calvin, *Institutio* (1539), fol. 2; cf. Calvin, *Institutio* (1559), I.i.3; on the Pauline ordering of the 1539 *Institutes*, see chapter 7; cf. Packer, "Calvin the Theologian," pp. 157–59 with Lefranc, "Calvin et l'eloquence française," p. 29.

58. Calvin, *Institutio* (1539), fol. 12; cf. Calvin, *Institutio*(1559), I.viii.1.

59. Cf. Ronald S. Wallace, "Calvin's Approach to Theology," in *The Challenge of Evangelical Theology: Essays in Approach and Method*, ed. Nigel Cameron (Edinburgh: Rutherford House, 1987), pp. 137–41, and John H. Leith, "Calvin's Theological Method and the Ambiguity in His Theology," in *Reformation Studies: Essays in Honor of Roland H. Bainton*, ed. Franklin H. Littell (Richmond: John Knox, 1962), pp. 111–13.

60. I owe this point to a conversation with Prof. Timothy Wengert. Cf. John B. Payne, Albert Rabel, and Warren S. Smith, "The Paraphrases of Erasmus: Origin and Character," in *Collected Works of Erasmus*, vol. 42 (Toronto: University of Toronto Press, 1984), p. xv, on Erasmus's apparent distinction between short *annotationes* or "philological notes" and the "continuous theological exposition" of the *commentarius*, with Kenneth Hagen, "What Did the Term *Commentarius* Mean to Sixteenth-Century Theologians?" in *Théorie et practique de l'exégèse*, ed. Irena Backus and Francis Higman (Geneva: Droz, 1990), pp. 13–38. If Hagen is correct that there

was no absolutely standardized sense of *commentarius* in the sixteenth century, Calvin appears to have followed the more Erasmian sense of the term. See also Basil Hall, "Calvin and Biblical Humanism," *Huguenot Society Proceedings* 20 (1959–64), p. 205.

61. E. David Willis, "Persuasion in Calvin's Theology," in *Calvin and Christian Ethics*, papers and responses presented at the Fifth Colloquium on Calvin and Calvin Studies, sponsored by the Calvin Studies Society, May 8–9 1985, ed. Peter De Klerk (Grand Rapids, Mich.: Calvin Studies Society, 1987), p. 83; cf. William J. Bouwsma, "Calvin and the Renaissance Crisis of Knowing," *Calvin Theological Journal* 17/2 (1982), pp. 190–211; Bouwsma, "Calvinism as *Theologia Rhetorica*," in *Calvinism as Theologia Rhetorica*, ed. W. Wuellner (Berkeley, Calif.: Center for Hermeneutical Studies, 1986), p. 14, n.1; Bouwsma, *John Calvin*, pp. 2–5, 113–127. But note the significant counter in Cornelis Augustijn, "Calvin und der Humanismus," in *Calvinus Servus Christi*, ed. W. H. Neuser (Budapest: Presseabteilung des Ráday-Kollegiums, 1988), pp. 127–42, where Calvin's approach to classical pagan literature is distinguished from that of many humanists; and cf. the similar conclusions in Donald T. Williams, "John Calvin: Humanist and Reformer. The Influence of Calvin's Early Humanism on His Work as a Christian Theologian," *Trinity Journal* (Spring 1976), pp. 67–78; also note B. J. van der Walt, "Renaissance and Reformation: Contemporaries but Not Allies," in *Calvinus Reformator: His Contribution to Theology, Church and Society* (Potchefstroom: Potchefstroom University for Christian Higher Education, 1982), pp. 85–92; and Don H. Compier, "The Independent Pupil: Calvin's Transformation of Erasmus' Theological Hermeneutics," *Westminster Theological Journal* 54 (1992), pp. 217–33. Calvin's opposition to some forms of humanism was also heavily documented by J. Bohatec, *Budé und Calvin: Studien zur Gedankenwelt des französischen Frühhumanismus* (Graz: Herman Bohlaus, 1950), pp. 121–240; also see Bohatec, "Calvin et humanisme," *Revue Historique* 183 (1938), pp. 207–41, and 185 (1939), pp. 71–104.

62. Parker, *John Calvin*, p. 105.

63. Parker, *John Calvin*, p. 105; cf. the similar remarks in B. Gerrish, *Grace and Gratitude: The Eucharistic Theology of John Calvin* (Minneapolis: Fortress Press, 1993), p. 18. The problem in both cases appears to be the assumption that Melanchthon's approach to *loci* was identical with that of Erasmus—and that Calvin sought a cohesion and order beyond the bounds of the *locus* method, whether as early as 1539 (Parker) or in 1559 (Gerrish). But Melanchthon's approach to the *locus* method was, from the outset, to identify the proper method and order of the topics. In this Calvin certainly followed Melanchthon.

64. See, chapter 7, "Establishing the *Ordo docendi . . .*" for a discussion of Melanchthonian influence on the order and structure of the *Institutes*. For Calvin's personal relationship with Melanchthon, see J. T. Hickman, "The Friendship of Melanchthon and Calvin," in *Westminster Theological Journal* 38 (1975–6), pp. 152–65; also see August Lang, "Melanchthon und Calvin," in *Reformation und Gegenwart. Gesammelte Aufsätze vornehmlich zur Geschichte und zum Verständnis Calvins und der Reformierten Kirche*, ed. Lang (Detmold: Meyersche Hofbuchhandlung, 1918), pp. 88–135; and note the section "Calvin and Melanchthon" in Philip Schaff, *History of the Christian Church* (repr. Grand Rapids, Mich.: Eerdmans, 1953), VIII, pp. 385–98.

65. Melanchthon, *Dispositio orationis in epistola Pauli as Romanos* (1529), in *CR* 15, col. 445.

66. Melanchthon, *Commentarii in Epistolam Pauli ad Romanos*, in *CR* 15, col. 499.

67. Cf. Calvin, *Institution* (1541), "Argument du livre," fol. A2r with Calvin, *Institutio* (1539), "Epistola ad Lectorem," fol. *1v; cf. *Institutes* (1559/McNeill-Battles), I, pp. 4–5, 7–8.

68. Calvin, *Institution* (1541), "Argument du livre," fol. A2r; and see the discussion of this religious and lingiustic context in Lefranc, *Grands écrivains français*, pp. 331–33.

69. This oddity in the 1541 text has led some scholars to hypothesize the existence of a French translation of the 1536 *Institutes*: thus, Jacques Pannier, "Une Première Institution française dès 1537?" *Revue d'Histoire et de Philosophie Religieuses*, 8 "Ein französische Ausgabe der ersten (1928), pp. 513–34; also Wilhelm Niesel and Peter Barth, *Institutio Calvins*," in *Theolo-*

gische Blätter, 7/1 (1928), pp. 2–10. The majority of scholars, however, have not accepted the hypothesis: see *CO* 3, pp. xxi–xxii; Marmelstein, *Étude comparative*, pp. 30; Benoit, "Introduction," in *Institution de la religion chrestienne*, I, pp. 12–13; and Wendel, *Calvin*, pp. 113–14. See also Calvin to François Daniel, 13 October 1536, in *CO*, col. (*Letters*, I, p. 45): "I was kept continually occupied on the French version of my little book." The comment may refer to a projected translation of the entire *Institutes*, but it could just as easily indicate either the independent publication of the letter to Francis I or the catechetical portion of what became the *Instruction et confession de foy* of 1537.

70. Cf. Marmelstein, *Étude comparative*, pp. 35–50; and Benoit, "History and Development," pp. 105–06.

71. See Lefranc, *Grands écrivains français*, pp. 336–38 for a survey of the "successive editions" of the *Insitutes*, with emphasis on the development of the French text.

72. Calvin to Viret, 23 August 1542, in *CO* 11, col. 431 (*Letters* I, p. 346).

73. Calvin to Farel and Viret, in *CO* 13, col. 477–78: i.e., letter 1319 (*CTS Tim., Titus, Philemon*, pp. 275–76); cf. his similar description of his role in Calvin, *Reply to Cardinal Sadolet*, in *CO* 5, col. 385–86 (*Tracts*, I, p. 26).

74. Calvin to Cordier, in *CO* 11, col. 525–26: i.e., letter 1345 (*CTS Phil., Col., Thess.*, p. 234).

75. Calvin, *Comm. in priorem Epist. ad Corinthios*, in *CO* 49, col. 297 (*CTS Corinthians* I, p. 37).

76. Ibid., in *CO* 49, col. 304 (*CTS Corinthians* I, p. 46).

77. Cf. the comments in Parker, *Calvin's New Testament Commentaries*, p. 85.

78. Calvin, *Defensio . . . adv. calumn. Pighii*, in *CO* 6, col. 229–30 (*Bondage and Liberation*, pp. 3–4); cf. Melanchthon to Calvin (May 11, 1543), in *CO* 11, cols. 538–42. Calvin certainly knew, before he drafted his response to Pighius, of his disagreement over grace and free choice with Melanchthon, inasmuch as Melanchthon's synergistic approach was already evident in the 1535 *Loci communes*. Pighius had also noted Melanchthon's divergence from Calvin (*CO* 6, col. 250–01; *Bondage and Liberation*, p. 29).

79. Calvin, *Defensio . . . adv. calumn. Pighii*, in *CO* 6, col. 229–30 (*Bondage and Liberation*, p. 3).

80. *Jehan Calvin aux Lecteurs* [*Préface de la Somme de Melanchthon 1546*], in *CO* 9, cols. 847–50. Also see Rodolphe Peter, "Calvin, traducteur de Mélanchthon," in *Horizons européens de la Réforme en Alsace*, ed. Marijn de Kroon and Marc Lienhard (Strasburg: Istra, 1980), pp. 119–33, on Calvin's probable work as the translator.

81. *Iehan Calvin aux Lecteurs*, *CO* 9, col. 847–48; cf. Calvin to Melanchthon 27 August 1554, in *CO* 15, col. 215–17 (*Letters*, III, pp. 61–66); and see discussion in chapter 7.

82. Calvin to Farel, 1 September, 1549, in *CO* 13, col. 374 (*Letters*, II, p. 247).

83. Calvin to Queen Elizabeth, *CO* 17, col. 414: i.e., letter 3000 (*CTS Isaiah* I, p. xvi).

84. Calvin to Dryander, 7 March 1550, in *CO* 13, col. 536 (*Letters* II, pp. 265–6).

85. Calvin, *Commentarii in Isaiam Prophetam, Praefatio* in *CO* 36, col. 19 (*CTS Isaiah* I, pp. xxvi–xxvii).

86. Cf. Calvin, *Institutio* (1539), fol. 225–44 with Calvin, *Institutio* (1559), II.vii.2 (an entirely new section on the promises of the Law) and II.vii.12, ad fin (added comments on the promise of grace that belongs to the third use of the Law, as taught in Psalms).

87. Calvin, *In Evang. Ioh. Commentarius*, argumentum, in *CO* 47, p. viii, col. 1 (*CTS John* I, p. 22).

88. Cf. "Calvin to the . . . Church of Zurich," in the *Consensus Tigurinus* (1554), (*Tracts*, II, p. 201).

89. Calvin, *In Evang. Ioh. Commentarius*, argumentum, in *CO* 47, p. viii, col. 1–2 (*CTS John* I, p. 22).

90. See Irena Backus, "Church, Communion and Community in Bucer's Commentary on the Gospel of John," in *Martin Bucer: Reforming Church and Community*, ed. D. F. Wright (Cambridge: Cambridge University Press, 1994), pp. 62–3.

91. Calvin, *Secunda defensio . . . contra Westphali calumnias*, in *CO* 9, col. 47 (*Tracts*, II, p. 248).

92. Beza to Calvin, 21 January 1552, in *Correspondence de Théodore de Bèze*, I, pp. 82–83.

93. Jean Calvin, *Vingtdeus sermons . . . auxquels est exposé le Pseaume cent dixneufieme, contenant pareil nombre des huictains* (Geneva: Iean Gerard, 1554), in *CO* 32, col. 481–752; also note *Two and Twentie Sermons of Maister Iohn Calvin, in which Sermons is most religiously handled, the hundredth and nineteenth Psalme of David, by eight verses aparte, according to the Hebrewe Alphabet*, trans. Thomas Stocker (London, 1580; reissued, Audubon, NJ: Old Paths Publications, 1996).

94. Calvin, *Comm. in II Timotheum*, in *CO* 52, col. 384: "institutio formandae vitae."

95. Calvin, *Vingtdeus sermons . . . auxquels est exposé le Pseaume cent dixneufieme*, in *CO* 32, col. 453–54.

96. Ibid., in *CO* 32, col. 482–83, 492, 494, 496, 633, et passim. The themes of "school" and the "ABC" are common in Calvin's sermons: also see, for example, Calvin, *Sermons sur le livre de Moyse, nommé Deutéronome*, sermon 146, 192, in *CO* 28, col. 267–68 and *CO* 29, col. 121 (*Sermons on Deut.*, p. 903, col. 1; p. 1192, col. 1); Calvin, *Sermons sur l'Epistre S. Paul apostre aux Galatiens*, sermon 5, in *CO* 50, col. 329 (*Sermons upon . . . Galatians*, p. 95); Calvin, *Sermons sur les deux Epistres S. Paul à Timothée, et sur l'Epistre à Tite* (Geneva: 1561), sermon 13 on II Tim. 2:16–18, in *CO* 54, col. 161 (*Sermons . . . on the Epistles of S. Paule to Timothie and Titus*, p. 814, col. 1); cf. Parker, *Calvin's Preaching*, pp. 25–29.

97. Calvin, *In Lib. Psalmorum Comm.*, in *CO* 31, col. 34–35 (*CTS Psalms* I, p. xlviii–xlix); and cf. James Luther Mays, "Calvin's Commentary on the Psalms: the Preface as Introduction," in *Calvin Studies IV*, ed. John H. Leith and W. Stacy Johnson (Davidson, N.C.: Colloquium on Calvin Studies, 1988), pp. 96–97.

98. Mays, "Calvin's Commentary on the Psalms," p. 98.

99. Calvin, *In Lib. Psalmorum Comm.*, *Calvinus lectoribus*, in *CO* 31, col. 17 (*CTS Psalms* I, p. xxxviii); note the similar sentiment in the Genesis commentary, Calvin, *In primum Mosis Comm.*, in *CO* 23, col. 239 (*CTS Genesis* I, p. 451): Calvin insists on following the "order of the text" rather than give a summary of the meaning of circumcision.

100. Calvin, *In Lib. Psalmorum Comm.*, *Calvinus lectoribus*, in *CO* 31, col. 35 (*CTS Psalms* I, p. xlix).

101. Calvin, *In Lib. Psalmorum Comm.*, *Calvinus lectoribus*, in *CO* 31, col. 13 (*CTS Psalms* I, p. xxxv).

102. Calvin, *Institutio* (1559), *Iohannes Calvinus lectori*, fol. 2r (*CO* 2, col. 1–2; *Institutes/ Battles*, p. 3).

103. Cf. Marmelstein, *Étude*, pp. 5–24, 60–66 with Wendel, *Calvin*, pp. 118–19 and De Greef, *Writings of John Calvin*, p. 201.

104. The 1551 and subsequent French editions (1553, 1554, 1557) augment the 1550 Latin text with materials, including a sizable discussion of the bodily resurrection, not added to the Latin until 1559 despite the reissuing of the Latin text in 1553 and 1554: *Institution* (1551), chap. VIII, §221–3; cf. Gilmont, *Bibliotheca Calviniana*, I, p. 422 with DeGreef, *Writings of John Calvin*, p. 201, and Wendel, *Calvin*, pp. 117–18.

105. Cf. the summary of differences made by the seventeenth century Dutch translator, as surveyed in R. Peter and J. F. Gilmont, *Bibliotheca Calviniana*, II (Geneva: Droz, 1991–94) p. 757.

106. Colladon's editorial letter found in Iohannes Calvinus, *Institutio christianae religionis* (Lausanne: Franciscus Le Preux, 1576) appears to indicate that his major work was with the

French text of 1560 and that his index of theological *loci* was originally done for the French edition, albeit first published in Latin; cf. Gilmont, *Bibliotheca Calviniana,* II, pp. 762–3.

107. Calvin, *Praelect. in lib. proph. Danielis,* in *CO* 18, col. 615 (*CTS Daniel* I, p. lxiv).

108. Ibid., *CO* 18, col. 615 (*CTS Daniel* I, p. lxiv).

109. Calvin, *Praelect. in lib. proph. Danielis . . . Calvinus piis Gallis,* in *CO* 18, col. 615–16 (*CTS Daniel* I, p. lxv).

110. Calvin, *Praelect. in lib. proph. Danielis,* in *CO* 18, col. 620 (*CTS Daniel* I, p. lxxi).

111. Ibid., in *CO* 18, col. 632–34 (*CTS Daniel* I, p. lxxv).

112. Ibid., in *CO* 18, col. 622 (*CTS Daniel* I, p. lxxiii); cf. Richard A. Muller, "The Hermeneutic of Promise and Fulfillment in Calvin's Exegesis of the Old Testament Prophecies of the Kingdom," in *The Bible in the Sixteenth Century,* ed. and intro. by David C. Steinmetz (Durham, N.C.: Duke University Press, 1990), pp. 68–82.

113. Cf. the comments in V. Forestier, *Calvin: Exégète de l'Ancien Testament,* (Lausanne: Georges Bridel, 1873) pp. 9–11.

114. Note that Calvin did not himself view his harmony of Exodus, Leviticus, Numbers, and Deuteronomy (1563) as a work radically distinct from the Genesis commentary (1554): the *Harmony* appeared for the first time in *Mosis libri V cum Ioannis Calvini Commentariis: Genesis seorsum; reliqui quatuor in formam harmoniae digesti* (Geneva, 1563): Calvin, in other words, published a second edition of his Genesis commentary with the first edition of the *Harmony* as a full commentary on the Pentateuch but, unlike his predecessors in the Protestant exegetical tradition, conflated the last four books in order to avoid duplication of comment. Cf. the discussion in De Greef, *Writings of John Calvin,* pp. 104–06.

115. Cf. Calvin, *Harm. ex tribus Evang.,* in *CO* 43, col. 4 (*CTS Evangelists* I, pp. xxxix–xl) with Calvin, *Mosis libri in formam harmoniae, Praefatio,* in *CO* 24, col. 5–6 (*CTS Harm. Moses* I, p. xiv).

116. Calvin, *Mosis libri in formam harmoniae, Praefatio,* in *CO* 24, col. 5–6 (*CTS Harm. Moses* I, pp. xiv-xv).

117. Ibid., in *CO* 24, col. 5–6 (*CTS Harm. Moses* I, p. xv).

118. Calvin's language here, with its interest in establishing the proper "scope" and *methodus* of the text in order that the reader not "wander" (*vagetur*), is a direct reflection of the 1539 preface to the *Institutes*; cf. the discussion in chapter. 6.

119. Cf. Calvin, *Institutio* (1559), II.viii.

120. Viz., *Mosis libri V cum Ioannis Calvini Commentariis: Genesis seorsum; reliqui quatuor in formam harmoniae digesti* (Geneva, 1563).

121. Calvin, *In primum Mosis Comm. . . . Dedicatio,* in *CO* 20, col. 121 (*CTS Genesis* I, p. liii).

122. See chapters 6–9.

CHAPTER THREE

An earlier, shorter form of this essay appears in Wilhelm H. Neuser and Brian G. Armstrong (eds.), *Calvinus Sincerioris Religionis Vindex: Calvin as Protector of the Purer Religion* (Kirksville, Mo.: Sixteenth Century Journal Publishers, 1997), pp. 247–66.

1. The *disputatio,* as it passed into the later Middle Ages and the Renaissance, did alter slightly in form: rather than pose an initial *quaestio,* the later academic *disputatio* began with a *thesis*: see the discussion in A. J. Kunz, *Gods kennis en wil volgens de jonge Gomarus: de plaat van Gods kennis en wil in de predestinatieleer van de jonge Gomarus (1599–1609)* (Utrecht: Faculteit der Godgeleerdheid, n.d), also Anthony Kenny, "Disputations of the Theologians," in *The Cambridge History of Later Medieval Philosophy,* ed. N. Kretzmann, A. Kenny, J. Pinborg, and E. Stump

(Cambridge: Cambridge University Press, 1982), pp. 21–26; and Brian Lawn, *The Rise and Decline of the Scholastic "Quaestio disputata"—With Special Emphasis on Its Use in the Teaching of Medicine and Science* (Leiden: E. J. Brill, 1993). Cf. John Schneider, *Philip Melanchthon's Rhetorical Construal of Biblical Authority* (Lewiston: Edwin Mellen, 1990), pp. 73–75; W. Van 't Spijker, *Principe, methode en functie van de theologie bij Andreas Hyperius* [Apeldoornse Studies, 26] (Kampen: J. H. Kok, 1990); Ian McPhee, "Conserver or Transformer of Calvin's Theology? A Study of the Origins and Development of Theodore Beza's Thought, 1550–1570," Ph.D. dissertation, Cambridge University, 1979), pp. xv–xviii; John Patrick Donnelly, *Calvinism and Scholasticism in Vermigli's Doctrine of Man and Grace* (Leiden: E. J. Brill, 1975), p. 193; Peter Fraenkel, *De l'écriture à la dispute. Le cas de l'Académie de Genève sous Théodore de Bèze* (Lausanne: Revue de Théologie et de Philosophie, 1977), pp. 5–7, 36–39; Irena Backus, "L'Enseignement de la logique à l'Academie de Genève entre 1559 et 1565," *Revue de Théologie et de Philosophie* 111 (1979), pp. 153–63; William T. Costello, *The Scholastic Curriculum at Early Seventeenth-Century Cambridge* (Cambridge, Mass.: Harvard University Press, 1958), pp. 15–35; Mark H. Curtis, *Oxford and Cambridge in Transition, 1558–1642: An Essay on Changing Relations Between the English University and English Society* (Oxford: Clarendon Press, 1959), p. 96; and Stephen Spencer, "Reformed Scholasticism in Medieval Perspective: Thomas Aquinas and François Turrettini on Incarnation," Ph.D. dissertation, Michigan State University, 1988, pp. 88–95.

2. Thus, Heiko A. Oberman, *Forerunners of the Reformation* (New York: Holt, Rinehart & Winston, 1966); Oberman, *The Harvest of Medieval Theology: Gabriel Biel and Late Medieval Nominalism*, rev. ed. (Grand Rapids, Mich.: Eerdmans, 1967); Oberman, *Masters of the Reformation: Emergence of a New Intellectual Climate in Europe*, trans. Dennis Martin (Cambridge: Cambridge University Press, 1981); and Oberman, "The Shape of Late Medieval Thought: The Birthpangs of the Modern Era," in *The Pursuit of Holiness*, ed. C. Trinkaus and H. Oberman pp. 3–25; Lewis Spitz, "Humanism and the Protestant Reformation," in *Renaissance Humanism*, ed. Albert Rabil Jr. (Philadelphia: University of Pennsylvania Press, 1988), vol. 3, pp. 381–411. See also James H. Overfield, *Humanism and Scholasticism in Late Medieval Germany* (Princeton, N.J.: Princeton University Press, 1984), pp. 59–60, 94–100, 329–30; Overfield, "Scholastic Opposition to Humanism in Pre-Reformation Germany," in *Viator* 7 (1976), pp. 391–420; Jean-Claude Margolin, *Humanism in Europe at the Time of the Renaissance*, trans. John L. Farthing (Durham, N.C.: Labyrinth Press, 1989), pp. 2–6, 21–39, 41–52; cf. Charles Trinkaus, "Italian Humanism and Scholastic Theology," in *Renaissance Humanism*, ed. Albert Rabil Jr., vol. 3, pp. 327–48, and John F. D'Amico, "Humanism and Pre-Reformation Theology," in ibid., pp. 349–79; also note Charles Trinkaus, *In Our Image and Likeness: Humanity and Divinity in Italian Humanist Thought*, 2 vols. (Chicago: University of Chicago Press, 1970), pp. 60–61, 332–33.

3. Note that the underlying problem of Erika Rummel, *The Humanist-Scholastic Debate in the Renaissance and Reformation* (Cambridge, Mass.: Harvard University Press, 1995) is its insistence on looking at what humanists said in polemic against scholastics rather than either examining the broader usage of the term *scholasticus* or recognizing how the polemic of the day tended to ignore the extent of the common ground on which the combatants stood.

4. Armand Aime LaVallee, "Calvin's Criticism of Scholastic Theology," Ph.D. dissertation, Harvard University, 1967, p. 237. La Vallee's work largely confines itself to an analysis of Calvin's criticism of the scholastics without moving on to the issue of positive appropriations.

5. LaVallee, "Calvin's Criticism of Scholastic Theology," pp. 237–41.

6. Karl Reuter, *Das Grundverständnis der Theologie Calvins* (Neukirchen: Neukirchner Verlag, 1963), pp. 35–36.

7. Alexandre Ganoczy, *La Bibliothéque de l'Academie de Calvin* (Geneva: Droz, 1969), pp. 104, 107.

8. LaVallee, "Calvin's Criticism of Scholastic Theology," pp. 242–49; Alexandre Ganoczy,

Le Jeune Calvin: Génèse et évolution de sa vocation réformatrice (Wiesbaden: F. Steiner, 1966); in translation, *The Young Calvin*, trans. David Foxgrover and Wade Provo (Philadelphia: Westminster, 1987), pp. 173–78.

9. Cf. Karl Reuter, *Vom Scholaren bis zum jungen Reformator* (Neukirchen: Neukirchner Verlag, 1981), with A. N. S. Lane, "Calvin's Use of Bernard of Clairvaux," in *Bernard von Clairvaux: Rezeption und Wirkung im Mittelalter und in der Neuzeit*, ed. Kaspar Elm (Wiesbaden: Harrassowitz Verlag, 1994), pp. 303–32; and note also Lane, "Bernard of Clairvaux: A Forerunner of Calvin?" in *Bernardus Magister: Papers Presented at the Noncentenary Celebration of the Birth of Saint Bernard of Clairvaux, Kalamazoo, Michigan, 10–13 May, 1990*, ed. John R. Sommerfeldt (Kalamazoo, Mich.: Cistercian Publications, 1991), pp. 533–45.

10. Thomas F. Torrance, *The Hermeneutics of John Calvin* (Edinburgh: Scottish Academic Press, 1988); cf. Alister E. McGrath, "John Calvin and Late Medieval Thought. A Study in Late Medieval Influences upon Calvin's Theological Development," *Archiv für Reformationsgeschichte* 77 (1986), pp. 58–78, for an attempt to balance Reuter's and Torrance's approach with Ganoczy's findings by hypothesizing a somewhat generalized early influence of the *via moderna* and what McGrath calls a *schola Augustiniana moderna* on Calvin's thought. McGrath's argument, in effect, supports Reuter and Torrance without recourse to John Major; see the trenchant critique of McGrath in Heiko A. Oberman, *Initia Calvini: The Matrix of Calvin's Reformation* (Amsterdam: Koninklijke Nederlandse Akademie van Wetenschappen, 1991), p. 14.

11. David C. Steinmetz, "Calvin and the Absolute Power of God," *Journal of Medieval and Renaissance Studies* 18/1 (Spring 1988), pp. 65–79; Steinmetz, "Calvin Among the Thomists," *Biblical Hermeneutics in Historical Perspective* (Grand Rapids, Mich.: Eerdmans, 1991), pp. 198–214; Susan E. Schreiner, "Through a Mirror Dimly: Calvin's Sermons on Job," in *Calvin Theological Journal* 21 (1986), pp. 175–193; Schreiner, "Exegesis and Double Justice in Calvin's Sermons on Job," *Church History* 58 (1989), pp. 322–38; Schreiner, *Where Shall Wisdom Be Found? Calvin's Exegesis of Job from Medieval and Modern Perspectives* (Chicago: University of Chicago Press, 1994); John Lee Thompson, "The Immoralities of the Patriarchs in the History of Exegesis: A Reappraisal of Calvin's Position," *Calvin Theological Journal* 26 (1991), pp. 9–46; Oberman, *Initia Calvini*, pp. 11–17; Jelle Faber, "Nominalisme in Calvijns preken over Job," in *Een sprekend begin*, ed. R. ter Beek et al. (Kampen: Uitgeverij Van den Berg, 1993), pp. 68–85.

12. Cf., for example, Paul Vignaux, "Nominalisme," s.v. in *Dictionnaire de théologie catholique*, vol. II/I, cols. 717–84; Vignaux, *Justification et prédestination au XIVe siècle: Duns Scot, Pierre d'Auriole, Guillaume d'Occam, Grégoire de Rimini* (Paris: E. Leroux, 1934); and Vignaux, *Nominalisme au XIVe siècle* (Montreal: Institute D'Études Médiévales, 1948); Heiko A. Oberman, *Archbishop Thomas Bradwardine: A Fourteenth-Century Augustinian. A Study of His Theology in its Historical Context* (Utrecht: Kemink & Zoon, 1958); Oberman, *The Harvest of Medieval Theology: Gabriel Biel and Late Medieval Nominalism*, rev. ed. (Grand Rapids, Mich.: Eerdmans, 1967); Oberman, *Masters of the Reformation: Emergence of a New Intellectual Climate in Europe*, trans. Dennis Martin (Cambridge: Cambridge University Press, 1981); Oberman, "Some Notes on the Theology of Nominalism with Attention to Its Relation to the Renaissance," *Harvard Theological Review* 53 (1960), pp. 47–76; Francis Oakley, "Pierre D'Ailly and the Absolute Power of God: Another Note on the Theology of Nominalism," *Harvard Theological Review* 56 (1963), pp. 59–73; and William J. Courtenay, "Nominalism in Late Medieval Religion," in *The Pursuit of Holiness*, ed. C. Trinkhaus and H. Oberman, pp. 26–59; and Courtney. "The Dialectic of Omnipotence in the High and Late Middle Ages," in *Divine Omniscience and Omnipotence in Medieval Philosophy*, T. Rudavsky (Dordrecht: Reidel, 1985), pp. 243–269; cf. the collection of Courtenay's essays, *Covenant and Causality in Medieval Thought: Studies in Philosophy, Theology, and Economic Practice* (London: Variorum Reprints, 1984).

13. Cf. Steinmetz, "Calvin and the Absolute Power of God," pp. 77–79, with Faber, "Nominalisme in Calvijns preken over Job," pp. 84–85.

14. Schreiner, " 'Through a Mirror Dimly', pp. 175–93; Schreiner, *Where Shall Wisdom Be Found*, pp. 91, 152–55, et passim; and David C. Steinmetz, "Calvin among the Thomists," pp. 198–214.

15. On Lyra's exegesis, its place in the development of the biblical commentary, and its significant use of Aquinas's exegetical work, see Ceslaus Spicq, *Esquisse d'une histoire de l'exégèse latine au moyen âge* (Paris: J. Vrin, 1944), pp. 335–42; also F. Vernet, "Lyre, Nicolas de" s.v. in *Dictionnaire de théologie catholique*, 11/1, cols. 1410–22.

16. Oberman, *Initia Calvini*, pp. 117–21; Schreiner, *Where Shall Wisdom Be Found*, pp. 106, 115.

17. Paul Helm, "Calvin (and Zwingli) on Divine Providence," *Calvin Theological Journal* 29/2 (1994), pp. 388–405.

18. See Heiko A. Oberman, "The Case of the Forerunner," in Heiko, *Forerunners of the Reformation* (New York: Holt, Rinehart & Winston, 1966).

19. Cf. Steinmetz, "Calvin and the Absolute Power of God," pp. 66, 73–79.

20. Cf. Schreiner, "Exegesis and Double Justice," pp. 332–34.

21. Cf. Brian G. Armstrong, *Calvinism and the Amyraut Heresy: Protestant Scholasticism and Humanism in Seventeenth-Century France* (Madison: University of Wisconsin Press, 1969), p. 32; Armstrong, "The Changing Face of French Protestantism: The Influence of Pierre Du Moulin," in *Calviniana: Ideas and Influence of Jean Calvin*, ed. Robert V. Schnucker (Kirksville, Mo.: Sixteenth-Century Journal Publishers, 1988), pp. 145–49; S. van der Linde, "Het 'Griekse' Denken in Kerk, Theologie en Geloofspraktijk," *Theologia Reformata* 28 (1985), p. 260.

22. Cf. David Knowles, *The Evolution of Medieval Thought* (New York: Vintage Books, 1962), p. 87, with J. A. Weisheipl, "Scholastic Method," in *NCE*, 12, p. 1145; G. Fritz and A. Michel, "Scholastique," in *Dictionnaire de théologie catholique*, 14/2, col. 1691; and Armand Maurer, *Medieval Philosophy* (New York: Random House, 1962), p. 90.

23. Cf. Oberman, *Thomas Bradwardine*, pp. 101–02, 120; Oberman, *Harvest of Medieval Theology*, pp. 30–56, 96–105; Oberman, "Some Notes on the Theology of Nominalism," pp. 56–68; Richard A. Muller, *God, Creation and Providence in the Thought of Jacob Arminius: Sources and Directions of Scholastic Protestantism in the Era of Early Orthodoxy* (Grand Rapids, Mich.: Baker Book House, 1991), pp. 184–85, 190–91, 202–05, 228–29.

24. John Calvin, *Praelect. in proph. minores*, CO 42, col. 187–88 (*CTS Minor Prophets* I, pp. xxvi–xxvii); cf. Parker, *Calvin's Preaching*, p. 132.

25. *Leges Academiae Genevensis* (Geneva: Stephanus, 1559; facsimile repr. Geneva: J. G. Fick, 1859), fol. c.i, verso; also *L'Ordre du College de Geneve*, in ibid., fol. c.i, verso.

26. Cf. *Leges Academiae Genevensis*, fol. c.ii, recto–c.iii, recto; with *L'Ordre du College de Geneve*, fol. b.ii, recto–verso; b.iii, verso with the discussion in Irena Backus, "L'enseignement de la logique à l'Académie de Genève entre 1559 et 1565," *Revue de Théologie et de Philosophie* 111 (1979), pp. 153–63.

27. The text of Beza's address is found in *Leges Academiae Genevensis*, fol. a.iii, recto–b.ii, recto, and also in *Le Livre du recteur de l'Académie de Genève*, ed. S. Stelling-Michaud, 6 vols. (Geneva: Droz, 1959–80), I, pp. 64–65. Cf. Gillian Lewis, "The Geneva Academy," in *Calvinism in Europe, 1540–1620*, ed. A. Pettegree, A. Duke, and G. Lewis (Cambridge: Cambridge University Press, 1994), p. 39.

28. Cf. Andreas Hyperius, *De theologo, seu de ratione studii theologici* (Basel: Oporinus, 1556, 1559), p. 398.

29. See *Renaissance Student Life: The Paedologia of Petrus Mosellanus*, trans. and intro. by Robert Francis Seyboldt (Chicago: University of Illinois Press, 1927).

30. Mathurin Cordier, *Colloquiorum scholasticorum libri IIII, ad pueros in sermone Latino paulatim exercendos* (Geneva: Stephanus, 1564); cf. Aloys Bömer, *Die lateinischen Schülergespräche der Humanisten*, 2 vols. (Berlin, 1897–99; repr. Amsterdam: P. Schippers, 1966); L. Massebieau,

Les colloques scolaires du seizième siècle, et les auteurs, 1480–1570 (Paris: J. Bonhoure, 1878; repr. Geneva: Slatkine, 1968); and Massebieau, *Répertoire des ouvrages pédagogiques du XVIe siècle* (Paris: J. Bonhoure, 1886). On Cordier, see Jules Le Coultre, *Maturin cordier et les origines de la pédagogie protestante dans les pays de langue française (1530–1564)* (Neuchatel: Secrétariat de l'Université, 1926), and Charles Delormeau, *Un Maître de Calvin: Mathurin Cordier, l'un des créateurs de l'enseignement secondaire moderne 1479–1564* (Neuchatel: Éditions H. Messeiller, 1976).

31. *De laude vitae scholasticae oratio, CR* 11, col. 298–306.

32. On the confluence of "scholastic" and "humanist" approaches in the sixteenth century, see Charles B. Schmitt, *Aristotle and the Renaissance* (Cambridge, Mass.: Harvard University Press, 1983), pp. 15–25.

33. Stephanus Szegedinus, *Theologiae sincerae loci communes de Deo et Homine perpetuis Tabulis explicati et scholasticorum dogmatis illustrati* (Basel: Conrad Valdkirchium, 1588). [The standard topics of sound theology concerning God and Humanity explained in running tables and illustrated with scholastic doctrinal formulae]

34. See, for example, Antoine Chandieu, *De verbo Dei scripto . . . Praefatio de vera methodo theologice simul et scholastice disputandi,* in *Opera theologica* (Geneva: Le Preux, 1593) with Johann Heinrich Alsted, *Theologia scholastica didactica exhibens locos communos theologicos methodo scholastica* (Hanoviae: Conrad Eifrid, 1618) and cf. Donald W. Sinnema, "Antoine De Chandieu's Call for a Scholastic Reformed Theology (1580)," in *Later Calvinism: International Perspectives,* ed. W. Fred Graham (Kirksville, M.: Sixteenth-Century Journal Publishers, 1994), pp. 159–90, with Muller, *Post-Reformation Reformed Dogmatics,* I, pp. 76–77, 258–67, 273–74, 297–98.

35. Ganoczy, *The Young Calvin,* p. 176; cf. LaVallee, "Calvin's Critique of Scholastic Theology," pp. 237–41.

36. Ganoczy, *The Young Calvin,* pp. 177–78.

37. LaVallee, "Calvin's Criticism of Scholastic Theology," p. 249. One such work was Gabriel Biel's *Collectorium,* which not only was used at the Sorbonne but was commented on by the Scotist Jérôme de Hangest, prior of the Sorbonne in 1513; Hangest also commented on the fourth book of the *Sentences.* Nonetheless, as LaVallee noted, we have no evidence that Calvin ever examined it. (Nor is it at all clear whether this Jérôme de Hangest was related to the bishops of Noyon.) The difficulty with the hypothesis, obviously, lies in the identification of the work or works that Calvin read. On the faculty and doctors of the Sorbonne, see James K. Farge, *Biographical Register of Paris Doctors of Theology, 1500–1536* (Toronto: Pontifical Institute of Medieval Studies, 1980); on Hangest, pp. 218–21; also see Farge, *Orthodoxy and Reform in Early Reformation France: The Faculty of Theology of Paris* (Leiden: E. J. Brill, 1985). And, of course, there was Iohannes Maior, *In sententiarum I–IV* (Paris, 1509–11): Farge, *Register,* p. 309, cites only the commentaries on books I, II, and IV, but Stegmüller indicates commentaries in all four books: Fridericus Stegmüller, *Repertorium Commentariorum in sententias Petri Lombardi,* 2 vols. (Würzburg: Ferdnand Schöningh, 1947), I, pp. 226–27.

38. But see the cautionary comments concerning the breath of Calvin's reading list in David C. Steinmetz, *Calvin in Context* (New York: Oxford University Press, 1995), pp. 73, 99, 136, and A. N. S. Lane, "The Sources of Calvin's Citations in His Genesis Commentary," in *Interpreting the Bible: Historical and Theological Studies in Honour of David F. Wright,* ed. Lane (Leicester: Apollos, 1997), pp. 55–83.

39. See Calvin, *Institutio* (1559), *Iohannes Calvinus lectori,* fol. 2v; I.i.3, ad fin.

40. Cf. the argument of chapter 6 with Beryl Smalley, *The Study of the Bible in the Middle Ages* (Notre Dame: University of Notre Dame Press, 1964), 63–64, and with Smalley, "The Bible in the Medieval Schools," in *The Cambridge History of the Bible,* 3 vols. (Cambridge: Cambridge University Press, 1963–70), II, pp. 197–98, and see also Yves M.-J. Congar, *A History of Theology,* trans. Hunter Guthrie (Garden City, N.Y.: Doubleday, 1968), pp. 79–80.

41. Cf. chapter 4.

42. Calvin, *Institutio* (1559), I.xvi.9: "Quoniam tamen longe infra providentiae Dei altitudinem subsidit mentis nostrae tarditas, adhibenda est quae eam sublevet distinctio"; i.e., the distinctions between "necessity *secundum quid*" and "absolute necessity" or between "consequent necessity" and a "necessity of the consequence," distinctions that were "not without reason invented in the schools"—thus, ibid., "Unde iterum videmus, non temere in scholis inventas fuisse distinctiones de necessitate secundum quid, et absoluta; item consequentis et consequentiae. . . ."

43. Ibid., II.xvii.1: "Quum ergo de Christi merito agitur, non statuitur in eo principium; sed conscendimus as Dei ordinationem, quae prima causa est. . . . Atque ita inscite opponitur Christi meritum misericordiae Dei. Regula enim vulgaris est, quae subalterna sunt, non puganre."

44. Ibid. II.xvii.2: "Haec distinctio colligitur ex plurimis scripturae locis."

45. Ibid., III.viii.11: "paucis definiendum est quid inter philosophicam ac christianam patientiam intersit."

46. Lyle D. Bierma, " 'Remember the Sabbath Day . . . ': Ursinus' Exposition of Exodus 20: 8–11," in *Biblical Interpretation in the Era of the Reformation*, ed. R. A. Muller and J. L. Thompson pp. 277–78, citing Calvin, *Institutio* (1536), *CO* 1, col. 37 (Battles, p. 24); cf. Calvin *Institutio* (1559), II.viii.34, where the argument is repeated, but without reference to the "sophists." There is no evidence that Calvin had direct acquaintance with the thought of Aquinas. As Oberman points out, the occasional "thomistic" accents found in Calvin can be better explained by the influence of the Dominican-trained Bucer, who had included *disputationes* on dogmatic themes in his commentaries—works that Calvin most surely read: see Oberman, "Initia Calvini," p. 11, esp. note 14.

47. Calvin, *Institutio* (1559), III.xxiii.2: "Neque tamen commentum ingerimus absolutae potentiae: quod sicuti profanum est, ita merito detestabile nobis esse debet. Non fingimus Deus exlegem, qui sibi lex est . . . Dei autem voluntas non modo ab omni vitio pura, sed summa perfectionis regula, etiam legum omnium lex est"; cf. the discussion by Steinmetz, "Calvin and the Absolute Power of God," pp. 65–79. On the history of the concept, see William J. Courtenay, *Capacity and Volition: A History of the Distinction of Absolute and Ordained Power* (Bergamo: P. Lubrina, 1990). Cf. Jean Calvin, *Sermons sur le Livre de Iob*, in *CO* 34, 331–44; cf. John Calvin, *Sermons of Maister Iohn Calvin, upon the Book of Iob* (London, 1574), especially sermon 88 (pp. 412–416); and see the discussion in Schreiner, *Where Shall Wisdom Be Found*, pp. 110–20.

48. Calvin, *Sermons sur le Livre de Iob*, *CO* 34, col. 339: "Et de fait, quand ces docteurs Sorboniques disent, que le Dieu a une puissance absolue, c'est un blaspheme diabolique qui a esté forgé aux enfers"; cf. Calvin, *Sermons on Job*, p. 415, col. 1:44–45.

49. Ibid., in *CO* 34, col. 336: "Or en cela Iob blaspheme Dieu: car combien que la puissance de Dieu soit infinie, si est-ce que de la faire ainsi absolue, c'est imaginer en luy une tyraine, et cela est du tout contraire à sa maiestè, car nostre Seigneur ne veut point estre puissant qu'il ne soit iuste: et ce sont choses inseparables, que sa iustice et sa puissance"; cf. Calvin, *Sermons on Iob*, p. 414, col. 1:2–5.

50. Ibid., *CO* 34, col. 334: "Voila donc comme il y a une iustice plus parfaite que celle de la Loy"; cf. Calvin, *Sermons on Iob*, p. 413, co. 1:31–32.

51. Ibid., *CO* 34, col. 340: "Il faut donc dire que Dieu a une puissance infinie, laquelle toutes fois est la regle de toute iustice: car c'est deschirer Dieu par pieces, quand nous le voudrons faire puissant, et qu'il ne sera plus iuste"; cf. Calvin, *Sermons on Iob*, p. 415, col. 1:42–49.

52. Cf. Calvin, *Comm. in Isaiam* [41:18–19], in *CO* 37, col. 47–48 (*CTS Isaiah* III, p. 267).

53. Calvin, *Institutio* (1559), III.xxiv.17: "quamvis multiplex sit Dei voluntas quoad sensum nostrum, non tamen eum hoc et illud in se velle, sed propria sapientia sua varie multiplice . . . attonitos reddere sensus nostros, donec cognoscere nobis dabitur mirabiliter eum velle quod nunc videtur esse voluntas ejus adversum."

54. Ibid., I.xvii.2: "sed arcanam Dei providentiam reverenter suspicere jubeat. hujus quoque altitudinis elogium ponitur in libro Job, quod mentes nostras humiliet."

55. Ibid., I.xviii.1, 3: "Tergiversando itaque effugiunt, Dei tantum permissu, non etiam voluntate hoc fieri. . . . [3] Unde [Augustinus] exclamat: magna opera Dei, exquisita in omnes voluntates eius (Psal.111:2); ut miro et ineffabili modo non fiat praeter ejus voluntatem quod etiam contra ejus fit voluntatem: quia non fieret si non sineret; nec utique nolens sinit, sed volens, nec sineret bonus fieri male, nisi omnipotens etiam de malo facere posset bene."

56. Ibid., III.ii.1–2: "Imo quum in scholis de fide disputant, Deum ejus objectum simpliciter vocando, evanida speculatione . . . miseras animas rapiunt transversum magis quam ad scopum dirigant. Nam quum Deus lucem inaccessam habitat, Christum occurrere medium necesse est. . . . Ergo hoc malum, ut aliis innumera, Scholasticis acceptum referri par est, qui velut obducto velo Christum texerunt, in cujus intuitum nisi recta intenti simus, per multos labyrinthos semper vagari contingent"; cf. II.vi.4.

57. Cf. Melanchthon, *Loci communes* (1521) in *CR* 21, col. 160–64, and see chapter 9 on the possibile derivation of Calvin's argument from Melanchthon.

58. P. Parthenius Minges, *Ioannis Duns Scoti doctrina philosophica et theologica*, (Quaracchi: Collegium S. Bonaventurae, 1930), I, pp. 509–10.

59. Cf. Oberman, *Dawn of the Reformation*, pp. 193–94.

60. See the summary of the medieval discussion of theology as practical or speculative in, for example, Jean de Paris, *Commentaire sur les Sentences*, édition critique par Jean-Pierre Muller, 2 vols. (Rome: Herder, 1961), *Prooemium*, q. 8 (pp. 22–28); Gregorius Ariminensis, *Super primum et secundum Sententiarum* (Venice, 1522; repr. St. Bonaventure, N.Y.: Franciscan Institute, 1955), *prol.*, q. 5, art. 1–3.; and cf. R. A. Muller, *Post-Reformation Reformed Dogmatics* (Grand Rapids, Mich.: Baker Book House, 1987–93), I, pp. 225–26, with Minges, *Scoti Doctrina Philosophica et Theologica*, I, pp. 515–20.

61. See Hugo de S. Victore, *De sacramentis Christiange fidei prol.* 2 (*PL* 176, col. 183); Aegidius Romanus, *Primus sententiarum* (Venice: Octauianus Scotus, 1521), *prol.* 1, q. 3; Gregorius Ariminensis, *Super primum et secundum Sententiarum* (Venice: Luceantonius, 1522; repr. St. Bonaventure, N.Y.: Franciscan Institute, 1955), *prol.*, q. 4, art. 1–2.

62. Johannes Altenstaig, *Vocabularius theologiae* (Hagenau: Heinrich Gran, 1517), s.v. *obiectum theologiae*. Unfortunately, there is no reference to Altenstaig in Ganoczy's *Bibliothèque de l'Académie de Calvin.*

63. Calvin, *Institutio* (1559), III.ii.2: "Praeterquam vero quod caliginosa sua definitione totam vim fidei deterunt ac fere exinaniunt. . . ."

64. Cf. Simon Pieter Dee, *Het Geloofsbegrip van Calvijn* (Kampen: J. H. Kok, 1918), pp. 30–36; Walter E. Stuermann, *A Critical Study of Calvin's Concept of Faith* (Ann Arbor, Mich.: Edwards Brothers, 1952), pp. 62–65; P. Lobstein, "La Connaissance réligieuse d'après Calvin," *Revue de Théologie et de Philosophie* 42 (1909), pp. 53–110; and chapter 9.

65. Calvin, *Institutio* (1559), III.ii.33: "Unde etiam liquet fidem humana intelligentia multo superiorem esse. Nec satis fuerit mentem esse Dei spiritu illuminatum, nisi et ejus virtute cor obfirmetur ac fulciatur."

66. Ibid., III.ii.33: "In quo tota terra Scholastici aberrant, qui in fidei consideratione nudum ac simplicem ex notitia assensum arripiunt, praeterita cordis fiducia et securitate. . . . quanta sit in percipiendis Dei mysteriis human hebetudo, partim quad ad firmam illam stabilemque cordis constantiam, hoc est, praecipuam fidei partem, non respiciunt."

67. Thomas Aquinas, *De Veritate*, xiv.1 and xxvii. 3, ad. 12, in *Sancti Thomae Aquinatis Doctoris Angelici Opera Omnia* Ad fidem optimarum editionum accurate recognita, 25 vols. (Parma, 1852–73), vol. 9; translated in *St. Thomas Aquinas: Theological Texts*, selected and trans. with notes by Thomas Gilby (Durham, N.C.: Labyrinth Press, 1982), pp. 195, 198.

68. Peter Lombard, *Sententiae*, III, d.23, c.4, s.1, citing Augustine, *In Ioannem euangelium tractatus*, in *CCL* 36. 29.6: "Aliud est enim credere in Deum, aliud credere Deo, aliud credere Deum. Credere Deo, est credere vera esse quae loquitur: quod et mali faciunt; et nos credimus homini, sed non in hominem. Credere Deum, est credere quod ipse sit deus; quod etiam mali faciunt. Credere in Deum, est credendo amare, credendo in eum ire, credendo ei adhaerere et eius membris incorporari"; cf. the variant form of the statement in Thomas Aquinas, *Summa theologiae*, IIa IIae, q.2, a. 2.

69. Peter Lombard, *Sententiae*, III, d. 23, c. 2, following Hebrews 11:1–2; ibid., III, d.23, c.3, s.4: "Haec est fundamentum . . . per quam Christus habitat *in cordibus.*"

70. See P. Parthenius Minges, *Scoti doctrina philosophica et theologica*, II, pp. 464–65.

71. On the "théologiens Sorboniques" see James K. Farge, *Biographical Register of Paris Doctors of Theology, 1500–1536, Subsidia Medievalia*, 10 (Toronto: Pontifical Institute of Medieval Studies, 1980) and Farge, *Orthodoxy and Reform in Early Reformation France: The Faculty of Paris, 1500–1536* (Leiden: E. J. Brill, 1980).

72. Cf. Erasmus, *Ratio seu methodus compendio perveniendi ad veram theologiam*, in *Ausgewählte Werke*, ed. Hajo Holborn and Annemarie Holborn (Munich: C. H. Berk, 1933), pp. 282, 285, 301, 304.

73. A complete collation of these texts is found in section "A" of the appendix at the end of the chapter.

74. For example, II.iii.13; III.xv.7; III.xviii.8; III.xviii.9; IV.xix.24. See the texts in part "B" of the appendix at the end of the chapter.

75. *CO* 7, cols. 1–44. Calvin's texts contain the articles of the Sorbonne doctors. Also see the French in the *Recueil des opuscules*, cols. 531–71, and cf. the discussion in Wulfert de Greef, *The Writings of John Calvin: An Introductory Guide*, trans. Lyle D. Bierma (Grand Rapids, Mich.: Baker Book House, 1993), pp. 159–60.

76. See Richard C. Gamble, "Calvin's Theological Method: The Case of Caroli," in *Calvin: Erbe und Auftrag. Festechrift für Wilhelm Heinrich Neuser zum 65. Geburtstag*, ed. Willem Van 't Spijker (Kampen: Kok Pharos, 1991), pp. 130–37.

77. Oberman, *Initia Calvini*, pp. 39–43.

78. See Francis Higman, *Censorship and the Sorbonne: A Bibliographical Study of Books in French Censured by the Faculty of Theology in the University of Paris, 1520–1551* (Geneva: Droz, 1979), pp. 23–45.

79. Bonaventure, III *Sent.* d. 19, a. 2, q. 1, ad. 1.

80. Duns Scotus, III *Sent.* d. 19, q. unica: "unde tandem concludit quod Christus dicitur mediator non secundum divinam sed secundum humanam in qua illa suscepit quibus nos toti trinitati reconciliat ut passionem mortemque . . ." but "quod mediatoris officio congruit cum medium sapiat proprietatem utriusque extremorum."

81. Biel, *Collectorium* III, d. xix, q. unica, art. 3, dubium 4.

82. Cf. Calvin, *Institutio* (1559), II.xiv.3, 6 with Joseph Tylenda, "Christ the Mediator: Calvin versus Stancaro," *Calvin Theological Journal* 8 (1973), pp. 5–16, 131–57.

83. Ibid., II.xvii.1; cf. François Wendel, *Calvin: The Origins and Development of His Religious Thought*, trans. Philip Mairet (New York: Harper & Row, 1963), pp. 227–232.

84. Ibid., I.xvi.8; cf. III.xxi.7; and note Calvin, *Comm. in Epist. ad Romanos* [11:34], in *CO* 49, col. 231: "Tenenda vero est quam nuper attuli distinctio inter arcanum Dei consilium et voluntatem in scriptura patefactam"; also Calvin, *Comm. in quatuor Pauli Epist.* [Eph. 3:11], *CO* 51, 183: "fuisse aeternum semperque fixum decretum, sed quod debuerit in Christo sanciri, quia in ipso statutum erat"; Calvin, *In Evang. Ioh. Commentarius* [6:40], in *CO* 47, col. 147: "Quod si Deus fide servari vult quos elegit et aeternum suum decretum hoc modo sancit ac exsequitur, quisquis non contentus Christo de aeterna praedestinatione curiose inquirit, quantum in se est, praeter Dei consilium salvus esse appetit. Electio Dei per se occulta est et arcana: eam Dominus

vocatione qua nos dignatur patefacit"; and Calvin, *In Evang. Ioh. Commentarius* [10:16], *CO* 47, 244: "Nam arcanum Dei consilium, quo ordinati sunt ad vitam homines, tandem suo tempore patefacit vocatio."

85. Calvin, *Institutio* (1559), I.xvi.9; II.xii.1.

86. Ibid., I.xvi.9, cited earlier, note 42; cf. the identical use of the example of Christ's bones in Calvin's treatise of 1552, *De aeterna Dei praedestinatione*, in *CO* 8, col. 354, as an explanation of the kinds of necessity.

87. Note Ioannes Oecolampadius, *Annotationes piae ac doctae in Evangelium Ioannis* (Basel: Bebel & Cratander, 1533), fol. 356v, grounding the preservation of Christ's bones on God's eternal decree; and Wolfgang Musculus, *Commentariorum in evangelistam Ioannem* (Basel: Ioannes Hervagius, 1548), pp. 440–41, on the providential preservation of Christ's bones unbroken.

88. Cf. Calvin, *In Evang. Ioh. Commentarius*, in *CO* 47, col. 421–22 (*CTS John* II, pp. 239, 241–42).

89. Calvin, *Institutio* (1559), II.xii.1: "De necessitate si quaeritur, non simplex quidem (ut vulgo loquuntur) vel absoluta fuit: sed manavit ex caelesti decreto, unde pendebat hominum salus."

90. Cf. Seeberg's analysis of Scotus' argumentation, *Textbook of the History of Doctrines*, trans. Charles Hay (Grand Rapids, Mich.: Baker Book House, 1952), II, pp. 156–157.

91. See Pieter A. Verhoef, "Luther's and Calvin's Exegetical Library," in *Calvin Theological Journal* 3 (1968), pp. 5–20; cf. Steinmetz, "John Calvin on Isaiah 6: A Problem in the History of Exegesi's," *Interpretation* 36 (1982), pp. 160–63.

92. Calvin, *Institutio* (1559), I.x.2: "Ubi animadvertamus ejus aeternitatem *kai autousian*, magnifico illo nomine bis repetito"; cf. I.xiii.23, of Christ: "Nam quum ubique ponatur nomen Jehovae, sequitur deitatis respectu ex se ipso esse."

93. John Calvin, *Mosis reliqui libri quatuor in formam harmoniae, digesta a Ioanne Calvino: cum eiusdem commentariis*, in *CO* 24, col. 43–44: "Futurum verbi tempus legitur Hebraice: Ero qui ero: sed quod praesenti aequipollet, nisi quod designat perpetuum durationis tenorem. Hoc quidem satis liquet, Deum sibi uni asserere divinitatis gloriam, quia sit a se ipso ideoque aeternus: et ita omnibus creaturis det esse, vel subsistere. Neque enim vulgare quidquam vel commune aliis de se praedicat, sed aeternitatem vendicat propriam solius Dei, idque ut pro sua dignitate celebretur. Proinde continuo post neglecta ratione grammaticae, idem verbum primae personae loco substantivi usurpat, et verbo tertiae persone annectit: ut admiratio subeat animos, quoties incomprehensibilis essentiae fit mentio. Etsi autem de haec aeternitate magnifice disserunt philosophi, et Plato constanter affirmet, Deum proprie esse *to on*, hoc tamen elogium non scite neque ut decet, in suum usum accommodant, nempe unicum esse Dei absorbeat quas cunque imaginamur essentias: deinde ut accedat simul summum imperium et potestas gubernandi omnia. . . . Ergo ut solide apprehendamus unum Deum, scire primum necesse est, quidquid in coelis est vel in terra, precario suam essentiam vel subsistentiam ab uno qui solus vere est, mutuari. Ex illo autem esse nascitur et posse: quia si Deus omnia virtute sustinet, arbitrio quoque suo regit"; cf. *CTS Harmony* I, pp. 73–74; and note the similar comments in *Zwingli's On the Providence of God*, in Huldrych Zwingli, *On Providence and Other Essays*, ed. W. J. Hinke (Durham, N.C.: Labyrinth Press, 1983), p. 147.

94. Aquinas, *Summa theologiae*, I, q.2, a.3: "Sed contra est quod dicitur, Exodi 3:14, ex persona Dei: *Ego sum qui sum*"; cf. Aquinas, *Summa contra gentiles*, I.23.9–10: "Deus autem est primum ens, quo nihil est prius. Dei igitur essentia est suum esse. [10] Hanc autem sublimem veritatem Moyses a Domino est edoctus: qui cum quaeret a Domino, *Exod*. 3:13–14, dicens, *Si dixerit ad me filii Israel, Quod nomen eius? quid dicam eis?* Dominus respondit: *Ego sum qui sum. sic dices filiis Israel: Qui est misit me ad vos*, ostendens suum proprium nomen esse QUI EST. Quodlibet autem nomen est institutum ad significandum naturam seu essentiam alicuius rei. Unde relinquitur quod ipsum divinum esse est sua essentia vel natura."

95. Aquinas, *Disputationes, II: De Potentia*, 1, cited in Thomas Gilby, *St. Thomas Aquinas, Theological Texts* (Durham, N.C.: Labyrinth Press, 1982), p. 35.

96. Bonaventure, *Itinerarium mentis in Deum*, V.2, 8; trans. José de Vinck in *The Works of Bonaventure*. 5 vols. (Paterson, N.J.: St. Anthony Guild, 1960), 5, pp. 43, 46.

97. John Duns Scotus, *A Treatise on God as First Principle*, trans. and with a commentary by Allan B. Wolter (Chicago: Franciscan Herald Press, 1966), I.1: "Dominus Deus noster, Moysi servo tuo, de tuo nomine filiis Israel proponendo, a te Doctore verissimo sciscitanti, sciens quid posset de te concipere intellectus mortalium, nomen tuum benedictum reserans, respondisti: EGO SUM, QUI SUM. Tu es verum esse, tu es totum esse."

98. Calvin, *Commentarius in Iohannis Apostoli epistolam*, CO 55, col. 310 (CTS, p. 173).

99. Ibid., *CO* 55, col. 310 (CTS, p. 173).

100. Ibid., *CO* 55, col. 310: "Qui hanc absurditatem volebant effugere, dixerunt, sufficienter pro toto mundo passum esse Christum: sed pro electis tantum efficaciter. Vulgo haec solutio in scholis obtinuit" (CTS, p. 173); cf. Lombard, *Sententiae in IV libris distinctae*, III, d. xx, c. 5.1: "Christus ergo est sacerdos idemque hostia et pretium nostrae reconciliationis, qui se in ara crucis non diabolo, sed Deo Trinitati obtulit, pro omnibus quantum ad pretii sufficientiam, sed pro electis tantum quantum ad efficaciam, quia praedestinatis tantum salutem effecit." Also note the *Glossa* on Heb. 5:9, *causa salutis aeternae omnibus obtemperantibus sibi*: "Tantum enim valet eius passio quod omnibus sufficit ad salutem" in *PL* 192, col. 438 B. See, further, Arthur M. Landgraf, *Dogmengeschichte der Fruhscholastik*, 4 vols. in 8 (Regensburg: F. Pustet, 1952–56), II/2, pp. 329–58.

101. Ibid., *CO* 55, col. 310: "Ego quamquam verum esse illud dictum fateor:nego tamen praesenti loco quadrare. Neque enim consilium Iohannis, quam toti ecclesiae commune facere hoc bonum" (*CTS*, p. 173).

102. Nicholas of Lyra, *Postillae perpetuae in Veteris et Novum Testamentum*, 5 vols. (Rome: Conradus Sweynheym and Arnoldus Pannartz, 1471–72), in loc.: "nam seipsum obtulit pro nostra expiatione, non pro nostris autem tantum: sed etiam pro totius mundi s. quantum ad sufficientiam, sed pro electis tantum: quantum ad efficaciam."

103. John Calvin, *Commentarii in Isaiam prophetam* 28:22, in *CO* 36, col. 479: "*Alienum* hoc opus dici ideo nonnulli putant, quod nihil magis Dei proprium sit, quam miseri atque ignoscere peccatis nostris . . . alienamque veluti personam et naturae ipsius adversam induere" (*CTS Isaiah* II, pp. 298–99).

104. Calvin, *Commentarii in Isaiam prophetam* 28:22, in *CO* 36, col. 479.

105. Nicholas of Lyra, *Postillae perpetuae*, in loc. "punire autem convenit ei per accidens, s. propter hominum maliciam ideo subditur alienum opus eius, etc."

106. See Schreiner, "Through a Mirror Dimly," pp. 179, 186; Schreiner, "Exegesis and Double Justice," pp. 327, 329, 331, 337–38; cf. Steinmetz, "John Calvin on Isaiah 6," pp. 159, 61.

107. Calvin could have had access to the *Biblia sacra cum glossis, interlineari et ordinaria, Nicolai Lyrani Postilla et Moralitatibus, Burgensis additionibus, & Thoringi replicis* (Lyons: Antoine Vincent, 1545) and the works of Denis the Carthusian, as identified in Ganoczy, *Bibliothèque de l'Académie*, pp. 183, 189. Some doubt has been cast on Calvin's use of Lyra in his commentary on Genesis by Lane, who notes that parallels between Calvin and Lyra can be accounted for by Calvin's use of Luther's lectures on Genesis: see Lane, "The Sources of Calvin's Citations in his Genesis Commentary," in *Interpreting the Bible*, ed. Lane, p. 76.

108. Cf. Lombard, *Sententia*, II, d.24, s.5; Aquinas, *Summa theologiae*, I, q.83, a.3. Note LaVallee, "Calvin's Criticism of Scholastic Theology," pp. 267–69, where the author offers a collation of translations showing the "interchangeability of terms" such as *adversarii* and *Papistes*, *scholastici* and *Sorbonnistes* in Calvin's *Institutes*. In this and the following citations from the *Institutes*, I have followed John Calvin, *Institutes of the Christian Religion of John Calvin: 1539, Text and Concordance*, ed. Richard F. Wevers, 4 vols. (Grand Rapids, Mich.: Meeter Center for

Calvin Studies, 1988); *Institutio christianae religionis* (1559), in *Ioannis Calvini opera quae supersunt omnia*, 59 vols., ed. Guilielmus Baum, Eduardus Cunitz, and Eduardus Reuss (Brunswick: Schwetschke, 1863–1900), vols. 29–30; *Institution de la religion chrestienne de Calvin*, texte original de 1541, réimprimé sous la direction de Abel Lefranc par Henri Chatelain et Jacques Pannier (Paris: Librairie Honoré Champion, 1911); and Calvin, *Institution de la religion Chrestienne* (Geneva: Crespin, 1560). I have also consulted *Institution de la religion chrétienne*, 4 vols. (Geneva: Labor et Fides, 1955–58). In addition, while recognizing the methodological problem, I have cited for the sake of further comparison some of the scholastic doctors noted in the apparatus of modern editions of the *Institutes*.

109. For example, the reference to "scholastici" and "scolastiques" was not present in 1539/41; cf. Lombard, *Sententiae*, II, d.25, s.8.

110. Cf. Aquinas, *Summa theologiae*, I, qu.83, a.3

111. Lombard, *Sententiae*, II, d.24, c.5; Aquinas, *Summa theologiae*, II/1, q.109, a.1–2; Duns Scotus, *In Sent.*, I, d. 17, q.2, a.2; q.3, a.19.

112. Aquinas, *Summa theologiae*, II/1, q.108, a.4; II/2, qq.184, 186.

113. Text added in 1559, no parallel in 1539/41; cf. Lombard, *Sententiae*, III, d.18; Bonaventure *In Sent.*, III, d.8; Aquinas, *Summa theologiae*, III, q.59, a.3.

114. Not found in 1539/41.

115. N.B., "sophistis" drops out of the Latin text in 1559. Cf. Lombard, *Sententiae*, III, d. 25, c. 1–4; Alexander of Hales, *Summa theologicae*, III, q. 82, memb. 4, a.1; Bonaventure, *In Sent.*, III, d.25, a.1, q.3; Aquinas, *Summa theologiae*, II/2, q.2, a. 5–8; Biel, *Collectorium*, III, d.25, q.1, a.1, nota 2.

116. The "in scholis" = "sorbonistes" appears only in 1559/60 but is textually related to the polemic of the 1539/41 text, as found in the preceding citation (III.ii.1–2)—thus, (1539): "qui praeterquam quod calignosa sua definitione totam vim eius deterunt: dum nugatorium fidei formatae et informis definitionem totam eius deterunt"; 1541: "lezquelz, oultre ce qu'liz amoyndrissent la vertu d'icelle par leur obscure et tenebreuse diffinition, en adjoustant je ne scay quelle distinction frivole de la foy formée et informe . . ."; Cf. Lombard, *Sententiae*, III, d. 23, c.4; Aquinas, *Summa theologiae*, II/2, q. 4, a.3.

117. Cf. Bonaventure, *In Sent.*, IV, d.20, pars. 1; Aquinas, *Summa theologiae*, II/1, q.112, a.5.

118. Cf. Lombard, *Sentences*, III, d.23, c.9; d.25, c.5; Bonaventure, *In Sent.*, III, d.36, q.6.

119. Cf. Lombard, *Sententiae*, IV, d.14, s.1

120. Cf. ibid., IV, a.17, s.1–4; Aquinas, *Summa theologiae*, III, suppl., q.6, a.2–3.; Biel, *Collectorium*, IV, d.17, q.1, a.1.

121. Ibid., III, d.19, s.4; Aquinas, *Summa theologiae*, III, q. 83, a.4.

122. Italicized phrases appear for the first time in 1559/60. Cf. Aquinas, *Summa theologiae*, II/1, q.112, a.3; Bonaventure, *In Sent.*, I, d.41, a.1, q.2.

123. These phrases are lacking in 1539/41: they appear for the first time in 1543. Cf. Aquinas, *Summa theologiae*, II/1, q.113, a.1.

124. Cf. Biel, *Collectorium*, II, d.27, q.1, a.2; Aquinas, *Summa theologiae*, III, supp., q.25, a.1.

125. Cf. Duns Scotus, *In Sent.*, I, d.17, q.3; Occam, *In Sent.*, I, d.17, q.1.

126. Lombard, *Sententiae*, I, d.40, s.4.

127. The phrase belongs to the 1536 text.

128. Cf. Lombard, *Sententiae*, IV, d.1, s.1; Aquinas *Summa theologiae*, III, q.62, a.6; II/1, q.101, a.2.

129. Not found in 1539/41; the reference is certainly to the "Ego Berengarius" mentioned in IV.xvii.12; cf. Alexander of Hales, *Summa theologicae*, IV, q.40, memb.3, a.7; Bonaventure, *In Sent.*, IV, d.10, q.1, a.4; Biel, *Collectorium*, IV, d.10, q.1.

130. Added in 1559, no parallel found in 1339/411. Cf. Lombard, *Sententiae*, III, d.22, c.3.
131. Phrase absent from the 1541 French text.
132. Cf. Lombard, *Sententiae*, IV, d.22, c.3; and note the similar differences of usage in III.iv.15—(1559): "Quid romanenses theologi?"; (1560): "Qu'en est-il des théologiens papistes?"; III.iv.17—(1559): "juxta istorum formulas dissecabant"; (1560): "selon les distinctions des docteurs confessionaires" ["istorum" refers to the "romanenses theologi" of III.iv.15.]

CHAPTER FOUR

This essay has also appeared in *Sixteenth Century Journal.*

1. The definitive study for all editions of Calvin's works published during his lifetime is Rodolphe Peter and Jean-François Gilmont, *Bibliotheca Calviniana. Les oeuvres de Jean Calvin publiées au xvie siècle: Écrits théologiques, littéraires et juridiques,* 2 vols. [1532–1564] (Geneva: Droz, 1991–94); cf. John Calvin, *Opera quae supersunt omnia,* ed. G. Baum, E. Cunitz, and E. Reuss (Brunswick: Schwetschke, 1863–1900); *Catalogus operum Calvini chronologicus,* in vol. 59, cols. 461–99, Benjamin B. Warfield, "On the Literary History of Calvin's Institutes," in John Calvin, *Institutes of the Christian Religion,* trans. John Allen, 7th ed. (Philadelphia: Presbyterian Board of Christian Education, 1936), pp. xxx–xxxi, and Olivier Fatio, "Présence de Calvin à l'époque de l'orthodoxie réformée: Les abrégés de Calvin à la fin du 16e et au 17e siècle," in *Calvinus Ecclesiae Doctor,* ed. W. H. Neuser [Die Referate des Internationalen Kongresses für Calvinforschung vom 25 bis 28 September 1978 in Amsterdam] (Kampen: J. H. Kok, 1980), pp. 171–207. I must offer a word of thanks to the H. Henry Meeter Center for Calvin Studies at Calvin College and Seminary, without the resources of which—namely, virtually all of the editions of Calvin's *Institutes* published between 1536 and 1667, plus the later editions and translations—this essay could not have been written.

2. Brian G. Armstrong, *Calvinism and the Amyraut Heresy: Protestant Scholasticism and Humanism in Seventeenth-Century France* (Madison: University of Wisconsin Press, 1969).

3. Modern efforts—subsequent to the editorial work of the *Corpus Reformatorum*—at understanding the structure and argument of the *Institutes* include Julius Köstlin, "Calvin's *Institutio* nach Form und Inhalt, in ihrer geschlichtlichen Entwicklung," *Theologische Studien und Kritiken* 41 (1868), pp. 7–62, 410–86; Edward A. Dowey, *The Knowledge of God in Calvin's Theology* (New York: Columbia University Press, 1952); Dowey, "The Structure of Calvin's Theological Thought as Influenced by the Two-fold Knowledge of God," in *Calvinus Ecclesiae Genevensis Custos,* ed. W. H. Neuser [Die Referate des Internationalen Kongresses für Calvinforschung. Vom 6 bis 9 September 1982 in Genf] (Frankfurt am Main: Peter Lang, 1984), pp. 135–48; T. H. L. Parker, *The Doctrine of the Knowledge of God: A Study in the Theology of John Calvin* (1952; rev. ed. Grand Rapids, Mich.: Eerdmans, 1959); Ford Lewis Battles, "Calculus fidei," in *Calvinus Ecclesiae Doctor,* ed. W. H. Neuser, pp. 85–110; Brian G. Armstrong, "The Nature and Structure of Calvin's Theology: Another Look," in *John Calvin's Institutes: His Opus Magnum,* ed. B. van der Walt (Potchefstrom: Institute for Reformational Studies, 1986), pp. 55–81; Armstrong, "*Duplex cognitio Dei,* Or? The Problem and Relation of Structure, Form, and Purpose in Calvin's Theology," in *Probing the Reformed Tradition: Historical Essays in Honor of Edward A. Dowey, Jr.,* ed. Elsie Anne McKee and Brian G. Armstrong (Louisville: Westminster/John Knox, 1989), pp. 135–53.

4. *Institutio christianae religionis, Ioanne Calvino Authore, quae ad superiores editiones hac postrema, omnium emendatissima locupletissimaque, recens adita sunt . . .* (Geneva: Ioannes le Preux, 1590), is the earliest edition in which I have found the *argumenta;* they are repeated in subsequent Genevan editions and are found also in various Dutch editions, including the Amsterdam *Opera* of 1667. From thence they were transmitted to the Tholuck edition in the nineteenth century and to the two older English translations namely, Allen and Beveridge: cf. *Joannis Calvini Institutio*

christianae religionis . . . curavit A. Tholuck, 2 vols. (Edinburgh: T. & T. Clark, 1874), I, pp. 21–24, 31, 167, 369; II, p. 199, Johannes Calvinus, *Institutie ofte Onderwijsinghe in de christelicke Religie* . . . over-geset door Wilhelmus Corsmannus (1650), reissued with an intro. by A. Kuyper (Doesburg: J. C. van Schenk Brill, 1889) and, also with corrections by J. H. Landwehr (Rotterdam: D. Bolle, 1912); and John Calvin, *Institutes of the Christian Religion*, trans. John Allen, 2 vols., 3rd ed. (Philadelphia: Presbyterian Board of Publication, 1841), I, pp. 41–46, 220–21, 483–84, II, 219–20, and Calvin, *Institutes of the Christian Religion*, trans. Henry Beveridge, 2 vols. 1845; repr. Grand Rapids, Mich.: Eerdmans, 1994, I, pp. 27–30, 36, 208, 461; II, p. 278. The *argumenta* are not, however, reproduced in the *Ioannis Calvini Opera quae supersunt omnia*, ed. G. Baum, E. Cunitz, and E. Reuss (Brunswick, 1863–1900), the *Calvini Opera Selecta*, ed. P. Barth and W. Niesel, 5 vols. (Rev. ed. Munich: Christian Kaiser, 1952–62), or the *Institutes of the Christian Religion*, ed. John T. McNeill, trans. Ford Lewis Battles, 2 vols. (Philadelphia: Westminster, 1960).

5. *Institutio christianae religionis, Ioanne Calvino authore. Quae ad superiores editiones hac postrema, omnium emendatissima locupletissimaque* (Geneva: Johannes Le Preux, 1590). I originally identified the crucial edition in which the apparatus was gathered as having been printed in 1585, based on the date on the title page of a Le Preux octavo edition at the Meeter Center: cf. my "In the Light of Orthodoxy: The 'Method and Disposition' of Calvin's *Institutio* from the Perspective of Calvin's Late Sixteenth-Century Editors," in *Sixteenth Century Journal*, 28/4 (1997), pp. 1203–29. The *Admonitio ad lectorem* in this volume, however, is dated 1590. The volume is also identical in all respects, the title page being excepted, to the 1592 Le Preux octavo printing, and appears to be a variant of the 1592 printing. This conclusion leaves the 1590 folio Le Preux edition as the point at which the apparatus was completed. I owe thanks to Irena Backus, Marc Vial, and Jean-François Gilmont for their help in resolving this issue.

6. Cf. the comments in Calvin, *Institutes* (McNeill/Battles), I, pp. xix–xx, where McNeill identifies the headings used to subdivide the chapters as new in his edition and indicates that the subheadings associated with the numbered sections of the *Institutes* were largely taken from the modern German translation of Otto Weber, with a few being added by McNeill himself. No mention is made by McNeill of the existence of the older apparatus—although he elsewhere expresses admiration for Launeus's work (see ibid., pp. xlvii–xlix).

7. The *Corpus Reformatorum* does refer to the various indices and materials in the prolegomena (*CO* 1, pp. xlviii), noting that they were not by Calvin and were therefore "banished"—with two exceptions, the index from the first edition (Basel, 1536: cf. *CO* 1, cols. 249–52) and the Colladon index of *loci*. The Colladon index does not appear, however, in the 1559 edition, but only a list, based on Colladon's index of *loci*, of the major heads without any reference to their parts or details concerning contents (*CO* 2, pp. 5–6); the Colladon index is found in its French version following the text of the 1560 French *Institution* (*CO* 4, cols. 1169–1238). Thus, none of the older apparatus for the Latin text apears in *CO*.

8. Johannes Calvin, *Unterricht in der christlichen Religion*, bearbeitet und übersetzt von Professor D. E. F. Müller (Neukirchen: Moers, 1909).

9. Johannes Calvijn, *Institutie, of Onderwijzing in de christelijke Godsdienst*, naar de laatste Uitgave in mei 1864, door de Prof. G. Baum, E. Cuniz en E. Reuss, 3 vols. (Kampen: G. Ph. Zalsman, 1865–68); Johannes Calvijn, *Institutie, of Onderwijzing in de christelijke Godsdienst*, uit het in vertaald door Dr. A. Sizoo (Delft: W. D. Meinema, 1931); Jean Calvin, *Institution de la religion chrestienne*, edition critique avec introduction, notes et variants publiée par Jean-Daniel Benoit, 5 vols. (Paris: J. Vrin, 1957–63).

10. Cf. Johannes Calvin, *Unterricht in der christlichen Religion: Institutio christianae religionis*, übersetzt und bearbeitet von Otto Weber (Neukirchen: Moers, 1936); Jean Calvin, *Institution de la religion chrétienne*, edition nouvelle publiée par La Société Calviniste de France, 4 vols. (Geneva: Labor et Fides, 1955–58).

11. Cf. Ioannes Calvinus, *Institutio totius christianae religionis* (Geneva: Ioannes Gerardus, 1550); Calvinus, *Institutio christianae religionis* (Geneva: Robertus Stephanus, 1553).

12. *Institutio christianae religionis, in libros quatuor nunc primum digesta, certisque distincta capitibus, ad aptissimam methodum: aucta etiam tam magna accessione ut propemodum opus novum haberi possit* (Geneva: Robertus Stephanus, 1559; Strasbourg: Wendelin Rihel, 1561); *Institutio christianae religionis in libros quatuor . . :* (Geneva: Antonius Rebulius, 1561). McNeill indicates that the Rebulius edition adds a new index: cf. Calvin, *Institutes* (McNeill/Battles), p. xxxix— but its index is actually only a version of the original Colladon index of *loci* that appears in virtually all of the editions of the *Institutes* from 1559 on. It is the case, however, that the 1559 Stephanus and the 1561 Rihel editions were folios and the entirely reset Rebulius edition is an octavo—perhaps the first octavo edition of the 1559 Latin text. The French of Colladon's index appears for the first time in Jean Calvin, *Institution de la religion chrestienne* (Geneva: Jean Crespin, 1560); it can also be found in *CO* 4, cols. 1169–1238. The attribution of the index to Colladon rests on the comment in Colladon's introduction to the 1576 Lausanne edition, "addimus autem nonnulla in Indice nostro per locos communes descripto," and on the vague statement in the introductory *admonitio* of the 1590 J. le Preux edition that the marginalia are based on Colladon's work in earlier editions (the index to *loci* being the only anonymous element of the apparatus). The Latin title of the index reads "Index in Institutionem christianae religionis a Io. Calvino conscriptam"—grammatically attributing the *Institutes* but not the index to Calvin. The 1574 edition of Norton's English translation, in which the index appears for the first time, however, attributes it directly to Calvin: "A Table of the Matters Entreated of in this Booke, disposed in the forme of common places, wherein is briefely rehearsed the summe of the Doctrine concerning every poynte taught in the Booke before at large, collected by the Author." In either case, the index is close to Calvin both in a personal sense and in its choice of words, which frequently reflect and even excerpt phrases from the 1559 text.

13. Jean Calvin, *Institution de la religion chrestienne. nouvellement mise en quatre livres: et distinguée par chapitres, en ordre et methode bien propre . . .* (Geneva: Jean Crespin, 1560).

14. *Institution de la religion chrestienne* (Geneva: Jacques Bourgeois, 1562) and *Institutio christianae religionis* (Geneva: Perrinus, 1568, 1569); cf. R. Peter and J.-F. Gilmont, *Bibliotheca Calviniana* (Geneva: Droz, 1991–94), II, pp. 903–8. Peter and Gilmont offer (pp. 905–07) the text of Marlorat's letter and (pp. 899–926) survey the many French editions of the *Institutes* published in 1562—some of which do not include the Marlorat materials; cf. *Institutio christianae religionis . . . indices duo locupletissimi: alter rerum insignium: alter vero locorum sacrae Scripturae qui in his Institutionibus obiter explicantur* (Geneva: Robertus Stephanus, 1568). Note the description of the Marlorat indices to the 1562 French text in *CO* 3, p. xlii, noting both an "indice . . . des matieres" and an "indice contenant les passages de la Bible . . ." and cf. the discussion in Calvin, *Institutes* (McNeill/Battles), I, pp. xxxix–xl. The editors of the *Calvini Opera* indicate (*CO* 3, p. xlvii) that they have included Marlorat's "Table des matières" at the end of the *Institution*; what appears at this location, however, are two indices, first a "Table ou brief sommaire des principales matieres" (*CO* 4, cols. 1169–1238), which is in fact the French version of the Colladon index, which had already been offered in the 1560 French edition of Crespin, and, second, the Marlorat "Indice des matieres" (*CO* 4, cols. 1239–60).

15. *Institutio christianae religionis* (Geneva: Franciscus Perrinus, 1568, 1569).

16. Cf. the comments in Bunnie, *Institutio christianae religionis, a Ioanne Calvino conscripta, compendium simul, ac methodi enarratio, per Edmundum Bunnium* (Antwerp: Aegidius Radaeus, 1582), fol. 5v–6v, and Fatio, "Présence de Calvin," pp. 176–84, on the compendia of Bunnie, Delaune, and Molichius, pp. 189–99, on the compendia by Olevianus, Piscator, and Colonius. Fatio does not mention Jerome Zanchi, *Compendium praecipuorum capitum doctrinae christianae*, in Zanchi's *Operum theologicorum* (Heidelberg, 1617), vol. 8, a work based on the third rescension 1543/5 of the *Institutes*. Examination of these compendia, apart from the impact of Bunnie,

Delaune, and Olevian on the apparatus of the *Institutes*, is beyond the compass of this essay but, as Fatio indicates, would be of considerable significance for the analysis of late-sixteenth- and seventeenth-century understanding of Calvin's thought. Rather, moreover, than follow Fatio's analysis of the compendia themselves, we direct our attention here to the way in which several of the compendia were drawn into the text-history of the apparatus and marginalia of the *Institutes*.

17. Cf. Bunnie, *Compendium*, fol. 5v–6v.

18. On the text and text-history of the *Institutes*, see Köstlin, "Calvin's *Institutio* nach Form und Inhalt," pp. 7–21, 33–60; Abel Lefranc, "Introduction," in *Institution de la religion chrestienne de Calvin*, texte original de 1541 (Paris: Librairie Honoré Champion, 1911), pp. 1*–57*; Warfield, "Literary History," pp. xvii–xxxiii; François Wendel, *Calvin: The Origins and Development of His Religious Thought*, trans. Philip Mairét (New York: Harper & Row, 1963), pp. 112–22; and Jean-Daniel Benoit, "The History and Development of the *Institutio*: How Calvin Worked," in *John Calvin: A Collection of Distinguished Essays*, ed. Gervase E. Duffield (Grand Rapids, Mich.: Eerdmans, 1966).

19. John Calvin, *Institutio christianae religionis . . . additi sunt nuper dou indices, hac postrema editione longè quam anteà castigatores, ab Augustino Marlorato pridem collecti . . .* (London: Thomas Vautrollerius, 1576); note that the title page reference to the two added Marlorat indices yields three indices in the Vautrollier *Institutio*, given the presence of the Colladon index of *loci* as well; also see J. C. Whitebrook, "Calvin's *Institute of Christian Religion* in the Imprints of Thomas Vautrollier," *Transactions of the Congregational Historical Society* 12 (1933–36), pp. 199–200. The *argumenta* are acknowledged in the preface as the work of Edmund Bunnie, whose *Compendium* or abridgement of the *Institutes* also appeared from Vautrollerius in the same year: *Institutio christianae religionis, a Ioanne Calvino conscripta, compendium simul, ac methodi enarratio, per Edmundum Bunnium* (London: Thomas Vautrollerius, 1576); cf. Fatio, "Présence de Calvin," p. 174. The Colladon and the Marlorat indices had not been translated for the first two printings of *The Institution of Christian Religion, wrytten in Latine by maister Iohn Calvin, and translated into Englysh according to the author's last edition* [trans. Thomas Norton] (London: Reinolde Wolfe & Richarde Harison, 1561, 1562), which includes only a brief two-page listing of the "heads" or titles of the *loci* from Colladon. The indices finally appeared in translation in 1574. The system of internal cross-references appears to be unique to the Vautrollerius edition, although the Vautrollerius/Bunnie marginalia do pass over into the Norton translation.

20. *Institutio christianae religionis, a Ioanne Calvino conscripta, compendium simul, ac methodi enarratio, per Edmundum Bunnium* (London: Thomas Vautrollerius, 1576), trans. as *The Institutions of Christian Religion, written by that reverend father, D. Iohn Calvin, compendiously abridged by Edmund Bunnie* (London: Thomas Dawson, 1578, 1580); also, *Institutio christianae religionis, a Ioanne Calvino conscripta, compendium simul, ac methodi enarratio, per Edmundum Bunnium* (Antwerp: Aegidius Radaeus, 1582); cf. the discussion in Calvin, *Institutes* (McNeill/Battles), I, p. xlviii, with Warfield, "Literary History," pp. xxxiv–xxxv. McNeill offers a description of various compendia of the *Institutes* but does not examine the relationship of the compendia to the sixteenth-century apparatus. The relationship between various sixteenth-century abridgements of the *Institutes* and elements of the apparatus is noted in Fatio, "Présence de Calvin," pp. 174–76, 191–92, and the Vautrollier editions are described at length in Whitebrook, "Calvin's *Institute of Christian Religion*," pp. 197–212. On another aspect of the work of Bunnie, see Brad S. Gregory, "The 'True and Zealouse Seruice of God': Robert Parsons, Edmund Bunny, and *The First Booke of the Christian Exercise*," *Journal of Ecclesiastical History* 45/2 (April 1994), pp. 238–68.

21. I am hesitant to describe all architectonic charts of the late sixteenth century, without qualification, as Ramist. Whereas the charts offered by Bunnie and, equally so, those provided by Launeus (see note 27) are horizontal and characterized by frequent bifurcation—as are Ramist charts—they carefully oblige the material, so that, when the subject is not amenable to bifurcation,

the division can be three- or fourfold. In addition, the Bunnie and the Launeus charts are not characterized by an overtly stated "either/or" division, typical of Ramist logic. They are, thus, little different from the Agricolan charts of the early sixteenth century: cf., for example, the chart of the Decalogue given with the 1525 Strasburg catechism in Ferdinand Cohrs, *Die Evangelischen Katechismusversuche vor Luthers Enchiridion*, 5 vols. (Berlin: A Hofmann, 1900–1907; repr., 2 vols., Hildesheim and New York: George Olms, 1978), I, p. 119.

22. Cf. *Institutio christianae religionis . . . compendium simul, ac methodi enarratio, per Edmundum Bunnium*, III.ii, ad init.

23. *Institutio christianae religionis, Ioanne Calvino authore. Quae ad superiores editiones hac postrema, omnium emendatissima locupletissimaque* (Geneva: Iohannes Le Preux, 1590).

24. *Ioannis Calvini Operum omnium theologicorum* (Geneva: Vignon & Chouet, 1617): *Institutio* in volume VI.

25. *Ioannis Calvini noviodunensis Opera omnia, in novem tomos digesta* (Amsterdam: Johann Jacob Schipper, 1667–71): *Institutio* in volume IX.

26. Note that the Allen translation includes only Olevian's *Methodus et dispositio* and Bunnie's four primary *argumenta*; Beveridge offers these tools plus the Bunnie/J. Le Preux initial argument-analysis for the longer chapters, a somewhat edited form of the 1590 J. Le Preux marginalia set as a chapter synopsis just prior to the text of each chapter, and a set of one hundred "aphorisms" summarizing the entire *Institutio*. The Beveridge translation, therefore, offers the most extensive translation of the sixteenth-century apparatus.

27. *Institutio christianae religionis, ab ipso authore anno 1559, & in libros quatuor digesta. . . . Cum Indice per locos communes opera N. Colladonis tunc contexto. Additi sunt postea duo Indices ab augustino Marlorato collecti anno 1562, ut testatur eius epistola: quorum prior res praecipuas; posterior, in ea expositos copiosissimae sacrae Scripturae locos continet. . . . Accesserunt autem hac editione, breves summae in singularum sectionum margine, quoad eius fieri potuit, & collationes diversorum locorum eiusdem Calvini, tum in Institutione, tum in variis Commentariis, sed praecipue in opusculis eis compluribus: quaedam etiam annotata tam ex veteribus, quam in recentioribus scriptoribus. Et hac quidam concinnabat hoc anno N. Collado . . . epistola ad doctissimum virum Blasium Marcuardum . . .* (Lausanne: Franciscus Le Preux, 1576).

28. *Institutio christianae religionis* (Lausanne, 1576), fol. **j; and see Peter and Gilmont, *Bibliotheca Calviniana*, II, pp. 711, 762–63 for comments on and a French translation of portions of the letter; much of the text also appears in the prolegomena to the *Institutio* in *CO* 1, p. xli. Colladon appears to have had a major hand in the final edition of the 1560 French translation of the *Institutes* and identifies himself as the author of its topical index, implying the priority of the French over the Latin version of the index: the textual relationship between the Latin and the French indices of *loci* is a subject for further investigation, although a preliminary examination indicates that they are virtually identical, while the presence of page as well as book, chapter, and section references in the Latin appear to indicate its prior relationship to the 1559 Latin edition (page references do not appear in the French index of 1560). In any case, the French index of theological topics is an effort distinct from the Marlorat indices of biblical passages or *loci* also found in these editions.

29. *Institutio christianae religionis, ab ipso authore in anno 1559, & in libros quatuor digesta, certisque distincta capitibus ad aptissimam methodum . . .* (Lausanne: Franciscus Le Preux, 1576, 1577), cf. at IV.xvii.33.

30. Cf. *Institutio christianae religionis* (Geneva: Le Preux, 1590, 1607; Geneva: Vignon & Chouet, 1617; Leiden: David Lopez de Haro, 1654; Amsterdam: Schipper, 1667); also in *Institution de la religion chrestienne . . . traduite par Charles Icard* (Bremen: Herman Brauer, 1713); and note the translation in *Institutes* (Beveridge), II, pp. 677–89.

31. *Institutionis christianae religionis a Ioanne Calvino conscriptae, Epitome in qua adversariorum obiectionibus breves ac solidae responsiones annotantur per Gulielmum Launeum* (London:

Thomas Vautrollerius, 1583); also, Launevs, *Editio secunda emendatior: Tabulis etiam & indice multo facilioribus & locupletioribus* (London: Thomas Vautrollerius, 1584); translated as *An Abridgement of the Institution of Christian Religion, written by M. Iohn Caluin*, trans. Christopher Fetherstone (Edinburgh: n.p., 1585, 1586, 1587); cf. the discussion in Warfield, "Literary History," p. xxxv, and Whitebrook, "Calvin's *Institute of Christian Religion*," pp. 207–11, for a detailed description of Delaune's and Fetherstone's work.

32. The aphorisms appeared separately in translation as *An hundred Aphorismes . . . summarily containing the matter and method of Maister Calvines Institutions* (London, 1596).

33. Cf. *Institutionis christianae religionis . . . Epitome* (London, 1583), *Generalis tabula totius institutionis*, unpaginated, fol. 1–4 of the table, the main divisions of Books I and II. Cf. the discussion in Calvin, *Institutes* (McNeill/Battles), I, pp. xlviii–xlix.

34. *Institutio christianae religionis* (1590), *Centum aphorismi quatuor librorum Institutionis christianae religionis summam & seriem breviter complectens*, located after Calvin's prefaces and after the basic *argumentum*, but before the beginning of book I.

35. Cf. Calvin, *Institutes*, II.i.1 with Dowey, *The Knowledge of God in Calvin's Theology*, pp. 41–2. The question of whether the "twofold knowledge of God" is in fact the fundamental structural concept of the *Institutes* has been questioned by Parker, *The Doctrine of the Knowledge of God*, (London, 1952; rev. ed. Grand Rapids, Mich: Eerdmans, 1959), pp. 119–21, who argued that the Apostle's Creed provides with its fundamental theme and ordering principle. We will return to this question from a sixteenth-century perspective later in this chapter.

36. Calvin, *Institutio christianae religionis* (1590), *Admonitio ad lectorum*.

37. Cf. *Institutio christianae religionis . . . compendium simul, ac methodi enarratio, per Edmundum Bunnium*, IV.ix, ad init. (no division of the chapter into its parts) with *Institutio christianae religionis* (1590), IV.ix, ad init. (summary and tripartite division of the chapter).

38. For example, *Institutio christianae religionis* (1590), IV.ix.3, margin: "Obiectio. In Ecclesia remanet veritas nisi inter pastores, 1 Concilia. Ies. 56:10. Resp. 1. ex vet. testamento ostendens Pastores vacuos fuisse Spiritu scientia & veritatis. Ose. 9:8." Also, ibid., IV.ix.4, margin: "Resp. 2. ex Novo Testamento, ubi praedictum est nostrum seculum ab eo malo immune haud futurum. 2 Pet. 2:1."

39. See Hans Joachim Bremme, *Buchdrucker und Buchhändler zue Zeit der Glaubenskämpfe: Stuien zur Genfer Druckgeschichte, 1565–1580* (Geneva: Droz, 1969), pp. 194–95.

40. Caspar Olevianus, *Institutionis religionis Christianae epitome ex Institutiones Ioh. Calvini excerpta* (Herborn: Christophorus Corvinus, 1586).

41. Köstlin, "Calvin's *Institutio* nach Form und Inhalt," p. 56, mistakenly assumes that the *argumenta* first appeared in the Amsterdam (Schipper) edition of 1667 that was used as a basis for Tholuck's nineteenth-century edition.

42. Calvin, *Institutio christianae religionis, Joannis Calvinus lectori*; cf. the discussion of this issue in chapter 1.

43. Calvin, *Institutio christianae religionis* (1559–90), *index*: "Rectè & proprie dici Christum nobis promeritum esse gratiam Gei & salutem: ubi ostenditur Christum non instrumentum duntaxat esse vel ministrum salutis, sed authorem & principem: neque ita loquendo obscurari Dei gratiam, quia non opponitur meritum Christi misericordiae Dei, imò ab ea dependet. & quae subalterna sunt, non pugnant, lib. 2, cap. 17, sect. 1. / Haec distinctio meriti Christi & gratiae Dei probatur es pluribus Scripturae locis, sect. 2. / Afferentur multa Scripturae testimonia, ex quibus certò & solidè colligitur, Christum sua obedientia verè nobis gratiam apud Patrem acquisisse ac promeritum esse, sect. 3.4.5. / Stultam esse curiositatem, quaerere an aliquid Christus sibi ipse meruerit: temerarium verò, asserere, sect. 6"; cf. Calvin, *The Institution of the Christian Religion* (London, 1574), Table. Note that the chapter-analysis in *Institutio christianae religionis* (Geneva, 1590) follows Colladon's grouping of sections 3–5 into a subdivision of the chapter; cf. Bunnie, *Compendium* (1582), at II.xvii. Note also that, as in other places, the Colladon index

frequently rests on Calvin's text: thus, the Colladon summary of section one reflects *Institutio,* II.xvii.1: "ex mera Dei misericordia, et simul interveniat Christi meritum, quod Dei misericordiae subjicitur"; the summary of section 2 is based on the first sentence of *Institutio,* II.xvii.2: "Haec distinctio colligitur ex plurimis scripturae locis"; of sections 3–5 on the first words of *Institutio,* II.xvii.3: "Quod autem Christus sua obedientia nobis gratiam apud patrem acquisierit ac promeritus sit"; and of section 6 on the phrasing of *Institutio,* II.xvii.5: "non minus stulta est curiositas, quam temeraria definitio ubi hoc idem asserunt."

44. Cf. Thomas F. Torrance, *The Hermeneutics of John Calvin* (Edinburgh: Scottish Academic Press, 1988), pp. 51–52, 66–68 and Marjorie O'Rourke Boyle, *Erasmus on Language and Method in Theology* (Toronto: University of Toronto Press, 1977), pp. 75–83.

45. Calvin, *Institutio christianae religionis* (Geneva: Stephanus, 1559), *Joannis Calvinus lectori.*

46. Cf. John Calvin, *Commentaries on the Epistle to the Romans,* Argumentum, in *CO* 49, cols. 1, 5 (*CTS Romans,* pp. xxix–xxx, xxxiv–xxxv).

47. Calvin, *Institutio christianae religionis* (1590), *Methodus et dispositio.*

48. Cf. Parker, *Calvin's Doctrine of the Knowledge of God,* p. 118, and Warfield, "Literary History," pp. xix–xx; Benoit, "History and Development of the *Institutio,*" p. 109; Köstlin, "Calvin's *Institutio* nach Form und Inhalt," pp. 55–58, offers a partial critique of the *argumentum,* drawing attention to the fact that the four books of the *Institutes* reflect more than the simple credal pattern—which is, in any case, a three-part model.

49. Cf. Calvin, *Institutio christianae religionis* (Lausanne: Franciscus Le Preux, 1577), where Colladon's phrase also appears in the marginalia.

50. Calvin, *Institutio christianae religionis* (1559), *Index:* "unde tum precandi fiducia, tum tranquillitas piis conscientiis oritur"; also cf. the adaptation in Bunnie, *Compendium* (1582): "non modo precandi fiduciam, sed etiam tranquillitatem piis conscientiis oriri." And cf. Calvin, *Institutio christianae religionis* (Lausanne, 1577), where Colladon's phrase also appears in the marginalia.

51. Cf. Bunnie, *Compendium* (1582): "Denique Papistas in hoc caput doctrinae peccare, qui in Missis suis Christum se immolare iactitant."

52. Bunnie, *Compendium* (1585), omits *argumentum* for this chapter.

53. Cf. Bunnie, *Compendium* (1582): "ut negent Deum quenquam reprobare, puerilem esse" with Launeus, *Epitome* (1584), margin: "Quos Deus reprobat."

54. Cf. Calvin, *Institutio* (Lausanne, 1577), margin: "Exceptio adversariorum refutantur."

55. Cf. Ibid., margin: "Altera exceptio adversariorum solvitur."

56. Cf. Ibid., margin: "Hic & sec.3.4.5. ostenditur, frustra litigare cum Deo reprobos, quum Deus nihil ipsis debeat, nihil non iustè velit, & ipsi suae damnationis iustas causas in se reperiant. Impiorum obiectio, & adversus eam muniuntur piae mentes sancta Dei voluntatis reverentia."

57. Cf. ibid., margin: "Profanum commentum. Absolutae potentia."

58. Cf. ibid., margin: "Obiectionis impiorum repetitio: & ad eam responsio."

59. The phrase "aequissima justitiae ratione" is found in Calvin, *Instititui christianae religionis,* III.xxiii.3—and was abstracted by Bunnie.

60. Cf. Calvin, *Institutio* (Lausanne, 1577), margin: "Excpetio impiorum ad superius responsum eorum obiectioni: & solutio exceptionis, hic & sec. 5. Vide & non ab similem impiorum obiectionem sec. 6. Vide & sect. 9."

61. Cf. ibid., margin: "Obiectio impiorum non valde disimilis illi, quae est sect.4."

62. Cf. Calvin, *Institutio christianae religionis* (1559), *Index:* "cur Deus ea vitio imputaret hominibus quorum necessitatem illis sua praedestinatione imposuit" and Bunnie, *Compendium* (1582): "Cur ea vitio Deus imputaret hominibus, quorum necessitatem sua praedestinatione imposuit." And note Calvin, *Institutio christianae religionis,* III.xxiii.6: "Cur ea vitio Deus imputaret hominibus, quorum necessitatem sua praedestinatione imposuit? Quid enim faceret?"

63. Cf. ibid., "Respondetur ad sacrilegiam interrogationem. . . ."

64. Cf. Calvin, *Institutio* (Lausanne, 1577), margin: "Obiectionis nodus expeditur, hic & sec.8.9."

65. Cf. Bunnie, *Compendium* (1582): "tertiam a Valla mutuatam approbat."

66. Cf. Richard A. Muller, "*Duplex cognitio dei* in the Theology of Early Reformed Orthodoxy," in *Sixteenth-Century Journal* 10/2 (Summer 1979), pp. 51–61.

67. As cited, in Calvin's time, in Johannes Altenstaig, *Vocabularius theologiae* (Hagenau: Heinrich Gran, 1517), s.v. *obiectum theologiae*.

68. Calvin, *Institutio christianae religionis* (1590) *Centum aphorismi*: "1. Vera hominis sapientia sita est in congnitione Dei Creatoris & Redemptoris. 2. Haec cognitio est nobis insita. . . . 3. Sed tale semen corrumpitur. . . . 4. Aliunde etiam est comparata: nempe totius mundi fabrica, & sacris scripturis."

69. Calvin, *Institutio christianae religionis* (1590) *Centum aphorismi*: "Cognitio Dei Redemptoris colligitur ex lapsu hominis, & ex materiali redemptionis causa."

70. Dowey, *The Knowledge of God in Calvin's Theology*, pp. 217–18.

71. Cf. Parker, *The Doctrine of the Knowledge of God*, pp. 119–21, and Dowey, "The Structure of Calvin's Theological Thought," pp. 142–48.

72. Cf. Launeus, *Epitome* (1584), *Generalis tabula*, first chart.

73. Köstlin, "Calvin's *Institutio* nach Form und Inhalt," pp. 55–58; Wendel, *Calvin*, p. 121; Dowey, "*The Knowledge of God in Calvin's Theology*, pp. 42–3; Dowey, "The Structure of Calvin's Thought," pp. 142–43.

74. Calvin, *Institutio christianae religionis* (1590), *Methodus et dispositio*: "Primus articulus Symboli Apostolici est de *Deo Patre*. . . . Sic primus liber est de cognitione Dei, quatenus est Creator, conservator et gubernator rerum omnium et singularum. Docet, et quae sit vera Creatoris notitia, et in quem finem tendat. . . ."

75. Ibid.: "Ideo in Symbolo sequitur, *Et in Jesum Christum*. . . . Ita et auctr noster in secundo Institutionis libro tractat de congnitione Dei, quateuns est Redemptor in Christo, ducite hominem ad Christum Mediatorem, ostenso hominis lapsu. . . ."

76. Ibid.: "Quamdiu Christus a nobis separatus est, nihil nobis prodest. Quamobrem ei inseri oportet, ut in palmites viti. Ideo post doctrina de Christo, in tertia Symboli parte sequitur *Et in spiritum Sanctum*: utpote qui est vinculum unionis inter nos et Christum."

77. Ibid.: "Quoniam autem Spiritus Sanctus non omnes homines Christo inserit, seu fide donat, et quos ea donat, non sine mediis ordinarie donat, verum utitur ad eam rem praedicatione Evangelii et Sacramentum usu, cum totius disciplinae administratione." Note that Olevianus' phraseology respects Calvin's unwillingness to place discipline on the same level as Word and Sacrament as a necessary mark of the church.

78. Much recent scholarship has pointed to relationship between scholastic and humanistic developments in the late fifteenth and sixteenth centuries: see, for example, James H. Overfield, *Humanism and Scholasticism in Late Medieval Germany* (Princeton, N.J.: Princeton University Press, 1984), pp. 59–60, 94–100, 329–30; Overfield, "Scholastic Opposition to Humanism in Pre-Reformation Germany," *Viator* 7 (1976), pp. 391–420; Lewis Spitz, "Humanism and the Protestant Reformation," in *Renaissance Humanism*, ed. Albert Rabil Jr. (Philadelphia: University of Pennsylvania Press, 1988), III, p. 393; and John F. D'Amico, "Humanism and Pre-Reformation Theology," in ibid., III, pp. 367–68.

79. See Quirinus Breen, "John Calvin and the Rhetorical Tradition," in Breen, *Christianity and Humanism: Studies in the History of Ideas* (Grand Rapids, Mich.: Eerdmans, 1968), pp. 107–29; and note E. David Willis, "Rhetoric and Responsibility in Calvin's Theology," in *The Context of Contemporary Theology: Essays in Honor of Paul Lehmann*, ed. Alexander McKelway and E. David Willis (Atlanta: John Knox Press, 1974), pp. 43–45, where too much distinction is made between late medieval logic and the rhetorical tradition of Christian humanism and too little distinction between method and content. As Dowey rightly commented, "Recognizing the

humanistic-rhetorical-juristic elements in Calvin's work appears, at present state, not to revolutionize the understanding of his teaching" ("The Structure of Calvin's Theological Thought," p. 137).

80. See Anthony Kenny, "Disputations of the theologians," in *The Cambridge History of Later Medieval Philosophy*, ed. N. Kretzmann, A. Kenny, J. Pinborg, and E. Stump (Cambridge: Cambridge University Press, 1982), pp. 21–6, and Brian Lawn, *The Rise and Decline of the Scholastic "Quaestio disputata"—With Special Emphasis on Its Use in the Teaching of Medicine and Science* (Leiden: E. J. Brill, 1993); and note A. J. Kunz, *Gods kennis en wil volgens de jonge Gomarus: de plaat van Gods kennis en wil in de predestinatieleer van de jonge Gomarus (1599–1609)* (Utrecht: Faculteit der Godgeleerdheid, n.d), to which I am grateful for this point.

81. Calvin, *Institutio christianae religionis* (1590), II.xiv, ad init.: "Duae sunt praecipuae partes hujus capitis: I. Doctrina de duabus in Christo naturis unicam personam efficientibus breviter traditur sec. 1–4. II. Serveti haereses naturarum in Christo distinctionem et divinae filii naturae aeternitatem tolentes, refelluntur sec. 5–8." Cf. Bunnie, *Compendium* (1582): "Primum doctrinam de duabus in Christo naturis breviter tradit, 1–4. Deinde contra exitialem quendam Serveti errorem de Filiatione Christi, aciem instruit, 5–8."

82. Ibid., II.xiv, margin: "Prima pars, demonstrans duas esse in Christo naturas, divinam & humanam. / confirmatio, per similitudinem, qua sumpta est à coniunctione corporis & anima. / Application similitudinis."

83. Ibid., II.xiv, margin: "Secunda confirmatio, à testimoniis Scripturae desumpta, quae utriusque naturae divine nempe & humana distinctionem declarant. / De communicatione proprietatum, testimonia."

84. Ibid., II.xiv, margin: "Tertia confirmation, à testimoniis quae utriusque nathrae coniunctionem ostendunt. / Regula in hac disputatione obervatum digna."

85. Ibid., II.xiv, margin: "Utilitas & usus superioris doctrinae de coniunctione & distinctione utriusque naturae in Christo. / Adversus Nestorianos duplicem Christum fingentes. / Item adv. Eutychianos utramque naturam confundentes ac destruentes. / Utrique meritò ab Ecclesia damnati."

86. Ibid., II.xiv, margin: "Altera pars capitis, qua nominatim Serveti, Filii Dei deitatem et utriusque naturae in eodem veritatem pernegantis, haereses refelluntur. / Generalis responsio, seu suma orthodoxa doctrina de Christo. / Unio hypostatica, quid. / 1. Obiectio Serveti adv. aertenam Christi deitatem.; sh Responsio. / 2. Obiectio. Responsio."

87. Ibid., II.xiv, margin: "3. Obiectio. / Responsio. / Christus verus, naturalis, & unicus filius: qua nota à filiis adoptivis, id est ab omnibus Dei in eodem Christo electis descernitur. / Duplex Christi filiatio: Dei videlicet, & hominis."

88. Ibid., II.xiv, margin: "4. Obiectio. / Responsio. / Confirmatio à testimoniis veterum Theologorum.

89. Ibid., II.xiv, margin: "Conclusio superiorum obiectionum, consequens horrendum inducens, quasi ex traduce Dei humanam naturam habet Christus. / Alia pestilentes Serveti errores cur non refelluntur.; sh Summa horum errorum & eorundem impietas breviter perstricta. / Impuri illius haeretici scopus." Calvin indicates in his text why he does not here refute other heresies of Servetus: he has written a separate treatise against the heretic (the *Defensio orthodoxae fidei sacrae Trinitatis adversus prodigiosus errores Michaelis Serveti Hispani*).

90. Calvin, *Institutes* (Beveridge), II.xiv.4.

91. Cf. Calvin, *Institutio christianae religionis* (1559–90), *index*: "tamen utile est attendere, ad soluendos plurimus nodos, & vitiandos errores Nestorii, Eutychis."

92. Calvin, *Institutes* (Beveridge), II.xiv.5

93. Calvin, *Institutes* (McNeill/Battles), II.xiv.5, 6; cf. Calvin, *Unterricht* (Weber), II.xiv.5: "Christus is von Ewigkeit her Gottes Sohn" and 6: "Christus als Gottessohn und Menschensohn."

94. Cf. Calvin, *Institutio christianae religionis* (1590), II.xii (against Osiander); III.xxii (the

doctrine of election: N.B., §8, an objection from the fathers; §9, an objection from Aquinas; §10, a contemporary objection); III.xxiii (refutation of objections to the doctrine of reprobation); IV.xvii (on the Lord's Supper) with the same chapters in Calvin, *Institutes* (Beveridge), and Calvin, *Institutes* (McNeill/Battles). McNeill does indicate "objections . . . answered" at II.xii.4, omits such reference at III.xxii.8–10, identifies objections in III.xxiii, and notes controversies without reference to formal structure in IV.xvii. Weber omits references to objections and answers at II.xii.4 and III.xiii.8–10, but notes them in III.xxiii and IV.xvii.

95. Cf. Peter Fraenkel, *De l'écriture à la dispute. Le cas de l'Académie de Genève sous Théodore de Bèze* (Lausanne: Revue de Théologie et de Philosophie, 1977), pp. 5–7, 36–39; Irena Backus, "L'Enseignement de la logique à l'Academie de Genève entre 1559 et 1565," *Revue de Théologie et de Philosophie* 111 (1979), pp. 153–63; William T. Costello, *The Scholastic Curriculum at Early Seventeenth-Century Cambridge* (Cambridge, Mass.: Harvard University Press, 1958), pp. 15–35; Mark H. Curtis, *Oxford and Cambridge in Transition, 1558–1642: An Essay on Changing Relations Between the English University and English Society* (Oxford: Clarendon Press, 1959), p. 96; and note the use of a highly formalized structure of question, answer, objections, and replies in Zacharias Ursinus, *Doctrinae christianae compendium* (London: Henricus Midletonus, 1586)—the lectures on the Heidelberg Catechism, offered by Ursinus ca. 1564ff.

96. Wendel, *Calvin*, p. 122.

97. Williston Walker, *John Calvin: The Organizer of Reformed Protestantism (1509–1564)* (1906; repr. with a bibliographical essay by John T. McNeill, New York: Schocken, 1969), p. 434.

98. Cf., for example, Thomas F. Torrance, *Calvin's Doctrine of Man* (Grand Rapids, Mich.: Eerdmans, 1957); Paul Van Buren, *Christ in Our Place: The Substitutionary Character of Calvin's Doctrine of Reconciliation* (Edinburgh: T. & T. Clark, 1957); Ronald S. Wallace, *Calvin's Doctrine of the Word and Sacrament* (Grand Rapids, Mich.: Eerdmans, 1957); Wallace, *Calvin, Geneva and the Reformation: A Study of Calvin as Social Reformer, Churchman, Pastor and Theologian* (Grand Rapids, Mich.: Baker Book House, 1988); Brian A. Gerrish, *Grace and Gratitude: The Eucharistic Theology of John Calvin* (Minneapolis: Fortress Press, 1993).

CHAPTER FIVE

1. William J. Bouwsma, *John Calvin: A Sixteenth-Century Portrait* (New York: Oxford University Press, 1988); cf. Bouwsma's earlier (and, to a certain degree, alternative) understanding of Calvin as participating in an epistemic or noetic crisis: "Calvin and the Renaissance Crisis of Knowing," *Calvin Theological Journal* 17/2 (1982), pp. 190–211.

2. Cf. Edward A. Dowey, "A Review of William J. Bouwsma's *John Calvin: A Sixteenth-Century Portrait*," in Dowey, *The Knowledge of God in Calvin's Theology*, 3rd ed. (Grand Rapids, Mich.: Eerdmans, 1994), pp. 270–74, and I. John Hesselink, "Reactions to Bouwsma's Portrait of 'John Calvin'," in *Calvinus Sacrae Scripturae Professor: Calvin as Confessor of Holy Scripture. Die Referate des Internationalen Kongresses für Calvinforschung vom 20. bis 23. August 1990 in Grand Rapids* ed. Wilhelm H. Neuser (Grand Rapids, Mich.: Eerdmans, 1994), pp. 209–13, where an account is given of several major reviews of Bouwsma's work. The most notable negative has been sounded recently in T. H. L. Parker, *Calvin: An Introduction to His Thought* (Louisville: Westminster/John Knox Press, 1995), p. 11, note 7: "Professor Bouwsma's programme is based on Kant's claim (by implication) to know Plato better than Plato knew himself (p. 5). On this basis an author can mean anything that we want him to mean. Calvin said A; he thought he meant A; our more sophisticated eyes can spot the tell-tale signs which show that, influenced unawares by X and Y, he really meant B. This seems to me the end of meaningful commerce with the past (or with the present either); supply 'Professor Bouwsma' for 'Calvin' in the previous sentence, and then where are we?"

3. William J. Bouwsma, "Anxiety and the Formation of Early Modern Culture," in *After the Reformation: Essays in Honor of J. H. Hexter*, ed. Barbard C. Malament (Philadelphia: University of Pennsylvania Press, 1980), pp. 215–46.

4. Bouwsma, *Calvin*, pp. 32–3.

5. Ibid., p. 34.

6. Ibid., p. 33.

7. Ibid., pp. 45–46.

8. Ibid., p. 48.

9. Ibid., p. 230.

10. Ibid., p. 231.

11. Note the similar dichotomizing approach in William J. Bouwsma, "The Two Faces of Humanism: Stoicism and Augustinianism in Renaissance Thought," in *Itinerarium Italicum: The Profile of the Italian Renaissance in the Mirror of its European Transformations*, ed. Thomas A. Brady and Heiko A. Oberman (Leiden: E. J. Brill, 1975), pp. 4, 52–58: here Bouwsma offers an equally unsatisfactory distinction between an Augustinian line of biblical Christianity more characteristic of the Reformation and a Stoic line of paganizing humanism belonging more exclusively to the Renaissance. Note that neither Calvin nor Erasmus obliges this pattern.

12. Francis Higman, "Linearity in Calvin's Thought," *Calvin Theological Journal* 26 (1991), pp. 109; cf. Higman, *The Style of John Calvin in His French Polemical Treatises* (London: Oxford University Press, 1967), pp. 83–102 (on Calvin's syntax).

13. Heiko A. Oberman, *Initia Calvini: The Matrix of Calvin's Reformation* (Amsterdam: Koninklijke Nederlandse Akademie van Wetenschappen, 1991), pp. 19–30.

14. Hermann Bauke, *Die Probleme der Theologie Calvins* (Leipzig: J. C. Hinrichs, 1922), pp. 16–19; also note Henry J. Weber, "The Formal Dialectical Rationalism of Calvin," *Papers of the American Church History Society* 8 (1928), pp. 19–41, which served to present Bauke's arguments to an American audience.

15. Bouwsma, *Calvin*, pp. 45–46.

16. Ibid., pp. 46–47.

17. Cf. Calvin, *Institutio* (1559), III.ii.2–3 with I.vi.3 and I.xiii.21.

18. I have included in the notes, however, references to various other locations in Calvin's works where uses of "labyrinth" and "abyss" occur that are similar to particular applications in the text of the *Institutes*.

19. Calvin, *Institutio* (1559), I.vii.5; xiii.14; xvii.2 [five times]; II.ii.24; xvi.9, 11; III.ii.18, 35; iv.16, 18 [three times], 22; xvii.5; xx.4; xxiii.5 [two times]; xxiv.3, 4 [two times]; xxv.12; IV.xvii.25.

20. Ibid., I.v.12; vi.3; xiii.21; III.ii.2, 3; vi.2; viii.1; xix.7; xxi.1; xxv.11; IV.vii.13, 22.

21. Ibid., III.xxi.1.

22. The literary and or rhetorical use of imagery of labyrinth and abyss has received detailed attention in Henry Kahane and Renée Kahane, "Christian and Un-Christian Etymologies," *Harvard Theological Review* 57 (1964), pp. 23–38 (part 1, "Abyss"); Alfred Doppler, *Der Abgrund: Studien zur Bedeutungsgeschichte eines Motivs* (Graz and Vienna: Böhlau, 1968); Victorino Capanaga, "El Hombre-Abismo, segun San Augustin," *Augustinus* 20 (1975), pp. 225–52; John E. Steadman, *The Hill and the Labyrinth: Discourse and Certitude in Milton and His Near-Contemporaries* (Berkeley: University of California Press, 1984); Penelope Reed Doob, *The Idea of the Labyrinth from Classical Antiquity Through the Middle Ages* (Ithaca N.Y.: Cornell University Press, 1990).

23. Jean Calvin, *Institution de la religion Chrestienne* (Geneva, 1541), fol. A1v–A2v, and the translation in Calvin, *Institutes* (McNeill Battles), I, p. 7, where the text is erroneously placed in the 1560 edition.

24. Cf. J. W. Marmelstein, *Étude comparative des textes latin et français de l'Institution* (Gron-

ingen: J. B. Wolters, 1923), pp. 35–50; also see Jean-Daniel Benoit, "The History and Development of the *Institutio*: How Calvin Worked," in *John Calvin*, ed. Gervase E. Duffield (Grand Rapids/Eerdmans, 1966), pp. 105–6.

25. Calvin, *Institutio* (1559), I.v.12.

26. Ibid., I.vi.3.

27. Ibid., I.xiii.21; Calvin, Sermon 8 on I Corinthians [10:19–24], *CO* 49, col. 680.

28. Cf. Doob, *The Idea of the Labyrinth*, pp. 64–91, for discussion of a large selection of nearly identical partistic uses of the labyrinth motif and, further, ibid., pp. 53, 64, 70–77, 100–01, 124–28, 130–33, 261, 279–86, 299–304, for specific comment on the Theseus-Christ parallel.

29. Commentary on II Peter 1:19 (*CO* 55, col. 457; *CTS Catholic Epistles*, p. 388); cf. the use of labyrinth in Calvin, *Commentary on Isaiah*, 59:10 (*CO* 37, col. 343; *CTS Isaiah*, IV, p. 256).

30. Calvin, *In Lib. Psalmorum Comm.*, in *CO* 31, col. 200 (*CTS Psalms* I, p. 320, "labyrinths and crooked bypaths": "labyrinths" is not in the Latin text of *CO*).

31. Calvin, *Institutio* (1559), III.ii.2–3; cf. the similar reference to the "labyrinth" of human traditions in John Calvin, *Comm. in quatuor Pauli Epist.*, [*Colossians*, 2:21], in *CO* 52, col. 114 (*CTS*, p. 200), where Calvin indicates "snare" (*laqueus*) as a synonym for "labyrinth."

32. Calvin, *Institutio* (1559), III.ii.3; cf.Calvin, *Defensio sanae et orthodoxae doctrinae de servitute et liberatione humani arbitrii*, in *CO* 6, col. 240 (also Calvin, *The Bondage and Liberation of the Will*, p. 77).

33. Cf. Hippolytus, *Refutation of All Heresies*, X.1 (*ANF* 5, p. 140); Prudentius, *Apotheosis*, line 203 (*CCSL* 126, p. 84); Jerome, *Praefatio*, in *Eusebii Pamphili Chronici canones Latine vertit, adavxit, ad sua tempora produxit S. Eusebius Hieronymus*, ed. J. K. Fotheringham (London: Humphrey Milford, 1923) p. 4, ll. 4–5; Augustine, *De Civitate Dei*, XVIII.13 (*CCSL* 48, p. 604), and the discussions in Doob, *Idea of the Labyrinth*, pp. 76–82.

34. Ambrose, *Expositio Psalmi CXVIII*, 8.31 (*CSEL*, 62, p. 168).

35. Augustine, *De Civitate Dei*, XII.14 [13], 18 [17], 21 [20] (*CCSL* 48, pp. 368, 374, 378).

36. Augustine, *Contra Academicos*, III.iv.7 (*CSEL* 63, p. 51), Jerome, *Contra Ioannem Hiersolymitanum*, 14 (*PL* 23, col. 382); Boethius, *Philosophiae consolatio*, III.xii (prosa).30 (*CCSL* 94, p. 62).

37. Calvin, *Institutio* (1559), III.vi.2; cf. Calvin, *Commentary on I Peter* 1:14, 18, in *CO* 55, cols. 222, 224 (*CTS Catholic Epistles*, pp. 46, 50).

38. Calvin, *Institutio* (1559), III.viii.1.

39. Bouwsma, *Calvin*, pp. 45–46.

40. Seneca, *Epistulae morales*, trans. Richard Gummere (3 vols. London: Heinemann, 1925), I, pp. 286–91.

41. Gregory of Nyssa, *Oratio catechetica magna*, 35, in *PL* 45, col. 87–8B (*NPNF* ser. 2, vol. 5, pp. 502–3).

42. Johannes Comenius, *The Labyrinth of the World and the Paradise of the Heart*, trans. Count Lützow (1901; repr. New York: Arno Press, 1971).

43. Calvin, *Institutio* (1559), III.xix.7 (Allen); note the parallel use of "abyss" to indicate the confusion of error in John Calvin, *Advertissement tresutile du grand proffit . . . inventoire de . . . reliques*, in *CO* 6, col. 441.

44. Cf. I.i.1–2 with Calvin, *In Lib. Psalmorum Comm.*, in *CO*, col. (*CTS Psalms* I, p. 320): "a man's life cannot be ordered aright unless it is framed according to the law of God . . . without this he can only wander in labyrinths and crooked bypaths." Also cf. the discussions in Dowey, *The Knowledge of God in Calvin's Theology*, pp. 41–49; Paul Lobstein, "La Connaissance réligieuse d'après Calvin," *Revue de Théologie et de Philosophie* 42 (1909), pp. 53–110; and T. H. L. Parker, *The Doctrine of the Knowledge of God: A Study in the Theology of John Calvin* (London, 1952; rev. ed. Grand Rapids, Mich.: Eerdmans, 1959), pp. 11–13.

45. Oberman, *Initia Calvini*, pp. 29–30.

46. Calvin, *Institutio* (1559), III.xxi.1.

47. Cf. Bernardino Ochino, *De labyrinthi, hoc est, De libero aut servo arbitrio, de divina praenotione, destinatione, et libertate disputatio* (Basel: Petrus Perna, 1561) and Theodore Beza, *Tabula praedestinationis* (Geneva, 1555), VII, par. 3; and note the discussion in Glen Garfield Williams, "The Theology of Bernardino Ochino" (Ph.D. dissertation, Eberhard-Karls-Universität, Tübingen, 1955), of Ochino's use of "labyrinth" as a metaphor for the dangers of speculation over against the certainty of faith (pp. 35–36); and note also the comparison of Ochino's thought with Calvin's, given the strong parallels as well as the significant difference over reprobation (pp. 56–62).

48. Calvin, *Institutio* (1559), III.xxv.11.

49. Augustine, *Contra academicos*, III.iv.7 (*CSEL* 63, p. 50); cf. Doob, *The Idea of the Labyrinth*, pp. 88–89. Note that earlier, in the same treatise, Augustine had drawn on the image of Daedalus, the architect of the labyrinth of Knossos, building wings to escape the island of Crete.

50. Calvin, *Institutio* (1559), IV.vii.13.

51. Ibid.

52. Ibid., IV.vii.22.

53. Ibid., IV.viii.

54. Ibid., I.vii.5.

55. Ibid., I.xvii.2, citing Deut. 30:12–14; the divine "abyss" is neutral here—but it can also be a very positive depth, like the depth of divine goodness of mercy: cf. Calvin, Sermon 9 on Job [2:7–10] (*CO* 33, col. 128; *Sermons on Job*, p. 42, col. 1:41).

56. Ibid., I.xiii.14.

57. Ibid., II.xvi.9, citing Zechariah 9:11.

58. Ibid., II.xvi.11; cf. the understanding of hell or Sheol as abyss in Sermon 73 on Job [20:1–7] (*CO* 34, cols. 150, 152; *Sermons on Job*, p. 345, col. 1:13, 2:15, where the translation simply gives "hell").

59. Ibid., II.ii.24.

60. Ibid., II.ii.26.

61. Ibid., III.ii.18.

62. Ibid., III.xx.4.

63. Ibid., III.xxv.12.

64. Christopher Marlowe, *The Tragical History of the Life and Death of Dr. Faustus*, Ed. Basil Ashmore (London: Blandford Press, 1948), Act. V, scene 2, ll. 150–54; which is itself a reflection of Revelation 6:16 [GB]: "the Kings of the earth . . . said to the mountaines and rockes, 'Fall on us, and hide us from the presence of him that sitteth on the throne, and from the wrath of the Lambe.'"

65. Calvin, *Institutio* (1559), III.ii.15. Cf. Joel R. Beeke, *Assurance of Faith: Calvin, English Puritanism, and the Dutch Second Reformation* (New York: Peter Lang, 1991), pp. 49–78. Beeke well argues that the seeming contradiction between the "firm conviction" of faith and the lingering probelem of unbelief is resolved eschatologically for Calvin.

66. For example, Calvin, *Institutio* (1559), III.ii.15, 18.

67. For example, ibid., III.ii.18; the other, III.ii.35, is treated later.

68. Ibid., III.iv.16.

69. Ibid., III.iv.22.

70. Augustine, *Adnotationes in Iob liber unus*, 38 (*CSEL* 28/2, pp. 604–05).

71. Calvin, *Institutio* (1559), III.iv.18.

72. Ibid., III.xvii.5; cf. Calvin, *Comm. in utramque Pauli Epist. ad Tim.*, in *CO* 52, col. 326 (*CTS*, p. 158): I Tim. 6:7, "Gurges est inexplebilis nostra cupiditas"; Sermon 26 on Job [6:24–30], where the abyss or pit of sin is also defined as a confusion from which only the utterly

recalcitrant are not delivered by divine enlightenment (*CO* 33, col. 324; *Sermons on Job*, p. 122, col. 2:2).

73. Augustine, *Enarrationes in Psalmos*, 134.16 (*CCSL* 40, p. 1949).

74. Calvin, *Institutio* (1559), III.ii.35; citing Augustine, *Sermons*, cxxxi.2,3; clv.5 (*PL* 38, 730, 905); cf. also Augustine, *Confessions*, trans. and intro. by R. S. Pine-Coffin (Baltimore: Penguin, 1961), IV.4: "Deus meus, et quam investigabilis abyssus iudiciorum"; also, ibid., XIII.2, 12.

75. Calvin, *Institutio* (1559), III.xxiii.5.

76. Ibid., III.xxiv.3.

77. Ibid., III.xxiv.4.

78. Augustine, *In Iohannis euangelium tractatus*, tract. 53, par. 6 (*CCL* 36, p. 455): ideo cum quaestiones huiusmodi in medium uenerint, quare alius sic, alius autem sic; quare ille deo deserente excaecetur, ille deo adiuuante illuminetur, non nobis iudicium de iudicio tanti iudicis usurpemus, sed contremiscentes exclamemus cum apostolo: o altitudo diuitiarum sapientiae et scientiae dei! quam inscrutabilia sunt iudicia eius, et inuestigabiles uiae eius! unde dictum est in psalmo: iudicia tua, sicut multa abyssus." Cf. Fulgentius Ruspensis, *De veritate praedestinationis et gratiae Dei*, I.18 (*CCSL* 91A, p. 469); Fulgentius Ruspensis, *Ad Trasamundum libri III*, II.1 (*CCSL* 91, p. 121).

79. N. B. Calvin, *Institutio* (1559), III.xxi.1 (labyrinth); xxiii.5 and xxiv 4 (abyss).

80. Ibid., III.xxiv.4.

81. Ibid., IV.xvii.25.

82. Bouwsma, *Calvin*, p. 34.

83. Cf. Ludwig Köhler, *Old Testament Theology*, trans. A. S. Todd (Philadelphia: Westminster, 1957), pp. 88–89, and Gerhard von Rad, *Genesis: A Commentary*, trans. John H. Marks (Philadelphia: Westminster, 1961), pp. 47–51, 125–26 and Edmond Jacob, *Theology of the Old Testament*, trans. Arthur Heathcote and Philip Allcock (New York: Harper & Row, 1958), pp. 140–45, 148, 170, 178, 193, 216, 237, 264–65, 282, 299, 304, 318–19, 336–37.

84. Cf. the discussion in Frank Egleston Robbins, *The Hexaemeral Literature: A Study of the Greek and Latin Commentaries on Genesis* (Chicago: University of Chicago Press, 1921), pp. 7–8, 68, 80. Note that the word *tehom* occurs some nineteen times in the Old Testament: Gen. 1:2; 7:11; 8:2; 49:25; Deut. 33:13; Job 38:30; 41:32 (Vg. 41:23); Ps. 36:6 (Vg. 35:7); 42:7 (Vg. 41: 8); 104:6 (Vg. 103:6); 148:7; Prov. 8:28 (Vg. 8:27); Is. 51:10; 63:13; Ez. 26:19; 31:4, 15; Amos 7:4; and Hab. 3:10 and is without exception translated as *abyssus* in the Vulgate. Calvin varies his translation, sometimes rendering *tehom* as *voragine*, chasm (Gen 1:2; 7:11; Deut. 33:13; Job 38:30; 41:23; Is. 51:10), sometimes as *abyssus* (Gen 8:2; 49:25; Ps. 36:7; 42:8; 104:6; 148:7; Is. 63:13; Amos 7:4; Hab 3:10).

85. Cf. Joachim Jeremias, "Abyssos" and "Hades," s.v. in *Theological Dictionary of the New Testament*, ed. Gerhard Kittel, trans. and ed. Geoffrey W. Bromiley (Grand Rapids, Mich.: Eerdmans, 1964–76), I, pp. 9–10, 146–49; Hans Bietenhard, "Hell, Abyss, Hades, Ghenna, Lower Regions," s.v. in *The New International Dictionary of New Testament Theology*, ed. Colin Brown (Grand Rapids, Mich.: Zondervan, 1975–79).

86. Translated from *The Bible of John Calvin, Reconstructed from the Text of His Commentaries*, compiled by Richard F. Wevers (Grand Rapids, Mich.: Digamma, 1994), in loc.: "Abyssus ad abyssum clamat ad vocem canalium tuorum: omnes fluctus tui et omnes illuviones tuae super me transierunt"

87. Calvin, *In Lib. Psalmorum Comm.*[42:8], in *CO* 31, col. 431 (*CTS Psalms* II, p. 139).

88. Augustine, *Enarrationes in Psalmos*, 41:13–14 (*CCSL* 38, pp. 470–71; *NPNF* 1 ser. VIII, p. 136); cf. Capanaga, "El Hombre-Abismo, segun San Augustin," pp. 225–52.

89. Calvin, *In primum Mosis Comm.* [1:2], in *CO* 23, cols. 15–16 (*CTS Genesis* I, p. 73).

90. Ibid., [8:21], in *CO* 23, col. 140 (*CTS Genesis* I, p. 285); cf. 1:2; 3:17 (*CO* 23, cols. 16, 72–73; *CTS Genesis* I, pp. 74, 172–74).

91. Augustine, *Confessions*, XIII.ii [3], xxi [30] (*CCSL* 27, pp. 243, 258; and note the continuance of the metaphor in Evagrius Monachus, *Altercatio legis inter Simonem Iudaeum et Theophilum Christianum* (*CSEL* 45, pp. 47–48): "Sicut Genesi dicit: Et erant tenebrae super abyssos de dixit Deus: Fiat lux! Abyssus enim quid intelligitur nisi corda hominum tenebris."

92. Calvin, *In primum Mosis Comm.*, in *CO* 23, col. 118–19, 133 (*CTS Genesis* I, p. 248–50, 272–73).

93. Cf. Calvin, *Sermons sur Job*, sermon 34 and 96 (pp. 156, col. 2, 450, col. 2–451, col. 1) and Calvin, *Praelect. in lib. Ieremiae*, in *CO* 37, col. 632–33 (*CTS Jeremiah* I, pp. 296–97).

94. Bouwsma, *Calvin*, p. 33 (Bouwsma's italics).

95. Calvin, *In Lib. Psalmorum Comm.*, in *CO* 31, col. 328 (*CTS Psalms* I, p. 544).

96. Bouwsma, *Calvin*, p. 46.

97. Calvin, *Sermons sur Deutéronome*, Sermon 41 [5:21], in *CO* 26, col. 383.

98. Cf. E. R. Dodds, *Pagan and Christian in an Age of Anxiety* (New York: Norton, 1970) and Bouwsma, "Anxiety and the Formation," pp. 215–46, Bouwsma, *John Calvin*, pp. 49–65, et passim, and W. H. Auden, *The Age of Anxiety: A Baroque Eclogue* (New York: Random House, 1947); note also Leonard Bernstein, Symphony No. 2: "The Age of Anxiety" (inspired by Auden).

99. Calvin to Christopher Fabri [Libertet], 11 September [1534/35?], in *CO* 10, col. 52 (*Letters*, I, p. 43).

100. Calvin, *Institutio* (1559), II.ii.14 (Allen): "Ipsarum porro artium inventio aut methodica traditio."

101. Cf. Philip Melanchthon, *Elementa rhetorices*, in *CR* 13, col. 573, and Neal W. Gilbert, *Renaissance Concepts of Method* (New York: Columbia University Press, 1960), pp. 119–28.

102. Melanchthon, *Elementa rhetorices*, col. 573: "ac significat hoc loco *methodos* rectam viam seu ordinem investigationis et explicationis, sive simplicium quaestionum, sive propositionum. . . . Methodus est habitus, videlicet scientia, seu ars, viam faciens certa ratione, id est, quae quasi per loca invia et obsita sentibus, per rerum confusionem, viam invenit et aperit, ac res ad propositum pertinentes, eruit ac ordine promit."

103. Calvin, *Institutio* (1559), IV.xix.13, ad fin: "omnibus denique esset quaedam velut methodus doctrinae Christianae."

104. Calvin, *In Lib. Psalmorum Comm.*, in *CO* 31, col. 200 (*CTS Psalms* I, p. 320).

105. Calvin, *Institutio* (1559), III.xxv.11: "hoc sit nobis viae compendium, contentos esse speculo et aenigmate donec cernemus facie ad faciem."

106. Cf. Philip Melanchthon, *Loci communes theologici*, *CR*, 21, col. 886: "spinosae disputationes"; cf. Philip Melanchthon, *Loci communes theologici 1543*, trans. J. A. O. Preus (St. Louis: Concordia, 1992), p. 158.

107. Calvin, *Institutio* (1559), IV.xvii.36.

108. André Malan Hugo, "The Spiritual and Intellectual Background," in *Calvin's Commentary on Seneca's De Clementia*, p. *43.

109. Millet, *Calvin et la dynamique de la parole*, (Paris: Librairie Honoré Champion, 1992), p. 673; cf. Ford Lewis Battles, *Calculus Fidei*, in *Calvinus Ecclesiae Doctor*, Die Referate des Internationalen Kongresses für Calvinforschung vom 25 bis 28 September 1978 in Amsterdam, ed. W. H. Neuser (Kampen: Kok, 1980), pp. 90–98.

110. Higman, *The Style of John Calvin*, pp. 86–88.

111. Millet, *Calvin et la dynamique de la parole*, (Paris: Librairie Honoré Champion, 1992), p. 673.

112. Higman, *The Style of John Calvin*, pp. 104–05, 122.

113. Thus, Pierre Viret, *De la vraye et fausse religion, touchant les voeus et les serments illcites*

. . . (Geneva: J. Rivery, 1560), and Viret, *Exposition de la doctrine de la foy chrestienne, touchant la vraye cognoissance & le vray service de Dieu* (Geneva: J. Rivery, 1564).

114. Desiderius Erasmus, *Adages*, II.x.51, in *Collected Works of Erasmus*, vol. 34, trans. Margaret Mann Phillips, annotated by R. A. B. Mynors (Toronto: University of Toronto Press, 1992), p. 147.

115. Luther to Spalatin, 15 February 1518 in *WaBr* I, 146.59–60.

116. Desiderius Erasmus, *De libero arbitrio*, ed. and trans. by E. Gordon Rupp, in collaboration with A. N. Marlow, in *Luther and Erasmus: Free Will and Salvation* (Philadelphia: Westminster, 1969), p. 38.

117. Melanchthon, *Loci theologici, CR*, 21, cols. 661–62; cf. Philip Melanchthon, *Loci communes 1543*, trans. J. A. O. Preus (St. Louis: Concordia, 1992), p. 45.

118. Melanchthon, *Loci theologici, CR*, 21, cols. 644, 887; cf. Melanchthon, *Loci communes* (trans. Preus), p. 36, 158.

119. See Sidonius Apollinaris, *Poems and Letters*, 2 vols., trans., intro., and notes by W. B. Anderson (Cambridge, Mass.: Harvard University Press, 1936–65), *Epistulae*, 2, 5; 9, 13; cf. *Oxford Latin Dictionary*, s.v., "inextricabilis," "inextricabilia," "labyrinthus."

120. Bernardino Ochino, *De labyrinthi*; Ochino, cf. *Sermons of Barnardine Ochyne (to the Number of 25) Concerning the Predestination and Election of God* (London: John Day, ca. 1570).

121. Beza, *Tabula praedestinationis*, VII, par. 3.

122. Calvin, *Institutio* (1559), IV.x.6.

123. Ibid., Joannis Calvinus lectori: "siquidem religionis summam omnibus partibus sic mihi complexus esse videor, et eo quoque ordine digessisse. . . ."

124. Calvin, *Institutio* (1559), I.i.3.

125. Ibid., I.v.ix: "rectissimam Dei quaerendi viam et aptissimum ordinem".

126. Ibid., III.iii.1.

127. Calvin, *In Lib. Psalmorum Comm.*, ad lectorem, in *CO* 31, col. 33 (*CTS Psalms* I, p. xlix).

128. One rare example of such pairing occurs in Calvin's sermon no. 174 on Deuteronomy [31:9–14], in *CO* 38, col. 617: but here the terms "labyrinth" and "abyss" are not only identical in meaning, they both point to a mistaken claim of the "papists"—who warn people not to read Scripture because it is an unintelligible labyrinth, such that when the unlearned read its pages they plunge into an abyss. On the contrary, Calvin writes, God gave his law not only to the tribe of Levi but to all people—not only for men but also for women and little children.

129. Cf. Calvin to Farel, 27 October 1540; Calvin to Viret, 1 March 1541, in *CO* 11, cols. 90–93, 167–69 (*Letters*, II, pp. 201–14, 230–33). The letter to Farel (*CO* 11, col. 91) does refer to Geneva as a *gurges* or whirlpool.

CHAPTER SIX

1. On the method and development of Calvin's *Institutes*, see Julius Köstlin, "Calvin's *Institutio* nach Form und Inhalt, in ihrer geschlichtlichen Entwicklung," *Theologische Studien und Kritiken* 41 (1868), pp. 7–62, 410–86; Emil Doumergue, *Jean Calvin, les hommes et les choses de son temps*, 7 vols. (Lausanne: G. Bridel, 1899–1917), IV, pp. 1–17; Benjamin B. Warfield, "On the Literary History of Calvin's Institutes," in John Calvin, *Institutes of the Christian Religion*, trans. John Allen, 7th ed. (Philadelphia: Presbyterian Board of Christian Education, 1936), pp. xxx–xxxi; Wilhelm Niesel, *The Theology of Calvin*, trans. Harold Knight (London: Lutterworth, 1956; repr. Grand Rapids, Mich.: Baker Book House, 1980), pp. 9–21, 246–54; François Wendel, *Calvin: The Origins and Development of His Religious Thought*, trans. Philip Mairet (New York: Harper & Row, 1963), pp. 111–49; Jean-Daniel Benoit, "The History and Development of the *Institutio*: How Calvin Worked," in *John Calvin*, ed. Gervase E. Duffield (Grand Rapids/:

Eerdmans/ 1966), pp. 102–17; Brian G. Armstrong, "*Duplex cognitio Dei*, Or? The Problem and Relation of Structure, Form, and Purpose in Calvin's Theology," in *Probing the Reformed Tradition: Historical Essays in Honor of Edward A. Dowey, Jr.*, ed. Elsie Anne McKee and Brian G. Armstrong (Louisville: Westminster/John Knox, 1989), pp. 135–53; and note the related perspective in Armstrong, "The Nature and Structure of Calvin's Thought According to the *Institutes*: Another Look," in *John Calvin's Institutes: His Opus Magnum*, ed. B. van der Walt (Potchefstrom: Institute for Reformational Studies, 1986), pp. 55–81.

2. Armstrong, "The Nature and Structure of Calvin's Thought," p. 57.

3. William J. Bouwsma, *John Calvin: A Sixteenth-Century Portrait* (New York: Oxford University Press, 1988), pp. 5, 238, note 24, citing Calvin, *Institutio* (1559), I.i.3; cf. Bouwsma, "The Spirituality of John Calvin," in *Christian Spirituality: High Middle Ages and Reformation*, ed. Jill Raitt (New York: Crossroad, 1987), pp. 318–19.

4. Armstrong, "*Duplex cognitio Dei*, Or? The Problem and Relation of Structure, Form, and Purpose in Calvin's Theology," p. 136.

5. Serene Jones, *Calvin and the Rhetoric of Piety* (Louisville: Westminster/John Knox, 1995), p. 195.

6. Brian G. Armstrong, "Exegetical and Theological Principles in Calvin's Preaching, with Special Attention to his Sermons on the Psalms," in *Ordentlich und Fruchtbar: Festschrift für Willem van t'Spijker*, ed. Wilhelm Neuser and Herman Selderhuis (Leiden: J. J. Groen en Zoon, 1997), p. 193; also note the bland, one-sided picture of Calvin offered in Randall C. Zachman, "Theologian in the Service of Piety: A New Portrait of Calvin," *Christian Century* (April 23–30, 1997), pp. 413–18—in fact, hardly new: cf., for example, G. E. Müller, "Calvin's Institutes of the Christian Religion as an Illustration of Christian Living," *Journal of the History of Ideas* 4 (1942), pp. 287–300, and H. W. Simpson, "*Pietas* in the *Institutes* of Calvin," in *Our Reformational Tradition: A Rich Heritage and Lasting Vocation*, ed. B. J. van der Walt (Potchefstroom: Institute for Reformational Studies, 1984), pp. 179–91.

7. Bouwsma, *John Calvin*, p. 5; cf. William Bouwsma, "Calvin and the Renaissance Crisis of Knowing," *Calvin Theological Journal* 17/2 (1982), p. 208: "The absence of system was, I think, a matter of principle for Calvin." Bouwsma here speaks of "the oddly informal organization" of the *Institutes* and of Calvin's "rejection of the notion of theology as a systematic discipline."

8. John Dillenberger, *Contours of Faith: Changing Forms of Christian Thought* (Nashville: Abingdon, 1969), p. 39, cited in Bouwsma, *John Calvin*, p. 276, note 100.

9. Wendel, *Calvin*, pp. 146–47.

10. Doumergue, *Jean Calvin*, IV, pp. 2, 9; cf. Brian Gerrish, *Grace and Gratitude: The Eucharistic Theology of John Calvin* (Minneapolis: Fortress Press, 1993), pp. 14–18.

11. Ferdinand Loofs, *Leitfaden der Dogmengeschichte* (Halle: M. Niemeyer, 1896), p. 882.

12. Reinhold Seeberg, *Textbook of the History of Doctrines*, trans. Charles Hay, 2 vols. (Grand Rapids, Mich.: Baker Book House, 1952), II, p. 394.

13. Cf. John H. Leith, "Calvin's Theological Method and Ambiguity in his Theology," in *Reformation Studies: Essays in Honor of R. H. Bainton*, ed. F. Littell (Richmond, Va.: John Knox, 1962), pp. 106–14, and Ronald S. Wallace, "Calvin's Approach to Theology," in *The Challenge of Evangelical Theology: Essays in Approach and Method*, ed. Nigel Cameron (Edinburgh: Rutherford House, 1987), pp. 123–50.

14. Cf. T. H. L. Parker, *The Doctrine of the Knowledge of God: A Study in the Theology of John Calin* (London, 1952; rev. ed. Grand Rapids, Mich.: Eerdmans, 1959), p. 2; I. John Hesselink, "The Development and Purpose of Calvin's Institutes," in *Reformed Theological Review* 24 (1965), p. 69.

15. Joannes Calvinus, *Christianae religionis institutio, totam fere pietatis summam, et quicquid est in doctrina salutis cognitu necessarium, complectens: omnibus pietatis studiosis lectu dignissimum*

opus, ac recens editum (Basel: Platter & Lasius, 1536); cf. the description of this edition in Rodolphe Peter and Jean-François Gilmont, *Bibliotheca Calviniana. Les oeuvres de Jean Calvin publiées au xvie siècle: Écrits théologiques, littéraires et juridiques,* 2 vols. [1532–1564] (Geneva: Droz, 1991–94), I, pp. 35–39.

16. Cf. Benoit, "History and Development," p. 103.

17. John Calvin, *Institutio christianae religionis nunc vere demum suo titulo respondens* (Strasbourg: Wendelin Rihel, 1539); cf. Peter and Gilmont, *Bibliotheca Calviniana,* I, pp. 58–64.

18. Cf. Jean Calvin, *Institution de la religion chrestienne: en laquelle est comprinse une somme de pieté, et quasi tout ce qui est necessaire a congnoistre en la doctrine de salut* (Geneva: du Bois, 1541), and Jean Calvin, *Institution de la religion chrestienne: composée en Latin par Jehan Calvin, et translatée en francoys par luymesme: en laquelle est comprise une somme de toute la chrestienté* (Geneva: Jean Girard, 1545), and cf. Peter and Gilmont, *Bibliotheca Calviniana,* I, pp. 187–189 (1545), 420–23 (1551), 487–90 (1553), 528–29 (1554); II, 638–41 (1557); 759–63 (1560).

19. Note that the title of Calvin's early (Basel: n.p., 1538) catechism was simply *Catechismus, sive christianae religionis institutio.*

20. Doumergue, *Calvin,* I, p. 593; so, too, Benoit, "History and Development," pp. 102–04.

21. T. H. L. Parker, *John Calvin: A Biography* (Philadelphia: Westminster, 1975), p. 72.

22. Calvin, *Institutio* (1539), *Epistola ad lectorem,* fol. *1v; cf. Calvin, *Institutes* (1559/Battles), I, p. 4.

23. Cf. Paul C. Böttger, *Calvins Institutio als Erbauungsbuch: Versuch einer literarischen Analyse* (Neukirchen: Neukirchner Verlag, 1990), pp. 9, 79–82.

24. T. H. L. Parker, *Calvin: An Introduction to His Thought* (Louisville: Westminster/John Knox, 1995), p. 5.

25. See further in chapter 7.

26. John Calvin, *Catechismus, sive christianae religionis institutio* (Basel: n.p., 1538); cf. Wulfert De Greef, *The Writings of John Calvin: An Introductory Guide,* trans. Lyle D. Bierma (Grand Rapids, Mich.: Baker Book House, 1993), p. 132.

27. John Calvin, *Le Catéchisme de l'église de Genève, c'est a dire le Formulaire d'instruire les enfants en la chrestienté* (1541–42; Geneva: J. Girard, 1545), in *CO* 6, col. 1–134; cf. De Greef, *Writings of John Calvin,* p. 132.

28. Cf. the discussion of the catechisms and the development of the 1539 edition in chapter 7.

29. Martin Luther, *Catechismus maior* in *Concordia triglotta: Libri symbolici Ecclesiae Lutheranae* (St. Louis: Concordia, 1921), p. 574B: "Praesentis huius opusculi sermonem haud alio animo elaboravimus, ut esset institutio puerorum aque simplicium. Hinc apud veteres lingua Graeca catechismus dictus est, quae vox puerilem institutionem significat." Note the similar identification of *institutio* as *paedogogia* in Philip Melanchthon, *De modo et arte concionandi,* in *Supplementa Melanchthoniana,* ed. Paul Drews and Ferdinand Cohrs, 5 vols. (Frankfurt: Minerva, 1968), vol. 5, p. 49. Cf. Joseph C. McClelland, "Renaissance in Theology: Calvin's 1536 Institutio—Fresh Start or False," in *In Honor of John Calvin, 1509–64,* ed. E. J. Furcha(Montreal: McGill University Press, 1987), pp. 161–62.

30. On Calvin's classical and humanist sources see Ford Lewis Battles, "The Sources of Calvin's Seneca Commentary," in *John Calvin: A Collection of Distinguished Essays,* ed. Gervase E. Duffield (Grand Rapids, Mich.: Eerdmans /, 1966), pp. 38–66; the introductory essays in *Calvin's Commentary on Seneca's De Clementia* with intro., trans., and notes by Ford Lewis Battles and André Malan Hugo (Leiden: E. J. Brill, 1969); Quirinus Breen, *John Calvin: A Study in French Humanism* (Grand Rapids, Mich.: Eerdmans, 1931); Breen, "John Calvin and the Rhetorical Tradition," in Breen, *Christianity and Humanism: Studies in the History of Ideas* (Grand

Rapids, Mich.: Eerdmans, 1968), pp. 107–29; Charles Partee, *Calvin and Classical Philosophy* (Leiden: E. J. Brill, 1977); and Olivier Millet, *Calvin et la dynamique de la parole: Etude de rhétorique réformée* (Paris: Librairie Honoré Champion, 1992).

31. Melanchthon, *Theologica institutio*, in *CR* 21, col. 49–60.

32. Calvin, *Institutio* (1539), "Epistola ad Lectorem," fol. *1v: "Porro hoc mihi in isto labore propositum fuit, sacrae Theologiae candidatos ad divini verbi lectionem ita preparare & instruere, ut & facilem ad eam aditum habere, & inoffenso in ea gradu pergere queant: siquidem religionis summam omnibus partibus sic mihi complexus esse videor, & eo quoque ordine digessisse, ut si quis eam recte tenuerit, ei non sit difficile, statuere, & quid potissimum quaerere in scriptura, & quem in scopum, quicquid in ea continetur, referre debeat. Itaque hac veluti strata via, si quas posthac scripturae enarrationes edidero, quia non necesse habebo de dogmatibus longas disputationes instituere, & in locos communes evagari, eas compendio semper adstringam." This interest in the establishment of a right method or order for the sake of avoiding "wandering" remained central to Calvin, as evidenced in the language of his preface to the *Harmony of the Last Four Books of Moses: CO* 24, col. 5–6.

33. Cf. Parker, *Calvin: An Introduction* pp. 6–8, and Parker, *Calvin's New Testament Commentaries*, pp. 53–54 and Compier, "The Independent Pupil: Calvin's Transformation of Erasmus' Theological Hermeneutics," *Westminster Theological Journal* 54 (1992), p. 231.

34. Calvin, *Institution* (1541/Lefranc), "Argument du present livre," p. iii; cf. the translation in Calvin, *Institutes* (1559/Battles), I, p. 7. McNeill/Battles incorrectly identify this passage as from the 1560 French edition—which is in fact the first French *Institution* in which the passage *does not* appear but is replaced by a French version of Calvin's famous "letter to the reader."

35. Calvin, *Institution* (1541/Lefranc), *Argument*, p. iii; cf. the translation in Calvin, *Institutes* (1559/Battles), I, p. 7.

36. Calvin, *Institutio* (1539), fol. 2: *ordo recte dicendi;* cf. Calvin, *Institutio* (1550), I.3: *ordo recte docendi; Institutio* (1559), I.i.3: *ordo recte docendi;* III.iii.1: *ratio docendi series.*

37. Philip Melanchthon, *Brevis discendae theologiae ratio*, in *Philippi Melanchthonis opera quae supersunt omnia*, ed. C. G. Bretschneider and H. E. Bindseil, 28 vols. (Halle/Braunschweig, 1844-), cols. 455–62; Melanchthon, *Elementa rhetorices*, in *CR*, 13, cols. 423–26, 451–54 (on *loci communes*), 573–78 (on method); Heinrich Bullinger, *Ratio studiorum, sive de institutione eorum, qui studia literarum sequuntur, libellus aureus. Accessit eodem dispositio locorum communium, tam philosophicorum, quam theologicorum. Item, Christianae fidei perspicue & breviter proposita quaedam axiomata . . .* (Zürich: Froschaver, 1527); Andreas Hyperius, *De theologo, seu de ratione studii theologici, libri IIII* (Basel: Oporinus, 1556, 1559); and on Hyperius see W. van 't Spijker, *Principe, methode en functie van de theologie bij Andreas Hyperius*, Apeldoornse Studies 26 (Kampen: J. H. Kok, 1990). Some reference must be made to the sixteenth-century understanding of "method." As Melanchthon indicates (*CR* 13, col. 573), *methodus* derives from the Greek *meta*, "after" or "beyond," and *hodos*, "way," and indicates, therefore, a "proper and direct way" (*rectam et compendiariam viam*) through materials, designed specifically to establish "the order of investigation and explication." The term applies, therefore, to the "method and disposition" of an entire work and also to the pattern of argument and the procedure of investigation or instruction followed within the chapters and the subsections of a larger essay. Also see Neal W. Gilbert, *Renaissance Concepts of Method* (New York: Columbia University Press, 1960). There remains disagreement concerning Bullinger's influence on Calvin: cf. T. H. L. Parker, *Commentaries on the Epistle to the Romans 1532–1542* (Edinburgh: T. & T. Clark, 1986), p. 74, and Fritz Büsser, "Bullinger as Calvin's Model in Biblical Exposition: An Examination of Calvin's Preface to the Epistle to the Romans," in *Calvin and Hermeneutics*, ed. Richard C. Gamble (New York: Garland, 1992), pp. 434–65.

38. Cf. Wendel, *Calvin*, p. 111; Pierre Imbart de la Tour, *Les Origines de la réforme*, 4 vols. [I. *La France moderne;* II. *L'Église catholique et la crise de la renaissance;* III. *L'Évangelisme (1521–*

1538); IV. *Calvin et l'Institution Chrétienne*] (Paris: Hachette/Firmin-Didot, 1905–35), IV, p. 55; T. H. L. Parker, *The Doctrine of the Knowledge of God: A Study in the Theology of John Calvin* (London, 1952; rev. ed. Grand Rapids, Mich.: Eerdmans, 1959), p. 3; and Jane Dempsey Douglass, *Women, Freedom, and Calvin* (Philadelphia: Westminster, 1985), p. 45; and note the rather bald statement of Alister McGrath, *A Life of John Calvin* (Oxford: Blackwell, 1990), pp. 145–46.

39. Imbart de la Tour, *Les origines de la réforme,* IV, p. 55.

40. Parker, *Knowledge of God,* p. 3; cf. Parker, *Calvin: An Introduction,* p. ix—where this assumption provides the basis for presenting an introduction to Calvin's theology based virtually entirely on the *Institutes.*

41. Paul T. Fuhrmann, "Calvin: Expositor of Scripture," *Interpretation* 6 (1952), p. 207.

42. Parker does note the relationship, *An Introduction,* pp. 6–9, but does not emphasize the division of labor—with the result that the 1559 *Institutes* remains the primary index to the whole of Calvin's thought.

43. Richard Stauffer, "Un Calvin méconnu: Le prédicateur de Genève," *Bulletin de la Societé d'Histoire du Protestantisme Français* 123 (1977), pp. 186–87, 190.

44. Elsie Anne McKee, "Exegesis, Theology, and Development in Calvin's *Institutio*: A Methodological Suggestion," in *Probing the Reformed Tradition: Historical Studies in Honor of Edward A. Dowey, Jr.,* ed. Brian G. Armstrong and Elsie A. McKee (Louisville: Westminster/John Knox, 1989), pp. 154–172; cf. Parker, *Calvin: An Introduction,* pp. 6–8, 16–17, 29.

45. A point missed in Simpson, "*Pietas* in the *Institutes* of Calvin," pp. 179–91; and cf. Wilhelm Neuser, "The Development of the *Institutes* 1536 to 1559," in *John Calvin's Institutes: His Opus Magnum,* ed. B. J. van der Walt (Potchefstrom: Institute for Reformational Studies, 1986), p. 36, to the effect that the *Institutes* of 1536 was "certainly no children's catechism" and already more "an outline of dogmatics than a catechism." The phrase *pietatis summa* does occur in *Institutes,* IV.x.1, but in the context of a polemic against the Roman claim that "they establish the whole of religion and the sum of piety" in a church filled with impiety and corrupt worship. This argument, moreover, establishes the context for the concentration of references to the exercise of piety in *Institutio* (1559), IV.xx–xix.

46. T. H. L. Parker, *Calvin's New Testament Commentaries* (London: SCM/Grand Rapids, Mich: Eerdmans, 1971), pp. 50–54.

47. Cf. David C. Steinmetz, "Calvin and Melanchthon on Romans 13:1–7," *Ex Auditu* 2 (1986), pp. 74–81; and Richard A. Muller, "Calvin, Beza and the Exegetical History of Romans 13," in *Calvin and the State: Papers and Responses Presented at the Seventh and Eighth Colloquia on Calvin & Calvin Studies,* ed. Peter De Klerk (Grand Rapids, Mich: Calvin Studies Society, 1993), pp. 139–70.

48. Cf. Simpson, "*Pietas* in the *Institutes* of Calvin," pp. 179–91. Note the similar problem in Sou-Young Lee, "Calvin's Understanding of Pietas," in *Calvinus Sincerioris Religionis Vindex,* ed. Wilhelm Neuser and Brian G. Armstrong (Kirksville, Mo.: Sixteenth-Century Journal Publishers, 1997), pp. 225–26.

49. Cf. Calvin, *Institutio* (1559), for *doctrina,* for example, Joannes Calvinus lectori; III.ii.13; IV.i.5; xx.2; *exercitia,* for example, IV.i.5; xx.16, 20, 29; xiv.19; xviii.13; xix.3; *studium,* for example, II.vii.1; viii.16; III.iii.2; x.5; IV.ix.8; xvii.43; xx.1.

50. These usages are often lost to the reader of the standard translations, which seldom render the term *disputatio* as "disputation" and therefore lose the technical implication of Calvin's usage.

51. Calvin, *Institutio* (1559), III.xix.1: "Poterat superior de sacramentis disputatio apud dociles et sobrios hoc obtinere."

52. Ibid., III.xv.7: "Supra, quum de libero arbitrio disputatio esset."

53. Ibid., III.iii.1: "Ergo duobus illis capitibus omissis, jejuna et mutila erit adeoque prope inutilis quaelibet de fide disputatio."

54. For example, Ibid., I.xiv.19; II.ii.1; ii.27; xiii.3; III.xi.6; xii.1; xix.15; xxi.4; xxii.4; IV.ii.12; iv.4; v.1; xix.3; xx.8.

55. John Calvin, *Institutio* (1550), II, "De cognitione hominis, ubi de peccato originali . . . ; cf. Calvin, *Disputatio de cognitione hominis* (Geneva: Crispin, 1552); so, also, *CO* 8, p. xvi, and De Greef, *Writings of John Calvin*, p. 201. Note also the use of a literary form of *disputatio* in Pierre Viret, *Disputationes chrestiennes* (Geneva: J. Gérard, 1552).

56. Cf., for example, Calvin, *Institutio* (1559), I.xiii.24; II.xiv.9; III.xi.18; xvii.2; xviii.7; xxiv.15; IV.xi.2; xiv.14, 15; xx.5.

57. Ibid., II.viii.12.

58. Ibid., I.xiii.24.

59. Ibid., IV.viii.1.

60. Cf. Calvin, *Institutes* (1559/Beveridge, Battles), IV.viii.1

61. McKee, "Exegesis, Theology, and Development," p. 156.

62. Cf. the discussion *dicta probantia* in Richard A. Muller, *Post-Reformation Reformed Dogmatics. II. Holy Scripture: the Cognitive Foundation of Theology* (Grand Rapids, Mich: Baker Book House, 1993), pp. 525–40.

63. See Neuser, "The Development of the *Institutes* 1536 to 1559," p. 35. Neuser analyzes well the language of *compendium* used in the 1536 *Institutes* and the parallel between *compendium* and *summa*, but he overlooks the issue of *loci* and *disputationes* (cf. ibid., pp. 42–43).

64. Note the absence of a full doctrine of creation in Calvin, *Institutio* (1559), I.xiv-xvi— but see Calvin, *In primum Mosis Comm.*, 1:1–2:25, *CO* 23, col. 13–52; and cf. the length of Calvin's exposition of the law, *Institutio* (1559), II.viii with the exposition in Calvin, *Mosis libri in formam harmoniae*, in *CO* 24, col. 209–728; and see further, chapter 8.

65. Parker, *Calvin's New Testament Commentaries*, pp. 50–54.

66. Cf. ibid., pp. 33–35.

67. Thus, for example, the commentary on Gen. 3:1, 6, refers to *Institutio* (1559), II.1.3 on original sin; the commentary on I Tim. 3:8 refers to the discussion of the diaconate in *Institutio* (1559), II.1.4–6, a section on which Calvin labored from 1539 to 1559. Also see the reference to *Institutio* (1559), II.xi, in the comment on Deut. 29:29 (*CO* 24, col. 256), where Calvin explicitly identifies the discussion of the perpetuity of the Law in the *Institutes* as the more extensive treatment and the comment following Deut 10:12–13 (*CO* 24, col. 728), where Calvin references his discussion of the use of the law in *Institutio* (1559), II.vii. Cf. the commentaries on Romans 3:21; I Cor. 1:1; 3:9; 5:5; 10:11; Eph. 6:2; I Tim. 2:6; 4:14; I Peter 1:20, where Calvin also refers to the *Institutes*.

68. Cf. Eugène Thionville, *De la théorie des lieux communs dans les Topiques d'Aristote et des principales modifications, qu'elle a subies jusque à nos jours* (Paris: J. Vrin, 1855); A. Gardeil, "La Notion du lieu théologique," *Revue des Sciences Philosophiques et Théologiques* (1908), pp. 51–73, 246–276, 484–505; Gardeil, "La Topicité," *Revue des Sciences Philosophiques et Théologiques* (1911), pp. 750–757; and Gardeil, "La certitude probable," *Revue des Sciences Philosophiques et Théologiques* (1911), pp. 237–266, 441–85. Also note Joan Lechler, *Renaissance Concepts of Commonplace* (New York: Pageant, 1962) and Peter Mack, *Renaissance Argument: Valla and Agricola in the Traditions of Rhetoric and Dialectic* (Leiden: E. J. Brill, 1993).

69. Philip Melanchthon, *Topica, cum commentariis Boetheii*, in *CR* 16, col. 807.

70. References in the following discussion are to Rudolf Agricola, *De inventione dialectica libri omnes et integri et recogniti* (Cologne: Ioannes Gymnicus, 1539); see Lisa Jardine, "Inventing Rudolf Agricola: Cultural Transmission, Renaissance Dialectic, and the Emerging Humanities," in *The Transmission of Culture in Early Modern Europe*, ed. A. Grafton and A. Blair (Philadelphia: University of Pennsylvania Press, 1990), pp. 39–86; and Jardine, "Ghosting the Reform of Rhetoric: Erasmus and Agricola Again," in Peter *Renaissance Rhetoric*, ed. Peter Mack, (London: St. Martin's Press, 1994), pp. 27–45.

71. Rudolf Agricola, *De inventione dialectica*, pp. 2, 3, 9; cf. Anton Dumitriu, *History of Logic*, 4 vols. (Tunbridge Wells, Kent: Abacus Press, 1977), II, p. 232; also note A. Faust, "Die Dialektik R. Agricolas: Ein Beitrag zur Charakteristik des deutschen Humanismus," *Archiv für Geschichte der Philosophie* 34 (1922), pp. 118–135.

72. See Eleonore Stump, *Dialectic and Its Place in the Development of Medieval Logic* (Ithaca, N.Y., and London: Cornell University Press, 1989), p. 156.

73. Agricola, *De inventone dialectica*, II.ii (p. 193): "ars probabiliter de qualibet re proposita disserendi"; cf. Quirinus Breen, "The Terms '*Loci communes*' and '*Loci*' in Melanchthon," in Breen, *Christianity and Humanism: Studies in the History of Ideas* (Grand Rapids, Mich: Eerdmans, 1968), pp. 93–7.

74. Cf. Agricola, *De inventione dialectica*, p. 1: "Oratio . . . primum & proprium habere videtur officium, ut doceat aliquid eum qui audit. . . . Hoc in praesentia dixisse sufficiat, posse docere orationem, ut non moveat, non delectet: movere aut delectare, ut non doceat, non posse"; with Augustine, *De doctrina christiana*, IV.27–28; and see John Monfasani, "Humanism and Rhetoric," in *Renaissance Humanism: Foundations, forms, and Legacy*, ed. Albert Rabil, Jr. (3 vols. (Philadelphia: University of Pennsylvania Press, 1988), III, pp. 171–77, 196–203.

75. See Arno Seifert, *Logik zwischen Scholastik und Humanismus: Das Kommentarwerk Johann Ecks* (Munich: Wilhelm Fink, 1978), pp. 26–28, 39–42; cf. Dumitriu, *History of Logic*, II, pp. 224–25, 230–33.

76. Stump, *Dialectic and Its Place in the Development of Medieval Logic*, p. 3.

77. Alain of Lille, *Regulae theologicae*, in *PL* 210, col. 621, and Erasmus, *De ratione studii ac legendi interpretandique auctores (On the Method of Study)*, in *Collected Works of Erasmus*, (Toronto: University of Toronto Press, 1978), xxiv, p. 676 and Erasmus, *Ratio seu methodus compendio ad veram theologiam* (1519) in *Desiderius Erasmus Roterodamus Ausgewählte Werke* ed. Hajo Holborn and Annemarie Holborn (Munich: C. H. Beck, 1933), p. 291; cf. Manfred Hoffmann, *Rhetoric and Theology: The Hermeneutic of Erasmus* (Toronto: University of Toronto Press, 1994), pp. 25, 37–38, 49–51, 151–56; Melanchthon, *Loci communes*, in *CR* 21 cols. 83 (1521), 347–49 (1535/6), and note Erika Rummel, *The Humanist-Scholastic Debate in the Renaissance and Reformation* (Cambridge, Mass.: Harvard University Press, 1995), p. 143.

78. Agricola, *De inventione dialectica*, II.1 (p. 179) and II.2 (p. 193).

79. Melanchthon, *Elementa rhetorices*, col. 424–26; cf. the discussion in Breen, "The Terms 'Loci Communes' and 'Loci' in Melanchthon," pp. 99–105 and Robert Kolb, "Teaching the Text: The Commonplace Method in Sixteenth Century Lutheran Biblical Commentary," *Bibliothèque d'Humanisme et Renaissance* 49 (1987), pp. 571–85, esp. pp. 576–78. Note how this approach is carried out also in Otho Brunfels, *Loci in acta apostolorum* (Strasbourg: n.p., 1528). Also see the discussion of Melanchthon's rhetoric in John W. O'Malley, "Content and Rhetorical Forms in Sixteenth-Century Treatises on Preaching," in *Renaissance Eloquence*, ed. James J. Murphy (Berkeley: University of California Press, 1983), pp. 241–43.

80. Melanchthon, *Loci communes* (1543), in *CR* 21, col. 603–104; cf. Timothy J. Wengert, "Philip Melanchthon's 1522 Annotations on Romans and the Lutheran Origins of Rhetorical Criticism," in *Biblical Interpretation in the Era of the Reformation*, ed. Richard A. Muller and John L. Thompson (Grand Rapids, Mich.: Eerdmans, 1996), pp. 135–37.

81. Cf. Olivier Millet, *Calvin et la dynamique de la parole*, pp. 44–45.

82. Cf. Agricola, *De inventione dialectica*, II.19 (pp. 283–85).

83. Ford Lewis Battles, "Calculus Fidei," in *Calvinus Ecclesiae Doctor*, ed. W. H. Neuser, [Die Referate des Internationalen Kongresses für Calvinforschung vom 25 bis 28 September 1978 in Amsterdam] (Kampen: J. H. Kok, 1980), pp. 85–110, note p. 93 on Ramus; and cf. Millet, *Calvin et la dynamique de la parole*, pp. 117, 120, 879.

84. Cf. Agricola, *De inventione dialectica*, I.iv (p. 25).

85. Battles, "Calculus fidei," pp. 91–98.

86. Cf. Agricola, *De inventione dialectica*, II.xix, "Quomodo confirmandae argumentationes" (pp. 283–87) on the division of truth from falsehood; contra Parker, *Calvin's Preaching*, pp. 131–32.

87. Breen, "John Calvin and the Rhetorical Tradition," pp. 111, 122–24.

88. Stump, *Dialectic and Its Place in the Development of Medieval Logic*, pp. 136–52.

89. Calvin, *Comm. in quatuor Pauli Epist.* [Galatians 3:10–11; 4:22], in *CO* 50, col. 208, 236–37 (*CTS* I, pp. 88–89, 136). Note that the syllogisms in 3:10–11 are filled out by Calvin from enthymematic arguments in the text.

90. Cf. Millet, *Calvin et la dynamique de la parole*, pp. 30–34.

91. Melanchthon, *Elementa rhetorices*, cols. 595–612 (on the syllogism), 616–20 (on the enthymeme); contra Breen, "John Calvin and the Rhetorical Tradition," pp. 122–24.

92. Agricola, *De inventione dialectica*, II.19 (p. 280): "*loci communes (ut rhetores vocant) non sunt aliud quam maiores ratiocinationum propositiones*"; thus, continues Agricola, if we wished to show that a certian Coelius should be condemned, we might show that he was a poisoner—given that rational process recognized, as a major or universal proposition, in this case, the *locus*, that all poisoners are to be condemned (pp. 280–81); cf. Stump, *Dialectic and Its Place in the Development of Medieval Logic*, p. 139, with reference to Peter of Spain.

93. Melanchthon, *Elementa rhetorices*, col. 452: "Etenim fere in omni probatione, maior nascitur ex aliquo communi loco.... Ac voco locos communes ... in omni doctrinae genere praecipua capita, quae fontes et summam artis continent." Cf. Lechler, *Renaissance Concepts of the Commonplaces*, pp. 74–75.

94. "Calvinus Grynaeo," in *CO* 10, col. 402–3. As Pannier points out, *brevitas* can equally well be paired with *claritas* or *sinceritas* in Calvin's approach: see Jacques Pannier, *Calvin écrivain. Sa place et son rôle dans l'histoire de la langue et de la littérature française*, 2nd ed. (Paris: Fisch bacher, 1930), pp. 10–11. These often cited terms, *brevitas* and *facilitas*, must be understood, *contra* the view of Battles and Gamble, as stylistic or rhetorical and methodological rather than as hermeneutical principles. They cannot, in other words, be seen as Calvin's grounds for ruling out the "allegorical" exegesis of Origin or Augustine: see F. L. Battles, "Introduction" in *John Calvin's Sermons on the Ten Commandments*, trans. Benjamin W. Farley (Grand Rapids Mich.: Baker Book House, 1980), p. 7; and Richard Gamble, "*Brevitas et facilitas:* Toward an Understanding of Calvin's Hermeneutic," *Westminster Theological Journal* 47 (1985), pp. 1–17; Gamble, "Exposition and Method in Calvin," *Westminster Theological Journal* 49 (1987), pp. 153–165; and Gamble, "Calvin as Theologian and Exegete," *Calvin Theological Journal* 23 (1988), 189–91.

95. See Cicero, *Rhetoricae libri duo*, I.20 [§28]: "narratione ... oportet ... tres habere res: ut brevis, ut aperta, ut probabilis sit"; Quintillian, *Institutionis oratoriae*, IV.2.31–32: "esse lucidam, brevem, veri similem"; and note Augustine, *De doctrina christiana libri*, IV.ii.3. Cf. Benoit Girardin, *Rhétorique et théologie* (Paris: Beauchesne, 1979), p. 229, and Eugene F. Rice Jr., "The Humanist Idea of Christian Antiquity: Lefèvre d'Étaples and His Circle," in *French Humanism, 1470–1600*, ed. Werner L. Gundersheimer (New York: Harper & Row, 1969), p. 167–68.

96. Andreas Hyperius, *De theologo, seu de recte studii theologici, libri IIII*, p. 398; also see Hyperius, *De formandis concionibus sacris, seu de interpretatione scripturarum populari, libri II* (Marburg: A. Colbius, 1553); I owe these citations to a paper by Donald Sinnema, "The Distinction Between Scholastic and Popular: Andreas Hyperius and Reformed Scholasticism," delivered at the Sixteenth-Century Studies Conference, October 1996; on Hyperius's method, also see Olivier Fatio, "Hyperius plagié par Flacius: La destinée d'une méthode exégetique," in *Histoire de l'exégèse au XVIe siècle*, ed. O. Fatio and P. Fraenkel (Geneva: Droz, 1978), pp. 362–81. And see chapter 3, "Scholasticism in Calvin," for further documentation of positive "humanistic" usages of "scholastic" and related terms.

97. See "Budaeus to the Reader," in John Calvin, *Commentaries on the Twelve Minor Prophets*,

CO 42, cols. 185–88 (*CTS Minor Prophets* I, pp. xxvi–xxvii); cf. Parker, *Calvin's Old Testament Commentaries*, pp. 20–21.

98. Cf. Heinrich Bullinger, *In omnes apostolicas epistolas, divi videlicet Pauli XIIII. et VII. canonicas commentarii* (Zürich: Froschauer, 1537), p. 101, "De magistratu," and Calvin, *Commentaries on the First Epistle of Peter*, Argument (CTS, pp. 21–23).

99. Wolfgang Musculus, *Loci communes theologiae sacrae* (Basel: Iohannes Hervagius, 1560, 1563).

100. For example, Wolfgang Musculus, *In divi Pauli Epistolas ad Philippenses, Colosenses, Thessalonienses ambas & primum ad Timotheum commentarii* (Basel: Iohannes Hervagius, 1565), pp. 47–48 (on the problem of works and merits over aginst salvation through faith); Musculus, *In Epistolam D. Apostoli Pauli ad Romanos commentarii* (Basel: Sebastianum Henric Petri, 1555), pp. 165–67 (*observatio* and *appendix* dealing with issue of God's mercy and foreknowledge) 196–97 (*quaestio* and *observatio* on the divine gift of the Spirit); and Musculus, *In Evangistam Matthaeum commentarii tribus tomos digesti* (Basel: n.p., 1544), pp. 497–504 (two *loci* on the nature of divine precepts), 504–05 (on infant baptism and the Lord's supper). On Musculus's exegesis, see Craig S. Farmer, *The Gospel of John in the Sixteenth Century: The Johannine Exegesis of Wolfgang Musculus* (New York: Oxford University Press, 1997).

101. See chapter 7.

102. Cf. McKee, "Exegesis, Theology, and Development," p. 154–55.

103. Cf. Kolb, "Teaching the Text," pp. 571–85.

104. See the discussion in chapter 8.

105. Calvin, *Commentarius in librum Psalmorum*, "Calvinus . . . lectoribus," in *CO* 31, col. 33.

106. Ibid., in

107. See chapter 2, "Of Prefaces . . ." for a discussion of Calvin's approach to the *Harmony of the Last Four Books of Moses.*

108. Cf. Köstlin, "Calvin's *Institutio* nach Form und Inhalt," p. 21.

109. Calvin, *Institutio* (1539), VIII: "De praedestinatione & providentiae Dei," fol. 244–71, and see chapter 8.

110. Thus, cf. Calvin, *Institutio* (1550), II.6–7; VII.8–10; X.4–5 and Calvin, *Institutio* (1559), I.xv.3–5; II.xii.5–7; III.xi.5–12, respectively, where 1559 additions reflect polemic against Andreas Osiander, *An filius Dei fuerit incarnandus* (1550): note that, from a purely chronological perspective, Calvin could have included his polemics against Osiander in his commentary on the Gospel of John (1553) or in the *Harmony of the Evangelists* (1555). The Trinity is an instance of a doctrine elaborated by Calvin at great length but never developed on a comparable scale in the *Institutes.* cf. Calvin, *Institutio* (1559), I.xiii, and John Calvin, *Defensio orthodoxae fidei de sacra Trinitate, contra prodigiosos errores Michaelis Serveti*, in *CO* 8, cols. 453–644.

111. See further discussion in chapter 8.

112. Cf. Calvin, *Comm. in Epist. ad Romanos* [8:28–9:33] in *CO* 49, col. 158–94 (*CTS Romans*, pp. 314–80) and cf. David C. Steinmetz, "Calvin Among the Thomists," in *Biblical Hermeneutics in Historical Perspective* (Grand Rapids, Mich.: Eerdmans, 1991), pp. 198–214, on Calvin's exegesis of the passage.

113. Calvin, *Institutio* (1559), IV.xx.32; cf. Muller, "Calvin, Beza and the Exegetical History of Romans 13," p. 154.

114. Cf. Calvin, *In Evang. Ioh. Commentarius*, in *CO* 47, col. 2 (*CTS John* I, p. 26), and Calvin, *Institutio* (1559), II.xiv.7–8: as the sixteenth-century apparatus indicated, the entire chapter takes the form of a disputation.

115. Ibid., II.xii.

116. Osiander's treatise *An filius Dei fuerit incarnandus* (1550) appeared before most of Calvin's commentaries on the texts disputed during the course of the polemic, but reference to

Osiander is lacking even from commentaries on the texts identified in *Institutio* (1559), II.xii.4–7, as crucial to the debate: thus, cf. the comments on I Tim. 1:15; II Tim. 1:9 in Calvin, *Comm. in utramque Epist. ad Tim.*, in *CO* 52, col. 259–61, 352–53 (*CTS Timothy*, pp. 38–40, 194–96); John 1:9–11, 14; 3:16; 5:25; 11:25 in Calvin, *In Evang. Ioh. Commentarius*, in *CO* 47, col. 8–10, 13–16, 63–66, 117–18, 262 (*CTS John*, I, pp. 37–40, 44–48, 122–26, 205–06, 435–36).

117. On the first point, see the suggestive essay by Armstrong, "*Duplex cognitio Dei*, Or? The Problem and Relation of Structure, Form, and Purpose in Calvin's Theology," pp. 136–137.

118. Cf. Parker, *The Doctrine of the Knowledge of God, pp. 34–36 and Muller, PRRD*, I, pp. 185–86.

119. Cf. the commentary on Exodus 3:14 (the divine essence and self-existence; *CO* 24, col. 43–44; *CTS Harmony* I, pp. 73–74) with Numbers 23:18 (unchangeability / immutability; *CO* 25, col. 282–83; *CTS Harmony* IV, pp. 210–12), Exodus 20:18 (majesty; *CO* 24, col. 204; *CTS Harmony* IV, p. 331)

120. See the discussion in chapter 8.

121. Cf. Parker, *Calvin's New Testament Commentaries*, pp. 14–17, 27–29; Parker, *Calvin's Old Testament Commentaries* (Edinburgh: T. & T. Clark, 1986), pp. 9, 14–15, 29–32.

122. See chapter 8.

123. Cf. Susan E. Schreiner, *Where Shall Wisdom be Found*, (Chicago: University of Chicago Press, 1994), pp. 91–155 and Schreiner, "Exegesis and Double Justice in Calvin's Sermons on Job," *Church History* 58 (1989), pp. 322–38, who demonstrates the importance of the Job sermons as a source of Calvin's theology.

124. David C. Steinmetz, *Calvin in Context* (New York: Oxford University Press, 1995), p. 19.

125. See, for example, A. N. S. Lane, "Calvin's Use of the Fathers and the Medievals," *Calvin Theological Journal* 16 (1981), pp. 149–205; Lane, "Calvin's Sources of St. Bernard," *Archiv für Reformationsgeschichte* 67 (1982), pp. 258–78; Lane, "Calvin's Use of Bernard of Clairvaux," in *Bernhard von Clairvaux: Rezeption und Wirkung im Mittelalter und in der Neuzeit*, ed. Kaspar Elm (Wiesbaden: Harrassowitz, 1994), pp. 303–32; Lane "The Sources of Calvin's Citations in his Genesis Commentary," in *Interpreting the Bible*, ed. Lane (Leicester: Apollos, 1997), pp. 47–97; and Richard C. Gamble, "Sources of Calvin's Genesis Commentary: A Preliminary Report," in *Archiv für Reformationsgeschichte* 84 (1993), pp. 206–21.

126. Cf. the problematic approach in Brian A. Gerrish, *Grace and Gratitude*, pp. 103, 126, 144, discussed in my review in *The Journal of Religion* 75/1 (1995), pp. 119–21.

CHAPTER SEVEN

1. In this essay, I have followed the text of Calvin's *Institutio christianae religionis* (1559) as found in in *Ioannis Calvini opera quae supersunt omnia*, 59 vols. (vols. 29–87 of *Corpus Reformatorum*), ed. Guilielmus Baum, Eduardus Cunitz, and Eduardus Reuss (Brunswick: Schwetschke, 1863–1900), vols. 1–2. I have also consulted John Calvin, *Institutes of the Christian Religion* [1536], trans. Ford Lewis Battles, rev. ed. (Grand Rapids: Eerdmans, 1986); Calvin, *Institutes of the Christian Religion* [1559], ed. John T. McNeill, trans. Ford Lewis Battles, 2 vols. (Philadelphia: Westminster, 1960); Calvin, *Institutes of the Christian Religion*, trans. John Allen, 2 vols., 3rd ed., rev. (Philadelphia: Presbyterian Board of Publication, 1841); and Calvin, *Institutes of the Christian Religion*, trans. Henry Beveridge, 2 vols. (repr. Grand Rapids: Eerdmans, 1989), with emendation as necessitated by the Latin original. On the text and text-history of the *Institutes*, see Wilhelm Baum, Eduard Cunitz, and Eduard Reuss, "Prolegomena," in *CO* 1, pp. xxi–lviii; Baum et al., "Introduction," in *CO* 3, pp. vii–xlvii; Julius Köstlin, "Calvin's *Institutio* nach Form und Inhalt, in ihrer geschlichtlichen Entwicklung," *Theologische Studien und Kritiken* 41 (1868), pp. 7–62, 410–486; Albert Autin, *L'Institution chrétienne de Calvin* (Paris: Société Française d'Éditions

Littéraires et Techniques, 1929); J. W. Marmelstein, *Étude comparative des textes latin et français de l'Institution* (Groningen: J. B. Wolters, 1923); Benjamin B. Warfield, "On the Literary History of Calvin's Institutes," in John Calvin, *Institutes of the Christian Religion*, trans. John Allen, 7th ed. (Philadelphia: Presbyterian Board of Christian Education, 1936), pp. xxx–xxxi; Jacques Pannier, *Calvin écrivain. Sa place et son rôle dans l'histoire de la langue et de la littérature française*, 2nd ed. (Paris: Fischbacher, 1930); Pannier, *Recherches sur la formation intellectuelle de Calvin* (Paris: Alcan, 1931); Pannier, "Notes historiques et critiques sur un chapitre de l'*Institution* écrit Strasbourg (1539)," in *Reuve d'Histoire et de Philosophie Religieuses* (1934), pp. 206–29; Pannier, "Introduction" in John Calvin, *Institution de la religion chrestienne* (1541), I, pp. vii–xxxi; Jean-Daniel Benoit, "Introduction," in Jean Calvin, *Institution de la religion chrestienne* (Paris: J. Vrin, 1957ff.), I, pp. 8–17; Benoit, "The History and Development of the *Institutio*: How Calvin Worked," in *John Calvin: A Collection of Distinguished Essays*, ed. Gervase E. Duffield (Grand Rapids: Eerdmans Press, 1966), pp. 102–17; and J. I. Packer, "Calvin the Theologian," in ibid., pp. 149–75; also note the discussions in François Wendel, *Calvin: The Origins and Development of His Religious Thought*, trans. Philip Mairet (New York: Harper & Row, 1963), pp. 144–46; T. H. L. Parker, *John Calvin: A Biography* (Philadelphia: Westminister, 1975), pp. 34–37, 72–74, 129–32; Parker, *Calvin: An Introduction to His Thought* (Louisville: Westminister/John Knox, 1995) pp. 4–10; Wilhelm H. Neuser and Brian G. Armstrong, "The Development of the *Institutes* 1536 to 1559," in *John Calvin's Institutes: His Opus Magnum*, ed. B. J. van der Walt (Potchefstrom: Institute for Reformational Studies, 1986), pp. 33–54; and Alister E. McGrath, *A Life of John Calvin* (Oxford: Blackwell, 1990), pp. 136–44.

2. On the 1536 *Institutes*, see Alexandre Ganoczy, *The Young Calvin*, trans. David Foxgrover and Wade Provo (Philadelphia: Westminster, 1987), pp. 133–238; August Lang, "The Sources of Calvin's Institutes of 1536," *Evangelical Quarterly* 8 (1936), pp. 131–40; and note Lang, "Luther und Calvin" and "Melanchthon und Calvin," in *Reformation und Gegenwart. Gesammelte Aufsätze vornehmlich zur Geschichte und zum Verständnis Calvins und der reformierten Kirche*, ed. Lang (Detmold: Meyersche Hofbuchhandlung, 1918), pp. 72–87 and 88–135; Jacques Pannier, "Une Première 'Institution' française dès 1537?" John Calvin, *Épitre à tous amateurs de Jésus-Christ*, ed. J. Pannier (Paris: Fischbacher, 1929); H. W. Simpson, "The *Editio Princeps* of the *Institutio Christianae Religionis*, 1536 by John Calvin," in *Calvinus Reformator: His Contribution to Theology, Church and Society* (Potchefstroom: Potchefstroom University for Christian Higher Education, 1982), pp. 26–32; E. David Willis, "The Social Context of the 1536 Edition of Calvin's *Institutes*," in *In Honor of John Calvin, 1509–64*, Papers from the 1986 International Calvin Symposium, McGill University, ed. E. J. Furcha (Montreal: McGill University, 1987), pp. 133–53; Joseph C. McLelland, "Renaissance in Theology: Calvin's 1536 *Institutio*—Fresh Start or False?" in ibid., pp. 154–74; and Ford Lewis Battles, "Introduction," in *Institutes* (1536), pp. xxxviii–xl. Also to be noted here is the recent translation of Barth's 1922 lectures: Karl Barth, *The Theology of John Calvin*, trans. G. W. Bromiley (Grand Rapids, Mich.: Eerdmans, 1995) which (pp. 157–226) surveys the 1536 *Institutes*. The previously noted studies by Köstlin and Benoit focus on the 1559 *Institutes*, and it has been characteristic of theological studies of Calvin's work to cite the 1559 edition nearly exclusively: for example, Adam Mitchell Hunter, *Teaching of Calvin: A Modern Interpretation*, 2nd ed. (London: James Clarke, 1950); Wilhelm Niesel, *Theology of Calvin*, trans. Harold Knight (London: Lutterworth, 1956); Parker, *Calvin: An Introduction*.

3. For example, see the excellent introduction in *Institution de la religion chrestienne de Calvin*, texte original de 1541, réimprimé sous la direction de Abel Lefranc par Henri Chateain et Jacques Pannier (Paris: Librairie Honoré Champion, 1911); Jean Calvin, *Épitre au roi François Ier: Préface de la première édition française de l'Institution de la religion chrétienne 1541*, avec introduction et notes par Jacques Pannier (Paris: Fischbacher, 1927); Calvin, "Notes historiques et critiques sur un chapitre de l'*Institution* écrit à Strasbourg (1539)," pp. 206–29; Fritz Büsser, "Elements of

Zwingli's Thought in Calvin's *Institutes*," in *In Honor of John Calvin, 1509–64*, ed. Furcha pp. 1–27; also note the fine discussion of the 1539 and 1543 editions with reference to Calvin's debate with the Anabaptists in Willem Balke, *Calvin and the Anabaptist Radicals*, trans. William J. Heynen (Grand Rapids, Mich.: Eerdmans, 1981), pp. 97–122, 155–68; Balke also examines the 1536 and 1559 texts (pp. 39–71; 209–11).

4. Notable exceptions—and model efforts to examine the strata of the *Institutes* with reference to one particular doctrine—are Harro Höpfl, *The Christian Polity of John Calvin* (Cambridge: Cambridge University Press, 1982), and Barbara Pitkin, "What Pure Eyes Could See: Faith, Creation, and History in John Calvin's Theology," Ph.D. dissertation, University of Chicago, 1994.

5. Calvin, *Institutio* (1559), Joannes Calvinus lectori; cf. *Institutes* (1559/Beveridge), p. 24.

6. Thus, e.g., Alister McGrath, *A Life of John Calvin* (Oxford: Blackwell, 1990), pp. 145–46; Parker, *Calvin: An Introduction*, p. ix; cf. P. Lobstein, "L'oeuvre dogmatique de Calvin," in *Etudes sur la pensée et l'oeuvre de Calvin*, ed. Lobstein (Nevilly: Editions de "La Cause," 1927), p. 100.

7. Cf. Parker, *John Calvin*, p. 105.

8. Calvin, *Institutio* (Basel: Platter and Lasius, 1536), fol. 42, 102, 157, 200, 285, 400, respectively. Still the most detailed comparative synopsis of the various editions of the *Institutes* is that offered by the editors of the *Calvini Opera*: *CO* 1, pp. li–lviii.

9. Thus, A. Lefranc, "Introduction," in *Institution de la religion chrestienne de Calvin* (1541), pp. 11–12; Autin, *L'Institution Chrétienne de Calvin*, p. 77; Neuser, "Development and Structure," pp. 33, 38–39; McGrath, *Life of Calvin*, p 137. But note the very carful evaluation of the extent of Luther's theological inluence in Willem van 't Spijker, "The Influence of Luther on Calvin According to the *Institutes*," in *John Calvin's Institutes: His Opus Magnum*, ed. B. Van der Walt, et al. (Potchefsttroom: Institute for Reformational Studies 1986), pp. 83–105.

10. Cf. Barth, *Theology of Calvin*, p. 41. See the early Reformation catechisms in Ferdinand Cohrs, *Die Evangelischen Katechismusversuche vor Luthers Enchiridion*, 5 vols. (Berlin: Hofmann, 1900–1907; repr., 5 vols. in 2, Hildesheim and New York: George Olms, 1978): note Bugenhagen's catechism for Braunschweig (1528), III, pp. 67ff., and Kaspar Loener, *Unterricht des Glaubens* (1529), III, pp. 462ff. It is clear, however, that the order—Law, Creed, Lord's Prayer—characteristic of Luther's catechisms and of Calvin's 1536 *Institutes* was not universally followed.

11. See Martin Luther, *Catechesis minor*, in *Concordia Triglotta: Libri symbolici Ecclesiae Lutheranae, Germanice-Latine-Anglice* (St. Louis: Concordia Publishing House, 1921), pp. 560–61. Edward F. Meylan, "The Stoic Doctrine of Indifferent Things and the Conception of Christian Liberty in Calvin's *Institutio Religionis Christianae*," *Romanic Review* 28 (1937), pp. 138–39, identified the discussion of Christian freedom of the 1536 *Institutes* and the separate chapter on the subject in the 1539 edition as an adaptation of the chapter of the same name found in Melanchthon's *Loci communes*.

12. Cf. H. Obendiek, "Die *Institutio* Calvins als 'Confessio' und 'Apologie,' " in *Theologische Aufsätze. K. Barth zum 50 Geburtstag* ed. Ernst Wolf (Munich: Kaiser, 1936), pp. 417–31; and Barth, *Theology of John Calvin*, pp. 158–59.

13. See, chapters 2 and 6.

14. Calvin to Farel, 27 October 1540, in *CO* 11, col. 90–93 (*Letters*, I, p. 212).

15. Cf. Battles, "Preface," in *Catechismus* (1538), pp. iv–v.

16. Note that "human traditions" is subsumed under Cap. XIV, *De potestate ecclesiastica* in Calvin, *Institutio* (1539), fol. 371–78 and becomes a separate, new chapter only in 1543: Calvin, *Institutio* (1543), cap. XIII (fol. 337–50).

17. Cf. John Calvin, *L'Institution puérile de la doctrine chrestienne faicte par manière de dyalogue* (1541) in *Opera Selecta*, 2, pp. 152–56; Calvin, *Le Catéchisme de l'église de Genève, c'est a dire le formulaire d'instruire les enfants en la chrestienté* (1541–42; Geneva: Jean Girard, 1545) and *Ca-*

techismus ecclesiae genevensis, hoc est formula erudiendi pueros in doctrina Christi (Strasbourg: Wendelin Rihel, 1545), in *CO* 6, cols. 1–146; translation in *Tracts* 2, pp. 33–94. Note that the Jean Girard 1545 edition of the *Catéchisme* is the earliest known exemplar.

18. Calvin, *Institutio* (Strasbourg: 1539), fol. 1, 17, 58, 97, 157, 186, 225, 244, 272, 296, 305, 327, 353, 360, 378, 393, 414, respectively.

19. Parker, *Calvin: An Introduction,* p. 5.

20. Contra Battles, "Calculus Fidei," in *Interpreting John Calvin,* ed. Robert Benedetto (Grand Rapids, Mich.: Baker Book House, 1996), pp. 147–50 and Battles, "Introduction" in *Institutes: 1536 Edition,* pp. xxxiv–xxxvi. Note, also, that the phrase *duplex cognitio Dei* or *duplex cognitio Domini,* although implied in the McNeill/Battles translation of *Institutes,* I.ii.1, "Of the resulting twofold knowledge of God we shall now discuss the first aspect; the second will be dealt with in its proper place," is not actually found in Calvin's Latin, which reads, ". . . hinc duplex emergit eius cognitio: quarum nunc prior tractanda est, altera deinde suo ordine sequitur." The phrase can, of course, be inferred from the chapter—as, indeed, from the titles of Books I and II of the *Institutes,* "De cognitione Dei Creatoris" and "De cognitione Dei Redemptoris"—and it remains a useful way of characterizing the relationship between the arguments of Books I and II.

21. Cf. Parker, *John Calvin,* pp. 73–74.

22. Calvin, *Institutio* (1536), fol. 40: "Summa fere sacrae doctrinae duabus his partibus constat, Cognitione Dei, ac nostri."

23. Cf. Calvin, *Institutio* (1536), fol. 40, and Calvin, *Institutio* (1539), I, ad init. (fol. 1): "Tota fere sapientiae nostrae, quae vera demum ac solida sapientia censeri debeat, duabus partibus constat: cognitione Dei, & nostri"; II, ad init. (fol. 17): "Non sine causa, veteri proverbio, tantopere homini commendata semper fuit cognitio ipsius"; and note Calvin, *Institutio* (1559), I.i.1, ad init; II.i.1, ad init.

24. Cf. Calvin, *Institutio* (1536), fol. 299–358, and Calvin, *Institutio* (1539), V, fol. 157–86.

25. Calvin, *Institutio* (1536), i.e., cap. 6 (fol. 400–514); cf. Calvin, *Institutio* (1539), i.e., cap. XIII–XV (fol. 353–93) and cap. XVII (fol. 414–34). On this new final chapter see Jacques Pannier, "Notes historiques et critiques sur un chapitre de l'*Institution* écrit à Strasbourg (1539)," pp. 206–29.

26. Calvin, *Institutio* (1539), cap. 7, 8.

27. See the discussion in chapter 6.

28. For a basic description and location of the several catechisms, see Wulfert De Greef, *The Writings of John Calvin An Introductory Guide,* trans. Lyle D. Bierma (Grand Rapids, Mich.:Baker Book House, 1993), pp. 124–25, 131–33; also see M. B. van't Veer, *Catechese en catechetische stof bij Calvijn* (Kampen: Kok, 1941).

29. John Calvin, *Catechism or Institution of the Christian Religion,* trans. and intro. by Ford Lewis Battles (Pittsburgh:Pittsburgh Theological Seminary, 1972; rev. 1976); cf. Battles, "Calculus Fidei," in *Interpreting John Calvin,* p. 159.

30. See chapter 2.

31. See chapter 6.

32. Desiderius Erasmus, *Ratio seu methodus compendio perveniendi ad veram theologiam* [1519], in *Desiderius Erasmus Roterodamus Ausgewählte Werke,* ed. Hajo Holborn and Annemarie Holborn (Munich: C. H. Beck, 1933). Cf. the analyses of this work in Albert Rabil Jr., *Erasmus and the New Testament, The Mind of a Christian Humanist* (1972; repr. Lanham, Md.:University Press of America), pp. 103–13 and Manfred Hoffmann, *Rhetoric and Theology:The Hermeneutic of Erasmus* (Toronto: University of Toronto Press, 1994), pp. 32–39.

33. Cf. Erasmus, *Ratio seu methodus compendio perveniendi ad veram theologiam,* in *Ausgewählte Werke,* ed. Hajo Holborn and Annemarie Holborn (Munich: C. H. Beck, 1933), p. 291.

34. Note Cornelius Augustijn, *Erasmus: His Life, Works, and Influence*, trans. J. C. Grayson (Toronto: University of Toronto Press, 1991), pp. 133, 196, where the author argues for the direct methodological impact of Erasmus on Melanchthon.

35. Büsser, "Elements of Zwingli's Thought in Calvin's *Institutes*," p. 3–9; cf. Lang, "The Sources of Calvin's Institutes of 1536," pp. 132, 137; Reinhold Seeberg, *Textbook of the History of Doctrines*, trans. Charles Hay (Grand Rapids, Mich.: Baker Book House, 1952), II, pp. 393–94.

36. Huldrych Zwingli, *De vera et falsa religione commentarius*, in *Opera completa editio prima*, ed. Melchior Schuler and Johannes Schulthess (-Zurich: Schulthess & Höhr, 1829–42), III, pp. 155–72, the *loci de vocabulo religionis, Inter quos constet religio, de Deo* and *De homine*.

37. Calvin, *Institutio* (1539), fol. 1: "Utra autem alteram praecedat, ac ex se pariat, non facile discernere"; cf. Calvin, *Institutio* (1559), I.i.1.

38. Calvin, *Institutio* (1539), fol. 2: "Utcunque tamen Dei nostrique notitia mutuo inter se nexu sint colligatae: ordo recte dicendi postulat, ut de illa, priore disseramus loco, tum hanc tractandam postea descendamus"; cf. Calvin, *Institutio* (1559), I.i.3, ad fin.

39. Zwingli, *De vera et falsa religione commentarius*, in *Opera* II, pp. 155, 166 (*Commentary*), pp. 58, 75.

40. Huldrych Zwingli, *In catabaptistarum strophas elenchus*, in *CR* 93/1, cols. 164–69; also see the translation, *Refutation of the Tricks of the Anabaptists*, in *Ulrich Zwingli (1484–1531): Selected Works*, ed. Samuel Macaulay Jackson (Philadelphia: University of Pennsylvania, 1972), pp. 234–35.

41. Cf. Calvin, *Institutio* (1539), VII (fol. 225ff.); Calvin, *Institutio* (1559), II.x–xi, note especially II.x.2. See the discussion Zwingli's views on covenant and testament in Lyle D. Bierma, *German Calvinism in the Confessional Age:The Covenant Theology of Caspar Olevianus* (Grand Rapids, Mich.:Baker Book House, 1997), pp. 32–35, 44, 48; and note Jack W. Cottrell, "Covenant and Baptism in the Theology of Huldreich Zwingli," Th.D. dissertation, Princeton Theological Seminary, 1971.

42. See Calvin to Melanchthon, 18 June 1550, in *CO* 13, col. 593–96 (*Letters*, II, pp. 274–74); Calvin to Melanchthon, 27 August 1554, Calvin to Vermigli, 27 August 1554, and Calvin to Sleidanus, 27 August 1554, in *CO* 15, col. 215–17, 219–21 (*Letters*, III, pp. 58, 60, 61–63). On the tensions between Calvin and Melanchthon, see D. Fischer, "Calvin et la Confession d'Augsbourg," in *Calvinus Ecclesiae Genevensis Custos*, ed. W. H. Neuser (Frankfurt am Main: Peter Lang, 1984), pp. 247–66.

43. Cited without reference in Philip Schaff, *History of the Christian Church*, 3rd ed., rev.; 8 vols. (1910; repr. Grand Rapids, Mich.:Eerdmans, 1979), VIII, p. 384. The compliment is often noted, but to my knowledge with no reference better than Schaff.

44. Cf. the reference to Castellio's use of Melanchthon in *Response à certaines calomnies et blasphemes*, in *CO* 58, col. 202.

45. Cf. Pannier, "Introduction," in *Institution de la religion chrestienne* (1541), pp. xxiv–xxv; Autin, *L'Institution Chrétienne de Calvin*, pp. 85–113; and Köstlin, "Calvins *Institutio* nach Form und Inhalt," pp. 9, 11–13, 33–41; Emil Doumergue, *Jean Calvin, les hommes et les choses de son temps*, 7 vols. (Lausanne:G. Bridel, 1899–1927), II, p. 545; IV, pp. 2–5; Warfield, "Literary History," pp. xvii–xix; Benoit, "History and Development," pp. 103–04. Köstlin (pp. 39–41) explicitly notes the differences between Calvin, *Institutio* (1539), and Melanchthon, *Loci communes* (1535/6), in the understanding of predestination but makes no reference to the issue of order and method.

46. Jacques Pannier, *Recherches sur la formation intellectuelle de Calvin jusqu' à sa conversion* (Paris: Alcan, 1931), pp. 60–61.

47. Cf. August Lang, "Melanchthon und Calvin," pp. 95–96; Lang, "The Sources of Calvin's Institutes," pp. 135–36; Doumergue, *Jean Calvin*, II, pp. 545–61; and Wendel, *Calvin*, pp. 134–

35. Lang explicitly states that the resemblances between places in the *Institutes* and the teachings of Melanchthon indicated in cross-references to the *Opera selecta* "do not amount to proofs," while Doumergue appears to see Melanchthon's influence waning in 1539, given the theological disagreements between Calvin and Melanchthon over predestination.

48. Köstlin, "Calvin's *Institutio*," pp. 11–12.

49. Cf. Willem Van 't Spijker, "De Invloed van Bucer op Calvijn blijkens de Institutie," *Theologia Reformata* 28 (1985), pp. 29–33, Lang, "The Sources of Calvin's Institutes," pp. 139–41, and Wendel, *Calvin*, pp. 135, 141.

50. *Jehan Calvin aux Lecteurs [Préface de la Somme de Melanchthon 1546]*, in *CO* 9, cols. 847–50.

51. Heinrich Bullinger, *De testamento seu foedere Dei unico & aeterno . . . brevis expositio* (Zürich:Froschauer, 1534); Bullinger, *De scriptura sanctae authoritate, certitudine, firmitate et absoluta perfectione . . . libri duo* (Zürich:Froschauer, 1538); also see Charles S. McCoy and J. Wayne Baker, *Fountainhead of Federalism: Heinrich Bullinger and the Covenantal Tradition*, with a translation of *De testamento seu foedere Dei unico et aeterno* (Lousville: Westminster/John Knox, 1991).

52. See Anthony Hoekema, "Calvin's Doctrine of the Covenant of Grace," *Reformed Review* 15 (1962), pp. 1–12; Hoekema, "The Covenant of Grace in Calvin's Teaching," *Calvin Theological Journal* 2 (1967), pp. 133–161; Lyle D. Bierma, "Federal Theology in the Sixteenth Century: Two Traditions?" *Westminster Theological Journal* 45 (1983), pp. 304–21; Bierma, "Covenant or Covenants in the Theology of Olevianus," *Calvin Theological Journal* 22 (1987), pp. 228–50; and Bierma, "The Role of Covenant Theology in Early Reformed Orthodoxy," *Sixteenth-Century Journal* 21/3 (1990), pp. 453–462; contra J. Wayne Baker, *Heinrich Bullinger and the Covenant: The Other Reformed Tradition* (Athens:Ohio University Press, 1980).

53. See Peter Alan Lillback, "The Binding of God: Calvin's Role in the Development of Covenant Theology," Ph.D. dissertation, Westminster Theological Seminary, 1985.

54. Melanchthon, *Loci communes theologici, CR* 21, cols. 192–206 (1521), 453–56 (1535), 800–16 (1543).

55. Calvin, *Institutio* (1539), VII, fol. 226: "Patrum omnium foedus adeo substantia & re ipsa nihil 'a nostro differt, ut unum prorsus atque idem sit. Administratio tamen variat"; cf. Calvin, *Institutio* (1559), II.x.2.

56. Melanchthon, *Loci communes theologici* (1543), in *CR* 21, col. 800; cf. *Loci communes* (1535/6) in *CR* 21, col. 453: "Lex Moysi ad certum populum ac tempus certum pertinuit, tamen legem naturae omnem esse gentium communem, et ad omnes aetates pertinere . . . Rursus Evangelium, hoc est, promissio reconciliationis propter Christum, etiam ad omnes aetates pertinet . . ."

57. See Edmond Grin, "L'unité des deux Testaments selon Calvin," *Theologische Zeitschrift* 17 (1961), pp. 175–86, for an analysis of Calvin's exposition. The broader question of the the-ological content of Calvin's chapters on the similarly and distinction of the testaments remains to be examined: if Melanchthon's *Loci communes* provide the context for Calvin's addition of the chapter on this sbuject in 1539, the question of the influences on Calvin's own formulation remains, inasmuch as some of Calvin's argument within the *locus* reflects his Reformed trajectory—viz., the influence of Zwingli and Bullinger—rather than the theology of Melanchthon.

58. Cf. Melanchthon, *Loci communes* (1521), col. 81; (1535/6), col. 253–54); (1543) col. 603–04, and Zwingli, *De vera et falsa religione commentarius*, in *Opera* III, pp. 147–55 (*Commentary*, pp. 54–55).

59. Melanchthon, *Loci communes theologici, CR* 21, col. 254 (1533) and 349 (1535).

60. Cf. Zwingli, *De vera et falsa religione commentarius*, in *Opera* III, pp. 191, 199, 203, *Evangelium, De poenitentia*, and *De lege*, respectively.

61. See Melanchthon, *Declamatio de studio doctrinae Pauli*, in *CR* 11, col. 43–51; Melanch-thon, *Theologiae studiosis Philippus Melanchthon S.* [viz., Melanchthon's preface to the *Operationes in Psalmos*], in *WA* 5, pp. 24–25; Luther, *Vorrede auff die Epistel S. Pauli an die Roemer, WADB*

5, p. 1, "diese Epistel ist das rechte Heubtstueck des newen Testaments"; also note the *Oratio de Paulo Apostolo, habita a Christophoro Iona*, in *CR* 11, col. 626: "Dixi de genere doctrinae, quod Paulus maxime illustravit, ac de aliis quibusdam doctrinae locis"; and cf. the discussion in John Schneider, *Philip Melanchthon's Rhetorical Construal of Biblical Authority* (Lewiston Canada:Edwin Mellen, 1990), pp. 100–01, 167–81.

62. *CR* 15, cols. 441–92. See the discussion of the relationship between Calvin's *Commentarius* and Melanchthon's *Dispositio* in Richard A. Muller, "*Scimus enim quod lex spiritualis est*: Melanchthon and Calvin on the Interpretation of Romans 7:14–23," in *Philip Melanchthon (1497–1560) and the Commentary*, ed. Timothy J. Wengert and M. Patrick Graham (Sheffield: University of Sheffield Academic Press, 1997), pp. 216–37; and see Joel Edward Kok, "The Influence of Martin Bucer on Calvin's Interpretation of Romans: A Comparative Case Study," Ph.D dissertation, Duke University, 1993), pp. 168, 171–73, which balances the influence of Bucer against that of Melanchthon, concluding that in "significant instances, Calvin's interpretation of Romans is closer to Melanchthon's than to Bucer's."

63. *CR* 21, col. 49–60.

64. *CR* 21, col. 81–228.

65. See the excellent study of Melanchthon's rhetorical analysis of Romans in Rolf Schäfer, "Melanchthon's Hermeneutik im Römerbrief-Kommentar von 1532," *Zeitschrift für Theologie und Kirche* 60 (1963), pp. 216–35.

66. See the detailed analysis of this section of Melanchthon's commentaries in Timothy J. Wengert, "Philip Melanchthon's 1522 Annotations on Romans and the Lutheran Origins of Rhetorical Criticism," in *Biblical Interpretation in the Era of the Reformation*, ed. Richard A. Muller and John L. Thompson (Grand Rapids, Mich.: Erdmans, 1996), pp. 131–35.

67. Note that although Calvin did not follow Melanchthon in identifying offense or scandal as a *locus* separate from Christian liberty in his *Institutes*, he certainly included the topic—understanding it as a subtopic within the *locus* on Christian liberty: see Calvin, *Institutio* (1539), pp. 357–58; cf. Calvin, *Institutio* (1559), III.xix.10–13, and note also IV.x.22. Calvin also wrote a separate treatise on the subject: *De scandalis* in *CO* 8, cols. 1–84.

68. See Philip Melanchthon, *Loci communes theologici* in *Opera quae supersunt omnia*, 28 vols., ed. C. G. Bretschreider (Brunswick: Schwetschke, 1834–1860), vol. 21; and Philip Melanchthon, *Loci communes theologici* (1521), trans. Lowell Satre, in *Melanchthon and Bucer*, ed. Wilhelm Pauck (Philadelphia: Westminster, 1969); also Philip Melanchthon, *Loci communes 1543*, trans. J. A. O. Preus (St. Louis: Concordia, 1992).

69. For example, McGrath, *Life of John Calvin*, p. 139.

70. Cf. Wengert, "Philip Melanchthon's 1522 Annotations" pp. 135–36, and the arguments in chapter 2 on Calvin's *Épitre aux tous amateurs* and his *Comentary on Romans*.

71. Melanchthon, *Loci theologici* (1535), in *CR* 21, col. 453–54.

72. Ibid., cols. 450–53.

73. Cf. chapter 2.

74. Theodore Beza, *Tabula praedestinationis* (Geneva, 1555), VIII, par. v. in *Tractations theologicae*, 3 vols. (Geneva: Jean Crispin/Eustathius Vignon, 1570–82).

75. Calvin, *Institutio* (1559), II.vii.6–12; cf. Calvin, *Institutio* (1536), in *CO* 1, cols. 49–51; *Institutio* (1539), III, fol. 91–94; Calvin, *Institution* (1541); and Melanchthon, *Loci communes* (1536), in *CR* 21, cols. 405–07. There is no clear distinction of uses of the law to be found either in Zwingli's *Commentarius* or in Bullinger's *De testamento*: at most the reader could infer two uses, a civil and a theological.

76. Cf. Melanchthon, *Loci communes* (1535/6), in *CR* 21, cols. 405–06: following the order civil, pedagogical, normative, with Calvin, *Institutio* (1536), in *CR* 1, cols 49–51, arguing for the order pedagogical, civil, and normative use.

77. Calvin moved the discussion of the three uses of the law to the beginning of his exposition

of the law only in the 1559 edition of the *Institutes* (II.vii.6–12): see the *Synopsis Editionum Institutionis Calvinianae* in *CO* 1, p. lii.

78. The older scholarship has obscured the issue of Melanchthon's formal or structural influence by its emphasis on the substantive differences between Melanchthon's and Calvin's doctrine of predestination: cf. Köstlin, "Calvin's *Institutio* nach Form und Inhalt," pp. 39–41.

79. Cf. Basil Hall, "Calvin Against the Calvinists," in *John Calvin: A Collection of Distinguished Essays,* ed. Gervase E. Duffield (Grand Rapids Mich.: Eerdmans, 1966), pp. 24, 27; cf. Barth, *Church Dogmatics,* II/2, pp. 76–93, 111.

80. McGrath, *Life of John Calvin,* p. 138; William J. Bouwsma, "Calvinism as *Theologia Rhetorica,*" in *Calvinism us Theologica Rhetorica,* ed. Wilhelm Wuellner (Berkeley: Center for Hermeneutical Studies, 1986), p. 11; cf. the similar comments in Parker, *John Calvin,* p. 105.

81. The original version of the work is Heinrich Bullinger, *Summa christlicher religion* (Zürich: Froschauer, 1556), translated into Latin as *Compendium christianae religionis* (Zürich, 1559) and into English as *Commonplaces of Christian Religion* (London: Henry Bynneman, 1575). Cf. the descriptions of the document in Muller, *Christ and the Decree: Christology and Predestination in Reformed Theology from Calvin to Perkins,* vol. 2 (Durham, N.C.: Labyrinth Press, 1986; paperback ed., Grand Rapids, Mich.: Baker Book House, 1988), pp. 39–44; and Edward A. Dowey, "Heinrich Bullinger as Theologian: Thematic, Comprehensive, Schematic," in *Calvin Studies V,* Proceedings of the Eighth Colloquium on Calvin Studies (Davidson College, Davidson, N.C., January 19–20, 1990), pp. 41–60.

82. Cf. Zwingli, *Commentarius* (*Commentary,* pp. 260–67)—following the sacraments and marriage, before the invocation of saints and merit.

83. Melanchthon, *Loci communes* (1535/6), in *CR* 21, col. 128–28.

84. Cf. Parker, *The Doctrine of the Knowledge of God,* p. 118 and John Calvin, *The Catechism of the Church of Geneva,* in *Calvin: Theological Treatises,* ed. J. K. S. Reid (Philadelphia: Westminster, 1954), p. 93: "into how many parts shall we divide this confession? Into four principal parts. . . . The first refers to God the Father; the second concerns his Son Jesus Christ, and also includes the entire sum of man's redemption. The third part concerns the Holy Spirit; the fourth the church and the divine benefits vouchsafed to it."

85. *Institutio totius christianae religionis* (Geneva: Ioannes Gerardus, 1550); cf. Roddphe Peter and Jean-François Gilmont, *Bibliotheca Calviniana,* 2 vols. (Geneva: Droz, 1991–94), I, pp. 372–74. Peter and Gilmont cite the anonymous editor's introductory comment to the index and note the question of the authorship of the index.

86. *Institution de la religion chrestienne* (Geneva: Jean Girard, 1551).

87. The words "order and" appear only in the French: *Institutio christianae religionis, in libris quatuor nunc primum digesta, certisque distincta capitibus, ad aptissimam methodum: aucta etiam tam magna accessione ut prope-modum opus novum habere possit* (Geneva: Stephanus, 1559); *Institution de la religion chrestienne nouvellement mise en quatre livres: et distinguée par chapitres, en ordre et méthode bien propre: Augmentée aussi de tel accroissement qu'on la peut presque estimer un livre nouveau* (Geneva: Crespin, 1560).

88. Calvin, *Institutio* (1559), Ioannes Calvinus lectori, in *CO* 2, col. 1.

89. On the *duplex cognitio Dei* see the classic study of Edward A. Dowey, *The Knowledge of God in Calvin's Theology* (New York: Columbia University Press, 1952; 3rd ed., Grand Rapids, Mich.: Eerdmans, 1994) and note Cornelis P. Venema, "The 'Twofold Knowledge of God' and the Structure of Calvin's Theology," *Mid-America Journal of Theology* 4 (1988), pp. 156–82.

90. Packer, "Calvin the Theologian," pp. 157–59.

91. Benoit, "The History and Development of the *Institutio,*" p. 109.

92. Cf. Melanchthon, *Loci communes,* XV and XVI in *CR* 21, col. 920ff. and 925ff. Note that the 1536 *Loci* had included these chapters but had placed them further on in the sequence, following *De scandalo: CR* 21, col. 519ff. and col. 524ff.

93. Cf. Benoit, "The History and Development of the *Institutio*," pp. 111–12.

94. Parker, *The Doctrine of the Knowledge of God*, p. 119; Parker, *John Calvin*, p. 131.

95. Dowey, *Knowledge of God*, p. 45

96. Parker, *Calvin's Doctrine of the Knowledge of God*, pp. 118–21.

97. Ibid., p. 120.

98. Battles, "Calculus Fidei," in *Interpreting John Calvin*, p. 159.

99. Cf. Parker, *The Doctrine of the Knowledge of God*, p. 120 and Dowey's somewhat labored attempt to explain this placement in relation to the *duplex cognitio* in *Knowledge of God in Calvin's Theology*, p. 151.

100. Calvin, *Catechismus, sive christianae religionis institutio* (Based: n.p., (1538), chapters 13–19.

101. Cf. Dowey, *Knowledge of God in Calvin's Theology*, pp. 211–12; Hall, "Calvin Against the Calvinists," p. 27; Barth, *Church Dogmatics*, II/2, pp. 80–88.

102. *Synopsis Editionum Institutionis Calvinianae*, in *CO* 1, pp. lv–lvi.

103. Cf. Calvin, *Institutio* (1550), XIV.38–41, 42–51 and *Institutio* (1559), I.xvi.4–9; xvii.3–14; and Calvin, *Institutio* (1550), VI.49–51, and *Institutio* (1559), I.xvi.1–3.

104. Calvin, *Catechismus, sive christianae religionis institutio*, cap. 13, *De electione et praedestinatione*, preceded by cap. 12, *Christum fide a nobis apprehendi* and followed by cap. 14 and 15, *Quid sit vera fides* and *Fides donum Dei*. The credal exposition begins at cap. 20.

105. Calvin, *Institutio* (1536), II (p. 151); Calvin, *Institutio* (1539), pp. 153–55; Calvin, *Institutio* (1550), VIII.220–24.

106. Calvin, *Institutio* (1559), I.i, iii–x, are based on Calvin, *Institutio* (1550), I.1–38, while Calvin, *Institutio* (1559), I.xi–xvii, are based on sections drawn from Calvin, *Institutio* (1550), II, III, VI, and XIV.

107. Note that the "addition" of the chapter on vows in 1543 was an actual addition of material—but also to be understood as a development of the Melanchthonian-Pauline order of topics.

108. Calvin, *Institutio* (1559), Ioannes Calvinus lectori, in *CO* 2, col. 1.

109. Cf. Olevian, "Methodus et dispositio," in Calvin, *Institutio* (1585), fol. **iii, verso. Note that the traditional Augustinian exegesis of Romans 7 as pertaining to the life of the believer leads directly to the systematic conclusion that sin must be discussed in the context of the doctrines related to redemption.

110. Cf. Gulielmus Launeus [William DeLaune], *Institutionis christianae religionis . . . Epitome* (London: Thomas Vautrollerius, 1583), *Generalis tabula totius institutionis*, unpaginated, fol. 1–4 of the table; Dowey, *Knowledge of God in Calvin's Theology*, pp. 41–42, et passim.

111. A fairly significant and as yet unanswered question, however, concerns the contents of those portions of the 1550 text that were either excised entirely or condensed and substantially rewritten as as result of the shuffling and editing process that took place in 1559: a notable example occurs in the movement from the two discussions of God's providential governance in Calvin, *Institutio* (1550), IV.49–53; XIV.38–41, to the chapter in Calvin, *Institutio* (1559), I.xvi.

CHAPTER EIGHT

1. In particular, note Iohannes Calvinus, *Institutio christianae religionis* in *Ioannis Calvini Opera Selecta*, ed. Peter Barth and Wilhelm Niesel (Munich: Chr. Kaiser, 1928–36), vols. III–V; and John Calvin, *Institutes of the Christian Religion*, 2 vols. ed. John T. McNeill, trans. Ford Lewis Battles, (Philadelphia: Westminster, 1960).

2. Calvin, *Institutio* (1539), Epistola ad Lectorem, fol. *1v: "Itaque hac veluti strata via, si quas posthac Scripturae enarrationes edidero. . . ."

3. Cf. Calvin, *Institutio* (1539), Epistola ad Lectorem, fol. *1v; cf. Calvin, *Institutio* (1559/ Battles), I, pp. 4–5.

4. Cf. the interesting juxtaposition of Calvin's view of Scripture from the *Institutes* with his view of Scripture elicited from his sermons in Parker, *Calvin's Preaching*, pp. 1–16.

5. Note that *OS* carefully places in brackets *in the text* only what Calvin places in the margin and allocates all other references to its own apparatus—while McNeill/Battles rushes in where *OS* feared to tread, placing *all* citations in the text, including those identified only by modern editors—and, of course, McNeill/Battles adds its own subsection headings, largely following Otto Weber, another point on which *OS* is guiltless.

6. There are actually sixty-eight references noted in the McNeill/Battles index, but the reference to a citation of Job 14:26 in *Institutes* (1559/Battles), III.xiv.19, is a typographical error: the citation is actually from Proverbs 14:26, as rightly indicated at that point in the text. Note that the Barth/Niesel edition includes as bracketed citations in the text of the *Institutes* only those references present in the margins of Calvin's original and offers references to texts only alluded to (and not cited) by Calvin in its apparatus; McNeill/Battles places all biblical references in brackets in the text and all patristic and medieval references (whether found in the original text or not) into the footnotes. This procedure, together with the tendency to add quotations marks and elipses not found in the original, yield a highly questionable product. From a purely textual perspective, the older translations (Norton, Allen, and Beveridge) are preferable.

7. Note that the various editions of the *Institutes* up to the 1550 Latin and the 1551 French cite only chapters of biblical books in the marginal apparatus: in the 1559 Latin and the 1560 French editions, Calvin (or his editorial assistants) added the verse numbers from the Stephanus Bible.

8. See Bruce M. Metzger, *The Text of the New Testament: Its Transmission, Corruption, and Restoration*, 3rd, enlarged ed. (New York: Oxford University Press, 1992), p. 104, on the introduction of versification in 1551 by Stephanus.

9. Cf. the comments on Calvin's manner of citation of Bernard and the fathers in A. N. S. Lane, "Calvin's Use of Bernard of Clairvaux," in *Bernhard von Clairvaux: Rezeption und Wirkung im Mittelalter und in der Neuzeit*, ed. Kaspar Elm (Wiesbaden: Harrassowitz Verlag, 1994), pp. 307–08.

10. Calvin explicitly notes the presence of *loci* in his preface to *Comm. in priorem Epist. ad Corinthios*, in *CO* 49, col. 304 (*CTS Corinthians* I, p. 46).

11. See Melanchthon, *Elementa rhetorices*, col. 452: "Ac voco locos communes, non tantum virtutes et vicia, sed in omni doctrinae genere praecipua capita, quae fontes et summam artis continent": the terms *fontes argumentorum* and *capita doctrinae* reflect the Ciceronian models, rooted in Aristole's identification of the proper subjects of dialectical and rhetorical syllogisms as topics or lines of argument, used by Agricola, *De inventione dialectica*, II.ii, and Melanchthon, *Elementa rhetorices*, in *CR* col. 428, 451–52; cf. Aristotle, *Rhetoric*, I.2 (1358a, 10ff) and II.23– 24 (1397a, 6–1402a, 25); Cicero, *De Inventione*, I.24, 26, 29, 30; and see Joan Lechler, *Renaissance Concepts of the Commonplace* (New York: Pageant, 1962), pp. 147–48, 154ff.

12. Cf., for example, Calvin, *Institutio* (1559), III.xx.1, citing Rom. 8:26 and 10:14, and Calvin, *Comm. in Epist. ad Romanos* (1540), fol. 221, 291–92; cf. *CO* 49, col. 156, 203, where 8:26–27 and 10:14–17 are identified as units: note that the verse numbers, given so prominently in *CO*, are not in Calvin's original—which appeared before Stephanus's versification of the Bible.

13. Cf., for example, Calvin, *Institutio* (1559), III.iv.35, citing Jer. 5:3, and the extended comment on the verse in Calvin, *Praelect. in lib. Ieremiae*, in *CO* 37, col. 608–11 ; also cf. Calvin, *Institutio* (1559), II.vii.2, citing Rom. 10:4 and II Cor. 3:6, and Calvin, *Comm. in Epist. ad Romanos*, in *CO* 49, col. 196, and Calvin, *Comm. in Epist. ad Corinthios*, in *CO* 50, col. 39–41;

and Calvin, *Institutio* (1559), III.xx.35, citing Rom. 9:3 and Calvin, *Comm. in Epist. ad Romanos*, in *CO* 49, col. 170–71.

14. This sense of the "*ad fontes*," albeit modified by the Melanchthonian understanding of Romans as the source not only of the materials for the *loci* but also of the *loci* themselves, surely derives from Erasmus: "Ego studiis meis nihil aliud conatus sum quam ut bonas litteras pane sepultas apud nostrate excitarem: deinde ut mundum plus satis tribuentem Iudaicis ceremoniis ad verae et Evangelicae pietatis studium expergefacerem: postremo ut studia theologiae scholastica, nimium prolapsa ad inanium quaestiumcularum argutias, ad divinae Scripturae fontes revocarem" in *Opus Epistolarum Des. Erasmi Roterodami*, 12 vols. ed. P. S. Allen et al. (Oxford: Clarendon Press, 1906–47), IV, p. 439.

15. Note that considerations of genre must become an integral part of the debate over the perceived disjunction between the *Institutes* and Calvin's exegetical works: cf. Kemper Fullerton, *Prophecy and Authority: A Study in the History of Doctrine and Interpretation of Scripture* (New York: Macmillan, 1919), pp. 133–64, and the counter argument in David L. Puckett, *John Calvin's Exegesis of the Old Testament* (Louisville: Westminster/John Knox, 1995), pp. 43–4 and the conclusions of Elsie Ann McKee, "Exegesis, Theology, and Development," in Calvin's "*Institutio*," in *Probing the Reformed Tradition: Historical Studies in Honor of Edward A. Dowey, Jr.*, ed. Brian G. Armstrong and Elsie A. Mckee (Louisville: Westminster/John Knox, 1989), pp. 155–6, 168.

16. Thus, Lobstein could note a far greater "historical" or contextual interest in the commentaries than in the sermons: see his "Calvin considéré comme prédicateur," *Études sur la pensée et l'oeuvre de Calvin*, ed. Lobstein (Neuilly: Editions de "La Cause," 1927), pp. 31–32; but note Danièle Fischer, "L'Élément historique dans la prédication de Calvin: Un aspect original de l'homilétique du Réformateur," *Revue d'Historie et de Philosophie Religieuses* 64 (1984), pp. 365–86, where a different issue, that of illustrative historical allusion, is taken up.

17. See the discussion in A. Ganoczy and S. Scheld, *Die Hermeneutic Calvins* (Wiesbaden: F. Steiner, 1983), pp. 111, 118; cf. B. Girardin, *Rhétorique et théologie*, m(Paris: Beauchesne, 1979), pp. 228–30.

18. Cf. Quintilian, *Institutio oratoria*, X.1; Melanchthon, *Elementa rhetorices*, in *CR* 13, col. 452, 480–81 and Millet, *Calvin et la dynamique de la parole* (Paris: Librairie Honoré Champion, 1992), pp. 759–62, and Hoffmann's characterization of this procedure in Erasmus in *Rhetoric and Theology* (Toronto: University of Toronto Press, 1994), pp. 51, 75, 145–47. And note Calvin's own use of the term in his *De clementia*, 17.11 (p. 56), 42.4 (p. 114), 43.39 (p. 118); cf. Girardin, *Rhétorique et théologie*, p. 229, on the "correction" of dialectical *brevitas* with rhetorical *perspicuitas*.

19. Cf. the comments in Lobstein, "Calvin considéré comme prédicateur," in *Études*, pp. 39–43.

20. Jean Calvin, *Sermons sur les deux Epistres S. Paul à Timothée, et sur l'Epistre à Tite* (Geneva: 1561), sermon 13 on II Tim. 2:16–18, in *CO* 54, col. 153–54; also note *Sermons of M. John Calvin, on the Epistles of S. Paule to Timothie and Titus*, trans. L. T. (London: G. Bishop and T. Woodcoke, 1579), p. 806, col. 2.

21. Cf. J. Bohatec, *Budé und Calvin* (Graz: Herman Böhlaus, 1950), pp. 121–240, on Calvin's "humanist" opponents, and Richard C. Gamble, "*Brevitas et facilitas*," Westminster Theological Journal 47 (1985), pp. 10–13; François Wendel, *Calvin* trans. Philip Mairet (New York: Harper & Row, 1963), pp. 34–35.

22. Calvin, *Institutio* (1539), fol. 13, see also *Institutio* (1559), I.viii.1: "tanto intervallo superent," literally, "surpass by such a margin." Note that François Wendel, *Calvin et l'humanisme* (Paris: Presses Universitaires de France, 1976), pp. 64–65, follows Bohatec in understanding this passage as a sign of Calvin's rupture with the form of humanism represented by Guillaume Budé, *De transitu hellenismi ad christianismum* (Paris: R. Stephanus, 1535); cf. Bohatec, *Budé und*

Calvin, pp. 121–47. Henri Strohl, *La Pensée de la Réforme* (Neuchâtel: Delachaux et Niestle, 1951), pp. 78–79, sees the context as the more immediate classicism of Johann Sturm's academy in Strasbourg, while Pannier, *Institution* (1541/Pannier), I, p. 310, draws a positive parallel with a passage in Lefèvre's *Quincuplex Psalterium.*

23. Calvin, *Sermons sur les deux Epistres S. Paul à Timothée, et sur l'Epistre à Tite*, sermon 6 on II Tim. 1:13–14, in *CO* 54, col. 70 (*Sermons of M. John Calvin, on the Epistles of S. Paule to Timothie and Titus*, p. 754, col.1).

24. Contra William J. Bouwsma, "Calvinism as *theologia rhetorica*," in *Calvinism as Theologica Rhetorica*, ed. William Wuellner (Berkeley: Center for Hermeneutical Studies, 1986), p. 12; see Melanchthon, *Elementa rhetorices*, in *CR* 13, col. 453; on Melanchthon's emphasis on edification in his use of the rhetorical *genus didascalicum* see O'Malley, "Content and Rhetorical Forms in Sixteenth-Century Treatises on Preaching," in *Renaissance Eloquence*, ed. James J. Murphy (Berkley: University of California Press, 1983), pp. 242–3.

25. Cf. Budé's comments in Calvin, *Praelect. in proph. min.*, in *CO* 42, col. 187–88 (*CTS Minor Prophets* I, pp. xxvi–xxvii). Also note Erwin Mülhaupt, *Die Predigt Calvins: ihre Geschichte, irhe Form, und irhe religiösen Grundgedanken* (Berlin: De Gruyter, 1931), pp. 17–18, on the Reformers' tendency to preach through entire books as an echo of the medieval university: the church becomes the *schola.*

26. Cf. T. H. L. Parker, *Calvin's Preaching* (Louisville: Westminster/John Knox, 1992), pp. 87–89 and Benjamin W. Farley, "Recurring Hermeneutical Principles in Calvin's Sermons, Polemical Treatises, and Correspondence," in *Calvin as Exegete: Papers and Responses Presented at the Ninth Colloquium on Calvin and Calvin Studies*, ed. Peter De Klerk (Grand Rapids, Mich.: Calvin Studies Society, 1995), p. 69.

27. Jean Calvin, *Sermons sur l'Epistre S. Paul apostre aux Galatiens* (Geneva, 1563): in *CO* 50, col. 269–696; 51, col. 1–136. Also note *Sermons upon the Epistle of Saint Paule to the Galatians*, trans. Arthur Golding (London, 1574; reissued Audubon, N.J.: Old Paths Publications, 1995). Calvin also turned to the Epistle to the Galatians in two *congrégations*, delivered in November 1562 (Gal. 2:11–16) and May 1563 (2:15–21). The *congrégations* are based on longer units of text (cf. the sermons on 2:11–14; 14–16; 15–16; 17–19; and 20–21) but are also somewhat shorter than any of Calvin's sermons on these texts. The method, however, is similar: as distinct from the approach in his commentaries, Calvin follows the text of Galatians and amplifies it through the use of theological argumentation and reflection on a wide variety of texts from other places in Scripture. See the text in Jean Calvin, *Deux congrégations et exposition du catéchisme*, première réimpression de l'édition de 1563 avec une introduction par Rodolphe Peter (Paris: Presses Universitaires de France, 1964).

28. Calvin, *Comm. in quatuor Pauli Epist.* [3:10–11], in *CO* 50, col. 208–09 (*CTS* I, pp. 88–9): Note that, in the commentary, Calvin identifies not Paul's citation from Deut. 27:26 but only Paul's syllogistic use of the point, whereas in the sermon, the syllogism is not directly noted, but the citation from Deuteronomy is identified and elaborated at some length from the Old Testament.

29. Cf. Calvin, *Sermons sur . . . Galatiens*, *CO* 50, cols. 287–302, and Calvin, *Comm. in epist ad Galatas*, in *CO* 50, cols. 170–71.

30. Calvin to Somerset, 22 October 1548, in *CO* 13, cols. 70–71 (*Selected Works . . . Letters*, II, p. 190).

31. Calvin, *Sermons sur le livre de Moyse, nommé Deutéronome*, sermon 49, in *CO* 26, col. 473–74 (*Sermons on Deut.*, p. 292, col. 1): see Richard Stauffer, "L'homilétique de Calvin," in *Communion et communication* (Geneva: Labor et Fides, 1978), pp. 59–60, taking exception to the comments in Paul Henry, *The Life and Times of John Calvin, the Great Reformer*, 2 vols., trans. Henry Stebbing (New York: Robert Carter, 1851), I, pp. 433–35. Henry assumed that the demand for extemporaneity also indicated, as he states with specific reference to Calvin's sermons

on Job, that Calvin preached "without preparation." Clearly, however, Calvin was objecting not to mental and spiritual preparation for preaching but to the preaching of formally prepared and set sermons by an undereducated clergy.

32. Cf. Calvin, *Sermons sur . . . Galatiens, CO* 50, cols. 469–82, and Calvin, *Comm. in epist ad Galatas,* in *CO* 50, cols. 203–04.

33. I must differ here with Stauffer, "L'homilétique de Calvin," p. 61, who extends Calvin's emphasis on *brevitas* to the sermons, albeit only on the textual evidence of Calvin's comments concerning his commentaries and Mülhaupt's comparison of the length of Calvin's sermons with those of Farel and Viret: cf. Mülhaupt, *Die Predigt Calvins,* p. 16. Comparison with the few surviving sermons of Pierre Viret—e.g., *Quatre sermons français sur Esaïe 65, mars 1559,* ed. Henri Meylan (Lausanne: G. Bridel, 1961)—is inconclusive. The 7000–8000-word length of Viret's sermons parallels the word length of Calvin's longest, ca. 7000 words, in the Isaiah sermons. Differences in length, particularly the comparative brevity of earlier sermon transcripts, are best attributed to the varying skill of the stenographers. See Francis M. Higman, "Introduction" in Jean Calvin, *Sermons sur le Livre d'Esaïe Chapitres 30–41* (Neukirchen-Vluyn: Nerkirchner Verlag, 1995), pp. vi–viii, xxiii. In any case, Calvin did not claim that *brevitas* ought to be characteristic of all written forms.

34. Cf. Calvin, *Institutio* (1559), III.ii.1–43, noting the polemic against implicit faith in sections 1–6 and the full definition in section 7.

35. Cf. Calvin, *Sermons sur . . . Galatiens, CO* 50, cols. 633–44 (citation from col. 636) and Calvin, *Comm. in epist. ad Galatas,* in *CO* 50, cols. 236–40.

36. A similar comparison is made between Calvin's commentary and his sermon on 2 Timothy 3:16 in Brian G. Armstrong, "Exegetical and Theological Principles in Calvin's Preaching," in *Ordentich und Fruchtbar,* ed. Wilhelm H. Neuser and Herman Selderhuis Eleiden: J. J. Groen et Zoon, 1997), p. 197.

37. T. H. L. Parker, *Calvin's Old Testament Commentaries,* (Edinburgh: T. & T. Clarle, 1986), p. 14; and cf. T. H. L. Parker, *Calvin's Preaching* (Edinburgh: T. & T. Clark/ (Louisville: Westminster/John Knox, 1992), pp. 57–60.

38. John Calvin, *Exposition sur l'Épître de Sainct Iudas apostre de nostre Seigneur Iésus Christ* (Geneva: Jean Girard, 1542); Parker, *Calvin's Preaching,* pp. 61–62.

39. E.g., Calvin, *Institutes,* II.vii.8, largely from 1539, and also entirely based on Rom. 3:19 and 11:32; thus, too, the additions to *Institutes,* II.vii.18, viz., a sentence on the unwillingness of the unregenerate to obey the law and another on the same problem among the "children of God" before they have been called, neither of which cites a text but both of which look to the substance of Rom. 1. In *Institutes,* II.vii.18, Calvin also adds a reference to I Tim. 1:9–10, on which he had not yet commented.

40. Cf. Benoit, "History and Development," pp. 110–12.

41. John Calvin, *Defensio sanae et orthodoxae doctrinae de servitute et liberatione humani arbitrii adversus calumnias Alberti Pighii Campensis* (Geneva, 1543), in *CO* 6, col. 225–404; in translation: John Calvin, *The Bondage and Liberation of the Will: A Defense of the Orthodox Doctrine of Human Choice against Pighius,* ed. A. N. S. Lane, trans. G. I. Davis, *Texts and Studies in Reformation and Post-Reformation Thought,* vol. 2 (Grand Rapids: Baker Book House, 1996).

42. John Calvin, *Exposition sur les deux Epistres de S. Pierre et l'Epistre de S. Iude* (Geneva, 1545).

43. John Calvin, *Commentarii in priorem Epistolam Pauli ad Corinthios* (Strasbourg, 1546); Calvin, *Commentarii in secundum Pauli Epistolam ad Corinthios* (Geneva, 1548); and note the publication of the French version of the commentaries on both I and II Corinthians, Geneva, 1547: the French of II Corinthians appeared before the Latin.

44. John Calvin, *Commentarii in epistolam ad Titum* (Geneva, 1550); Calvin, *Commentaire de M. Iean Calvin sur l'Epistre de Saint Jacques* (Geneva, 1550); cf. Wulfert De Greef, *The Writings*

of John Calvin: An Introductory Guide, trans. Lyle D. Bierma (Grand Rapids, Mich: Baker Book House, 1993), pp. 98–9.

45. Parker, *Calvin's Preaching,* p. 62.

46. John Calvin, *Deux sermons faitz en la ville de Genève* (Geneva, 1546), comprising sermons on Psalms 115 and 124; and Calvin, *Quatre sermons traictans des matières fort utiles pour nostre temps . . . avec briefve exposition du Psaume LXXXVII* (Geneva, 1552), comprising sermons on Psalm 6:4, Hebrews 13:13, and Psalm 27:4, probably from 1549, and the somewhat later exposition of Psalm 87.

47. See Parker, *Calvin's Preaching,* pp. 60–64, 179; De Greef, *Writings of John Calvin,* pp. 110–12. Raguenier recorded ninety-one sermons on Jeremiah 29–51, and there is a manuscript of twenty-five sermons on Jeremiah 15–18.

48. On the chronology of Calvin's preaching see Parker, Calvin's Preaching, pp. 150–57, 163–71; also note Parker's earlier work, *The Oracles of God: An Introduction to the Preaching of John Calvin* (London: Lutterworth, 1962), pp. 27–44, 160–62; and Mülhaupt, *Die Predigt Calvins,* pp. 1–24.

49. On this latter point see P.-D. Nicole and C. Rapin, "De l'exégèse à l'homilétique, evolution entre le Commentaire de 1551, les sermons de 1558 et le commentaire de 1559 sur le prophète Esaïe," in *Calvinus Ecclesiae Genevensis Custos,* ed. Wilhelm H. Neuser (Frankfurt am Main: Peter Lang, 1984), pp. 159–62.

50. Calvin to Farel, July 1550 and Calvin to Farel, 19 August 1550, in *Letters* II, pp. 277–78, 278–79.

51. *Congrégation faite en l'eglise de Genève par M. Iean Calvin; en laquelle la matiere de l'election eternelle de Dieu fut sommairement et clairement par luy deduite et ratifiée d'un commun accord par ses freres ministres* (Geneva: Vincent Bres, 1562), in *CO* 8, col. 91–138 (Note that the *Congrégation* was delivered orally on December 18, 1551). The *Congrégation* is translated in *Calvinism by Calvin; being the Substance of Discourses delivered by Calvin and the other Ministers of Geneva on the Doctrines of Grace,* trans. and intro. by R. Govett (London: James Nisbet, 1840).

52. John Calvin, *De aeterna Dei praedestnatione* (Geneva, 1552), in *CO* 8, col. 249–366, trans. as *Concerning the Eternal Predestination of God,* trans. and intro. by J. K. S. Reid (London: James Clarke, 1961), p. 50, and Calvin, *Calvin's Calvinism: Treatises on the Eternal Predestination of God and the Secret Providence of God,* trans. Henry Cole (London, 1856; repr. Grand Rapids, Mich.: Reformed Free Publishing Association, n.d.), pp. 13–186, 223–56.

53. John Calvin, *Brevis responsio Io. Calvini ad diluenda nebulonis cuiusdam calumnias* (Geneva, 1557), in *CO* 9, col. 257–66, trans. as *A Brief Reply in Refutation of the Calumnies of a Certain Worthless Person,* in Calvin, *Calvin's Calvinism,* pp. 187–206; John Calvin, *Calumniae nebulonis cuiusdam, quibus odio et invidia gravare conatus est doctrinam Ioh. Calvini de occulta Dei providentia. Ioannis Calvini ad easdem responsio* (Geneva, 1558), in *CO* 9, cols. 269–318, trans. as *On the Secret Providence of God,* in Calvin, *Calvin's Calvinism,* pp. 257–350; and *Response à certaines calomnies et blasphèmes, dont quelsques mains s'efforcent de rendre de la doctrine de la prédestination de Dieu odieuse,* appended to the *Traité de la prédestination* (Geneva, 1560): *CO* 58, col. 198–206.

54. For example, the commentaries on Gen. 3:1 and 6; Deut. 10:12–13; 29:29; Romans 3:21; I Cor. 1:1; 3:9; 5:5; 10:11; Eph. 6:2; I Tim. 2:6; 3:8; 4:14; I Peter 1:20.

55. On the movement from the Deuteronomy sermons to the *Harmony on the Last Four Books of Moses* see Wulfert De Greef, "Das Verhältnis von Predigt und Kommentar bei Calvin, dargestellt an den Deuteronomium Kommentar und den Predigten," in *Calvinus Servus Christi,* ed. Wilhelm H. Neuser (Budapest: Presseabteilung des Ráday-Kollegiums, 1988), pp. 195–204; on the increased precision of Calvin's reading of the Hebrew of Genesis brought about by the movement from sermons to commentary, see Max Engammare, "Calvin connaissait-il la Bible?

Les citations de l'Écriture dans ses sermons sur la Genèse," *Bulletin de la Societé d'Histoire du Protestantisme Français* 141 (1995), pp. 163–83.

56. Nicole and Rapin, "De l'exégèse à l'homilétique," pp. 159–62.

57. The remainder of Calvin's exegetical work, the commentaries or lectures on Daniel (1561), Jeremiah (1563), Lamentations (1563), the *Harmony of the Last Four Books of Moses* (1563), Joshua (1564), and Ezekiel [chapters 1–19] (1565), appeared after the final edition of the *Institutes*.

58. Discussion of biblical themes a. d issues that do not appear as *loci* in the *Institutes* follows later in this chapter.

59. Calvin, *Institutio* (1559), III.xx.1. (The NcNeill/Battles edition cites here two other verses from Romans 8 [15 and 16], which were undoubtedly in Calvin's mind at this point but which do not appear in the original marginal apparatus of the 1559 *Institutes*.)

60. Calvin, *Institutio* (1559), III.xx.28.

61. Calvin, *Institutio* (1559), III.xx.9; Calvin also cites the text of Matt. 9:2, "Your sins are forgiven you," but does not identify the citation marginally.

62. Cf. Calvin, *Comm. in Epist. Canonicas*, in *CO* 55, col. 306–07 (*CTS Catholic Epistles*, pp. 167–68).

63. Calvin, *Institutio* (1559), III.xx.11; cf. Calvin, *Comm. in Epist. Canonicas*, in *CO* 55, col. 430–32 (*CTS Catholic Epistles*, pp. 355–57).

64. Calvin, *Institutio* (1559), III.xx.11, *ad fin*, citing Rom. 10:14, 17. But note that Calvin did edit and augment the Romans Commentary in 1551 and 1556.

65. See notes 39, 49, 50, 51.

66. Calvin, *Institutio* (1559), III.xxi.4, *ad fin*.

67. For example, Calvin, *Institutio* (1559), I.xvi.1, elaborating on the reference to Acts 17: 28 only passingly noted in Calvin, *Institutio* (1550), VI.51; also, *Institutio* (1559), I.xvi.4, adding substantive comment on (but without explicit citation of) Gen. 22:8; cf. Calvin, *Institutio* (1550), XIV.38.

68. Calvin, *Institutio* (1559), III.xxii.6, cf. the use of Acts 2:23 and I Pet. 1: 2, 19–20.

69. Cf. Calvin, *Institutio* (1559), III.xxii.7, and the comments on John 6:37, 39, 44–45, 70; 10:28–29; 13:18; 17:6, 9, 11–12: Calvin, *In Evang. Ioh. Commentarius*, in *CO* 47, col. 145–46, 149–50, 163, 249–50, 310–12, 378–83 (*CTS John* I, pp. 251–54, 256–59, 280, 415–16; II, pp. 63–65, 170–77).

70. Cf. Calvin, *Institutio* (1559), III.xxii.10, and the comments on Isaiah 43:22; 49:1; 54: 13; 56:3; 65:2: Calvin, *Comm. in Isaiam*, in *CO* 37, col. 97–98, 190–91, 275–77, 295–96, 417–18 (*CTS Isaiah*, pp. 402, 435; II, pp. 123, 232; III, pp. 345–6; IV, pp. 8, 146–47, 179, 378–80).

71. Calvin, *Institutio* (1559), III.xxi.5, citing Deut. 32:8–9; 4:37; 7:7–8; 10:14–15; 23:5; Psalm 47:7; Deut. 9:6; Psalm 100:3; 95:7; 105:6; 44:3; 33:12; 1 Sam. 12:22; Psalm 65:4; Is. 14:1; 41:9, respectively.

72. Calvin, *Institutio* (1559), III.xxi.6, citing Psalm 78:67–68; 147:20; Mal. 1:2–3. NcNeill adds a reference to Rom. 9:13 to the citation from Malachi, but this is not in Calvin's original.

73. Cf. Susan E. Schreiner, *Where Shall Wisdom Be Found* (Chicago: University of Chicago Press, 1994), pp. 91–93.

74. Note that Calvin's response to Bolsec, the *Congrégation . . . de l'élection éternelle de Dieu* of 1551, attacks the "papist" and "Sorbonnist" theologians who not only pervert the doctrine of election but fail to acknowledge the congruity of election with the justice of God (*CO* 8, col. 102, 107–08, 110–11, 115). What is more, Calvin concludes his argument with the example of Job (*CO* 8, col. 116). These themes are developed at length with particular reference to the "Sorbonnists" in the Job sermons of 1554.

75. Cf., for example, Calvin, *Institutes*, I.xiv.17, 19 (allusions from 1543); I. xvii.8 (citation

from 1539); II.iv.2 (general reference from 1539); III.xii.1 (two citations and several allusions from 1539); III.xii.5; xiv.16; xvii.9; xx.28 (single citations from 1539).

76. Calvin, *Institutes*, I.xvii.2, citing Job 26:14; 28:21, 28.

77. Calvin, *Institutes*, I.xvlii.1, 3: no verses are actually noted in either place, but allusions are to Job 1:6 and 21.

78. Calvin, *Institutes*, III.xiv.15. This theme of *duplex iustitia* also resounds throughout the Job sermons.: see Susan E. Schreiner, "Exegesis and Double Justice in Calvin's Sermons on Job," *Church History* 58 (1989), pp. 322–338.

79. Calvin, *Institutio* (1559), I.xiii.8, 22 (against Servetus); I.xiii.23 (against Gentile); II.xii.4–7 (against Osiander); added materials in II.xiv.5–8 (against Servetus). Textual and topical relationships between these explicit attacks on Servetus and Gentile as well as the other trinitarian additions to the 1559 *Institutes* (e.g., I.xiii.6, 10, 20, 24–29 and editorial additions to I.xiii.1, 2, 3, 5, 7, 9, 11, 14, 16, and 17) and Calvin's polemical treatises against these writers remain to be examined.

80. Cf. John Frederick Jansen, *Calvin's Doctrine of the Work of Christ* (London, 1956), pp. 101–03.

81. Calvin, *Institutes*, I.x.2, commenting on Exodus 34:6–7; ibid., I.xiii.23; and cf. the discussion of divine attributes in ibid., I.x.2.

82. Calvin, *Mosis libri in formam harmoniae*, in *CO* 24, col. 43–44 (*CTS Harm. Moses* I, pp. 73–74).

83. Calvin, *In Lib. Psalmorum Comm.*, in *CO* 31, col. 88 (*CTS Psalms* I, p. 94).

84. Ibid., in *CO* 31, col. 788 (*CTS Psalms* III, p. 350).

85. Ibid., in *CO* 31, col. 833–34; *CO* 32, col. 71–72 (*CTS Psalms* III, p. 462; IV, p. 121).

86. Ibid., in *CO* 32, col. 715 (*CTS Psalms* III, p. 213)

87. Calvin, *Institutes*, I.xiv.2.

88. Calvin, *In primum Mosis Comm.*, in *CO* 23, col. 14–51 (*CTS Genesis* I, pp. 69–137).

89. Cf. Anthony Hoekema, "Calvin's Doctrine of the Covenant of Grace," *Reformed Review* 15 (1962), pp. 1–12; Hoekema, "The Covenant of Grace in Calvin's Teaching," *Calvin Theological Journal* 2 (1967), pp. 133–61; and Lyle D. Bierma, "Federal Theology in the Sixteenth Century: Two Traditions?" *Westminster Theological Journal* 45 (1983), pp. 304–21; on the preface to Olivetan's New Testament, see chapter 2. Neither these texts nor Calvin's method has been considered by J. Wayne Baker, *Heinrich Bullinger and the Covenant: The Other Reformed Tradition* (Athens: Ohio University Press, 1980), pp. 193–98, 258–60; Baker, "Heinrich Bullinger, the Covenant, and the Reformed Tradition in Retrospect" in *Calvin Studies VIII: The Westminster Confession in Current Thought*, ed. John H. Leith (Davidson, N.C.: Colloquium on Calvin Studies, 1996), pp. 72–73. It is ironic that Baker cites Bullinger's commentaries and sermons from the time of the *Second Helvetic Confession* (ibid., pp. 67–68) to prove, despite the language and focus confession itself, that the confession fits into a context of covenant theology and then, at the same time, refuses to examine Calvin's commentaries and sermons and bases his assertion that Calvin held no concept of a conditional or two-sided covenant solely on the *Institutes*.

90. Similarly, despite the obvious importance of a doctrine of covenant to his theology, Bullinger did not take the step of including a specific *locus* on covenant in his synopses of the basic topics of Christian theology—the *Compendium*, the *Decades*, or the *Second Helvetic Confession*. Cf. Baker, "Heinrich Bullinger, the Covenant, and the Reformed Tradition in Retrospect," pp. 62–65, 67, where this lacuna is acknowledged but not duly factored into the argument. Bullinger did include covenant as a topic, however, in his early *loci communes sacri*, published as the second part of his *Ratio studiorum* (1527) but not in his unpublished *Institutionum* of 1531: see Edward A. Dowey, "Heinrich Bullinger as Theologian: Thematic, Comprehensive, Schematic,

in *Calvin Studies V*, ed. John H. Leith (Davidson, N.C.: Colloquium on Calvin Studies, 1990), pp. 50–52.

91. Cf. Calvin, *Institutio* (1559), II.x.11, in the original of which there are *no* texts explicitly cited, but rather a multitude of unidentified allusions to Genesis 12–22, and Calvin, *In primum Mosis Comm.*, cap. 12–22, in *CO* 23, cols. 176, 180, 183, 194, 211–16, 235, 237–40, 276, 312 (*CTS Genesis* I, pp. 346, 353, 358, 376, 404–12, 445, 449–52, 510, 561–62).

92. Calvin, *In primum Mosis Comm.*, 17:1–23, in *CO* 23, col. 232–48 (*CTS Genesis* I, pp. 441–65); Calvin, *Sermons sur le V. livre de Moyse*, in *CO* 25, col. 694; 28, col. 288–93, 308–09; trans. as *Sermons of M. Iohn Calvin upon the Fifth Book of Moses called Deuteronomie* trans. Arthur Golding (London, 1583; repr. Edinburgh: Banner of Truth, 1987), col. 46a, 913b–915b, 923–24; Calvin, *In Lib. Psalmorum Comm.*, 78:34ff.; 132:12, in *CO* 31, col. 734; 32, col. 348–49 (*CTS Psalms* III, pp. 253–54; V, pp. 154–56); and cf. Hoekema, "The Covenant of Grace in Calvin's Teaching," pp. 133–61.

93. Contra J. T. McNeill in *Institutes* (1559/Battles), II.x, note 1, this is not the place where "Calvin unfolds the doctrine of covenant." McNeill and Baker (*Heinrich Bullinger and the Covenant*, pp. 194–97) both assume, contrary to Calvin's chapter titles, that *Institutio* (1559), II.x–xi, is a discusion of covenant and/or the primary *locus* of Calvin's doctrine of the covenant.

94. Calvin, *In primum Mosis Comm.*, 17:7–8 in *CO* 23, col. 237–39 (*CTS Genesis* I, pp. 447–51).

95. Cf. Calvin, *Institutes*, II.vii, ix–xi (II.vii.12 on the third use specifically) and Calvin, *Harmony of the Four Last Books of Moses*, in *CO* 24, col. 725–28; *CO* 25, col. 5–58 (*CTS Pentateuch* I, pp. 196–289 passim on the use, sanctions, and promises of the law). Calvin here broke with his own rule and present a short *locus* on the "use of the law" in his commentary (*CO* 24, cols. 725–28, but he also cross-referenced it to the collateral discussion in *Institutes*, II.vii.

96. Leonard Trinterud, "The Origins of Puritanism," *Church History* 20 (1951), pp. 37–57; cf. Baker, *Heinrich Bullinger and the Covenant*, pp. 193–98; Baker, "Heinrich Bullinger . . . in Retrospect," pp. 72–73.

97. Contra Philip C. Holtrop, *The Bolsec Controversy on Predestination, from 1551 to 1555*, Vol. I, parts 1–2 (Lewiston: Edwin Mellen, 1993), p. 847.

98. Charles Partee, *Calvin and Classical Philosophy* (Leiden: E. J. Brill, 1977).

99. Edward A. Dowey, *The Knowledge of God in Calvin's Theology* (New York: Columbia University Press, 1952; 3rd expanded ed. Grand Rapids, Mich.: Eerdmans, 1994), pp. 215–16.

100. Calvin, *In Ezech. praelectiones*, in *CO* 40, col. 47 (*CTS Ezekiel* I, p. 87).

101. Cf. Calvin, *Institutio* (1559), I.xiv.21; xvi.1, 4; xvii.2.

102. Note his denial of the concept of "permission" in *Institutio* (1539), fol. 253; cf. *Institutio* (1559), III.xxiii.8 [from 1539]; also note I.xviii.1–3 [largely from 1559]; the similar denial in *Brevis responsio Io. Calvini ad diluenda nebulonis cuiusdam calumnias* (1557), in *CO* 9, col. 260; and his grudging acceptance of its Augustinian form in *Calumniae nebulonis cuiusdam . . . Calvini de occulta Dei providentia* (1558), in *CO* 9, cols. 291, 295–300.

103. Calvin, *In Ezech. praelectiones*, in *CO* 40, col. 48–49 (*CTS Ezekiel* I, p. 89).

104. Irena Backus, " 'Aristotelianism' in Some of Calvin's and Beza's Expository and Exegetical Writings on the Doctrine of the Trinity, with Particular Reference to the Terms *ousia* and *hypostasis*," in *Histoire de l'exégèse au XVIe siècle*, ed. Olivier Fatio and Pierre Fraenkel (Geneva: Droz, 1978), pp. 251–60.

105. Note the similar conclusion with regard to still other issues reached by Douglas Kelly, "Varied Themes in Calvin's 2 Samuel Sermons and the Development of His Thought," in *Calvinus Sincerioris Religionis Vindex*, ed. Wilhelm H. Neuser and Brian G. Armstrong (Kirkville, Mo.: Sixteenth-Century Journal Publishers, 1997 pp. 209–24.

CHAPTER NINE

An earlier form of this essay appeared in *Calvin Theological Journal* 25/2 (November 1990), pp. 207–224.

1. Cf. e.g., P.-E. Massot, *La Notion de la foi d'après l'Institution chrétienne de Calvin* (Montauban: J. Vidallet, 1871), pp. 11–13; Benjamin Blondiaux, *De la notion de la foi d'après l'Institution chrétienne de Calvin* (Montauban: J. Vidallet, 1874), pp. 11–14; Simon Pieter Dee, *Het Geloofsbegrip van Calvijn* (Kampen: J. H. Kok, 1918), pp. 30–36; Peter Brunner, *Vom Glauben bei Calvin* (Tübingen: J. C. B. Mohr, 1925), pp. 116–22; Walter E. Stuermann, *A Critical Study of Calvin's Concept of Faith* (Ann Arbor, Mich.: Edwards Brothers, 1952), pp. 62–65; also see P. Lobstein, "La Connaissance réligieuse d'après Calvin," *Revue de théologie et de philosophie* 42 (1909): 53–110, and reissued in the author's *Études sur la pensée et l'oeuvre de Calvin* (Neuilly: Éditions de "La Cause," 1927), pp. 113–53; Paul Wernle, *Der evangelische Glaube nach den Hauptschriften der Reformatoren*, Band III, *Calvin* (Tübingen: J. C. B. Mohr, 1919), pp. 217–20; Emil Doumergue, *Jean Calvin, les hommes et les choses de son temps*, 7 vols. (Lausanne: G. Bridel, 1899–1917), iv, 239–62; Edward A. Dowey, *The Knowledge of God in Calvin's Theology* (New York, 1952; 3rd ed. Grand Rapids, Mich.: Eerdmans, 1994), pp. 153–72; John Newton Thomas, "The Place of Natural Theology in the Thought of John Calvin," in *Journal of Religious Thought* 15 (1958), pp. 107–09; François Wendel, *Calvin: The Origins and Development of His Religious Thought*, trans. Philip Mairet (New York: Harper & Row, 1963), p. 241.

2. *Catechisme* (1541), in *Ioannis Calvini opera quae supersunt omnia*, 59 vols., ed. G. Baum, E. Cunitz, and E. Reuss (Brunswick: Schwetschke, 1863–1900), vi, col. 43: "une certaine et ferme cognoissance."

3. Calvin, *Institutio* (1539), fol. 99: "divinae erga nos benevolentiae firman certamque cognitionem"; *Institution* (1541/Lefranc), p. 191: "une ferme et certaine congnoyssance de la bonne volunté de Dieu envers nous"; cf. *Institutio* (1559), III.ii.7.

4. Calvin, *Institutio* (1536), II, fol. 103.

5. Ibid., II, fol. 103: "Hoc vero est, non modo verum reputare id omne, quod de Deo ac Christ vel scriptum est, vel dicitur: sed spem omnem ac fiduciam in uno Deo ac Christo reponere."

6. Calvin, *Catechismus, sive christianae religionis institutio* (1538), cap. 14 (pp. 17–18): "fides autem Christiana, non nuda aut Dei cognitio . . . quae in cerebro volutata cor minime afficiat. . . . Sed firma est ac solida cordia fiducia, qua in Dei misericordia, per Evangelium nobis promissa, secure acquiescimus."

7. Heribert Schützeichel, *Die Glaubenstheologie Calvins* (Munich: Max Hueber, 1972), pp. 133–44; and Susan E. Schreiner, "The Spiritual Man Judges All Things: Calvin and the Exegetical Debates About Certainty in the Reformation," in *Biblical Interpretation in the Era of the Reformation*, ed. Richard A. Muller and John L. Thompson (Grand Rapids, Mich.: Erdmans, 1996), pp. 208–14.

8. Victor A. Shepherd, *The Nature and Function of Faith in the Theology of John Calvin* (Macon, Ga.: Mercer University Press, 1983), pp. 16–20.

9. Werner Krusche, *Das Wirken des Hl. Geistes nach Calvin* (Göttingen: Vandenhoeck & Ruprecht, 1957), p. 51.

10. R. T. Kendall, *Calvin and English Calvinism to 1649* (New York: Oxford University Press, 1978), pp. 19, 29, 34. For a shortened form of Kendall's thesis, see his essay "The Puritan Modification of Calvin's Theology," in *John Calvin: His Influence in the Western World*, ed. W. Stanford Reid (Grand Rapids, Mich.: Zondervan, 1982), pp. 197–214. Kendall's book has been heavily critiqued by W. Stanford Reid, (*Westminster Theological Journal* 43 (1980), pp. 155–64, by Paul Helm, *Calvin and the Calvinists* (Carlisle, Pa.: Banner of Truth, 1982), and by George W. Harper, ("Calvin and English Calvinism to 1649: A Review Article," *Calvin Theological Journal*, 20/2 (1985), pp. 255–62).

11. Kendall, *Calvin and English Calvinism*, p. 19.

12. Ibid., p. 19.

13. Calvin, *Institutio* (1559), III.ii.14.

14. Ibid., III.i.4.

15. Blondiaux, *De la notion de la foi*, pp. 14–15; Massot, *La notion de la foi*, pp. 14–16.

16. Doumergue, *Jean Calvin*, IV, pp. 250–51.

17. Lobstein, "La Connaissance," in *Études*, pp. 114, 117, 123, 139; cf., also, Charles Partee, "Calvin and Experience," *Scottish Journal of Theology* 26 (1973), pp. 169–81, and Willem Balke, "The Word of God and Experientia according to Calvin," in *Calvinus Ecclesiae Doctor*, ed. W. H. Neuser (Kampen: J. H. Kok, 1980), pp. 19–31, for careful discussions of the experiential dimension of faith in Calvin's theology that preserves Calvin's own distinction between the "knowledge of faith" (*scientia fidei*) and the "knowledge of experience" (*scientia experimentalis*) in general.

18. Dee, *Geloofsbegrip*, pp. 8–9, 36–7, 40–2.

19. Ibid., pp. 54–57.

20. John H. Leith, *John Calvin's Doctrine of the Christian Life*, foreword by Albert C. Outler (Louisville: Westminster/John Knox Press, 1989), pp. 91–92 (cited here inasmuch as this fine study is the publication of Professor Leith's doctoral dissertation of 1949 and stands in dialogue with the "older" scholarship).

21. Arvin Vos, *Aquinas, Calvin, and Contemporary Protestant Thought: A Critique of Protestant Views of the Thought of Thomas Aquinas* (Grand Rapids, Mich.: Eerdmans, 1985), p. 35. Vos, however, does not study Calvin's view of the interrelationship of intellect and will in faith, nor does he address the problem through the eyes of the historical discussion of and debate over Calvin's view of faith: his work is, intentionally and with good reason, a contemporary demand for a balanced Protestant appreciation of Aquinas by way of a comparison between Aquinas' thought and Calvin's.

22. Brian G. Armstrong, "*Duplex cognitio Dei*, Or? The Problem and Relation of Structure, Form, and Purpose in Calvin's Theology," in *Probing the Reformed Tradition: Historical Essays in Honor of Edward A. Dowey, Jr.*, ed. Elsie Anne McKee and Brian G. Armstrong (Louisville: Westminster/John Knox, 1989), p. 139; and note the related perspective in Armstrong, "The Nature and Structure of Calvin's Theology: Another Look," in *John Calvin's Institutes: His Opus Magnum*, ed. B. van der Walt (Potchefstrom: Institute for Reformational Studies, 1986), pp. 55–81.

23. Schreiner, "The Spiritual Man Judges All Things," pp. 207–08.

24. Cf. the groundbreaking discussion of development in Calvin's doctrine of faith in Barbara Pitkin, "What Pure Eyes Could See: Faith, Creation, and History in John Calvin's Theology," Ph.D. dissertation, University of Chicago, 1994, pp. 13–15.

25. Dee, *Geloofsbegrip*, pp. 14–20.

26. Cf. Etienne Gilson, *The Christian Philosophy of St. Thomas Aquinas*, trans. L. K. Shook (New York: Random House, 1956), pp. 242–44, and Frederick C. Copleston, *Aquinas* (Baltimore: Penguin, 1955), pp. 184–85.

27. Karl Reuter, *Das Grundverständnis der Theologie Calvins* (Neukirchen: Neukirchner Verlag, 1963); Thomas F. Torrance, "Knowledge of God and Speech about Him According to John Calvin," in *Theology in Reconstruction* (London: Oxford University Press, 1965). But note the pointed critique of Reuter's approach in Alexandre Ganoczy, *The Young Calvin*, trans. David Foxgrover and Wade Provo (Philadelphia: Westminster, 1987), pp. 173–78: Calvin appears to have arrived rather late at his Scotistic opinions rather than having learned them from John Major when a student in Paris, as Reuter and Torrance suppose. Note that Dee recognized the Franciscan parallel as well: Dee, *Geloofsbegrip*, pp. 54–57.

28. See Vernon Bourke, *Will in Western Thought: A Historical-Critical Survey* (New York: Sheed & Ward, 1964); Hannah Arendt, *The Life of the Mind*, 2 vols. (New York: Harcourt,

Brace, Jovanovich, 1978), pp. 85–146; Wilhelm Kahl, *Die Lehre vom Primat des Willens bei Augustinus, Duns Scotus und Descartes* (Strassbourg: Trübner, 1886); and Bernardine M. Bonansea, "Duns Scotus Voluntarism," in *John Duns Scotus, 1265–1965,* ed. Ryan and Bonansea (Washington: CUA Press, 1965), pp. 83–121.

29. Gilson, *The Christian Philosophy of St. Thomas Aquinas,* p. 244; cf. "Cognitio," in Roy J. Deferrari et al., *A Lexicon of St. Thomas Aquinas* (Washington: CUA Press, 1949), pp. 164–68, noting in particular the contrast (p. 166) between *cognitio intellectiva seu intellectualis* and *cognitio sensitiva seu sensibilis;* and note *cognitio affectiva.*

30. See Thomas Aquinas, *Summa theologiae* (Madrid: Biblioteca Auctores Cristianos, 1951), IIa IIae, q.2, art.2; q.4, art.2; cf. the discussion in Vos, *Aquinas and Calvin,* pp. 16–17, 35.

31. On the relation and cooperation of intellect and will and on the formal primacy of will despite its use of intellective knowledge (*cognitio intellectiva*), see Bernardino Bonansea, *Man and His Approach to God in John Duns Scotus* (Lanham, Md.: University Press of America, 1983), pp. 66–68; also see the discussion and text of Scotus in *Duns Scotus on the Will and Morality,* selected, and trans., and intro. by Allan B. Wolter (Washington, D.C.: Catholic University of America Press, 1986), pp. 35–38, 145–75; cf. Bonansea, "Duns Scotus' Voluntarism," pp. 98, 100, 114–20; P. Parthenius Minges, *Ioannis Duns Scoti doctrina philosophica et theologica quoad res praecipuas proposita et exposita,* 2 vols. (Quaracchi: College of St. Bonaventure, 1930), I, pp. 270–71, 284–99; and Efrem Bettoni, *Duns Scotus: The Basic Principles of his Philosophy,* trans. Bernardino Bonansea (Washington: CUA Press, 1961), pp. 93–117.

32. Calvin, *Institutio* (1536), II, fol. 103: "non modo Deum & Christum esse credimus: sed etiam in Deum credimus & Christum, vere ipsum pro Deo nostro, ac Christum pro salvatore agnoscentes."

33. Ibid., II, fol. 104.

34. Cf. Philip Melanchthon, *Loci communes theologici* (1521), in *CR* 21, col. 163: "Est itaque fides, non aliud nisi fiducia misericordiae divinae. . . . Ea fiducia benevolentiae, seu misericordiae dei cor primum pacificat. . . . Alioqui quo ad non credimus, nono est in corde sensus misericordiae dei" and Huldrych Zwingli, *De vera et falsa religione commentarius,* in *CR* 90, p. 760. Note the discussion in W. P. Stephens, *The Theology of Huldrych Zwingli* (Oxford: Clarendon Press, 1986), pp. 162–64.

35. Calvin, *Catechismus, sive christianae religionis institutio* (1538), pp. 17–18: "Fides autem Christiana, non nuda aut Dei cognitio, aut scripturae intelligentia putanda est, quae in cerebro voluntata cor minime afficiat: qualis solet esse opinio earum, quae probabili ratione nobis confirmantur. Sed firma est ac solida cordis fiducia, qua in Dei misericordia, per Evangelium nobis promissa, secure acquiescimus."

36. Cf. Philip Melanchthon, *Loci communes theologici* (1535), *CR* 21, col. 422: "Fides significat haud dubie in hac causa apud Paulam fiduciam misericordiae promissae propter Christum. . . . certe omnes articulos fidei complectimur, et historiam de Christo referimus ad illum articulum, qui beneficium Christi commemorat, remissionem peccatorum. Complectitur ergo fiducia illa et notitiam de Christo filio Dei, et voluntatis seu habitum seu actionem, qua vult et accipit promissionem Christi, atque ita acquiescit in Christo." See above, chapter 7, this volume, and cf. T. H. L. Parker, *Commentaries on the Epistle to the Romans, 1532–1542* (Edinburgh: T & T. Clark, 1986), p. 188.

37. Cf. Heinrich Bullinger, *The Decades of Henry Bullinger, Minister of the Church of Zurich,* 4 vols., ed. Thomas Harding (Cambridge: Cambridge University Press, 1849–52), I.iv (I, pp. 81–83, 88).

38. Heinrich Bullinger, *In Pauli ad Romanos Epistolam . . . Commentarius* (Zurich: Froschauer, 1533); also found in Bullinger, *In omnes apostolicas epistolas, divi videlicet Pauli XIIII. et VII. canonicas commentarii* (Zürich: Froschauer, 1537).

39. Bullinger, *In Pauli ad Romanos,* fol. 73r.

40. Ibid., fol. 132r: "cum cordis mentio fit integritas & animi synceritas requiritur, hypocrisis excluditur." Note here also the association of *cor* with *animus*.

41. Calvin, *Institutio* (1539), fol. 99: "Itaque aliunde & mentem illuminari, & cor obfirmari convenit, quo Dei verbum plenum apud no fidem obtineat. Nunc iusta fides definitio mobis constabit, si dicamus, esse Divina erga nos benevolentiae firmam certamque cognitionem: quae gratuitam in Christo, per spiritum sanctam & revelatur mentibus nostris, & cordibus obsignatur"; cf. *Instution* (1541/Lefranc), p. 191: "Parquoy il faut que l'entendement de l'homme suit d'ailleurs illuminé, et le coeur confermé, devant que la parolle de dieu obtienne pleine Foy en nous. Maintenant nous avons une pleine deffinition de la Foy: si nous determinons, que c'est une ferme et certaine congnoyssance de la bonne volunté de Dieu envers nous: laquelle estant fondée sur la promesse gratuite donné en Jesus christ, est revelée à nostre entendement, et scellée en nostre coeur par le Sainte Esprit"; and note *Institutio* (1559), III.ii.7.

42. Calvin, *Comm. in Ep. ad Romanos*, in *CO* 49, col. 89, 202 (*CTS Romans*, pp. 189, 393), commenting on Romans 5:2 and 10:10.

43. Ibid., in *CO* 49, col. 202 (*CTS Romans*, p. 393).

44. Calvin, *Institutio* (1539), II, fol. 22–23 and *Institutio* (1559), I.xv.7; II.ii.2; cf. Calvin's commentaries on I Thess. 5:23: "Quoniam autem duae praecipuae sunt animae facultates, intellectus et voluntas" (*CO* 52, col. 179); Phil. 4:7: "Scriptura animam hominis, quoad facultates, in duas partes solet dividere, mentem et cor: mens intelligentiam significat, cor autem omnes affectus: aut voluntates. Ergo haec duo nomina totam animam comprehendunt. . . ." (*CO* 52, col. 61–62); this basic anthropology appears also in Calvin's Old Testament commentaries, albeit with a profound sensitivity to the differences between the Hebrew usage and the Latin: cf. Psalm 3:2–3, "anima sedem affectuum mihi significat" (*CO* 31, col. 53), just as *mens* can indicate the *sedes rationis*, cf. the commentary on Matt. 22:37 (*CO* 45, col. 611); Psalm 119:34: "Da mihi intellectum ut servem et toto corde custodiam. Totis autem cordis fit mentio . . ." (*CO* 32, col. 229); 139:7: "*Spiritus* non simpliciter pro virtute hic ponitur, ut plerumque in scripturis: sed pro mente et intelligentia" (*CO* 32, col. 379). On Calvin's doctrine of the will, see John H. Leith, "The Doctrine of the Will in the *Institutes of the Christian Religion*," in *Reformatio Perennis: Essays on Calvin and the Reformation in Honor of Ford Lewis Battles*, ed. B. A. Gerrish, in collaboration with Robert Benedetto (Pittsburgh: Pickwick Press, 1981), pp. 49–66.

45. Calvin, *Institutio* (1539), II, fol. 22; Calvin, *Institutio* (1559), II.i.8–9; iii.1; and cf. the commentary on Psalm 119:37, "Et certe scimus labem originalis peccati non tantum residere in aliqua parte hominis, sed possidere totam animam et corpus" (*CO* 32, col. 220).

46. Calvin, *Institutio* (1539), II, fol. 23: "subesse duas humanae animae partes quae quiden praesenti institutio convniant. Intellectum et voluntatem. Sit autem officium intellectus, inter objecta discernere, prout unumquodque probandum, aut improbandum visum fuerit: Voluntas autem eligere & sequi quod bonum intellectus dictaverit: aspernari ac fugere, quod ille improbarit. . . . Satis sit nobis, intellectum esse quasi animae ducem et gubernatorem. Voluntatem in illius nutum semper respicere, & iudicium in suis desideriis expectare"; virtually unchanged in Calvin, *Institutio* (1559), I.xv.7. Note also Calvin's indication of a prelapsarian priority of intellect in *Institutio* (1559), I.xv.8.

47. Calvin, *Institutio* (1539), II, fol. 23: "Porro quam sit, ad dirigendam voluntatem, intellectus, gubernatio, mox videbitur."

48. In 1559, Calvin would drastically rearrange this material, removing the initial discussion of original sin to what had become book II and then dividing the discussion of the will into a prelapsarian presentation of the priority of the intellect and a postlapsarian discussion of the problem of the fallen will in relation to intellect and affections or appetites. Note the alteration of the comment in Calvin, *Institutio* (1559), I.xv.7: "Porro quam certa nunc sit ad dirigendam voluntatem intellectus gubernatio, alibi videbitur"—where "mox" becomes "alibi"—accommo-

dating the reference to the dispersion of the subsequent argument to the postlapsarian discussion of human nature in II.ii.12–26.

49. Calvin, *Institutio* (1539), II, fol. 23; Calvin, *Institutio* (1559), I.xv.7, citing *Nichomachean Ethics*, VI.2.

50. Calvin, *Institutio* (1539), II, fol. 23; cf. Calvin, *Institutio* (1559), I.xv.7.

51. Calvin, *Institutio* (1539), II, fol. 23; cf. Calvin, *Institutio* (1559), II.ii.3. Note that the displacement of this portion of the original chapter in the 1559 order renders the point somewhat more difficult to recover.

52. Cf. Aquinas, *Summa theologiae*, Ia, q. 80, art. 2; q. 83, art. 3–4; Aquinas, *On the Soul*, trans. John Patrick Rowan (St. Louis: B. Herder, 1949), art. 8, obj. 11–12, resp. 11–13 (pp. 162–63, 172–73); and see Gilson, *The Christian Philosophy of St. Thomas Aquinas*, pp. 243–44.

53. Johannes Duns Scotus, *Opus Oxoniense*, lib. III, dist. 33, nota 9, in *Opera*, ed. Wadding (Paris: Vives, 1891–95), xv, col. 446b; cf. Minges, *Scoti doctrina*, I, pp. 276–77; and *Duns Scotus on the Will and Morality*, pp. 160–72; cf. Bonansea, *Man and His Approach to God*, pp. 54–56, noting instances of all three terms, including a reference to will as *appetitus intellectivus* in the *Reportata Parisiensia*.

54. Bonansea, "Duns Scotus' Voluntarism," p. 99; Bettoni, *Duns Scotus*, p. 84.

55. Minges, *Scoti doctrina*, I, pp. 277–78.

56. Cf. the discussion in Etienne Gilson, *The Christian Philosophy of St. Augustine*, trans. L. E. M. Lynch (New York: Random House, 1967), pp. 132–34.

57. Calvin, *Institutio* (1539), II, fol. 35; cf. Calvin, *Institutio* (1559), II.ii.26–27; and note the identification of the intellect as governor or *hegemonikon* in Calvin, *Defensio sanae et orthodoxae doctrinae de servitute et liberatione humani arbitrii*, in *CO* 6, col. 285–86 (also John Calvin, *The Bondage and Liberation of the Will: A Defense of the Orthodox Doctrine of Human Choice Against Pighius*, ed. A. N. S. Lane, trans. G. I. Davis (Grand Rapids, Mich.: Baker Book House, 1996), p. 77.

58. Calvin, *Institutio* (1539), II, fol. 24; cf. Calvin, *Institutio* (1559), II.ii.3.

59. Calvin, *Institutio* (1539), II, fol. 23; cf.Calvin, *Institutio* (1559), II.ii.2.

60. Calvin, *Institutio* (1539), II, fol. 38; cf. Calvin, *Institutio* (1559), II.iii.5, and note Calvin, *Institutio* (1539), fol. 35; *Institutio* (1559), II.ii.26. Note that Battles renders *Nihil ergo hoc ad arbitrii libertatem, an homo sensu naturae ad bonum appetendum feratur* as "Therefore whether or not man is impelled to seek after the good by an impulse of nature has no bearing upon the freedom of the will" when the text argues that the natural inclination toward the good cannot be used as an argument for "freedom of choice."

61. Cf. Augustine, *De libero arbitrio*, I.i.1; III.i.2; III.xvi.46; III.xvii.49, and *Retractationes*, I.viii.1–6; *De spiritu et littera*, cap. 52–53, 57–58, 60; and *Contra duas epistolas Pelagianorum*, cap. 4, 5, 7; and Martin Luther, *The Bondage of the Will*, in *Luther's Works*, 56 vols., ed. Jaroslav Pelikan and Helmut Lehmann (St. Louis: Concordia/Philadelphia: Fortress Press, 1955ff), xxxiii, pp. 37–40, 64–67.

62. Cf. Calvin, *Institutio* (1539), II, fol. 35; Calvin, *Institutio* (1559), II.ii.26; Calvin, *Institutio* (1539), II, fol. 38, 40; Calvin, *Institutio* (1559), II.iii.5, 8.

63. For example, Calvin, *Institutio* (1539), II, fol. 23; Calvin, *Institutio* (1559), I.xv.7.

64. Calvin, *Institutio* (1539), II, fol. 34; cf. Calvin, *Institutio* (1559), II.ii.24.

65. Calvin, *Institutio* (1539), II, fol. 31; cf. Calvin, *Institutio* (1559), II.ii.18.

66. Calvin, *Institutio* (1539), II, fol. 38; cf. Calvin, *Institutio* (1559), II.iii.5.

67. Calvin, *Institutio* (1539), II, fol. 39; cf. Calvin, *Institutio* (1559), II.iii.6.

68. Calvin, *De servitute et liberatione humani arbitrii*, in *CO* 6, col. 279–80; also see Calvin, *The Bondage and Liberation of the Will*, pp. 67–69; and cf. A. N. S. Lane, "Did Calvin Believe in Free Will?" *Vox Evangelica* 12 (1981), pp. 79–80.

69. Calvin, *Institutio* (1559), II.ii.6: "Voluntatem dico aboleri, non quatenus est voluntas: quia in hominis conversione integrum manet quod primae est naturae: creari etiam novam dico, non ut voluntas esse incipiat, sed ut vertatur ex mala in bonam": new text in 1559—cf. Calvin, *Institutio* (1539), II, fol. 39. On the essential freedom of the will in the Augustinian tradition and the relation of this concept to grace (and predestination) see Etienne Gilson, *The Spirit of Medieval Philosophy*, trans. A. H. C. Downes (New York: Scribner, 1936), pp. 306–09.

70. Calvin, *Institutio* (1539), II, fol. 105; cf. Calvin, *Institutio* (1559), III.ii.33. One section derives from 1539 and 1559, but the text cited here derives from the 1539 stratum exclusively.

71. Calvin, *Institutio* (1539), II, fol. 105; cf. Calvin, *Institutio* (1559), III.ii.33.

72. Calvin, *Institutio* (1539), II, fol. 105; cf. Calvin, *Institutio* (1559), III.ii.33.

73. Cf. the polemic against "scholastic" conceptions of faith that fail to emphasize certainty in Calvin, *Commentarii ad Romanos*, in *CO* 49, col. (*CTS Romans*, p. 173), commenting on Romans 4:16. Note also the parallels between Calvin's initial polemic against implicit faith in the 1539 stratum of the *Institutes* (III.ii.2–3), citing Romans 10:10, and the argument in Calvin, *Commentarii ad Romanos* in *CO* 49, col. 206–07 (*CTS Romans*, pp. 401–102), commenting on Romans 10:17; also see Melanchthon, *Loci communes* (1521), in *CR* 21, cols. 160–2, 164.

74. Cf. Calvin, *Sermons sur . . . Galatiens* [3:3–5], *CO* 50, col. 479–82.

75. Calvin, *Institutio* (1539), II, fol. 106; Calvin, *Institutio* (1559), III.ii.34.

76. Calvin, *Comm. Eph.*(1:13), in *CO* 51, col. 153.

77. Note that *animus* can indicate either the rational soul as such or the seat of the feelings or affections—so that, when used by itself, it can mean either the soul or the volitional-affective faculty. This is surely the case in Calvin, *Institutio* (1536), II, fol. 104, where faith is defined as "firma animi persuasio." When paired with *mens*, however, the term ought surely to be understood as the seat of the other faculty, and as roughly synonymous with *cor.*

78. Calvin, *Institutio* (1539), II, fol. 106: "Neque enim si in summo cerebro volutatur Dei verbum, fide perceptum est; sed ubi in imo corde radices egit . . ."; cf. Calvin, *Institutio* (1559), III.ii.36; and note the virtually identical language of *Institutio* (1539), I, fol. 7: "Atque hic quidem observandum est, invitari nos ad Dei noticiam, non quae inani speculatione contineatur: sed quae solida furura sit & fructuosa, si percipiatur a nobis," to which Calvin, *Institutio* (1539), I.v.9 adds "radicemque agat in corde," perhaps reflecting the 1539 language of chapter II; also see Dowey, *The Knowledge of God in Calvin's Theology*, pp. 24–28; cf. Vos, *Aquinas and Calvin*, pp. 7, and Leith, *John Calvin's Doctrine of the Christian Life*, pp. 91–93.

79. Calvin, *Institutio* (1559), I.v.9.

80. Cf. Melanchthon, *Loci communes* (1521), in *CR* 21, cols. 161–63; and Calvin, *Comm. in Epist. ad Romanos*, in *CO* 49, col. 202 (*CTS Romans*, p. 393), which parallels the language of the *Institutes.*

81. Cf. Calvin, *Institutio* (1559), I.iv.4; I.xv.6–7; Calvin, *Institutio* (1539), I, fol. 23; *Institutio* (1559), II.ii.2, adding "in mente et corde sitas esse animae facultates." And note Stuermann, *A Critical Study*, pp. 85–86.

82. Cf. the commentary on Matt. 22:37, "Hebraeos sub voce *cordis* mentem interdum notare, praesertim ubi animae coniungitur" (*CO* 45, col. 611) with the commentary on Deuteronomy 6:5, where Calvin notes the difference between Hebrew and Greek usage, "Cordis nomen hoc loco, ut alibi, non pro sede affectuum, sed pro intelligentia sumitur. Itaque supervacuum fuisset addere *dianoian* quod fecerunt evangelistae, nisi ambiguitas tollendae causa. Nam quia Graecis non perinde usitata est haec significatio . . ." (*CO* 24, col. 724). Cf. also the commentary on Ps. 86:11, "cor suum formari in Dei obsequium, et in eo constanter stabiliri postulat: quia sicuti mens nostra luce indiget, sic voluntas rectitudine. . . . Nam quum sint duae eius facultates, utraque se destitui fatetur David, lumen spiritus sancti caecitati mentis suae opponens: et cordis rectitudinem affirmans merum esse Dei donum" (*CO* 31, col. 795–96) and on Ps. 119:34, as

cited in note 21. Vos takes note of Calvin's vocabulary in this regard but makes no attempt to work out the relationships between the language of the faculty psychology and the terms (Latin and French) that Calvin actually uses in his exegesis of the Old and New Testaments (*Aquinas and Calvin,* pp. 7–8).

83. Cf. Sermon on Deut. 6:4–9, *CO* 25, col. 433–34.

84. Sermon on Deut. 6:4–9: "Or nous voyons qu'en nos ames il y a premierement la vertu de penser, quand nous concevons les choses pour iuger, pour discerner: voila la premiere faculté de l'ame. C'est qu'apres avoir veu les choses, nous entrons en deliberation, et iugement, nous concluons ceci ou cela. . . . Et puis il y a l'Ame, non point seulement pour la vie, mais c'est un moyen entre les pensees, et le coeur. Car le coeur emporte les affections, les desirs, les volontez: c'est autre chose de penser une chose, et de l'appeter . . ." (*CO* 25, col. 434).

85. Commentary on Matt. 22:37 (*CO* 45, col. 611).

86. Commentary on Phil. 4:7 (*CO* 52, col. 61–62), cited in note 30.

87. Calvin, *Institutio* (1559), II.ii.2, ad init.

88. Commentary on Ps. 86:11, "quo adhaeret cor hominis Deo ubi a spiritu regitur: et inquietudinem qua aestuat, hucque et illuc rapitur, quamdiu fluctuat inter suos affectus" (*CO* 31, col. 795).

89. Calvin, *Institutio* (1539), XVII, fol. 416: "Non enim linguae est doctrina, sed vitae, nec intellectu memoriaque duntaxat apprehenditur, ut reliquae disciplinae, sed tum recipitur demum ubi *animam totam* possidet, sedemque et receptaculum invenit, in intimo cordis affectu" [my italics]; cf. *Institutio* (1559), III.vi.4.

90. Calvin, *Institutio* (1539), II, fol. 105; cf. Calvin, *Institutio* (1559), III.ii.33.

91. Cf. Calvin, *Institutio* (1539), I, fol. 22–23; Calvin, *Institutio* (1559), I.iv.4; I.v.9, and the commentaries on John 9:31, "quod Deus non exaudiat nisi a quibus vere et sincero corde vocatur. . . . In summa, nemo ad Deum orandum rite est comparatus, nisi qui cor fide purgatum habet" (*CO* 47, col. 230); and Ps. 37:7, "Prosequitur eandem doctrinam, nempe ut patienter et moderate feramus quidquid inquietare animos nostros solet. . . . nam ut affectus nostri Deo obstrepunt, ita fides in placidum obsequium nos componens, tumultus omnes in cordibus nostris compescit" (*CO* 31, col. 369).

92. See Melanchthon, *Loci communes* (1521), in *CR* 21, col. 163; ibid., (1535/6), in *CR* 21, col. 422.

93. Commentary on I John 2:27, "Non enim fides nuda est ac frigida Christi apprehensio, sed vivus et efficax potentiae eius sensus"; and cf. the previous comments, "In summa, non alio spectat quam as stabiliendam eorum fidem . . . dum eam cordibus nostris obsignat, ut certo sciamus Deum loqui. Nam quum in Deum respicere debeat fides, solus ipse sibi testis esse potest, ut cordibus nostris persuadeat . . ." (*CO* 55, col. 328).

94. Cf. Calvin, *Institutio* (1559), III.ii.33.

95. Reginald Garrigou-Lagrange, *The Theological Virtues,* 2 vols. trans. Thomas à Kempis Reilly (St. Louis: Herder, 1965), I, pp. 273–74.

96. Garrigou-Lagrange, *The Theological Virtues,* I, p. 270; and note, in particular, Aquinas, *Summa contra gentiles,* III.xl.2.

97. Aquinas, *Summa theologiae,* IIa IIae, q. 2, art. 2 and q. 4, art. 2; cf. Garrigou-Lagrange, *The Theological Virtues,* I, p. 159, 270–71.

98. Cf. Aquinas, *Summa theologiae,* Ia, q. 82, art. 2; IIIa, q. 92, art.1, and Gilson, *The Christian Philosophy of St. Thomas Aquinas,* pp. 242–44, and James E. O'Mahony, *The Desire of God in the Philosophy of St. Thomas Aquinas* (Toronto: Longmans, Green, 1929), pp. 190–94, 206–18.

99. Scotus, *Opus oxoniense,* lib. IV, dist. 49, q. 4, nota 4; cf. Minges, *Scoti doctrina,* I, p. 702.

100. Calvin, *Institutio* (1559), III.ii.33; and note I.v.9; III.ii.36, together with the commen-

taries on Ps. 86:11 (cited in, note 76); and 119:37, "imo pravitatem quam dixit proximo verso regnare in hominum cordibus, ad externos quoque sensus extendit: ac si diceret morbum concupiscendi non in animis moso latere, sed diffusum esse per omnes partes . . ." (*CO* 32, col. 230).

101. Commentary on I Cor. 13:12–13 (*CO* 49, col. 514–15).

102. Cf. Calvin, *Institutio* (1559), I.ii.1: "persuasi simus fontem omnium bonorum esse"; Calvin, *Institutio* (1559), 3.25.2: "De summo fine bonorum anxie disputarunt olim philosophi, atque etiam inter se certarunt; nemo tamen, excepto Platone, agnovit summum hominis bonum esse eius coniunctionem cum Deo," and the commentary on Ps. 18:2, "Notandum vero est, amorem Dei tanquam praecipuum pietatis caput hic poni: quia nulla re melius colitur Deus" (*CO* 31, col. 170).

103. See Ganoczy, *The Young Calvin*, pp. 173–78, 209–10.

104. See chapter 3, "Scholasticism in Calvin."

105. Calvin, *Institutio* (1559), III.ii.33: "In quo, tota terra, scholastici aberrant: qui in fidei consideratione nudum ac simplicem e notitia assensum arripiunt . . ." (identical with 1539); *Institution* (1560), III.ii.33: "En laquelle chose les Theologiens Sorboniques faillent trop lourdement: qui pensent que la Foy soit un simple consentement à la parolle de Dieu . . ." (identical with 1541).

106. Cf. Calvin, *Institutio* (1559), III.ii.14 with III.ii.8.

107. Cf. Calvin, *Institutio* (1559), III.i.4; III.ii.33–35, 41–43; III.ii.1–2.

108. Cf. the conclusions in Richard A. Muller, "The Priority of the Intellect in the Soteriology of Jacob Arminius," *Westminster Theological Journal* 55 (1993), pp. 55–72.

CHAPTER TEN

1. See Charles B. Schmitt, *Aristotle and the Renaissance* (Cambridge, Mass.: Harvard University Press, 1983), pp. 15–27.

2. Cf. J. Bohatec, *Calvin et l'humanisme* (Paris: Revue Historique, 1939), pp. 5–7, 48–50; François Wendel, *Calvin et l'humanisme* (Paris: Presses Universitaires de France, 1976), pp. 63–72.

3. Paul Vignaux, *Luther, commentateur des sentences* (Paris: J. Vrin, 1935), pp. 24–30.

4. Andreas Hyperius, *Methodus theologiae* (Basel: Oporinus, 1567), pp. 2–6.

5. Wolfgang Musculus, *Loci communes sacrae theologiae* (Basel: Ioannes Hervagius, 1573), cap. xlii, xliv, xlv.

6. S. van der Linde, "Gereformeerde Scholastiek IV: Calvijn," *Theologia Reformata* 29 (1986), pp. 244–66.

7. Beryl Smalley, "The Bible in the Medieval Schools," in *Cambridge History of the Bible*, 3 vols. (Cambridge: Cambridge University Press, 1963–70), II, pp. 197–98; cf. Yves M.-J. Congar, *A History of Theology*. trans. Hunter Guthrie (Garden City, N.Y.: Doubleday, 1968), pp. 79–80; Johannes Beumer, *Die theologische Methode*, in *Handbuch der Dogmengeschichte*, ed. A. Grillmeier, M. Schmaus, and L. Scheffczyk (Freiburg in Breisgau: Herder, 1972), pp. 72–73; J. Van der Ploeg, "The Place of Holy Scripture in the Theology of St. Thomas," in *Thomist* 10 (1947), pp. 404–07; for a sense, at least, of the books available to Calvin and others, see Alexandre Ganoczy, *La Bibliothéque de l'Académie de Calvin* (Geneva: Droz, 1969).

8. Cf. Erwid Mülhaupt, *Die Predigt Calvins: Ihre Geschichter, ihre form und ihre religiösen Grundgedanken* (Berlin: DeGruyter, 1931), pp. 17–18 with Parker, *Calvin's Preaching*, pp. 80, 132.

9. See John Calvin, *Vingt deux sermons sur le Pseaume cent dix neufieme*, in *CO* 32, col. 453–4; also note David C. Steinmetz, "The Scholastic Calvin," in *Protestant Scholasticism: Essays in Reassessment*, ed. Carl Trueman and R. Scott Clark (London: Paternoster, forthcoming); and cf. Parker, *Calvin's Preaching*, pp. 25–29.

10. Calvin, *Institutio* (1539), *Epistola ad lectorem*, fol. *1r.

11. Contra the undifferentiated appeal to "Ciceronian" rhetoric in Serene Jones, *Calvin and the Rhetoric of Piety* (Louisville: Westminster/John Knox, 1995).

12. John Dillenberger, *Contours of Faith: Changing Forms of Christian Thought* (Nashville Tenn.: Abingdon, 1969), p. 39.

13. Hermann Bauke, *Das Problem des Theologie Calvins* (Leipzig: J. C. Hinrichs, 1922), pp. 16–19.

14. Wilhelm H. Neuser and Brian G. Armstrong, "The Development of the *Institutes* 1536 to 1559," in *John Calvin's Institutes: His Opus Magnum*, ed. B. J. van der Walt (Potchefstromi: Institute for Reformational Studies, 1986) pp. 36–39, and T. H. L. Parker, *The Doctrine of the Knowledge of God: A Study in the Theology of John Calvin* (Rev. ed. (Grand Rapids, Mich.: Eerdmans, 1959), pp. 117–21.

15. See Francis Higman, "Linearity in Calvin's Thought," *Calvin Theological Journal* 26/1 (1991), pp. 100–110; and note Melanchthon, *Loci communes theologici* (1536), in *CR* 21, col. 254.

16. Bartholomaus Keckermann, *Systema sacrosanctae theologiae, tribus libris adornatum* (Hanoviae: Gulielmus Antonius, 1602); also found in Keckermann's *Operum omnium quae extant*, 2 vols. (Geneva: Petrus Aubertus, 1614), appended to vol. II, separate pagination.

17. For example, Johannes Marckius, *Christianae theologiae medulla didactico elenctica* (Amsterdam: Gerardus Borstius, 1690); Johann Heinrich Heidegger, *Corpus theologiae christianae*, 2 vols. (Zurich: D. Gessner, J. N. Bodmer, 1700) and Heidegger, *Medulla theologiae christianae* (Zurich: D. Gessner, 1696) and *Medulla medullae theologiae christianae* (Zürich: D. Gessner, 1697).

18. Thus, for example, Edward Leigh, *A Systeme or Body of Divinity* (London: William Lee, 1664), and Samuel Maresius, *Collegium theologicum sive systema breve universae theologiae comprehensum octodecim disputationibus* (Groningen: Franciscus Boronchorst 1645).

19. Thus, Cicero, *Epistolae ad Q. Fratrem*, 2.13.4, speaks of the *corpus omnis Romani iuris*.

20. For example, Maresius, *Collegium theologicum*, and Johannes Marckius, *Sylloge dissertationum philologico-theologicarum, ad selectos quosdam textus Veteris Testamenti* (Leiden: Petrus Van der Aa, 1717).

21. As, for example, Johannes Marckius, *Christianae theologiae medulla didactico elenctica*, and Marckius, *Compendium theologiae christianae didactico-elencticum* (Groningen: Francisus Bronchorst 1686).

22. Thus, Wolfgang Musculus, *Loci communes*; Andreas Hyperius, *Methodus theologiae*; Peter Martyr Vermigli, *P. M. Vermilii loci communes* (London: Ioannes Kyngston, 1576); Johannes Polyander, et al. *Synopsis purioris theologiae, disputationibus quinquaginta duabus comprehensa.* (Leiden: Elsevir, 1625); Friedrich Spanheim, *Disputationum theologicarum syntagma. Pars prima: Disputationum theologicarum miscellanearum; Pars secunda: Anti-Anabaptistica controversia* (Geneva: Chouet, 1652).

23. Cf. Richard A. Muller, *Christ and the Decree: Christology and Predestination in Reformed Theology from Calvin to Perkins* (Durham, N.C.: Labyrinth Press, 1986), pp. 1–10, 175–82, and Muller, *Post-Reformation Reformed Dogmatics*, 2 vols. (Grand Rapids, Mich.: Baker Book House, 1987–93), I, pp. 82–87.

24. On Lombard's theology and its context see Marcia L. Colish, *Peter Lombard*, 2 vols. (Leiden: E. J. Brill, 1994).

25. Cf. Robert Kolb, "Teaching the Text: The commonplace Method in Sixteenth-century Biblical Commentary," *Bibliothèque d'Humanisme et Renaissance* 49 (1987), pp. 571–85, and A. Muller, *Post-Reformation Reformed Dogmatics*, I, pp. 251–258.

26. For example, E. David Willis, "Rhetoric and Responsibility in Calvin's Theology," in *The Context of Comtemporary Theology*, ed. Alexander McKelway and E. David Willis (Atlanta:

John Knox Press, 1974), p. 43, and Willis, "Persuasion in Calvin's Theology," in *Calvin and Christian Ethics*, ed. Peter De Klerk (Grand Rapids, Mich.: Calvin Studies Society, 1987), p. 83.

27. Cf. Philip Melanchthon, *Loci communes* (1521) and *Loci praeciupi theologici* (1543), in *Opera quae supersunt omnia*, 28 vols., ed. C. G. Bretschreider (Brunswick: Schwetschke, 1834–60), vol. 21; Musculus, *Loci communes sacrae theologiae*; Hyperius, *Methodus theologiae*; Martin Chemnitz, *Loci theologici*, ed. Polycarpleyser 3 pts. (Frankfurt: Johannes Spies, 1591–94); Vermigli, *P. M. Vermilii loci communes*.

28. *CO* 9, col. 848; cf. François Wendel, *Calvin: The Origins and Development of His Religious Thought*, trans. Philip Mairet (New York: Harper & Row, 1963), pp. 134–5.

29. Melanchthon, *Loci communes theologici* (1536), in *CR* 21, col. 254.

30. The phrase "ordo recte docendi" appears in Calvin, *Institutio* (1559), I.i.3; but cf. Joannis Calvinus lectori: "siquidem religionis summam omnibus partibus sic mihi complexus esse videor, et eo quoque ordine digessisse . . ."; *Institutio* (1559), III.iii.1: "ratio et docendi series" and IV.x.6: "nunc studebo totam summam quo potero optimo ordine colligere."

31. Armstrong, *Calvin and the Amyraut Heresy: Protestant Scholasticism and Humanism in Seventeent-Century France*, (Madison: University of Wisconsin Press, 1969), pp. 34–4.

32. Cf. the formal similarities noted in Paul C. Böttger, *Calvin's Institutio als Erbauungsbuch: Versuch einer literarischen Analyse*. (Neukirchen: Neukirchner Verlag, 1990), p. 81.

33. Cf. Beryl Smalley, *The Study of the Bible in the Middle Ages* (Notre Dame: University of Notre Dame Press, 1964), 63–64, and Smalley, "The Bible in the Medieval Schools," in *The Cambridge History of the Bible*, 3 vols. (Cambridge: Cambridge University Press, 1963–70), II, pp. 197–98; see also Congar, *A History of Theology*, pp. 79–80.

34. Cf. Paul Oskar Kristeller, *Renaissance Thought: The Classic, Scholastic, and Humanist Strains* (New York: Harper & Row, 1961), p. 116; James H. Overfield, *Humanism and Scholasticism in Late Medieval Germany* (Princeton, N.J.: Princeton University Press, 1984), pp. 59–60, 94–100, 329–30, and Overfield, "Scholastic Opposition to Humanism in Pre-Reformation Germany," *Viator* 7 (1976), pp. 391–420.

35. See Gerhard Ebeling, "The Meaning of 'Biblical Theology,' " in *Word and Faith*, trans. J. Leitch (London: SCM, 1963), pp. 79–97; John Sandys-Wunsch and Laurence Eldredge, "J. P. Gabler and the Distinction Between Biblical and Dogmatic Theology: Translation, Commentary and Discussion of His Originality," *Scottish Journal of Theology* 33 (1980), pp. 133–58.

36. John T. McNeill, in *Institutes* (1559/Battles), p. 428, note 1; J. Wayne Baker, *Heinrich Bullinger and the Covenant: The Other Reformed Tradition* (Athens: Ohio University Press, 1980), p. 197, cf. pp. 193–98.

37. Cf. Muller, *God, Creation and Providence in the Thought of Jacob Arminius: Sources and Directions of Scholastic Protestantism in the Era of Early Orthodoxy* (Grand Rapids, Mich.: Baker Book House, 1991), pp. 15–51, for discussion and further bibliography.

38. Cf. the survey in Richard A. Muller, s.v. "Orthodoxy, Protestant" in *Encyclopedia of the Reformed Faith*, ed. Donald McKim (Louisville: Westminster/John Knox Press, 1992).

39. *Calvin*, p. 122.

40. Cf. Steinmetz, "Calvin and the Absolute Power of God," *Journal of Medieval and Renaissance Studies* 18/1 (Spring 1988), pp. 65–66, 77–79; Steinmetz, "Calvin Among the Thomists," in *Biblical Hermeneutics in Historical Perspective* (Grand Rapids, Mich.: Eerdmans, 1991), pp. 210–14; Thompson, "The Immoralities of the Patriarchs in the History of Exegesis: A Reappraisal of Calvin's Position, *Calvin Theological Journal* 26 (1991)," pp. 40–41; Susan E. Schreiner, "Exegesis and Double Justice in Calvin's Sermons on Job," *Church History* 5 (1989), pp. 327, 329–38; Schreiner, "Through a Mirror Dimly: Calvin's Sermons on Job," *Calvin Theological Journal* 21 (1986), pp. 179, 185.

41. Cf. Jill Raitt, *The Eucharistic Theology of Theodore Beza: Development of the Reformed Doctrine* (Chambersburg, Pa.: American Academy of Religion, 1972); Raitt, "The Person of the

Mediator: Calvin's Christology and Beza's Fidelity," *Occasional Papers of the Society for Reformation Research* 1 (December 1977), pp. 53–80; Tadataka Maruyama, *The Ecclesiology of Theodore Beza: The Reform of the True Church* (Geneva: Droz, 1978); and Richard A. Muller, "Christ in the Eschaton: Calvin and Moltmann on the Duration of the *Munus Regium*," *Harvard Theological Review* 74/1 (1981), pp. 31–59.

42. Cf. Leith's comments on Niesel's christocentric interpretation of Calvin in "Calvin's Theological Method and Ambiguity in His Theology," in *Reformation Studies: Essays in Honor of R. H. Bainton*, ed. F. Littell (Richmond, Va.: John Knox, 1962), p. 111.

43. For example, Dowey's claims that the 1559 *Institutes* divides into two primary parts and not four, that the arrangement of topics in *Institutes*, Book II, evidenced Calvin's partial assimilation of his own fundamental ordering principle, and that "book II really begins only in chapter vi" (*The Knowledge of God in Calvin's Theology* [New York: Columbia University Press, 1952; 3rd ed., Grand Rapids, Mich.: Eerdmans, 1994], pp. 41, 45.

BIBLIOGRAPHY

ABBREVIATIONS

CCL	*Corpus Christianorum, Series Latina.*
CO	*Ioannis Calvini Opera quae supersunt omnia*
CR	*Corpus Reformatorum*
CSEL	*Corpus scriptorum ecclesiasticorum latinorum*
CTS	Calvin Translation Society
NPNF	*Nicene and Post Nicene Fathers*
PG	*Patrologia Graeca*, ed. J. P. Migne
PL	*Patrologia Latina*, ed. J. P. Migne
WA	*D. Martin Luthers Werke. Kritische Gesamtausgabe*
WABR	*D. Martin Luthers Werke . . . Briefwechsel*
WADB	*D. Martin Luthers Werke . . . Deutsche Bibel*
CCL	*Corpus Christianorum. Series Latina. Turnholti, Typographi Brepols, 1953ff.*
CSEL	*Corpus Scriptorum Ecclesiasticorum Latinorum. Vienna: Academia Litterarum Caesarae Vindobonensis, 1866ff.*
NPNF	*A Select Library of Nicene and Post-Nicene Fathers. Ed. Philip Schaff and Henry Wace. First Series, 14 vols. Second Series, 14 vols. New York: Christian Literature Co., 1886–1900.*
PG	*Patrologia Graeca Cursus Completus. Ed. J.-P. Migne. 161 vols. Paris: Vives, 1857–66.*
PL	*Patrologia Latina Cursus Completus. Ed. J.-P. Migne. 221 vols. Paris: Vives, 1844–55.*

WA   *D. Martin Luthers Werke; kritische Gesamtausgabe. 108 vols. to date. Weimar, H. Bohlau, 1883– .*

Erasmus, Desiderius. *The Collected Works of Erasmus,* Ed. R. J. Schoeck, B. M. Corrigan, et al. Toronto: University of Toronto Press, 1974ff.

Opera omnia. See Duns Scotus.

Opera Selecta

WORKS OF CALVIN

Sixteenth-Century Texts and Translations

Brevis responsio Io. Calvini ad diluenda nebulonis cuiusdam calumnias (Geneva, 1557). Trans. as *A Brief Reply in Refutation of the Calumnies of a Certain Worthless Person,* in Calvin, *Calvin's Calvinism,* pp. 187–206.

Calumniae nebulonis cuiusdam, quibus odio et invidia gravare conatus est doctrinam Ioh. Calvin de occulta Dei providentia. Ioannis Calvini ad easdem responsio (Geneva, 1558), in *CO* 9 cols. 269–318. Trans. as *On the Secret Providence of God,* in Calvin, *Calvin's Calvinism,* pp. 257–350.

Le Catéchisme de l'église de Genève, c'est a dire le Formulaire d'instruire les enfants en la chrestienté. 1541–42; Geneva: Jean Girard, 1545.

Catechismus ecclesiae genevensis, hoc est formula erudiendi pueros in doctrina Christi. Strasbourg: Wendelin Rihel, 1545.

Catechismus, sive christianae religionis institutio. Basel: n.p., 1538.

Christianae religionis institutio, totam fere pietatis summam, et quicquid est in doctrina salutis cognitu necessarium, complectens: omnibus pietatis studiosis lectu dignissimum opus, ac recens editum. Basel: Platter & Lasius, 1536.

Commentaire de M. Iean Calvin sur l'Epistre de Saint Jacques. Geneva, 1550.

Commentarii in priorem Epistolam Pauli ad Corinthios. Strasbourg, 1546.

Commentarii in secundum Pauli Epistolam ad Corinthios. Geneva, 1548.

Congrégation faite en l'eglise de Genève par M. Iean Calvin; en laquelle la matiere de l'election eternelle de Dieu fut sommairement et clairement par luy deduite et ratifiée d'un commun accord par ses freres ministres. Geneva: Vincent Bres, 1562.

Deux sermons faitz en la ville de Genève. Geneva, 1546.

Exposition sur les deux Epistres de S. Pierre et l'Epistre de S. Iude. Geneva, 1545.

Exposition sur l'Épitre de Sainct Iudas apostre de nostre Seigneur Iésus Christ. Geneva: Jean Girard, 1542.

Institutie ofte Onderwijsinghe in de christelicke Religie... over-geset door Wilelmus Corsmannus (1650), reissued with an intro. by A. Kuyper. Doesburg: J. C. vanSchenk Brill, 1889.

Institutio christianae religionis, a Ioanne Calvino conscripta, compendium simul, ac methodi enarratio, per Edmundum Bunnium. London: Thomas Vautrollerious, 1576.

Institutio christianae religionis nunc vere demum suo titulo respondens. Strasbourg: Wendelin Rihel, 1539.

Institutio totius christianae religionis. Geneva: Ioannes Gerardus, 1550.

Institutio christianae religionis. Geneva: Robertus Stephanus, 1553.

Institutio christianae religionis, in libros quatuor nunc primum digesta, certisque distincta capitibus, ad aptissimam methodum: aucta etiam tam magna accessione ut propemodum opus novum haberi possit. Geneva: Robertus Stephanus, 1559; Strasbourg: Wendelin Rihel, 1561.

Institutio christianae religionis in libros quatuor..... Geneva: Antonius Rebulius, 1561.

Institutio christianae religionis. Geneva: Perrinus, 1568, 1569.

Institutio christianae religionis . . . indices duo locupletissimi: alter rerum insignium: alter vero loco-rum sacrae Scripturae qui in his Institutionibus obiter explicantur. Geneva: Robertus Ste-phanus, 1568.

Institutio christianae religionis . . . additi sunt nuper dou indices, hac postrema editione longè quam anteà castigatores, ab Augustino Marlorato pridem collecti. . . . London: Thomas Vautrollerius, 1576.

Institutio christianae religioni, ab ipso authore in anno 1559, & in libros quatuor digesta, certisque distincta capitibus ad aptissimam methodum. . . . Lausanne: Franciscus Le Preux, 1576, 1577.

Institutio christianae religionis, Ioanne Calvino authore. Quae ad superiores editiones hac postrema, omnium emendatissima locupletissimaque. Geneva: Iohannes Le Preux, 1590.

L'Institution puérile de la doctrine chrestienne faicte par manière de dyalogue (1541) in Opera Selecta, 2, pp. 152–56.

Institution de la religion chrestienne: en laquelle est comprinse une somme de pieté, et quasi tout ce qui est necessaire a congnoistre en la doctrine de salut. Geneva: Michel du Bois, 1541.

Institution de la religion chrestienne: composée en Latin par Jehan Calvin, et translatée en francoys par luymesme: en laquelle est comprise une somme de toute la chrestienté. Geneva: Jean Girard, 1545.

Institution de la religion chrestienne. . . . Geneva: Jean Girard, 1551.

Institution de la religion chrestienne. . . . Geneva: Jean Girard, 1553.

Institution de la religion chrestienne. . . . Geneva: Philibert Hamelin, 1554.

Institution de la religion chrestienne. . . . Geneva: François Iaquy, Antoine Davodeau, & Iaques Bourgeois, 1557.

Institution de la religion chrestienne. Nouvellement mise en quatre livres: et distinguée par chapitres, en ordre et methode bien propre. . . . Geneva: Crespin, 1560.

Institution de la religion chrestienne. Geneva: Jacques Bourgeois, 1562.

Institution de la religion chrestienne . . . traduite par Charles Icard. Bremen: Herman Brauer, 1713.

The Institution of Christian Religion, wrytten in Latine by maister Iohn Calvin, and translated into Englysh according to the author's last edition. Trans. Thomas Norton. London: Reinolde Wolfe & Richarde Harison, 1561, 1562.

Ioannis Calvini Opera omnia theologica in septem tomos digesta. Geneva: Vignon & Chouet, 1617.

Ioannis Calvini noviodunensis Opera omnia, in novem tomos digesta. Amsterdam: Johann Jacob Schipper, 1667–71.

Joannis Calvini Institutio christianae religionis . . . curavit A. Tholuck, 2 vols. Edinburgh: T & T. Clark, 1874.

Leges Academiae Genevensis. Geneva: Stephanus, 1559; facsimile repr. Geneva: J. G. Fick, 1859.

Mosis libri V cum Ioannis Calvini Commentariis: Genesis seorsum; reliqui quatuor in formam har-moniae digesti. Geneva: H. Stephanus, 1563.

Quatre sermons traictans des matieres fort utiles pour nostre temps . . . avec briefve exposition du Psaume LXXXVII. Geneva, 1552.

Recueil des opuscules. C'est à dire, petits traictez de M. Iean Calvin. 2nd ed. Geneva: Iacob Stoer, 1611.

Sermons of M. Iohn Calvin upon the Fifth Book of Moses called Deuteronomie. Trans. Arthur Golding. London: Henry Middleton, 1583; facsimile repr. Edinburgh: Banner of Truth, 1993.

Sermons sur l'Epistre S. Paul apostre aux Galatiens. Geneva, 1563. *Sermons sur le Livre d'Estaïe Chapitres 30–41.* Neukirchen-Vluyn: Nerkirchner Verlag, 1995.

Sermons of Maister Iohn Calvin, upon the Book of Iob. London: George Bishop, 1574.

Sermons upon the Epistle of Saint Paule to the Galatians. Trans. Arthur Golding. London, 1574; reissued, Audubon, N.J.: Old Paths Publications, 1995.

Sermons sur l'Epistre aux Ephesiens Geneva: Jean-Baptiste Pinereul, 1562.

Sermons sur les deux Epistres S. Paul à Timothée, et sur l'Epistre à Tite. Geneva: Conrad Badius, 1561.

Sermons of M. John Calvin, on the Epistles of S. Paule to Timothie and Titus. Trans. L. T. London: G. Bishop and T. Woodcoke, 1579.

Thirteen Sermons of Maister Iohn Calvin, Entreating of the Free Election of God in Iacob, and of Reprobation in Esau. A treatise wherein every Christian may see the excellent benefites of God towardes his Children, and his marvellous iudgements towards the reprobate. Trans. Iohn Fielde. London, 1579; reissued, Audubon, N.J.: Old Paths Publications, 1996.

Two and Twentie Sermons of Maister Iohn Calvin, in which Sermons is most religiously handled, the hundredth and nineteenth Psalme of David, by eight verses aparte, according to the Hebrewe Alphabet. Trans. Thomas Stocker. London, 1580; reissued Audubon, N.J.: Old Paths Publications, 1996.

Vingtdeus sermons . . . auxquels est exposé le Pseaume cent dixneufieme, contenant pareil nombre des huictains. Geneva: Iean Gerard, 1554.

Modern Editions and Translations

The Bible of John Calvin, Reconstructed from the Text of his Commentaries. Comp. Richard F. Wevers. Grand Rapids, Mich.: Digamma, 1994.

The Bondage and Liberation of the Will: A Defense of the Orthodox Doctrine of Human Choice Against Pighius. Ed. A. N. S. Lane. Trans. G. I. Davis [*Texts and Studies in Reformation and Post-Reformation Thought*, vol. 2]. Grand Rapids Mich.: Baker Book House, 1996.

Calvinism by Calvin; being the Substance of Discourses delivered by Calvin and the other Ministers of Geneva on the Doctrines of Grace. Trans. and intro. R. Govett (London: James Nisbet, 1840). [A translation of *Congrégation faite en l'eglise de Genève par M. Iean Calvin; en laquelle la matiere de l'election eternelle de Dieu fut sommairement et clairement par luy deduite et ratifiée d'un commun accord par ses freres ministres.*]

Calvin's Calvinism: Treatises on the Eternal Predestination of God and the Secret Providence of God. 2 vols. in 1 Trans. Henry Cole. London: Wertheim and Mackintosh, 1856–57; repr. Grand Rapids, Mich.: Reformed Free Publishing Association, n.d.

Calvin's Commentary on Seneca's De Clementia. Trans., intro. and notes by Ford Lewis Battles and André Malan Hugo. Leiden: E. J. Brill, 1969.

Calvin: Theological Treatises. Trans, intro., and notes by J. K. S. Reid. Philadelphia: Westminster, 1954.

Catechism or Institution of the Christian Religion. Trans. and intro. Ford Lewis Battles. Pittsburgh: Pittsburgh Theological Seminary, 1972; rev. ed., 1976.

Le Catéchisme français de Calvin, publiée en 1537, reimprimé pour la première fois, avec deux notices par Albert Rilliet and Théophile Dufour. Geneva: H. Georg, 1878.

Commentaries of John Calvin. 46 vols. Edinburgh: Calvin Translation Society, 1844–55; repr. Grand Rapids, Mich.: Baker Book House, 1979.

Concerning the Eternal Predestination of God. Trans. and intro. J. K. S. Reid. London: James Clarke, 1961. (Also *A Treatise on the Eternal Predestination of God.* Trans. Henry Cole. In Calvin, *Calvin's Calvinism* [London, 1856], pp. 5–206.)

A Defense of the Secret Providence of God. Trans Henry Cole. In Calvin, *Calvin's Calvinism* (London, 1856), pp. 207–350.

Deux congrégations et exposition du catéchisme. Première réimpression de l'édition de 1563 avec une introduction par Rodolphe Peter. Paris: Presses Universitaires de France, 1964.

Épitre a tous amateurs de Jésus-Christ: Préface à la traduction française du Nouveau Testament par Robert Olivetan (1535) . . . avec Introduction sur une édition française de l'Institution dès 1537? Ed. Jacques Pannier. Paris: Fischbacher, 1929.

Épitre au roi François Ier: Préface de la première édition française de l'Institution de la religion chrétienne, 1541. Texte publié, pour la première fois, d'après l'exemplaire de la Bibliothèque Nationale, avec Introduction et Notes par Jacques Pannier. Paris: Fischbacher, 1927.

Institutes of the Christian Religion (1536). Trans. and annot. Ford Lewis Battles. Rev. ed. Grand Rapids, Mich.: Eerdmans, 1986.

Institutes of the Christian Religion of John Calvin: 1539, Text and Concordance. 4 vols. Ed. Richard F. Wevers. Grand Rapids, Mich.: Meeter Center for Calvin Studies, 1988.

Institutes of the Christian Religion [1559]. 2 vols. Trans. John Allen. Philadelphia: Presbyterian Board of Christian Education, 3rd rev. ed., 1841; 7th ed., 1936.

Institutes of the Christian Religion (1559). 2 vols. Trans. Henry Beveridge. Edinburgh, 1845; repr. Grand Rapids, Mich.: Eerdmans, 1989.

Institutes of the Christian Religion (1559). 2 vols. Ed. John T. McNeill. Trans. Ford Lewis Battles. Philadelphia: Westminster, 1960.

Institutie, of Onderwijzing in de christelijke Godsdienst. Naar de laatste Uitgave in mei 1864, door de Prof. G. Baum, E. Cuniz, en E. Reuss. 3 vols. Kampen: G. Ph. Zalsman, 1865–68.

Institutie, of Onderwijzing in de christelijke Godsdienst. Uit het in vertaald door Dr. A. Sizoo. Delft: W. D. Meinema, 1931.

Institution de la religion chrestienne de Calvin. Texte original de 1541 réimprimé sous la direction de Abel Lefranc par Henri Chatelain et Jacques Pannier. Paris: Librairie Honoré Champion, 1911.

Institution de la religion chrestienne [1541]. Ed. J. Pannier. Paris, 1936–39.

Institution de la religion chrestienne [1560], édition critique avec introduction, notes et variants publiée par Jean-Daniel Benoit. 5 vols. Paris: J. Vrin, 1957–63.

Institution de la religion chrétienne. Edition nouvelle publiée par La Société Calviniste de France. 4 vols. Geneva: Labor et Fides, 1955–58.

L'Institution puérile de la doctrine chrestienne faicte par manière de dyalogue (1541) in *Opera Selecta,* vol. 2, pp. 152–56

Ioannis Calvini opera quae supersunt omnia. 59 vols. Ed. Guilielmus Baum, Eduardus Cunitz, and Eduardus Reuss. Brunswick: Schwetschke, 1863–1900. [*CO,* vols 1–59 = *CR,* vols. 29–87]

Preface to the Homilies of Chrysostom. Trans. John H. McIndoe. *Hartford Quarterly* 5 (1965), pp. 19–26.

Selected Works of John Calvin: Tracts and Letters. Ed. Henry Beveridge and Jules Bonnet. 7 vols. Grand Rapids, Mich.: Baker Book House, 1983.

Supplementa Calviniana. Sermons inédits. Ed. Erwim Mühlhaupt et al. 8 vols. to date. Neukirchen: Neukirchner Verlag, 1936–.

Treatises against the Anabaptists and against the Libertines. Trans. and ed. Benjamin Wirt Farley. Grand Rapids, Mich.: Baker Book House, 1982.

Unterricht in der christlichen Religion. Bearbeitet und übersetzt von Professor D. E. F. Müller. Neukirchen: Moers, 1909.

Unterricht in der christlichen Religion: Institutio christianae religionis. Übersetzt und bearbeitet von Otto Weber. Neukirchen: Moers, 1936.

EARLY WORKS, TRANSLATIONS, AND CRITICAL EDITIONS

Aegidius Romanus. *Opus super secundo libro sententiarum.* Venice: Luca di Domenico, 1482.

———. *Primus sententiarum . . . correctus a reveredo magro Augustino Montifalconio.* Venice: Octauianus Scotus, 1521.

Agricola, Rudolf. *De inventione dialectica libri omnes et integri et recogniti.* Cologne: Ioannes Gymnicus, 1539.

Alain of Lille. *Regulae theologicae,* in *PL* 210.

Alexander of Hales. *Summa theologica.* 4 vols. Quaracchi: Collegium S. Bonaventurae, 1924–58.

Alsted, Johann Heinrich. *Theologia scholastica didactica, exhibens locos communos theologicos methodo scholastica.* Hanover: Conrad Eifrid, 1618.

Altenstaig, Johannes. *Vocabularius theologiae.* Hagenau: Heinrich Gran, 1517.

Ambrose. *Expositio Psalmi XCVIII*, 8.31. *CSEL*, 62, p. 168.

Aristotle. *The Basic Works of Aristotle.* Ed. and intro. Ricgard McKeon. New York: Random House, 1941.

———. *The Rhetoric and Poetics of Aristotle.* Intro. and notes by Friedrich Solmsen. New York: Random House, 1954.

Augustine, Aurelius. *Adnotationes in Iob liber unus*, 38. *CSEL* 28/2, pp. 604–05.

———. *De Civitate Dei*, XVIII.13. *CCL* 48, p. 604.

———. *Confessionum libri tredecim*, in *CCL* 27.

———. *Confessions.* Trans. and intro. by R. S. Pine-Coffin. Baltimore: Penguin, 1961.

———. *Contra duas epistolas Pelagianorum libri IV*, in *CSEL* 60.

———. *De doctrina christiana libri IV*, in *CCL* 32.

———. *De libero arbitrio libri III*, in *CCL* 29.

———. *De spiritu et littera ad Marcellum liber I*, in *CSEL* 60.

———. *Enarrationes in Psalmos*, in *CCL* 38–40.

———. *In Iohannis euangelium tractatus*, in *CCL* 36.

———. *Retractationes*, in *CCL* 37.

Beza, Theodore. *Confessio christianae fidei.* Geneva: Jean Bonnefoy, 1560; London: Thomas Vautrollerius, 1575.

———. *Correspondence de Théodore de Bèze.* Ed. H. Aubert, F. Aubert, H. Meylan, A. Dutour, et al. Geneva: Droz, 1960– .

———. *L'Histoire de la vie et mort de [M. Iean Calvin].* In ———. *Commentaires de M. Iean Calvin, sur le livre de Iosué.* Geneva: François Perrin, 1564. [*CO* 21, col. 1–50]

———. *Ioannis Calvini Epistolae . . . eiusdem I. Calvini Vita.* Geneva: Petrum Santandreanum, 1575. [The *Vita* is also found in *CO* 21, col. 119–172.]

———. *Summa totius christianismi, sive descriptio & distributio causarum salutis electorum & exitii reproborum, ex sacris literis collecta. [Tabula praedestinationis].* 1555; in *Tractationes theologicae*, vol. 1, pp. 170–205.

———. *Tractationes theologicae.* 3 vols. Geneva: Jean Crispin/Eustathius Vignon, 1570–82.

La Bible, qui est toute la Saincte Escriture du Vieil et du Nouveau Testament: autrement l'anciene & la Nouvelle Alliance. Le tout reveu & conferé sur les textes Hebrieux et Grecs par les Pasteurs & Professerus de l'Eglise de Geneve. Geneva: Pierre et Iaques Chouët, 1638.

Biblia sacra cum glossis, interlineari et ordinaria, Nicolai Lyrani Postilla et Moralitatibus, Burgensis additionibus, & Thoringi replicis. Lyons: Antoine Vincent, 1545.

Biel, Gabriel. *Collectorium circa quattuor libros sententiarum.* Tübingen, 1501; critical ed., Tübingen: Mohr, 1973–.

Bonaventure. *Breviloquium.* In *Opera omnia*, vol. 5.

———. *Commentarius in IV libros sententiarum.* In *Opera omnia*, vols. 1–4.

———. *Opera omnia.* 10 vols. Quaracchi: Collegium S. Bonaventurae, 1882–1902.

———. *The Works of Bonaventure.* 5 vols. Trans. José de Vinck. Paterson, N.J.: St. Anthony Guild, 1960.

Brunfels, Otho. *Loci in acta apostolorum.* Strasbourg: n.p., 1528.

Bucer, Martin. *Enarratio in Evangelion Iohannis.* Ed. Irena Backus. Leiden: E. J. Brill, 1988.

———. *Metaphrases et enarrationes perpetuae Epistolarum D. Pauli Apostoli . . . Tomus primus . . . in Epistolam ad Romanos.* Strasbourg: Wendelin Rihel, 1536.

———. *Résumé sommaire de la doctrine chretienne.* Texte établi et traduit par François Wendel. Paris: Presses Universitaires de France, 1951.

Budé, Guillaume. *De transitu hellenismi ad christianismum.* Paris: R. Stephanus, 1535.

Bullinger, Heinrich. *Compendium christianae religionis decem libris comprehensum.* Zurich: Froschauer, 1556.

———. *Confessio et exposition simplex orthodoxae fidei.* Zurich: Froschauer, 1566; text in Schaff, *The Creeds of Christendom,* vol. 3, pp. 233–306.

———. *The Decades of Henry Bullinger.* Ed. Thomas Harding. Trans. H.I. 4 vols. Cambridge: Cambridge University Press, 1849–52.

———. *In omnes apostolicas epistolas, divi videlicet Pauli XIIII. et VII. canonicas commentarii.* Zurich: Froschauer, 1537.

———. *In Pauli ad Romanos Epistolam . . . Commentarius.* Zurich: Froschauer, 1533.

———. *Ratio studiorum, sive de institutione eorum, qui studia literarum sequuntur, libellus aureus. Accessit eodem dispositio locorum communium, tam philosophicorum, quam theologicorum. Item, Christianae fidei perspicue & breviter proposita quaedam axiomata.* Zurich: Froschauer, 1527.

———. *De scripturae sanctae authoritate, certitudine, firmitate et absoluta perfectione . . . libri duo.* Zurich: Froschauer, 1538.

———. *Sermonum decades quinque.* Zurich: Froschauer, 1552.

———. *Summa christlicher religion.* Zurich: Froschauer, 1556. (Translated into Latin as *Compendium christianae religionis* [1559] and into English as *Commonplaces of Christian Religion* [London: Henry Bynneman, 1575].)

———. *De testamento seu foedere Dei unico et aeterna . . . brevis expositio.* Zurich: Froschauer, 1534.

Bunnie, Edmund. *Institutio christianae religionis, a Ioanne Calvino conscripta, compendium simul, ac methodi enarratio, per Edmundum Bunnium.* Antwerp: Aegidius Radaeus, 1582.

———. *The Institutions of Christian Religion, written by that reverend father, D. Iohn Calvin, compendiously abridged by Edmund Bunnie.* London: Thomas Dawson, 1578, 1580.

Chandieu, Antoine. *De verbo Dei scripto. . . . Praefatio de vera methodo theologice simul et scholastice disputandi.* In *Opera theologica.* Geneva: Le Preux, 1593.

Chemnitz, Martin. *Loci theologici,* ed. Polyarp Leyser, 3 pts. Frankfurt: Johannes Spies, 1591–94.

Cicero. *Ad C. Herrenium libri quattuor de arte rhetorica.* In *Scripta quae manserunt omnia,* pars I/1.

———. *Epistolae ad Q. Fratrem,* 2.13.4.

———. *M. Tullii Ciceronis scripta quae manserunt omnia.* Recognovit C. F. W. Mueller. 5 parts in 11 vols. Leipzig: B. G. Teubner, 1898–1910.

———. *Rhetoricae libri duo. Qui sunt de inventione rhetorica.* In *Scripta quae manserunt omnia,* pars. I/1.

Colladon, Nicholas. *Vie de Jean Calvin.* Geneva: François Perrin, 1564. [*CO* 21, col. 51–118]

Comenius, Johannes. *The Labyrinth of the World and the Paradise of the Heart.* Trans. Count Lützow. 1901; repr. New York: Arno Press, 1971.

Cordier, Mathurin. *Colloquiorum scholasticorum libri IIII, ad pueros in sermone Latino paulatim exercendos.* Geneva: Stephanus, 1564.

Daneau, Lambert. *Christianae isagoges ad christianorum theologorum locos communes, libri II.* Geneva: E. Vignon, 1583.

Duns Scotus, Johannes. *Duns Scotus on the Will and Morality.* Selected, trans., and intro. Allan B. Wolter. Washington, D.C.: Catholic University of America Press, 1986.

———. *Opera omnia.* Edito nova iuxta editonem Waddingi. 26 vols. Paris: Vives, 1891–95.

———. *Opus Oxoniense* (Scotus's Oxford commentary on Lombard's Sentences). In *Opera Omniá,* vols. 8–21.

———. *A Treatise on God as First Principle.* Trans. and with a commentary by Allan B. Wolter Chicago: Franciscan Herald Press, 1966.

Erasmus, Desiderius. *The Collected Works of Erasmus.* Ed. R. J. Schoeck, B. M. Corrigan, et al. Toronto: University of Toronto Press, 1974– .

————. *De libero arbitrio.* Ed. and trans. E. Gordon Rupp, in collaboration with A. N. Marlow. In *Luther and Erasmus: Free Will and Salvation.* Ed. E. Gordon Rupp and Philip S. Watson. Philadelphia: Westminster, 1969.

————. *Ratio seu methodus compendio perveniendi ad veram theologiam* [1519]. In *Desiderius Erasmus Roterodamus Ausgewählte Werke.* Ed. Hajo Holborn and Annemarie Holborn. Munich: C. H. Beck, 1933.

————. *De ratione studii ac legendi interpretandique auctores* (On the Method of Study). Ed. Craig R. Thompson. In *Collected Works of Erasmus.* Vol. 24 Toronto: University of Toronto Press, 1978.

Eusebius Pamphilius. *Eusebii Pamphili Chronici canones Latine vertit, adavxit, ad sua tempora produxit S. Eusebius Hieronymus.* Ed. J. K. Fotheringham. London: Humphrey Milford, 1923.

Evagrius Monachus. *Altercatio legis inter Simonem Iudaeum et Theophilum Christianum,* in *CSEL* 45.

Fulgentius Ruspensis. *Ad Trasamundum libri III,* in *CCSL* 91.

————. *De veritate praedestinationis et gratiae Dei,* in *CCSL* 91A.

Gregorius Ariminensis. *Super primum et secundum Sententiarum.* Venice: Luceantonius, 1522; repr. St. Bonaventure, N.Y.: Franciscan Institute, 1955.

Heidegger, Johann Heinrich. *Corpus theologiae christianae, exhibens doctrinam veritatis.* 2 vols. Zurich: J. H. Bodmer, 1700.

————. *Medulla medullae theologiae christianae.* Zurich: D. Gessner, 1697.

————. *Medulla theologiae christianae.* Zurich: D. Gessner, 1696.

Hippolytus. *Refutation of All Heresies,* X.1. ANF 5, p. 140.

Hugo, André Malan. "The Spiritual and Intellectual Background," in *Calvin's Commentary on Seneca's De Clementia,* p. *43.

Hugo de S. Victore, *De sacramentis christianae fidei,* in *PL* 176, cols. 173–618.

————. *Summa sententiarum septem tractatibus distincta,* in *PL* 176, cols. 41–174.

Hyperius, Andreas. *De formandis concionibus sacris, seu de interpretatione scripturarum populari, libri II.* Marburg: A. Colbius, 1553.

————. *De theologo, seu de ratione studii theologici.* Basel: Oporinus, 1556, 1559.

————. *Methodus theologiae, sive praecipuorum Christianae religionis locorum communium, libri tres.* Basel: Oporinus, 1567.

Jean de Paris. *Commentaire sur les Sentences.* Edition critique par Jean-Pierre Muller. 2 vols. Rome: Herder, 1961.

Jerome, *Praefatio.* In *Eusebii Chronici canones Latine vertit, adavxit, ad sua tempora produxit S. Eusebius Hieronymus,* ed. J. K. Fotheringham (London: Humphrey Milford, 1923).

Keckermann, Bartholomaus. *Operum omnium quae extant.* 2 vols. Geneva Petrus Aubertus, 1614.

————. *Systema sacrosanctae theologiae, tribus libris adornatum.* Hanover: Gulielmus Antonius, 1602.

Launeus, Gulielmus [William DeLaune]. *An Abridgement of the Institution of Christian Religion, written by M. Iohn Caluin.* Trans. Christopher Fetherstone. Edinburgh: n.p., 1585, 1586, 1587.

————. *An hundred Aphorismes . . . summarily containing the matter and method of Maister Calvines Institutions.* London: Thomas Vautrollerius, 1596.

————. *Institutionis christianae religionis a Ioanne Calvino conscriptae, Epitome in qua adversariorum obiectionibus breves ac solidae responsiones annotantur per Gulielmum Launeum.* London: Thomas Vautrollerius, 1583; *Editio secunda emendatior: Tabulis etiam & indice multo facilioribus & locupletioribus.* London: Thomas Vautrollerius, 1584.

Leigh, Edward. *A Systeme or Body of Divinity*. London: William Lee, 1662; 1664.

Luther, Martin. *Catechismus maior* in *Concordia triglotta: Libri symbolici Ecclesiae Lutrheranae*. St. Louis: Concordia, 1921.

———. *D. Martin Luthers Werke. Kritische Gesamtausgabe*. 66 vols. Weimar: Hermann Böhlaus Nachfolger, 1883–1987.

———. *Luther's Works*. 56 vols. Ed. Jaroslav Pelikan and Helmut Lehmann. St. Louis: Concordia / Philadelphia: Fortress Press, 1955–86.

Marckius, Johannes. *Christianae theologiae medulla didactico elenctica*. Amsterdam: Gerardus Borstius, 1690.

———. *Compendium theologiae christianae didactico-elencticum*. Groningen: Francisus Bronchorst, 1686.

———. *Sylloge dissertationum philologico-theologicarum, ad selectos quosdam textus Veteris Testamenti*. Leiden: Petrus Van der Aa, 1717.

Maresius, Samuel. *Collegium theologicum sive systema breve universae theologiae comprehensum octodecim disputationibus*. Groningen: Franciscus Bronchorst, 1645.

Marlowe, Christopher. *The Tragical History of Dr. Faustus, in a special version . . . including the 1592 edition of "The History of the Damnable Lide and Deserved Death of Doctor John Faustus*. Ed. Basil Ashmore. London:Blandford Press, 1948.

Melanchthon, Philip. *Elementa rhetorices*, in *CR* 13, col. 573.

———. *Loci communes theologici* (1521). Trans. Lowell Satre. In *Melanchthon and Bucer*. Ed. Wilhelm Pauck. Philadelphia: Westminster, 1969.

———. *Loci communes theologici*. Wittenberg, 1521, 1536, 1543.

———. *Loci communes 1543*. Trans. J. A. O. Preus. St. Louis: Concordia, 1992.

———. *De modo et arte concionandi*, in *Supplementa Melanchthoniana*, vol. 5.

———. *Philippi Melanchthonis opera quae supersunt omnia*. 28 vols. Ed. C. G. Bretschneider and H. E. Bindseil. Halle/Braunschweig: C. A. Schwetschke, 1834–1860. [*CR*, vols 1–28]

———. *Supplementa Melanchthoniana*. Ed. Paul Drews and Ferdinand Cohrs. 5 vols. Frankfurt: Minerva, 1968.

Mosellanus, Petrus. *Renaissance Student Life: The Paedologia of Petrus Mosellanus*. Trans. and intro. Robert Francis Seyboldt. Chicago: University of Illinois Press, 1927.

Musculus, Wolfgang. *Commentariorum in Evangelistam Ioannem*. Basel: Iohannes Hervagius, 1548.

———. *Commonplaces of Christian Religion*. 2nd ed. London: Henry Bynneman, 1578.

———. *In divi Pauli Epistolas ad Philippenses, Colosenses, Thessalonienses ambas & primum ad Timotheum commentarii*. Basel: Iohannes Hervagius, 1565.

———. *In Epistolam D. Apostoli Pauli ad Romanos commentarii*. Basel: Sebastianum Henric Petri, 1555.

———. *In Evangistam Matthaeum commentarii*. Basel: n.p., 1544.

———. *Loci communes Sacrae theologial*. Basel: Iohannes Hervagius, 1560, 1561, 1573.

Nicholas of Lyra. *Postillae perpetuae in Veteris et Novum Testamentum*. 5 vols. Rome: Conradus Sweynheym and Arnoldus Pannartz, 1471–72.

Ochino, Bernardino. *De labyrinthi, hoc est, De libero aut servo arbitrio, de divina praenotione, destinatione, et libertate disputatio*. Basel: Petrus Perna, 1561.

———. *Sermons of Barnardine Ochyne (to the Number of 25) Concerning the Predestination and Election of God*. London: John Day, ca. 1570.

Oecolampadius, Ioannes. *Annotationes piae ac doctae in Evangelium Ioannis*. Basel: Bebel & Cratander, 1533.

Olevianus, Caspar. *Institutionis religionis Christianae epitome ex Institutiones Ioh. Calvini excerpta*. Herborn: Christophorus Corvinus, 1586.

Peter Aureole. *Scriptum super primum sententiarum.* 2 vols. Ed. Eligius M. Buyaert. St. Bonaventure, N.Y.: Franciscan Institute, 1952.

Peter Lombard. *Sententiae in IV libris distinctae.* Editio tertia. 2 vols. Grottaferrata: Collegium S. Bonaventurae ad Claras Aquas, 1971–81.

Polyander, Johannes et al. *Synopsis purioris theologiae, disputationibus quinquaginta duabus comprehensa ac conscripta per Johannem Polyandrum, Andream Rivetum, Antonium Walaeum, Antonium Thysium.* Leiden: Elsevir, 1625.

Prudentius, *Apotheosis,* line 203 (*CCSL* 126, p. 84).

Quintillian. *M. Fabi Quintiliani Institutionis oratoriae, libri XII.* 2 vols. Ed. Ludovicus Rademacher. Leipzig: B. G. Teubner, 1907–11.

Sidonius Apollinaris, Caius Sollius Modestus. *Poems and Letters.* 2 vols. Trans., intro., and notes by W. B. Anderson. Cambridge: Harvard University Press, 1936–65.

Spanheim, Friedrich. *Disputationum theologicarum syntagma. Pars prima: Disputationum theologicarum miscellanearum; Pars secunda: Anti-Anabaptistica controversia.* Geneva: Chouet, 1652.

Stelling-Michaud, S., ed. *Le Livre du recteur de l'Académie de Genève.* 6 vols. Geneva: Droz, 1959–80.

Szegedinus, Stephanus. *Theologiae sincerae loci communes de Deo et Homine perpetuis Tabulis explicati et scholasticorum dogmatis illustrati.* Basel: Conrad Valdkirchium, 1588.

Thomas Aquinas. *On the Soul.* Trans. John Patrick Rowan. St. Louis: B. Herder, 1949. *St. Thomas Aquinas: Theological Texts.* Selected and trans. with notes by Thomas Gilby. Durham, N.C.: Labyrinth Press, 1982.

Summa theologiae. Cura Fratrum eiusdem Ordinis. 5 vols. Madrid: Biblioteca Auctores Cristianos, 1951.

Ursinus, Zacharias. *Doctrinae christianae compendium.* London: Henricus Midletonus, 1586.

Vermigli, Peter Martyr. *The Common Places of Peter Martyr.* Trans. Anthony Marten. London: Henry Denham, 1583.

———. *In epistolum s. Pauli apostoli ad Romanos . . . commentarii.* Basel: Petrus Perna, 1558.

———. *Loci communes.* Zurich: Froschauer, 1580.

———. *P. M. Vermilii loci communes.* London: Ioannis Kyngston, 1576; 2nd. ed., London: Thomas Vautrollerius, 1583.

Viret, Pierre. *De la vraye et fausse religion, touchant les voeus et les serments illcites . . .* Geneva: J. Rivery, 1560.

———. *Disputationes chrestiennes.* Geneva: J. Gérard, 1552.

———. *Exposition de la doctrine de la foy chrestienne, touchant la vraye cognoissance & le vray service de Dieu.* Geneva: J. Rivery, 1564.

———. *Exposition familière sur le Symbole des Apostres.* Geneva: J. Brés, 1560.

———. *Quatre sermons français sur Esaïe 65, mars 1559.* Ed. Henri Meylan. Lausanne: G. Bridel, 1961.

———. *A Verie Familiare Exposition of the Apostles Crede.* London: J. Day, n.d. [1548?].

Zwingli, Huldrych. *Commentary on True and False Religion.* Ed. Samuel M. Jackson and Clarence N. Heller. 1929; repr. Durham, N.C.: Labyrinth Press, 1981.

———. *Huldrici Zuinglii Opera completa editio prima.* Ed. Melchior Schuler and Johann Schulthess. 8 vols. in 6 Zurich: Schulthess & Höhr, 1829–42

———. *In catabaptistarum strophas elenchus,* in *CR* 93.

———. *Sämtliche Werke. Unter Mitwerkung des Zwingli-Vereins in Zürich.* 14 vols. Ed. Emil Egli et al. Leipzig: Heinsius, 1905– . [Vols. 88ff of the *Corpus Reformatorum.*]

———. *Ulrich Zwingli (1484–1531): Selected Works.* Ed. Samuel Macaulay Jackson. Philadelphia: University of Pennsylvania Press, 1972.

———. *De vera et falsa religione commentarius* (1525). In *Opera,* vol. 3.

LATER WORKS

Anderson, Marvin W. *Peter Martyr, A Reformer in Exile (1542–1562): A Chronology of Biblical Writings in England and Europe.* Nieuwkoop: DeGraaf, 1975.

————. "Theodore Beza: Savant or Scholastic?" *Theologische Zeitschrift* 43/4 (1987), pp. 320–332.

Arendt, Hannah. *The Life of the Mind.* 2 vols. New York: Harcourt, Brace, Jovanovich, 1978.

Armstrong, Brian G. *Calvinism and the Amyraut Heresy: Protestant Scholasticism and Humanism in Seventeenth-Century France.* Madison: University of Wisconsin Press, 1969.

————. "The Changing Face of French Protestantism: The Influence of Pierre Du Moulin." In *Calviniana: Ideas and Influence of Jean Calvin,* ed. Robert V. Schnucker (Kirksville, Mo.: Sixteenth Century Journal Publishers, 1988), pp. 145–49.

————. "*Duplex cognitio Dei,* Or? The Problem and Relation of Structure, Form, and Purpose in Calvin's Theology." In *Probing the Reformed Tradition: Historical Essays in Honor of Edward A. Dowey, Jr.,* ed. Elsie Anne McKee and Brian G. Armstrong (Louisville, Ky.: Westminster/John Knox, 1989), pp. 135–53.

————. "Exegetical and Theological Principles in Calvin's Preaching, with Special Attention to his Sermons on the Psalms." In *Ordentlich und Fruchtbar,* ed. Wilhelm H. Neuser and Herman Selderhuis, (Leiden: J. J. Groen en Zoon, 1997), pp. 191–203.

————. "The Nature and Structure of Calvin's Theology: Another Look." In *John Calvin's Institutes: His Opus Magnum,* ed. B. van der Walt (Potchefstroom: Institute for Reformational Studies, 1986), pp. 55–81.

Auden, W. H. *The Age of Anxiety: A Baroque Eclogue.* New York: Random House, 1947.

Augustijn, Cornelis. "Calvin und der Humanismus," in *Calvinus Servus Christi,* ed. W. H. Neuser (Budapest: Presseabteilung des Ráday-Kollegiums, 1988), pp. 127–42.

————. *Erasmus: Der Humanist als Theologe und Kirchenreformer.* Leiden: E. J. Brill, 1996.

————. *Erasmus: His Life, Works, and Influence.* Trans. J. C. Grayson. Toronto: University of Toronto Press, 1991.

Autin, Albert. *L'Institution chrétienne de Calvin.* Paris: Société Française d'Éditions Littéraires et Techniques, 1929.

Ayers, Robert H. "The View of Medieval Exegesis in Calvin's *Instiutes,*" *Perspectives in Religious Studies* 7/3 (1980), pp. 188–93.

Backus, Irena. " 'Aristotelianism' in Some of Calvin's and Beza's Expository and Exegetical Writings on the Doctrine of the Trinity, with Particular Reference to the Terms *ousia* and *hypostasis.*" In *Histoire de l'exégèse au XVIe siècle,* ed. Olivier Fatio and Pierre Fraenkel, pp. 251–60.

————. "Church, Communion and Community in Bucer's Commentary on the Gospel of John." In *Martin Bucer: Reforming Church and Community,* ed. D. F. Wright (Cambridge: Cambridge University Press, 1994), pp. 62–3.

————. "The Fathers in Calvinist Orthodoxy: Partistic Scholarship." In *The Reception of the Church Fathers in the West,* ed. Backus (Leiden: E. J. Brill, 1997), vol. 2, pp. 839–66.

————. "L'Enseignement de la logique à l'Academie de Genève entre 1559 et 1565," *Revue de Théologie et de Philosophie* 111 (1979), pp. 153–63.

Backus, Irena, ed. *The Reception of the Church Fathers in the West: From the Carolingians to the Maurists.* 2 vols. Leiden: E. J. Brill, 1997.

Backus, Irena, and Chimelli, Claire. *Le Vraie Piété: Divers traités de Jean Calvin et confession de foi de Guillaume Farel.* Geneva: Droz, 1986.

Backus, Irena, and Higman, Francis, eds. *Théorie et practique de l'exégèse.* Geneva: Droz, 1990.

Baker, J. Wayne. *Heinrich Bullinger and the Covenant: The Other Reformed Tradition.* Athens: Ohio University Press, 1980.

————. "Heinrich Bullinger, the Covenant, and the Reformed Tradition in Retrospect." In *Calvin Studies VIII*, ed. John H. Leith (Davidson, N.C.: Colloquium on Calvin Studies, 1996), pp. 58–75.

Baldwin, Claude-Marie Halbritter. "Calvin s'attaque à la persécution: Une étude comparative de son style français." Ph.D. dissertation, Michigan State University, 1984.

Balke, Willem. *Calvin and the Anabaptist Radicals.* Trans. William J. Heynen. Grand Rapids Mich.,: Eerdmans, 1981.

————. "The Word of God and Experientia according to Calvin." In *Calvinus Ecclesiae Doctor*, ed. W. H. Neuser (Kampen, J. H. Kok, 1980), pp. 19–31.

Barnaud, Jean. "L'Institution de la religion chrétienne," *Études Théologiques et réligieuses* 13/2 (1938), pp. 94–116.

————. *Pierre Viret, sa vie et son oeuvre.* 1911; repr. Nieuwkoop: DeGraaf, 1973.

Barth, Karl. *The Theology of John Calvin.* Trans. G. W. Bromiley. Grand Rapids Mich.: Eerdmans, 1995.

Battles, Ford Lewis. "Calculus Fidei." In Battles, *Interpreting John Calvin* ed. Robert Benedetto (Grand Rapids, Mich.: Baker Book House, 1996), pp. 139–78. [Also in *Calvinus Ecclesiae Doctor*, ed. W. H. Neuser, pp. 85–110.]

————. "The Future of Calviniana." In *Renaissance, Reformation, Resurgence*, ed. Peter De Klerk (Grand Rapids, Mich.: Calvin Theological Seminary, 1976), pp. 133–73.

————. *Interpreting John Calvin.* Ed. Robert Benedetto. Grand Rapids, Mich.: Baker Book House, 1996.

————. "Introductio." In *John Calvin's Sermons on the Ten Commandments*, trans. Benjamin W. Farley. (Grand Rapids, Mich.: Baker Book House, 1980).

————. "The Sources of Calvin's Seneca Commentary." In *John Calvin: A Collection of Distinguished Essays*, ed. Gervase Duffield (Grand Rapids, Mich: Eerdmans, 1966), pp. 38–66.

Bauke, Hermann. *Die Probleme der Theologie Calvins.* Leipzig, J. C. Hinrichs, 1922.

Baumgartner, Antoine. *Calvin hébraïsante et interprète de l'Ancien Testament.* Paris: Fischbacher, 1899.

Beeke, Joel R. *Assurance of Faith: Calvin, English Puritanism, and the Dutch Second Reformation.* New York: Peter Lang, 1991.

Bell, M. Charles. "Calvin and the Extent of Atonement," *Evangelical Quarterly* 55 (April 1983), pp. 115–23.

————. "Was Calvin a Calvinist?" *Scottish Journal of Theology* 36/4 (1983), pp. 535–40.

Benoit, Jean-Daniel. "Calvin à Strasbourg." In *Calvin à Strasbourg: Quatre etudes publiée à l'occasion de l'arrivée de Calvin à Strasbourg* (Strasbourg: Editions Fides, 1938), pp. 11–36.

————. "The History and Development of the Institutio: How Calvin Worked." In *John Calvin: A Collection of Distinguished Essays*, ed. Gervase E. Duffield (Grand Rapids, Mich.: Eerdmans, 1966), pp. 102–17.

Bentley, Jerry H. *Humanists and Holy Writ: New Testament Scholarship in the Renaissance.* Princeton, N.J.: Princeton University Press, 1983.

Bettoni, Efrem. *Duns Scotus: The Basic Principles of his Philosophy.* Trans. Bernardino Bonansea. Washington: CUA Press, 1961.

Beumer, Johannes. *Die theologische Methode.* In *Handbuch der Dogmengeschichte*, ed. A. Grillmeier, M. Schmaus, and L. Scheffczyk. Freiburg in Breisgau: Herder, 1972.

Bierma, Lyle D. "Covenant or Covenants in the Theology of Olevianus," *Calvin Theological Journal* 22 (1987), pp. 228–50.

————. "The Covenant Theology of Caspar Olevian." Ph.D. dissertation, Duke University, 1980.

————. "Federal Theology in the Sixteenth Century: Two Traditions?" *Westminster Theological Journal* 45 (1983), pp. 304–21.

————. *German Calvinism in the Confessional Age: The Covenant Theology of Caspar Olevianus.* Grand Rapids, Mich.: Baker Book House, 1997.

————. " 'Remember the Sabbath Day . . . ': Ursinus' Exposition of Exodus 20:8–11." In *Biblical Interpretation in the Era of the Reformation*, ed. R. A. Muller and J. L. Thompson (Grand Rapids, Mich.: Eerdmans, 1995), pp. 272–91.

————. "The Role of Covenant Theology in Early Reformed Orthodoxy," *Sixteenth Century Journal*, 21/3 (1990), pp. 453–62.

Bietenhard, Hans. "Hell, Abyss, Hades, Ghenna, Lower Regions." In *The New International Dictionary of New Testament Theology*, ed. Colin Brown. Grand Rapids, Mich.: Zondervan, 1975–79.

Bizer, Ernst. *Frühorthodoxie und Rationalismus.* Zurich: EVZ Verlag, 1963.

————. "Die reformierte Orthodoxie und der Cartesianismus," *Zeitschrift für Theologie und Kirche* 55 (1958), pp. 306–72.

Blaser, Klauspeter. *Calvins Lehre von den drei Ämtern Christi.* Zurich: EVZ Verlag, 1970.

Blondiaux, Benjamin. *De la notion de la foi d'après l'Institution chrétienne de Calvin.* Montauban: J. Vidallet, 1874.

Boegner, Marc. *Les Catéchismes de Calvin: Étude d'histoire et Catéchétique.* Pamiers: L. Labrunie, 1905.

Bohatec, J. *Budé und Calvin: Studien zur Gedankenwelt des französischen Frühhumanismus.* Graz: Herman Böhlaus, 1950.

————. *Calvin et humanisme.* Paris: Revue Historique, 1939 [from *Revue Historique* 183 (1938), pp. 207–41, and 185 (1939), pp. 71–104].

Bömer, Aloys. *Die lateinischen Schülergespräche der Humanisten . . . Quellen für die Schul- und Universitätsgeschichte des 15. und 16. Jahrhunderts.* 2 vols. Berlin, 1897–99; repr. Amsterdam: P. Schippers, 1966.

Bonansea, Bernardino. *Man and His Approach to God in John Duns Scotus.* Lanham, Md.: University Press of America, 1983.

————. "Duns Scotus' Voluntarism." in *John Duns Scotus, 1265–1965*, ed. J. K. Ryan and B. Bonansea. (Washington, D.C.: CUA Press, 1965), pp. 83–121.

Böttger, Paul C. *Calvins Institutio als Erbauungsbuch: Versuch einer literarischen Analyse.* Neukirchen: Neukirchner Verlag, 1990.

Bourke, Vernon. *Will in Western Thought: A Historical-Critical Survey.* New York: Sheed & Ward, 1964.

Bouwsma, William J. "Anxiety and the Formation of Early Modern Culture." In *After the Reformation: Essays in Honor of J. H. Hexter*, ed. Barbard C. Malament (Philadelphia: University of Pennsylvania Press, 1980), pp. 215–46.

————. "Calvin and the Renaissance Crisis of Knowing," *Calvin Theological Journal* 17/2 (1982), pp. 190–211.

————. "Calvinism as *Theologia Rhetorica.* In *Calvinism as Theologia Rhetorica*, ed. Wilhelm Wuellner (Berkeley, Calif.: Center for Hermeneutical Studies, 1986), pp. 1–21.

————. *John Calvin: A Sixteenth Century Portrait.* New York: Oxford University Press, 1988.

————. "The Spirituality of John Calvin." In *Christian Spirituality: High Middle Ages and Reformation*, ed. Jill Raitt (New York: Crossroad, 1987), pp. 318–19.

————. "The Two Faces of Humanism: Stoicism and Augustinianism in Renaissance Thought." In *Itinerarium Italicum: The Profile of the Italian Renaissance in the Mirror of Its European Transformations*, ed. Thomas A. Brady and Heiko A. Oberman (Leiden: E. J. Brill, 1975), pp. 3–60.

Bray, John S. *Theodore Beza's Doctrine of Predestination.* Nieuwkoop: DeGraaf, 1975.

Breen, Quirinus. *John Calvin: A Study in French Humanism.* Grand Rapids, Mich.: Eerdmans, 1931.

————. "John Calvin and the Rhetorical Tradition." In *Christianity and Humanism: Studies in the History of Ideas* (Grand Rapids, Mich.: Eerdmans, 1968), pp. 107–29.

————. "The Terms '*Loci communes*' and '*Loci*' in Melanchthon," in *Christianity and Humanism: Studies in the History of Ideas* (Grand Rapids, Mich.: Eerdmans, 1968), pp. 93–97.

Bremme, Hans Joachim. *Buchdrucker und Buchhändler zur Zeit der Glaubenskämpfe: Studien zur Genfer Druckgeschichte, 1565–1580*. Geneva: Droz, 1969.

Brunner, Peter. *Vom Glauben bei Calvin*. Tübingen: J. C. B. Mohr, 1925.

Büsser, Fritz. "Bullinger as Calvin's Model in Biblical Exposition: An Examination of Calvin's Preface to the Epistle to the Romans." In *In Honor of John Calvin, 1509–64*, ed. E. J. Furcha (Montreal: McGill University Press, 1987), pp. 64–95.

————. "Calvin's Institutio: Einige Gedanken über ihre Bedeutung," *Zwingliana* 11/2 (1059), pp. 93–105.

————. "Elements of Zwingli's Thought in Calvin's *Institutes*." In *In Honor of John Calvin, 1509–64*, ed. E. J. Furcha, (Montreal: McGill University Press, 1987), pp. 1–27.

Butin, Philip W. *Revelation, Redemption, and Response: Calvin's Trinitarian Understanding of the Divine-Human Relationship*. New York: Oxford University Press, 1995.

Capanaga, Victorino. "El Hombre-Abismo, segun San Augustin," *Augustinus* 20 (1975), pp. 225–52.

Chomarat, Jacques. *Grammaire et rhétorique chez Erasmus*. 2 vols. [Les Classiques de l'humanisme. Etudes, vol. 10]. Paris: Belles Lettres, 1981.

Clark, Mary T. *Augustine, Philosopher of Freedom: A Study in Comparative Philology*. New York: Desclée, 1958.

Clavier, Henri. "Calvin commentateur biblique." in *Études sur le calvinisme*, ed. H. Clavier (Paris: Fischbacher, 1936), pp. 99–144.

Cohrs, Ferdinand. *Die Evangelischen Katechismusversuche vor Luthers Enchiridion*. 5 vols. Berlin: A. Hofmann, 1900–1907; repr., 2 vols., Hildesheim: George Olms, 1978.

Colish, Marcia L. *Peter Lombard*. 2 vols. Leiden: E. J. Brill, 1994.

Compier, Don H. "The Independent Pupil: Calvin's Transformation of Erasmus' Theological Hermeneutics," *Westminster Theological Journal* 54 (1992), pp. 217–233.

Congar, Yves M.-J. *A History of Theology*. Trans. Hunter Guthrie. Garden City, N.Y.: Doubleday, 1968.

Copleston, Frederick C. *Aquinas*. Baltimore: Penguin, 1955.

Costello, William T. *The Scholastic Curriculum at Early Seventeenth-Century Cambridge* (Cambridge, Mass.: Harvard University Press, 1958.

Cottrell, Jack W. "Covenant and Baptism in the Theology of Huldreich Zwingli." Th.D. dissertation, Princeton Theological Seminary, 1971.

Courtenay, William J. *Capacity and Volition: A History of the Distinction of Absolute and Ordained Power*. Bergamo: P. Lubrina, 1990.

————. *Covenant and Causality in Medieval Thought: Studies in Philosophy, Theology, and Economic Practice*. London: Variorum Reprints, 1984.

————. "The Dialectic of Omnipotence in the High and Late Middle Ages." In Rudavsky, *Divine Omniscience and Omnipotence in Medieval Philosophy* (Dordrecht: Riedel, 1985), ed.? pp. 243–269.

————. "Nominalism in Late Medieval Religion." In *The Pursuit of Holiness in Late Medieval Religion* (Leiden: E. J. Brill, 1974), ed. C. Trinkhaus and H. Oberman pp. 26–59.

Courvoisier, Jacques. "La haute école de Genève au 16e siècle d'après le discours de Théodore de Bèze," *Theologische Zeitschrift*, 35 (1979), pp. 169–76.

Cremeans, Charles D. *The Reception of Calvinistic Thought in England*. Urbana: University of Illinois Press, 1949.

Curtis, Mark H. *Oxford and Cambridge in Transition, 1558–1642: An Essay on Changing Relations between the English University and English Society.* Oxford: Clarendon Press, 1959.

D'Amico, John F. "Humanism and Pre-Reformation Theology." In *Renaissance Humanism,* ed. Albert Rabil Jr. (Philadelphia: University of Pennsylvania Press, 1988), vol. 3, pp. 349–79.

Dantine, Johannes. "Das christologische Problem in Rahmen der Prädestinationslehre von Theodor Beza," *Zeitschrift für Kirchengeschichte,* 77 (1966), pp. 81–96.

———. "Les Tabelles sur la doctrine de la prédestination par Théodore de Bèze," *Revue de théologie et de philosophie* 16 (1966), pp. 365–77.

Davies, Rupert E. *The Problem of Authority in the Continental Reformers: A Study in Luther, Zwingli, and Calvin.* London: Epworth, 1946.

De Greef, Wulfert. "Das Verhältnis von Predigt und Kommentar bei Calvin, dargestellt an den Deuteronomium Kommentar und den Predigten." In *Calvinus Servus Christi,* ed. W. H. Nevser (Budapest: Presseabteilung des Ráday-Kollegiums, 1988), pp. 195–204.

———. *The Writings of John Calvin: An Introductory Guide.* Trans. Lyle D. Bierma. Grand Rapids, Mich.: Baker Book House, 1993.

De Jong. Peter Y., ed. *Crisis in the Reformed Churches: Essays in Commemoration of the Great Synod of Dort, 1618–1619.* Grand Rapids, Mich.: Reformed Fellowship, 1968.

De Klerk, Peter. "Calvin Bibliography," published annually in *Calvin Theological Journal,* beginning with vol. 6 (1971).

De Klerk, Peter, ed. *Calvin and Christian Ethics.* Papers and responses presented at the Fifth Colloquium on Calvin and Calvin Studies, May 8–9, 1985. Grand Rapids, Mich.: Calvin Studies Society, 1987.

———, ed. *Calvin and the Holy Spirit.* Papers and responses presented at the Sixth Colloquium on Calvin and Calvin Studies, May 6–7, 1987. Grand Rapids, Mich.: Calvin Studies Society, 1989.

———, ed. *Calvin and the State.* Papers and responses presented at the Seventh and Eighth Colloquia on Calvin and Calvin Studies, October 26–29, 1989, and May 8–9, 1991. Grand Rapids, Mich.: Calvin Studies Society, 1993.

———, ed. *Calvin as Exegete.* Papers and responses presented at the Ninth Colloquium on Calvin and Calvin Studies, May 20–22, 1993. Grand Rapids, Mich.: Calvin Studies Society, 1995.

———, ed. *Renaissance, Reformation, Resurgence.* Papers and responses presented at the Colloquium on Calvin and Calvin Studies, April 22–23, 1976. Grand Rapids, Mich.: Calvin Theological Seminary, 1976.

Dee, Simon Pieter. *Het Geloofsbegrip van Calvijn.* Kampen: J. H. Kok, 1918.

Delormeau, Charles. *Un Maître de Calvin: Mathurin Cordier, l'un des créateurs de l'enseignement secondaire moderne 1479–1564.* Neuchatel: Éditions H. Messeiller, 1976.

DeVries, Dawn. *Jesus Christ in the Preaching of Calvin and Schleiermacher.* Louisville, Ky.: Westminster/John Knox Press, 1996.

Dictionnaire de théologie catholique. Ed. A. Vacant et al. 23 vols. Paris: Letouzey et Ane, 1923–50.

Dielhe, Albrecht. *The Theory of Will in Classical Antiquity.* Berkeley: University of California Press, 1982.

Dillenberger, John. *Contours of Faith: Changing Forms of Christian Thought.* Nashville, Tenn.: Abingdon, 1969.

Dodds, E. R. *Pagan and Christian in an Age of Anxiety: Some Aspects of Religious Experience from Marcus Aurelius to Constantine.* New York: Norton, 1970.

Dolfen, Christian. *Die Stellung des Erasmus von Rotterdam zur scholastischen Methode.* Osnabrück: Meinders & Elstermann, 1936.

Donnelly, John Patrick. *Calvinism and Scholasticism in Vermigli's Doctrine of Man and Grace.* Leiden: E. J. Brill, 1975.

———. "Calvinist Thomism," *Viator* 7 (1976), pp. 441–45.

———. "Italian Influences in the Development of Calvinist Scholasticism," *Sixteenth Century Journal* 7/1, pp. 81–101.

———. "Response to Jacques Lefèvre d'Étaples: From Philosophy to Sola Scriptura." In *Renaissance, Reformation, Resurgence,* ed. Peter De Klerk, (Grand Rapids, Mich.: Calvin Theological Seminary, 1976), pp. 49–57.

Doob, Penelope Reed. *The Idea of the Labyrinth from Classical Antiquity Through the Middle Ages.* Ithaca, N.Y.: Cornell University Press, 1990.

Doppler, Alfred. *Der Abgrund: Studien zur Bedeutungsgeschichte eines Motivs.* Graz: Böhlau, 1968.

Douglass, Jane Dempsey. *Women, Freedom, and Calvin.* Philadelphia: Westminster, 1985.

Doumergue, Emil. *Jean Calvin, les hommes et les choses de son temps.* 7 vols. Lausanne: G. Bridel, 1899–1927.

Dowey, Edward A. "Heinrich Bullinger as Theologian: Thematic, Comprehensive, Schematic." In *Calvin Studies V,* ed. John H. Leith, (Davidson, N.C.: Colloquium on Calvin Studies, 1992), pp. 41–60.

———. *The Knowledge of God in Calvin's Theology.* New York: Columbia University Press, 1952; 3rd exp. ed., Grand Rapids, Mich.: Eerdmans, 1994.

———. "The Structure of Calvin's Theological Thought as Influenced by the Two-fold Knowledge of God." In *Calvinus Ecclesiae Genevensis Custos,* ed. W. H. Neuser (Frankfurt am Main: Peter Lang, 1984), pp. 135–48.

Duckert, Armand. *Théodore de Bèze: Prédicateur.* Geneva: Romet, 1891.

Duffield, Gervase E. *John Calvin: A Collection of Distinguished Essays.* Grand Rapids, Mich.: Eerdmans, 1966.

Dumitriu, Anton. *History of Logic.* 4 vols. Tunbridge Wells, Kent: Abacus Press, 1977.

Ebeling, Gerhard. "The Meaning of 'Biblical Theology.' " In *Word and Faith,* trans. J. Leitch (London: SCM, 1963), pp. 79–97.

Eliott, Mark W. "Calvin the Hebraiser?" In *Interpreting the Bible,* ed. A. N. S. Lane (Leicester: Apollos, 1997), pp. 99–112.

Emmen, Egbert *Christologie van Calvijn.* Amsterdam: H. J. Paris, 1935.

Engammare, Max. "Calvin connaissait-il la Bible? Les Citations de l'Écriture dans les sermons sur la Genèse," *Bulletin de la Societé d'Histoire du Protestantisme Français* 141 (1995), pp. 163–84.

———. "Calvin Incognito in London: The Rediscovery in London of sermons on Isaiah," *Proceedings of the Huguenot Society* 26/4 (1996), pp. 453–62.

———. "Joannes Calvinus trium linguarum peritus? La question de l'Hébreu," *Bibliothèque d'Humanisme et Renaissance* 58 (1996), pp. 35–60.

———. "Le Paradis à Genève. Comment Calvin prèchait-il la chute aux Genevois?" *Études Théologiques et Religieuses* 69 (1994), pp. 329–47.

Engel, Mary Potter. *John Calvin's Perspectival Anthropology.* Atlanta: Scholars Press, 1988.

Faber, Jelle. "Nominalisme in Calvijns preken over Job." In *Een sprekend begin,* ed. R. ter Beek et al. (Kampen: Uitgeverij Van den Berg, 1993), pp. 68–85.

Farge, James K. *Biographical Register of Paris Doctors of Theology, 1500–1536.* Toronto: Pontifical Institute of Medieval Studies, 1980.

———. *Orthodoxy and Reform in Early Reformation France: The Faculty of Theology of Paris, 1500–1543.* Leiden: E. J. Brill, 1985.

Farley, Benjamin W. "Recurring Hermeneutical Principles in Calvin's Sermons, Polemical Treatises, and Correspondence." In *Calvin as Exegete,* ed. Peter De Klerk (Grand Rapids, Mich.: Calvin Studies Society (1995) pp. 69–87.

Farmer, Craig S. *The Gospel of John in the Sixteenth Century: The Johannine Exegesis of Wolfgang Musculus.* New York: Oxford University Press, 1997.

Fatio, Olivier. "Hyperius plagié par Flacius: La destinée d'une méthode exégetique." In *Histoire del exégèse au XVIe siècle,* ed. Olivier Fatio and Pierre Fraenkel Geneva: Droz, 1978), pp. 362–81.

———. "Présence de Calvin à l'époque de l'orthodoxie réformée: Les abrégés de Calvin à la fin du 16e et au 17e siècle." In (ed.), *Calvinus Ecclesiae Doctor,* ed. W. H. Neuser (Kampan: J. H. Kok, 1980), pp. 171–207.

Fatio, Olivier, and Fraenkel, Pierre, ed. *Histoire del exégèse au XVIe siècle.* Textes du Colloque International tenu à Genève en 1976. Geneva: Droz, 1978.

Faust, A. "Die Dialektik R. Agricolas: Ein Beitrag zur Charakteristik des deutschen Humanismus," *Archiv für Geschichte der Philosophie* 34 (1922), pp. 118–35.

Fischer, Danièle. "Calvin et la Confession d'Augsbourg." In *Calvinus Ecclesiae Genevensis Custos,* ed. ed. W. H. Neuser (Frankfurt am Main: Peter Lang, 1984), pp. 245–71.

———. "L'Élément historique dans la prédication de Calvin: Un aspect original de l'homilétique du Réformateur," *Revue d'Historie et de Philosophie Religieuses* 64 (1984), pp. 365–86.

Forestier, Victor. *Calvin: Exégète de l'Ancien Testament.* Lausanne: Georges Bridel, 1873.

Forstman, H. J. *Word and Spirit: Calvin's Doctrine of Biblical Authority.* Stanford: Stanford University Press, 1962.

Foxgrover, David. "John Calvin's Understanding of Conscience." Ph.D. dissertation, Claremont Graduate School, 1978.

———. " 'Temporary Faith' and the Certainty of Salvation," *Calvin Theological Journal* 15 (1980), pp. 220–32.

Fraenkel, Peter, *De l'écriture à la dispute. Le cas de l'Académie de Genève sous Théodore de Bèze.* Lausanne: Revue de Théologie et de Philosophie, 1977.

———. *Testimonia Patrum: The Function of the Patristic Argument in the Theology of Philip Melanchthon.* Geneva: Droz, 1961.

Fritz, G., and Michel, A. "Scholastique," s.v. in *Dictionnaire de théologie catholique.*

Fuhrmann, Paul T. "Calvin: Expositor of Scripture," *Interpretation* 6 (1952), pp. 188–209.

Fullerton, Kemper. *Prophecy and Authority: A Study in the History of the Doctrine and Interpretation of Scripture.* New York: Macmillan, 1919.

Furcha, E. J., ed. *In Honor of John Calvin, 1509–64.* Papers from the 1986 International Calvin Symposium. Montreal: McGill University, Press, 1987.

Gaberel, Jean Pierre. *Histoire de l'Église de Génève depuis le commencement de la Reformation jusqu'à nos jours.* 3 vols. Geneva: J. Cherbuliez, 1858–62.

Gamble, Richard C. "*Brevitas et facilitas:* Toward an Understanding of Calvin's Hermeneutic," *Westminster Theological Journal* 47 (1985), pp. 1–17.

———. "Calvin as Theologian and Exegete: Is There Anything New?" *Calvin Theological Journal* 23 (1988), pp. 178–94.

———. "Calvin's Theological Method: The Case of Caroli." In *Calvin: Erbe und Auftrag,* ed. Willem van 't Spijker (Kanipan: Kok Pharos, 1991), pp. 130–37.

———. "Exposition and Method in Calvin," *Westminster Theological Journal* 49 (1987), pp. 153–65.

———. "Sources of Calvin's Genesis Commentary: A Preliminary Report," *Archiv für Reformationsgeschichte* 84 (1993), pp. 206–21.

Ganoczy, Alexandre. *La Bibliothéque de l'Académie de Calvin.* Geneva: Droz, 1969.

———. *Calvin, théologien de l'Église et du ministère.* Paris: Editions du Cerf, 1964.

———. *Le jeune Calvin: Genèse et évolution de sa vocation réformatrice.* Wiesbaden: F. Steiner, 1966.

———. *The Young Calvin*. Trans. David Foxgrover and Wade Provo. Philadelphia: Westminster, 1987.

Ganoczy, Alexandre, and Müller, Klaus. *Calvins Handschriftlighe Annotationen zu Chrysostomus: Ein Beitrag zur Hermeneutik Calvins*. Wiesbaden: F. Steiner, 1981.

Ganoczy, Alexandre, and Scheld, Stefan. *Die Hermeneutik Calvins: Geistesgeschichtliche Voraussetzungen und Grundzüge*. Wiesbaden: F. Steiner, 1983.

Gardeil, A. "La Certitude probable," *Revue des Sciences Philosophiques et Théologiques* (1911), pp. 237–66, 441–85.

———. "La Notion du lieu théologique," *Revue des Sciences Philosophiques et Théologiques* (1908), pp. 51–73, 246–76, 484–505.

———. "La Topicité," *Revue des Sciences Philosophiques et Théologiques* (1911), pp. 750–57.

Gardy, Frédéric, and Dufour, Alain, eds. *Bibliographie des oeuvres théologiques, littéraires, historiques et juridiques de Théodore de Bèze*. Geneva: Droz, 1960.

Garrigou-Lagrange, Reginald. *The Theological Virtues*. 2 vols. Trans. Thomas à Kempis Reilly. St. Louis: Herder, 1965.

Geisendorf, Paul-F. *Théodore de Bèze*. Geneva: Laboret et Fides, 1949.

Gerrish, Brian A. "Biblical Authority and the Continental Reformation," *Scottish Journal of Theology*, 10 (1957), pp. 337–60.

———. *Grace and Gratitude: The Eucharistic Theology of John Calvin*. Minneapolis: Fortress Press, 1993.

Gessert, Robert A. "The Integrity of Faith: An Inquiry into the Meaning of Law in the Thought of John Calvin," *Scottish Journal of Theology* 13 (1960), pp. 133–71.

Gilbert, Neal W. *Renaissance Concepts of Method*. New York: Columbia University Press, 1960.

Gilby, Thomas. *St. Thomas Aquinas, Theological Texts*. Durham, N.C.: Labyrinth Press, 1982.

Gilson, Etienne. *The Christian Philosophy of St. Augustine*. Trans. L. E. M. Lynch. New York: Random House, 1967.

———. *The Christian Philosophy of St. Thomas Aquinas*. Trans. L. K. Shook. New York: Random House, 1956.

———. *The Spirit of Medieval Philosophy*. Trans. A. H. C. Downes. New York: Scribner, 1936.

Girardin, Benoit. *Rhetorique et théologie. Calvin: L'Epître au Romains*. Paris: Beauchesne, 1979.

Gonin, Louis. *Les Catéchismes de Calvin et d'Ostervald: Étude historique et comparative*. Montauban: J. Granié, 1893.

Graham, W. Fred. "Calvin and the Political Order: An Analysis of Three Explanatory Studies." In *Calviniana: Ideas and Influence of John Calvin*, ed. Robert V. Schnucker, vol. 10, *Sixteenth-Century Essays and Studies* (Kirksville, Mo.: Sixteenth Century Publishers, 1988), pp. 51–61.

Gregory, Brad S. "The 'True and Zealouse Seruice of God': Robert Parsons, Edmund Bunny, and *The First Booke of the Christian Exercise*," *Journal of Ecclesiastical History* 45/2 (April 1994), pp. 238–68.

Grin, Edmond, "L'Unité des deux Testaments selon Calvin," *Theologische Zeitschrift* 17 (1961), pp. 175–86.

Haas, Guenther H. *The Concept of Equity in Calvin's Ethics*. Waterloo, Ontario: Wilfrid Laurier University Press, 1997.

Hagen, Kenneth. "What Did the Term *Commentarius* Mean to Sixteenth-century Theologians?" In *Théorie et practique de l'exégèse*, ed. Irena Backus and Francis Higman (Geneva: Droz, 1990), pp. 13–38.

Hagenbach, Karl R. *A History of Christian Doctrines*. 3 vols. Trans. E. H. Plumptre. 3 vols. Edinburgh: T. & T. Clark, 1880–81.

Hall, Basil. "Calvin against the Calvinists." In *John Calvin: A Collection of Distinguished Essays*, ed. Gervase E. Duffield (Grama Rapids, Mich.: Eerdmans, 1966), pp. 19–37.

————. "Calvin and Biblical Humanism," *Huguenot Society Proceedings* 20 (1959–64), pp. 195–209.

Harper, George W. "Calvin and English Calvinism to 1649: A Review Article," *Calvin Theological Journal* 20/ 2 (1985), pp. 255–62.

Hauser, Henri. *Études sur la Réforme française.* Paris: Alphonse Picard et Fils, 1909.

Hazlett, W. Ian P. "Calvin's Latin Preface to His Proposed French Edition of Chrysostom's Homilies: Translation and Commentary." In *Humanism and Reform: The Church in Europe, England, and Scotland, 1400–1643. Essays in Honour of James K. Cameron,* ed. James Kirk (Oxford: Basil Blackwell, 1991), pp. 129–50.

Helm, Paul. *Calvin and the Calvinists.* Carlisle, Pa.: Banner of Truth, 1982.

————. "Calvin (and Zwingli) on Divine Providence," *Calvin Theological Journal* 29/2 (1994), pp. 388–405.

Henry, Paul. *The Life and Times of John Calvin, the Great Reformer.* 2 vols. Trans. Henry Stebbing. New York: Robert Carter, 1851.

Hesselink, I. John. *Calvin's Concept of the Law.* Allison Park, Pa.: Pickwick Publications, 1992.

————. "The Development and Purpose of Calvin's Institutes," *Reformed Theological Review* 24 (1965), pp. 65–72.

————. "Reactions to Bouwsma's Portrait of 'John Calvin'." In *Calvinus Sacrae Scripturae Professor,* ed. W. H. Neuser (Grand Rapid, Mich.: Eurdt mans, 199 pp. 209–13.

Higman, Francis. *Censorship and the Sorbonne: A Bibliographical Study of Books in French Censured by the Faculty of Theology in the University of Paris, 1520–1551.* Geneva: Droz, 1979.

————. "Introduction." In Jean Calvin, *Sermons sur le Livre d'Esaïe Chapitres 30–41* (Neukirchen-Vluyn: Nerkirchner Verlag, 1995)

————. "Linearity in Calvin's Thought," *Calvin Theological Journal* 26 (1991), pp. 100–10.

————. *The Style of John Calvin in His French Polemical Treatises.* London: Oxford University Press, 1967.

Hoekema, Anthony. "Calvin's Doctrine of the Covenant of Grace," *Reformed Review* 15 (1962), pp. 1–12.

————. "The Covenant of Grace in Calvin's Teaching," *Calvin Theological Journal* 2 (1967), pp. 133–61.

Hoenderdaal, Gerrit Jan. "The Life and Struggle of Arminius in the Dutch Republic." In *Man's Faith and Freedom: The Theological Influence of Jacob Arminius.* New York: Abingdon Press, 1973.

Hoffmann, Manfred. *Rhetoric and Theology: The Hermeneutic of Erasmus.* Toronto: University of Toronto Press, 1994.

Hollweg, Walter. *Heinrich Bullingers Hausbuch.* Neukirchen: Kreis Moers, 1956.

Holtrop, Philip C. *The Bolsec Controversy on Predestination, from 1551 to 1555.* Vol. I, parts 1–2. Lewiston, Canada: Edwin Mellen, 1993.

Hoogland, Marvin P. *Calvin's Perspective on the Exaltation of Christ in Comparison with the Post-Reformation Doctrine of the Two States.* Kampen: J. H. Kok, 1966.

Höpfl, Harro. *The Christian Polity of John Calvin.* Cambridge: Cambridge University Press, 1982.

Hughes, Philip Edgcumbe. "Jacques Lefèvre d'Étaples: From Philosophy to Sola Scriptura." In *Renaissance, Reformation, Resurgence,* ed. Peter De Klerk (Grand Rapids, Mich.: Calvin Theological Seminary, 1976), pp. 33–47.

Hunter, Adam Mitchell. *The Teaching of Calvin: A Modern Interpretation.* London: James Clarke, 1950.

Imbart de la Tour, Pierre. *Les Origines de la réforme.* 4 vols. [I. *La France moderne;* II. *L'Église catholique et la crise de la renaissance;* III. *L'Évangelisme (1521–1538);* IV. *Calvin et l'Institution Chrétienne*] Paris: Hachette/Firmin-Didot, 1905–35.

Jacob, Edmond. *Theology of the Old Testament.* Trans. Arthur Heathcote and Philip Allcock. New York: Harper & Row, 1958.

Jacobs, Paul. *Prädestination und Verantwortlichkeit bei Calvin.* Neukirchen: Kreis Moers, 1937.

Jansen, John Frederick. *Calvin's Doctrine of the Work of Christ.* London: J. Clark, 1956.

Jardine, Lisa. "Inventing Rudolf Agricola: Cultural Transmission, Renaissance Dialectic, and the Emerging Humanities." in *The Transmission of Culture in Early Modern Europe,* ed. A. Grafton and A. Blair (Philadelphia: University of Pennsylvania Press, 1990), pp. 39–86.

———. "Ghosting the Reform of Rhetoric: Erasmus and Agricola Again." In *Renaissance Rhetoric,* ed. Peter Mack (London: St. Martin's Press, 1994), pp. 27–45.

Jeremias, Joachim. "Abyssos" and "Hades," s.v. in *Theological Dictionary of the New Testament,* ed. Gerhard Kittel, trans. and ed. Geoffrey W. Bromiley. 15 vols. Grand Rapids, Mich.: Eerdmans, 1964–76.

John Calvin's Institutes: His Opus Magnum. Proceedings of the Second South African Congress for Calvin Research, July 31–August 3, 1984. Potchefstroom: Institute for Reformational Studies, 1986.

Jones, Serene. *Calvin and the Rhetoric of Piety.* Louisville, Ky.: Westminster/John Knox, 1995.

Kahane, Henry, and Kahane, Renée. "Christian and Un-Christian Etymologies," *Harvard Theological Review* 57 (1964), pp. 23–38.

Kahl, Wilhelm. *Die Lehre vom Primat des Willens bei Augustinus, Duns Scotus und Descartes.* Strassburg: Trübner, 1886.

Kelly, Douglas. "Varied Themes in Calvin's 2 Samuel Sermons and the Development of His Thought." In *Calvinus Sincerioris Religionis Vindex,* ed. (Kirlesville, Mo.: Sixteenth Century Journal Publishers, 1997), pp. 209–24.

Kempff, D. *A Bibliography of Calviniana, 1959–1974.* Leiden: E. J. Brill, 1975.

Kendall, R. T. *Calvin and English Calvinism to 1649.* New York: Oxford University Press, 1979.

———. "The Puritan Modification of Calvin's Theology." In *John Calvin: His Influence in the Western World,* ed. W. Stanford Reid (Grand Rapids, Mich.: Zondervan, 1982), pp. 197–214.

Kenny, Anthony. "Disputations of the Theologians." In *The Cambridge History of Later Medieval Philosophy,* ed. N. Kretzmann, A. Kenny, J. Pinborg, and E. Stump (Cambridge: Cambridge University Press, 1982).

Kickel, Walter. *Vernunft und Offenbarung bei Theodor Beza.* Neukirchen: Neukirchner Verlag, 1967.

Kingdon, Robert M. "The First Expression of Theodore Beza's Political Ideas," in *Archiv für Reformationsgeschichte,* 46 (1955), pp. 88–99.

Klooster, Fred H. *Calvin's Doctrine of Predestination.* Calvin Theological Seminary Monograph Series, 3. Grand Rapids, Mich.: Calvin Theological Seminary, 1961.

Knowles, David. *The Evolution of Medieval Thought.* New York: Vintage Books, 1962.

Koch, Ernst. *Die Theologie der Confessio Helvetica Posterior.* Neukirchen: Neukirchner Verlag, 1968.

Köhler, Ludwig. *Old Testament Theology.* Trans. A. S. Todd. Philadelphia: Westminster, 1957.

Kohls, Ernst Wilhelm. *Die Theologie des Erasmus.* 2 vols. Basel: F. Reinhardt, 1966.

Kok, Joel Edward. "The Influence of Martin Bucer on Calvin's Interpretation of Romans: A Comparative Case Study." Ph.D dissertation, Duke University, 1993.

Kolb, Robert. "Teaching the Text: The Commonplace Method in Sixteenth-century Lutheran Biblical Commentary," *Bibliothèque d'Humanisme et Renaissance* 49 (1987), pp. 571–85.

Köstlin, Julius. "Calvin's *Institutio* nach Form und Inhalt, in ihrer geschlichtlichen Entwicklung," *Theologische Studien und Kritiken* 41 (1868), pp. 7–62, 410–86.

Kraus, Hans Joachim. "Calvin's Exegetical Principles," *Interpretation* 31 (1977), pp. 329–41.

Kristeller, Paul Oskar. *Renaissance Thought: The Classic, Scholastic, and Humanist Strains*. New York: Harper & Row, 1961.

Krusche, Werner. *Das Wirken des Hl. Geistes nach Calvin*. Göttingen: Vandenhoeck & Ruprecht, 1957.

Kunz, A. J. *Gods kennis en wil volgens de jonge Gomarus: de plaat van Gods kennis en wil in de predestinatieleer van de jonge Gomarus (1599–1609)*. Utrecht: Faculteit der Godgeleerdheid, n.d.

Landgraf, Arthur M. *Dogmengeschichte der Fruhscholastik*, 4 vols. in 8. Regensburg: F. Pustet, 1952–56.

Lane, Anthony N. S. "Bernard of Clairvaux: A Forerunner of Calvin?" In *Bernardus Magister*, ed. John R. Sommerfeldt (Kalamazoo, Mich.: Cistercian Publications, 1993), pp. 533–45.

———. "Calvin's Doctrine of Assurance," *Vox Evangelica*, 11 (1979), pp. 32–54.

———. "Calvin's Sources of St. Bernard," *Archiv für Reformationsgeschichte* 67 (1982), pp. 258–78.

———. "Calvin's Use of Bernard of Clairvaux." In *Bernhard von Clairvaux: Rezeption und Wirkung im Mittelalter und in der Neuzeit*, ed. Kaspar Elm (Wiesbaden: Harrassowitz Verlag, 1994), pp. 303–32.

———. "Calvin's Use of the Fathers and the Medievals," *Calvin Theological Journal* 16 (1981), pp. 149–205.

———. "Did Calvin Believe in Free Will?" *Vox Evangelica* 12 (1981), pp. 79–80.

———. "Did Calvin Use Lippoman's *Catena in Genesim*?" *Calvin Theological Journal* 31/2 (1996), pp. 404–19.

———. "Justification in Sixteenth-Century Patristic Anthologies." In *Auctoritas Patrum: Contributions on the Reception of the Church Fathers in the 15th and 16th Century*, ed. Leif Grane, Alfred Schindler, and Markus Wriedt (Mainz: Verlag Philipp von Zabern, 1994), pp. 69–95.

———. "The Sources of Calvin's Citations in his Genesis Commentary." In *Interpreting the Bible*, ed. Lane (Leicester: Apollos, 1997), pp. 47–97.

Lane, A. N. S., ed. *Interpreting the Bible: Historical and Theological Studies in Honour of David F. Wright*. Leicester: Apollos, 1997.

Lang, August. "Luther und Calvin." In *Reformation und Gegenwart*, ed. Lang (Detmold: Meyersche Hofbuchhandlung, 1918), pp. 72–87.

———. "Melanchthon und Calvin." In *Reformation und Gegenwart*, ed. Lang (Detmold: Meyersche Hofbuchhandlung, 1918), pp. 88–135.

———. *Reformation und Gegenwart: Gesammelte Aufsätze vornehmlich zur Geschichte und zum Verständnis Calvins und der reformierten Kirche*. Detmold: Meyersche Hofbuchhandlung, 1918.

———. "The Sources of Calvin's Institutes of 1536," *Evangelical Quarterly* 8 (1936), pp. 131–40.

LaVallee, Armand Aime. "Calvin's Criticism of Scholastic Theology." Ph.D. dissertation, Harvard University, 1967.

Lawn, Brian. *The Rise and Decline of the Scholastic "Quaestio disputata"—With Special Emphasis on Its Use in the Teaching of Medicine and Science*. Leiden: E. J. Brill, 1993.

Le Coultre, Jules. *Maturin Cordier et les origines de la pédagogie protestante dans les pays de langue française (1530–1564)*. Neuchatel: Secrétariat de l'Université, 1926.

Lechler, Joan. *Renaissance Concepts of Commonplace*. New York: Pageant, 1962.

Lee, Sou-Young. "Calvin's Understanding of Pietas." In *Calvinus Sincerioris Religionis Vindex*, ed. Brian G. Armstrong Whilhelm H. Neuser and (Kirksnlle, Mo.: Sixteenth Century Journal Publishers, 1997), pp. 225–40.

Lefranc, Abel, *Calvin et l'éloquence française*. Paris: Fischbacher, 1934.

———. *Grands écrivains français de la Renaissance*. Paris: Librairie Honoré Champion, 1914.

———. "Introduction," in *Institution de la religion chrestienne de Calvin*: Texte original de 1541 réimprimé sous la direction de Abel Lefranc par Henri Chatelain et Jacques Pannier (Paris: Librairie Honoré Champion, 1911), pp. 1*–57*.

———. *La Jeunesse de Calvin*. Paris: Fischbacher, 1888.

Leith, John H. "Calvin's Theological Method and Ambiguity in His Theology." In *Reformation Studies: Essays in Honor of R. H. Bainton*, ed. F. Littell (Richmond, Va.: John Knox, 1962), pp. 106–14.

———. "The Doctrine of the Will in the *Institutes of the Christian Religion*." In *Reformatio Perennis: Essays on Calvin and the Reformation in Honor of Ford Lewis Battles*, ed. by B. A. Gerrish, in collaboration with Robert Benedetto (Pittsburgh: Pickwick Press, 1981), pp. 49–66.

———. *John Calvin's Doctrine of the Christian Life*. Foreword by Albert C. Outler. Louisville, Ky.: Westminster/John Knox Press, 1989.

Leith, John H, ed. *Calvin Studies V*. Davidson, N.C.: Colloquium on Calvin Studies, 1990.

———, ed. *Calvin Studies VI*. Davidson, N.C.: Colloquium on Calvin Studies, 1992.

———, ed. *Calvin Studies VIII*. Davidson, N.C.: Colloquium on Calvin Studies, 1996.

Leith, John H., and Johnson, W. Stacy, eds. *Calvin Studies IV*. Davidson, N.C.: Colloquium on Calvin Studies, 1988.

Lewis, Gillian. "Calvinism in Geneva in the time of Calvin and Beza, 1541–1608." In *International Calvinism, 1541–1715*, ed. Menna Prestwich (Oxford: Oxford University Press, 1985), pp. 39–70.

———. "The Geneva Academy." In *Calvinism in Europe, 1540–1620*, ed. Andrew Pettegree, et al (Cambridge: Cambridge University Press, 1994), pp. 35–63.

Lillback, Peter Alan. "The Binding of God: Calvin's Role in the Development of Covenant Theology." Ph.D. dissertation; Westminster Theological Seminary, 1985.

Lobstein, P. "Calvin considéré comme prédicateur." In *Études sur la pensée et l'oeuvre de Calvin*, ed. Lobstein (Neuilly: Éditions de "La Cause," 1927), pp. 15–49.

———. "La Connaissance religieuse d'après Calvin," *Revue de Théologie et de Philosophie* 42 (1909), pp. 53–110. [Also found in the author's *Études*, pp. 113–53.]

———. "Les Commentaires de Calvin," in *Études*, ed. Lobstein pp. 169–76.

———. "Les Sermons de Calvin sur le livre de Job," in *Études*, ed. Lobstein pp. 51–67.

———. "L'Oeuvre dogmatique de Calvin," in *Études*, ed. Lobstein, pp. 97–111.

———. *Études sur la pensée et l'oeuvre de Calvin*. Neuilly: Éditions de "La Cause," 1927.

Locher, Gottfried W. *Die Theologie Huldrych Zwinglis im Lichte seiner Christologie*, I. *Die Gotteslehre*. Zurich: Zwingli-Verlag, 1952.

Loofs, Ferdinand. *Leitfaden der Dogmengeschichte*. Halle: M. Niemeyer, 1896.

Mack, Peter. *Renaissance Argument: Valla and Agricola in the Traditions of Rhetoric and Dialectic*. Leiden: E. J. Brill, 1993.

Margolin, Jean-Claude. *Humanism in Europe at the Time of the Renaissance*. Trans. John L. Farthing. Durham, N.C.: Labyrinth Press, 1989.

Marmelstein, J. W. *Étude comparative des latin et français de l'Institution*. Groningen: J. B. Wolters, 1923.

Martin, Alain-Georges. "La place de la Trinité dans l'Institution chrétienne de Calvin," *Revue Réformée* 30 (September 1979), pp. 131–49.

Maruyama, Tadataka. *The Ecclesiology of Theodore Beza: The Reform of the True Church*. Geneva: Droz, 1978.

Massebieau, L. *Les Colloques scolaires du seizième siècle, et leurs auteurs, 1480–1570*. Paris: J. Bonhoure, 1878; repr. Geneva: Slatkine, 1968.

————. *Répertoire des ouvrages pédagogiques du XVIᵉ siècle*. Paris: J. Bonhoure, 1886.

Massot, P.-E. *La Notion de la foi d'après l'Institution chrétienne de Calvin*. Montauban: J. Vidallet, 1871.

Maurer, Armand. *Medieval Philosophy*. New York: Random House, 1962.

Mays, James Luther. "Calvin's Commentary on the Psalms: The Preface as Introduction," in *Calvin Studies IV*, ed. John H. Leith and W. Stacy Johnson, (Davidson, N.C.: Colloguium on Calvin Studics, 1988), pp. 96–97.

McClelland, J. C. "The Reformed Doctrine of Predestination according to Peter Martyr," *Scottish Journal of Theology* 8 (1955), pp. 255–71.

————. "Renaissance in Theology: Calvin's 1536 Institutio—Fresh Start or False?" In *In Honor of John Calvin, 1509–64*, ed. E. J. Furcha (Montreal: McGill University Press, 1987), pp. 154–74.

————. *Visible Words of God*. Edinburgh: Oliver & Boyd, 1957.

McCoy, Charles S., and Baker, J. Wayne. *Fountainhead of Federalism: Heinrich Bullinger and the Covenantal Tradition*, with a translation of *De testamento seu foedere Dei unico et aeterno*. Louisville, Ky.: Westminster/John Knox, 1991.

McGrath, Alister E. "John Calvin and Late Medieval Thought: A Study in Late Medieval Influences upon Calvin's Theological Development," *Archiv für Reformationsgeschichte* 77 (1986), pp. 58–78.

————. *A Life of John Calvin*. Oxford: Blackwell, 1990.

McIndoe, John I. "John Calvin, Preface to the Homilies of Chrysostom," *Hartford Quarterly Review* (Winter 1965), pp. 18–26.

McKee, Elsie Anne. "Exegesis, Theology, and Development in Calvin's *Institutio*: A Methodological Suggestion." In *Probing the Reformed Tradition: Historical Studies in Honor of Edward A. Dowey, Jr.*, ed. Brian G. Armstrong and Elsie A. McKee (Louisville, Ky.: Westminster/John Knox, 1989), pp. 154–172.

McNeill, John T. "Thirty Years of Calvin Study," *Church History* 17 (1948), pp. 207–40. Reprinted, with a preface and a second part, carrying the references forward to 1968, in W. Walker, *John Calvin* (1969).

McPhee, Ian. "Conserver or Transformer of Calvin's Theology? A Study of the Origins and Development of Theodore Beza's Thought, 1550–1570." Ph.D. dissertation, Cambridge University, 1979.

Meijering, E. P. "The Fathers in Calvinist Orthodoxy: Systematic Theology," in *The Reception of the Church Fathers in the West*, ed. Irena Backus (Leiden, E. J. Brill, 1997), vol. 2, pp. 867–88.

Metzger, Bruce M. *The Text of the New Testament: Its Transmission, Corruption, and Restoration*. 3rd, enl. ed. New York: Oxford University Press, 1992.

Meylan, Edward F. "The Stoic Doctrine of Indifferent Things and the Conception of Christian Liberty in Calvin's *Institutio Religionis Christianae*," *Romanic Review* 28 (1937), pp. 135–45.

Meylan, Henri. *D'Érasme à Théodore de Bèze: Problèmes de l'Eglise et de l'Ecole chez les Réformés*. Geneva: Droz, 1976.

Millet, Olivier. *Calvin et la dynamique de la parole. Étude de rhétorique réformée*. Paris: Librairie Honoré Champion, 1992.

Minges, P. Parthenius. *Ioannis Duns Scoti doctrina philosophica et theologica quod res praecipuas proposita et exposita*. 2 vols. Quaracchi: Collegium S. Bonaventurae, 1930.

Monfasani, John. "Humanism and Rhetoric." In *Renaissance Humanism*, ed. Albert Rabil Jr. (Philadelphia: University of Pennsylvania Press, 1988), pp. 171–235.

Mooi, R. J. *Het Kerk- en Dogmahistorisch Element in de Werken van Johannes Calvijn*. Wageningen: H. Veenman & Zonen, 1965.

Mozley, J. B. *A Treatise on the Augustinian Doctrine of Predestination*. 2nd ed. New York: E. P. Dutton, 1878.

Mülhaupt, Erwin. *Die Predigt Calvins: Ihre Geschichte, ihre Form und ihre religiösen Grundgedanken*. Berlin: DeGruyter, 1931.

Müller, G. E. "Calvin's Institutes of the Christian Religion as an Illustration of Christian Living," *Journal of the History of Ideas* 4 (1942), pp. 287–300.

Muller, Richard A. "Calvin and the Calvinists: Assessing Continuities and Discontinuities Between the Reformation and Orthodoxy, Part I," *Calvin Theological Journal* 30/2 (November 1995), pp. 345–75; "Part II," *Calvin Theological Journal*, 31/1 (April 1996), pp. 125–60.

———. "Calvin, Beza and the Exegetical History of Romans 13." In *Calvin and the State*, ed. Peter De Klerk (Grand Rapids, Mich.: Calvin Studies Society, 1993), pp. 139–170.

———. "Calvin's *Argument du livre* (1541), An Erratum to the McNeill/Battles *Institutes*," *Sixteenth Century Journal*, 29/1 (1998), pp. 35–8.

———. *Christ and the Decree: Christology and Predestination in Reformed Theology from Calvin to Perkins*. Studies in Historical Theology. Vol. 2. Durham, N.C.: Labyrinth Press, 1986; paperback ed., Grand Rapids, Mich.: Baker Book House, 1988.

———. "Christ in the Eschaton: Calvin and Moltmann on the Duration of the *Munus Regium*," *Harvard Theological Review* 74/1 (1981), pp. 31–59.

———. "*Duplex cognitio dei* in the Theology of Early Reformed Orthodoxy," *Sixteenth Century Journal* 10/2 (April 1979), pp. 51–61.

———. "Fides and Cognitio in Relation to the Problem of Intellect and Will in the Theology of John Calvin," *Calvin Theological Journal* 25/2 (November 1990), pp. 207–24.

———. *God, Creation and Providence in the Thought of Jacob Arminius: Sources and Directions of Scholastic Protestantism in the Era of Early Orthodoxy*. Grand Rapids, Mich.: Baker Book House, 1991.

———. "The Hermeneutic of Promise and Fulfillment in Calvin's Exegesis of the Old Testament Prophecies of the Kingdom." In *The Bible in the Sixteenth Century*, ed. and intro. David C. Steinmetz (Durham, N.C.: Duke University Press, 1990), pp. 68–82.

———. "Orthodoxy, Protestant" s.v. in *Encyclopedia of the Reformed Faith*, ed. Donald McKim. Louisville, Ky.: Westminster/John Knox Press, 1992.

———. *Post-Reformation Reformed Dogmatics*. 2 vols. Grand Rapids, Mich.: Baker Book House, 1987–93.

———. "Scholasticism in Calvin: A Question of Relation and Disjunction." In *Calvinus Sincerioris Religionis Vindex*, ed. Wilhelm H. Neuser and Brian G. Armstrong (Kirksville, MO.: Sixteenth Century Journal Publishers, 1997), pp. 247–66.

———. "*Scimus enim quod lex spiritualis est*: Melanchthon and Calvin on the Interpretation of Romans 7:14–23." In *Philip Melanchthon (1497–1560) and the Commentary*, ed. Timothy J. Wengert and M. Patrick Graham (Sheffield: Sheffield Academic Press, 1997), pp. 216–37.

Muller, Richard A., and Bradley, James E. *Church History: An Introduction to Research, Reference Works, and Methods*. Grand Rapids, Mich.: Eerdmans, 1995.

Muller, Richard A., and Thompson, John L., eds. *Biblical Interpretation in the Era of the Reformation: Essays Presented to David Steinmetz in Honor of His Sixtieth Birthday*. Grand Rapids, Mich.: Eerdmans, 1996.

Murray, John. *Calvin on Scripture and Divine Sovereignty*. Grand Rapids, Mich.: Eerdmans, 1960.

———. "Calvin on the Extent of the Atonement," *Banner of Truth* 234 (March 1983), pp. 20–22.

———. "Calvin's Doctrine of Creation," *Westminster Theological Journal* 17, (1954/55), pp. 21–43.

Nauert, Charles, Jr. *Humanism and the Culture of Renaissance Europe*. Cambridge: Cambridge University Press, 1995.

Neander, Johann August Wilhelm. *Lectures on the History of Christian Dogmas*. 2 vols. Trans. J. Ryland. London: Bohn, 1858.

Neuser, Wilhelm H. "Calvin's Conversion to Teachableness." In *Calvin and Christian Ethics*, ed. Peter De Klerk (Grand Rapids, Mich.: Calvin Studies Society, 1987), pp. 57–77.

Neuser, Wilhem H., ed. *Calvinus Ecclesiae Genevensis Custos*. Die Referate des Internationalen Kongresses für Calvinforschung. Vom 6 bis 9 September 1982 in Genf. Frankfurt am Main: Peter Lang, 1984.

———, ed. *Calvinus Ecclesiae Doctor*. Die Referate des Internationalen Kongresses für Calvinforschung vom 25 bis 28 September 1978 in Amsterdam. Kampen: J. H. Kok, 1980.

———, ed. *Calvinus Sacrae Scripturae Professor: Calvin as Confessor of Holy Scripture*. Die Referate des Internationalen Kongresses für Calvinforschung vom 20. bis 23. August 1990 in Grand Rapids. Grand Rapids, Mich.: Eerdmans, 1994.

———, ed. *Calvinus Servus Christi*. Die Referate des Internationalen Kongresses für Calvinforschung vom 25 bis 28 August 1986 in Debrecen. Budapest: Presseabteilung des Ráday-Kollegiums, 1988.

Neuser, Wilhelm H., and Armstrong, Brian G. "The Development of the *Institutes* 1536 to 1559." In *John Calvin's Institutes: His Opus Magnum*, ed. B. J. van der Walt (Potchefstroom: Institute for Reformational Studies, 1986), pp. 33–54.

Neuser, Wilhelm H., and Armstrong, Brian G., eds. *Calvinus Sincerioris Religionis Vindex: Calvin as Protector of the Purer Religion*. Die Referate des Internationalen Kongresses für Calvinforschung, vom 13. bis 16. September in Edinburgh. Kirksville, Mo.: Sixteenth Century Journal Publishers, 1997.

———, ed. *Calvinus Theologus*. Die Referate des Internationalen Kongresses für Calvinforschung vom 16 bis 19 September 1974 in Amsterdam. Neukirchen: Neukirchner Verlag, 1976.

Neuser, Wilhelm, and Selderhuis, Herman, ed. *Ordentlich und Fruchtbar: Festschrift für Willem van 't Spijker* Leiden: J. J. Groen en Zoon, 1997.

Nicole, P.-D., and Rapin, C. "De l'exégèse à l'homilétique, evolution entre le Commentaire de 1551, les sermons de 1558 et le commentaire de 1559 sur le prophète Esaïe." In *Calvinus Ecclesiae Genevensis Custos*, ed. Wilhelm H. Neuser (Frankfurt am Main: Peter Lang, 1984), pp. 159–62.

Niesel, Wilhelm. *Calvin Bibliographie, 1901–1959*. Munich: Kaiser, 1961.

———. *The Theology of Calvin*. Trans. Harold Knight. London: Lutterworth, 1956; repr. Grand Rapids, Mich: Balor Book House, 1980.

Niesel, Wilhelm, and Barth, Peter. "Ein französische Ausgabe der ersten *Institutio Calvins*", in *Theologische Blätter* (1928), pp. 2–10.

Nixon, Leroy. *John Calvin: Expository Preacher*. Grand Rapids, Mich.: Eerdmans, 1950.

Nuovo, Victor. "Calvin's Theology: A Study of its Sources in Classical Antiquity." Ph.D. dissertation, Columbia University, 1964.

Oakley, Francis. "Pierre D'Ailly and the Absolute Power of God: Another Note on the Theology of Nominalism," *Harvard Theological Review* 56 (1963), pp. 59–73.

Obendiek, H. "Die *Institutio* Calvins als 'Confessio' und 'Apologie.' " In *Theologische Aufsätze. K. Barth zum 50 Geburtstag* ed. Ernst Wolf. (Munich: Kaiser, 1936), pp. 417–31.

Oberman, Heiko A. *Archbishop Thomas Bradwardine: A Fourteenth-Century Augustinian. A Study of His Theology in Its Historical Context*. Utrecht: Kemink & Zoon, 1958.

———. "*Subita conversio*: The Conversion of John Calvin." In *Reformiertes Erbe, Festschrift für Gottfried W. Locher zu seinem 80. Geburtstag*, ed. H. A. Oberman, E. Saxer, A. Schindler, and H. Stucki, *Zwingliana* 19/2 (1992), pp. 279–95.

————. *The Dawn of the Reformation: Essays in Late Medieval and Early Reformation Thought.* Edinburgh: T. & T. Clark, 1986.

————. "The 'Extra' Dimension in the Theology of Calvin," *Journal of Ecclesiastical History* 21 (1970), pp. 43–64.

————. *Forerunners of the Reformation.* New York: Holt, Rinehart Winston, 1966.

————. *The Harvest of Medieval Theology: Gabriel Biel and Late Medieval Nominalism.* Rev. ed. Grand Rapids, Mich.: Eerdmans, 1967.

————. *Initia Calvini: The Matrix of Calvin's Reformation.* Amsterdam: Koninklijke Nederlandse Akademie van Wetenschappen, 1991.

————. "John Calvin: The Mystery of His Impact." In *Calvin Studies VI*, ed. John H. Leith p. 1–14. (Davidson, N.C.: Colloquium on Calvin Studies, 1992),

————. *Masters of the Reformation: Emergence of a New Intellectual Climate in Europe.* Trans. Dennis Martin. Cambridge: Cambridge University Press, 1981.

————. "The Shape of Late Medieval Thought: The Birthpangs of the Modern Era." In *The Pursuit of Holiness*, ed. C. Trinkaus and H. Oberman (Leiden: E. J. Brill, 1974), pp. 3–25

————. "Some Notes of the Theology of Nominalism," *Harvard Theological Review* 53 (1960), pp. 47–76.

O'Mahony, James E. *The Desire of God in the Philosophy of St. Thomas Aquinas.* Toronto: Longmans, Green, 1929.

O'Malley, John W. "Content and Rhetorical Forms in Sixteenth-Century Treatises on Preaching." In *Renaissance Eloquence*, ed. James J. Murphy (Berkeley: University of California Press, 1983), pp. 238–52.

Otten, Hans. *Calvins theologische Anschauung von der Prädestination.* Munich: Chr. Kaiser Verlag, 1938.

Overfield, James H. *Humanism and Scholasticism in Late Medieval Germany.* Princeton, N.J.: Princeton University Press, 1984.

————. "Scholastic Opposition to Humanism in Pre-Reformation Germany," *Viator* 7 (1976), pp. 391–420.

Packer, J. I. "Calvin the Theologian." In *John Calvin: A Collection of Distinguished Essays*, ed. Gervase E. Duffield (Grand Rapids, Mich.: Eerdmans, 1966), pp. 149–75.

Pannier, Jacques. *Calvin à Strasbourg.* Strasbourg: Imprimerie Alsacienne, 1925.

————. *Calvin écrivain. Sa place et son rôle dans l'histoire de la Langue et de la littérature française.* 2nd ed. Paris: Fischbacher, 1930.

————. "De la préréforme à la réforme. A propos des deux dernières publications de Lefevre d'Étaples," *Revue d'Histoire et de Philosophie Religieuses* 15 (1935), pp. 530–47.

————. "Introduction," in John Calvin, *Institution de la religion chrestienne* (1541), vol. 1, pp. vii–xxxi.

————. "Notes historiques et critiques sur un chapitre de l'*Institution* écrit à Strasbourg (1539)," *Revue d'Histoire et de Philosophie Religieuses* 14 (1934), pp. 206–229.

————. *Recherches sur l'évolution religieuse de Calvin jusqu' à sa conversion.* Strasbourg: Librairie Istra, 1924.

————. *Recherches sur la formation intellectuelle de Calvin.* Paris: Alcan, 1931.

————. "Une Première Institution française dès 1537?" *Revue d'Histoire et de Philosophie Religieuses* 8 (1928), pp. 513–34.

Parker, T. H. L. "The Approach to Calvin," *Evangelical Quarterly* 16 (1944), pp. 165–72.

————. *Calvin: An Introduction to His Thought.* Louisville, Ky.: Westminster/John Knox, 1995.

————. *Calvin's New Testament Commentaries.* London: SCM/Grand Rapids, Mich.: Eerdmans, 1971.

————. *Calvin's Old Testament Commentaries.* Edinburgh: T. & T. Clark, 1986.

————. "Calvin the Exegete: Change and Development." In *Calvinus Ecclesiae Doctor*, ed. W. H. Neuser (Kampen: J. H. Kok, 1980), pp. 33–46.

————. *Commentaries on the Epistle to the Romans 1532–1542*. Edinburgh: T. & T. Clark, 1986.

————. *The Doctrine of the Knowledge of God: A Study in the Theology of John Calvin*. London, 1952; rev. ed. Grand Rapids, Mich.: Eerdmans, 1959.

————. *John Calvin: A Biography*. Philadelphia: Westminster, 1975.

————. *The Oracles of God: An Introduction to the Preaching of John Calvin*. London: Lutterworth, 1962.

————. *Calvin's Preaching*. Louisville, Ky.: Westminster/John Knox Press, 1992.

————. "The Sources of the Text of Calvin's New Testament," *Zeitschrift für Kirchengeschichte* 73 (1962), pp. 272–98.

Partee, Charles. *Calvin and Classical Philosophy*. Leiden: E. J. Brill, 1977.

————. "Calvin and Experience," *Scottish Journal of Theology* 26 (1973), pp. 169–81.

————. "Calvin's Central Dogma Again," *Sixteenth Century Journal*, 18 (1987), pp. 191–99.

Payne, John B. *Erasmus: His Theology of the Sacraments*. Richmond, Va.: John Knox Press, 1970.

Pelkonen, J. P. "The Teaching of John Calvin on the Nature and Function of the Conscience," *Lutheran Quarterly* 21 (1969), pp. 24–88.

Peter, Rodolphe. "Calvin and Louis Budé's Translation of the Psalms." In *John Calvin: A Collection of Distinguished Essays*, ed. Gervase Duffield (Grand Rapids, Mich.: Eerdmans, 1966), pp. 190–209.

————. "Calvin, traducteur de Mélanchthon." In *Horizons européens de la Réforme en Alsace*, ed. Marijn de Kroon and Marc Lienhard (Strasbourg: Istra, 1980), pp. 119–33.

————. "The Geneva Primer or Calvin's Elementary Catechism," in *Calvin Studies* ed. John H. Leith (Davidson, N.C.: Colloquium on Calvin Studies, 1990), vol. 5, pp. 135–61.

————. "Jean Calvin prédicateur, notice bibliographique à propos d'un ouvrage récent," in *Revue d'Histoire et de Philosophie Religieuses* 52 (1972), pp. 111–17.

————. "Rhétorique et prédication selon Calvin," *Revue d'Histoire et de Philosophie Religieuses* 55 (1975), pp. 249–72.

Peter, Rodolphe, and Gilmont, Jean-François. *Bibliotheca Calviniana. Les oeuvres de Jean Calvin publiées au xvi⁴ siècle: Écrits théologiques, littéraires et juridiques*. 2 vols. [1532–1564] Geneva: Droz, 1991–94.

Peterson, Robert A. *Calvin's Doctrine of the Atonement*. Phillipsburg, N.J.: Presbyterian and Reformed Publishing, 1983.

Pitkin, Barbara. "Imitation of David: David as a Paradigm for Faith in Calvin's Exegesis of the Psalms," *Sixteenth Century Journal* 24/4 (1993), pp. 843–63.

————. "What Pure Eyes Could See: Faith, Creation, and History in John Calvin's Theology." Ph.D. dissertation, University of Chicago, 1994.

Plattard, Jean. *La Renaissance de lettres en France de Louis XII à Henri IV*. Paris: Librairie Armand Collin, 1925.

————. "Le Beau 'style' de Calvin," *Bulletin de l'Association Guillaume Budé* 62 (January 1939), pp. 22–29.

————. " 'L'Institution chrestienne' de Calvin, premier monument de l'éloquence française," *Revue des Cours et Conférences* 37 (1935/6), pp. 495–501.

Postema, Gerald. "Calvin's Alleged Rejection of Natural Theology," *Scottish Journal of Theology* (1971), pp. 423–34.

Prestwich, Menna, ed. *International Calvinism, 1541–1715*. Oxford: Oxford University Press, 1985.

Puckett, David L. *John Calvin's Exegesis of the Old Testament*. Louisville, Ky.: Westminster/John Knox, 1995.

Quistorp, Heinrich. *Calvin's Doctrine of the Last Things*, trans. Harold Knight. Richmond, Va.: John Knox Press, 1955.

Rabil, Albert, Jr. *Erasmus and the New Testament: The Mind of a Christian Humanist.* 1972; repr. Lanham, Md.: University Press of America, 1993.

Rabil, Albert, Jr., ed. *Renaissance Humanism: Foundations, Forms, and Legacy.* 3 vols. Philadelphia: University of Pennsylvania Press, 1988.

Raitt, Jill. "Beza, Guide for the Faithful Life," *Scottish Journal of Theology* 39/1 (1986), pp. 83–107.

———. *The Eucharistic Theology of Theodore Beza: Development of the Reformed Doctrine.* Chambersburg, Pa.: American Academy of Religion, 1972.

———. "The Person of the Mediator: Calvin's Christology and Beza's Fidelity," *Occasional Papers of the Society for Reformation Research*, 1 (December 1977), pp. 53–80.

Rainbow, Jonathan H. *The Will of God and the Cross: An Historical and Theological Study of John Calvin's Doctrine of Limited Redemption.* Allison Park, Pa.: Pickwick Publications, 1990.

Rakow, Mary. "Christ's Descent into Hell: Calvin's Interpretation," *Religion in Life* 43 (1974), pp. 218–26.

Reid, J. K. S. *The Authority of Scripture: A Study of Reformation and Post-Reformation Understanding of the Bible.* London: Methuen, 1962.

———. "The Office of Christ in Predestination." *Scottish Journal of Theology* 1 (1948), pp. 5–19, 166–83.

Reist, Benjamin A. *A Reading of Calvin's Institutes.* Louisville, Ky.: Westminster/John Knox Press, 1991.

Reuter, Karl. *Das Grundverständnis der Theologie Calvins.* Neukirchen: Neukirchner Verlag, 1963.

———. *Vom Scholaren bis zum jungen Reformator.* Neukirchen: Neukirchner Verlag, 1981.

Rice, Eugene F. Jr. "The Humanist Idea of Christian Antiquity: Lefèvre d'Étaples and His Circle." In *French Humanism, 1470–1600*, ed. Werner L. Gundersheimer (New York: Harper & Row, 1969), pp. 163–80.

Robbins, Frank Egleston. *The Hexaemeral Literature: A Study of the Greek and Latin Commentaries on Genesis.* Chicago: University of Chicago Press, 1921.

Rorem, Paul. "Calvin and Bullinger on the Lord's Supper: Part I. The Impasse," *Lutheran Quarterly* NS 2 (1988), pp. 155–84.

———. "Calvin and Bullinger on the Lord's Supper: Part II. The Agreement," *Lutheran Quarterly* NS 2 (1988), pp. 357–89.

Roussel, Bernard. "Histoire de l'église et histoire de l'exégèse au XVIe siècle," *Bibliothèque d'Humanisme et Renaissance* 37 (1975), pp. 181–92.

Rummel, Erika. *The Humanist-Scholastic Debate in the Renaissance and Reformation.* Cambridge, Mass.: Harvard University Press, 1995.

Sandys-Wunsch, John, and Eldredge, Laurence. "J. P. Gabler and the Distinction between Biblical and Dogmatic Theology: Translation, Commentary and Discussion of His Originality," *Scottish Journal of Theology* 33 (1980), pp. 133–58.

Schäfer, Rolf. "Melanchthon's Hermeneutik im Römerbrief-Kommentar von 1532," *Zeitschrift für Theologie und Kirche* 60 (1963), pp. 216–35.

Schaff, Philip. *The Creeds of Christendom: With a History and Critical Notes.* 3 vols. 6th ed. rev. and enl. New York: Harper & Row, 1931; repr. Grand Rapids, Mich.: Baker Book House, 1983.

Schaff, Philip. *History of the Christian Church.* repr. Grand Rapids, Mich.: Eerdmans, 1953.

Schmitt, Charles B. *Aristotle and the Renaissance.* Cambridge, Mass.: Harvard University Press, 1983.

Schneider, John. *Philip Melanchthon's Rhetorical Construal of Biblical Authority.* Lewiston, Canada: Edwin Mellen, 1990.

Schreiner, Susan E. "Exegesis and Double Justice in Calvin's Sermons on Job," *Church History* 58 (1989), pp. 322–38.

———. "The Spiritual Man Judges All Things: Calvin and the Exegetical Debates about Certainty in the Reformation." In *Biblical Interpretation in the Era of the Reformation*, ed. Richard A. Muller and John L. Thompson, (Grand Rapids, Mich.: Eerdmans, 1996), pp. 189–215.

———. *The Theater of His Glory: Nature and the Natural Order in the Thought of John Calvin.* Durham, N.C.: Labyrinth Press, 1991.

———. "Through a Mirror Dimly: Calvin's Sermons on Job," *Calvin Theological Journal* 21 (1986), pp. 175–93.

———. *Where Shall Wisdom Be Found? Calvin's Exegesis of Job from Medieval and Modern Perspectives.* Chicago: University of Chicago Press, 1994.

Schützeichel, Heribert. *Die Glaubenstheologie Calvins.* Munich: Max Hueber, 1972.

Schwarz, W. *Principles and Problems of Biblical Translation: Some Reformation Controversies and Their Background.* Cambridge: Cambridge University Press, 1955.

Schweizer, Alexander. "Die Entwickelung des Moralsystems in der reformierten Kirche," *Theologische Studien und Kritiken* 32 (1850), pp. 5–78, 288–327, 554–580.

———. *Die Glaubenslehre der evangelisch-reformierten Kirche, dargestellt und aus den Quellen belegt.* 2 vols. Zurich: Orell, Füssli, 1847.

———. *Die Protestantischen Centraldogmen in ihrer Entwicklung innerhalb der reformierten Kirche.* 2 vols. Zurich: Orell, Füssli, 1854–56.

Seeberg, Reinhold. *Textbook of the History of Doctrines.* 2 vols. Trans. Charles Hay. Grand Rapids, Mich.: Baker Book House, 1952.

Seifert, Arno. *Logik zwischen Scholastik und Humanismus: Das Kommentarwerk Johann Ecks.* Munich: Wilhelm Fink, 1978.

Selinger, Suzanne. *Calvin Against Himself: An Inquiry in Intellectual History.* Hamden, Conn.: Archon, 1984.

Shedd, W. G. T. *A History of Christian Doctrine.* 2 vols. New York: Scribner, 1889; repr. Minneapolis: Klock & Klock, 1978.

Shepherd, Victor A. *The Nature and Function of Faith in the Theology of John Calvin.* Macon, Ga.: Mercer University Press, 1983.

Shuger, Debora K. *Sacred Rhetoric: The Christian Grand Style in the English Renaissance.* Princeton, N.J.: Princeton University Press, 1988.

Siegel, Jerrold E. *Rhetoric and Philosophy in Renaissance Humanism.* Princeton, N.J.: Princeton University Press, 1968.

Simpson, H. W. "The *Editio Princeps* of the *Institutio Christianae Religionis*, 1536 by John Calvin." In *Calvinus Reformator: His Contribution to Theology, Church and Society* (Potchefstroom: Potchefstroom University for Christian Higher Education, 1982), pp. 26–32.

———. "*Pietas* in the *Institutes* of Calvin." In *Our Reformational Tradition: A Rich Heritage and Lasting Vocation*, ed. B. J. van der Walt (Potchefstroom: Institute for Reformational Studies, 1984), pp. 179–91.

Sinnema, Donald W. "Antoine de Chandieu's Call for a Scholastic Reformed Theology (1580)." In *Later Calvinism: International Perspectives*, ed. W. Fred Graham (Kirksville, Mo.: Sixteenth Century Journal Publishers, 1994), pp. 159–90.

———. "The Distinction between Scholastic and Popular: Andreas Hyperius and Reformed Scholasticism." Paper delivered at the Sixteenth Century Studies Conference, St. Louis, October 1996.

Smalley, Beryl. *The Study of the Bible in the Middle Ages.* Notre Dame, Ind.: University of Notre Dame Press, 1964.

———. "The Bible in the Medieval Schools." In *The Cambridge History of the Bible*, 3 vols., ed,

P. Ackroyd, C. Evans, G. W. H. Lampe, and S. L. Greenslade (Cambridge: Cambridge University Press, 1963–70), vol. 2, pp. 197–98.

Smits, Luchesius. *Saint-Augustine dans l'oeuvre de Jean Calvin*. 2 vols. Assen: Van Gorcum, 1957–58.

Spencer, Stephen. "Reformed Scholasticism in Medieval Perspective: Thomas Aquinas and François Turrettini on Incarnation." Ph.D. dissertation, Michigan State University, 1988.

Spicq, Ceslaus. *Esquisse d'une histoire de l'exégèse latine au moyen âge*. Paris: J. Vrin, 1944.

Spitz, Lewis. "Humanism and the Protestant Reformation." in *Renaissance Humanism*, ed. Albert Rabil Jr. (Philadelphia: University of Pennsylvania Press, 1988), vol. 3, pp. 381–411.

Stauffer, Richard. *Dieu, la Création et la Providence dans le prédication de Calvin*. Bern: Peter Lang, 1978.

———. "L'homilétique de Calvin." In *Communion et communication* (Geneva: Labor et Fides, 1978).

———. *Interprétes de la Bible: Études sur les réformateurs du XVIe siècle*. Paris: Beauchesne, 1980.

———. "Les Sermons inédits de Calvin sur le livre de la Genèse," *Revue de Théologie et de Philosophie*, 3 ser., 15 (1965), pp. 26–36.

———. "Un Calvin méconnu: Le prédicateur de Genève," *Bulletin de la Societé d'Histoire du Protestantisme Français* 123 (1977), pp. 184–203.

———. "Un Texte de Calvin inconnu en français: Le sermon sur le Psaume 46:1–6," *La Revue Reformée* 15 (1964), pp. 1–15.

Steadman, John E. *The Hill and the Labyrinth: Discourse and Certitude in Milton and His Near-Contemporaries*. Berkeley: University of California Press, 1984.

Stegmüller, Fridericus. *Repertorium Commentariorum in sententias Petri Lombardi*. 2 vols. Würzburg: Ferdnand Schöningh, 1947.

Steinmetz, David C. "Calvin Among the Thomists." In *Biblical Hermeneutics in Historical Perspective*, M. Burrows and P. Rorem (Grand Rapids, Mich.: Eerdmans, 1991), pp. 198–214.

———. "Calvin and Abraham: The Interpretation of Romans 4 in the Sixteenth Century," *Church History* 57 (1988), pp. 443–55.

———. "Calvin and His Lutheran Critics," *Lutheran Quarterly* 4/2 (1990), pp. 100–18.

———. "Calvin and Melanchthon on Romans 13:1–7," *Ex Auditu* 2 (1986), pp. 74–81.

———. "Calvin and the Absolute Power of God," *Journal of Medieval and Renaissance Studies* 18/1 (Spring 1988), pp. 65–79.

———. "Calvin and the Divided Self of Romans 7." In *Augustine, the Harvest, and Theology (1300–1650)*. ed. K. Hagen (Leiden: E. J. Brill, 1990), pp. 300–13.

———. "Calvin and the Monastic Ideal." In *Anticlericalism in Early Modern Europe* ed. K. Hagen (Leiden: E. J. Brill, 1991).

———. "Calvin as an Interpreter of Genesis." In *Calvinus Sincerioris Religionis Vindex*, ed. Wilhelm H. Neuser and Brian G. Armstrong (Kirksville, Mo.: Sixteenth Century Journal Publishers, 1997), pp. 53–66.

———. *Calvin in Context*. New York: Oxford University Press, 1995.

———. "John Calvin on Isaiah 6: A Problem in the History of Exegesis," *Interpretation* 36 (1982), pp. 156–170.

———. *Misericordia Dei: The Theology of Johannes von Staupitz in Its Late Medieval Setting*. Leiden: E. J. Brill, 1968.

———. *Reformers in the Wings*. Philadelphia: Fortress Press, 1971.

———. "The Scholastic Calvin," in *Protestant Scholasticism: Essays in Reappraisal* ed. Carl Trueman and R. Scott Clark (London: Paternoster, forthcoming).

———. "The Superiority of Pre-Critical Exegesis," *Theology Today* 37 (1980), pp. 27–38.

———. "The Theology of Calvin and Calvinism." In *Reformation Europe: A Guide to Research*, ed. Steven E. Ozment (St. Louis: Center for Reformation Research, 1982), pp. 211–32.

Stelling-Michaud, S., ed. *Le Livre du recteur de l'Académie de Genève*, 6 vols. Geneva: Droz, 1959–80.

Stephens, W. P. *The Theology of Huldrych Zwingli*. Oxford: Clarendon Press, 1986.

Strohl, Henri. "La Méthode exégétique des Réformateurs." In *Le Problème biblique dans le Protestantisme*, ed. J. Boisset (Paris: Presses Universitaires de France, 1955), pp. 87–104.

———. *La Pensée de la Réforme*. Neuchâtel: Delachaux et Niestle, 1951.

Stuermann, Walter E. *A Critical Study of Calvin's Concept of Faith*. Ann Arbor, Mich.: Edwards Brothers, 1952.

Stump, Eleonore. *Dialectic and Its Place in the Development of Medieval Logic*. Ithaca, N.Y.: Cornell University Press, 1989.

Thionville, Eugène. *De la théorie des lieux communs dans les Topiques d'Aristote et des principales modifications, qu'elle a subies jusque á nos jours*. Paris: J. Vrin, 1855.

Thomas, John Newton. "The Place of Natural Theology in the Thought of John Calvin," *Journal of Religious Thought* 15 (1958), pp. 107–36.

Thompson, John Lee. *John Calvin and the Daughters of Sarah: Women in Regular and Exceptional Roles in the Exegesis of Calvin, His Predecessors and His Contemporaries*. Geneva: Droz, 1992.

———. "The Immoralities of the Patriarchs in the History of Exegesis: A Reappraisal of Calvin's Position," *Calvin Theological Journal* 26 (1991), pp. 9–46.

———. "Patriarchs, Polygamy and Private Resistance: John Calvin and Others on Breaking God's Rules," *Sixteenth Century Journal* 25/1 (1994), pp. 3–28.

Todd, William Newton. "The Function of the Patristic Writings in the Thought of John Calvin." Th.D. dissertation, Union Theological Seminary, New York, 1964.

Torrance, James B. "The Incarnation and 'Limited Atonement,'" *Scottish Bulletin of Evangelical Theology* 2 (1984), pp. 32–40.

Torrance, Thomas F. *Calvin's Doctrine of Man*. Grand Rapids, Mich.: Eerdmans, 1957.

———. "Calvin's Doctrine of the Trinity," *Calvin Theological Journal*, 25/2 (November 1990), pp. 165–93.

———. *The Hermeneutics of John Calvin*. Edinburgh: Scottish Academic Press, 1988.

———. "Knowledge of God and Speech about Him According to John Calvin." In Torrance, *Theology in Reconstruction* (London: Oxford University Press, 1965), pp. 76–98.

Trinkaus, Charles. *In Our Image and Likeness: Humanity and Divinity in Italian Humanist Thought*. 2 vols. Chicago: University of Chicago Press, 1970.

———. "Italian Humanism and Scholastic Theology." In *Renaissance Humanism*, ed. Albert Rabil Jr. (Philadelphia: University of Pennsylvania Press, 1988), vol. 3, pp. 327–48.

Trinterud, Leonard. "The Origins of Puritanism," *Church History* 20 (1951), pp. 37–57.

Tylenda, Joseph. "Calvin's First Reformed Sermon? Nicholas Cop's Discourse," *Westminster Theological Journal* 38 (1975/76), pp. 300–18.

———. "The Calvin-Westphal Exchange. The Genesis of Calvin's Treatises Against Westphal," *Calvin Theological Journal* 9 (1974), pp. 182–209.

———. "Christ the Mediator: Calvin versus Stancaro," *Calvin Theological Journal* 8 (1973) 5–16, 131–57.

———. "Girolami Zanchi and John Calvin," *Calvin Theological Journal* 10 (1975), pp. 101–41.

Van Buren, Paul. *Christ in Our Place: The Substitutionary Character of Calvin's Doctrine of Reconciliation*. Edinburgh: T. &. T. Clark, 1957.

van der Linde, S. "Gereformeerde Scholastiek IV: Calvijn," *Theologia Reformata* 29 (1986), pp. 244–66.

———. "Het 'Griekse' Denken in Kerk, Theologie en Geloofspraktijk," *Theologia Reformata* 28 (1985), pp. 248–68.

Van der Ploeg, J. "The Place of Holy Scripture in the Theology of St. Thomas," *Thomist* 10 (1947), pp. 398–422.

Van der Walt, Bahrend Johannes. "Was Calvin a Calvinist or Was/Is Calvinism Calvinistic?" In *Our Reformational Tradition: A Rich Heritage and Lasting Vocation*, ed. T. van der Walt, L. Floor, et al. (Potchefstroom: Potcheftstroom University for Christian Higher Education, 1984), pp. 369–77.

———. "Renaissance and Reformation: Contemporaries but Not Allies." In *Calvinus Reformator: His Contribution to Theology, Church and Society* (Potchefstroom: Potchefstroom University for Christian Higher Education, 1982), pp. 85–92.

Van der Walt, Barend Johannes, Pont, A. D., and Van der Walt, J. *John Calvin's Institutes: His Opus Magnum.* Potchefstroom: Institute for Reformational Studies, 1986.

Van Oort, Johannes. "John Calvin and the Church Fathers." In *The Reception of the Church Fathers in the West: From the Carolingians to the Maurists*, 2 vols., ed. Irena Backus, (Leiden: E. J. Brill, 1997), pp. 661–700.

Van Schelven, A. A. "Beza's *De Iure Magistratuum in Subidos*," *Archiv für Reformationsgeschichte* 45 (1954), pp. 62–81.

Van 't Spijker, Willem. "De Invloed van Bucer op Calvijn blijkens de Institutie," *Theologia Reformata* 28 (1985), pp. 15–34.

———. "The Influence of Luther on Calvin According to the *Institutes*." In *John Calvin's Institutes: His Opus Magnum* ed. B. Vander Walt et al. (Potchefstroom: Institute for Reformational Studies, 1986), pp. 83–105.

———. *Principe, methode en functie van de theologie bij Andreas Hyperius* (Apeldoornse Studies, 26). Kampen: J. H. Kok, 1990.

Van 't Spijker, Willem, ed. *Calvin: Erbe und Auftrag. Festechrift für Wilhelm Heinrich Neuser zum 65. Geburtstag.* Kampen: Kok Pharos, 1991.

van 't Veer, M. B. *Catechese en catechetische stof bij Calvijn.* Kampen: Kok, 1941.

Venema, Cornelis P. "Heinrich Bullinger's Correspondence on Calvin's Doctrine of Predestination, 1551–1553," *Sixteenth Century Journal* 17/4 (1986), pp. 435–50.

———. "The 'Twofold Knowledge of God' and the Structure of Calvin's Theology," *Mid-America Journal of Theology* 4 (1988), pp. 156–82.

Verhoef, Pieter A. "Luther's and Calvin's Exegetical Library," *Calvin Theological Journal* 3 (1968), pp. 5–20.

Vernet, F. "Lyre, Nicolas de" s.v. in *Dictionnaire de théologie catholique*, 11/1, cols. 1410–22.

Vignaux, Paul. *Justification et prédestination au XIVᵉ siècle: Duns Scot, Pierre d'Auriole, Guillaume d'Occam, Grégoire de Rimini.* Paris: E. Leroux, 1934.

———. "Nominalisme," s.v. in *Dictionnaire de théologie catholique*, vol. II/I, cols. 717–784.

———. *Luther, commentateur des sentences.* Paris: J. Vrin, 1935.

———. *Nominalisme au XIVᵉ siècle.* Montreal: Institute D'Études Médiévales, 1948.

Vischer, Wilhelm. "Calvin exégète de l'Ancien Testament," *La Revue Reformée* 18 (1967), pp. 1–20.

Von Rad, Gerhard. *Genesis: A Commentary.* Trans. John H. Marks. Philadelphia: Westminster, 1961.

Vos, Arvin. *Aquinas, Calvin, and Contemporary Protestant Thought: A Critique of Protestant Views of the Thought of Thomas Aquinas.* Grand Rapids, Mich.: Eerdmans, 1985.

Walchenbach, John R. "John Calvin as Biblical Commentator: An Investigation into Calvin's Use of John Chrysostom as an Exegetical Tutor." Ph.D. dissertation, University of Pittsburgh, 1974.

Walker, Williston. *John Calvin: The Organizer of Reformed Protestantism (1509–1564).* 1906; repr., with a bibliographical essay by John T. McNeill, New York: Schocken, 1969.

Wallace, Ronald S. *Calvin, Geneva and the Reformation: A Study of Calvin as Social Reformer, Churchman, Pastor and Theologian.* Grand Rapids, Mich.: Baker Book House, 1988.

———. "Calvin's Approach to Theology." In *The Challenge of Evangelical Theology: Essays in Approach and Method,* ed. Nigel Cameron (Edinburgh: Rutherford House, 1987), pp. 123–50.

———. *Calvin's Doctrine of the Christian Life.* Edinburgh: Oliver & Boyd, 1959.

———. *Calvin's Doctrine of the Word and Sacrament.* Grand Rapids, Mich.: Eerdmans, 1957.

Warfield, Benjamin B. "Calvin's Doctrine of God," (Philadelphia: Presbyterian and Reformed Publishing, 1956), In "Calvin's Doctrine of the Knowledge of God," and "Calvin's Doctrine of the Trinity." In *Calvin and Augustine,* ed. Samuel Craig (Philadelphia: Presbyterian and Reformed Publishing, 1956), pp, 133–185, 29–130, and 189–284.

———. "On the Literary History of Calvin's Institutes." In John Calvin, *Institutes of the Christian Religion,* trans. John Allen, 7th ed. (Philadelphia: Presbyterian Board of Christian Education, 1936), pp. xxx–xxxi.

Weber, Henry J. "The Formal Dialectical Rationalism of Calvin," *Papers of the American Church History Society* 8 (1928), pp. 19–41.

Weisheipl, J. A. "Scholastic Method," s.v. in *New Catholic Encyclopedia.* 15 vols. (New York: McGraw Hill, 1967), vol. 12, pp. 1145–6.

Wendel, François. *Calvin et l'humanisme.* Paris: Presses Universitaires de France, 1976.

———. *Calvin: The Origins and Development of His Religious Thought.* Trans. Philip Mairet. New York.: Harper & Row, 1963.

Wengert, Timothy J. *Philip Melanchthon's "Annotationes in Johannem" in Relation to Its Predecessors and Contemporaries.* Geneva: Droz, 1987.

———. "Philip Melanchthon's 1522 Annotations on Romans and the Lutheran Origins of Rhetorical Criticism." In *Biblical Interpretation in the Era of the Reformation,* ed Richard A. Muller and John L. Thompson (Grand Rapids, Mich.: Eerdmans, 1996), pp. 118–140.

———. " 'We Will Feast Together in Heaven Forever': The Epistolary Friendship of John Calvin and Philip Melanchthon." In *Melanchthon in Europe: His Work and Influence Beyond Wittenberg,* ed. Karin Maag (Grand Rapids: Baker Book House, 1999), pp. 19–44.

Wernle, Paul. *Der evangelische Glaube nach der Hauptschriften der Reformatoren.* 3 vols. Tübingen: J. C. B. Mohr, 1919.

Whitebrook, J. C. "Calvin's *Institute of Christian Religion* in the Imprints of Thomas Vautrollier," *Transactions of the Congregational Historical Society* 12 (1933–36), pp. 199–200.

Williams, Donald T. "John Calvin: Humanist and Reformer. The Influence of Calvin's Early Humanism on His Work as a Christian Theologian," *Trinity Journal* (Spring 1976), pp. 67–78.

Williams, Glen Garfield. "The Theology of Bernardino Ochino." Ph.D. dissertation, Eberhard-Karls-Universität, Tübingen, 1955.

Willis, E. David. *Calvin's Catholic Christology: The Function of the So-called Extra Calvinisticum in Calvin's Theology.* Leiden: E. J. Brill, 1966.

———. "Persuasion in Calvin's Theology." In *Calvin and Christian Ethics,* ed. Peter De Klerk (Grand Rapids, Mich.: Calvin Studies Society, 1989), pp. 83–94.

———. "Rhetoric and Responsibility in Calvin's Theology." In *The Context of Contemporary Theology: Essays in Honor of Paul Lehmann,* ed. Alexander McKelway and E. David Willis (Atlanta: John Knox Press, 1974), pp. 43–63.

———. "The Social Context of the 1536 Edition of Calvin's *Institutes.*" In *In Honor of John Calvin, 1509–64,* ed. E. J. Furcha (Montreal: McGill University Press, 1987), pp. 133–53.

Woudstra, Marten H. "Calvin Interprets 'What Moses Reports': Observations on Calvin's Commentary on Exodus 1–19," *Calvin Theological Journal* 21 (1986), pp. 151–74.

————. *Calvin's Dying Bequest to the Church: A Critical Evaluation of the Commentary on Joshua* (Calvin Theological Seminary Monograph Series, 1). Grand Rapids, Mich.: Calvin Theological Seminary, 1960.

————. "The Use of 'Example' in Calvin's Sermons on Job." In *Bezield Verband: Opstellen aangeboden aan Prof. J. Kamphuis* ed. M. Arntzen, (Kampen: J. H. Kok, 1984), pp. 344–51, 456–58.

Wright, David F. "Calvin's Pentateuchal Criticism: Equity, Hardness of Heart, and Divine Accommodation in the Mosaic Harmony Commentary," *Calvin Theological Journal* 21 (1986), pp. 33–50.

Wyatt, Peter. *Jesus Christ and Creation in the Theology of John Calvin.* Allison Park, Pa.: Pickwick Publications, 1996.

Zachman, Randall C. "Theologian in the Service of Piety: A New Portrait of Calvin," *Christian Century* (April 23–30, 1997), pp. 413–18.

INDEX